THE RIGHT IN FRANCE FROM THE THIRD REPUBLIC TO VICHY

The Right in France from the Third Republic to Vichy

KEVIN PASSMORE

OXFORD
UNIVERSITY PRESS

OXFORD
UNIVERSITY PRESS

Great Clarendon Street, Oxford, OX2 6DP,
United Kingdom

Oxford University Press is a department of the University of Oxford.
It furthers the University's objective of excellence in research, scholarship,
and education by publishing worldwide. Oxford is a registered trade mark of
Oxford University Press in the UK and in certain other countries

First Edition published in 2013

Impression: 1

British Library Cataloguing in Publication Data
Data available

ISBN 978–0–19–965820–6

Printed in Great Britain by
MPG Books Group, Bodmin and King's Lynn

For Garthine

Acknowledgements

If I remember correctly, I began writing this book some seventeen years ago. Already in the late 1990s, the volume of scholarly work on conservatism and the right was enormous, and since then it has increased dramatically. I have tried to keep up with it, and a book like this is especially reliant on the work of others. Indeed, my debt to some historians' work goes beyond conventional acknowledgement in footnotes: the work of Michel Dobry, Philippe Levillain, Gilles Le Béguec, Nicholas Roussellier, François Monnet, and David Bensoussan, to name just some, has been especially influential. Inevitably, I have sometimes disagreed with their interpretations, and to avoid over-complication of the narrative I have not always made that explicit. As for those whose research has received insufficient attention, I hope that they will understand that one has to stop at some point—the necessity of doing so makes me all the more conscious that this is *a* history of the right in the Third Republic and Vichy—not *the* history.

Over the years, I have also received help from a great number of institutions, scholars, librarians, archivists, and friends. I gratefully acknowledge financial support from the Arts and Humanities Research Council (Research Leave Scheme, AH/F003048/1), the British Academy (Small Personal Research Grants, 1995, 2003, 2007), and the Scouloudi Foundation in association with the Institute of Historical Research (Research Awards, 2000, 2007). I have also received generous financial support from the School of History, Archaeology, and Religion at Cardiff University, and special thanks are due to my colleagues in the History department, who covered for me during periods of research leave.

I owe a debt to librarians and archivists at the Bibliothèque nationale de France and Archives nationales. The late Monsieur Gilles de La Rocque kindly allowed me to consult the Fonds La Rocque, and the donors of the Fonds Ribot and Fonds Deschanel gave me permission to consult those papers, all held at the Archives nationales.

I would like to thank Christopher Wheeler at Oxford University Press for his patient support for this project from its inception, and Emma Barber for her patient editorial work.

I would like to thank Orla Smyth, Chloé Faucillon, and Thomas Daum for the hospitality they provided in Paris. I have learned much from my postgraduate students at Cardiff, in particular Chris Millington, Mark Pitchford, and Joe Starkey, and from presentations to several seminars at the École des hautes etudes en sciences sociales in Paris. Ian Dennis drew the maps, and was as patient as ever with my frequent alterations. A number of colleagues and friends have read parts of the manuscript: Magali Della Sudda, Lloyd Bowen, Jackie Clarke, Julian Jackson, Chris Millington, Mary Vincent, Garthine Walker, and Julian Wright. Special thanks are due to Lloyd Bowen, Jackie Clarke, Karen Adler, and Laura Downs. Over innumerable lunches and dinners, in Cardiff and Paris, I have learned an enormous amount from them, and this book bears the imprint of their ideas.

Lastly, I am enormously thankful to Joe and Emily Passmore for putting up with the financial drain resulting from frequent trips to France, and above all my wife, Garthine Walker. She has followed this project from its inception, and is an inspiration as a person, colleague, and historian.

Contents

Abbreviations

ABBREVIATIONS USED IN THE FOOTNOTES

AN	Archives nationales
ANFAM	Archives nationales. Fonds Millerand
ANFL	Archives nationales. Fondes Lamy
ANFLM	Archives nationales. Fonds Louis Marin
ANFLR	Archives nationales. Fonds La Rocque
ANFM	Archives nationales. Fonds Mackau
ANFR	Archives nationales. Fonds Ribot
ANFT	Archives nationales. Fonds Tardieu
ANFXR	Archives nationales. Fonds Rochefoucauld
ANPG	Archives nationales. Police générale
APP	Archives de la préfecture de police
BNF	Bibliothèque nationale de France
EHESS	École des hautes études en sciences sociales
IEP	Institut d'études politiques
JOCD	*Journal officiel. Chambre des députés*
JOS	*Journal officiel. Sénat*

ABBREVIATIONS USED IN THE TEXT

ACJF	Association catholique de la jeunesse française
ADCM	Association de défense des classes moyennes
AF	Action française
AL	Action libérale
ALP	Action libérale populaire
ANEE	Association nationale d'expansion économique
ANO	Alliance nationale de l'Ouest
ANOD	Association nationale pour l'organisation de la démocratie
ANPAPF	Alliance nationale pour l'accroissement de la population française
ANR	Action nationale républicaine
ARD	Alliance (républicaine) démocratique
ARS	Action républicaine et sociale
CFTC	Confédération française des travailleurs chrétiens
CGPF	Confédération générale de la production française (from 1936, Confédération générale du patronat français)
CGSCM	Confédération générale des syndicats des classes moyennes
CGT	Confédération générale du travail
CGTU	Confédération générale du travail unitaire
CIPF	Confédération de l'intelligence et de la production française
CNE	Conseil national économique
CPEE	Centre polytechnicien d'études économiques (formerly X-Crise, 1931)
CPRN	Centre de propagande des républicains nationaux
CRCI	Comité républicain du commerce, de l'industrie, et de l'agriculture

CSAR	Comité secret d'action révolutionnaire
DC	Démocratie chrétienne
DRAC	Ligue des droits du religieux ancien combattant
ERD	Entente républicaine démocratique
EVP	Équipes volantes de propagande
FC	Fédération des contribuables
FCM	Filles du Cœur de Marie
FDG	Fédération des gauches
FICF	Fédération des industriels et des commerçants français (Fédération Lebon)
FN	Front national
FNC	Fédération nationale catholique
FNCR	Fédération nationale des combattants républicains
FR	Fédération républicaine
FRB	Fédération régionaliste bretonne
FRF	Fédération régionaliste française
GQG	Grand Quartier Général
JAC	Jeunesse agricole chrétienne
JACF	Jeunesse agricole chrétienne féminine
JOC	Jeunesse ouvrière chrétienne
JOCF	Jeunesse ouvrière chrétienne féminine
JP	Jeunesses patriotes
JR	Jeunesse royaliste
LDN	Ligue des droits de la nation
LDP	Ligue des patriotes
LFF	Ligue des femmes françaises
LPDF	Ligue patriotique des françaises
LPF	Ligue de la patrie française
LRN	Ligue républicaine nationale
NCO	Non-Commissioned Officer
NRF	Nouvelle revue française
OCM	Organisation civile et militaire
PAPF	Parti agraire et paysan français
PCF	Parti communiste français
PDP	Parti démocrate populaire
PNB	Parti nationaliste breton (1911–14), Parti national breton (1934–44)
PPF	Parti populaire français
PR	Proportional representation
PRD	Parti républicain démocrate
PRDS	Parti républicain démocrate et social
PRNS	Parti républicain nationale et social
PSF	Parti social français
PSN	Parti socialiste national
QR	Quatrième république
RPF	Rassemblement du peuple français
SFIO	Section française de l'internationale ouvrière (Parti socialiste)
SIS	Syndicat des ingénieurs salariés
SPF	Syndicats professionnels français
UCAD	Union des Comités d'action défensive
UF	Union fédérale

UFC	Union de la France chrétienne
UFSF	Union française pour le suffrage des femmes
UIE	Union des intérêts économiques
UN	Union nationale
UNC	Union nationale des combattants
UNSA	Union nationale des sydicats agricoles
UNVF	Union nationale pour le vote des femmes
UPR	Union patriotique républicaine
URB	Union régionaliste bretonne
URD	Union républicaine démocratique
USE	Union du sud-est
USIC	Union sociale des ingénieurs catholiques
USIF	Union des syndicats d'ingénieurs français
USSR	Union of Soviet Socialist Republics
VN	Volontaires nationaux

Maps

Map of departments
Pas-de-Calais
Nord
Somme
Seine-Inférieure
Aisne
Ardennes
Oise
Moselle
Manche
Calvados
Eure
Seine-et-Oise
Marne
Meuse
Meurthe-et-Moselle
Bas-Rhin
Finistère
Côtes-du-Nord
Orne
Seine-et-Marne
Ille-et-Vilaine
Mayenne
Eure-et-Loir
Aube
Haute-Marne
Vosges
Morbihan
Sarthe
Loiret
Yonne
Haute-Saône
Haut-Rhin
Territoire de Belfort
Loire-Inférieure
Maine-et-Loire
Indre-et-Loire
Loir-et-Cher
Côte-d'Or
Doubs
Cher
Nièvre
Deux-Sèvres
Vendée
Vienne
Indre
Saône-et-Loire
Jura
Allier
Haute-Savoie
Ain
Creuse
Charente-Inférieure
Charente
Haute-Vienne
Puy-de-Dôme
Loire
Rhône
Savoie
Corrèze
Isère
Cantal
Haute-Loire
Dordogne
Gironde
Ardèche
Drôme
Hautes-Alpes
Lot
Lozère
Lot-et-Garonne
Aveyron
Alpes-Maritimes
Tarn-et-Garonne
Basses-Alpes
Vaucluse
Landes
Gard
Tarn
Gers
Hérault
Haute-Corse
Bouches-du-Rhône
Var
Haute-Garonne
Basses-Pyrénées
Aude
Hautes-Pyrénées
Ariège
Corse-du-Sud
Pyrénées-Orientales

Map 1

1

Introduction

2 OCTOBER 1888

On a bitter autumn night, two figures wearing false beards, with their collars turned up, slipped into General Boulanger's house through the tradesmen's entrance. One was the worldly Marquis de Breteuil, advisor to the pretender to the French throne and friend of the Prince of Wales; the other was the austere Catholic, Comte Albert de Mun. In the dining room, they joined Boulanger, whom they found wrapped comfortably in fine furs, and two more conspirators: Arthur Meyer, editor of the Royalist *Le Gaulois*, and the recently widowed duchesse d'Uzès, sole inheritor of the Veuve Cliquot champagne fortune. Since 1887, Boulanger, the darling of the Radical Republicans, had been engaged in a demagogic campaign to make the Third Republic more democratic. Yet some months previously, his emissaries had secretly informed Royalists that Boulanger might favour restoration of the monarchy. In return, Royalists clandestinely financed his electoral campaign, d'Uzès contributing much of the money. The plotters dined chez Boulanger in the hope of securing solid support from the General himself.

Breteuil found the dinner a trial: Boulanger too obviously revelled in tasteless luxury purchased with Royalist money, and he horribly resembled the social-climbing hero of Guy de Maupassant's recently published *Bel-Ami*. Boulanger's failure to anticipate that the Catholics, de Mun and d'Uzès, could not eat meat on a Friday did not improve the atmosphere. The guests did not like or respect each other, and only Meyer, whom Breteuil saw as 'cunning, and not Jewish for nothing', kept the conversation going. The meal over, the guests retreated to a freezing greenhouse-like structure to smoke, where they vainly attempted to extract a commitment from the General. D'Uzès, Breteuil recorded, silently devoured with her eyes the handsome Boulanger—a notorious womanizer.[1]

8 FEBRUARY 1924

Thirty-six years later, the moderate conservative President of the Council of Ministers, Raymond Poincaré, was defending in the Chamber of Deputies his project for emergency powers to reduce government spending and raise taxes, and thus

[1] Henri de Breteuil, *La Haute société: journal secret, 1886–1889* (Paris, 1979), May and 5 October 1888.

deal with the disastrous financial legacy of the Great War. The left pressed hard, using the religious question to divide the anticlerical Poincaré from his right-wing Catholic allies. As often happened in the parliament of the Third Republic, where brandishing revolvers was not unknown, proceedings quickly degenerated. Amid screaming, insults, and threats, the right accused the left of complicity with the German enemy. A Royalist proposed cutting deputies' salaries, while the Socialists demanded 100 per cent income tax on deputies' earnings outside the Chamber. At one point, the notoriously touchy Poincaré stalked out of the Chamber, ostensibly because the country 'had nothing to gain from such debates'; perhaps because a deputy had insinuated that as a member of pre-war governments, Poincaré shared responsibility for the defeats of August 1914.

Poincaré also faced pressure from his right. Although the latter approved the government's attempt to force Germany to pay reparations through occupation of the Rühr, it was less enamoured of his domestic policies, and doubtless did not like his endorsement of secularism in the present debate. When the Royalist Magne spoke against tax rises and proposed faster implementation of cuts, Poincaré and his partisans accused him of echoing Communist attacks on a patriotic government. Poincaré's fellow Lorraine deputy, the nationalist Désiré Ferry, urged Poincaré to support Magne's amendment, provoking the premier to invoke corridor rumours about right-wing plots, and to threaten to campaign against Ferry in the coming elections.

'Look, I'd rather you didn't vote for me', Poincaré declared, and he urged the Catholic and nationalist right not to endorse him publicly while intriguing in the corridors.

The sitting over, Ferry approached Poincaré, all but provoking the latter to a duel: 'If you insist on what you have been saying, I shall be obliged to do as M. Bracke did (involved in an incident on the previous day); I shall send you my seconds.'

'At your service', Ferry replied, 'but allow me to explain: I do not doubt your word, but the words reported to you'. Another Lorraine nationalist, Édouard de Warren, joined in, while yet another deputy was sent packing from a discussion 'between Lorrainers'. Eventually, the deputies agreed to disagree.[2]

16 NOVEMBER 1935

Rallies in left-wing strongholds of the anti-parliamentary, nationalist league, the Croix de feu, often provoked disorder, and such was the case in industrial Limoges. Since the previous winter, the league had held military-style mobilizations, in which dozens, sometimes thousands, of motor vehicles transported activists to destinations that were often revealed only in the course of the journey. At Limoges, the mobilization ended with a private meeting in a riding school. The Socialist senator-mayor and deputy led a Popular Front counter-demonstration, which, in spite of the rain, attracted at least 2,000 people. They advanced on the riding school

[2] Archives nationales 317 AP 168, Fonds Marin, Minute, 8 February 1924.

chanting 'La Rocque for the firing squad', and the two sides exchanged projectiles across a police cordon. In the darkness, around 1,000 Croix de feu left the hall without incident, leaving some 200 inside, confronting a roughly equal number of demonstrators. The remaining Croix de feu refused to leave, whether out of bravado, confusion, or fear is unclear. Whatever the case, they vainly telephoned the local dragoon barracks for help. The Prosecutor concluded that a group of demonstrators had broken through the barrier, and that the Croix de feu had fired a 'salvo' with their revolvers, doubtless because in the pitch black they believed themselves to be under direct attack. The Prosecutor added that since some counter-demonstrators had been seen holding revolvers, it was highly likely that they had fired back. Nobody died, but about a dozen people on each side were injured with bullets, or with sharp objects and clubs in the hand-to-hand that followed.[3]

Both sides claimed that they had acted defensively. *L'Humanité*, the Communist organ, reported that the counter-demonstrators wanted merely 'to boo the French Hitlerists', while a moderately left-wing newspaper noted that the left would not have dreamed of organizing a rally in the chic Parc Monceau—one can indeed imagine the response of the police.[4] Colonel de La Rocque, president of the Croix de feu, explained that his members had responded to a systematic campaign to entangle his movement in local skirmishes, and thus neutralize it. Given the evidence that the police had gathered, he could not avoid admitting implicitly that his followers had fired, but claimed that they had responded in a framework of discipline, under his own responsibility, and in legitimate self-defence, not as 'individuals'. His Limoges section leader told the police that he was pleased that his comrades had disobeyed his orders not to bring weapons, for that saved them from massacre.[5] The right-wing weekly, *Gringoire*, complained that the Popular Front was systematically denying patriots the right to assemble, and that the thousands of attacks suffered by nationalists over the last years could have been avoided if the Communists encountered men such as the Croix de feu leader in Limoges. It lauded another right-wing group that had promised to revenge itself on three opponents for each of its own that was harmed. However, *Gringoire* felt that La Rocque's policy of avoiding confrontation had failed, and that other leagues had shown more 'bottle' [cran].[6] A few weeks later, La Rocque's parliamentary representative proposed mutual disarmament of left and right, to the fury of *Gringoire* and its ilk.

HISTORIOGRAPHY

From a present-day perspective, these episodes self-evidently belong to the histories of the 'right' and perhaps also to that of the 'extreme' right. It is less obvious that they belong to that of 'conservatism', and matters were even more complex for

[3] Archives nationales, BB^{18} 2959, 24 February, 24 March 1936; Jacques Nobécourt, *Le colonel de La Rocque (1885–1946), ou les pièges du nationalisme chrétien* (Paris, 1997), 327–8.

[4] *L'Humanité*, 17 November 1935; *La République*, 19 November 1935.

[5] *Le Flambeau*, 23 November 1935. [6] *Gringoire*, 22 November 1935.

protagonists. They reserved the term 'right' for opponents of the Republic, especially Monarchists, and used it interchangeably with 'extreme right'. Moderate Republicans such as Poincaré never saw themselves as 'right-wing', while the Croix de feu claimed to be neither left nor right. Poincaré might have accepted the label 'conservative', but so also did the moderately left-wing Radical-Socialists. Moreover, from the 1880s Monarchists had appropriated the term *conservateur* as a way to appeal to Republicans and mask dynastic disputes in their own ranks. An obscure quarrel in the southern department of the Hérault shows how important the choice of labels could be. Royalist purists there saw two deputies' use of the label 'conservateur' in the 1919 elections as a capitulation to Republicanism:

> MM de Guibal and de Rodez have permitted *L'Éclair* to call them 'conservatives', and this old-fashioned term has been restored to honour on their behalf. Some say that until now 'conservative' has been a synonym for 'Monarchist', but that opinion provokes protest from *L'Éclair*. 'Conservatives' are 'Monarchists'? Come on!' it says, 'A Progressist [Moderate] Republican is a conservative and the great majority of Radicals are terribly conservative'. Whoa, eminent confrere! Do you think that Union national voters sent MM de Guibal, de Rodez and even M de Magallon to the Chamber so that they could be conservative in the same way as your Républicains de gauche [Moderate Republicans] and your Radicals . . .? For the great majority, if not all of them, that would be disappointing.[7]

Certainly, that Moderate Republicans, right, and extreme right all claimed to be conservative allowed them periodically to unite, but that did not prevent any of them from allying when it suited with elements of the left. Monarchists conspired with Boulanger, while Poincaré echoed the left's anticlericalism. Indeed, it is impossible to identify an interest or idea that united these groups as a category: neither nationalism, religion, nor anti-communism could do that, while the Poincaré incident hints at the importance of regional divisions too. Neither were conservatives uniformly misogynist. True, a sense of male honour is evident in Breteuil's dismissal of the duchesse d'Uzès, the recourse to the duel, and in the Croix de feu's desire not to back down before Communism. Yet Anne d'Uzès was an accomplished artist, and as a feminist, she would contribute to transforming the place of women in right-wing politics—thus preparing the way for massive female involvement in the Croix de feu.

Given the difficulties of definition, it is more realistic to chart protagonists' deployment of labels such as 'right', 'centre', and 'conservative' as weapons in conflicts among themselves and against the left, without ruling out alliances with the latter. The course of these struggles, in which impulses towards both unity and disunity were always present, depended on context. Moreover, 'high politics' were entangled with class, gender, religious, and regional divisions in society, and so are vitally important to understanding our subject. My book therefore takes issue with the prevalent historiographical assumption that day-to-day politics were secondary to more fixed underlying dispositions.

[7] *Le Midi nouveau*, 30 November 1919. Quoted in Philippe Secondy, *La Persistance du Midi blanc* (Perpignan, 2006), 205.

Indeed, the 'traditional' political history of the rational intentions of great men has never dominated the historiography of the French right. Even Charles Seignobos, who imported 'German' scientific history into France, assumed that durable regional 'temperaments' determined political allegiances. The first serious study of the right, André Siegfried's *Tableau politique de la France de l'ouest sous la Troisième République* (1913) also saw political conflicts as iterations of near-static regional temperaments and psychologies. In 1946, François Goguel reaffirmed the importance of deep mental structures in his examination of the parties of 'order' and 'movement', as he preferred to call the right and left.[8]

After 1945, the Fondation Nationale des Sciences Politiques (FNSP, Sciences Po) institutionalized this history of temperaments; Siegfried would be its first president and Goguel would occupy the post in the 1970s. From Seignobos to Goguel and beyond, these powerful figures represented what Gérard Noiriel calls 'government intellectuals'. Their task was to teach 'realist' statecraft, the art of the possible, reconciling order and progress, through the study of history and the unique national psychology. This aspiration had been integral to the conservative political culture that I shall examine in this book, and Sciences Po's predecessor, the École libre des sciences politiques, had been a significant component of that culture.[9]

Noiriel's claim that there was an opposition between the political history of Sciences Po and the social history of the *Annales* is less convincing. Actually, the *Annales*' dismissal of political history *per se* and its political rivalry with Sciences Po obscured their agreement that historians should focus on deep mentalities and corresponding social structures. Perhaps Noiriel forgot that Siegfried had been a founding member of the *Annales* board. Moreover, the *Annales* had borrowed the notion of 'mentality' from the ethnologist Lucien Lévy-Bruhl, whose understanding of the concept owed much to the 'crowd theory' that conservatives espoused.[10]

René Rémond and his Critics

René Rémond lies at the confluence of conservative political culture and its scholarly history. He had been active in Catholic youth groups in the 1930s, began teaching at Sciences Po in 1947, and succeeded Goguel as president of the FNSP in 1981. His magisterial *La Droite en France de 1815 à nos jours*, first published in 1954 and thrice revised, highlighted the persistence of temperaments, but unlike Goguel, he claimed that there were three distinct right-wing mentalities. He contended

[8] François Goguel, *La Politique des partis sous la IIIe République* (Paris, Seuil), 1946; Jean-François Sirinelli, 'Des Droites et du politique', in Jean-François Sirinelli (ed.), *Histoire des droites en France*, i: *Politique* (Paris, 1992), xviii–xxii.

[9] Gérard Noiriel, *Les Fils maudits de la République. L'Avenir des intellectuels en France* (Paris, 2005), 105–20.

[10] Jacques Le Goff, 'Les Mentalités. Une Histoire ambigüe', in Jacques Le Goff and Pierre Nora (eds), *Faire l'histoire*, iii: *Nouveaux objets* (Paris, 1974), 76–94.

that following the Revolution of 1789, three irreducible right-wing tendencies crystallized, 'each with its own system of thought, temperament, and clientele'. It is worth describing their origins in some detail, for as an account of the pre-history of the period studied in this book, it retains much validity.[11]

The first temperament, 'Legitimism', was loyal to the elder branch of the Bourbon dynasty. It emerged from intransigent Monarchist opposition to the Revolution and solidified as 'Ultraroyalism' under the Bourbon Restoration (1814–1830). It was Monarchist, Catholic, and traditionalist, advocating organic hierarchy and deference. The second strand, Orleanism, originated in the liberal opposition to the Bourbon Restoration. It won power with the Revolution of 1830 and placed the younger Orléans branch of the royal family on the throne of the 'July Monarchy' (1830–1848). In government, the Orleanists were opposed from the right by the Legitimists, yet were themselves conservative. The Orleanists admired the constitutional Monarchy of 1789–1792 and advocated rule by the talented (the wealthy) under a restricted suffrage in a liberal-capitalist society. In 1848, their refusal to extend the franchise precipitated revolution and the establishment of the Second Republic.[12]

Surprisingly, in April 1848, the Orleanists, Legitimists, and conservative Republicans won a majority in the Constituent Assembly. They united in the 'Party of Order', without, Rémond argues, burying their fundamental differences. In December, they helped Prince Louis-Napoléon win the Presidency of the Republic, in the belief that he would be their creature. They inadvertently revitalized the third strand in the right: Bonapartism.

This temperament combined authoritarianism, anti-parliamentarianism, and nationalism with universal suffrage and the claim to be neither left nor right. Louis-Napoléon soon emancipated himself from the Party of Order. In December 1851, he carried out a *coup d'état*, and a year later proclaimed himself Napoléon III. He maintained universal suffrage as a conquest of the Revolution and used administrative favour to win peasant support. Yet since the regime began by suppressing a peasant rising in defence of the Republic, it had to rely on conservative Orleanists for much of its administrative personnel. In its final years, the Empire encountered opposition from a loose coalition of Orleanists, Republicans, and a few Legitimists, who demanded greater powers for parliament. In January 1870, Napoléon III conceded much ground to his critics, inaugurating the Orleanist-dominated Liberal Empire. A few months later, the regime collapsed in military defeat at the hands of Germany.[13]

This narrative may be disputed. In the 1790s, Legitimists were already divided between ultras and constitutionalists. Rémond says little of manifestations of popular Legitimism in the 'White Terror' of 1815 and Abbé Genoude's movement of the 1840s, or of popular Bonapartism. Yet his account of the pre-1870 period is less controversial than his major contention—that all three tendencies survived the decline of Monarchism and persisted into the present. Legitimism became integrist

[11] René Rémond, *Les Droites en France*, fourth revised edition (Paris, 1982).
[12] Rémond, *Les Droites*, 46–98. [13] Rémond, *Les Droites*, 99–121.

Catholicism; Orleanism survived as elitist-but-democratic conservatism; while Bonapartism resurfaced in the anti-parliamentary leagues and later in Gaullism.

Rémond's model proved enormously influential, and commentators still use it to categorize politicians.[14] It marked the multi-contributor *Histoire des droites en France* (1993), largely a product of Sciences Po. Significantly, its editor, Rémond's pupil, Jean-François Sirinelli, sought to heal the misunderstanding between historians and political scientists (implicitly the *Annales* and Sciences Po). He cited Siegfried and Rémond as proof that political history could be approached structurally.[15] Most contributors used Rémond's method, even if they proposed new temperaments. Later works also use Rémond's method to identify centrist and extreme-right temperaments.[16] Gilles Richard argues that there were no less than eleven political mentalities, which sometimes crystallized as the right.[17]

Rémond rightly argues that no common denominator united the right—more on that later. Yet there are problems with his schema. New movements were not simply variations within discrete traditions, but made from diverse materials. For instance, *fin-de-siècle* Nationalism was more than an avatar of Bonapartism; it combined Moderate Republicanism, Christian Democracy, and Royalism, not to mention ideas from outside the political sphere proper (from Darwinism to Latinist literary criticism). Moreover, traditions overlapped: the frontier between Orleanism and Bonapartism was as porous as that between Bonapartism and Republicanism. There were many discontinuities, including the passage of eastern France from left to right and of the southwest from Bonapartism to Radicalism. In the 1890s and 1900s, the Progressists re-conquered some urban areas from the left. In the Vendée, there was considerable variation in voting within broadly stable areas.[18] Finally, French and 'foreign' traditions were not hermetically sealed from each other. Conservatives meditated and adapted ideas and practices from Swedish social democracy, the British Conservative Party, Fascism, and elsewhere.

Another difficulty is that Rémond relies on a modernization teleology, in which the role of the 'great man' is essential. Legitimism was 'traditional', so it inevitably declined with modernization; Orleanism was more modern because it accepted capitalism, but its reliance on pre-industrial 'notables' ultimately made it traditional too. Bonapartism is more complex, for in the Third Republic 'notables' captured it, but in Gaullism its supposedly purer, modern version re-emerged; it broke notable power and modernized the right. For Rémond, de Gaulle was 'realistic'

[14] *Le Figaro* 14 October 2007; Nick Hewlett, 'Nicolas Sarkozy and the legacy of Bonapartism: the French presidential and parliamentary elections of 2007', *Modern & Contemporary France* 15, no. 4 (2007), 405–22.

[15] Jean-François Sirinelli, 'Des Droites et du politique', in *Histoire des droites*, i: xxv–xxvii.

[16] Rosemonde Sanson, *L'Alliance républicaine démocratique. Une Formation du centre (1901–1920)* (Rennes, 2003); François Roth (ed.), *Les Modérés dans la vie politique française (1870–1965)* (Nancy, 2000); Matthias Bernard, *La Guerre des droites. De L'Affaire Dreyfus à nos jours* (Paris, 2007).

[17] Gilles Richard, 'Réflexions sur le clivage droite(s)-gauche(s) à l'aube du XXIe siècle', *Vingtième siècle* 90 (April–June 2006), 155–68.

[18] Jean-Clément Martin, 'Signification des votes et comportement social en Vendée, XIXème et XXème siècles', in *Les Agriculteurs aux urnes* (Paris, 1990), unpaginated.

because he was 'too conscious of the force of things, of the movement of history, to believe it possible to go back on the changes that time has wrought'. Like all 'great men', De Gaulle understood the course of history, so his policies were 'realistic' rather than 'ideological'.[19] Here too the boundary between historians and their protagonists is blurred, for right-wing critics of the Third Republic also saw their proposed reforms as 'realistic' remedies to objective faults.

The sociologist Stanley Hoffmann systematized the view that the Third Republic had failed to modernize. He graduated from Sciences Po in 1948, and subsequently moved to Harvard, adding a Parsonian social science inflection to the backwardness thesis, confirming that international comparison had been intrinsic to the social and historical sciences in both countries since Tocqueville. Hoffmann argued that French people combined individualist materialism with subservience to authority, and so (unlike Americans) they could not form associations to look after their own interests. Instead, they expected 'notables' to intercede with the government to grant them favours; notables dominated parliament and so politics was concerned with personalities and materialism rather than programmes. Modern parties were impossible. Since the government protected special interests, the economy could not modernize, and the French people were 'Malthusian' in their refusal to innovate or have babies.[20] In conformity with the notion that the elite modernizes first, only a few heroic failures, who suffered for contesting received ideas, were conscious, like de Gaulle, of historical necessity. Under the shock of defeat, modernizing ideas progressed in both Vichy and the Resistance.[21]

Advocates of the failed modernization thesis fit the right into their story differently. For some, the left sabotaged the right's desire for modernity: Odile Rudelle blames the Machiavellian Clemenceau (a 'great villain') for preventing the emergence of a Republican conservative party in the 1880s.[22] Michel Winock argues that after 1919 the right accepted its place in a two-party system, while the left remained stuck in anachronistic antipathies inherited from the Revolution.[23] More commonly, historians agree with Rémond that backward-looking notables dominated the right, with the partial exception of the heirs of Bonapartism. This negative estimate is especially common in the historiography of party organization. Raymond Huard argues that the upheaval of the French Revolution provoked a lasting fear of parties among conservatives. Only with the emergence of Gaullism did they recognize the 'inevitability' of what Huard calls a 'universal' process

[19] Rémond, *Les Droites*, 317.

[20] Stanley Hoffman, 'The French political community', in Stanley Hoffman et al. (eds), *In Search of France* (New York, 1963), 1–117.

[21] François Monnet, *Refaire la République: André Tardieu, une dérive réactionnaire, 1876–1945* (Paris, 1993), 131, 172; Marjorie M. Farrar, *Principled Pragmatist: The Political Career of Alexandre Millerand* (New York and Oxford, 1991), 305–9; Julian Wright, 'Social reform, state reform, and Aristide Briand's moment of hope in France, 1909–1910', *French Historical Studies* 28, no. 1 (Winter 2005), 31–67.

[22] Odile Rudelle, *La République absolue. Aux Origines de l'instabilité de la France contemporaine* (Paris, 1982).

[23] Michel Winock, *La Fièvre hexagonale. Les Grandes crises politiques 1871–1968* (Paris, 1986), 193–238.

possessed of a 'profound continuity...beyond the accidents of political life'.[24] Other historians have identified precursors of modernizing Gaullism in the Third Republic—notably the Parti social français (PSF) of the late 1930s.[25]

The problems of modernization theory are well known. It selects elements from historical change, such as rationalization, specialization, industrialization, urbanization, and democracy, and presents them as inevitable and normative. Anything else is traditional, anachronistic, or dysfunctional. Modernization then becomes an extra-historical, objective force, to which societies must adapt. Great men recognize that before anyone else, so they fight against the grain only for history (academics, *faute de mieux*) to vindicate them. Scholars judge countries, parties, and people according to how 'modern' they were. In effect, the initial *choice* of features of change becomes a *standard* from which to derive the meaning of conservative politics, at the expense of protagonists' own conceptions.

A related difficulty with Rémond's approach is its essentialism. This criticism might seem misplaced given his insistence that the right has no fixed meaning, and that groups coalesced as 'the right' only in specific contexts, in opposition to other groups. Doubtless, this insight owed something to Rémond's encounter with the anti-positivism of Pierre Duhem and Henri Poincaré in the Catholic milieu he frequented as a youth. However, that same milieu was equally concerned to deny any affinities between moderate conservatism and fascism, and so essentialism reappears in Rémond's individual strands of the right (and in his approach to fascism).

Consequently, his temperaments work only so long as the right actually was organized around fidelity to the three pretenders. As a reviewer in *Annales* commented, 'from 1880, the unfolding of the argument becomes a little problematic; under the Third Republic, the right is doubltess too complex'.[26] As his story progresses, Rémond saves his definitions only by excluding more and more 'incidental' detail. For instance, only by assuming that their attitudes to democracy were secondary can he establish affinities between Orleanism and the interwar centre or between the PSF and Gaullism. Actually, 'secondary' features may be vitally important in context. Identical difficulties undermine Mathias Bernard's claim that the moderate and extreme right were categorically different.[27]

Essentialism is especially evident in the debate on whether the leagues of the 1930s were Bonapartist, as Rémond argued, or fascist as his critics maintain. Both sides construct definitions that make some features of fascism and the leagues essential and others superficial. Accordingly, Rémond argues that the leagues essentially wished to preserve social hierarchy, whereas fascism was essentially a 'revolutionary ideology'; consequently, similarities between the leagues and fascism

[24] Raymond Huard, *La Naissance du parti politique en France* (Paris, 1996), 18–21, 263–5, 315–19; W.D. Irvine, *French Conservatism in Crisis: The Republican Federation of France* (Baton Rouge, 1979), xviii; François Audigier, 'L'Alliance démocratique de 1933 à 1937 ou l'anachronisme en politique', *Vingtième siècle* 47 (July–September 1995), 147–57.

[25] Jean-Paul Thomas, 'Droite et rassemblement du PSF au RPF, 1936–1948. Hommes, réseaux, cultures: Rupture et continuités d'une histoire politique', thèse de doctorat, IEP Paris, 2002.

[26] Robert Mandrou, review of René Rémond, *La Droite en France de 1815 à nos jours* (Paris, 1954), in *Annales ESC* 10, no. 4 (October–December 1955), 606–7.

[27] Bernard, *La Guerre des droites*.

were merely a 'roman whitewash'.[28] Using the same method, but reaching an opposite conclusion, Robert Soucy concurs that the leagues were conservative, but since he redefines fascism as conservative too, the leagues become fascist.[29]

Finally, Rémond left little room for non-elite conservatism. Like many historians, he emphasized the leadership of notables who depended upon their personal status and provision of services rather than their ideas. He saw Orleanism and Legitimism as 'oligarchic' and stressed the triumph of conservative over radical Bonapartism. The top-down approach is still more explicit in Sirinelli's history. His three volumes deal successively with political strategies for the conquest of power and political ideas, then with the 'cultures' (leagues, parties, salons, the press) through which these ideas are transmitted to the 'sensibilities' that unconsciously regulate political behaviour. One moves thus from the rational elite to the irrational mass. Sirinelli's history includes little on working-class conservatism and still less on women.[30]

Marxism

Rémond's implicit target was the Marxist view that conservatives were ultimately united in defence of capitalism. Nevertheless, his account of the pre-1890s history largely matches the Marxist one: for both, Orleanists represented finance capital and Legitimists the landed aristocracy. Marxists differed in arguing that from the 1890s, the bourgeoisie and aristocracy merged in opposition to Socialism. To counter the objection that the Dreyfus Affair fractured this coalition, Herman Lebovics maintained that capitalists now felt secure enough to leave government to the petty-bourgeois Radical-Socialist Party. For Lebovics, these 'basic compromises' remained in place until the 1930s, when economic crisis and the revival of the left provoked the bourgeoisie to turn to the leagues and then Vichy. Although not a Marxist, Robert Soucy argues that through authority and repression the leagues pursued the same conservative ends as the parliamentary right.[31]

Again, essentialism is a problem: Lebovics and Soucy implicitly assume that the primary purpose of the right is to defend property, and so they define contrary behaviour as rhetorical or circumstantial. For instance, Lebovics underplays religious conflict within the right. Undeniably, conservatives often united against Socialism. Yet they agreed less often on the nature of the threat or the solution to the problem; sometimes, the very intensity of anti-socialism increased the stubbornness with which they defended Catholic or secular responses, and they were tempted to use anti-communism as a weapon against rival conservatives. Another difficulty is that this version of Marxism leaves little room for non-capitalists to

28 Rémond, *Les Droites*, 206–8.

29 Robert Soucy, *French Fascism: The Second Wave* (Newhaven, 1995).

30 Sirinelli, 'Des Droites et du politique', xxxvi–xlii.

31 Herman Lebovics, *The Alliance of Iron and Wheat in the Third French Republic 1860–1914: Origins of the New Conservatism* (Baton Rouge, 1988); Sanford Elwitt, *The Third Republic Defended: Bourgeois Reform in France, 1880–1914* (Baton Rouge, 1986); Roger Martelli, *Peut on connaitre la droite? Cahiers d'histoire de l'institut Maurice Thorez*, 20–1 (1977), 15–19.

influence the course of right-wing history. Lawyers and intellectuals speak for the economic ruling class, while workers and the petty bourgeoisie internalize ideas that are objectively inimical to their interests.

Cultural Approaches

The linguistic turn had mixed consequences for the history of conservatism. It reinforced antipathy to political history, which seemed to depend upon a naïve belief in the rational, male, bourgeois individual—even though that conviction had never dominated the historiography of the French right. Poststructuralist-influenced historians have largely ignored the history of conservatism *per se*, but the Foucauldian emphasis upon the power of discourses to define truth and marginalize dissidence recalled the Marxist theory of ideology. Thus, four years after the appearance of his classically Marxist history of conservative politics in the 1890s, Lebovics published a path-breaking cultural study of 'true France', without abandoning the notion that ideology served the interests of capitalism.[32] Furthermore, Foucauldian history sometimes inherited the Marxist assumption of functional unity within the ruling class: for instance, Mary-Louise Roberts' account of the perceived gender crisis of the 1920s assumes an undifferentiated anti-feminism on right and left.[33] Certainly, politicians used ideas to include and exclude, but we should not assume that the rank and file ingested them uncritically. Moreover, discourses were not pure expressions of 'power', but of dialogue and conflict between their authors, their sources, and their audience.

Notwithstanding, cultural history has much to offer the history of conservatism. It widens our sense of what is relevant to politics: unacknowledged prejudices about gender and race along with discourses from other fields, including biology, management science, and military strategy, shaped conservatism. And cultural historians have shown that the distinction between elite and popular knowledge was far from watertight.

Moreover, cultural approaches show that conservatives (and their opponents) shared many analytical categories and participated in a common political culture, yet used its categories differently. For instance, they did not respond to Socialism in a manner determined by allegedly objective interests: Catholics and secularists understood Socialism differently and imagined different solutions. I therefore use the concept of political culture differently also to Serge Berstein, whose method is rooted in an older functionalist sociological tradition. Berstein allows for the multiplicity of political cultures in a given society, but argues that one of them is dominant because it corresponds to the expectations of the majority. Thus, he views Republicanism in that sense, as 'quasi-consensual', and able to shape the other major traditions. Only minority traditions stand outside it. For Berstein, the Republican tradition is not fixed because it 'adapts' to new circumstances, but that

[32] Herman Lebovics, *True France: The Wars Over Cultural Identity, 1900–1945* (Ithaca, 1992).

[33] Mary-Louise Roberts, *Civilization Without Sexes: Reconstructing Gender in Postwar France, 1917–1927* (Chicago, 1994).

implies that its essence must remain the same.[34] In fact, the most widely accepted categories could be understood and used very differently.

The 'Classificatory Struggle'

Recently, some historians have combined chronology with attention to the use of language and cultural and social capital for advantage. They draw on Pierre Bourdieu's notion of competition within a field, particularly as elucidated by the political scientist, Michel Dobry.[35] Rather than seek to classify conservative movements, Bourdieusians examine the use of categories in a 'classificatory struggle'.[36]

From this perspective, the conventional use of categories and definitions carries three dangers. The first is conflation of historians' own categories with those of contemporaries—to assume, for instance, that a model of conservatism allows us to discern the meaning of political action for protagonists. The second is to suppose that categorization explains the actual history or 'ultimate meaning' of a given movement. It cannot do so because things excluded from the definition will also be important. The motives of people within a movement are never reducible to the category: nobody acts simply as a liberal or a fascist, but also as a mother or father, Catholics or Protestant, or as an anticlerical, bourgeois, or aristocrat, and much more. Degree of commitment varies from vague sympathy or paper membership through marching in demonstrations to fanatical adhesion. In effect, the classificatory fallacy involves the elevation of some features of a given organization into a definition, which is then used to characterize other elements as contextual variations. Thirdly, categorization obscures the multiple connections between different movements. People may belong to more than one movement; movements may collaborate with others, and ideologies may be shared. A major theme of this book is that conservatives participated in a common culture, shared with parts of the left, which each reworked in given contexts.

Of course, historians must define the boundaries of their object of study, but they must remember that they *choose* these limits from many possibilities. Since their object does not exist prior to studying it, it can have no essential quality. Rather, historians must make clear what their own choice includes and excludes. We saw that Rémond explained the concept of the right in precisely this way, but he abandoned that insight when discussing his individual mentalties.[37]

Bearing these points in mind, I use the anachronistic term 'conservative' to refer collectively to all the groups included in my study. That is *my* category, to which I do not ascribe a core meaning. I have included in my study all parties to the right of the Radical-Socialists, but I could have added the 'conservative' Radical-Socialists

[34] Serge Berstein, 'Nature et fonction des cultures politiques', in *Les Cultures politiques en France* (Paris, 1999), 7–31 at 20.

[35] Michel Dobry (ed.), *Le Mythe de l'allergie française au fascisme* (Paris, 2003); Michel Dobry, 'Février 1934 et la découverte de l'allergie française à la révolution fasciste', *Revue française de sociologie* 30, no. 4 (July–December 1989), 511–33.

[36] Laurent Kestel, 'De la conversion en politique. Genèse et institutionnalisation du Parti populaire français, 1936–1940', thèse de doctorat, Paris I, 2006.

[37] Rémond, *Les Droites*, 24–31.

or restricted my attention to those who accepted the right-wing label. Furthermore, contemporaries used the term 'conservative' differently. To make that clear, I use the French term, '*conservatisme*' when appropriate, and I explore its meaning for protagonists, as I do other terms.

For instance, returning to the problem with which we began, the notion that the right and centre shared a fundamental conservatism imposes our own categories on the past, and/or aligns us with those Third Republican politicians who believed that the centre *ought to* recognize its fundamental community of beliefs with the right. Some centrists agreed, but others countered that true conservatism entailed opposition to the extremes of left and right. Both sides (like some historians) claimed that what in reality were choices, were rooted in the mentality of the people. Whereas 'conservative' is a historiographical device, I use the term 'right' to refer only to those who assumed the label themselves, that is to say Monarchists and certain Catholics and nationalists. To designate Republican conservatives, I usually use their own terms—notably 'Progressist' and 'centre'. In both cases, I chart the contradictory meanings of the terms, and the strategies each used to incorporate or exclude others.

I treat the question of fascism likewise. Certainly, historians may ask what the leagues had in common with Fascism and Nazism. Yet however many similarities or dissimilarities they find, they will not identify the leagues' essence or explain their history, for other elements not included in the comparison were important too. To say that the Croix de feu belonged with Nazism in the category of fascism requires regarding as secondary the greater violence of the Italian Fascist movement and the Nazi's biological antisemitism, both of which were vital to the histories of those movements. Categorization also obscures the heterogeneity of the leagues. As Soucy demonstrates, the leagues cooperated with the parliamentary right, but they also shared features with left-wing movements.

Breaking with the classificatory logic does not then mean that we can write what we like. We must investigate empirically the diverse motives that brought people to a movement, their divergent understandings of what it stood for, and how they used labels as political interventions. We may ask how conservative movements perceived other movements and how they incorporated selected elements of foreign movements into French contexts.[38] We must also explore overlaps, ideological, organizational, and personal between movements, including between right and left.

CONSERVATIVE CULTURES

This book combines Rémond's emphasis on the diversity of conservative traditions with cultural historians' recognition of a shared political culture extending into the left, with Marxists' emphasis on the importance of anti-socialism, and with the

[38] Bruno Goyet, 'La "Marche sur Rome". Version originale sous-titré. La Réception du fascisme en France dans les années 20', in *Le Mythe*, 69–105.

Bourdieusian concept of categorical struggle. Conservatives (and their opponents) inscribed conflicting traditions, including those identified by Rémond and more, into common categories, usually shaped by collective psychology, in pursuit of aims that sometimes conflicted and sometimes converged with those of others. Furthermore, the contested nature of political culture, coupled with the contradictions of elite ideologies and their vulnerability to misinterpretation, enabled non-elite groups to shape conservatism.

The Elite and the Mass

Beginning with this shared culture, all conservatives assumed a strongly gendered and racialized opposition between the 'mass' and the 'elite', a notion that in the 1890s would be systematized in Gustave Le Bon's 'crowd psychology'. The mass was materialist, passive, and fond of routine, but was liable to unpredictable outbursts; it could not assimilate knowledge rationally, so it learned through the repetition of images and simple ideas, and it admired strong men. Consequently, demagogues could exploit the mass. Yet if the elite channelled mass passion into nationalism or religion, it could be a force for good. The elite was not immune from passions, but used reason and self-control to direct idealism into positive action; if it 'knew' the mass, it could draw inspiration from it, ensure the predominance of virtuous instincts within the mass and prevent demagogues from leading it astray. Knowledge of the history and morals of the people permitted the elite to adopt 'realistic' policies, free from ideology, in accordance with the national psychology and the movement of history (recall Rémond's depiction of de Gaulle). These categories survived because they were sufficiently flexible—and unfalsifiable—to explain any situation.

The left too assumed the elite–mass dichotomy, and nothing illustrates its appeal to politicians better than mutual depiction of left and right as 'demagogues'.[39] Thus, the Republicans believed that the masses were vulnerable to manipulation by priests and so needed the guidance of teachers and Prefects. Likewise, Socialists despaired at workers' preference for alcohol and sport over politics and endeavoured to create a working-class elite. Communists expected a vanguard party to raise the proletariat above materialism. Conservatives countered that left-wing activists were demagogues because they were insufficiently detached from the mass. A genuine elite possessed inherited worth, or had demonstrated talent in business, cultural, or military fields. It had acquired practical knowledge, which it coupled with a generalist education, to be contrasted with the abstract, half-baked, book-learning of leftists. The conservative elite understood the mass, but was sufficiently detached from it to represent the nation.

Beyond that, conservatives agreed neither on the characteristics of the mass nor of the elite. Was 'the people' inherently Catholic, Monarchist, conservative, or nationalist? Conservatives idealized variously the aristocrat or bourgeois, the

[39] Christopher E. Forth, *The Dreyfus Affair and the Crisis of French Manhood* (Baltimore, 2006), 103–36; Mark Meyers, 'Feminizing fascist men: crowd psychology, gender, and sexuality in French antifascism, 1929–1945', *French Historical Studies* 29, no. 1 (Winter 2006), 109–42.

country gentleman living on his estates or the businessman, the star of the Paris Bar or the provincial lawyer, the Catholic or the anticlerical. Monarchy, a professional senate, parliamentarianism, dictatorship, a strong presidency, proportional representation, management science, and the anti-parliamentary league were all means to secure the pre-eminence of the elites. Party organization made sense in this context rather than in relation to an ahistorical standard of modernity: parties were either a means to *exclude* the masses from direct involvement in politics or to manipulate them.

That brings me to popular conservatism. A problem for this book is that it often relies upon secondary works that unwittingly accept the elite–mass distinction (via the concepts of *mentalité* or hegemony). Some historians assume that conservative elites owed electoral success to monopolization of charity and employment opportunities, to their prestige, and to their propagation of religion. In fact, where deference existed, it is hard to say whether it was cause or consequence of popular conservatism. Also, recipients of charity did not necessarily see it in the same way as the giver. The Bourdieusian approach is not without danger either, for it holds that only intellectuals reflect on the nature of a field.

In view of these difficulties, the book focuses largely upon organized groups, while showing that popular conservatism was intrinsic to the remaking of conservatism. Ordinary conservatives used ruling ideas creatively, with degrees of intentionality that varied historically. They could do so because elite ideologies were contradictory; they were not pure expressions of a singular point of view, but of multiple and varied sources and of dialogue with an intended audience. They were also open to misinterpretation.[40]

Some studies of popular conservatism are helpful, notably the portrait of popular Bonapartism in Alain Corbin's brilliant *Village of the Cannibals* (1992). In my own work on the Rhône, I argued that conservatives could not rely simply on 'notability', for ordinary conservatives had their own ideas and did not necessarily 'internalize' the values of their betters. Above all, two decades of research illuminate the role of women in conservative politics. It combines attention to agency and the chronology of women's history with the cultural methods of gender history. It explores the misogyny of the male leadership of the right together with its contradictions, and relates it to the activism of women and the resources available to them.[41]

Tradition and Modernity

Conservatives also shared the categories of tradition and modernity, which were closely related to the elite–mass dichotomy, for the elite acquired its ability to

[40] Michel de Certeau, *La Culture de l'ordinaire* (Paris, 1978); Quentin Skinner, *Visions of Politics* (Cambridge, 2002).

[41] For instance Magali Della Sudda, 'Une Activité politique féminine conservatrice avant le droit de suffrage en France et en Italie. Socio histoire de la politisation des femmes catholiques au sein de la Ligue patriotique des françaises (1902–1933) et de l'Unione fra le donne cattoliche d'Italia (1909–1919)', thèse de doctorat, EHESS Paris, 2007.

master its passions through the accumulation of virtues through the generations—a notion taken from evolutionary biology. Whereas historians often seek to brand conservative movements as traditional, modern, or a mixture of both, I examine protagonists' use of these labels and the meanings that they gave them. We shall see that the most ardent traditionalists saw progress as unavoidable, while no prophet of progress wished to efface all traditions. Indeed, most conservatives believed that tradition must underpin change so that it did not turn into anarchy (another lesson of collective psychology), and more generally that a successful society (and individual) required a proper harmony of opposites, such as practicality and idealism, activism and submission to the common good. As they did with elite and mass, conservatives constructed understandings of traditional and modern from a variety of materials in particular contexts, including crowd psychology, military tactics, regional mentalities, gender, racial and class difference, child development, human biology, Social Darwinism, and Lamarckianism. From this perspective, we may see, for instance, that the clerical/anticlerical struggle was not one of tradition against modernity, but of struggle over resources in the present.

Narratives

The core purpose of this book is to fit successive reinventions of the right into a meaningful narrative without resorting to Rankean political history or to modernization teleologies. I do not therefore seek to reduce the history of conservatism to a single chronology, for historical periods, like any categories, are matters of perspective and choice, which illuminate some things and obscure others. Readers may detect at least three narrative rhythms in the book.

First, periods of relative unity and disunity alternated. Unity was greatest in 1873–1874, when monarchists united behind Moral Order; in 1884–1886, in the movement for 'conservatisme'; in the late 1890s behind the conservative Republican, Jules Méline, and from 1910 to 1924, culminating in 1919 in the Bloc national. In 1926–1932, as the 'Républicains nationaux', conservatives came close to achieving the dream of a 'united party on the British model'. Conservative disunity ensured the failure to restore the monarchy in 1873, and was especially evident in conflicts following the Pope's endorsement of the Republic in 1892 (the Ralliement) and during the Dreyfus Affair. The experience of the Bloc national provoked much discord among conservatives, while in the 1930s, anti-communism was insufficient to bring them together. Indeed, conservative unity did not neatly coincide with the seriousness of the threat from the left.

Secondly, whereas historians often depict the story of conservatism in relation to a process of modernization (or failed modernization), involving formalization of party structure and broadening participation, I propose a three-stage alternative. From the 1870s to the early 1900s, Royalists and Bonapartists drew upon informal popular conservatism, which included women as well as men. In contrast, Moderate Republicans and Orleanists sought to confine political action to election campaigns and parliamentary debate. Then, from around 1906 to 1924, conservatives in general adopted the Moderate Republican model of small, informal committees, dominated by upper-class men, and popular conservatism declined. From the mid 1920s, conservative activism revived in protest at the alleged failure of the Bloc national. It took various forms, ranging from the restructuring of parliamentary conservative parties through the re-emergence of Christian Democracy, to anti-parliamentary leagues. Catholic women returned to political activism, as did other groups that considered themselves unrepresented in older parties. In all three stages, conservatives conceived their organizational methods in terms of collective psychology and sought to perpetuate elite leadership. Yet non-elite conservative groups were able to use these same categories in their own way. Crowd theory saw the elite as male, bourgeois, and perhaps military, but conservative workers, women, and others endeavoured to represent themselves as elites and thus to reconfigure conservatism.

Without forgetting that each of these threads has its own history, I shall weave them into the familiar narrative—my third chronology. My chapters explore the decline of Monarchism, Boulangism, the Ralliement, the Dreyfus Affair, the Union sacrée, the Bloc National, the re-emergence of the leagues in the mid 1920s and the 1930s, and the crystallization of conservatism around right-wing Radicalism in the final years of the regime. In each, I show what brought conservatives together, and the limits of their alliance. In particular, I show that the shared categories—elite and mass, competence and generalism—crossed with interconnected and contradictory traditions, many of them not intrinsically conservative, or even political, informed each of these remakings. We shall see, for instance, that the concept of 'organization'—a key way to secure elite hegemony—changed quite radically with each of these reinventions. Of course, alternative chapter structures would have produced a different history. However, my subject is the ways in which conservatives dealt with a succession of challenges and reinvented themselves in diverse forms, and it has the advantage of showing that conservatives both confronted similar problems and participated in common cultures and put them to different, often contradictory uses.

2

Moral Order (1870–1884)

Fusion (of royal families): Still hoping!

Gustave Flaubert, *Dictionnaire des idées reçues* (1880)

In the winter of 1870–1871, the terms 'conservative' and 'right' coincided. Defeat at the hands of the invading German armies had carried off the Second Empire and big-city crowds had acclaimed the revived Republic. On the left, Jacobins and Socialists, especially in Paris, demanded war to the death against the Germans and their alleged aristocratic friends in France; on the right, Monarchists and Moderate Republicans increasingly felt that only peace could prevent revolution. On 28 January 1871, the Moderate Republican majority in the Provisional Government concluded an armistice, and in elections to a National Assembly, held on 8 February, the peace party won handsomely, with a near majority for the Royalists, comprising around 200 Legitimists and 180 Orleanists. In May, the government suppressed the Parisian rebels, now organized in the Commune, at the cost of thousands of deaths. The Third Republic threatened to be as short-lived as its equally bloody predecessors had been.

Yet Royalists proved powerless to restore the monarchy. Orleanists and Legitimists could not surmount their differences, while already on 2 June the Republicans won ninety-nine out of 150 seats in by-elections necessitated by the election of many Deputies in multiple departments. Moderate Republicans allied to the Radicals and cleverly combined democracy and anticlericalism with the claim that the Republic was a conservative force for order, and that Monarchists were subversives.

For five years, the Monarchist majority struggled to preserve elite leadership in these difficult circumstances. The majority oscillated between the centre and right. At first, centrism prevailed, which meant cooperation of constitutional Monarchists with the very moderately Republican Centre gauche. The alliance was based, in the language of the time, on the 'honnêtes gens', those Republicans and Monarchists who placed order above particular constitutional arrangements. In the 'Pacte de Bordeaux', so named because the Assembly was meeting in the city, the majority shelved the question of the regime pending the occupiers' departure and restoration of the national finances. Adolphe Thiers, former July Monarchy minister, became 'Chef du pouvoir exécutif de la République française'. On 1 March, the Assembly ratified the peace treaty and ceded Alsace-Lorraine to Germany. Restoration of the monarchy seemed impossible because in July the Legitimist pretender, the Comte de Chambord, reaffirmed his opposition to parliamentarianism, which

Orleanists held dear. Consequently, on 31 August 1871, the Assembly made Thiers 'President of the French Republic', on condition that he reaffirmed the Pacte de Bordeaux. The centre strategy failed because Monarchists feared that it would lead to definitive establishment of the Republic. In January 1872, Thiers pronounced clearly for the Republic and in the following months, the Republicans won more by-elections.

On 24 May 1873, following the victory of a Radical in Paris, fearful Royalists provoked Thiers into resignation. Marshal MacMahon, of indeterminate dynastic loyalty, became president, and announced a policy of 'Moral Order'. The Orleanist Duc Albert de Broglie became Prime Minister and promised a 'politique de droite'. Neither MacMahon nor Broglie abandoned the desire to reconcile 'honest men' above dynastic questions, and thus to unite Monarchists with Moderate Republicans. Yet they sought to do so under an authoritarian government. The Interior Minister sacked officials, transferred teachers, suspended newspapers, and restricted civil funerals, which were symbols of Republican secularism. Meanwhile, Chambord's reconciliation with the Orleanist Comte de Paris at Frohsdorf on 4–5 August seemingly made restoration possible. Many Orleanists accepted restoration in the expectation that the Comte de Paris would soon succeed the aging and childless Chambord. Contrary to rumour, Chambord wanted the throne; he ordered a Lieutenant-General's uniform and a Legion of Honour rosette sporting a fleur-de-lis in place of the eagle.[1]

Historians no longer see Chambord's refusal to compromise as solely responsible for the failure of restoration. The Centre gauche, essential for parliamentary approval, resolutely opposed it, while many Orleanists preferred a conservative republic to a Bourbon restoration and were conscious of the unpopularity of the monarchy in the country.[2] Those Orleanists who did favour restoration reassured themselves and the Centre gauche that Chambord did not endanger the gains of the 1789 Revolution, chiefly parliamentary government. In response, Ultralegitimists proclaimed precisely that Chambord 'would end the perversion of 1789'. On 27 October, Chambord 'clarified' his position. He reaffirmed his attachment to the white flag and neglected to mention a constitution. Restoration was impossible.[3]

Broglie turned back to the centre, and his relations with the right declined to the point where he suspended the Catholic and Legitimist *L'Univers*, and forbade mayors and functionaries to go to England to celebrate the majority of the Bonapartist

[1] Charles de Dreux-Brézé, *Notes et souvenirs pour servir à l'histoire du parti royaliste, 1872–1883*, fourth edition (Paris, 1899), 67–74.

[2] A. Hélot, *Journal politique de Charles Lacombe*, 2 vols (Paris, 1907), 25 October 1873; Gabriel de Broglie, *L'Orléanisme* (Paris, 1980); Stéphan Rials, *Le Légitimisme* (Paris, 1983); Hervé Robert, *L'Orléanisme* (Paris, 1992); Jean-Paul Bled, *Les Lys en exil, ou la seconde morte de l'Ancien régime* (Paris, 1992); Louis Girard, *Les Libéraux français, 1814–1875* (Paris, 1985), 230–64; Alan Grubb, *The Politics of Pessimism: Albert de Broglie and Conservative Politics in the Early Third Republic* (Newark, DE, 1996), 153–4, 161–2.

[3] *Le Soleil*, 23–29 October 1873; Kerdrel to de Meaux, 10 October 1873, in Vicomte de Meaux, *Souvenirs politiques (1871–1877)* (Paris, 1905), 151, 168: *Lacombe*, 19 October 1873; Bernard Ménager, *La Vie politique dans le Nord 1852–1877*, 3 vols (Lille, 1983), 1147–8.

Prince Impérial. Hoping to create a provisional regime dominated by Royalists, Broglie secured MacMahon's election as president for seven years (le Septennat), and proposed a strong senate. He proved unable to consolidate this arrangement because a revival of Bonapartism provoked some Royalists to conclude that the only way to curb both Bonapartism and radical Republicanism was to establish a conservative parliamentary republic. This was not the first time that constitutional Monarchists and Moderate Republicans would unite against the extremes. Yet that would never be the only option available, and that problematizes any attempt to pin down the content of conservative politics.

INTERPRETATIONS

Inevitably, René Rémond argues that 'between the benches of the Orleanists and Legitimists ran an abyss'. Yet to show the persistence of his three temperaments after the emergence in the 1890s of Republican conservatism, he has to posit the prior merging of Orleanists and Legitimists around their common identity as 'notables'.[4] Thus, Rémond rejoins the widely held view that 'notables' constituted a single ruling elite united in defence of hierarchy, which was undermined by modernization and democratization. In this view, the political divisions of Monarchism were superficial.[5] The 'notables thesis' rightly emphasizes that all Monarchists, including Bonapartists, wished to preserve the rule of 'the best'. Well before Le Bon systematized crowd theory, Monarchists assumed the elite–mass distinction, often conceptualized using the metaphor of the helmsmen, steering the ship of state through dangerous waters. The image starkly opposed the active elite and the passive mass.

The notables thesis misses the complex political, cultural, and social issues surrounding the meanings of the elite and mass. There was some truth in the Marxist view that the Orleanist and Legitimist division corresponded to that between the bourgeoisie and aristocracy respectively, even if defined as much culturally and religiously as economically. Bonapartists, meanwhile, both assumed class superiority and differentiated themselves from Royalists by means of militarist nationalism. Moreover, far from being social egalitarians, the Republicans too were elitist. They envisaged the advent of a new ruling class led by moderately anticlerical Parisian lawyers, allied to provincial professionals, businessmen, and rural bourgeois, who defined themselves in opposition to 'feudal privilege'.[6] These rival claimants to elite status struggled for the helm: Chambord saw himself as the only pilot able to steer the ship to port, while the

[4] René Rémond, *Les Droites en France*, fourth revised edition (Paris, 1982), 125.

[5] Robert R. Locke, *French Legitimists and the Politics of Moral Order in the Early Third Republic* (Princeton, 1974), 173–5; Stephen D. Kale, *Legitimism and the Reconstruction of French Society 1852–1883* (Baton Rouge, 1992); John Rothney, *Bonapartism after Sedan* (New York, 1969); Bernard Ménager, *Les Napoléons du peuple* (Paris, 1988), 261–309.

[6] Philip Nord, *The Republican Moment: Struggles for Democracy in Nineteenth-Century France* (Cambridge, MA, 1995).

Bonapartist, Jules Amigues, claimed that France would not board Republican or Royalist boats—for him, the mass possessed a limited power of choice.[7]

Consequently, Monarchists' views of democracy were more complex than the notables thesis—or the maritime metaphor—implies. Monarchists did not believe it possible to rule against the people, however irrational its beliefs, and so they redefined democracy rather than reject it. On the one hand, Bonapartists and Legitimist Ultras counterpoised popular politics to parliamentarianism. Bonapartists argued that the people themselves must choose the dynasty, while the Legitimists mobilized popular religion. On the other hand, Orleanists and moderate Legitimists advocated channelling extra-parliamentary populism, whether of the extreme left or right, into the regulated legal processes of parliamentary elections, thus ending the cycle of insurrection, bloodbath, and reaction. Ultimately, some constitutional Monarchists saw the Republican parliamentary version of this idea as a lesser evil than Bonapartism. Contradictions in Monarchists' view of the mass further complicated matters. The Commune universally horrified them, as it did many Republicans, and they saw it as another manifestation of the feminine lability of the mass, personified in the figure of the *pétroleuse* (female arsonist).[8] Yet they also felt that feminine values of self-sacrifice and charity could reconcile the classes. That implied mobilization of women outside the home, which potentially undermined the masculine identity of the elite and provided elite women with a stake in Monarchism. Indeed, ordinary people did not espouse Monarchism simply out of deference and materialism. They had their own reasons for doing so, and sometimes their agendas undermined their leaders' efforts to build an alliance with rival Monarchist factions. I shall now place these conflicts in the context of the social, intellectual, and political changes of the Second Empire and after.

MONARCHISM IN CONTEXT

France in 1871 was a predominantly peasant society, but market relations were important in the countryside and industrial capitalism advanced in railways, metallurgy, and textiles. Simultaneously, the Empire witnessed expansion of education, professions, and bureaucracy. These twin developments happened within a society divided by the succession of regimes, religion, and class, so there was no simple conflict between old and new; rather, social change simultaneously promoted Republicanism and popular conservatism and reconfigured divisions between and within Monarchist families. Change was not, as the notables thesis assumes, an external force to which Monarchists reacted. Rather, competition and convergences between Monarchists and Republicans helped make the modern world. For instance, to counter Republican democracy, Legitimists used railways and newspapers to mobilize the Catholic people in great pilgrimages.

[7] Dreux-Brézé, *Notes*, 132–7; Jules Amigues, *A Ceux qui se disent conservateurs. On demande un dictateur* (Paris, 1873), 4–7.

[8] Gay L. Gullickson, *Unruly Women of Paris* (New York, 1996).

Take first divisions among Monarchist leaders. There is *some* truth in the Marxist equation of Monarchism with land and Orleanism with big business. If there was a big business *party*, it was the Republican Centre gauche, which included some ex-Orleanists with ties to monarchy. For instance, the Centre gauche Auguste Casimir-Perier (father of the future President) was brother-in-law to the Orleanist leader, Gaston d'Audiffret-Pasquier; they possessed adjoining mansions in Paris and both sat on the board of the Anzin coal company.[9] There was little difference in business support for Legitimists and Orleanists, at 9 and 8 per cent respectively. However, Orleanists like Alfred Deseilligny of the Decazeville coal company and Legitimist moderates such as Denis Benoist d'Azy were more active in company management than Ultras, who largely confined themselves to investment. Family businessmen were more numerous amongst Orleanists (16 per cent) than Legitimist moderates (13 per cent) and Chevaux-Légers (1 per cent). Thus business largely preferred liberals (Moderate Republicans, moderate Legitimists or Orleanists). Yet the relationship was historical rather than automatic, for religion mattered too. In the Nord, the longer-established linen and wool industries espoused liberal Legitimism, while *parvenu* cotton manufacturers were predominantly Orleanist or very moderately Republican.[10]

The landed aristocracy preferred Monarchism, but Monarchism was not exclusively aristocratic or landed.[11] In the National Assembly, the pre-1789 aristocracy constituted 55 per cent of Legitimist deputies and 22 per cent of Orleanists. Forty-two per cent of Legitimists were large landowners, compared to 22 per cent of Orleanists. Among the Chevaux-Légers, the proportion of aristocrats (pre-and post-1789) reached 75 per cent.[12] These differences were even sharper in some conseils généraux.[13] Bonapartism too was dominated by the landed aristocracy, but it included bourgeois figures such as the father of Pierre Taittinger, who in the 1920s would blend Bonapartism with fascism.[14]

The aristocracy did not constitute a feudal class in the Marxist sense that it appropriated surplus from the peasantry through political coercion. It was capitalist in that it offered land for rent or employed wage labour or sharecroppers to produce goods for the market. Yet the aristocracy remained distinctive. It responded to loss of legal privilege by using inherited advantages—land, *chateaux*, and titles—to distinguish itself from the bourgeoisie and maintain its prestige among the peasantry. This strategy was compatible with co-option from the bourgeoisie, although noble marriages

[9] Jean Garrigues, 'Les Réseaux d'influence du Centre gauche (1870–1879)', in François Roth (ed.), *Les Modérés dans la vie politique française (1870–1965)* (Nancy, 1998), 29–40.

[10] Ménager, 'La Vie politique', 1048–50, 1146–7, 1156.

[11] Locke, *French Legitimists*, 74–5; Jacques Gadille, *La Pensée et l'action politique des évêques français au début de la Troisième République*, 2 vols (Paris, 1967), i, 26–7.

[12] Louis Girard, René Gossez, and Antoine Prost (eds), *Les Conseillers généraux en 1870* (Paris, 1967), 139; Locke, *French Legitimists*, 70.

[13] Michel Denis, 'Un Aspect du conservatisme en Bretagne au début de la Troisième République. Le Monarchisme libéral', *Annales de Bretagne* 77, nos. 2–3 (1970), 391–495; Denis, *Les Royalistes*, 462–4.

[14] Jean Quellien, *Bleus blancs, rouges. Politique et élections dans le Calvados 1870–1939* (Caen, 1986), 153; Jean Philippet, 'Le Temps des ligues. Pierre Taittinger et les Jeunesses patriotes', thèse de doctorat, IEP Paris, 2000, 105.

were predominantly endogamous.[15] There were divisions within the nobility. The Napoleonic nobility penetrated Parisian society, but rarely provincial salons. The wealthy nobles of Franche-Comté, divided between Orleanism and Legitimism, participated in a national network; lacking a strong landed base and distrusted by the peasantry, they used multiple residence, spas, and seasons to define themselves.[16] Breton lesser nobles relied more on land and titles than on geographical mobility. Memories of the Vendée reinforced these 'backwoods' nobles' sense of alienation.[17]

Under the Empire, the expansion of Catholic education divided both bourgeoisie and aristocracy, for it simultaneously provoked re-Christianization and anticlericalism. Whereas Victor de Broglie, a chief minister of the July Monarchy, had been a deist, his son Albert, the Moral Order premier, was a liberal Catholic. Louis Veuillot, editor of the ultramontane *L'univers*, was the son of a freethinker.[18] The importance of religion can be seen in the cases of two lawyer-deputies and personal friends from Saint-Omer: the unbeliever joined the Centre gauche while the Catholic preferred the Orleanist Centre droit.[19] Broadly, the bourgeoisie comprised an anticlerical majority and a substantial Catholic minority, while Monarchists divided into a Catholic majority and free-thinking minority. Liberal Catholicism was more common in the bourgeoisie, while ultramontanism seduced more aristocrats, especially after the Emperor's backing for Italian unity had outraged Legitimist defenders of the Pope.

A glance at the broader conservative constituency confirms that the notables thesis wrongly assumes the passivity of ordinary conservatives. Thus, although the Empire appointed mayors, it allowed room for village democracy. Often, that concession unintentionally promoted Republicanism, but since the administration sometimes sided with councils against notables and priests, it sustained popular Bonapartist dislike of aristocrats too. In the Orne in 1866, Baron Mackau, the official candidate, defeated the Orleanist Audiffret-Pasquier, even though the latter had the support of most of the local aristocracy.[20] Imperial interventionism also caused the expansion of a class of minor officials with a stake in Bonapartism, which survived into the Republic.

[15] Claude-Isabelle Brelot, *La Noblesse réinventée. Nobles de Franche-Comté de 1814 à 1870*, 2 vols (Paris, 1992); Claude-Isabelle Brelot (ed.), *Noblesses et villes, 1780–1950. Actes du colloque de Tours, 17–19 mars 1994* (Tours, 1995); André-Jean Tudesq, 'Les Survivances de l'Ancien régime. La Noblesse dans la société française de la première moitié du XIXe siècle', in D. Roche and C.E. Labrousse (eds), *Ordres et classes* (Paris, 1973), 199–214; Ralph Gibson, 'The French nobility in the nineteenth century—particularly in the Dordogne', in Jolyon Howorth and Philip G. Cerny (eds), *Elites in France: Origins, Reproduction, Power* (London, 1981), 5–45.

[16] Brelot, *La Noblesse*, *passim*.

[17] Jean-Clément Martin, *La Vendée et la mémoire (1800–1980)* (Paris, 1989), 114; Denis, 'Un Aspect', 396; Stephen Kale, 'French legitimists and the politics of abstention', *French Historical Studies* 20, no. 4 (Fall 1997), 665–701.

[18] Denis, *Les Royalistes*, 399–407; Kale, *Legitimism*, 80–4.

[19] Jean-Marc Guislin, 'Centre droit et Centre gauche à travers l'itinéraire politique de deux parlementaires modérés, Louis Martel et Auguste Paris', in *Les Modérés*, 29–40.

[20] Roger Magraw, 'The conflicts in the villages', in Theodore Zeldin (ed.), *Conflicts in French Society* (London, 1970), 169–227; Barnett Singer, *Village Notables in Nineteenth-Century France: Priests, Mayors, Schoolmasters* (Albany, NY, 1983); Éric Phélippeau, *L'Invention de l'homme politique moderne. Mackau, l'Orne, et la République* (Paris, 2002), 128–35.

Meanwhile, imperial reliance upon the Church to provide education and social services increased the political importance of religion for ordinary conservatives, especially women. The number of male clergy grew from 45,000 in 1830 to 75,000 in 1878 and the number of women from 31,000 in 1831 to 127,000 in 1878.[21] Recruitment from the peasantry and lower middle class increased, while bourgeois and noble women played an important role in education and charity. In associations such as the Béates of Haute-Loire and the Breton *Tiers Ordres*, women of all classes taught in schools and helped the poor and sick. The extension of the railway network and popular press permitted ultramontane Catholicism and Legitimism to come together in the great pilgrimages of the 1870s. These developments were politicized by the clerical/anticlerical conflict and by Catholics' conviction that female compassion was essential to overcoming class conflict, so horribly revealed in the Commune. In southern towns like Montpellier and Nîmes, Catholic–Protestant rivalry had long sustained inter-class Legitimism, and from mid century charitable works began to reinforce the Confréries de pénitents as the link between classes.[22] Ordinary people who owed their status and identity to Catholicism had a vested interest in dynastic politics and reinforced its divisions.

Conservatives could not use notoriety and wealth alone to mobilize 'vertical communities'. Certainly, in the small pre-1848 electorate, personal knowledge of the candidate was possible, and in the short campaign of 1870, Royalists may have had an advantage because they were better organized than their opponents were. However, since the advent of universal suffrage, candidates no longer knew all their electors. Given the imperfect secrecy of the ballot, pressure on tenants and employees remained possible.[23] For instance, in Alès (Gard), the Legitimist forgemaster Benoist d'Azy hired only Catholics.[24] Yet Republicans too used such methods,[25] and the remarkable diaries of a Breton peasant show that voters found ways to avoid coercion.[26] Anyway peasants' willingness to drink candidates' health did not prove deference. Even in conservative Ile-et-Vilaine, a Legitimist reported that

[21] Claude Langlois, 'Les Effectifs des congrégations féminines au XIXe siècle. De L'Enquête statistique à l'histoire quantitative', *Revue d'histoire de l'Église de France* 60, no. 164 (1974), 44–53.

[22] R. Marlin, 'La Droite à Besançon de 1870 à 1914', *Bulletin de la Faculté de lettres de Strasbourg* 44, no. 4 (1966), 413–23; Philippe Secondy, *La Persistance du Midi blanc* (Perpignan, 2006), 63–72; Jean-Pierre Landrévie, 'Le Tarn-et-Garonne de l'Empire à la République', *Annales du Midi* 84, no. 108 (1972), 283–312 at 303–4.

[23] In Pontivy (Morbihan) a local gentleman wrote: 'Monsieur the Viscount de Kergariou informs the tenants of Monsieur de Laussanne, Mme de Guélen and Mlle Coussin that he is charged by his relatives, the proprietors, to ensure that without exception all tenants vote for Monsieur the Comte de Mun. He is charged with surveying the execution of this order so that he can report to the proprietors, who will remember what happens.' Quoted in Eugen Weber, 'Comment la politique vint aux paysans: a second look at peasant politicization', *American Historical Review* 87, no. 2 (April 1982), 357–87, at 382. See also Grimaudière to Pocquet in B.-A. Pocquet du Haut-Jussé (ed.), *Légitimistes parlementaires. Correspondance politique de Barthélemy Pocquet, redacteur du Journal de Rennes, 1848–1878* (Paris, 1976), 144–6.

[24] Gérard Cholvy, 'Religion et politique en Languedoc méditerranéen et Roussillon à l'époque contemporaine', in *Droite et Gauche de 1789 à nos jours* (Montpellier, 1975), 33–75.

[25] Jean-Marc Guislin, *Le Travail parlementaire de l'Assemblée nationale de 1871 à travers les représentants du Pas-de-Calais* (Arras, 2004), 79–80.

[26] Jean-Marie Déguignet, *Mémoires d'un paysan Bas-breton* (Le Relecq-Kerhuon, 1999), 335–42.

there was no prejudice against the monarchy, but that the Royalist party had been unpopular for 150 years.[27] An Orleanist wrote that rumours of restoration caused even those he had hitherto considered 'good' to 'fear throne and alter'.[28]

Candidates were still chosen by their peers; in that respect, personal qualities still counted. Candidatures 'arose' from negotiation between committees, journalists, and perhaps the administration and/or bishop. This method persisted because only the wealthy could bear the cost of election—a Legitimist elected in an 1872 spent 6,000 francs. In 1876–1877, Monarchists benefited from Prefectoral support, but they also recruited specialist electoral agents, personal secretaries, and distributors of ballots. Wherever archives survive, they show careful charting of the opinions of electors. Bonapartists distributed tracts on a national scale and used photography (using montage to depict the sick Napoléon III on a horse).[29] Conservatives had to persuade often-sceptical electors to vote for them. Thus, the expansion and entrenchment of popular conservatism simultaneously sustained Monarchist hopes, constrained their freedom of action, and reinforced their divisions.

We must nevertheless be alive to the permeability of the boundaries between the Monarchist factions. For instance, Monseigneur Dupanloup, by tradition a moderate Legitimist, sat with the Orleanists. Each family possessed some affinities with rivals, and, in day-to-day politics, endeavoured to privilege similarities, while redefining conservatism in the process. Take, for instance, Ernest Renan. The great positivist scholar stood as a 'liberal' in 1869, and was close to the Orleanists. After 1870, he felt that restoration could unite Orleanist believers in historic right with Legitimist advocates of divine right. This anticlerical also accepted Catholic control of primary education, so long as the Church abandoned its dogmatic pretensions. Furthermore, Renan argued that since the monarchy, not the people, made France, government must be based on the traditional aristocratic ethos of force. He called for a new militarist aristocracy, including only those of the existing nobility whose titles withstood scholarly investigation.[30] I shall now turn my attention to the ways in which the different families struggled to define the elite, fight the Republicans, and capture the 'people'.

ORLEANISM

Renan's flexibility was typical of Orleanists. Many had supported the Empire, especially in its liberal incarnation. On its right, Orleanism was linked through liberal Catholicism to moderate Legitimism. On its left, many of the conservative Republican Centre gauche had once been Orleanists. Some of the 180 deputies of the Orleanist centre droit, like the pretender's uncle, the Duc d'Aumale, preferred a conservative republic to a Legitimist restoration.

[27] Grimaudière to Pocquet, March, 1876, in *Légitimistes parlementaires*, 144–6.

[28] Duc d'Audiffret-Pasquier, *La Maison de France et l'Assemblée nationale* (Paris, 1938), 139–44.

[29] Rothney, *Bonapartism*, 180–2; Phélippeau, *L'Invention*, 28–37, 176–81; François Pairault, *Monsieur le Baron. Eugène Eschassériaux, éminence grise du bonapartisme 1823–1906* (Paris, 2004), 188–9.

[30] Ernest Renan, *La Réforme intellectuelle et morale* (Paris, 1873).

This suppleness reflected a desire to convince conservatives that constitutional loyalties were less fundamental than shared commitment to the social order—a view allegedly inherent in 'honest men'. Dupanloup explained that to be a conservative 'it is not necessary to believe in God or in another life. It is sufficient to believe in one's field, vine, home, wife, children, daily bread, and boiled beef and vegetables', while Prime Minister Broglie hoped to 'reinforce the base of the social order' before founding a political 'edifice'.[31] The 'honest man' was both a self-representation and an intervention designed to unite conservatives, but in practice he appealed to moderate Legitimists and the Centre gauche, while excluding Bonapartist and Ultra populism.

The honest man was characterized first by having acquired a patrimony through merit and work. The noble Audiffret-Pasquier wrote to an Ultra, 'Through my work I have fashioned an honourable place that I owe to no-one, and I demand recompense from no-one for an attitude which was imposed on me by my conscience.'[32] Broglie explained that his second chamber would not be based on birth or fortune, 'but superiority of merit, services rendered, and intellectual and moral capital acquired through work'.[33] So although Orleanists agreed with Gambetta that legal equality trumped class, Broglie feared that the advent of the 'nouvelles couches' would end the 'ascendancy of the enlightened and superior classes' and provoke the triumph of 'ignorance and proscription of wealth'.[34] Individual sons of peasants and artisans might enter the ruling class, but it was closed to the lower classes collectively.[35] Whereas Ultralegitimists assumed that aristocracy was innately honourable, Orleanists held that an individual must conquer respect through engagement in the world.[36] Only those who had proved themselves by reaching the highest positions in the Church, magistracy, Army, or economy were fit to govern. They contrasted the Comte de Paris' familiarity with 'the social and political questions born out of the feverish activity of modern societies' with Chambord's exile.[37]

The belief in work dovetailed with the second characteristic of the honest man: his practical scientific outlook. Whereas older Orleanists deduced constitutional schemes from philosophical first principles, a new generation espoused the positivism of Hippolyte Taine and Renan. Taine especially contributed to the scientific study of government, holding that knowledge of the race, milieu, and moment should inform constitutional schemes, not abstractions. A typically positivist deputy

[31] Mgr. Dupanloup, *Du Devoir des honnêtes gens dans les élections* (Paris, 1871), 12; Speech of 22 July 1873, in *Discours du Duc de Broglie* (Paris, 1909), 101–2; *Le Soleil*, 24 September 1873.

[32] Audiffret-Pasquier to Maillé, July 1873, in *La Maison,* 115–17; Sudhir Hazareesingh, *From Subject to Citizen: The Second Empire and the Emergence of Modern French Democracy* (Princeton, NJ, 1998), 173; Michel Denis, *Les Royalistes de la Mayenne et le monde moderne (XIXe–XXe siècles),* Le Mans, Klincksieck, 1977, 422; Pierre-Auguste Callet, *Les Responsabilités. Lettres d'un gentilhomme de province à Mgr Le Comte de Chambord* (Paris, 1875); *Lacombe,* 21 August 1871; Hazareesingh, *From Subject to Citizen*, 167–71, 192–3.

[33] *Discours du Duc de Broglie*, 28 February 1873, 56.

[34] *Discours du Duc de Broglie,* 18 November 1872, 38.

[35] *Le Français*, 5 December 1880.

[36] Dupanloup, *Du Devoir des honnêtes gens*, 3–6; Callet, *Les Responsabilités*, 5–10, 17–18; Audiffret-Pasquier, *La Maison*, 6, 63.

[37] *Le Soleil*, 28 October 1873.

evoked astronomy: society, like the stars, required revolution (i.e. progress) in order.[38] *Mutatis mutandis*, the Orleanist scientist was neither a Legitimist obsessed by principle, nor a Republican lawyer possessed of paper qualifications. He was a 'gentleman-scholar', competent in the natural and human sciences, engaged in practical work, but with the leisure to reflect. In 1871, these principles were embodied in the École libre des sciences politiques, in which Taine and other Orleanists and conservative Republicans participated. Its head, Émile Boutmy, explained that the École would preserve the leadership of the leisured and cultivated in the 'age of number'.[39]

Thirdly, the honest man's practicality opposed him to anticlerical and Catholic fanaticism. He saw anticlericalism as a manifestation of the revolutionary spirit; Aumale saw Orleanism as 'monarchy without aristocracy and priests'. As liberals, Orleanists regarded religion as a matter of individual conscience, which should regulate political and social organization only in so far as behaviour should be moral. Broglie felt that priests could claim 'no superiority other than that of their virtues'—not as representatives of the Church.[40] Salvation depended on use of one's God-given talents.[41] The largely Catholic Orleanists refused to make religion the rallying point of an anti-Republican crusade, and responded cautiously to the secularization measures of 1880–1881.[42]

Thus, the Orleanists defined the elite through work, practicality, and avoidance of abstractions and extremes. The volatile, materialist people lacked those qualities, and so the suffrage should be restricted. Yet popular susceptibilities must set limits on government—hence the need to 'know' the national psychology. Thus, the elite knew that parliament actually governed, but the people would respect order only in the person of the king, for it understood only symbols. Similarly, while the wise knew that the tricolour was merely a flag, for the mass it represented the Revolution—Legitimists would have known that were they not isolated from the world.[43]

These ideas informed Orleanists' attitude to the workers. Orleanist businessmen used priests to staff company schools: at Decazeville, the Orleanist manager Deseilligny believed that Catholic education would stabilize the impulsive workforce. He constructed a cross-class alliance by invoking the industrial interest, investing in the hitherto failing coal and iron industries, and improving municipal infrastructure.[44] Deseilligny was an exception among Orleanists in his concern for workers, perhaps because he was well disposed to the Empire. After Deseilligny's death in 1875, Republicans capitalized on working-class discontent about wages and priestly interference. Anyway, the largely ultramontane clergy of the region could

[38] Callet, *Les Responsabilités*, 40–2, 44–6.

[39] Pierre Favre, *Naissances de la science politique en France (1870–1914)* (Paris, 1989), 25.

[40] *Discours du Duc de Broglie*, 114–15.

[41] Callet, *Les Responsabilités*, 11–12.

[42] Meaux, *Souvenirs*, 105–6; *Lacombe*, 5 October 1876, 5 May 1877.

[43] Callet, *Les Responsabilités*, 30–4, 44–6; *Le Soleil*, 28 February 1873.

[44] Donald Reid, *The Miners of Decazeville. A Genealogy of Deindustrialization* (Cambridge, MA, 1985), 64–71; Kale, *Legitimism*, 136.

not be relied upon; it attacked the Orleanist Duc de Decazes for his hostility to the restoration of the temporal power of the Pope and allied with rural Legitimists who disliked Deseilligny's industrialism.[45]

Orleanists had little to offer women either. One deputy maintained that women must 'spin wool and remain in the home'.[46] Only Dupanloup adopted more nuanced views, and he was close to Legitimism: education would sustain women's natural religiosity, innate gentleness, and domestic instincts in a fortified intellect.[47] Like many Catholics, he saw women as essential to the re-Christianization of men. His views had been shaped by a *féminisant* tendency in liberal Catholicism. Entire passages of his *Lettres* were inspired by his protégé, Netty du Boÿs.[48] Most Orleanists were horrified by Legitimist mobilization of women in pilgrimages.

Of all the Monarchists, Orleanists were most fearful of universal suffrage. They saw Republicans as demagogic manipulators of the prejudices and materialism of the mass, leading inevitably to revolution or Bonapartism.[49] They advocated restricted suffrage, but promised to govern in accord with the realities of the national character, using the symbols of monarchy and the Revolution to secure the allegiance of the mass. This strategy attracted better-off farmers and rural bourgeois in Normandy and parts of Brittany, who shared their attachment to the Revolution and order. Even there, attacks on universal suffrage lost votes to Bonapartists and Republicans.

Once Broglie judged restoration unlikely, he sought to create a republic without Republicans. A powerful upper house with the sole right to initiate legislation would prevail over a lower chamber, elected by 'reformed universal suffrage'. MacMahon would provide the essential symbol: 'a constitutional sovereign floating at a higher level above parties'.[50] This strategy was designed to counter Ultralegitimist and Bonapartist populism as much as Radicalism, and Orleanists and Moderate Republicans frequently allied against Bonapartists in by-elections.[51] Both also denounced the 'sensation' of the pilgrimages and the 'enormity' of Ultra pretensions, as did moderate Legitimists.[52]

[45] Reid, *The Miners*, 64–71; Patrice Lesueur, 'Quand le Haut Rouergue devenait Bonapartiste et le Bas Rouergue républicain et orléaniste', *Revue de Rouergue* 16 (1988), 523–84.

[46] Guy Blois, 'Les Partisans du roi à Clairac au début de la Troisième République (1870–1890)', *Revue de l'Agenais* 121 (1994), 605–10.

[47] Mgr. Dupanloup, *Lettres sur l'éducation des filles et sur les études qui conviennent aux femmes dans le monde* (Paris, 1902, first edition 1879). Broglie in *Le Français*, 12 December 1880.

[48] L. Desbords, 'Les Écrits de Mgr Dupanloup sur la haute éducation des femmes', in Françoise Mayeur and Jacques Gadille (eds), *Éducation et images de la femme chrétienne en France au début du XXe Siècle* (Paris, 1980), 25–40; J. Godel, 'De quelques femmes de lettres et de leur influence sur la pensée de Mgr Dupanloup', in *Éducation et images*, 47–60; Françoise Mayeur, 'Les Catholiques libéraux et l'éducation des femmes', in *Le Catholicisme libéral* (Grenoble, 1974), 421–44.

[49] Quoted in Girard, *Les Libéraux*, 235; Audiffret-Pasquier, *La Maison*, 37–8.

[50] 24 July 1874, in *Discours du Duc de Broglie*, 218; Callet, *Les responsabilités*, 5–10, 30–4.

[51] Guislin, 'Centre droit', 29–40; *Le Soleil*, 3 March, 12 October 1873.

[52] *Lacombe*, 22 September, 187; Alfred de Falloux, *Discours et mélanges politiques*, 2 vols (Paris, 1882), ii, 336–41.

MODERATE LEGITIMISM

In the National Assembly, the Legitimists split into two. Eighty Ultras, also known after the street (ironically, an impasse) in which they met as the 'Chevaux-Légers', refused constitutionalism. Another 120 formed the Réunion Colbert behind the Comte de Falloux. By 1874, there was a chasm between them—in 1876, Bishop Freppel of Angers, an Ultra deputy, excommunicated the liberal Falloux over a conflict concerning Church property. Moderates shared Orleanist constitutionalism, liberal Catholicism, and economic liberalism. Both Moderates and Orleanists distrusted Ultra populism almost as much as Republicanism and consequently both opposed universal suffrage, but sought a constitution in accordance with popular susceptibilities. Moderates differed from Orleanism in espousing 'associative' rather than individualist liberalism and in assigning religion a greater role in the regulation of social conflict. Their understanding of the nature of the ruling class differed accordingly. Also, Moderates 'associationist liberalism' provided potential openings for women, the clergy, and social reformers within the right.

Like all Monarchists, moderates endorsed the elite–mass distinction and saw Republicans as demagogues. One of them detested 'miserable lawyers', whose goal was 'not to conduct the nation's business naturally, simply, and honestly', but to 'show off their wit and conquer a more or less sham notoriety and popularity outside the Chamber'.[53] Moderates provide much of the historiographical evidence for the alleged merging of bourgeoisie and aristocracy, and they were the surest supporters of 'fusion' of the two royal families.

Yet moderate conceptions of the elite differed from that of their allies. Whereas Orleanists wanted to assimilate the aristocracy into the Third Estate, moderates sought a more equal alliance. A moderate deputy saw behind the Orleanist–Legitimist conflict 'the same old... struggle of bourgeois vanity against noble fatuity', and wished to 'calm these susceptibilities'.[54] While moderates evoked aristocratic honour, they saw legal privilege as incompatible with progress.[55] Charles Chesnelong, deputy and head of the Comités catholiques, felt that Broglie's proposed senate 'gave too much room to intellectuals and not enough to truly conservative and social influences'—landowners and natural social groupings. Whereas Orleanists favoured a suffrage based on age, residence, property, and/or wealth—theoretically open to any individual—moderates evoked the 'natural authorities' and preferred chambers of commerce, municipal welfare offices, parish councils, and fathers of families to elect deputies.[56]

Along with participation in civil society, honour underpinned individual worth. Like the Orleanists, moderates saw honour as attainable through manly engagement with the world—they dismissed Chambord as 'a wilful child who

[53] Locke, *French Legitimists*, 146–7, 201.

[54] Audiffret-Pasquier, *La Maison*, 157–8; Meaux, *Souvenirs*, 151.

[55] Louis d'Armailhac, *La Légitimité et le progrès, par un économiste* (Poitiers, 1871), 87–91; Kale, *Legitimism*, 37; Alfred de Meaux, *L'Assemblée nationale en 1872* (Paris, 1872), 5, 13.

[56] Falloux to Lacombe, 18 August and 4 September 1872, in *Lacombe*; Falloux 'De La Contre-révolution', 385–7; 'Du drapeau', 324, in *Discours*; Meaux, in *L'Assemblée nationale*, 17.

stubbornly demands the moon',[57] and admired the Orleanist princes for acting 'like princes'.[58] Schooling would provide an initiation to moral life, while leaving choice to the individual, and preparing men for modern society—not that of Saint-Louis.[59] Yet Falloux felt that Chambord believed too much in principles and the Orleanists too little.[60] Moderates valued military honour as much as Ultras did, seeing it both as a product of aristocratic breeding and as evidence of manly engagement with the world.

For different reasons, the moderates' followed the Orleanists in urging government in accordance with the national character. 'We do not have the right to concern ourselves only with our consciences', one of them said, 'we must provide France with institutions in accordance with the customs, penchants, pains, and *even the faults* of its past'.[61] That meant acceptance of the Revolution, which for one moderate was a 'beautiful moment in French history', bringing freedom of association (not of the individual), equality before the law, religious freedom, and elected assemblies. Moderates agreed that the people must identify with the regime through a symbol, for them the legitimate, but constitutional, monarchy. The regime must not depend on royal whim, but weakening royal prestige would undermine stability.[62]

Some saw Catholicism as more fundamental to the national character than monarchy—there lay a major difference with Orleanists—but they rejected the Ultras' theocracy. Moderates saw the dogma of the *Syllabus* as the 'stupid product of a cruel sect', but were as loyal to the Pope as any Ultra.[63] They sought the engagement of the clergy in the world, and aspired to conciliate Catholicism with 'modern society'. Some endorsed Dupanloup's distinction between the 'thesis', or principle, of anti-liberalism, and the 'hypothesis' of acceptance of liberalism in some cases.[64] Others saw Christianity as the true basis of liberty, and demanded a free church in a free society. They feared that too close an identification between Catholicism and politics would divide the faithful.[65]

In theory, Catholicism could flourish under any regime, and that potentially made a republic possible. Chesnelong felt that within limits his Comités catholiques could defend the Church within the Republic. Falloux went further, calling upon Moderate Republicans to 'baptise the beast'—catholicize the Republic.[66]

[57] La Borderie to Pocquet, 23 and 14 February 1874, in *Légitimistes parlementaires*, 169–70.

[58] Locke, *French Legitimists*, 32.

[59] Falloux, 'De L'Unité nationale', *Discours*, ii, 10–15, 39.

[60] Falloux to Lacombe, in *Lacombe*, 18 August 1872.

[61] Meaux, *Souvenirs*, 130–2 (author's italics); see also Falloux, 'Du Drapeau' and 'De La Contrerévolution', in *Discours*, ii, 319–44, 383–4.

[62] Armailhac, *La Légitimité*, 78; Chesnelong to Meaux, 11 September 1873, in Meaux, *Souvenirs politiques*, 159–69.

[63] Jean-Louis Ormières, 'Falloux et les catholiques libéraux (1848–1883)', in Bernard Plongeron (ed.), *Catholiques entre monarchie et république. Mgr Freppel en son temps* (Paris, 1995), 25–36.

[64] Girard, *Les Libéraux*, 213–23; Falloux, 'Du Contrerévolution', 371–4.

[65] Kerdrel to Pocquet, 26 April 1876, in *Légitimistes parlementaires*, 194; Falloux, 'Du Drapeau', 342–4; Charles Chesnelong, *Les Comités catholiques de France* (Paris, 1877), 3–4; Philippe Levillain, *Albert de Mun. Catholicisme français et catholicisme romain du syllabus au ralliement* (Rome and Paris, 1983), 683–4.

[66] Falloux, 'De L'Unité nationale', 88–93.

Such thinking opened the way to Christian Democracy or to 'Toryism', which meant defending property, family, and society within the regime.[67] Yet the obstacles to a constitutional conservatism were immense. One deputy feared that his ideal of 'the practice of the ten commandments of God under a representative regime' would provoke Orleanist merriment.[68]

This blend of Catholicism and liberalism informed moderates' view of the social question. Like Orleanists they saw religion as a means to propagate the work ethic and render tolerable the hardships of lower-class life, but were more interested in the social question. In fact, Social Catholicism owed as much to the moderates' blend of corporatism and associationist liberalism as to the Ultras' *noblesse oblige*. Falloux argued that since the economy obeyed immutable laws, the social question could not be resolved through the Ultra 'counterrevolution' or preaching resignation to the proletariat. He advocated instead Frédéric LePlay's eclectic social science.[69] Moderates saw in LePlay a means to reconcile progress and tradition, notably in his injunction to industrialists to manage their factories in a Christian spirit.[70]

Several Social Catholic businessmen sympathized with the moderates, including Benoist d'Azy (Forges d'Alais), Eugène Schneider (Le Creusot), and Léon Harmel (Val-de-Bois). These *patrons sociaux* used segregation of sexes in the factory and control over education and leisure in company towns to isolate workers from harmful influences and to moralize them. Employers enforced respect of the Sabbath (unless work was 'absolutely necessary') and personally attended baptisms, marriages, and funerals.[71] They drew on organicist ideas of hierarchy but did not seek to revive corporations. Rather, they urged the government to guarantee liberty for charities. They denounced Ultra anti-liberalism.[72]

Although moderates saw religion as underpinning necessary social inequality, their brand of Catholicism potentially threatened hierarchy. We have seen that Liberal Catholicism provided an outlet for du Boÿs' moderate feminism. Harmel, the most advanced Social Catholic, anticipated Christian Democracy. While he stressed the primacy of the employer, he granted workers' boards the right of consultation in management. He held that Catholic reforms would defeat Socialism, yet his seeming willingness to dilute employer authority worried the Ultra, Albert de Mun, who feared that Harmel's 'materialism' would contaminate workers with Revolutionary ideas, and subordinate the clergy to factory management.[73] For now, Harmel cut an isolated figure.

[67] La Borderie to Pocquet, 7 August 1872, and 23 and 24 February 1874, in *Légitimistes parlementaires*, 148–50, 164–6.

[68] Carron to Pocquet, 14 February 1873, B.-A. Pocquet du Haut-Jussé, 'Correspondance politique du colonel Carron', *Mémoires de la société d'histoire et d'archéologie de Bretagne* 40 (1960), 83–211 at 117.

[69] Falloux, 'De La Contre-révolution', 381–2.

[70] Alan Pitt, 'Frédéric LePlay and the family: paternalism and freedom in the French debates of the 1870s', *French History* 12, no. 1 (1998), 67–89.

[71] Maurice Aubry, *Le Travail des femmes dans les ateliers, manufactures et magasins* (Nancy, 1875).

[72] Gérard Noiriel, *Les Ouvriers dans la société française, XIXe–XXe siècle* (Paris, 1986), 77–82.

[73] Kale, *Legitimism*, 190–209, 310–16; Levillain, *Albert de Mun*, 413–44, 594–626; De Mun, 'Discours prononcé à la clôture de la troisième Assemblée générale des membres de l'Œuvre des cercles catholiques' (Paris, 1875), 101–5; Amadée de Margerie, *La Restauration de la France* (Nancy, 1872), 198–200.

In the National Assembly, moderate Legitimists were closer to Orleanism than to Ultracism. Moderates and Orleanists criticized the Ultras for unreflecting adhesion to principle; they advocated alliance of the bourgeoisie and aristocracy, representative government and moderate Catholicism. Both reluctantly accepted a non-monarchical regime so long as it preserved the rule of the 'best', limited the reach of popular sovereignty, and secured popular allegiance to the symbols of Revolution and monarchy. The moderates were more clerical, favoured a stronger executive, and were more interested in the social question than were the Orleanists. Their associationist liberalism provided openings for non-elite conservatives.

THE ULTRAS

Few Ultras believed that the privileges of the old-regime nobility could be re-established. However, they used economic and moral criteria to give it a special role. They contrasted the 'independence' of the landed aristocracy with the 'cupidity' of the bourgeoisie, and called for re-establishment of primogeniture, so that the aristocracy could regain its 'goods and blood'. They idealized influential rural families, involved in agriculture, devoted to local, perhaps national, government, and excluded civil servants, doctors, lawyers, and businessmen from their elite. This ruling class was divinely sanctioned: God made privileged individuals in the same way that he made oaks.[74]

Ultras accepted renewal of the nobility through co-option of those who 'lived nobly'—they always had. However, they were suspicious of the bourgeoisie as a class and evoked the 'mediocrity of the Third Estate'. They feared 'the ease with which industrial fortunes can be acquired' and that 'the influx of families without enthusiasm would prevent the modern nobility from becoming as influential as the old'. De Mun, the ex-soldier who emerged as the Ultras' most authoritative figure, believed the nobility to possess 'more blood' than other classes and to be more capable of good—so long as it abandoned hunting and cigars. Ultras felt that the future of the aristocracy depended on moral regeneration through Christianity, so non-Catholic landowners were effectively expelled from the ruling class: the elite must be characterized by 'firmness of principle'.[75]

Indeed, aristocratic Ultras assumed that they had been born with honour that made them innately superior to *roturiers*, and they must not lose it through unworthy actions. Honour meant the duty of the male heir to transmit property and moral worth down the generations. There was an element of knightly chivalry in this, evident both in the predilection for military careers and in the modelling of charitable organizations such as the Hospitalité Notre Dame de Salut upon the

[74] Gustave de Bernardi, *La Vérité divine. Christianisme et révolution* (Paris, 1870), 387–8; Antoine Blanc de Saint Bonnet, *La Légitimité* (Tournai, 1873), 327–8.

[75] Bernardi, *La Vérité*, 384; Blanc de Saint Bonnet, *La Légitimité*, 251; Levillain, *Albert de Mun*, 662–3; Amadée de Margerie, *La Restauration* (Nancy, 1872), 65–7.

Knights-Hospitallers.[76] Thus, Chambord's affection for the white flag was based on the assumption that he could lose his reputation by denying the principles upon which it rested.[77] 'Without my principle', he said, 'I am merely a fat man with a limp'.[78] Consequently, Ultras saw no value in certificates as qualifications for public service jobs. 'The capacity to govern', wrote an Ultra, 'is not visible and never has been'.[79] Indeed, high administrative positions should be unpaid.[80] Ultras used advantages that they had acquired through the generations, their lineage, and their social, economic, and cultural capital, to justify their right to govern in a society in which they lacked legal privilege.

Ultra obsession with principle and hierarchy dictated absolute hostility to 1789. The Revolution was a sin against the divine order that held in check the selfishness lurking in all people.[81] Yet rebellion was doomed to failure, for 'deicides inevitably became suicides'.[82] *Any* compromise with Revolutionary principles engendered decay. Consequently, Ultras condemned moderates and Orleanists for their impossible search for compromise between monarchy and national sovereignty.[83] De Mun claimed that only 'Catholic and Royalist counterrevolution' could confront revolution.[84]

Ultras were not unconditionally absolutist or even Monarchist. They accepted that Christianity could prosper as well under a republic as a monarchy—that was the Papal position. As aristocrats, they saw divine right as a threat to their own influence, and advocated decentralized power. However, following Catholic natural law doctrine, they argued that a people owed perpetual allegiance to whatever principle of authority it had chosen and that since the French had opted for monarchy 800 years previously, the National Assembly must proclaim unconditionally the return of Chambord. On this point, there was little difference between 'secular' Ultras whose primary loyalty was to the king and 'clericals' like de Mun, who reaffirmed in 1881 that Catholics must not endorse the Republic.[85]

Yet Ultras could not decide whether legitimacy resided principally in the monarchy or in the Church. Those who prioritized the monarchy were convinced that the king embodied the constitution, *including* 'le principe chrétien', and so restoration was enough to restore religion. 'The revolution', wrote an Ultra, has

[76] Elizabeth C. Macknight, 'Honor and the military', *Historical Reflections* 35, no. 3 (2009), 95–114; Ruth Harris, *Lourdes: Body and Spirit in the Secular Age* (London, 1999), 267–8.

[77] M.L. Brown, *The Comte de Chambord* (Durham, NC, 1967), 130.

[78] Marie de Roux, *Origines et fondation de la Troisième République* (Paris, 1906), 169.

[79] Jean-Baptiste-Victor Coquille, *La Royauté française* (Paris, 1874), 52, quoted in Hazareesingh, *From Subject to Citizen*, 105.

[80] Hazareesingh, *From Subject to Citizen*, 131–3.

[81] Bernardi, *La Vérité divine*, 339–50.

[82] Auguste Nicolas, *L'État sans dieu. Mal social de la France* (Paris, 1872), 23–4.

[83] Bernardi, *La Vérité*, 408–9; Kale, *Legitimism*, 322.

[84] Charles Molette, *Albert de Mun, 1872–1890. Exigence doctrinale et préoccupations sociales chez un laïc catholique d'apres des documents inédits* (Paris, 1970), 218.

[85] Bernardi, *La Vérité divine*, 339–43; De Margerie, *La Restauration*, 205–6, 300–7; Gustave Véran, *La Légitimité devant le catholicisme* (Paris, 1880); Kale, *Legitimism*, 319–20; Albert de Mun, *Dieu et le roi* (Paris, 1881); Levillain, *Albert de Mun*, 677–704; Kale, *Legitimism*, 315.

divided public opinion 'as the prism divides the rays of the sun. Suppression of the prism would restore the original white ray.' Monarchical Ultras feared subordination of the monarchical to the Christian cause.[86]

Clerical Ultras differed in seeing restoration as *insufficient* for national regeneration. De Mun argued that an austere Christian elite must regenerate society through perpetual affirmation of the *Syllabus*. His insistence upon the unity of the Catholic and Monarchical causes earned criticism from Monarchical Ultras for doubting Chambord's primacy.[87] De Mun's belief in public display of Catholicism fed into popular Catholicism, and that worried moderates and Orleanists, not to speak of Republicans.

The Catholic People

Ultras understood the distinction between elite and mass in religious terms. Emmanuel d'Alzon, founder of the Assumptionist Order, and Louis Veuillot, editor of *l'Univers*, celebrated the miracles and visions of popular piety, which they saw as an antidote to bourgeois rationalism. D'Alzon prided himself on his ability to speak to the people, while Veuillot had backed popular opposition to the civil and religious authorities' attempts to regulate the Lourdes shrine.[88] De Mun's Œuvre des cercles catholiques d'ouvriers (founded in 1871), was intended to be the nucleus of an elite-led popular movement for restoration. His efforts to reorganize the Legitimist party itself failed because Chambord and aristocrat-dominated departmental committees feared the rivalry of a party.[89] In fact, all Ultras believed in social hierarchy: d'Alzon, never forgot his aristocratic birth, while de Mun's Cercles were hierarchically organized. Yet Ultra leaders did not simply manipulate popular religion, for they believed in a timeless struggle of good and evil, prophesies, and cataclysms as much as ordinary Catholics did.

The Ultras' combination of hierarchy and populism was especially visible in the vogue for pilgrimages. Most spectacular was that of June 1873 to Paray-le-Monail, where in 1675 Christ had promised to reign over France if the king displayed the sacred heart on his banners. As the restoration campaign climaxed, Ultras claimed that the pilgrimage demonstrated that without Catholicism the people 'would no longer be a PEOPLE, but an agglomeration, not even a collection'. Whereas the Republican doctrine of popular sovereignty led to anarchy, the Catholic people were bound together in obedience to hierarchy, as in medieval times. Paray-le-Monail was a new 'crusade', uniting women with men, and workers with bourgeois.[90] At Lourdes, hierarchy was compatible with symbolic inversion, as the rich

[86] Véran, *La Légitimité devant le catholicisme.*

[87] De Mun, 'Discours prononcé, à la troisième Assemblée générale', 87–132.

[88] Harris, *Lourdes*, 214–13.

[89] De Mun, 'Discours prononcé à la troisième Assemblée générale', 87–132; Levillain, *Albert de Mun*, 492–536, 686–7.

[90] *L'Union*, 21–24 June 1873; Harris, *Lourdes*, 258; Raymond A. Jonas, 'Restoring a sacred centre-centre', *Historical Reflections* 20, no. 1 (Winter 1994), 95–123; Denis, *Les Royalistes*, 399–406.

carried the sick poor on stretchers. Yet some Catholics feared that the Virgin's predilection for communication with uncatechized peasant girls would undermine ecclesiastical authority. The liberal majority in the episcopate saw the Comités catholiques, which organized the pilgrimages, as a threat to their prerogatives.[91]

There were ambiguities in Ultra views of the social question too. They believed that charity would demonstrate that Christian fraternity was the true basis of relations between the classes and persuade the lower classes to accept their suffering.[92] Ultras were numerous in associations such as the industrialist Kolb-Bernard's Ordre de la Sainte-famille, which brought workers and employers of Lille together in worship, and Sociétés de Saint-Vincent de Paul, which offered religious instruction, food, and clothing to the unfortunate.[93] Yet whereas moderates and Orleanists did not contest market relations, Ultras expected the state to favour charity, and some saw industry as 'enslavement of the people'. Some argued that workers were entitled to the 'property of their labour' and that the rights of the employer should be correspondingly restricted. Others advocated compulsory corporations as a means to rigidify the social system and restrict industrialization. De Mun's opponents attacked him both as a Christian Socialist and as an advocate of the *ancien régime*.[94] Actually, he insisted on the guiding role of the 'elevated classes', a view that would lead to conflict with Christian Democrats in the 1890s. Nevertheless, the solidarity provided by de Mun's Œuvre des cercles contributed unintentionally to the emergence of Christian Democracy.

Women played an important role in Ultracism. Nuns and lay women constituted a significant proportion of pilgrims. Their involvement reflected the feminization of the clergy, but Ultra perceptions of gender roles mattered too. They saw the family as more important than the individual, and Legitimism as 'the extension of the family principle to the state'.[95] Consequently, the feminine sphere was larger for Ultras than for rival Monarchists, and Ultras accepted politicization of female activity, albeit delimited by 'female characteristics'. Thus, Ultras urged pious women to bring their unbelieving husbands back to the Church: 'the gentle and hidden method of domestic influence' would triumph over the husband's 'more supple mind'.[96] Likewise, women's natural religiosity and bounty would propagate the values that would reconcile the classes.[97] In 1879, de Mun attached a Comité des dames patronesses to the Œuvre des cercles, and urged members to preach the virtues of the movement.[98] Legitimist women promoted religious education in the villages of the Isère, and in the Haute-Loire they were the backbone of the Red Cross.

[91] Harris, *Lourdes*, 20, 42–3, 50–1; Jacques Gadille, 'Les Evêques de France', in Jacques Benoist (ed.), *Le Sacré-Coeur de Montmartre. Un Vœu national* (Paris, 1995), 59–65.

[92] Margerie, *La Restauration*, 195–204.

[93] Locke, *French Legitimists*, 186–97; Kale, *Legitimism*, 154–64.

[94] Blanc de Saint Bonnet, *La Legitimité*, 328–32; Hazareesingh, *Subject to Citizen*, 134; Levillain, *Albert de Mun*, 541–2, 594–603, 611, 621–2.

[95] Coquille, *La Royauté française*, quoted in Hazareesingh, *From Subject to Citizen*, 116.

[96] Margerie, *La Restauration*, 321–5.

[97] Margerie, *La Restauration*, 321–40; de Mun, 'Discours à la troisième Assemblée générale', 120–5.

[98] De Mun, 'Discours prononcé à l'Œuvre des cercles catholiques', 87–132; de Mun, *Allocution à l'Association des dames patronnesses du comité de l'œuvre* (Paris, 1879); Harris, *Lourdes*, 228–30.

These women were not simply the agents of men. In the Nord, bourgeois Legitimist women incorporated domesticity into an anti-materialist, conservative ideology that was at odds with their Republican husbands' liberalism. Their religiosity disrupted the strategies of moderate Royalists.[99]

Ultracism also provided leverage for the male clergy. Whether priests were able to play a part in politics depended upon their standing in local communities. In conservative Normandy, they were regarded with suspicion, and that fed into Orleanism or Bonapartism. In Brittany and in the Hautes-Pyrénées, the clergy were integral to village life; there had never been a tithe to set peasants against clergy, while the Republic seemed to represent conscription, taxation, and anticlericalism.[100] Democratization of village life had not undermined clerical influence, for widespread illiteracy—or lack of mastery of French—meant that peasants could not take over village administration. Clerical Legitimism prospered especially in Basque, Catalan, Breton, and Flemish regions.[101] The election of village councils by universal suffrage sometimes provided the 'priests' party' with popular sanction. Priests were also influential in southern towns like Nîmes and Montpellier, where conflict with Protestants had deep roots.[102]

Where the lower clergy favoured the Ultras and popular opinion backed it, the largely liberal and Gallican bishops found it difficult to enforce their wishes. In minority language regions episcopal authority over priests was notoriously fragile. In a by-election held in 1880 in Brest III, the clergy defied the moderate Bishop of Quimper by supporting the Ultra Bishop Freppel.[103] In the Hérault, the ultramontane clergy disliked their liberal vicars-general, but idolized the Ultra Bishop de Cabrières of Montpellier. The latter's intransigence owed something to his birth in a district of intense Catholic/Protestant conflict in the Gard.[104]

The clergy's alliance with Ultras was difficult. De Mun's plan to stand as a 'Catholic' at Pontivy in 1876 provoked Royalist fear of clerical independence. Local Royalists described the pro de Mun Cercles catholiques as 'theocratic and hardly Royalist', and claimed that the Bishop of Vannes supported de Mun because he wished to 'de-royalize his diocese' and forget that he was the son of a butcher.[105] For the moment, popular Catholicism was closest to the Ultras, without being unconditionally Royalist. It sometimes placed the Church above the monarchy, and in future it

[99] Magraw, 'The conflicts in the villages', 201–13; Auguste Rivet, *La Vie politique dans la Haute-Loire de 1815 à 1974* (Le Puy, 1979), 441–2; Bonnie Smith, *Ladies of the Leisure Class: The Bourgeoisie of Northern France in the Nineteenth Century* (Princeton, NJ, 1981).

[100] Caroline Ford, *Creating the Nation in Provincial France: Religion and Political Identity in Brittany* (Princeton, NJ, 1993), 78–96.

[101] Maurice Agulhon et al., *Les Maires en France du Consulat à nos jours* (Paris, 1986), 48; Yves Le Gallo, 'Aux Sources de l'anticléricalisme en Basse Bretagne. Un Recteur sous la Troisième République', *Bulletin de la Société archéologique du Finistère*, no. 99 (1972), 803–48.

[102] Cholvy, 'Religion et politique', 33–75.

[103] Étienne Cornut, *Monseigneur Freppel d'après des documents authentiques et inédits* (Paris, 1893), 286–95; Gadille, *La Pensée*, i, 163, 185–6; André Siegfried, *Tableau politique de la France de l'ouest sous la Troisième République* (Paris, 1964, first published 1913), 194.

[104] *Légitimistes parlementaires*, 189–90; Rivet, *La Vie politique*, 290; Secondy, *La Persistence*, 101–3.

[105] Levillain, *Albert de Mun*, 452–80.

would contribute to Christian Democracy. In some areas, popular Catholicism reinforced Bonapartism, which was equally frightening to moderate Royalists.

BONAPARTISM

Bonapartists never possessed more than thirty deputies in the Assembly, yet after 1873, they were neck-and-neck with Republicans in by-elections. In 1876, Bonapartists won twice as many seats as the Royalists. Historians' preoccupation with the longer-term decline of Bonapartism has caused them to underestimate this success. Moreover, they wrongly explain decline as the consequence of Bonapartism's absorption into notable-dominated Royalism.[106] Certainly, Prince Jérôme Bonaparte's Jacobin Republicanism was uninfluential, but we should not neglect the influence of authoritarian populism in the mainstream.

After 1870, this authoritarian populism revived because Orleanists largely deserted Bonapartism. The authoritarian democrat, Eugène Rouher, marginalized under the liberal Empire, now dominated, along with figures such as the Charentais Eugène Eschassériaux. These men had no sympathy with Royalism and saw the Empire as the only alternative to revolution. In January 1873, to ensure that Napoléon III was fit to ride into Paris, Bonapartist leaders pressured him to have the operation that killed him. The Emperor's demise confirmed the break with liberalism.[107]

Rouher's model was the Second Republic, in which Bonapartists had used the Royalists to defeat the Republicans, and then turned on the Royalists to establish the Empire. In 1873, Bonapartists helped the Royalists to overthrow Thiers, and Rouher defended 'order, religion, morality and the family' with Broglie;[108] then they unanimously opposed Chambord's restoration, and Orleanists were shocked to hear Rouher speak the language of the left. Subsequently, Bonapartists refused the Republican offer of alliance, but voted with them in the election of life senators in December 1875. In the 1876 elections, Rouher largely prevented absorption into the conservative alliance.[109] Those elections brought into parliament a new generation of intransigents, led by Paul de Cassagnac, who distrusted even the Bonaparte family for its experiment with liberalism. Cassagnac favoured the conservative alliance only in so far as it preserved imperialist chances, and condemned the 'white ghosts from the royal ossuary'.[110] After the 1876 elections, Rouher urged Bonapartists to support the most radical Republican proposals in order to show the impossibility of the Republic. This was too much for some Bonapartists, especially

[106] Ménager, *Les Napoléons*, 261–309; Rothney, *Bonapartism*, 175–85; Karen Offen, *Paul de Cassagnac and the Authoritarian Tradition in Nineteenth Century France* (New York, 1994), 27–45, 64–5, 75.

[107] Pairault, *Monsieur le Baron*, 169–70, 215.

[108] *L'Ordre*, 5 January 1873.

[109] Albert Duruy, *Comment les empires reviennent* (Paris, 1975), 94–9, 101–6; *L'Ordre*, 2 July 1873. See *Courrier de Bretagne*, 9 and 26 January 1876, for Bonapartist reservations regarding MacMahon in 1876.

[110] Cassaganac, *Empire ou royauté*, 5; Rothney, *Bonapartism*, 32–5.

the more conservative Bonapartist senators. Yet many Bonapartists voted in the National Assembly for municipal councils to elect mayors and for press freedom, thus provoking the *seize-mai* crisis. Nonetheless, Bonapartists allied with Royalists in the 1877 elections.[111]

Bonapartists had much in common with Royalists. They too belonged to the upper class and mocked the Republicans' lack of education, notoriety, experience, and moral authority. However, they differentiated themselves from Royalists by depicting themselves as an enlightened progressive elite, defined by military prowess and openness to business, but rooted in the countryside and the people. Their ideal ruling class was more self-consciously industrial and progressive than that of the Royalists. Some preferred large industry to small, and included science, the banks, and the civil service in their ruling class.[112] They also idealized the rural bourgeoisie and condemned the urban middle class, especially the 'vultures of the bar'. Post-Sedan Bonapartism posed as a rural reaction against the liberal Empire, imposed by the cities and the Parisian *literati*.[113]

Bonapartists also saw themselves as a national-military elite. Cassagnac's satirical account of an election campaign depicted the fictional Bonapartist candidate, Napoléon Vannes, like his creator, as the son of a country proprietor who had served as an officer under the first Napoléon and volunteered to fight as a common soldier in 1870. Cassagnac deployed class stereotypes against Royalists: the Orleanist candidate was a wealthy banker, worshipping profit and usury, who refused to sacrifice blood or money for the nation. The Legitimist was a talentless pseudo-aristocrat desperate to impress the local gentry and treasonable like his *émigré* ancestors. The Republican was a war profiteer.[114] Bonapartists defended Napoléon III's military reputation, accusing the Republicans of stabbing him in the back.[115] The Prince Impérial was allegedly ready, at 17 years of age, to mount his horse.[116]

With militarism went aggressive masculinity. Only the Radical Republicans rivalled them in readiness to duel for their honour—Cassagnac fought seventeen. To ensure respect for their sons, he wrote, fathers should put a sword in their hands. Orleanists, in contrast, believed that men were defined by self-mastery and reason, and so condemned the duel, while Catholics felt that the upper classes must set an example of Christian fraternity—Veuillot gave up duelling when he converted to ultramontanism.[117] Military virtue was linked to fatherhood. Cassagnac's satire contrasts the fertile Vannes with Republicans who had 'called for girls' while their country shed blood and with the Legitimist 'dry fruit' who marries a

[111] Pairault, *Monsieur le Baron*, 169–70, 215.

[112] *L'Ordre*, 10 January and 6 April 1873; Albert Duruy, *Comment les empires reviennent*, 39–61; Offen, *Cassagnac*, 51; Duruy, *Comment*, 27–9.

[113] *L'Ordre*, 1 July 1873; *Courrier de Bretagne*, 26 January 1876; Offen, *Cassagnac*, 28–9, 41.

[114] Paul de Cassagnac, *Bataille électorale. La Revanche du scrutin: Histoire de nulle part et partout* (Paris, 1875), 33–5, 63; Paul de Granier de Cassagnac, *Empire et royauté* (Paris, 1873), 30–4; *Le Pays*, 8 May 1874; *L'Ordre*, 10 August 1873; Rothney, *Bonapartism*, 30.

[115] *L'Ordre*, 5 January 1873; Offen, *Cassagnac*, 58–9.

[116] *L'Ordre*, 13 January 1873.

[117] *Le Pays*, 18 June 1874; Paul de Cassagnac, 'Preface', in Émile André, *Le Jeu de l'épée. Leçons de Jules Jacob* (Paris, 1887), xiii–xxvi.

'sterile girl'.[118] The other side of Bonapartist masculinity was a sharp assertion of women's maternal destiny. Napoléons I and III equated the size of a country's population with its weight in international affairs.[119] Bonapartists saw the falling birth rate as a sign of Roman decadence.[120]

Bonapartist military masculinity was inseparable from authoritarianism. In 1872, Cassagnac urged his constituents in the Gers to follow 'men who feel no peril and flinch at nothing to affirm [their] political rights'.[121] He gladly assumed the role of 'national policeman'. *L'Ordre* proclaimed that in the face of barbarian pillage, no 'interest [would be] defended by Chambord's pretended incarnation of "law"'; it asked the Legitimists 'where is your gendarme?'[122] Parliamentarianism was equally 'impotent', for Radicals and Communards inevitably exploited it.[123] When Cassagnac entered parliament, it was to 'respond to insult with insult'.[124]

The promise of order often attracted Royalists to Bonapartism, yet Bonapartism claimed to wield the sword in the interests of the people.[125] During the 1873 restoration campaign, Cassagnac and Eschassériaux reminded Legitimists that universal suffrage was a modern idea that could not be reversed. Heredity smoothed transmission of powers, but the people must choose the dynasty, and the sovereign must consult universal suffrage in the event of disagreement between himself and the nation. Cassagnac threatened Legitimists that if they attempted to enslave the nation then the party of the Empire, 'its whole body trembling,...will impose silence on the bad citizens, so that one can hear in all four corners of France *the great voice of the people, which is none other than the voice of God!*'.[126]

The Bonapartist strong man emerged from the people. Cassagnac described the Napoléons as 'your own kings, because they are of your own flesh and blood, *people* like you', whereas Royalists and Republicans despised the peasantry.[127] Gambetta's announcement of the arrival of the *nouvelles couches* was unnecessary, since the Empire had already established equality of opportunity. The Bonapartist elite comprised 'rural proprietors, dependent upon the conservation and improvement of their paternal inheritance, who were all sons of their own works'.[128]

Religion did not serve as a *terrain d'entente* with Royalism either, even though Bonapartism had become predominantly Catholic. With the exception of those

118 Cassagnac, *Bataille électorale*, 26–33.

119 Richard Tomlinson, 'The disappearance of France: French politics and the birthrate', *Historical Journal* 28, no. 2 (1985), 405–15.

120 *L'Ordre*, 7 January 1873.

121 Quoted in Offen, *Cassagnac*, 48–9.

122 Offen, *Cassagnac*, 54, 85; *L'Ordre*, 13 January 1873.

123 *Courrier de Bretagne*, 26 February 1876; *L'Ordre*, 11 January 1872; Offen, *Cassagnac*, 50–6; Rothney, *Bonapartism*, 38.

124 Offen, *Cassagnac*, 65.

125 Duruy, *Comment les empires reviennent*, 21–2.

126 Cassagnac, *Empire ou royauté*, 3–8, 15–18, 38–9. See also Cassagnac, *Bataille électorale*, 17–18; *L'Ordre*, 5 January 1873; *Journal de Bordeaux*, 10 January 1873; *Courrier de Bretagne*, 8 and 29 January 1876; Offen, *Cassagnac*, 53–6; François Pairault (ed.), *Mémoires d'un grand notable bonapartiste* (Pons, 2000), 169–70.

127 *L'Ordre*, 13 January and 10 August 1873; Cassagnac, *Bataille électorale*, 6–8; Offen, *Cassagnac*, 53–6.

128 *L'Ordre*, 15 July 1873. See also 5 January 1873.

from Protestant Charente-Inférieure, Bonapartists condemned anticlericalism and disavowed Jérôme's belief that only the Empire was strong enough to resist Rome.[129] Cassagnac stressed the generosity of the Empire to the Church and reminded electors that the Prince Imperial was a godson of the Pope. But whereas Legitimists saw religion as teaching Christian fraternity, Bonapartists evoked an avenging God.[130] They rejected divine right, opposed encroachment of the Church upon the civil authority, and criticized Legitimists for putting Church before country.[131] They feared that 'the exaggerations of Paray-le-Monail' would excite peasant anticlericalism.[132]

Bonapartists looked to the state rather than charity to establish class harmony. Even those who advocated alliance with the bourgeoisie argued that the changing world imposed new duties on the government, and called for the sponsorship of mutualist pensions and accident insurance, increased welfare spending, improved rural medicine, and public works. Rouher proposed an income tax, and Cassagnac endorsed the views of the populist Jules Amigues.[133] Such pronouncements confirmed Royalist suspicion that Bonapartists were 'hand in hand with the Communards'.[134] Bonapartists did not contest property in principle and they infantilized the people, yet their populism, statism, and social reformism challenged Royalists.

Popular Bonapartism

Bonapartist populism resonated most in the western and south-western countryside, especially from the Saumur region of Maine-et-Loire through Charente-Inférieure, Deux-Sèvres, Vienne, Indre, and the Dordogne to the Pyrénées in the south. Throughout this region Bonapartist peasants detested priests and nobles as heartily as Republicans did.[135] Many were fanatically devoted to the Emperor, fiercely egalitarian, and consumed with hatred for the rich. They believed that aristocrats and Republicans (the latter associated since 1848 with high taxes) were in league against the Emperor. In 1868, anticlerical and anti-noble disturbances swept through the west, triggered by fear that corn on the coat of arms of the new Bishop of La Rochelle signified restoration of the tithe. In August 1870, in the village of Hautfaye in the Dordogne, a group of peasants burned alive a young noble whom they accused of having shouted 'Vive la république!'.[136]

129 Offen, *Cassagnac*, 98–9.
130 Duruy, *Comment les empires reviennent*, 29; *L'Ordre*, 1 July 1873; Offen, *Cassagnac*, 52.
131 Duruy, *Comment les empires reviennent*, 29; *Courrier de Bretagne*, 16 February to 1 March 1876; Cassagnac, *Empire ou royauté*, 25, 52; *L'Ordre*, 10 August 1873.
132 Cassagnac, *Bataille électorale*, 38–41; *L'Ordre*, 10 August 1873; *Le Pays*, 26 July 1873; Offen, *Cassagnac*, 101.
133 Duruy, *Comment les empires reviennent*, 14–16, 34–6; Rothney, *Bonapartism*, 94–6, 246–7; *L'Ordre*, 4 September 1873.
134 *Lacombe*, 20 July 1875.
135 Landrévie, 'Le Tarn-et-Garonne', 300.
136 Alain Corbin, *Village of the Cannibals: Rage and Murder in France, 1870* (Cambridge, MA, 1992), 1–38.

In Charente-Inférieure, Eschassériaux's anticlericalism and endorsement of the Revolution struck a chord amongst the peasantry and he was instrumental in securing pardons for peasants convicted of offences related to the 1868 disturbances. He built an effective political machine thanks to his income from his extensive lands and his status as an imperial deputy. After 1873, he invoked imperial free trade—popular in a department where brandy exports were important. He accused Royalists of depriving the peasantry of the vote in order to restore the monarchy, and used the stab-in-the-back myth against Republicans.[137] In Gers, Cassagnac was not anticlerical, but local smallholding winegrowers loved his fierce anti-Royalism. He reputedly won a by-election in 1878 because peasants found him more revolutionary than the Republicans.[138]

Normandy, another Bonapartist bastion, was more conservative. In February 1871, the rural electorate voted overwhelmingly for wealthy Orleanist landowners. In peasant eyes, constitutional Monarchism had the advantage of simultaneously defending the Revolution and order. However, Orleanist compromises with Legitimists and opposition to universal suffrage gave it little chance of undermining Bonapartism in the longer term, for prosperous peasants combined attachment to property with fear of feudalism and the tithe. A Bonapartist tract demanded a 'revolutionary monarchy', able to reconcile popular and hereditary sovereignty. Bonapartists also competed with Republicans for the sympathy of the small peasant proprietors in the *bocage* of western Calvados, and Bonapartists alone addressed agricultural labourers' concerns.[139] Rather than multiply examples, suffice it to mention the Morvan region (Nièvre, Côte-d'Or, and Saône-et-Loire), where both Bonapartists and Republicans exploited the antipathy of small peasants to Legitimist forest owners, whom they accused of restricting peasants' rights to graze cattle and gather dead wood.[140]

Catholic Bonapartism did not necessarily signify conservatism. The Empire had defended popular religiosity—at Lourdes Empress Eugénie helped the locals resist the authorities' efforts to repress popular enthusiasm for Bernadette's vision.[141] In the Gers, Cassagnac depicted the people marching behind Bonapartist NCOs and 'white-haired priests', while in Calvados, Bonapartists insisted that Catholicism was a 'democratic religion'. In the previously mentioned Pontivy by-election, de Mun confronted the Bonapartist Abbé Cadoret, backed by many of the lower clergy. Cadoret denounced Republicans as town dwellers, contemptuous of peasant ignorance, and castigated de Mun as champion of the Jesuits and *ancien régime*. Cadoret foreshadowed Christian Democracy in tapping into regional

[137] Rothney, *Bonapartism*, 160–200; Jacques Gouault, *Comment la France est devenue républicaine 1870–1875* (Paris, 1954), 157–8.

[138] Offen, *Cassagnac*, 112.

[139] Quellien, *Bleus, blancs, rouges*, 22–43, 78–88, 123–4; Gabriel Désert, 'Les Paysans Bas Normands et la politique', *Annales de Normandie* 26, no. 3 (1976), 195–223; Ménager, *Les Napoléons*, 280.

[140] Alfred Massé, 'Les Partis politiques dans la Nièvre de 1871 à 1906', *Les Cahiers nivernais* 19 (April 1910), 1–86; Marcel Vigreux, *Paysans et notables du Morvan au XIXe siècle jusqu'en 1914* (Château-Chinon, 1987), 439–42, 586; Ménager, *Les Napoléons*, 229, 280, 301–2.

[141] Harris, *Lourdes*, 23–135.

Catholic identity. He portrayed himself as 'a priest, a man of the Morbihan, a son of the people', and invoked Christian equality. De Mun's partisans described Cadoret as a 'Communard'.[142]

Popular Bonapartism was weaker among workers, but significant in some areas. In Montauban, Catholic workers voted for a Catholic Bonapartist against the Protestant bourgeoisie.[143] In the 1877 election in the Nord, Amigues defeated a Republican industrialist partly thanks to an apocryphal letter from the Prince Imperial, urging his father to break with conservatism. In industrial Roubaix, Tourcoing, and the Anzin mining towns, Bonapartism expressed discontent against Republican and Orleanist employers. In Lille, in contrast, Republicans were more independent of business, and Bonapartism was correspondingly weak.[144] Many Bonapartist leaders viewed with suspicion Amigues' appeal to attend to workers' needs—Cassagnac excepted. Yet Bonapartists could not have done so without undermining their populist message to peasants, which depicted *all* the urban classes as united in a conspiracy against country dwellers.

CONCLUSION

On 5 February 1875, the votes of a few Orleanists ensured the passage of the Wallon amendment, which definitively established the Republic. Some constitutional Royalists had concluded that a conservative republic would dam the tide of Bonapartism and Radicalism. Once the Republic was agreed in principle, Orleanists and moderate Legitimists helped create a strong executive and senate, designed to preserve the rule of the best. Royalists soon regretted their actions. In the elections of 1876, the Republicans won 340 seats compared to 160 for Monarchists, including 94–110 Bonapartists, 50–60 Orleanists, and only 18–20 Legitimists. Gambetta was the obvious choice to head the government, but MacMahon called instead upon the Centre gauche. Following differences between deputies and the conservative Senate majority on press freedom and religion, MacMahon recalled Broglie to power in the coup of 16 May 1877 and then dissolved parliament.

In the ensuing campaign, the government transferred Prefects and Sub-Prefects and sacked civil servants. Through sponsorship of official candidates, it imposed unity on the right. Yet there was little agreement as to what victory would mean. MacMahon and Broglie wished to remain within the constitution. Audiffret-Pasquier wanted Aumale to become lieutenant-general. Cassagnac hoped to convert MacMahon's regime into an imperial state. Some Legitimists considered a *coup de force*, while the future *abbé démocrate*, Jules Lemire, saw MacMahon as 'an instrument of providence', defending Catholics against evil in the expectation of a king worthy to serve God.[145] The right did not produce a common platform;

142 See page 42; *Courrier de Bretagne*, 26 and 29 January, 16, 19, and 26 February, 1 March 1876.

143 Landrévie, 'Le Tarn-et-Garonne', 305–6.

144 Ménager, 'La Vie politique', 912–18, 1047–8, 1094, 1201, 1209, 1231–5; Ménager, *Les Napoléons*, 280–1; Rothney, *Bonapartism*, 78–100.

145 Fonds Mackau, 156 AP I 94 (dossier 2); Jean-Marie Mayeur, *L'Abbé Lemire. Un Prêtre démocrate 1853–1928* (Paris, 1968), 39.

MacMahon was quasi-mute. Locally, quarrels between Monarchist families continued.[146] The Republicans secured re-election of 321 of their 363 sitting deputies, but the right won only 180 seats (around 104 Bonapartists, 50 Legitimists, and 35 Orleanists). MacMahon was reduced to 'a good sign on a bad shop'.[147] In 1879, after the Republicans gained control of the Senate, he resigned.

The victorious Republicans carried out extensive purges of the administration and judiciary. Daniel Halévy spoke of a 'révolution des emplois'.[148] They sacked *fonctionnaires*, republicanized the Conseil d'État, and suspended hundreds of magistrates, while many more resigned. After the 1881 elections, the government began to secularize state schools and expelled religious orders. The purges reached down to road-menders in remote communes.[149]

For Monarchists, the advent of the 'nouvelles couches' signalled the domination of parliament by unknowns—men without 'experience' who had failed in professional life—bankrupt businessmen, lawyers without cases, and doctors without patients. Some hoped to unite the right in defence of the Church. In 1880, they created a Comité de défense religieuse under Chesnelong. Yet it was torn apart by conflict between Legitimists and their opponents. In the 1881 general elections, Monarchists were reluctant to stand; thanks to a high abstention rate, they dropped to 25 per cent of the vote and ninety seats.[150]

While one may only speculate as to what would have happened had Chambord proved flexible, the defeat of Monarchism was not exclusively attributable to him. Contrary to the view that Monarchist political divisions obscured deeper unity as notables, I have argued that his decision makes sense only in relation to disputes among Monarchists concerning the very shape of the ruling class and society more generally. Chambord thought in terms of divine right, aristocracy, and religion. Broglie endeavoured to unite Monarchists around order, but only Orleanists and moderate Legitimists understood order as he did. These constitutional Monarchists hoped that their insight into popular susceptibilities would allow them to govern on the nation's behalf. They sought to restrict the franchise, and reserve decision-making to the best, assembled in parliament.

Constitutional Monarchists believed that Ultra fanaticism excited the passions of the masses and destroyed the enlightened values upon which progress depended. Ultras responded that constitutional Monarchists' compromise with the Revolution led to anarchy. Orleanists and moderates attempted to incorporate conservative Bonapartism into the Moral Order majority, but feared its authoritarian populism. A Royalist newspaper in the Pas-de-Calais, asked whether 'the greater evil was the [Radical] chest infection of which one might be cured or the

[146] Martin Simpson, 'The death of Henri V: the Legitimists without the Bourbons', *French History* 15, no. 4 (2001), 378–99 at 391, 393.

[147] Kerdrel to Pocquet, 4 December 1877, in *Légitimistes parlementaires*, 200–2.

[148] Daniel Halévy, *La Fin des notables*, ii. *La République des ducs* (Paris, 1930), 378.

[149] Patrick Cabanel, 'La République contre les catholiques', in Marc-Olivier Baruch and Vincent Duclert (eds), *Les Serviteurs de l'état. Une Histoire politique de l'administration française* (Paris, 2000), 169–82; Jean-Pierre Machelon, *La République contre les libertés?* (Paris, 1976), 282–300.

[150] Levillain, *Albert de Mun*, 656–76.

[Bonapartist] tuberculosis that killed slowly'?[151] For their part, Bonapartists regarded Legitimists and Orleanists as unmanly enemies of the nation, too self-interested to provide the masses with the reforms or the master they required.

Monarchists were also constrained by the fact that economic growth, democratization of village life, and the expansion of the state and the clergy had strengthened popular conservatism. There were tensions between Royalists and the clergy, while women did not necessarily share the outlook of male Monarchists. Sometimes, Catholic and Bonapartist populism converged. Often, Bonapartism rivalled Republicanism as a vehicle for peasant populism. There were so many examples of Bonapartist voters preferring Republican to Royalist candidates in run-off elections that the Prefect of Côte du Nord urged a defeated Bonapartist to remain in the race in order to prevent a Republican victory.[152] One Bonapartist commented, 'Our good peasants are easy to lead when one leads them where they want to go.'[153]

The divisions of Monarchism explain the failure of restoration, but not necessarily its longer-term decline. No general explanation works: neither the erosion of notable power nor the appeal of Gambetta's conservatism. Of course, the Monarchist victory of 1871 depended on exceptional conditions, and Republican victories quickly revealed how much so. Yet where Monarchists resisted successfully, it was not because notable methods were more effective or because their constituencies were more backward. Orleanists retained influence in the more prosperous Norman countryside, while Legitimists won in areas such as the south, Brittany, and the Vendée, where Catholic–Protestant struggles or memories of the Chouannerie divided the population. Above all, Bonapartism represented a populist alternative to Republican democracy in the southwest and other areas.

Moreover, Monarchism was far from defeated. It retained considerable strength in the diplomatic corps, senior civil service, business, agriculture, and the Church. The aristocracy, women especially, remained faithful to the king. In 1885, Monarchists made substantial gains as '*conservatives*', revealing how uncertain popular allegiance remained. In 1889, with their Boulangist allies, they came close to victory.

151 Guislin, *L'Affirmation*, 89–90.

152 Gouault, *Comment la France est devenue républicaine*, 184, 188; Ménager, *Les Napoléons*, 297–8; Alain Corbin, *Archaïsme et modernité en Limousin au XIXe siècle* (Paris, 1975), 937–43.

153 Fernand Giraudeau, *Vingt ans de despotisme et quatre ans de liberté* (Paris, 1874), 65.

3

From *Conservatisme* to Boulangism (1884–1889)

> **General** is always 'brave'. Generally does what is not his job, such as ambassador, village councillor, or head of the government.
>
> Gustave Flaubert, *Dictionnaire des idées reçues* (1880)

Conservatisme has attracted little historical attention, even though it was central to Monarchist politics for years to come. It involved the difficult trick of setting aside dynastic ambitions without abandoning Monarchism, and of attacking the Opportunists (Moderate Republicans) for colonial misadventure, religious persecution, and financial mismanagement. In the 1885 elections, the strategy appeared fruitful. Under the leadership of Baron Armand de Mackau, the recently formed Union conservatrice gained 45 per cent of the vote on the first ballot. Thanks to alliance between Opportunists (as the Moderate Republicans were now known) and Radicals in the second round, the Republicans still won 383 seats. However, Monarchists concluded that the transfer of only half a million voters would bring victory. Furthermore, since the Chamber consisted of three equal blocks—Radical, Opportunist, and Monarchist—new possibilities and dilemmas emerged. Monarchists could ally with Opportunists in defence of the social order, but that carried the danger of republicanizing the right, and thus threatening the social order. Alternatively, they could ally with Radicals against Opportunism, but that too endangered order. Initially, neither option was possible, for the Opportunists continued their alliance with the Radicals, and to guarantee the latter's support, they gave General Georges Boulanger the post of War Minister.

Boulanger was the son of a Welsh noblewoman and a Breton lawyer. As the Marquis de Breteuil put it, his political convictions had never embarrassed him. He had been Bonapartist under the Empire; under Moral Order, he participated in pilgrimages and wrote obsequious letters to his former commander, the Duc d'Aumale. As War Minister, he initiated reform of conscription, long demanded by Radicals, and expelled the royal princes from the Army—Aumale included. In January 1896, he expressed sympathy for striking Decazeville miners. His dashing presence in the military review of 14 July, celebrated in Paulus' *café-concert* song, *En revenant d'la revue*, confirmed his popularity with Radicals. In April 1887, Boulanger's intemperate intervention in a frontier incident with Germany reinforced his standing among Radicals, but horrified Opportunists and Monarchists. To prevent Boulanger's return, Monarchists took the unprecedented step of supporting Rouvier's Opportunist cabinet, thus confining the Radicals to opposition.

Out of office, Boulanger endeavoured to win back the War Ministry, with the support of the Communard Henri de Rochefort's *L'Intransigeant*, Parisian Blanquistes, and Déroulède's Ligue des patriotes, while state employees petitioned in his favour. On 23 May, 38,457 people wrote Boulanger's name on their ballots in a Paris by-election. Alarmed, the government exiled Boulanger to a command in Clermont-Ferrand, provoking 20,000 demonstrators to delay his train's departure. Boulanger's fortunes improved in late November, when President Grévy resigned because his son-in-law, Daniel Wilson, had been selling honours. Radicals and Boulangists mobilized against the possibility that the Opportunist, Jules Ferry, might succeed Grévy. At this stage, Boulangists still opposed Opportunism from a Radical-Jacobin standpoint, and attacked Ferry for his alleged pro-monarchism.

Yet in October, unbeknown to his Radical backers, Boulanger's emissaries informed the pretender that if Monarchists helped him return to power, the General would restore the king. Boulanger also contacted the radical Bonapartist, Georges Thiébaud, and visited Prince Jérôme in Switzerland. On 26 February 1888, thanks to Thiébaud, Boulanger appeared on the ballot in multiple by-elections, although as a serving officer he was ineligible. He gained 55,000 votes in seven departments. On 15 March, the government released him from active duty, leaving him free to imitate Louis-Napoléon's use in 1848 of the plebiscitary potential of multiple candidacies and departmental list voting. He resigned after each victory, provoking new elections. He won in the Aisne, Dordogne, Nord (twice), Somme, and Charente-Inférieure.

Most Radicals deserted Boulanger as a danger to the regime, but a minority joined Thiébaud, Déroulède, and Rochefort in a Comité de protestation nationale, while a host of Boulangist committees emerged in Paris, mostly from Radicalism and its Socialist margin.[1] Meanwhile, Monarchists left Boulanger a clear field in by-elections and financed his campaigns. A secret Committee of three Orleanists, two pro-Orleanist Bonapartists, one Imperialist, and one Legitimist directed Monarchists' relations with Boulanger. Monarchists had thus embraced the third possibility opened up in 1885: alliance with the Radicals against parliament. On 29 January 1889, the strategy appeared to have worked, for Boulanger won spectacularly in Radical Paris. The myth developed that Boulanger was too timid to seize power. In fact, Boulangists confidently awaited victory in the general elections of September.

Historians disagree on whether Boulangism 'ultimately' belonged to the left or right, or represented a new radical nationalism, perhaps fascism.[2] For Odile Rudelle, Boulangism mobilized moderate electors, who were desirous of pacification within the Republic and tired of a political class that was unable to cast off

[1] For a survey of these organizations, see Bertrand Joly, *Nationalistes et conservateurs en France* (Paris, 2008), 49–54.

[2] Frederick Seager, *The Boulanger Affair: The Political Crossroads of France* (New York, 1968), 174; Zeev Sternhell, *La Droite révolutionnaire (1885–1914). Les Origines françaises du fascisme* (Paris, 1978).

anachronistic disputes.[3] For Zeev Sternhell, Boulangism originated in the extreme left's frustration with parliamentarianism, and its synthesis of nationalism and socialism looked forward to fascism. In contrast, Philippe Levillain demonstrated the extent of Monarchist involvement, which he attributed to the impasse of *conservatisme*, but was circumspect on the nature of the Boulangism.[4] William Irvine also emphasized Royalist participation, and detected conservative content under the surface of 'radical' Boulangism. He saw this conjunction of conservatism and extreme nationalism as proto-fascist.[5] Bertrand Joly depicted Boulangism as a disparate movement of those left out by political and social 'modernization', from Monarchists to artisans.[6]

There is truth in all these characterizations, but Boulangism cannot be reduced to any of them. I shall ask why different groups became involved in it and what they understood it to be, and I shall explore the strategies they employed in their struggles with allies and enemies. I shall also stress the complexity of the relationship between Boulangist leaders and their followers: Levillain and Irvine rightly illuminate Monarchist leaders' roles,[7] but I shall suggest that rank-and-file pressure pushed Monarchist leaders further down the authoritarian-populist road than they would otherwise have ventured, and transformed Monarchism in the process. Bonapartist attraction to Boulangism reinforced this radical populism, a dimension neglected by historians, in spite of Rémond's view that Boulangism was a form of Bonapartism.[8] Notwithstanding, one cannot reduce Boulangism to Bonapartism either, for both ideologies were disparate and contested, and the frontiers between Bonapartism, Royalism, Radicalism, Socialism, and Boulangism were indistinct. Historians have tended to discuss Monarchist and radical Boulangism separately. In fact, while there was no single Boulangism, emergence from a common culture facilitated collaboration in particular contexts.

BOULANGISM, RADICALISM, AND MONARCHISM IN POLITICAL CULTURE

To begin with, Boulangism drew upon the opposition of left and right to Orleanist and Opportunist parliamentarianism. We saw in the previous chapter that the Republicans and constitutional Monarchists who framed the constitution intended to channel social and political conflict into elections and parliamentary debate. They espoused an elitist conception of democracy: one might expect from the people only a general aspiration for good government, so long as Prefects, teachers,

[3] Odile Rudelle, *La République absolue. Aux Origines de l'instabilité de la France contemporaine* (Paris, 1982).

[4] Philippe Levillain, *Boulanger, fossoyeur de la monarchie* (Paris, 1982).

[5] W.D. Irvine, *The Boulanger Affair Reconsidered* (Oxford, 1989).

[6] Joly, *Nationalistes*, 116.

[7] Irvine, *The Boulanger Affair*, 106, 108, 152.

[8] René Rémond, *Les Droites en France*, fourth revised edition (Paris, 1982), 150–3.

officers, landowners, businessmen, justices, or priests, depending on political persuasion, guided its choice. Deputies would interpret the will of the people through reasoned debate, as sovereign individuals (so party discipline was alien to them). Furthermore, in reaction against the Empire's authoritarianism and the *seize-mai* coup, the Republicans established the primacy of parliament. The Président de la République was weak, while the Président du conseil des ministres was simply first among equals, possessed of his own ministry, lacking the coordinating role of the British Prime Minister (the difference is so vital that I shall use 'Président du conseil', not 'Prime Minister'). Parliament expected to be associated with day-to-day government.

Radicals rejected parliamentarianism in the name of the direct democracy, demonstrations, and strikes of traditional Republicanism. With some justice, they condemned the constitution as 'Orleanist'; they demanded partial renewals of the Chamber and suppression of the Senate, while Alfred Naquet, the future Boulangist, advocated the referendum and direct election of the president.[9] Some Radicals espoused the populism of Auguste Chirac and Numa Gilly (the latter a Radical, then Boulangist, deputy), who denounced manipulation of government and economy by the 'new feudalism' of big business, perhaps Jewish.[10] In the National Assembly, Radicals and Bonapartists had sometimes combined in opposition to Orleanist parliamentarianism; Naquet and others had joined Bonapartists in voting for a plebiscite.[11]

Monarchists criticized parliamentarianism for lacking authority and continuity; even Orleanists believed that strong government should balance parliamentarianism. Monarchists also saw parliamentarianism as excluding the talented from government, a view apparently confirmed by Republican purges of the judiciary and Army. Some Monarchists also attacked parliamentarianism in the name of Bonapartist and Catholic populism, and Boulangism would draw upon both forms of antiparliamentarism. Left and right also shared a catastrophic view of history in which bourgeois corruption would eventually produce popular insurrection and national redemption. In 1888–1889, Boulangists, Radicals, and the right each hoped to capture constitutional revisionism for themselves.[12]

Nationalism provided another potential meeting ground. Certainly, Radical *revanchism* worried Monarchists, for it reminded them of the Commune; Boulanger's warmongering incited Monarchists to back Opportunists against him in 1887.[13] Yet Monarchists were not immune from nationalism, even if they identified the nation with the Monarchy rather than the people. They believed that democracy had undermined military discipline, and that only a Monarchy could

[9] James R. Lehning, *To be a Citizen* (Ithaca, NY, 2001), 10–11.

[10] Patrick Hutton, 'The impact of the Boulangist crisis upon the Guesdist party at Bordeaux', *French Historical Studies* 7, no. 2 (Fall 1974), 226–44; Patrick Hutton, 'The Boulangist movement in Bordeaux politics', PhD Dissertation, University of Wisconsin, 1969.

[11] François Pairault, *Monsieur le Baron. Eugène Eschassériaux, éminence grise du bonapartisme 1823–1906* (Paris, 2004), 196–7.

[12] Rudelle, *La République*, 207–9.

[13] Henri de Breteuil, *La Haute société. Journal secret, 1886–1889* (Paris, 1979), 31 May 1887.

restore it and make revenge possible. De Mun advanced this case in a parliamentary speech, and evoked national glory so eloquently that the whole chamber rose and applauded.[14] De Mun's speech foreshadowed both Boulangism and the Ralliement in that he did not mention Monarchy. For the moment, most Monarchists were more orthodox. They held that revenge depended on alliance with monarchist Russia and Britain.[15] Yet the nationalist Déroulède introduced the idea of a Russian alliance into Republican circles. The populist wing of Monarchism was more explicitly *revanchard*. The Catholic *La Croix* preached revenge, even if suspicious of Radical *revanchism*; Bonapartists approved Boulanger's bellicosity from the start.[16]

Imperialism also represented common ground. Radicals and Monarchists both attacked Ferry's colonial misadventures, while endorsing colonialism in principle. Monarchist critics of the Tonkin reverse of 1885 were more concerned to highlight the Republic's incompetence than to attack colonialism itself. Édouard Hervé, director of the Monarchist *Le Soleil*, refused to abandon Tonkin, let alone the rest of Indochina, and insisted that France would take revenge at all costs, for in his view the honour of France was even more important to Monarchists than to Republicans. He rejected only Ferry's proposed march on Beijing. *Le Gaulois* pointed out that Monarchists put France above the king, and had shed blood at Tonkin under the Republican flag.[17]

Meanwhile, two developments politicized national identity and in ways that brought the extremes together. First, immigration became a political issue and was linked to economic nationalism. Although in the 1880s the economy was depressed, the decade witnessed the expansion of iron, steel, and coal production, while the Freycinet Plan of 1881 boosted railway and port construction. Thanks to the low birth rate and peasants' reluctance to work in industry, immigrants constituted a significant part of the new industrial workforce, while Parisian artisan industries also witnessed an influx of foreign workers. By 1881, more than a million foreigners resided in France. Politicians of left and right saw demands for restrictions on immigration as an ideal way to prove their sensitivity to voters' concerns during the economic depression.[18] Opportunists' opposition to controls fuelled the belief that they were unpatriotic. Immigration also coincided with a campaign on the part of textile and iron producers for tariff protection; it was cast as defence of 'national labour', in the hope of enlisting workers and defusing class struggle—even though employers generally defended free movement of labour.[19] On the left, Marxists often contradicted their internationalism in practice, while older Socialist and Radical traditions were nationalist anyway.

[14] Levillain, *Boulanger*, 33.

[15] Breteuil, *La Haute société*, 10 August, 14 October 1887.

[16] Irvine, *The Boulanger Affair*, 189, n. 23.

[17] *Le Soleil*, 31 March, 1 April 1885; *Le Gaulois*, 30 March 1885; Herman Lebovics, *The Alliance of Iron and Wheat in the Third French Republic 1860–1914: Origins of the New Conservatism* (Baton Rouge, 1988), 156–8.

[18] Gérard Noiriel, *The French Melting Pot: Immigration, Citizenship and National Identity*, tr. Geoffroy de Fourcade (Minneapolis, 1996).

[19] Lebovics, *The Alliance*, 51–73.

Secondly, June 1889 witnessed enactment of the first coherent law on nationality. Opportunists claimed that its provision for easier naturalization would compensate for the low French birth rate, overcome the labour shortage, and assimilate immigrants into the nation. Opportunists were not free from fear of the 'other', for they were determined to prevent the formation of autonomous ethnic communities on French soil and to refuse naturalization to those who allegedly only wanted public assistance. The Radicals were still more contradictory, for they demanded both easy naturalization and greater restrictions on foreign workers.[20] The right rarely contested the law in principle, but wished to make it more restrictive. The Monarchist Henri de Gavardie, who led opposition in the Senate, evoked the threat to French jobs and the danger of naturalizing undeserving characters, while mixing religious and racist definitions of France. Significantly, he claimed to speak for popular opposition to the law.[21] Xenophobia was also connected to the 1887 military service law, for many believed that children of foreigners avoided conscription and thus gained an advantage in the labour market. Boulanger's bellicosity intensified fears that immigrants were spies, and as War Minister, he extended surveillance of foreigners. The precise relationship of the nationality question to Boulangism is complex, but the potential for a meeting of extremes was present.

Meanwhile, racial science and Darwinism entered political discourse generally. Among Radicals, Clemenceau was especially fond of quoting Darwin, while Opportunists and constitutional Monarchists justified imperialism with racist arguments.[22] Renan and Taine, both advocates of constitutional Monarchism, pioneered the application of race to politics. Legitimists became less inclined to reject race science in the name of religion, and had recourse to Darwinist ideas—Gavardie spoke of workers as engaged in a 'struggle for life'.[23] Just as Barrès was adopting a blood-and-soil definition of the nation, expansion of the popular press, thanks to mechanization and the press law of 1881, nationalized racial stereotypes, and *faits divers* rubrics highlighted immigrant crime.

Monarchist and radical Boulangists also shared the elite–mass distinction, while constructing it differently. We have already noted Monarchists' belief that the Republic substituted the rule of mediocrity for elite government. Political failure caused them to question the qualities of their own leaders; Breteuil regretted the Orléans family's inability to 'speak to the people'.[24] These doubts reinforced the belief that the defeat of 1870–1871 was due to the emasculating effects of civilization upon the French elites, compared to the 'primitive' Germans. While Opportunists and constitutional Monarchists saw the team sports of English public schools as the antidote to degeneration, radicals of left and right hoped that gymnastics, fencing, and boxing would counter individualism and that contact with the people would

[20] *Journal officiel. Chambres des députés* (hereafter JOCD), 16 March 1889, 597.

[21] *Journal officiel. Sénat* (hereafter JOS), 11 February 1886, 123–4; Cécile Mondonico-Torri, 'Aux Origines du Code de la nationalité en France', *Le Mouvement social* 171 (1995), 31–46.

[22] Breteuil, *La Haute société*, 7 November 1886.

[23] JOS, 11 February 1886, 123–4.

[24] Breteuil, *La Haute société*, 25 July, 16 October 1887.

maintain the virility of the elite. This encounter with the people would be just sufficient to inoculate the elite against the dangers of sedentary civilization, without undermining its superiority.[25]

This logic makes sense of Boulanger's often-noted, but rarely analysed, reputation as a '*café-concert* general', for the *café-concert* provided another potential meeting point of left and right. The Duc de Broglie condemned Boulangism's music-hall ethos and likened compromise with it to frequentation of prostitutes.[26] Such dismissals reflected the widespread view that *café-concerts* epitomized the decadence and feminization of French culture. Yet bourgeois attitudes to the *café-concert* were complex, for the institution was shaped by popular resentments, censorship, and commercialization. Since the 1860s, large *café-concerts* on Haussmann's Grands Boulevards, of which the Chat noir (1881) and Folies Bergères (1882) were best known, had emerged alongside the host of less reputable establishments in working-class Paris. The former were 'respectable', but borrowed the dangerousness of the latter. Even the best *café-concert* permitted a degree of social mixing not possible in salon society. In the fashion for 'encanaillement' (slumming), the wealthy played at being part of the 'rabble', suffering the insults of *café-concert* performers, while occupying segregated spaces. Students, then exclusively upper class, were notoriously attracted to *café-concerts* of the lowest rank. Their elders were the heirs of the 'flâneurs', strollers on the boulevards, who observed crowds from a distance, while preserving their own autonomy, differentiating themselves from 'badauds', those who 'gawked' indiscriminately. Habitués of the *café-concert* mixed aristocratic *désinvolture* with popular wit and slang. Even the Prince of Wales could be insulted at the Chat noir. The Royalist, pro-Boulanger *Gaulois* endeavoured to convince its high-society audience of the sophistication of Paulus' songs.[27]

Boulangism was politicized *encanaillement*. In the 1880s, thanks to timid relaxation of censorship, *café-concert* songs began to broach controversial subjects. They mixed socialism, populism, anticlericalism, patriotism, xenophobia, and moral messages, lauding traditional femininity and rural life. Most of the songs were the work of unknown authors, perhaps government employees (a source of support for Boulangism), hiding behind anonymity. During the Boulanger crisis, the authorities continued to censor songs that mocked the government, while singers endeavoured to subvert censorship.[28] Boulangism was unofficially headquartered *chez* Durand on rue Royale. The General also attended the Chat noir. Leading Boulangists, such as Rochefort and Déroulède, combined politics with play- and song-writing. In the *café-concert,* Boulangists rubbed shoulders with Royalist aristocrats such as Boni de Castellane, dandy and boulevardier, and Radicals such as

[25] Christopher E. Forth, *The Dreyfus Affair and the Crisis of French Manhood* (Baltimore, 2006).

[26] Alan Grubb, *The Politics of Pessimism: Albert de Broglie and Conservative Politics in the Early Third Republic* (Newarck, 1996), 341.

[27] *Le Gaulois*, 26 June 1889; Gregory Shaya, 'The *flâneur*, the *badaud*, and the making of mass public in France, circa 1860–1910', *American Historical Review* 109, no. 1 (2004), 41–77; Concetta Condemi, *Les Cafés-concerts. Histoire d'un divertissement, 1849–1914* (Paris, 1992).

[28] Eva Kimminich, 'Chansons étouffées. Recherche sur les *Cafés concerts* au XIXe siècle', *Politix* 4, no. 14 (1991), 19–26.

Clemenceau.[29] While the Goncourts lamented that humming *En revenant d'la revue* had 'conquered the most intelligent and delicate mouths', pedlars sold the song in the villages.[30]

Duelling too allowed left and right to converge, and it too illuminates Boulangist conceptions of the elite–mass relationship. Catholics opposed the duel for its violence, while Moderate Republicans preferred rational debate. In contrast, the Bonapartist Cassagnac, the Radical Clemenceau, and the Boulangists Rochefort and Déroulède, fought numerous duels. For them, duelling was an intrinsic part of their right as men equal to other men to defend their honour. Duelling supposedly countered the physical degeneration that excessive civilization entailed, and so Boulangists criticized Republicans for avoiding duels and linked their lack of will to an excess of 'lard'.[31] The duel would also regulate violence so that men did not regress to a primitive state, and it would bring them together across political boundaries: Cassagnac attended the same *salle d'armes* as the Radical Arthur Ranc, and claimed that he would have been a Radical, had he not been a Bonapartist.[32]

In July 1888, the tubby Radical Président du conseil, Floquet, defeated Boulanger in a duel, provoked by his having called the General a 'pion de lycée' in a parliamentary debate. The quarrel illustrates both the common ground and the conflict between populisms: the debt to a common political culture does not mean that there was a 'fundamental' similarity between left and right Boulangists, for each saw the movement differently. Moreover, criticisms of parliament spread well beyond Boulangism, and some Opportunists shared it. Also, in different ways, the Opportunists were as racist as the Boulangists. Rather, in a particular context, particular groups privileged the common ground that potentially exists between any ideologies, and were transformed in the process.

MONARCHISM AND BOULANGISM

In 1886, Monarchists had little faith in the future of the Republic. Legitimists believed that no regime could survive unless based on divine law; Orleanists assumed that orderly progress depended on the allegiance of the masses to a monarchy; Bonapartists held that government could be based only on military authority and popular sovereignty. The Republicans were demagogues who exploited the materialism and passions of the febrile mass, from which they were insufficiently distant. The right believed a new Commune to be likely, and interpreted each ministerial crisis as a portent of collapse, in which the people's Monarchist instinct would reappear.

[29] Gustave Coquiot, *Les Cafés-concerts* (Paris, 1891); T.J. Clark, 'The Bar at the Folies-Bergères', in Jacques Beauroy, Marc Bertrand, and Edward T. Gargan (eds), *The Wolf and the Lamb: Popular Culture in France* (Saratoga, CA, 1977), 233–52, 243–4.

[30] Condemi, *Les Cafés-concerts*, 135–6; Michael Burns, *Rural Society and French Politics: Boulangism and the Dreyfus Affair, 1886–1900* (Princeton, 1982), 82.

[31] *L'Autorité*, 12 March 1889.

[32] Preface by Paul Cassagnac, Arthur Ranc, and Anatole de La Forge, in Émile André, *Le Jeu de l'épée. Leçons de Jules Jaco* (Paris, 1887), xiii–xxvi.

Monarchists were less certain how the regime would end. Should Monarchists palliate the abuses of the Republic through cooperation with Moderate Republicans, thus demonstrating their fitness to govern? Should they adopt the 'politique du pire'—aid the most extreme Republicans in order to bring events to their logical conclusion? Monarchists endorsed Boulangism because it seemingly portended catastrophe and a popular demand for order, and because alternatives appeared impossible. They also feared that a rival dynasty or non-Monarchist strong man might exploit the crisis.

The Pretenders

In 1873, a surplus of dynasties crippled Monarchism. Now there were more pretenders than dynasties. The Comte de Paris was hardly known in France, and his counsellors were somewhat dismissive of him. Breteuil claimed that the English looked down on the Orléans because of their creased hats and badly cut clothes.[33] Yet Paris was an intelligent man, who was prepared to compromise to achieve what he wanted. No rival matched his authority.

On 24 August 1883, Legitimist hopes died with the Comte de Chambord. Royalist Committees were dissolved. Moderate Legitimists, already close to Orleanism, rallied enthusiastically to Paris. By the end of the year, a new Royalist organization was in place, dominated by Orleanists and moderate Legitimists. Constitutional Monarchists displaced Ultras in bastions such as Maine-et-Loire and Morbihan.[34] A few Ultras, the Blancs d'Espagne, proclaimed the rights of the Spanish Bourbons to the throne. For them 'the Orleanist princes represent a political order and a system of government that is merely a form of the Revolution'.[35] Many Legitimists sought an alternative to politics in local government and charitable and professional associations, especially agricultural unions, which were to have a great future. Others turned to religious defence. *La Croix* at first suggested that the Pope should decide the succession according to each pretender's service to the Church. Subsequently, without rallying to the Republic, the Assumptionist journal announced a purely Catholic line.[36] Some Ultras rallied to Paris, one declaring, 'I, an intransigent White, who has never flagged, side with the party of the king of the barricades'.[37] De Mun concluded that Paris represented the best available hope for religion; indeed, he believed that Paris could not reign unless he embraced counterrevolution.[38]

[33] Breteuil, *La Haute société*, 14 November 1888, 7 May 1889.

[34] Philippe Levillain, *Albert de Mun. Catholicisme français et catholicisme romain du syllabus au ralliement* (Rome and Paris, 1983), 777–82.

[35] Arthur Loth, *Revue du monde catholique*, September 1884.

[36] Yves Marchasson, '*La Croix* et le ralliement', in René Rémond and Émile Poulat (eds), *Cent ans d'histoire de* La Croix (Paris, 1987), 69–106; Joseph A. Grenier, 'An apostolate of battle: *La Croix*, 1883–1890', *Catholic Historical Review* 67, no. 2 (1981), 214–35.

[37] Martin Simpson, 'The death of Henri V: The Legitimists without the Bourbons', *French History* 15, no. 4 (2001), 378–99, at 387.

[38] Levillain, *Albert de Mun*, 757–60, 766–7.

In June 1879, the 23-year-old Prince Imperial died in South Africa while serving with the British Army, just as he was building popularity in France. Bonapartism split between the followers of Prince Jérôme, who favoured an anticlerical authoritarian Republic, and his orthodox 18-year-old son, Victor. By 1884, Victor's supporters had accumulated sufficient money to ensure his independence and to control the Bonapartist press.[39] Yet in that year, Cassagnac embraced *n'importequisme*, or *solutionisme*: he would support whichever pretender acted first, on condition that he held a plebiscite. Cassagnac became a friend of Paris.[40] The three-way division of Bonapartism weakened it as an electoral force, but Boulangism would reveal untapped Bonapartist strength. For the moment, Orleanism was in the ascendant, even if it had adopted a Bonapartist air.

Conservatisme

That Mackau, the architect of *conservatisme* and president of the parliamentary Union des droites, was a convert to Orleanism from Bonapartism confirmed the point.[41] *Conservative* committees emerged in many departments while Royalist organizations went into hibernation.[42] In 1885, Mackau and Cassagnac agreed a common programme and secured the presentation of a single list in most constituencies. They eliminated too militant Monarchists from their lists and attracted a few representatives of the Centre gauche.

In the Orleanist spirit, *conservatisme's* guiding principle was that the psychology of the people was rarely Monarchist or clerical, but was innately conservative. Monarchists should therefore avoid dynastic references and demonstrate that the Republic could not protect conservative interests. Thus, *conservatisme* opposed both secularization of education and colonialism for its expense. Many candidates also embraced protectionism. Mackau hoped that Monarchism would win votes beyond its 'throne and altar' constituency and create an irresistible movement of anti-Republican opinion. *Conservatisme* potentially reconciled Orleanist parliamentarianism with moderate Legitimists' liberal Catholicism, Cassagnac's *solutionisme*, and Bonapartists' belief in universal suffrage.

There were tensions within *conservatisme* concerning religion and social policy. Leo XIII's encyclical *Nobilissima Gallorum Gens* (February 1884), without endorsing the Republic, advocated legal defence of religion, thus converging with Mackau's view that religion should be defended as one of several 'interests'. In effect, Mackau endorsed the liberal Catholic view that monarchy would permit the Church to flourish in a free society. Consequently, Ultralegitimists saw *conservatisme* as a

[39] Karen Offen, *Paul de Cassagnac and the Authoritarian Tradition in Nineteenth-Century France* (New York, 1994), 115–33, 150–2.

[40] Offen, *Paul de Cassagnac*, 146–7, 151–2.

[41] Archives nationales, Fonds Mackau 101/2 (hereafter ANFM, carton, dossier number) 8 February 1887; JOCD, 1–4 December (1883); Albert de Broglie (ed.), *Discours du Duc de Broglie* (Paris, 1909), 339–62; Comte d'Haussonville, *Un Programme de gouvernement* (Paris, 1882); Levillain, *Boulanger*, 60.

[42] Michel Denis, *Les Royalistes de la Mayenne et le monde moderne (XIXe–XXe siècles)* (Le Mans, 1977), 470–1.

rejection of their confessionalism. In mid 1884, Mackau went to the Vatican to discuss toning down the Ultra *L'Univers*, while Cassagnac endeavoured to restrain the intransigent Deputy-Bishop Freppel.[43] The *conservative* programme in the Mayenne included too many concessions to Republicanism for Legitimist liking.[44] There were also difficulties in Lyon, where, in 1879, clerics, businessmen, and academics of various Monarchist tendencies founded the *Nouvelliste de Lyon*. The newspaper, soon the most important right-wing daily in the region, backed *conservatisme* without hiding its hope that the Comte de Paris would return through a plebiscite. It endorsed the Republic's economic liberalism, but preferred de Mun's Catholic intransigence.[45]

In keeping with the *conservative* strategy, the *Nouvelliste* also tried to reach beyond the right's constituency through provision of local news and agricultural advice. Local studies suggest that campaigns for protectionism succeeded with cereal producers in Loir-et-Cher and Gironde. Condemnation of religious persecution paid off in Aveyron, Lozère, and Ardèche, where conflicts with Protestants fed popular Catholic resentment of Republican education policies, and where, at a time of economic hardship, the suppression of religious orders reduced employment opportunities.[46] Global analysis shows that the increase in the right's vote in 1885 was attributable partly to having presented more candidates and partly to transfer of votes from the very moderately Republican Centre gauche.[47]

For Rudelle, the 1885 elections displayed the electorate's desire for 'pacification', an aspiration transferred into Boulangism when politicians of left and right failed to recognize that. Thus, Rudelle provides yet another example of implicit historiographical acceptance of crowd theory. In fact, perceptions mattered more. Whatever its 'real' meaning, Monarchists interpreted the election in the light of their catastrophic view of history, and what they saw was polarization. Some therefore feared that *conservatisme* would turn Monarchism into a constitutional opposition, or cause voters to believe that Monarchists accepted the Republic, when the regime was actually collapsing. Consequently, in 1886, they refused to support the moderate Brisson government even though its programme was close to their own, and backed the Opportunists only when Boulanger seemed to threaten war and revolution. When Boulanger secretly approached the Monarchists, he pushed at an open door. For Monarchists, Boulangism offered connection with the innate popular desire for strong government, while continuing *conservatisme*'s acceptance of democracy. Three failed attempts to form a constitutional opposition confirm both Monarchists' hostility to the Republic and the impasse within which they found themselves when Boulanger approached them.

[43] Offen, *Paul de Cassagnac*, 148–50.

[44] Denis, *Les Royalistes*, 475–7.

[45] Louis de Vaucelles, *Le Nouvelliste de Lyon et la défense religieuse (1879–1889)* (Lyon, 1971), 48–53, 111–22.

[46] Georges Dupeux, *Aspects de l'histoire sociale et politique du Loir-et-Cher, 1848–1914* (Paris, 1962), 74–5; Hélène Lacaze, 'Le Boulangism en Gironde', *Revue historique de Bordeaux et du départment de la Gironde*, new series, 16 (1967), 71–85; Peter M. Jones, *Politics and Rural Society: The Southern Massif Central c. 1750–1880* (Cambridge, 1985), 213–14.

[47] Rudelle, *La République*, 116–57.

The Parti Catholique

On 15 September 1885, shortly before polling day, de Mun called for the formation of a party open to Catholics of any political persuasion. He renewed his appeal after the elections. He chose this course because following Chambord's death, he had failed to turn Royalist committees into a Catholic and Royalist party that would remain organizationally independent of the Comte de Paris; most Legitimists hated the Orléans too much to follow de Mun, while Paris feared a party that he did not control.[48] We have seen that de Mun opposed reduction of Catholic defence to one element in Mackau's *conservative* programme. He believed that Monarchists could exploit untapped reserves of Catholicism within the people.[49]

De Mun's party would organize Catholics behind a parliamentary group. It would recruit its 'cadres and spirit' from the Œuvre des cercles, form committees in all communes, and engage in permanent activism. It would 'raise the flag of Christ', make divine law the basis of its action, and attract people of all opinions and classes through social reforms. Although the party would include Catholic Republicans, it would not endorse the Republic. De Mun urged Catholics to prepare for 'decisive combat', and warned them to resist the Republicans even when they adopted an 'apparently' moderate stance. He still regarded monarchy as essential to Christian society, but saw Catholics rather than Monarchists as the core of his movement.[50]

Only fourteen deputies, largely from clerical Brittany, endorsed de Mun's appeal, foreshadowing Christian Democracy there. Within the Œuvre des cercles, the mercurial La Tour de Pin denounced the excessive role attributed to deputies in the putative party and placed his faith in the people alone.[51] De Mun's social reformism and clericalism alarmed other Monarchists. Mackau rightly saw the party as undermining *conservatisme*. Chesnelong, leader of the Catholic Committees, believed that de Mun would alienate liberal Catholics.[52] Vatican intervention, solicited by Mackau and perhaps Paris, forced de Mun to retract. The episode demonstrated the weakness of counterrevolutionary Monarchism and perhaps encouraged de Mun to see Boulangism as a last-ditch attempt to restore the monarchy. The populism of his scheme also represented a bridge to Boulangism—de Mun proclaimed the people to be 'the instrument and the end of electoral struggles'.

Raoul-Duval's 'Pre-Ralliement'

In August 1886, Edgard Raoul-Duval urged Monarchists and Opportunists to unite in a constitutional opposition and oppose 'all Socialist attacks on the family,

[48] Henri Rollet, *Albert de Mun et le Parti catholique* (Paris, 1947); Benjamin Martin, *Count Albert de Mun: Paladin of the Republic* (Chapel Hill, 1978), 58–62.

[49] Albert de Mun, *Discours du Comte Albert de Mun*, iii (2). *Discours politiques* (Paris, 1888), 321–4.

[50] De Mun, *Discours politiques*, 8 September, 3 November 1885, 325–38.

[51] Levillain, *Albert de Mun*, 848–9.

[52] Alexander Sedgwick, *The Ralliement in French Politics 1890–1898* (Cambridge, MA, 1965), 17–18.

property and individual rights'.[53] Raoul-Duval was not a maverick, but a typically Orléano-Bonapartist conservative. He differed in believing that a conservative Republican party could break the chain that led from Republicanism to anarchy, and in claiming that the alternative was not monarchy or Republic, but a conservative or radical republic. He was backed by a small group of deputies, the Monarchist *Figaro,* and, most interestingly, the Opportunist *La République française.* Yet most Republicans were hostile, not least because Raoul-Duval expected them to accept the right's 1885 programme. Most Monarchists found the notion of a conservative Republic unthinkable. The Orleanist *Gazette de France* reaffirmed its conviction that hereditary principle guaranteed order, and doubted whether Raoul-Duval was a conservative. *L'Univers* declared that the Republic was not a perfectible lesser evil, but an 'enemy', dedicated to the destruction of what remained of Christian society.[54]

The Rouvier Government

Paradoxically, the furore over Raoul-Duval's proposal had scarcely died down before Monarchists agreed to support Rouvier's Opportunist administration. Mackau, de Mun, and Cassagnac, with Paris' approval, put out feelers to the Opportunists in December 1886.[55] Their aim was to remove Boulanger, whom they feared for his Radicalism and because he might ruin their chances by taking power in the inevitable crisis. Mackau promised that in return for breaking with the Radicals, rejecting income tax, slowing secularization of schools, and concessions in public employment, Monarchists would cease to attack the regime. Rouvier accepted Monarchist support, and the conciliatory Eugène Spuller became Minister of Religion. On 16 October, Monarchists abstained for a conservative Republican in a by-election in the Orne.[56] Isolated voices proposed permanent alliance. The Orleanist Marquis de Castellane called for a change of men, not of regime, while de Mun hinted at approval for an authoritarian Republic.[57]

More typically, Mackau declared that *conservateurs* supported Rouvier 'without forgetting anything, without renouncing anything, faithful, on the contrary, to their past—because faithful to the interests of the country'.[58] Indeed, Monarchists feared that backing Rouvier would republicanize the right. The pretenders agreed. In August 1887, Victor rejected solutionism, and forbade Bonapartists to ally with Royalists unless given a fair share of seats. The next month, Paris declared that

[53] *Le Temps*, 22 August 1886.

[54] Rudelle, *La République*, 176–80; Jean El Gammal, 'Un Pré-Ralliement. Raoul-Duval et la droite républicaine, 1885–1887', *Revue d'histoire moderne et contemporaine* 29, no. 4 (October–December 1982), 599–621; Bernard Bodinier and Claude Cornu, 'Un Précurseur de la "droite républicaine". Edgard Raoul-Duval (1832–1887)', *Revue d'histoire moderne et contemporaine* 46, no. 4 (October–December 1999), 680–712; Offen, *Cassagnac*, 166; Sedgwick, *The Ralliement*, 18–20; Vaucelles, *Le Nouvelliste*, 122.

[55] ANFM 102/2, Paris to Mackau, 16 June 1887, 8 February 1888.

[56] Levillain, *Boulanger*, 29–37; Seager, *The Boulanger Affair*, 39–50.

[57] Seager, *The Boulanger Affair*, 82; Levillain, *Boulanger*, 33–4.

[58] *L'Année politique*, (Paris, 1887), 249.

Rouvier was a temporary palliative. Breaking with Orleanist tradition, he attacked parliamentarianism and advocated a strong monarchy legitimated by universal suffrage—Bonapartism!

Rank-and-file Monarchists were uncomfortable with the Rouvier expedient too. Legitimists had always been suspicious of *conservatisme* and now they saw none of the promised moderation in local functionaries' behaviour.[59] In any case, Royalist committees did not see their mission as the conquest of votes, but as displaying the royal flag, so that the people would rally to it when the regime collapsed. Alliance with Republicans compromised their ability to do that.[60] Then, Rouvier's fall in the midst of the Wilson scandal reminded Monarchists of the inevitability of the Republic's collapse. Even de Mun and Cassagnac, who preferred to keep Rouvier in office, wanted to intensify the crisis.[61]

The Turn to Boulanger

The failure of the Rouvier experiment left Monarchists without a strategy. Mackau later commented 'We were advancing in the dark; ignorant of what might be possible at the last moment and of what the interest of the right might be.'[62] Monarchists feared the consequences of *conservatisme*, rejected constitutional opposition, and a Catholic party. Furthermore, they had never been wholly adverse to military intervention in politics, and the many ex-officers in the Monarchist leadership felt some sympathy with Boulanger.[63] Even parliamentarians like Falloux and Audiffret-Pasquier forgot their constitutional scruples as the Republicans consolidated their power.[64] Many hoped that a 'constable', a French General Monck, might restore the monarchy.[65] Whereas monarchists envisaged a coup, the Bonapartist Thiébaud designed Boulanger's electoral strategy, and Cassagnac hoped that the people might rise up against the Republic.[66]

Ordinary Monarchists voted for Boulanger without waiting for a signal from their leaders. In February 1888, Breteuil commented that the 50,000 votes garnered by 'this apparently Republican general' came from rural conservatives. In Maine-et-Loire in February, Monarchists opted for the General against the explicit advice of their deputies.[67] Provincial Monarchists contrasted Boulanger's activism with the inertia of their own leadership. The Bonapartist *Écho de la frontière* pointed to Boulanger's victories in conservative communes and commented 'for the moment it

[59] ANFM 102/2, 8 February 1888; Offen, *Cassagnac*, 151, 160; Martin, *Count Albert de Mun*, 68–72; *Courrier de Tarn-et-Garonne*, August 1888; Rudelle, *La République*, 186; Vaucelles, *Le Nouvelliste*, 122.

[60] Simpson, 'The death of Henri V', 392–3.

[61] Offen, *Cassagnac*, 172–5; Levaillain, *Boulanger*, 52–4.

[62] ANFM 94/1, 12 August 1888.

[63] Rudelle, *La République*, 189.

[64] Levillain, *Boulanger*, 84.

[65] Adrien Dansette, *Du Boulangisme à la révolution dreyfusienne* (Paris, 1938), 115.

[66] Offen, *Cassagnac*, 141–4, 162.

[67] Breteuil, *La Haute société*, 10 February 1888 (the date of the entry precedes the elections to which it refers); Irvine, *The Boulanger Affair*, 78–9.

suffices that he is the opponent of Opportunism'.[68] The Jeunesse royaliste deserted *en masse* to Boulangism; everywhere Royalists attended Boulangist meetings in spite of instructions to the contrary from the Comte de Paris.[69] Discontent with moderate leadership was essential to right-wing support for Boulanger: in 1889, Abbé Lemire, the future Christian Democrat deputy, had confided to his diary, '"conservative" is not sufficiently bellicose and I will be delighted to write "revision"'.[70]

In the following years, except in Paris and possibly the Aisne, around two thirds of Boulanger's votes came from the right, and the General was defeated in left-wing departments.[71] Reliance on conservative votes increased with time. In the Nord, Boulanger won at least 60 per cent of his vote from the right on 15 April, and a considerably larger proportion on 19 August.[72] Monarchist leaders followed as much as they directed the movement. Mackau advised Paris that 'we will inevitably be forced to find a very similar electoral ground to that of the General if we do not want to be swept away by the Boulangist tide'.[73] The exhaustion of alternative strategies, expectation of catastrophe in the Republic, and pressure from below, pushed most, but not all, Monarchist leaders into Boulangism.

Orleanists and Boulangism

Anti-Boulangist Orleanists were most numerous among those removed from the practice of universal suffrage. They included senators and some of Paris' entourage, who regarded themselves as a 'government in waiting' and drew their legitimacy from allegiance to the pretender. For them, Royalists should simply sustain the Monarchist idea through periodic royal manifestos and symbolic candidatures, so that when the Republic collapsed the king would benefit. They criticized the inactivity of Royalist committees not because they wanted to create a modern electoral machine, but to preserve the purity of their ideal. Consequently, they also disliked the dilution of Royalism in *conservatisme* and even more in Boulangism. The pretender's advisor, the Comte d'Haussonville, warned that 'The deputies don't count; only the Monarchist party does.' The antipathy of the Orleanist generation of the 1870s, Broglie included, to Bonapartism reinforced their distrust of Boulangism.[74] In Lyon, Joseph Rambaud of the *Nouvelliste* belatedly accepted the need to profit from a 'necessary crisis', but felt that there were too many Jews and Masons in Boulanger's entourage to make him trustworthy, and did not back revisionist candidates in 1889.[75] Anti-Boulangists believed that popular Royalism remained strong.[76]

[68] *L'Anjou*, 28 February 1888; *L'Echo de la Frontière*, 20 March 1888.

[69] Irvine, *The Boulanger Affair*, 94, 107, 121; *L'Écho de la Frontière*, 31 March, 12 April 1888.

[70] Jean-Marie Mayeur, *L'Abbé Lemire. Un Prêtre démocrate 1853–1928* (Paris, 1968), 46.

[71] Burns, *Rural Society*, 88–101.

[72] Jacques Néré, 'Les Élections Boulanger dans le département du Nord', thèse complémentaire, University of Paris, 1959, 174–5, 193.

[73] ANFM 102/1, meeting of 16 April 1888; Mackau to Paris, 26 July 1889; *L'Autorité*, 20 April 1889, quoted in Seager, *The Boulanger Affair*, 232–3; *Le Soleil*, 11 October 1889.

[74] Irvine, *The Boulanger Affair*, 85–6, 90–5; P.-L. Target, *1889: Monarchie ou anarchie* (Paris, 1888); *Le Figaro*, 7 August 1888.

[75] Vaucelles, *Le Nouvelliste*, 117–20.

[76] ANFM 102/2, Mackau to Paris, 6 December 1888.

Pro-Boulanger Orleanists more pessimistically assumed that the people were fundamentally apolitical, but would accept the monarchy if a respected figure imposed his will. Pro-Boulangists were more common among deputies, who believed that election entitled them to speak for the Monarchist movement, and mocked Paris' entourage as 'the blackballees of universal suffrage'.[77] Pro-Boulangists had embraced *conservatisme* because they feared that explicitly Monarchist pronouncements would divide the right and frighten the people. Now they hoped to use Boulanger to win the 500,000 extra votes needed for a parliamentary majority.

If there was an element of instrumentalism in Orleanist strategies, engagement in Boulangism nevertheless reinforced the influence of authoritarian populism. Orleanists became more favourable to a *coup d'état*—in November 1887 Mackau and Martimprey raised no objection to Boulanger's proposed coup. In the early 1880s Édouard Hervé, editor of the Orleanist *Le Soleil*, spoke favourably of the plebiscite. The Comte de Paris declared in his *Instructions* of 15 September 1887 that the ancient pact between nation and the monarchy must be renewed through either a constituent assembly or a 'popular vote'. Breteuil remarked that Guizot would have veiled his face on hearing the grandson of 1830 speak thus.[78] Cassagnac concluded that monarchy and empire had merged.[79]

Breteuil spoke for a 'modern' democratic monarchy, and proclaimed himself the enemy of the Faubourg Saint-Germain and of those who could not separate God and king. Corruption, he said, reached the summit of the state and a wave of discontent had swept the country; universal suffrage would overthrow unworthy governments.[80] Mackau claimed that the 'deep layers of universal suffrage' had recognized conservative unity. In May 1888, he created the Ligue de la consultation nationale, intended to shift the initiative away from parliament and Royalist committees and enable Royalists to lead the revisionist movement in the country. Jules Auffray, its young secretary, criss-crossed France, demanding one million members for the league. With some justice, anti-Boulanger Orleanists attacked the league as a cover for Bonapartism.[81]

Orleanists also called upon women. In July 1888, they launched the Ligue de la Rose, modelled on the British Primrose League, open to men, and especially women, of all classes. The League would form 'an Army... of monarchical and democratic conservatism'. Women's involvement was justified in ways destined to become familiar. They would act through moral influence rather than rational

[77] ANFM 102/1, Mackau to Paris, 1 July 1888, 13 and 25 September 1888; Levillain, *Boulanger*, 77–8, 86–7; Dansette, *Boulangisme*, 178.

[78] Breteuil, *La Haute société*, 16 October 1887; Fonds Mackau 102, Mackau to Comtesse de Quinsonas, 14 September 1887.

[79] Dansette, *Boulangisme*, 161–2; Levillain, *Boulangisme*, 78–9; Irvine, *The Boulanger Affair*, 43–4; Breteuil, *La Haute société*, 17 September and 16 October 1887.

[80] Henri de Breteuil, *La Monarchie démocratique* (Paris, 1888); *La Monarchie moderne* (La Chatre, 1888); *La Haute société*, 23 October, 14–18 November 1888.

[81] A.F., Mackau, *L'Union, préface de la victoire* (Paris, 1889); Burns, *Rural Society*, 106–19; Fonds Mackau, 102 (dossier 2) Manifeste de la Ligue de la consultation national; *Courrier de Tarn-et-Garonne*, August 1888; *Moniteur de la Nièvre*, 29 September 1888; *Le Figaro*, 7 August 1888; ANFM 102/1 letters of Mackau to Paris, 1888.

persuasion; their engagement was an exceptional response to the dangers confronting their husbands and sons.[82] Nevertheless, this was a significant departure for Monarchism—Breteuil had previously condemned all female engagement in politics.[83] The formation of the league resulted partly from contact with Republican feminism through Boulangism and from rapprochement with Legitimism since Chambord's death. It represented an explicit politicization of the female networks of wealthy society. Furthermore, the Comtesse de Paris, patron of the league, was an unusual woman. Breteuil ridiculed her masculine dress, chain smoking, and habit of sinking endless glasses of brandy like a hussar officer whilst using expressions unusual in a woman, and of hunting wearing waders with a rifle slung over her shoulder.[84] The duchesse d'Uzès, whom we met in the Introduction to the book, was also a keen hunter.

Orleanists did not wholeheartedly embrace plebiscitary democracy. Paris belatedly opposed 'direct consultation of the nation' as 'a barely disguised capitulation to the doctrine of the "appeal to the people"'. Breteuil envisaged a constituent assembly, not a plebiscite. Orleanists did not adopt the anti-capitalism or antisemitism of the radical Boulangists. One finds the usual prejudices against Jews in Breteuil's diary, but they were mixed with admiration for the bankers Rothschild and Hirsch, who had provided much of the money that Royalists disbursed to Boulangists. Yet in the longer term, Boulangism reinforced some Orleanists' rapprochement with Bonapartism and weakened dynastic loyalty. Orleanist Boulangism represented both an attempt by Royalist leaders to mobilize the people 'from above', and to control a movement that had begun autonomously.

Legitimists and Boulangism

Legitimists were not conspicuous supporters of Boulanger for they were weak in the Chamber and Royalist committees. Nevertheless, Boulangism and Legitimism had a significant mutual impact. The Blancs d'Espagne were divided. Some believed that any compromise with the Revolution would corrupt the principles necessary to the recovery of France. Others backed Boulangism for its opposition to Orleanist parliamentarianism; they did not want Boulanger to restore Paris, but felt that since Don Carlos' accession to the throne was a distant prospect, the Republic should be rendered as 'wise, liberal, and honest as possible'.[85]

Mainstream Legitimists were equally uncertain. The Mayenne aristocracy were largely hostile, yet a Boulangist committee appeared in the department.[86] Bishop Freppel had little faith in Paris' Catholicism, and since 1885 he had represented a minority that considered it possible to defend religion within the Republic; he

[82] *Le Soleil*, 30 July 1888.

[83] Breteuil, *La Haute société*, 28 July 1886, 27 August, 28 October 1887, 31 January 1888, 27 February 1889.

[84] Breteuil, *La Haute société*, 25 March 1887.

[85] *Journal de Paris*, 27 January; Gustave Véran et al., *La Légitimité devant le Boulangisme* (Paris, 1889); *L'Univers*, 27 January 1889.

[86] Denis, *Les Royalists*, 481–2.

hoped that Boulangism might permit the election of a Catholic majority.[87] De Mun saw Boulangism as an unwitting instrument of providence, a popular rising against a government that did not conform to divine law, of which the Œuvre des Cercles might capture leadership.[88] De Mun also thought that Boulangism would overcome parliamentary opposition to social reform: the failure in May 1888 of a bill for compulsory accident insurance provoked him to condemn both the Opportunists and Monarchists' 'deadly, sterile reaction'. In 1889, at the counter-commemoration of the centenary of the Revolution at Romans, he presented the Œuvre des Cercles as part of a popular rebellion against liberalism. In angry exchanges with conservatives, he described reform as a terrain 'where we may join hands' with the Socialists, 'in a common sentiment of humanity and love for the people'.[89]

The turn to Social Catholicism accentuated economic antisemitism, notably in de Mun and La Tour du Pin's theoretical review, *L'Association catholique*. Elsewhere, Castellane remarked that charitable conservatives disliked materialist Jews.[90] The collapse in 1882 of the Union générale bank, which Legitimists had created as a rival to Protestant and Jewish banks, linked Catholic and economic antisemitism, and gave birth to the myth of the Rothschilds.[91] Under the headline 'La France juive', the Legitimist *L'Anjou* described Jews and Protestants as 'the kings of France'.[92] At the forefront of Catholic antisemitism was *La Croix*, which claimed after Boulanger's Paris victory that 'Freemasons and Jews have experienced a first-class squeeze'. This concoction of intransigent Catholicism, social reform, antisemitism, and populism would feed into the Christian Democracy of the 1890s.

Boulanger's defeat in Catholic Ardèche and his below average performance in Catholic Flanders in the much-analysed Nord department has perhaps obscured the importance of Catholic Boulangism.[93] Yet the willingness of rural voters to back Boulanger in Catholic Maine-et-Loire has already been noted; in Ardèche Boulanger won about half of the Catholic vote, and benefited from clerical support. De Mun reported in July 1889 that in Catholic Morbihan there was 'a general tendency in favour of Boulanger'. According to *L'Année politique*, the belief that the Republic was dying led many priests to back Boulanger.[94] The fact that Boulangists were rarely elected in rural Catholic constituencies owes more to a

[87] Étienne Cornut, *Monseigneur Freppel d'après des documents authentiques et inédits* (Paris, 1893), 354–8.

[88] ANFM 102/1, 16 April 1888 and de Mun to Mackau, 23 July 1888.

[89] *Discours et écrits divers du Comte Albert de Mun*, iv, 88–92, 17 June 1888; Robert Talmy, *Au Sources du catholicisme social. L'École de La Tour du Pin et l'encyclique* Rerum Novarum (Paris, 1963), 173.

[90] Marquis de Castellane, *La Politique conservatrice. Les Cahiers conservateurs en 1889* (Paris, 1889), 4.

[91] Jeannine Verdès-Leroux, *Scandale financier et antisémitisme catholique, le krach de l'Union générale* (Paris, 1969).

[92] *L'Anjou*, 8 March 1888; Verdès-Leroux, *Scandale financier*; Marc Angenot, *Ce que l'on dit des juifs en 1889* (Saint-Denis, 1989), 36–7, 63–6.

[93] Néré, 'Les Élections Boulanger', 132–6, 195–8.

[94] Daniel, *Année politique*, 1889, 186–8; Vaucelles, *Le Nouvelliste*, 119; Jones, *Politics and Rural Society*, 294. Jean Quellien, *Bleus, blancs, rouges. Politique et élections dans le Calvados 1870–1939* (Caen, 1986), 139–41.

shortage of Boulangist activists than to the indifference of the electorate—they were absent from the Morbihan countryside.[95] Like Bonapartism, Boulangism lacked wealthy men to represent it in such areas. Anyway, Boulanger had agreed not to present candidates in Monarchist constituencies.

Bonapartists and Boulangism

Bonapartism possessed obvious affinities with radical Boulangism. In spite of participation in *conservatisme*, Bonapartist populism persisted. Victoristes rejected Jérôme's Republican anticlericalism but were anti-Royalist, committed to the 'appel au peuple', and included the would-be prophet of working-class Bonapartism, Jules Amiges. Cassagnac too demanded an income tax and engaged in the *politique du pire*—he thought that amnestying the Communards would hasten the collapse of the regime.[96] Although lacking money and Deputies, Jérômistes retained support in the anticlerical Dordogne. Boulangism would reveal untapped reservoirs of popular Bonapartism.

Jérôme, Victor, and Cassagnac all hoped to profit from Boulangism.[97] In July 1887, well before the Royalist–Boulanger alliance was established, Cassagnac urged Boulanger to carry out a coup, only to drop him—temporarily—when he failed to act.[98] Bonapartists believed that 'willingly or unwillingly, [Boulanger] will be God's instrument for the realization of his will'.[99] They were too poor to fund Boulanger, but could offer votes and activism—Thiébaud was the inspiration for Boulanger's by-election campaign. Ideologically, both depended on the charismatic leader, opposed parliamentarianism, denounced the Opportunists as representatives of materialist liberalism, and advocated the plebiscite. Without being Socialist, both wished to 'do something' for the workers. Some even felt that Boulanger physically resembled the young Napoléon III.[100] The Comtesse Martel-Mirabeau, better known as Gyp, saw Boulanger's audacity, strength, and charisma as the epitome of Napoleonic masculinity. In the 1889 election campaign, she harangued crowds of peasants and workers in Normandy.[101] Gyp was typical of Bonapartists in associating openly with radical Boulangists. Thiébaud sat on the Comité de protestation nationale, and two more Bonapartists later joined him. In 1888, Bonapartists flooded into Déroulède's Ligue des patriotes and some gained positions of authority. With Déroulède, the Bonapartists formed the hard-line faction in the Boulangist leadership.[102]

95 Fonds Mackau 110 (dossier 2), de Mun to Mackau, 27 and 30 July 1889; Irvine, *The Boulanger Affair*, 97–8.

96 Offen, *Paul de Cassagnac*, 128–32, 139–40.

97 Offen, *Paul de Cassagnac*, 164–5.

98 *L'Autorité*, 11 and 15 July 1887.

99 *L'Écho de la frontière*, 20 March 1888.

100 Dansette, *Boulangisme*, 165.

101 Willa Z. Silverman, *Gyp: La dernière des Mirabeau* (Paris, 1995), 105–6.

102 Bertrand Joly, *Déroulède. L'Inventeur du nationalisme* (Paris, 1998), 144–7, 164–5, 206, 217–18, 240–2.

Some Bonapartists were open to the more novel themes of radical Boulangism. The Victoristes of Rouen set up a Boulangist newspaper, *L'Indépendant normande*, which echoed Boulanger's call for a Republic open to all shades of opinion, and declared that 'France must face up to two enemies: Germany without and the Jew within'.[103] Antisemitism also marked the Bonapartist daily, *Le Petit caporel*, which denounced Jewish monopolizers and claimed that foreigners were Boulanger's chief enemies.[104] Gyp wrote a puppet play in which Jewish financiers were condemned to the flames of hell.[105] The Bonapartist deputy Jean-Edmond Laroche-Joubert led the legislative campaign for a tax on foreign workers. Cassagnac opposed the political exploitation of antisemitism.

The best Boulangist electoral performances were in rural areas with Bonapartist traditions. These constituencies fell into three categories. In the first, Bonapartism was historically strong, but lacked leaders and money, as in Jérômiste Dordogne and the Nord. In the Gironde, in the absence of Bonapartist candidates, some peasants voted for Republicans rather than hated Royalists and then turned to Boulanger in 1889.[106] In Legitimist Mayenne, pockets of peasant Bonapartism were open to Boulangism.[107] In the second category, including Charente-Inférieure and Calvados, sitting Bonapartist deputies backed Boulanger. In Caen II, where Bonapartism alone addressed agricultural labourers, it mutated easily into Boulangism and contributed to the victory of the Bonapartist Fernand Engerand in 1889.[108] Thirdly, in some constituencies voters had oscillated between Bonapartism, Radicalism, and Socialism: in Nevers, an alliance of Radicals and Bonapartists, amongst whom woodcutters were prominent, elected an ex-Radical against a Royalist in 1889.[109] Even in the towns, where Bonapartism had been weak for years, there was a link with the far left. In Paris, the geography of Boulangist voting was similar to that for Louis-Napoléon in 1848 and the left subsequently. Boulanger did well among workers in Rennes, Lorient, Brest, and Bordeaux, and among the miners of the Nord and the textile workers of Roubaix-Tourcoing, all of whom had at one time been attracted to Bonapartism. Especially striking was the support of Cambrai weavers for Boulanger, since it was there that in 1877 the radical Bonapartist Amigues had won a surprise victory.[110]

Boulangism was not simply the reactivation of a subterranean Bonapartist mentality. The east and south, which had favoured Louis-Napoléon in 1848, largely

[103] Marcel Boivin, 'Le Boulangisme en Haute-Normandie', *Annales de Normandie* 26, no. 3 (1976), 225–62.

[104] Angenot, *Ce que l'on dit des juifs*, 73–4.

[105] Silverman, *Gyp*, 109.

[106] Hélène Lacaze, 'Le Boulangism en Gironde', *Revue historique de Bordeaux et du département de la Gironde*, new series, 16 (1967), 71–85.

[107] Denis, *Les Royalistes*, 481.

[108] François Pairault, 'Le Boulangisme dans les Charentes', *Revue de Saintonge et d'Aunis* 22 (1996), 89–117; Quellien, *Bleus, blancs, rouges*, 121.

[109] Alfred Massé, 'Les Partis politiques dans la Nièvre de 1871 à 1906', *Les Cahiers nivernais* 19 (April 1910), 1–86, at 57–71.

[110] Néré, 'Les Élections Boulanger', 159–62; Bernard Ménager, *Les Napoléons du peuple* (Paris, 1988), 344–6; Jean Garrigues, 'Les Élections législatives dans la Seine', mémoire de maîtrise, Paris X Nanterre, 1981; Pairault, 'Le Boulangisme', 89–117.

rejected Boulanger. Much depended upon the attitudes of Radical and Bonapartist deputies. Usually Bonapartist elites backed Boulanger, but where they opposed him, Boulangism was weaker: in the Charente by-election of 1888, the powerful Bonapartist Committee refused to stand aside for Déroulède, and on the second ballot, the Boulangists backed an Opportunist against the Bonapartist.[111] Boulangists were best able to awaken latent Bonapartist feeling where the General himself stood and where it was possible to put massive resources into by-elections.

The ambiguity of relations between Bonapartism and Radicalism underlined the malleability of populism, not in the sense of the 'volatility of the mass', but of the creative ways in which voters used the available possibilities. Moreover, the elites were as politically flexible as voters: Cassagnac expressed a mixture of hatred and admiration for the Radicals. The *Écho de la frontière*, published in the mining district of Valenciennes, reprinted articles by Radicals such as Pelletan and Rochefort on the need for institutional change and incited miners against Opportunist managers. The newspaper backed Boulanger from an early stage and miners voted for Boulanger in 1888.[112] Boulangism and Bonapartism emerged from the same matrix of populism as Radicalism.

RADICAL BOULANGISM

Those Radicals and Socialists—the majority—who abandoned Boulanger early in 1888 are relevant to the history of the movement but less so to that of the right. Those Radicals and Socialists who followed Boulanger to the end were immensely important to Boulangism's history. They dominated the Comité de protestation nationale and Parisian committees such as the ex-Radical Georges Laguerre's Ligue d'Action républicaine and the Fédération des républicains révisionnistes. Laguerre also managed the daily *La Presse*, which Mackau had purchased. Radicals controlled *La Cocarde*, which sold 200,000 copies of its first issue. Socialist Boulangists were prominent in Bordeaux, Nancy, and Paris, where the Blanquistes possessed an estimated 10,000 propagandists.[113] Boulangism won a significant minority of votes from the left.

Radical Boulangists presented the Royalist alliance as a means to include all parts of the nation in the Republic, and the historian Odile Rudelle agreed that Boulangism did indeed represent the French people's aspiration for 'pacification'.[114] Certainly, in his Tours speech, Boulanger demanded peace between clericals and anticlericals in the interests of national unity.[115] Yet radical Boulangists were well aware that Royalist sympathizers did not accept the Republic: hence *La Cocarde*'s warning that Royalists were wrong to see Boulangism as anti-Republican,

111 Burns, *Rural Society*, 101–5.
112 *Écho de la frontière*, 28 February, 1, 6, 15 March 1888.
113 Hutton, 'Popular Boulangism', 93–5; Sternhell, *La Droite révolutionaire*, 58–9.
114 Rudelle, *La République*, 233–4.
115 *La Cocarde*, 10 March 1889; *La Presse*, 10 June 1889.

while Boulanger claimed that restoration would mean civil war.[116] Boulangists felt closer to Bonapartists, who had often abandoned dynasticism: Déroulède maintained that the influx of Bonapartists into the Ligue des patriotes created 'an alliance of blues that will lead to the victory of the national party'.[117]Appeals to national unity were more an exercise in legitimation and an intervention in the internal politics of the Boulangist movement than a representation of the mind of the people.

The struggle within Boulangism problematizes attempts to judge its 'Republicanism', and anyway, Boulangism took the uncertainties of any political movement to new heights. One Parisian group refused to elaborate a programme and spoke only of the 'destruction that must precede reconstruction'.[118] Some remained faithful to Radical revisionism: Parisian shopkeeper Boulangists advocated unicameral direct democracy, while Boulanger himself evoked suppression of the Presidency of the Republic, and Parisian shopkeeper Boulangists advocated unicameral direct democracy.[119] More ambiguously, Boulanger, in a speech to the Bonapartist Committee of Nièvre, condemned dictatorship and monarchy, yet argued that parliamentary faults justified the 1851 coup.[120] His speech was incompatible with the Republicanism of the Republicans, but may have been inspired by Naquet's American-style presidentialism. It chimed equally well with Boulangist calls for suppression of intermediaries in economic and political life and for government by 'a single representative [commis], to whom orders will be given [by the people], and who will be revocable at will'.[121] Boulanger's views also resonated with Bonapartist demands for a non-monarchical plebiscitary regime. Given these uncertainties, we can say only that Republicanism had always been a contested ideology, and that Boulangism rejected parliamentarianism in favour of arrangements that were meant to bring government closer to the people. There were also more novel tendencies in radical Boulangism, for some embraced an authoritarian Republic and broke with Republican universalism to found an exclusive national populism.

Take Boulangist conceptions of the elite–mass relationship. If Boulangism was populist, it was not literally popular. It recruited leaders from the younger generation of the Republican elite. Laisant was a graduate of the École Polytechnique; Laur of the less-reputed École des Mines de Saint Etienne; Laguerre was a famous trial lawyer; Susini was a wealthy doctor who had practised in the United States; Dillon was a well-off businessman, and Naquet was a scientist. Ordinary activists were of similar origin to Republican equivalents: lawyers, small manufacturers and merchants, shopkeepers, artisans, white-collar workers, and some workers. In Roubaix, the Boulangist leader was a seminary-educated doctor from an artisan family;

[116] *La Cocarde*, 12 January 1889; *La Presse*, 10 July 1889.
[117] Quoted in Joly, *Déroulède*, 218; *La Presse*, 3 May 1889.
[118] Joly, *Nationalistes*, 36–43, 51.
[119] Philip Nord, *Paris Shopkeepers and the Politics of Resentment* (Princeton, 1986), 322–3.
[120] *L'Année politique*, 1888, 118; Naquet, *Discours de Marseille*.
[121] Georges de Labruyère (ed.), *La Cocarde*, 13 March 1888.

his committee was composed of shopkeepers and artisans.[122] These were the 'nouvelles couches' that Monarchists so detested.

The radical Boulangist leadership's conception of its relationship to the people was closer to the Radical Republican combination of electoralism and extra-parliamentary activism than to Opportunist parliamentarianism. It echoed the Radical conviction that the best of the people could rise, through education, to self-government. Boulangists also saw themselves as defending the defenceless. The languages of duelling were important in this respect. A Boulangist journalist's view that Président du conseil Floquet was heading for 'an electoral slap' casts the people, like the duellist, as an agent of retribution, restoring order where the government could not—just as the duel settled disputes in cases where the courts were inadequate.[123] Here the people, like the duellist, are conceived as masculine. However, Boulangists also saw themselves as acting on behalf of a feminine people, just as a duellist might defend female honour. Since women did not possess the independence required of the elite, they could not duel and needed male protection. Likewise, the people required a champion to defend its honour, if necessary with the sword. The Opportunists, in contrast, lacked the courage to defend the people—hence Ferry's alleged cowardice when confronted with a duel.

The languages of duelling converged with cultural tropes, popular and elite. *Café-concert* songs were populated with caricatures of the greedy bourgeois and the honest poor, the humble peasant and the 'gamin de Paris', forced to make his way in a corrupt and unfair world.[124] These dichotomies were transferred into politics through attacks on 'Ferry-famine' (a reference to alleged profiteering during the 1870 war). There was a residue here of early nineteenth-century melodramas, in which the dashing upper-class hero rescues the poor heroine from the clutches of the evil baron, a genre that persisted in romanticism. Highbrow literature showed some similar characteristics. Maurice Barrès' Boulanger novel *Le Jardin de Bérenice* (1890) explicitly feminized the people: Philippe, a young Boulangist candidate, fights a double battle with his Republican opponent, Simon, for the heart of the people and Bérenice, 'the incarnation of the popular soul'. Through Bérenice, Philippe understands the 'creative method of the masses', and communicates with the national past. However, the people need Philippe, for he combines reason with the ability to interpret their feelings. Philippe proves a better tribune of the people than the dry rationalist, Simon (a demagogue in terms of crowd theory). The same logic informs Naquet's conviction that the people demanded revision through Boulanger, 'a man' who understands popular feeling.[125]

[122] Joly, *Déroulède*, 84–5; Sternhell, *La Droite révolutionnaire*, 117–19; Peter Rutkoff, *Revanche and Revision: The Ligue des Patriotes and the Origins of the Radical Right in France 1882–1900* (Athens, 1981), 49–53; David M. Gordon, *Liberalism and Social Reform: Industrial Growth and Progressiste Politics in France, 1880–1914* (Westport, CT, 1996), 46; Nord, *Paris Shopkeepers*, 312–15.

[123] *La Cocarde*, 12 July 1888; André, *Le Jeu de l'épée*, xiii–xxvi.

[124] Kimminich, 'Chansons étouffées', 22–3.

[125] Alfred Naquet, *Discours au cercle révisionniste de Marseille* (Avignon, 1888), 57–67.

This new nationalism cast Boulanger as the possessor of special insight into the national character. Before 1888, Barrès had rejected nations and religions as constraints upon selfhood. He espoused Boulangism because he believed that the scientific rationalism of the Republicans stifled deeper truths, and that the Opportunists refused to honour those who recognized them—the symbolists generally and the theorist of biological race, Jules Soury, in particular. Influenced by Hartmann's idea of the unconscious, the symbolist quest for inner experience, and Soury's racism, Barrès concluded that participation in a popular movement and communion with the land enabled one to reach the inner self. He wrote that Republican science mocked the '"deep roots, the power of permanence" that some people are able to perceive in the countryside'.[126] However, Barrès did not deny the Revolutionary tradition, from which he retained the notion of a struggle of the people against parasitic politicians and bourgeois.

Paul Déroulède personified Boulangist nationalism. He entered politics as a follower of Gambetta, whom he idolized for his part in the 1870 war. In 1881, Gambetta's brief government gave him the task of organizing military education in the state schools. After Gambetta's overthrow, Déroulède formed the Ligue des Patriotes, a federation of pre-existing gymnastic and shooting clubs. Whereas Moderate Republicans saw schools and military service as a means to inculcate democratic values, Déroulède wanted to create a disciplined phalanx of citizens, motivated by a religion of 'la patrie'. He condemned democratic individualism, class struggle, and religious conflict for dividing the nation. He agreed with Renan that in 1870 feudal Prussia had demonstrated its superiority to egalitarian France. By 1885, Déroulède was looking for a strong man. In May 1888, he won control of the Ligue des patriotes from moderates.[127]

Boulangist nationalism accentuated the exclusionary potential within Republicanism. Rochefort saw Germans and Jews behind Opportunism and claimed that 35,000 Jews had been imported into France to vote against Boulanger in 1889.[128] Laur denounced Rothschild's manipulation of the economy.[129] *La Cocarde* described the notorious antisemite publicist Édoaurd Drumont as a 'sincere obsessive', and attacked the Royalist editor of *Le Gaulois*, Arthur Meyer, as 'a defender of a social order that permits the big banks, in other words a few families of which most are not native French, and which possess international ramifications, to enrich themselves at the expense of France'.[130] Around one third of Boulangist newspapers were antisemitic.[131] The pro-Boulanger Parisian shopkeepers' association, the Ligue syndicale, held that Jewish and German department store owners were bent on the destruction of the French people and that Opportunists and Radicals were

[126] Maurice Barrès, *Le Jardin de Bérenice* (Paris, 1890); *Le Figaro*, 19 May 1888; C. Stewart Doty, *From Cultural Rebellion to Counterrevolution: The Politics of Maurice Barrès* (Athens, 1976), 9–35.

[127] Zeev Sternhell, 'Paul Déroulède and the origins of modern French nationalism', *Journal of Contemporary History* 6, no. 4 (1971), 46–70; Rutkoff, *Revanche*.

[128] Roger L. Williams, *Henri Rochefort: Prince of the Gutter Press* (New York, 1970), 200–2; Angenot, *Ce que l'on dit des juifs*, 80–1.

[129] Angenot, *Ce que l'on dit des juifs*, 84–5; *La Cocarde*, 7, 8, 10 March 1889.

[130] *La Cocarde*, 17 March 1888.

[131] Angenot, *Ce que l'on dit des juifs*, 75–8.

indifferent to the defence of 'national labour'.[132] There were countervailing forces. Two Jews, Naquet and Eugène Mayer, sat on the Comité national; Déroulède and Boulanger opposed antisemitism. The antisemites Auguste Chirac and Drumont rejected Boulangism only because they believed that Jews controlled it.[133]

For some Boulangists, the notion that cosmopolitan capital employed foreign labour connected antisemitism with xenophobia. Attacks on foreign workers were a staple of the Boulangist newspaper, *La France*. In Bordeaux, strikes against Spanish workers prepared the way for Boulangism: Charles Dupon, vice-president of the bordelais Ligue des patriotes, created a League for the Protection of National Labour, and claimed that the fundamental conflict in society was between the French people and the cosmopolitan businessmen who siphoned off capital and poured foreign workers into France. Socialists and Radicals agreed.[134] In Nancy, Barrès attacked Opportunists for permitting foreign workers to take French jobs, and claimed that French workers had more in common with French capitalists than with Belgian workers.[135]

For radical Boulangists, a truly national government would look after all the people: waged labour, small traders, and artisans, all of whom were victims of a liberalism that left the weak to fend for themselves. There was disagreement over whether reform meant restoration of a pre-capitalist golden age, as it did for Barrès, or diffusion of technology, as it did for Laisant, or share ownership, as Naquet advocated. Whatever the case, this programme differed from Marxist Socialism, for it rested on class collaboration within the national community. When Laur invoked 'the mine for the miners', at Decazeville, he meant workers' participation in management; he evoked Republican fraternity, not class struggle. The Decazeville manager, Gambastide, stood for election as a Boulangist in 1889, promising to defend miners against competition from rural outwork. Other board members saw Gambastide as 'revolutionary', nonetheless.[136]

Boulangist Socialism may not conform to present-day notions, but in context it was not clearly distinct from the mainstream version. Both appealed interchangeably to the people and to workers, and both participated in the Parisian building strikes of 1888–1889. Boulangists rarely displayed the anti-Marxism that would later become important in the far right. Only the eclectic *Revue socialiste* displayed *some* hostility to Marxism as a 'German ideology'; others mocked the Marxist Jules Guesde more for his 'theoretical' stance than for the German or Jewish origins of his doctrine.[137] Neither did Boulangists echo the Bonapartists' threat to use the sword against the left. Whereas the radical right would later allege that revolutionaries

[132] Nord, *Paris Shopkeepers*, 302–50.

[133] Seager, *The Boulanger Affair*, 174–6.

[134] Lehning, *To be a Citizen*, 116–17; Hutton, 'The impact of the Boulangist crisis', 236–40.

[135] Doty, *Cultural Rebellion*, 56–61; William Serman, 'The nationalists of Meurthe-et-Moselle, 1888–1912', in Robert Tombs (ed.), *Nationhood and Nationalism in France: From Boulangism to the Great War* (London, 1991), 121–35; Angenot, *Ce que l'on dit des juifs*, 82–4; Gordon, *Liberalism and Social Reform*, 40–1.

[136] Donald Reid, *The Miners of Decazeville: A Genealogy of Deindustrialization* (Cambridge, MA, 1985), 101–9.

[137] Sternhell, *La Droite révolutionnaire*, 45–7.

manipulated and controlled moderate Socialists, Boulangists criticized revolutionaries for having capitulated to reformists and Republicans.[138]

For its part, Socialism included an enormous range of opinions, not clearly differentiated from Radicalism, Boulangism, or even Bonapartism. Initially, Socialists were almost universally attracted to Boulanger and largely abandoned him as he shifted to the right. The Possiblists were the first to turn against him, for they believed in the parliamentary path to Socialism. Marxists were more equivocal. Their leader, Guesde, refused to intervene in what he saw as a struggle within the bourgeoisie, while Paul Lafargue, Marx's son-in-law, felt that Boulanger represented popular opposition to Opportunism, and could be used by Socialists. In 1889, Lafargue stood as a Socialist Revisionist. In Bordeaux, Guesdists threw in their lot with Boulanger.[139] Socialist railway workers in Béziers and Roche-sur-Yonne, dockers in La Rochelle, Lorient, and Brest, miners in Nièvre and Decazeville, and textile workers in Flers and Fougères all enthusiastically backed Boulanger.[140] Radical Boulangist deputies in the Cher and Nièvre expressed the discontent of woodcutters, who had oscillated between Bonapartism and Radicalism.[141]

The followers of the late Auguste Blanqui were the closest of the Socialists to Boulangism. They espoused a working-class Jacobinism, advocating seizure of power by a revolutionary party on the back of an urban uprising. They addressed the 'people' rather than the industrial proletariat. They were anti-parliamentarian, nationalistic, xenophobic, and sometimes antisemitic. Blanquistes at first backed Boulanger in the hope that he might permit them to seize power. Then, while Édouard Vaillant denounced Boulangist Cæsarism, Henri Rochefort, together with Ernest Granger's faction of the Blanquiste Comité central révolutionnaire, became an integral part of the Boulangist movement.[142] In 1889, Boulangists were elected in Paris XV with Blanquiste votes, while in Lyon Blanquistes were elected as Boulangists.[143]

Radical Boulangism played a part in modifying the right's relationship to the 'woman question'. A few women were among left-wing converts to Boulangism. Marguerite Durand, a former actor (the stage again), came to Boulangism with her husband, Laguerre, and jointly ran *La Presse* with him. Another former actor, the Socialist Séverine (Caroline Rémy), wielded her sharp pen in the General's cause. After Boulangism collapsed, Durand and Séverine, having temporarily cut themselves off from their own milieu, wrote for conservative newspapers. They would

[138] *La Cocarde*, 1, 8, 9, 10 January 1889.

[139] Michel Winock, 'Socialism and Boulangism, 1887–89', in Edward J. Arnold (ed.), *The Development of the Radical Right in France: From Boulanger to le Pen* (London, 2000), 3–15; Sternhell, *La Droite révolutionnaire*, 174; Michel Winock, 'La Scission de Châtellerault et la naissance du parti "Allemaniste" (1890–1891)', *Le Mouvement social* 75 (April–June 1971), 33–62.

[140] Irvine, *The Boulanger Affair*, 104–6.

[141] Massé, 'Les Partis', 57–71; L.-H. Roblin, *Les Bûcherons du Cher et de la Nièvre, leurs syndicats* (Paris, 1903), 96–9, 314; Eugen Weber, 'Comment la politique vint aux paysans: a second look at peasant politicization', *American Historical Review* 87, no. 2 (April 1982), 357–87.

[142] Patrick Hutton, 'The role of the Blanquiste party in left-wing politics in France', *Journal of Modern History* 46, no. 2 (1974), 277–95.

[143] Sternhell, *La Droite révolutionnaire*, 53.

later collaborate on the women's newspaper, *La Fronde*. Ordinary women also attended Boulangist meetings, as they did Socialist gatherings. This presence converged with Boulangism's self-representation as a mass movement, synonymous with the nation itself, demonstrated through the mobilization of crowds of people. Women were present too in the crowds represented in the new popular press, of which the readership was often female.[144] Yet the Boulangist crowd perpetuated gender distinctions, preserving and expanding the reach of domesticity: women were welcomed because they suffered from Opportunist waste and taxes more than anyone.[145] In mobilizing women, Boulangism anticipated later movements of the extreme right, but unlike them, it did not combine participation with anti-feminism, just as anti-socialism did not accompany working-class involvement. Feminism was not yet a significant political issue—or even yet a word.

Radical Boulangism was a diverse movement. Some supporters, especially some of those who had come from Radicalism, remained close to their origins. Others, notably Barrès and Déroulède, contributed to the creation of a new, exclusive nationalism, based on the assumption of a passive people. Whereas Radicalism sometimes contradicted in practice its universalist discourse, Barrès broke explicitly with universalism, allied with advocates of dictatorship, and envisaged an exclusive, mobilized, national community.

CONCLUSION

Following Boulanger's victory in Paris, shocked Radicals and Opportunists united behind a new government under Pierre Tirard. It threatened Boulanger and his lieutenants with treason; it attempted to detach Monarchists from Boulanger by slowing down laicization and cracking down on the activities of the Boulangist left, notably in Parisian building strikes. Boulanger fled to Brussels. In the October 1889 elections, the alliance between Boulanger and the right functioned well, and only fraud prevented a Boulangist victory. Afterwards, the Monarchists dropped Boulanger while some radical Boulangists returned to Republicanism. Parisian shopkeepers renewed ties with Radicals, who now realized the danger of neglecting them.[146] After a few weeks of internal struggle, the Comité national disbanded. In 1891, Boulanger committed suicide over the grave of his mistress in Brussels. Ultimately, his story owed more to romanticism, in which good did not always triumph over evil, than to melodrama.

Notwithstanding, Boulangism produced a multiple legacy. In Bordeaux and among the woodcutters of Nièvre and Cher, Boulangism inadvertently encouraged proletarian autonomy. In Vendôme (Loir-et-Cher), the Boulangist newspaper reappeared in the 1890s under the Socialist label.[147] Bonapartism was the greatest

[144] Shaya, 'The *flâneur*', 70. [145] *La Cocarde*, 15 July 1888.

[146] Nord, *Paris Shopkeepers*, 347–8.

[147] Georges Dupeux, *Aspects de l'histoire sociale et politique du Loir-et-Cher, 1848–1914* (Paris, 1962), 517–18.

loser, for it dropped to thirty deputies in the 1889 parliament: many Bonapartists had stood as Boulangists, thereby losing enough Royalist support to ensure defeat. In the southwest, Boulangism helped detach the peasantry from Bonapartism, dispersing its electors between Moderate and Radical Republicanism.[148] Three Bonapartist deputies converted to Radicalism during the 1890s; when in 1901 Charles Ginoux-Defermon (Vendée) abandoned his plebiscitary tradition for Catholic Monarchism, part of his electorate turned to the left.[149]

Boulangism, especially in decline, gave birth to a radical right, which by the time of the Dreyfus Affair, would more clearly attack Socialism and feminism. In the 1890s, this strand of Boulangism was close to the new Christian Democratic movement. Christian Democrats and Boulangists would share antisemitism; already in the January 1890 Paris municipal elections, Boulangists supported antisemitic candidates in a futile effort to revive their fortunes.

Meanwhile, the need for endorsement from radical Boulangists, together with popular conservative Boulangism, forced Monarchism to 'democratize' its discourses and practices—hence the politicization of women's action, for instance. That did not mean that Monarchists had taken a step towards the Republic, for democratization was compatible with Monarchism. Moreover, their attraction to Boulangism stemmed from readiness to envisage a *coup d'état*, a catastrophic view of history, and the belief that Boulangism demonstrated the people's unconscious desire for strong government. That said, the 1889 defeat caused some Monarchists to revise their view of the Republic, for their enormous expectations had been disappointed. Cassagnac had written that the Paris election was 'the supreme battle that will decide our fate and after which, if we lose it, we must lock ourselves forevermore into the Republic...and abandon all hope from without'.[150] As it happened, Cassagnac never accepted the Republic, but others did.

[148] Pairault, 'Le Boulangisme', 110–16.

[149] David Bensoussan, *Combats pour une Bretagne catholique et rurale. Les Droites bretonnes dans l'entre-deux-guerre* (Paris, 2006), 181.

[150] *l'Autorité*, 2 January 1889.

4

The Ralliement (1890–1898)

> As for me, whose devotion to the Holy See cannot be doubted, I feel that the best means to demonstrate my filial respect is to signal some singular abuses of [the Pope's] word and to explain very simply the troubled situation that has resulted for us [Monarchists].
>
> Émile Keller, 14 October 1897

After the elections, Mackau told the Comte de Paris that without Boulangist help Monarchists would have gained only sixty seats. He took comfort from Bonapartist losses, yet he had forgotten neither his Bonapartist past nor his Boulanger moment; he hoped that if Royalists acted like 'democrats and men of action', not 'salon politicians', Bonapartist voters would turn to them. Mackau also warned of the right's 'lack of energy', and predicted acceptance of 'constitutionalism or something like it'.[1] He would not have said that a few months earlier. In 1889, when Ferry urged Monarchists to drop Boulanger in return for religious pacification, de Mun replied, 'Religious war has been the cement of your union... it is on you like the poisoned tunic of Nessus, you cannot escape it; it is burning you; it will destroy you'.[2] Monarchists believed the Republic to be unviable, but Boulanger's failure convinced some that its crisis would not be immediate.

On 13 October 1889, de Mun appealed for acceptance of the constitution. In March 1890, the Orleanist, and recently Boulangist, Jacques Piou, founded the fifteen-strong Droite constitutionnel parliamentary group. Still within the logic of *conservatisme* and Boulangism, Piou did not endorse the Republic, but declared that democracy was irreversible. In November, Cardinal Lavigerie of Alger, with Pope Leo XIII's approval, toasted the Republic. Three months later, the encyclical, *Au milieu des sollicitudes*, instructed Catholics to accept the Republic and join Opportunists in defending social order. If some Monarchists were resigned to 'constitutionalism', that is action within the regime, accepting the Republic in principle was another matter—this apparently minor distinction would become crucial to right-wing politics. De Mun and Mackau obeyed; Breteuil also did so, but withdrew from politics. Piou renamed his group the Droite républicaine and won support from around two thirds of the right. A small group of Catholic Republicans, notably Étienne Lamy, also embraced the Ralliement. The Comte d'Haussonville, the royal representative in France, spoke for the unrepentant.

[1] Archives nationales, Fonds Mackau, 156 AP I, 102/1, Mackau to Paris, 24 September, 17 October, 8 December 1889.

[2] Benjamin Martin, *Count Albert de Mun: Paladin of the Republic* (Chapel Hill, 1978), 81.

Although understandably doubtful of the sincerity of converts from Boulangism, the Opportunists generally welcomed the Ralliement. In March 1893, Charles Dupuy formed an Opportunist government with Droite républicaine support. Yet in the 1893 elections, Ralliés won only thirty-six seats, compared to Monarchists' sixty-five—de Mun, Lamy, and Piou were all defeated. In the new Chamber, the Opportunists were sufficiently numerous to ignore the Ralliés, but some nevertheless saw the right as a lesser evil than the Radicals. Under Jean Casimir-Perier the Opportunists reached out to the right; his Education Minister, Eugène Spuller, called for a 'new spirit' in Church–State relations. Succeeding governments inclined more towards the Radicals, and in November 1895, Léon Bourgeois formed the first ever Radical-dominated government, provoking an alliance of Opportunists and the right against it. In April 1896, after Bourgeois fell, Jules Méline formed a 'Progressist' (as the Opportunists became known) government with Rallié support. His ministry lasted until June 1898 and for some historians seemed to inaugurate constitutional conservatism and even constitute a second founding of the Republic.

Herman Lebovics argues that the convergence of Progressist big business with Monarchist landowners, united in opposition to working-class and peasant Radicalism, lay behind Méline's administration, and that protectionism played a key role in promoting trust between erstwhile opponents. The general tariff of 1893, which bore Méline's name, was intended to improve profits for business, landowners, and peasants, and provide security of employment for workers. Commitment to imperialism and to 'management' of the social question also united Republicans and ex-Monarchists.[3] Lebovics shares the assumption that the Third Republic failed to 'modernize' because its idealization of the peasantry sacrificed economic dynamism to social defence, but also assumes that 'modern' social concerns had displaced the 'traditional' religious question.[4]

In support of his thesis, Lebovics rightly points to the increase in number and scale of strikes, the foundation in 1892 of the Fédération des bourses du travail as the first national trade union structure, and in 1893 the election to Parliament of around forty Socialists. Yet it is hard to relate day-to-day politics to the intensity of the threat, let alone to perceptions of it, for anti-socialism had been integral to conservative politics for decades. The great Decazeville strikes of January 1886 and the strike wave of 1888–1889 did not deter Monarchists from using Boulangism against the Opportunists. Neither does the anti-Socialist thesis explain why, in 1898–1899, the Dreyfus Affair fractured the conservative alliance, for it coincided with another strike wave. Certainly, anti-socialism was essential to conservative politics, but that did not imply consensus on means or ends. Indeed, that opponents and advocates of the Ralliement accused each other of fomenting Socialism reveals the ubiquity of anti-socialism, its limits, and its use as a weapon in conflicts among conservatives.

[3] Herman Lebovics, *The Alliance of Iron and Wheat in the Third French Republic 1860–1914: Origins of the New Conservatism* (Baton Rouge, 1988); Sanford Elwitt, *The Third Republic Defended: Bourgeois Reform in France, 1880–1914* (Baton Rouge, 1986).

[4] Alexander Sedgwick, *The Ralliement in French Politics 1890–1898* (Cambridge, MA, 1965), 117, 153–5.

There were several reasons why Moderate Republicans and Monarchists understood the 'social question' differently. First, the co-existence in France of industry and agriculture and of large firms in coal, steel, engineering, and textiles with artisanal enterprises and peasant smallholdings presented several possibilities. Méline wished to use the peasantry as bulwark against Socialism, while others countered that large-scale industry would increase prosperity and defuse social tension. Secondly, it proved impossible to separate anti-socialism from the religious question. As mentioned in Chapter 2, the economy, state, and civil society expanded within a society already divided by religion, and indeed was partly a *consequence* of conflict between Catholics and secularists, for instance in education provision. Both Catholics and secularists were torn between recognition of common concerns and the conviction that their values, whether religious or secular, guaranteed social harmony and that those of their opponents undermined it.

Thirdly, Radicalism posed a distinct problem. Weakened in the cities by Socialism, Radicalism spread to the countryside, developing a network of rural bourgeois and petty bourgeois, Freemasons, municipal councillors, and journalists, often linked to the administration. The new generation of Radicals was more interested in social reform than its elders had been, and often allied with Socialists. The rise of village Radicalism intensified the clerical/anticlerical struggle and compounded Opportunist and Monarchist fears of levelling. Yet many Moderate Republicans sympathized with Radical anticlericalism, which in turn was inseparable from social issues.

Fourthly, the disputed meaning of the Ralliement posed a problem for conservatives. The Pope simultaneously endorsed a compromise with the Republicans to defend property, unity of Catholics in defence of their rights, and pursuit of social reform. His instructions provoked both the socially conservative and religiously flexible parliamentary Ralliement and a Christian Democratic movement that combined social reform, regionalism, women's activism, religious intransigence, and antisemitism. Christian Democracy thus compromised the parliamentary Ralliés' attempt to reach out to Moderate Republicans. Furthermore, Christian Democracy's virulent antisemitism opened it to Boulangists and Monarchists. The latter, as the quotation at the head of the chapter illustrates, claimed Papal backing too. Paradoxically, their fidelity to Monarchism did not prevent either insidious republicanization or absorption into a broader radical right.

Notwithstanding, the anti-socialism thesis works if we remember that it was inseparable from the religious and social conflicts, and that it was contradictory. There was much in Méline's programme to recommend it to the right, including protectionism, class collaboration under elite leadership, and the Russian Alliance, concluded in 1892–1894. Convergences between Progressists and Ralliés were strongest among liberal-conservative parliamentarians, lawyers, academics, and businessmen, linked by education and involvement in certain associations. Yet there remained many obstacles to the extension of the Ralliement into the country. That is not to say that enlightened elite policies were undermined by the backward mass, for the party leaders did not agree on the meaning of conservatism, and were themselves invested in the issues that divided the country.

PROGRESSISTS AND RALLIÉS IN POLITICAL CULTURE

In 1896, an Opportunist explained that 'the Socialist Party entered the scene at the moment when the old classification was ageing'. The Radicals, he continued, had broken with the individualism of 1789 and followed the revolutionaries, while 'the right sees the social peril and almost everywhere abandons its intransigence to defend the fundamental principles of a society in danger'.[5] In the southwest, the Marquis de Solages, head of the Carmaux mining company, responded to Socialist conquest of 'his' town by appealing to Progressists: 'The immediacy of the peril obliges regrouping all those who desire a regime of peace in liberty and justice.'[6] Rallié deputies were disproportionately involved in big business, which divided its loyalties between Ralliés, Progressists, and the Centre gauche. Rallié deputies were especially numerous in the industrial northeast, where Socialism was strong. Landowning deputies were less supportive of the Ralliement, but many later backed Méline.[7]

Sometimes Méline's backing for protectionism brought Republican and Monarchist business and landowning groups together. Three members of Piou's Droite constitutionnelle were members of Méline's tariff lobby, the Association de l'industrie française. In Mayenne, the Royalist Prince de Broglie (Albert's son) reluctantly attended a banquet of President Félix Faure on the grounds that Méline's 'allegedly moderate ministry' was 'allegedly concerned with agriculture, inspiring rightly or wrongly confidence in the rural population'.[8] Protectionism did not underpin Méline's coalition everywhere. It hardly counted in Aynard's Lyon or Eugène Motte's Roubaix, where free traders dominated; the pro-Méline Centre gauche was strongly anti-protectionist.[9] Méline's coalition may have held together because the government actually became more accommodating towards free traders. The free-trader *Journal des Débats*, close to the Centre gauche, claimed that Méline had 'grown up in office'.[10]

The evolution of Moderate Republicanism reinforced convergence. Boulangism discredited Opportunist leaders, particularly Ferry. The new 'Progressist' generation included figures who would dominate parliamentary life into the 1920s: Paul Deschanel,

[5] René Henry, 'Le Parti rural organisable et mobilisable', *Revue politique et parlementaire* 13 (1897), 14–36; Sedgwick, *The Ralliement*, 80–1.

[6] Rolande Trempé, 'Du Royalisme à la République, le "ralliement" du marquis de Solages, député de la deuxième circonscription d'Albi', *Annales du Midi* 71, no. 1 (1959), 59–70; Rolande Trempé, 'Une Campagne électorale étudiée d'après les archives privées', *Actes du 82ᵉ Congrès national des sociétés savantes, Bordeaux 1957* (1958), 471–90.

[7] David Shapiro, 'The Ralliement in the politics of the 1890s', in David Shapiro (ed.), *The French Right 1890–1919: Three Studies* (Cambridge, 1962), 13–46; Sedgwick, *The Ralliement*, 35.

[8] Michel Denis, *Les Royalistes de la Mayenne et le monde moderne (XIXᵉ–XXᵉ siècles)* (Le Mans, 1977), 497.

[9] D.M. Gordon, *Liberalism and Social Reform: Industrial Growth and Progressiste Politics in France, 1880–1914* (Westport, 1996), 41–63, 115–21; Jean-Marie Mayeur, *L'Abbé Lemire. Un Prêtre démocrate 1853–1928* (Paris, 1968), 106.

[10] Jean Garrigues, *La République des hommes d'affaires (1870–1900)* (Paris, 1997), 244–6; Joël Dubos, 'Organisation des réseaux modérés sous la IIIᵉ République: André Lebon, un homme à l'intersection des cercles du pouvoir', in François Roth (ed.), *Les Modérés dans la vie politique française (1870–1965)* (Nancy, 2000), 299–315 at 304–5.

Charles Jonnart, Louis Barthou, and Raymond Poincaré. Their allies in the older generation—René Waldeck-Rousseau, Édouard Aynard, Alexandre Ribot, and Jean Casimir-Périer—had avoided discredit because they had temporarily withdrawn from the *avant-scène* or were too conservative for inclusion in the governments of the 1880s. Several Progressists, like Poincaré, were of Orleanist parentage, and the Centre gauche was especially close to Orleanism. After 1885, the Opportunists' need for Radical support had excluded the Centre gauche from government, but in February 1889 it reformed as the Union libérale, presided by Henri Barboux. It opposed Boulangism and sought a united conservative party, including Monarchists; it counted fifty-two deputies in 1893.[11] The two generations were behind the Grand cercle républicain, formed in 1898 as an equivalent to English Tory clubs.

Republican and Rallié leaders also shared intellectual attitudes, even if that did not always facilitate practical collaboration. On that issue, I part company with Pierre Rosanvallon, who argues that 'modern' Republican social science was fundamentally different from traditionalist Monarchist thought, which was turned towards the preservation of a class 'threatened by the ascent of a new bourgeoisie'.[12] In fact, many Monarchists embraced the social science of the day, even if they used it differently to Progressists.

Both assumed the elite–mass distinction, with its organicist, racial, and gendered dimensions, as the influence of the Monarchist Hippolyte Taine on the conservative Republican Le Bon illustrated. In 1893, Taine concluded publication of *Les Origines de La France contemporaine*, his reflection on the preservation of elite rule in an age of mass bloodthirstiness. Soon afterwards, Le Bon published his seminal studies of the crowd and of Socialism.[13] Le Bon was then a very conservative Republican—anticlerical, scathing about the capacities of the crowd, and yet a defender of parliament as the best method of government.[14] Moderate Monarchists were as enamoured of organicism and Darwinism as were the Republicans. A writer in the Orleanist *Le Soleil* declared that 'Nature, in order to secure the conservation and progress of races, proceeds following the law known as the law of natural selection.'[15] We have seen that the École des sciences politiques institutionalized intellectual links between constitutional Monarchists and Progressists. Émile Boutmy, head of the School, promised that 'the latest discoveries relating to the descent of races and languages' would enable the elite to know the people.[16]

Le Bon's crowd theory systematized widely shared ideas. He argued that in the crowd, that is, democratic society in general, the individual merged into a collective mind and surrendered to passions, instincts, and materialism. Drawing on theories of hypnosis, he contended that the crowd was vulnerable to manipulation

[11] Garrigues, *La République*, 21–80; Gilles Le Béguec, 'Le Bâtonnier Barboux (1834–1910)', in *Barreau, politique et culture à la Belle Époque* (Limoges, 1993), 5–27.

[12] Pierre Rosanvallon, *Le Peuple introuvable* (Paris, 1998), 160.

[13] Gustave Le Bon, *La Psychologie des foules* (Paris, 1895); *La Psychologie du socialisme* (Paris, 1898).

[14] Robert Nye, *The Origins of Crowd Psychology: Gustave Le Bon and the Crisis of Mass Democracy in the Third Republic* (London, 1975); Benoît Marpeau, *Gustave Le Bon. Parcours d'un intellectuel, 1841–1931* (Paris, 2000), 95–146; Rosanvallon, *Le peuple*, 136–60.

[15] *Le Soleil*, 6 January 1893.

[16] Pierre Favre, *Naissances de la science politique en France (1870–1914)* (Paris, 1989), 32–5.

by demagogues. Le Bon equated the mass with the spinal cord rather than the brain; it was barely civilized, and was comparable to women and 'inferior' races. In contrast, the elite, through hereditary acquisition of acquired characteristics, 'mastered' its irrational impulses. Nonetheless, the elite's instinctive racial sense permitted it to understand the psychology of the mass, guide it rationally, and ensure predominance of national impulses in it. Le Bon cited Boulangism as an example of the danger of the mass, but above all had Socialism in mind, and so his ideas reinforced the anti-Socialist coalition. Collective psychology appealed also because it could be used as a weapon—rivals were demagogues who were too close to the mass—and because it permitted the ascription of fundamentally different contents to the national psychology.

Crowd theory reinforced shared views of the constitution. Both Ralliés and Progressists wished to preserve rational deliberation in parliament from the passions of the crowd—of left or right. For them, parliament was the terrain of the generally educated man, possessed of sufficient experience of life to know the mass, but detached enough to avoid demagogy and recognize the national interest. They condemned (mythical) average Republican deputies as demagogues who imported the materialism and passions of the mass into parliament. For the moment, most Progressists saw the re-establishment of *scrutin d'arrondissement* (two-round voting in arrondissment constituencies) in 1889 as sufficient to eliminate demagogues and ensure elite tutelage over the 'floating mass'.[17] A few suggested 'organizing' universal suffrage in order to give 'organic' structure to the formless mass, perhaps through Benoist's campaign for professional suffrage.[18] Such schemes brought Progressists close to the Ralliés, if more in debate than actual agreement. Progressists did not entirely overcome their fear that Ralliés threatened the regime. The latter did indeed favour constitutional reform, even if they were discreet on the matter for fear of appearing anti-Republican.

Progressists and Ralliés met also in responses to the social question. Whereas older Republicans believed that education and social mobility dissolved class barriers, many Progressists now accepted the permanence of classes and felt that the proletariat must be integrated into the system through inculcation of capitalist values and improvement of the race. Republicans became more open to the LePlayist social science in which constitutional Monarchists had long been interested. The engineer, Émile Cheysson, facilitated rapprochement by stripping LePlayism (always eclectic) of its reactionary Catholic flavour and developing the notion of social 'expertise', or 'social engineering'.[19] Drawing on crowd theory, Progressists and Ralliés saw Socialism as a regression to primitive collective society: Cheysson claimed that research in the colonies would expose the primitiveness of Socialism.[20]

[17] For instance, *Le Temps*, 8–12 February 1889.

[18] Ernest Naville, 'Les Objections à la représentation proportionnelle', *Revue politique et parlementaire*, 12 (1897), 43–58; Charles Benoist, *La Crise de l'état moderne* (Paris, 1895), 15–20; Gilles Le Béguec, 'L'Entrée au Palais-Bourbon. Les Filières privilégiées d'accès à la fonction parlementaire 1919–1939', Doctorat d'état, Paris X Nanterre, 1989, 170–4.

[19] Elwitt, *The Third Republic Defended*, 20–60.

[20] Janet Horne, *A Social Laboratory for Modern France: The Musée Social and the Rise of the Welfare State* (Chicago, 2002), 176.

Reformers also saw Socialism as a result of degeneration. Influenced by the non-Darwinist biologist, Jean-Baptise Lamarck, they believed that decay of the social organism derived from unremitting pressure from the milieu. 'Defects' in the mass—tuberculosis, alcoholism, syphilis, and smoking—could damage succeeding generations. The elites could counter degeneration so long as they respected the balance of the social organism; the elite would give organic structure to the mass.[21]

The Musée social, founded in 1894 as a centre for study of the social question, was the major institutional product of this convergence. It brought together Progressist politicians, social scientists, and businessmen, including Jules Siegfried and Léon Say, with Catholic 'experts' in the social question, notably Cheysson, LePlay's heir, Edmund Demolins, and the Comte de Chambrun, an unorthodox Catholic who was sympathetic to Protestants. The Musée was at that time close to the École libre des sciences politiques; only later did it attract a wider spectrum of reformers.[22]

The above developments reinforced Méline's anti-Socialist coalition. Yet dynasticism, religion, and the question of access to political and administrative power complicated matters. Legitimist deputies were largely opposed to the Ralliement. Among Monarchist deputies generally, opponents were older and had not forgotten the purges of the 1880s; they included many ousted magistrates.[23] Resentment of exclusion from political influence was common to all Monarchists, but some were closer to the circuits of power than others, and the development of the new Republican governing class in the 1880s was crucial to the fate of the Ralliement.

Governing Republicans were recruited through the Parisian medical and especially law faculties and Paris Bar. Those probationary lawyers who were selected annually as 'Secrétaires de stage' were guaranteed preferment, notably via ministerial cabinets. Poincaré, a former Secrétaire de stage, was typical of this milieu. From the 1890s, lawyers increasingly refined their training at the École libre des sciences politiques, which had acquired a near monopoly on recruitment to the senior administration by the end of the century.[24] Big business too was part of this network. Leading barristers often represented big firms—Poincaré worked for the chemical giant Saint-Gobain. Some lawyers were significant shareholders, while business families sent their sons into the professions and administration. In Lyon the Centre gauche network, in which businessmen and the liberal professions rubbed shoulders, included the Chamber of Commerce, the Société d'économie politique, the pro-imperialist Société de géographie, and the mutualist movement.[25] The local Progressist Deputy, Henry Fleury-Ravarin, was the grandson of a peasant and son of a businessman. He was educated at the Paris Law Faculty and École des sciences politiques, passing through the Conseil d'État and a ministerial

[21] Robert Nye, *Masculinity and Male Codes of Honour in Nineteenth-Century France* (Oxford, 1993), 74–88.

[22] Horne, *A Social Laboratory*, 99–140.

[23] Shapiro, 'The Ralliement', 27–36.

[24] Le Béguec, 'L'Entrée', 142–3; Philip Nord, *The Republican Moment: Struggles for Democracy in Nineteenth-Century France* (Cambridge, MA, 1995).

[25] Mathias Bernard, *La Dérive des modérés. La Fédération républicaine du Rhône sous la Troisième République* (Paris, 1998), 78–80.

cabinet, before winning election to the Chamber.[26] Poincaré held that the best way to defeat Socialism was to stuff parliament with 'the best qualified men, the industrialists, merchants, landowners, savants, lawyers, and all those who have the qualifications required to speak in the name of the moral and material interests of the country'.[27]

Radicals and Boulangists attacked Moderate Republicans for their proximity to the right, and there was some truth in the accusation. Yet Progressists were more suspicious of Catholics and Monarchists than the Radicals believed. Even the unimpeachably Republican Aynard, who possessed considerable economic and cultural capital, was excluded from government office because of his Catholicism. Monarchist deputies and notables were still more distrusted. Take the example of lawyers, who in 1881 constituted 27 per cent of Bonapartist deputies and 18 per cent of Royalists. Monarchist lawyers more often pled in provincial bars—Piou had practised in Toulouse—where they were part of a culture in which business, Church, the landowning aristocracy, and Army officers were prominent.[28] This society was strongest in the countryside, but also dominated certain provincial towns. In Montpellier, the Medical and Law Faculties, landowning aristocracy, and Church formed a cohesive Legitimist society.[29]

Both Monarchists and Ralliés resented their political marginality. Catholics could not become ministers, and were excluded even from low-level employment in the Education and the Interior Ministries, the Council of State, and prefectural corps. Down to village level, Prefects monitored the politics of civil servants and refused promotion to the disloyal.[30] They intervened in elections, especially in conservative departments, distributing favours and subsidies. Ralliés hoped to end this discrimination, and concessions were a touchstone of success of the Ralliement. Monarchists doubted that Ralliés could succeed, and anyway 'fairness' could hardly placate those who wanted a confessional regime. Méline did make some gestures to Catholics, but most ordinary Catholics perceived little change. Indeed, for Republicans the Ralliement made religion a *more* important marker of unreliability, as Monarchism became less visible. Furthermore, if Progressists toned down anticlericalism, they risked losing votes to Radicals—in 1893, Jonnart proposed concessions to Catholics constituents, but Radical pressure forced him to recant.[31]

Consensus on the social question was also limited. Republicans favoured partnership between public assistance and private charity, on condition that the latter abandoned confessionalism for science.[32] Some Catholics saw the Musée social as

26 Bernard, *La Dérive*, 37–9.

27 Paul Deschanel, *Comité national républicain du commerce et de l'industrie* (Paris, 1898), 6–9.

28 Jean Estèbe, *Les Ministres de la République* (Paris, 1982); Garrigues, *La République*, 327–30; Christophe Charle, *Les Élites de la République* (Paris, Fayard) 1987.

29 Philippe Secondy, *La Persistance du Midi blanc* (Perpignan, 2006), 163–4, 230–1.

30 Maurice Larkin, *Religion, Politics and Preferment in France since 1890* (Cambridge, 1995), 75–9; Christophe Voilliot, *Le Candidature officiel. Une Pratique d'État de la Restauration à la Troisième République* (Paris, 2005), 232–6.

31 Jean Vavasseur-Desperriers, *République et liberté. Charles Jonnart, une conscience républicaine* (Lille, 1996), 19; Le Béguec, 'L'Entrée', 59–64.

32 Christian Topalov, 'Les "réformateurs et leurs réseaux". Enjeu d'un objet de recherche', in *Laboratoires du nouveau siècle: La Nébuleuse réformatrice et ses réseaux en France, 1880–1914* (Paris, 1999), 14–16.

an agent of Protestantism and feminism, dedicated to the elimination of charity.[33] And although agricultural unions were generally regarded as an antidote to class conflict, they became another field of struggle between Republicans, conservatives, and Christian Democrats.[34] Conservative Catholics saw the purpose of rural banks as moral and religious education,[35] while Christian Democrats advocated independent peasant unions.

The shallowness of the Progressist–Rallié alignment was further complicated by divisions within each camp. The Musée social was divided between advocates of employer- and state-sponsored social reform. Aynard, the spokesman for liberals, saw mutualism as a *counterweight* to the state, and so regarded state subsidies as incipiently Socialist. He described de Mun as 'a state interventionist just as he is a religious interventionist'.[36] Aynard expressed a feeling among Progressists that Monarchists were not genuinely liberal, either economically or in religion. Divisions on the Rallié side were equally troublesome, for there was more than one Ralliement.

THE PAPAL RALLIEMENT

Leo XIII instructed Catholics to cooperate with the 'honnêtes gens' (the Progressists) and to use liberalism as justification for fair treatment. Yet he simultaneously urged them to strive for the construction of a Christian state, insisted that religion was the cement of society, and rejected the Church's subordination to common law. Indifference to the Church, he said, denied the divine basis of government authority. He ruled out a confessional party, but encouraged Catholics to mobilize against the anti-religious 'plot' (doubtless many readers imagined Jews, Protestants, and Freemasons).[37] The Pope's multiple objectives proved hard to reconcile, and undermined the Ralliement. If the Ralliés avoided religious controversy in the interests of compromise with the Progressists, they risked alienating those who followed Papal instructions to unite in defence of Catholic rights, even with Monarchists. The popular Catholic movement's outspoken attacks on the lay laws reinforced the Progressists' anticlericalism and discomfited the Ralliés.

Leo XIII's backing for social reform further complicated matters. In *Rerum novarum*, published seven months after the Toast d'Alger, he described the misery

[33] Françoise Blum, 'Le Comte de Chambrun, catholique, mécène des protestants', in Colette Chambelland and Pierre Rosanvallon (eds), *Le Musée social en son temps* (Paris, 1998), 27–41 at 28.

[34] Denis, *Les royalistes*, 453–5.

[35] Hubert Bonin, 'Crédit agricole et combat politique dans la Gironde à l'Ombre du XXe siècle', *Annales du Midi* 105, no. 201 (1993), 65–91; Louis Durand, 'Les Caisses rurales' and Hyacinthe de Gailhard-Bancel 'Les Syndicats agricoles', in *Compte-rendu général du Congrès national catholique de Reims* (Lille, 1897), 415–39, 446–559.

[36] Édouard Aynard, *Discours prononcés à la Chambre des députés pendant la législature de 1889 à 1893* (Paris, 1893), 4–5; Bernard, *La Dérive*, 67–70.

[37] Léon XIII, *Au Milieu des sollicitudes* (Evreux, 1892); *Lettre de S.S. Léon XIII à Monseigneur A.J. Fava* (Grenoble, 1892); Vicki Caron, 'Catholic political mobilization and antisemitic violence in fin de siècle France: the case of the Union nationale', *Journal of Modern History* 81, no. 2 (June 2009), 294–346 at 308.

of the poor as 'utterly undeserved', approved trade unionism, and advocated legislative correction of the abuses of liberal capitalism. This apparent qualification of property rights potentially undermined the anti-Socialist alliance with Progressists, while the insistence that reform must be guided by Catholic social teaching stirred up the religious question. Moreover, *Rerum novarum* did not disarm conservatives, for the Pope also condemned Socialism, endorsed private property, and advised charity for the rich and resignation for the poor.[38]

Meanwhile, Papal acceptance of the Republic, coupled with Social Catholicism and an injunction to mobilize against the lay laws provoked the emergence of a popular Catholic movement, which attacked parliamentary Ralliés as insufficiently Christian and 'social'. The course of the Ralliement depended on the interplay between divergent interpretations of Leo's objectives and Republican responses.[39] Furthermore, there was no clear line between acceptance and rejection of the Ralliement. Some opposed it altogether; some wanted to unite Monarchists on the 'constitutional ground' without accepting the Republic; others wanted an alliance between Ralliés and Progressists within the Republic. A division between social reformers and conservatives ran through both camps; each constructed the elite differently and attributed different qualities to the mass.

THE CONSERVATIVE RALLIEMENT

In March 1891, Cardinal Richard of Paris urged Catholics to defend religion 'on the constitutional terrain'—the second of the above options. Piou's Droite constitutionnelle at first followed this strategy. It included the Bonapartist Jules Delafosse, who saw the Ralliement as an opportunity to implement the Boulangist programme, and Royalists such as Charles Thellier de Poncheville. Piou refused alliance with the Opportunists—remarking in a Boulangist spirit that the people held the keys to the regime, not the Opportunists.[40] On 22 June, Chesnelong, Mackau, Breteuil, de Mun, and Haussonville, representing all the Monarchist tendencies, launched the Union de la France chrétienne (UFC). It did not accept the Republic, but espoused legal methods for Catholic defence and implicitly reserved the right to restore the monarchy.

Au milieu des sollicitudes forced dissolution of the UFC and conversion of the Droite constitutionnelle into the Droite républicaine. Yet the 'constitutional' strategy did not die. Indeed, its advocates could claim support from the Pope, given his instructions to fight 'masonic domination' of the Republic. Henceforth, creation of a Catholic party including Monarchists was right-wing Catholics' principal strategy. In October 1896, they held a conference in Reims to celebrate

[38] Christian Ponson, *Les Catholiques lyonnais et la Chronique sociale* (Lyon, 1979), 53–8.

[39] Ponson, *Les Catholiques*, 53–9; Sedgwick, *The Ralliement*, 40; Jean-Marie Mayeur, 'Congrès nationaux de la démocratie chrétienne', *Revue d'histoire moderne et contemporaine* 9 (July–September 1962), 171–206 at 178.

[40] Sedgwick, *The Ralliement*, 41–2, 48; Martin, *Albert de Mun*, 90–7.

the fourteen-hundredth anniversary of the baptism of Clovis. It was the first of three annual Congrès nationaux catholiques.

The Congrès espoused intransigent Liberal Catholicism, shading into integrism, updated with nationalism—as Abbé Bouvy put it, France was 'baptized at Reims and for centuries had been the right arm of God'. Abbé Gaudeau explained that society could not achieve peace, order, and 'the complete and worthy life of man' without the Church. Consequently, the Church had an imprescriptible right to spiritual liberty, and laws should maintain the principles of religion. Given that the majority of people were Catholic, anti-religious laws were tyrannical. Intolerance was necessary, for good and evil could not be placed on an equal footing. Gaudeau continued, in a passage in which social Darwinism reinforced intransigence:

> We must have the courage to admit that intolerance is necessary and legitimate. In the social as well as the philosophical order of things any organism that has the right to live has the right to be intolerant. The Church wants to live. The Church is a mother and there is nothing more legitimately intolerant than a mother.

In practical terms that meant independence for the clergy, defence of Catholic education, opposition to divorce, and final authority for the Church in matters touching the salvation of souls. Gaudeau spoke of liberty, but the Church would have special rights—it decided what the needs of the Catholic people were, and it alone would administer them. The Congrès' conceptions accorded well with *Le Nouvelliste de Lyon*'s view that since Monarchism provoked so much opposition, Catholics would be best served by an authoritarian-but-democratic clerical regime, respectful of the 'sacred laws of Christianity, morality, and the family'—a view that left little room for compromise with Moderate Republicans.[41]

The Congrès catholiques' conception of Church–State relations divided Catholics. First, whereas Christian Democrats believed that the lower clergy and laity must re-Christianize society by 'going to the people', conservatives held that the Church must reach society through the *state*—through 'the head of the social and political body'.[42] The Congrès assumed that the population was fundamentally Catholic, but had been subverted by Jews, Protestants, and Freemasons. It added the populist expectation that the Catholic people would rise up and 'suck from her breast the poison which is destroying [France]'. Catholic notables would guide this insurrection.[43] Inadvertently, this populism enlarged the space for radical Catholic groups. Secondly, the Reims congress denied that alliance with Republicans could defend religion. One speaker concluded a speech with the prayer 'God save us from the honest men'—those who cry to heaven about the misfortunes of the times, but happily go about their business and pleasure.[44]

[41] Vaucelles, *Le Nouvelliste*, 124.

[42] Abbé Bernard Gaudeau, 'Les Principes théologiques qui doivent régler les relations de l'Église avec la société civile en générale', in *Congrès national catholique de Reims*, 174–96.

[43] Sedgwick, *The Ralliement*, 96–8, 108.

[44] Louis Durand, 'Les Caisses rurales', 438–9.

THE PARLIAMENTARY RALLIEMENT

Piou's Droite républicaine aimed, precisely, to reach out to the 'honest men'. It started from the assumption that the electorate was democratic but conservative. Whereas Monarchists previously felt that Boulangism would channel the masses' innate conservatism into a democratic monarchy, Piou now felt that the electorate regarded restoration as a 'leap in the dark' and so was alienated from genuine conservatives. The Droite républicaine ceased to attack the regime, but still denounced the Republicans' financial profligacy and anticlericalism. It wanted a party open to all defenders of property who believed in freedom of conscience. In return for support, the government would revise the lay laws and permit Catholics to enter public office.[45] Piou intimated that the Droite républicaine might join a government willing to apply the *loi scolaire* fairly. Another Rallié called for a great party uniting 'the clergy, Moderate Republicans, conservatives of good faith and sincere patriots', which would detach Moderate Republicans from the Radicals.[46]

Parliamentary Ralliés were initially divided on social and religious questions. De Mun saw the Droite constitutionnelle as insufficiently Catholic and social. He organized a rival movement, the Ligue de propagande catholique et sociale, supported by the Association catholique de la jeunesse française (ACJF). He also revived the idea of a Catholic Party, now, thanks to *Rerum novarum*, with a more social bent.[47] He denied that the Church should serve as the *gendarme* of the rich, and called for a 'social Ralliement'. He flirted with antisemitism and in 1892 worked with the Radicals to pass a bill limiting women's working hours. Around one third of Rallié deputies backed de Mun, refusing for instance to endorse Progressist opposition to the right of railway workers to form unions.[48] The Royalist *Gazette de France* campaigned against de Mun in the elections of 1893 and contributed to his defeat by a Republican. De Mun returned to the Chamber in the by-election in Finistère in the following year as the deputy of the lower clergy, having been attacked by local Royalists as a 'Christian Socialist'.[49] Of course, de Mun was no less anti-Socialist than Piou. He declared that if the Republic did not become social and Catholic, pagan capitalism would give way to atheist Socialism.[50]

Ultimately de Mun backed Méline, for the appearance of Christian Democracy made Social Catholicism appear dangerous. Christian Democrats attacked noble leadership of Social Catholicism as a throwback to the *Ancien Régime*, whereas de Mun insisted that only the 'elevated classes' were sufficiently disinterested to

[45] André Reille, *Avant la bataille* (La Chapelle-Monteligeon, 1897), 2–3; Joseph Denais, *Jacques Piou. Un Apôtre de la liberté* (Paris, 1959), 58.

[46] Sedgwick, *The Ralliement*, 42–3, 47–8.

[47] Sedgwick, *The Ralliement*, 36; Martin, *Albert de Mun*, 90–7; Charles Molette, *Albert de Mun, 1872–1890: Exigence doctrinale et préoccupations sociales chez un laïc catholique d'après des documents inédits* (Paris, 1970), 170.

[48] Martin, *Albert de Mun*, 81, 84, 99–101; Sedgwick, *The Ralliement*, 41, 58–9; Molette, *Albert de Mun*, 330.

[49] Caroline Ford, *Creating the Nation in Provincial France: Religion and Political Identity in Brittany* (Princeton, 1993), 122–7.

[50] Martin, *Albert de Mun*, 96–8.

assuage class hostility. Likewise, de Mun preferred mixed unions of workers and employers to the autonomous workers' unions favoured by many Christian Democrats.[51] De Mun's position matched that of the pioneer of agrarian corporatism, Hyacinthe de Gailhard-Bancel, who dreamed of the day when peasants would look upon the château and say 'there's our star'.[52] In the absence of Piou and Lamy, beaten in 1893, de Mun, recently attacked as a Socialist, became leader of the Ralliés.

The Méline government apparently realized Rallié hopes for alliance with the Progressists. Some Catholics were appointed to senior administrative positions, while the lay laws were applied moderately—in 1898 the religious orders were more numerous than when secularization began in the 1880s. Yet Progressists and Catholics concluded no national alliance for the 1898 elections. The parliamentary Ralliés' social conservatism and readiness to moderate religious grievances allowed monarchists and Christian Democrats to pose as the champions of Catholics and/or the poor, and ultimately destroyed the Ralliement.

THE POPULAR RALLIEMENT

The Pope's dual endorsement of democracy and Social Catholicism precipitated the creation of a host of interlinked political, social, and charitable organizations.[53] Many were part of a broad Christian Democratic nebulous, which shared anti-capitalism, social reformism, intransigent Catholicism, antisemitism, corporatism, and the desire to 'go to the people'. Christian Democrats endorsed democracy, without necessarily viewing Republicans or the Republic positively. They were populists in that they counterpoised the people to the elite, and they differed sociologically from older right-wing groups. But their definition of the people as Catholic made possible alliance with conservatives, whose sense of exclusion from influence rendered them open to populism anyway.

Consequently, the Assumptionist nebulous, the most right-wing element of Christian Democracy, shaded into the Congrès nationaux catholiques, which refused to accept the Republic unless it repudiated *laïcité*. In 1883, Assumptionists founded *La Croix* (1883), an addition to its Bonne presse stable. Under the leadership of Pères Picard and Bailly, *La Croix* achieved a circulation of 173,500 in 1896 (including 25,000 priests), while *La Croix du dimanche* sold over 400,000 copies. The Assumptionists established groups dedicated to the diffusion of *La Croix*, from which emerged in January 1896 the Justice-Égalité Committees, which were electorally influential in spite of their small membership. *La Croix* abandoned Monarchism after Chambord's death, for it saw Orléanism as anti-Catholic and the Ralliement as a means to create a theocratic state inspired by the *Syllabus of*

[51] Martin, *Albert de Mun*, 104–14; Henri Rollet, *L'Action sociale des catholiques en France*, 2 vols (Paris, 1947), i, 388, 423–34; Mayeur, 'Congrès nationaux', 202.

[52] Gailhard-Bancel, 'Les Syndicats agricoles', 446–59.

[53] Ponson, *Les Catholiques lyonnais*, 60.

Errors.[54] *La Croix* backed Christian Democracy until 1898—breaking with it over secularism. Even before then, the Assumptionists cooperated with Monarchists so long as they put religion first.[55]

The second element of Christian Democracy was the Union nationale (UN), founded in 1893 by the turbulent populist, Abbé Garnier. It was a loose federation of electoral committees, cooperatives, friendly societies, banks, and agricultural unions, with around 12,500 members in the late 1890s. The UN was less theocratic than *La Croix* but equally antisemitic and more socially conservative.[56]

Thirdly, following *Rerum novarum*, Harmel reorganized the Reims branches of the Œuvre des cercles on a proletarian basis, thus contradicting de Mun's principle of aristocratic leadership. He founded the Démocratie chrétienne (DC), a network of *œuvres*, including trade unions, some of which excluded employers. In 1896 DC became a political party; open only to wage earners, it claimed 20,000 members.[57] It advocated a 'Christian Republic', in which Catholicism would be influential, but the Church would not govern. Nonetheless, DC was hardly less intransigent on religious matters than *La Croix*.[58] From 1896, all three strands participated in annual Christian Democrat congresses organized in Lyon on the initiative of the local UN.

Christian Democracy combined several strands in right-wing history with left-wing democracy and social reform. From Ultralegitimism it took clericalism, populism, and the injunction to live faith publicly. The Assumptionists had played a significant role in the Legitimist pilgrimages, while Garnier had also been a Legitimist.[59] From liberal Legitimism, Christian Democracy took the idea of reconciliation between the Church and the modern world. 'Liberal' Christian Democrats included Harmel, who had long opposed de Mun's 'counterrevolution', and abbé Lémire, who had abandoned his youthful Ultracism.[60]

Christian Democracy also owed a debt to Bonapartism and Boulangism, which reinforced its desire to 'do something' for the poor, hatred for Progressism, anti-parliamentarianism, and nationalism. Christian Democrats also echoed the antisemitism of Boulangism in its twilight.[61] One activist described the UN as the heir of Boulangism, while members of the UN rubbed shoulders with former Boulangists in the Ligue antisémitique, re-founded in 1897.[62] In Paris, the formerly

[54] J.A. Grenier, 'An apostolate of battle: *La Croix*, 1883–1890', *Catholic Historical Review* 67, no. 2 (1981), 214–35 at 215–16.

[55] Yves Marchasson, '*La Croix* et le Ralliement', in René Rémond and Émile Poulat (eds), *Cent ans d'histoire de* La Croix (Paris, 1987), 69–106; Christian Estève, 'Le Souvenir de la Révolution dans le Cantal. L'Exemple du Ralliement et son échec partiel', *Revue historique* 287, no. 581 (January–March 1992), 391–497; Mayeur, *Lemire*, 152–4; Danielle Delmaire, *Antisémitisme et catholiques dans le Nord pendant l'affaire Dreyfus* (Lille, 1991), 41–6.

[56] Stephen Wilson, 'Catholic populism in France at the time of the Dreyfus Affair: the Union nationale', *Journal of Contemporary History* 10, no. 4 (1975), 667–701.

[57] Rollet, *L'Action sociale*, 335–6.

[58] Mayeur, *Lemire*, 181–4, 235; Rollet, *L'Action sociale*, 184, 227, 342–9.

[59] Wilson, 'Catholic populism', 674, 679, 690.

[60] Ponson, *Les Catholiques lyonnais*, 61; Mayeur, *Lemire*, 143, 186–8.

[61] Ponson, *Les Catholiques lyonnais*, 62.

[62] Wilson, 'Catholic populism', 693; Bertrand Joly, 'Les Antidreyfusards avant Dreyfus', *Revue d'histoire moderne et contemporaine* 39 (April–June 1992), 198–221 at 212–14.

Boulangist shopkeepers' Ligue syndicale collaborated with the UN and with Harmel's Union fraternelle du commerce de l'industrie.[63] DC was strongest in the north-eastern proletarian towns that had backed Boulanger.

The Ralliement and *Rerum novarum* enabled ordinary Catholics, especially priests, to take on the leadership of right-wing movements, and thus break the monopoly of wealthy men. A government survey in 1893 showed that most priests accepted the Republic but not the lay laws.[64] Christian Democracy was especially strong where French-speaking bishops confronted insubordinate Breton-, Basque-, Flemish-, and Occitan-speaking clergy.[65] Indeed, Christian Democrats helped to democratize a regionalist movement hitherto dominated by aristocrats—Jean Charles-Brun, future regionalist leader, came to the movement through Christian Democracy.[66] In Finistère, Christian Democrats also benefited from the relative financial independence of the clergy and the support of the Social Catholic network centred upon the Quimper seminary.[67] Meanwhile, cheap American food imports reduced the viability of landed estates and weakened the nobility. In Mayenne, some priests exposed as forgeries the documents upon which aristocratic myths were based while others joined with prosperous farmers in sponsoring agricultural unions.[68]

The first clerical victory came in 1893, with Lemire's election in Hazebrouck (Nord) against a Republican backed by Rallié mining and landowning interests and the Archbishop.[69] In Brittany, in 1894, the clergy of Saint-Pol-de-Léon forced Royalists to accept de Mun's candidature in a by-election.[70] In 1897, in Brest II, the clergy successfully presented Abbé Gayraud against a Monarchist aristocrat.[71] In 1899, Abbé Trochu and Emmanuel Desgrées de Lou launched *L'Ouest-Éclair*, which linked Christian Democrats across Brittany. Conservative Catholics responded in 1901 with the publication of *Le Nouvelliste de Bretagne*, and the two became the 'brother enemies'.[72] Conservative Catholics usually won elections, but they had to incorporate Christian Democrat themes to do so, and so the split between liberal and social Ralliés was reinforced.[73]

Christian Democracy also radicalized the urban right. The UN in Lyon, the Prefect said, was spurned by 'calm and influential people'. In Paris, the Ligue syndicale moved towards Harmel's Union fraternelle, which denounced 'Jewish'

63 Nord, *Paris Shopkeepers*, 392–400.

64 Sedgwick, *The Ralliement*, 55.

65 Hudson C. Meadwell, '"Brittany Always". Ethnic collective action in Brittany during the Third Republic', PhD thesis, Duke University, 1988, 139–214, 255–62; Shapiro, 'The Ralliement', 45–6; E. Defoort, 'Jean-Marie Gantois dans le mouvement flamand en France (1919–1939)', in Christian Gras and Georges Livet (eds), *Régions et régionalisme en France du XVIIIe siècle à nos jours* (Paris, 1977), 327–36, 327–8.

66 Julian Wright, *The Regionalist Movement in France 1890–1914* (Oxford, 2003), 208.

67 Ford, *Creating the Nation*, 97–107; Mayeur, *Lemire*, 121.

68 Denis, *Les Royalistes*, 454, 462–4.

69 Mayeur, *Lemire*, 88–141.

70 See page 84.

71 Ford, *Creating the Nation*, 127–31.

72 Henri de Cadore, 'L'Ouest-Éclair et les deux Ralliements (1899–1930). Contribution à l'intégration des Catholiques de l'Ouest dans la République', in Michel Lagrée, Patrick Harismendy, and Michel Denis (eds), *L'Ouest-Éclair. Naissance et essor d'un grand quotidien régionale* (Rennes, 2001), 55–78.

73 Denis, *Les Royalistes*, 454, 462–4.

department stores.[74] From 1896, Harmel also began to address white-collar workers separately, a group that was numerous at the Christian Democracy congresses.[75] Since those educated in Catholic schools faced discrimination in state employment, they often worked in private-sector jobs. They saw Socialism as a threat to the Catholic values on which their status and promotion depended. Many clerks aspired to rise in the hierarchy, not overthrow it, but resented low wages and poor promotion opportunities.[76]

Christian Democrats' style exacerbated conservative fears. They used the accoutrements of popular religion, placed crucifixes and candles in windows on election days, mobilized local saints, traditions, and pilgrimages, and addressed crowds in minority languages.[77] Like Boulangists, Christian Democrats spoke at open public meetings—even de Mun restricted himself to private gatherings in Finistère in 1894—and used the mass circulation press. *La France libre* aimed to create an organization to rival the Socialists, with trained speakers able to contradict Socialist orators; the clergy would speak to the people in public meetings, just as Christ had spread the word in synagogues and markets.[78]

Whereas conservative Catholics believed that recapture of the state and repression of anticlericals would permit re-emergence of the people's innate Catholicism, Christian Democrats believed that the people must be reconverted. *L'Ouest-Éclair* claimed that France was no longer Catholic, but democratic, and so the faithful must re-conquer popular opinion.[79] Christian Democrats therefore urged the faithful to 'not be embarrassed by religion', 'unless you want the people to be embarrassed by it too'.[80] The *abbés démocrates* likened priests to missionaries in pagan countries.[81] Bishops saw that as evidence of Presbyterianism and democracy within the Church.[82]

Christian Democrats' social definition of democracy undermined the parliamentary Ralliement. For Lemire, democracy meant government '*by and through* the people', whereas for conservative Ralliés it entailed elite concern *for* the people. Like Legitimists, Christian Democrats rejected individualism as a manifestation of the Jewish and Protestant spirit of the Revolution, and rooted the individual in the natural communities, including the profession. The UN favoured factory councils, hours and wage regulation, pensions, and rights for mixed trade unions, but rejected state intervention.[83] DC preferred worker-only unions and accepted state

[74] Nord, *Shopkeeper Protest*, 367–72, 392–5.

[75] Mayeur, 'Congrès nationaux', 384–9; *Lemire*, 159.

[76] Lenard R. Berlanstein, *Big Business and Industrial Conflict in Nineteenth-Century France* (Berkeley, 1991), 228–57.

[77] *La France libre illustrée*, 16 February 1895; Mayeur, *Lemire*, 30, 60, 65, 100, 134; Yves Pourcher, *Les Maîtres de granit. Les Notables de Lozère du XVIIIe siècle à nos jours* (1987, 1987), 222, 240, 251–3; Jean El Gammal, 'Républicains et conservateurs en Lozère de 1885 à 1906: Luttes politiques et traditions historiques', in Jean-Paul Chabrol (ed.), *La Vie politique en Lozère, 1815–1939* (Mende, 1992), 232.

[78] Mayeur, *Lemire*, 120–1; Ford, *Creating the Nation*, 119–20; *La France libre illustrée*, 29 December 1894, 15 September 1895.

[79] De Cadore, '*L'Ouest-Éclair*', 58; *La Croix de Lyon*, 9 October 1892, cited in Ponson, *Les Catholiques lyonnais*, 59–60.

[80] *La France libre illustrée*, 16 March 1895.

[81] Mayeur, *Lemire*, 65–7.

[82] Mayeur, *Lemire*, 216.

[83] Wilson, 'Catholic populism', 677–8.

intervention.[84] The 1896 congress condemned capitalism on the grounds that it depended on the 'productiveness of money as money'.[85] Christian Democrats denounced critics who could not see 'that by trying to soften their selfishness and create an acceptable life for the workers we are carrying on the work of social pacification'.[86] Some conservatives understood, but others saw *any* limitation on property as incipiently Socialist.[87]

Christian Democrats defended the patriarchal family as another natural community. They attacked divorce and paid employment, yet defined women's tasks widely enough to give them a role that they lacked in the parliamentary Ralliement. *La Croix* created a Ligue de l'Ave Marie, in which women and children prayed for defence of the Church, and defended it in writing, conversation, and elections.[88] Many female charitable organizations, previously loyal to Legitimism, joined the Christian Democrat nebulous. Some local Christian Democrats formed women's committees.[89] Christian Democracy also broadened women's action socially, for in 1896 the first Catholic women's trade union appeared in Paris. *La France libre* urged women to defend the honour of their households by sending their husbands to the café if they insisted on reading 'immoral' journals such as the Rallié *Figaro*.[90] More adventurously and less typically, Marie Maugeret elaborated a Catholic familial feminism. She attended the national feminist congress of 1896—where she might have heard God described as the personification of evil—and afterwards founded *Le Féminisme chrétien*. Women's organizations undermined the parliamentary Ralliement because their clericalism frightened the Progressists. Indeed, clericalism provided common ground with opponents of the Ralliement.

Christian Democratic antisemitism had similar consequences. The extent of Catholic antisemitism is now well known to historians. Drumont's works attracted much praise and little criticism; Lemire found his *Testament d'un antisémite* to be exaggerated but 'sinisterly true'.[91] Many prominent antisemitic organizers and publicists were Catholic, and there was much overlap in membership between antisemitic and Christian Democrat leagues.[92] There were also ideological convergences. Christian Democrats blended a racial definition of Jewishness with religious and economic grievances against the government. They denied that antisemitism was religiously motivated, for they did not wish to endorse religious persecution. Rather they depicted Jews as enemies of the French nation, which for père Bailly, was 'a nation produced by God to serve him'; only a Catholic could be

[84] *La France libre illustrée*, 13 October 1895; Mayeur, *Lemire*, 120, 194–6, 199–200.

[85] Mayeur, 'Congrès nationaux', 189–91, 200–2.

[86] *La France libre illustrée*, 29 December 1894.

[87] Mayeur, *Lemire*, 144; Wilson, 'Catholic populism', 676–7.

[88] Marchasson, '*La Croix* et le Ralliement', 74, 85.

[89] Bernard, *La Dérive*, 57; Elwitt, *The Third Republic*, 75; Bonnie Smith, *Ladies of the Leisure Class: The Bourgeoisie of Northern France in the Nineteenth Century* (Princeton, 1981), 116–18.

[90] *La France libre illustrée*, 5 and 19 January 1895.

[91] Mayeur, *Lemire*, 84; Wilson, *Ideology*, 509–65; Caron, 'Catholic political mobilization', 294–310.

[92] Sternhell, *La droite Révolutionnaire*, 222–3; Caron, 'Catholic political mobilization', 320.

a true Frenchman.[93] Catholics could therefore accept the Republic, but must oppose its allegedly Jewish (and Masonic and Protestant) ruling class and laws. Christian Democrats also espoused economic antisemitism. For Lemire, 'Drumont is right when he campaigns against the Jewish notion of the superiority of money, which has caused devaluation of the farmer and farming.'[94] Although Christian Democrats rejected biological racism in principle, they saw the Jews as a hereditary race, denouncing, for instance, the 'scrofulous heredity' of a Jewish Radical.[95] Another favourite theme was that rabbinic power, sanctioned by the Talmud, preserved the Jewish race from assimilation.[96]

Christian Democrats did not share all the views of the antisemitic leagues. Lemire ensured the latter's exclusion from the 1897 Christian Democrat Congress. Yet antisemitism *per se* was not at issue; rather the antisemites refused to back Lemire's strategy of alliance with Progressists in the coming elections.[97] Lemire held that antisemitism was *insufficient* to resolve religious, social, and political problems. Christian Democrats also rejected physical attacks on Jews—but evoked extermination. They agreed with Drumont that measures ranging from boycotts of Jewish businesses through 'repression of certain financial practices' to withdrawal of citizenship, were necessary.[98]

Without erasing differences, antisemitism linked Christian Democrats to conservatives. Monarchists and even some bishops agreed with Drumont's charge that Rallié bishops had capitulated to Jews and Protestants.[99] Also attractive to conservatives was the notion that Jewish business rather than capitalism itself was responsible for social conflict: at the 1896 Congress, Garnier wanted condemnation only of 'pagan capitalism'. Yet conservatives feared that antisemitism would get out of hand. The category 'pagan' could also include Republican and even Catholic capitalists who did not conform to the Christian Democrats' idea of Christianity. Indeed, *La Croix*'s antisemitism shaded into a general attack on conservatism: the paper claimed that a conservative 'is an animal fattened by the Jew for his personal use; the Jew will chop him up when he feels the need'.[100] Whatever the case, some conservatives were alarmed. A conservative newspaper in the Nord admired Lemire's anti-socialism, but criticized 'his harsh words against Jewry and the exploiters'. The *Nouvelliste de Lyon* preferred religious to economic antisemitism.[101]

Christian Democracy complicated the task of those who wanted to unite Progressists and Ralliés against Socialism. Its clericalism agitated the divisive religious

[93] Caron, 'Catholic political mobilization', 299–30; Mayeur, *Lemire*, 198–9; Grenier, 'An apostolate of battle', 229–30; *La France libre illustrée*, 22 December 1895; Marchasson, '*La Croix* et le Ralliement', 69–106.

[94] *La France libre illustrée*, 13 October 1895.

[95] *La France libre illustrée*, 5 January 1895.

[96] *La France libre illustrée*, 24 July, 17 November 1895.

[97] Caron, 'Catholic political mobilization', 324.

[98] Mayeur, 'Congrès nationaux', 176–7; Abbé Gayraud, *Le Démocrates chrétiens* (Paris, 1899), 197–201; Wilson, 'Catholic populism', 693–4; Rollet, *L'action sociale*, 419–23.

[99] Wison, *Ideology*, 536–9.

[100] *La Croix*, 25 October 1890, cited in Marchasson, *La Croix*, 88–9.

[101] Mayeur, *Lemire*, 162.

question, while its social reformism alarmed Progressists, Ralliés, and Monarchists alike. Christian Democrats ridiculed Monarchists: *La France libre* dismissed those 'who see in a restoration the chance to lick the fatty reality of the present' and those 'who wait in calm contemplation of their navels for the king to come and do not believe it necessary to stir themselves when it's only God! They will neither use street methods, nor put their white hands in the callused hands of the people.' Lyonnais Monarchists warned the Archbishop of 'the grave danger' of Christian Democrat social doctrines, while Monarchist silk merchants forced the sacking of *Croix de Lyon* journalists who attacked their wage policy.[102] The Association des patrons catholiques du Nord, with episcopal backing, accused Lemire of paving the way for Socialism.[103] Yet Monarchists were attracted to the Christian Democrats' religious intransigence, anti-socialism, attacks on the Progressists, and sometimes their Social Catholicism. Monarchists financed the UN and Justice-Égalité and joined the latter. Even the DC included Monarchists.[104]

THE ANTI-RALLIEMENT

For Lamy, Monarchism meant mourning, not fidelity. His view was all the more poignant because the Comte de Paris' doctors had told him early in 1889 that he had only months to live. Although he survived until July 1894, he cut financial support for the Royalist organization in France and dismissed his departmental agents. His successor, the Duc d'Orléans, considered frivolous by some, defied expectations. He re-established a functioning, if sparse, organization, run by landowners, ex-officers, sacked magistrates, and members of the Société des agriculteurs. Monarchism retained considerable influence in local government, industry, and agriculture, academe, the press, and the Church.[105]

Monarchism survived firstly by exploiting the ambiguity of Papal declarations. Typically, the *Moniteur universelle* insisted that while the Pope forbade Catholics to foment civil war, they could advocate legal restoration.[106] Monarchists were open to the charge of ignoring Papal instructions to ally with Moderate Republicans, yet the Pope took time to clarify that point. Secondly, anti-socialism was as likely to sustain rapprochement with the Republicans as intransigence. Paris advised Mackau that when the social question 'has to be confronted head on, it will be recognized that by its very nature the Republic will be incapable of standing up to it'.[107]

[102] *La France libre illustrée*, 6 April 1895; Ponson, *Les Catholiques lyonnais*, 60; Mayeur, 'Congrès nationaux de la démocratie chrétienne', 174–5, 189–92.

[103] Mayeur, *Lemire*, 165–9.

[104] Rollet, *L'Action sociale*, 88–9; Mayeur, *Lemire*, 152, 161; Bernard, *La Dérive*, 56–7.

[105] Malcolm Anderson, 'The right and the social question in parliament', in David Shapiro (ed.), *The Right in France, 1890–1919: Three Studies* (Cambridge, 1962), 85–134, 88–90. In 1905, 45 per cent of the Independents were landowners; in 1914, 89 per cent of the Groupe des droites were landowners.

[106] *Le Moniteur universel*, 20 February 1892; *L'Éclair*, 14 October 1897.

[107] ANFM, 102/2, Paris to Mackau, 28 January, 2 March 1892; *Le Moniteur universel*, 10 June 1892; Secondy, *La Persistence*, 112–13.

Another Monarchist claimed that Socialism was hardly worse than Opportunism.[108] Pending favourable conditions, Monarchists husbanded resources, defended vital interests, and/or tried to hasten the collapse of the regime. Yet all these strategies potentially endangered the cause, absorbing them into either Republicanism or nationalism, or marginalizing them. By the 1890s, mourning was indeed an appropriate attitude for Monarchists to adopt.

Opponents of the Ralliement were particularly strong in the pretenders' entourage and Royalist committees. Paradoxically, they adopted a strategy that threatened republicanization. Certainly, royal representative Haussonville declared a quasi-Legitimist fidelity to principle and argued that 'honour' dictated resistance.[109] The debt to Chambord ended there, for as opponents of Boulangism, this group had rediscovered constitutional Monarchism. Eugène Dufeuille, head of the royal political office, argued that monarchy alone permitted the alternation in power of complementary, but mutually critical, parties. It alone prevented democratic levelling and ensured the pre-eminence of an elite characterized by a service ethos, measure, and compromise. He added that this elite would not be over-sensitive to the *point d'honneur* (the motive for a duel)—a criticism of extremist Monarchists, who were ever-ready to defend national honour with the sword.[110]

Dufeuille assumed that the Republic would inevitably collapse but was uncertain what would succeed it. Restoration required the support of all liberty-loving 'honest men', so Royalists must not alienate potential supporters by exaggerating the faults of the Republic—which would benefit Bonapartists and Socialists. For instance, Monarchist parliamentarians were moderate on the religious question: Haussonville argued that religion was dependent on private choice, and refused to isolate Catholic grievances from the conservative programme as a whole.[111] Broglie felt that conservative government within the Republic would merely show the irreparability of a 'faulty machine', yet supported 'sound measures' proposed by the Republicans. Haussonville saw no need for positive action: 'Conspiracy! What's the use? Events conspire for us and they are the best auxiliary.'[112] Such pronouncements led to suspicions that Orleanists did not want restoration.

For different reasons, Legitimists found it equally hard to sustain their Monarchism. It was not that they sympathized with the Ralliement. They shared less common ground with the Republicans, even if they were not entirely closed to contemporary social science, for organicism had precedents in counterrevolutionary thought, and Darwinism reinforced their belief in a struggle between good and evil.[113] They also assumed the elite–mass relationship, but conceived it on the model of the perfect, hierarchical society—the Church. The Montpellier Medical Faculty was known internationally for its defence of vitalism, which assumed the existence of a soul, against organicism.[114]

108 Joly, 'Le Parti royaliste', 338; Henri Rémy de Simony, *La République ouverte* (Paris, 1891).
109 Othenin d'Haussonville, *Discours à Nîmes* (Paris, 1891).
110 Eugène Dufeuille, *Réflexions d'un monarchiste* (Paris, 1901).
111 D'Haussonville, *Église et république*; Haussonville, 'Discours de Nîmes'; *Le Soleil*, 7, 8 January 1893.
112 Quoted in Callais, 'La Jeunesse royaliste', 565.
113 See page 84.
114 Secondy, *La persistance*, 230–1.

Given that Legitimists saw Orleanism as too close to Republicanism, they were equivocal about restoration. Some chose 'internal emigration'. Mayenne nobles, who almost universally rejected the Ralliement, became introverted. They opposed the scientific agriculture advocated by Republicans, for it undermined their relationship with the peasantry. They were outflanked by capitalist farmers and merchants, who brought both Progressism and Christian Democracy to the department.[115] Generally, Legitimists held aloof from the official Royalist organization, but in 1897 a number of them signed a collective letter denouncing the July Monarchy and recalling Chambord's intransigence.[116]

Other Legitimists took up the Pope's command to oppose anticlerical laws, while ignoring his instruction to do so in alliance with Moderate Republicans. *L'Éclair*, doubtless inspired by Cabrières, urged Catholics to unite, 'above politics', in order to fight anticlericalism legally, especially through the election of Catholic deputies. Cabrières relied on Marian devotion, the Sociétés de Saint-Vincent-de-Paul, and the Confréries de pénitents, all of which were led by wealthy 'hommes d'oeuvres', often noble, sometimes lawyers, and usually Monarchist.[117] Cabrières undermined the Ralliement because his organizations included Monarchists, and because he saw Radical and Moderate Republicans as equally anti-Catholic.[118] The Catholic strategy nevertheless also weakened Monarchism because it provided a space for Christian Democrats to challenge for leadership of the Catholic movement. Cabrières refused to publish *Rerum novarum*, while *La Croix méridionale* attacked the prelate's social conservatism and Monarchism.[119] Yet both Christian Democracy and Legitimism became entangled in a broader nationalist movement, undermining Monarchism from another angle.

Opposition to the Ralliement accentuated Monarchists' nationalism, which had developed in the Boulanger alliance. Denial of the Pope's right to direct French Catholics to accept the Republic, coupled with Republican attacks on Catholics' alleged loyalty to a 'foreign power', both accentuated Monarchists' nationalism.[120] The Droite royaliste declared that the form of government must be decided 'in France and among Frenchmen'. Monarchists also claimed that nationalism and religion derived from the same sacrifice of personal interests.[121] One Monarchist declared, 'in his resistance, each Catholic is a patriot'.[122]

Furthermore, many Monarchists saw antisemitism as a counter to Republican 'internationalism' and to discrimination against Catholics. The Indre-et-Loire deputy, Jules Delahaye, spoke at the antisemitic meeting of the 1896 Christian Democrat Congress, while in Bordeaux, one of the most virulent Royalist antisemites, the Comte de Eugène Lur-Saluces, formed a new 'Pacte de Bordeaux'

[115] Bernard, *La Dérive*, 49–50; Denis, *Les Royalistes*, 447–53, 468–70.

[116] François Callais, 'La Jeunesse royaliste, préfiguration de l'Action française', *Histoire, économie et société* 10, no. 4 (1991), 561–89 at 566–7.

[117] *L'Éclair*, 24 February 1892; Secondy, *La Persistence*, 109–25, 161–4.

[118] *L'Éclair*, 5 March 1892.

[119] Secondy, *La Persistence*, 120–5.

[120] *L'Éclair*, 22 January 1892.

[121] *L'Éclair*, 24 February 1892.

[122] *L'Éclair*, 14 October 1897.

with the left to keep the Progressists out of power.[123] The leaders of organized antisemitism, Drumont and the Marquis de Morès (who in 1897 founded the Ligue antisémitique), were both radicalized Catholic Royalists who wanted an alliance of Church and people to restore the traditional authorities. Morès' band was popular amongst the butchers of La Villette in the eighteenth arrondissement, where it was linked to anarchists and revisionist Socialists. Morès' departure for Africa in 1894, and his death in 1896, set back organized antisemitism. Its revival coincided with the establishment of the Méline government; in January 1897, Jules Guérin resuscitated the Ligue antisémitique with Drumont as honorary president. It soon had 20,000 members and it expanded substantially in the following year, for unlike its predecessors it spread to provincial cities and some rural areas, often sponsored by Monarchists, who claimed that the Jews had imposed the Republic on France and were responsible for falling farm prices.[124]

The evolution of Bonapartism reinforced radical nationalism. Victor's authority had been partially re-established, but as ever, Bonapartism lacked money and candidates, while many of his supporters envisaged a plebiscitary Republic.[125] Victor abandoned the conservative alliance following the death of Jérôme in 1891, but could not prevent the dispersal of his followers into radicalisms of various shapes. In 1894, in a by-election in Caen II, the Rallié Comte de Saint-Quentin, backed by Moderate Republicans, faced the Bonapartist Joret-Desclosières. The Prefect described the latter as 'a demagogue of the Imperialist-Boulangist type, who today describes himself as a Radical, and who will be supported by the whole agricultural lower class'.[126] Other Bonapartists joined demonstrations with Christian Democrats.[127] In Gers, where conflict with Protestants sustained popular Catholicism, Paul Cassagnac allied with the lower clergy against the Rallié Bishop and moved closer to Drumont.[128]

The recently founded Jeunesse royaliste (JR) combined radicalization with resistance to the decline of Monarchism, and thus paved the way for Action française (AF). The aristocrat Roger Lambelin founded the first Parisian group in 1888, only to see members desert to Boulangism. He was more successful in the following year, which saw the creation of a national federation. Unlike the Royalist leadership, the JR included Catholic Bonapartists and especially Legitimists. Lambelin possessed land in the Mayenne, had participated in the Œuvre des cercles, and admired Drumont. In 1893, General Charette, the one-time Papal Zouave, placed the JR

[123] Elisabeth Cazenave, 'L'Affaire Dreyfus et l'opinion bordelaise. Essai de méthodologie', *Annales du Midi* 84, no. 107 (1972), 63–76.

[124] Sternhell, *La Droite révolutionnaire*, 222–3; Caron, 'Catholic political mobilization', 306–8, 320; Nancy Fitch, 'Mass culture, parliamentary politics and modern antisemitism: the Dreyfus Affair in rural France', *American Historical Review* 97, no. 1 (February 1992), 66–84.

[125] David Bensoussan, *Combats pour une Bretagne catholique et rurale. Les Droites bretonnes dans l'entre-deux-guerres* (Paris, 2006), 182; Shapiro, 'The Ralliement', 13–46.

[126] Jean Quellien, *Bleus, blancs, rouges. Politique et élections dans le Calvados 1870–1939* (Caen, 1986), 57–8, 121–2.

[127] Bernard Ménager, 'Nationalists and Bonapartists', in Robert Tombs (ed.), *Nationhood and Nationalism in France: From Boulangism to the Great War* (London, 1991), 136–46.

[128] Offen, *Paul de Cassagnac*, 215–16; Maurice Bordes, 'La Vie religieuse du diocèse d'Auch sous la Troisième République', *Annales du Midi* 102, no. 191 (1990), 451–67.

under the sign of the 'cross and white cocade'. The JR was strong in southern white towns like Sète, Marseille, and Montpellier, where popular Legitimism thrived in competition with Protestantism.

The JR was not literally popular—Parisian sections included barristers from the Union monarchiste, one of the 'parties' within the elite debating circle, the Conférence Molé-Tocqueville.[129] Nevertheless, its radicalism frightened the Legitimist nobles of Mayenne. The JR leader in Montpellier attacked the Ralliés for their belief that 'the building would be fine once cleaned and inhabited by them'; in fact, 'the house needs re-building on other foundations'. Whereas Royalists traditionally felt that Monarchism would reappear in a crisis of the Republic, the JR set out to proselytize the people, just as Christian Democrats 'went to the people'. The league laid plans for the pretender's reappearance in France, and resisted Dufeuille's instructions to support Progressists in the 1898 elections, claiming that electoral action was 'secondary and relative'.[130]

Countless opportunities arose for Monarchists to embarrass the Ralliés. They ranged from a deduction from the salary of a bishop during an absence at Rome, to controversy over the taxation of religious orders (the *droits d'accroissement*).[131] Monarchists denounced the 'Freemasons in power' and the 'lukewarm' Catholics who sell their support to the government at a low price.[132] They also attacked Méline's social reforms: Charles Maurras, then taking his first steps in journalism, denounced 'state Socialism'; another journalist saw de Mun and the Progressist Deschanel as allies of the Socialists.[133] In 1897 some Monarchist deputies opposed credits for the President of the Republic's visit to Russia; those who voted in favour claimed that the alliance was not the work of the government, but of two nations responding to the mysterious forces of Providence.[134] Over half of Monarchists voted against the budget in March 1898 because of excessive taxation of religious orders and the 'electoral pillage' of France.[135]

While constitutional Monarchism remained influential, the activist tendency gained ground thanks to the meagreness of Méline's concessions to Catholics. The pretender officially supported Dufeuille, but from 1893, he patronized the JR, for it openly proclaimed its Royalism at a time when most dared not. In 1896, the pretender brushed aside criticisms from the head of the royal Consultative Committee, Audiffret-Pasquier, of his 'too-Bonapartist' declarations. In January 1898, the more activist Eugène Buffet replaced Dufeuille. Thus, Monarchists reinforced the Christian Democrats' challenge to the conservative Ralliement, and took a further step towards the radical right.

[129] Callais, 'La Jeunesse royaliste', 564; Denis, *Les Royalistes*, 486–9; Joly, 'Le Parti royaliste', 328–9.

[130] *La Gazette de France*, 15 March 1898; François Callais, 'La Jeunesse royaliste, préfiguration de l'Action française', *Histoire, économie et société* 10, no. 4 (1991), 561–89; Denis, *Les Royalistes*, 486–9; Joly, 'Les Antidreyfusards', 218–19; Secondy, *La Persistance*, 127–30.

[131] For instance, *L'Éclair*, 7, 21 January 1892.

[132] *L'Éclair*, 14 October 1897; *La Gazette de France*, 4–5 January 1898.

[133] *Le Soleil*, 6–9 July 1896.

[134] *L'Eclair*, 4 September 1897.

[135] Shapiro, *The Ralliement*, 40.

THE FÉDÉRATION ÉLECTORALE

In March 1896, the Pope charged Étienne Lamy with organizing the 1898 elections.[136] Lamy had been one of the 363 deputies opposed to the *seize-mai* coup of 1877, and led a small group of Catholic Republicans.[137] He had persuaded the Pontiff that de Mun's and Piou's pasts rendered them unpalatable to Progressists, and that only a Catholic Republican could unite Ralliés with Christian Democrats and campaign against the lay laws moderately enough not to alienate Progressists. Lamy's task was impossible, for his personal position summed up the weaknesses of the Ralliement more generally.

Lamy's strength was that he combined Catholicism with positioning in the liberal intellectual and cultural circles that connected conservative Republicans with moderate Monarchists. He had much in common with the Moderate Republican Ferdinand Brunetière, a recent convert to Catholicism and editor of the *Revue des Deux Mondes,* in which Lamy also wrote. Brunetière argued that Darwinism legitimated an elitist conservative society and even validated the doctrine of original sin. Lamy too was fond of using science to prove that society depended on religion; he elaborated a Catholic version of Le Bon's evolutionism, elite theory, and collective psychology.[138] He argued that the Republicans had rooted the regime in the popular psyche, so the right must accept the regime or risk irrelevance. Yet their historical destiny fulfilled, Republican vices would bring them down in favour of a new elite.

Lamy maintained that a 'virile' strategy must precipitate events, especially in a Republic, where the 'law of the fittest' prevailed. Monarchists, said Lamy, could not engage wholeheartedly in this struggle because they did not accept the regime—he contrasted the 'tenderness of [Piou's] adieus' to Monarchism with 'the chilliness of his new course'. Genuine Republicans should lead the right and demand repeal of the lay laws in the name of toleration and equality before the law.[139] Lamy sought a majority in which Catholics would 'rub shoulders with men of broad mind and goodwill', but was more favourable to the popular Ralliement than the parliamentarians were.[140]

By December 1896, Lamy had secured the support of all the major non-Royalist Catholic organizations. The Fédération électorale was announced officially in December 1897 at the Congrès national catholique. Lamy achieved some local success. In Lyon, a new generation of liberal lawyers and businessmen backed him. They won Progressist support and secured the election of one of their number to parliament.[141] Lamy also attracted those Christian Democrats who were most attached to the Republic; Lemire persuaded the Christian Democrat congress of

[136] Sedgwick, *The Ralliement*, 89–117.

[137] Charles Molette, *L'Action catholique de la jeunesse française, 1886–1907. Une Prise de conscience du laïcat catholique* (Paris, 1968), 151.

[138] *La politique nouvelle*, 8 February 1897.

[139] Étienne Lamy, 'Le Devoir des conservateurs', *Revue des Deux Mondes* 61 (1892), 512–36.

[140] Lamy, 'Le Devoir des conservateurs', 512–36; *La Politique nouvelle*, 8 February 1897; Sedgwick, *The Ralliement*, 90–1.

[141] Bernard, *La Dérive*, 41–9.

1897 to accept the Fédération's programme.[142] Such successes were rare. Lamy's Ligue de la Politique nouvelle was not a mass organization, and his status as leader was not publicly known until December 1897. He struggled to reconcile competing interpretations of the Ralliement.

Lamy was too secular and/or conservative for many Christian Democrats. He complained that 'this sudden, noisy, agitation' had awakened fear of 'government of priests', and excluded the *abbés démocrates* from the Fédération's 1897 Congress.[143] The Assumptionists endorsed the Republic and agreed to allow their Justice-Égalité committees to participate in the Fédération, but they would neither couch their grievances in the language of liberalism nor cut ties with Monarchists. Lamy dared not break with Justice-Égalité, for it alone kept the 'more ardent Catholics' in the fold. He asked the clergy to provide covert inspiration.[144] The Congrès catholiques also undermined Lamy, for they too placed Catholic unity above alliance with Progressists.[145] They attacked Méline, and demanded repeal, not just modification, of the lay laws. In Haute-Garonne the partisans of the Congrès catholiques joined the Fédération, but a deal with Progressists broke down thanks to fear that the administration would not keep its promise to back Piou's candidacy in the department.[146]

Lamy also gained little support from the parliamentary leaders of the Ralliement. Piou and de Mun did not share Lamy's desire to unite all Catholics, not least because they opposed Christian Democracy for its social radicalism and Catholic fundamentalism.[147] They were better placed than Lamy to bargain with Méline. Encouraged by rumours that Méline had agreed to reform the lay laws, Lamy initially accepted negotiation with the Progressists. Yet pressure from Justice-Égalité and others forced him to change his mind. In a speech of 18 April 1898, he berated the Progressists for their broken promises, and demanded reform of the lay laws as the condition of support for them.[148] Anyway, he had always condemned the Progressists' secular morality and discrimination against Catholics.[149] Lamy acknowledged that the religious question was intrinsic to all the major issues of the period: discrimination against Catholics undermined the quality of deputies and deprived parliament of legitimacy; international influence depended on missionaries; religion persuaded workers to await their reward in heaven for accepting the harshness of labour.[150]

In the elections the Assumptionists disbursed funds and supported candidates without consulting the Fédération. In previously mentioned Haute-Garonne, the local committee did not reveal Lamy's instruction that Catholics should support a Progressist on the second ballot. In Digne (Hautes-Alpes) Catholics allied with

142 *La Politique nouvelle*, 4 November 1897; Mayeur, 'Congrès nationaux', 171–206, 178–9, 186–7; Mayeur, *Lemire*, 217.

143 Mayeur, *Lemire*, 245.

144 Sedgwick, *The Ralliement*, 104–6.

145 Archives nationales, Fonds Lamy AN 333 AP 48/1 (hereafter ANFL, carton, dossier number), Bellomayre to Lamy, 15 February 1898.

146 ANFL, 48/1, Quilliau to Lamy, 29 April 1898.

147 Martin, *Albert de Mun*, 121–4.

148 *La Politique nouvelle*, 8, 15 March 1897.

149 *La Politique nouvelle*, 15 February 1897.

150 Lamy, *Les Catholiques et la situation présente*, 13–31.

Radicals against the Progressist Joseph Reinach, whom the Bishop denounced as a Panamiste and Jew.[151] Catholics in the country at large rejected compromise with the Progressists. Monarchists were torn between supporting conservative candidates and displaying their flag.[152]

Extra-parliamentary pressure undermined compromise on the Republican side too. In Côte d'Or Moderate Republicans voted for Radicals rather than Ralliés on second ballots. Many Progressist deputies who had supported Méline's moderation in parliament were intransigent in their constituencies, for they relied on Radical votes. Whereas Méline remained silent on the lay laws, Barthou, at the electorally crucial Ministry of the Interior, saw them as 'an integral and inalienable part of the Republican domain' and warned voters against 'the perfidious designs of those who would enter the Republic to destroy it'.[153] Centre gauche deputies, who had traditionally seen the lay laws as illiberal, now declared them inviolable, out of concern to differentiate themselves from the Ralliés.

Lamy's discomfiture was compounded by his own defeat on the first ballot. The Ralliés won thirty-eight seats—one more than in 1893. Royalists won forty-one seats and Bonapartists twelve. The Ralliés proved unable to convert parliamentary alliance into an electoral coalition with the moderates. Extremists were strengthened on both sides. Radicals and Socialists gained half a million votes, although this was not translated into seats. On the right, eighteen deputies were elected as antisemites. Many Progressists won only with Radical votes. The Fédération électorale broke up in disputes concerning the name of a re-launched organization, illustrating once more the loaded nature of political labels: should it be entitled 'Republican', as the Christian Democrats, UN, and Lamy wanted, or 'constitutional', as the Congrès nationaux catholiques, Justice-Égalité, and ACJF preferred?[154] When the Chamber reconvened, the Ralliés still backed Méline. But on 22 June 1898 sufficient Monarchists and Progressists voted with the Radicals to defeat him.

CONCLUSION

Lebovics argues that the return of the religious issue was possible after 1898 because anti-socialism was so well rooted in political culture.[155] In fact, the religious question revived precisely because it was entangled with class issues. Republicans and Catholics each saw their own values as essential to the defeat of Socialism. Méline declared that 'the best way to destroy revolutionary doctrines is to remain faithful to the ideals of justice and solidarity which are part of the Republican tradition'.[156] Catholics believed that secularism engendered Socialism and saw Catholic education as the antidote.

[151] ANFL, 48/1, Boissans to Lamy, 26 October 1897.

[152] *La Gazette de France*, 4–5 January 1898.

[153] Sedgwick, *The Ralliement*, 114–16, 144–6.

[154] Charles Molette, *L'Action catholique*, 238–9.

[155] Lebovics, *The Alliance*, 184–90.

[156] Quoted in André Daniel, *L'Année politique* (Paris, 1896), 163.

Neither was it easy to enlist the popular constituency of the right in an anti-Socialist alliance. Catholicism and anticlericalism were more than anachronistic throwbacks. They were part of collective identity, and were essential to the networks through which candidates became known locally and nationally, and were tied up with access to education and state employment. This was most obvious in areas of long-standing hostility between Catholics and Protestants, and it explains for example the resistance of the right in Montpellier to the Ralliement. Similar considerations applied in those parts of Brittany and the west where political alignments revolved around conflicts between whites, blues, and reds. Furthermore, obsession with the Socialist menace led to neglect of the right's broader constituency. For instance, Progressists defended protectionism on the grounds that small shopkeepers raised prices more than tariffs did, and refused to condemn department stores. Playing down the religious question estranged white-collar workers and women for whom religion was a condition of promotion and social action respectively.

Some of these groups initially turned to Christian Democracy, but by 1898 the movement was losing ground. Disputes concerning *laïcité* undermined the 1898 Christian Democratic Congress. In March 1899, the Vatican instructed priests to obtain episcopal authorization before speaking on social topics, and in January 1901 the Pope warned Christian Democrats of the dangers of Socialism. Already, Christian Democracy had given way to antisemitism and nationalism. Antisemitism was intrinsic to the Catholic movement, both to Christian Democracy and to Royalist opponents of the Ralliement.[157] Thus, the Dreyfus Affair did not represent the unprecedented irruption of antisemitism into politics. Rather, Alfred Dreyfus' conviction in 1894 and opposition to revision of his verdict were specific instances of a broader antisemitism that was intrinsic to the politics of the 1890s. The emergence of independent antisemitic leagues further radicalized the right and dealt another blow to the Ralliement.

Increasingly, antisemitism brought the popular Ralliement together with its conservative opponents. For Christian Democrats antisemitism was a means to distinguish between the Republic and its corrupt rulers, and was thus an intrinsic part of their campaign for a theocratic republic. Yet the violence of their antisemitism and attacks on the government brought them close to Royalists, for whom antisemitism represented a means to oppose the Ralliement itself, to express resentment at 'discrimination' against themselves, and later to attack Méline—intransigents claimed that he worked for the Dreyfusard 'syndicate'.[158] Christian Democrats thus faced a dilemma, which intensified in early 1898, when a series of antisemitic riots greeted the publication of Émile Zola's 'J'accuse', the first public manifestation of Dreyfusism. The UN tried to steer a middle way, maintaining its antisemitic rhetoric while condemning physical attacks on Jews, for violence clearly broke with Republican principles. That did not prevent it from losing support to antisemitic organizations.[159]

[157] Fitch, 'Mass culture', 66–84. [158] *La Gazette de France*, 3 February 1898.
[159] Caron, 'Catholic political mobilization', 325–8.

Increasingly, antisemitism united urban popular conservatism with aristocratic royalism. The riots of January and February involved all the major cities of France and two dozen smaller towns, mostly in right-wing constituencies, from Vannes (Morbihan) to Montpellier (Hérault). They were instigated by war veterans, sometimes the Army itself, the UN and other Catholic organizations, Royalist newspapers, and in Paris the Ligue antisémitique. Socially, the rioters were mainly students and petty bourgeois, especially clerks.[160] Three months later, eighteen antisemitic deputies were elected in metropolitan France, five of them representing cities, the rest in rural Royalist constituencies in the west and Brittany, the Massif Central, and the once Bonapartist southwest and southeast.[161] In 1898, the Comte Jean de Sabran-Pontevès, president of the Royalist committee of Indre-et-Loire, stood in Paris XIX as a Royalist antisemite. Supported by the butcher boys of La Villette, Sabran-Pontevès gained 4,000 votes on the second ballot. He contrasted his relative success with the failings of a Royalist leadership too concerned with 'salon society'.[162] Certainly there were tensions in the antisemitic movement. Drumont soon left Guérin's league. He was more comfortable with the largely Monarchist antisemitic deputies, whose parliamentary group he presided.[163] The street-fighters, including the butchers of La Villette, stayed with Guérin, yet Guérin happily took Royalist money.[164]

The Méline government failed to incorporate the right into the Republic, and precisely *because* it endeavoured to prioritize anti-socialism, it inadvertently precipitated the Dreyfus Affair.

[160] Wilson, *Ideology*, 106–20.

[161] Fitch, 'Mass culture', 55–95; Sternhell, *La Droite révolutionnaire*, 221–2.

[162] Joly, 'Le Parti royaliste', 351–2.

[163] Sternhell, *La Droite révolutionnaire*, 221–2.

[164] Joly, 'Les Antidreyfusards', 212–14.

5

Nationalism (1898–1900)

There is no Dreyfus Affair

Jules Méline, 4 December 1897

Méline's coalition was foundering before the elections. Prioritization of anti-socialism had provoked opposition from clericals, anticlericals, and social reformers, all of whom used antisemitism against the government. For monarchists, antisemitism permitted incitement of the people against the 'foreign' Republic without endangering family and property, and expressed resentment at discrimination against the 'competent'. Indeed, the condemnation for espionage of the Jewish staff officer Alfred Dreyfus, back in 1894, owed much to discontent among monarchist and aristocratic officers at new methods of recruitment to the General Staff. Older, largely Catholic officers from the St-Cyr military academy resented a new promotion system that favoured younger, more secular graduates of the École Polytechnique—such as Dreyfus.[1] Commandant Marquis Mercier du Paty de Clam, charged with the Dreyfus enquiry, thought that only 'Frenchmen of France' should occupy sensitive military positions; one of his superiors believed that for centuries Jews had been traitors.[2] For Christian Democrats, depiction of Republicans as the agents of a Jewish, Protestant, and Masonic conspiracy enabled them to demand a social and clerical Republic without seeming to attack the regime. The right had no monopoly on antisemitism. For Radicals, antisemitism permitted depiction of Méline as an agent of the cosmopolitan rich, and most Radicals were as Antidreyfusard as the right. Initially, the few Dreyfusards were closest to Progressism. Neither Émile Zola's open letter of January 1898 accusing the Army of victimizing Dreyfus, nor the novelist's subsequent trial and conviction, mobilized the left.

Only War Minister Godefroy Cavaignac's admission that Colonel Henry had fabricated evidence against Dreyfus polarized political opinion. The left saw the forgery as evidence of a military, monarchist, and Catholic conspiracy against the Republic, while the right defended the honour of the Army, and Cavaignac insisted that 'secret documents' proved Dreyfus' guilt. Some claimed that Cavaignac's exposure of the fraud proved the Army's disinterestedness, while Henry's suicide reinforced the belief that his forgery had been 'patriotic'.[3] The emergence of nationalist leagues

[1] Ruth Harris, *Dreyfus: Politics, Emotion and the Scandal of the Century* (New York, 2010), 62–4.
[2] Michael Burns, *Dreyfus* (London, 1992), 123; Jean-Denis Bredin, *L'Affaire*, (Paris, 1983), 13.
[3] *L'Éclair*, 2 September 1898.

further radicalized the right. Already in 1897, Jules Guérin's Ligue antisémitique had begun to attract Christian Democrats, and now the revival of anticlericalism in the Affair ruined the Christian Democrats' hopes of Christianizing the Republic. In September 1898, the Ligue des patriots (LDP) re-formed. In Paris, it was close to national-Socialist groups, including Parti républicain socialiste français, founded in 1898 by Rochefort and Francis Laur, and the Blanquiste Comité central révolutionnaire. In December 1898, Jules Lemaître and François Coppé founded the relatively moderate Ligue de la Patrie Française (LPF). Since October, Nationalists and monarchists had been predicting the end of the Republic, and in February 1899 Déroulède tried unsuccessfully to persuade a general to march on the presidential Palace. On 4 June, a Nationalist band, including de Mun's son, Bertrand, attacked President Loubet at the Auteuil racecourse.

Méline's efforts to confine the Affair to the judicial arena confirmed the left's suspicion that he was beholden to the right. Eventually, the Progressists split. On 22 June, one of them, René Waldeck-Rousseau, an unbelieving anticlerical, formed a government of 'Republican defence', backed by the Radicals and Socialists—once again, the left claimed to defend the existing order against right-wing subversion. Méline led conservative Progressists into opposition, and some embraced Nationalism. Albert de Mun, forgetting papal injunctions to defend religion in the name of justice (not to speak of doctrinal condemnation of suicide) donated publicly to the memorial fund for Henry and denounced the Dreyfusard 'syndicate'.

For some historians, religious and constitutional quarrels revived because politicians felt safe to pursue 'secondary' interests once Méline had stabilized the social order.[4] In fact, all these questions were inseparable. Monarchists and Christian Democrats attacked the parliamentary Ralliement precisely because they felt that it *encouraged* Socialism, and continued social unrest confirmed that fear. Exposure of the Henry forgery coincided with strikes in the railway and building industries, while the Confédération général du travail (CGT) preached anti-militarism and the insurrectionary general strike. What is more, Méline's successor, Brisson, revived the income tax proposal—precisely the issue which had precipitated unity behind Méline. The inclusion of the Socialist, Alexandre Millerand, in the Waldeck-Rousseau government intensified anti-socialism. Conservatives frequently equated Drefusardism with Socialism. The Nationalist Thiébaud saw the strikes and the Brisson government's (hesitant) Dreyfusism as two consequences of its subservience to the lodges, synagogues, and consistories, while Royalists argued that Dreyfusardism was a pretext to undermine the Army and foment a new Commune.[5] The new Nationalist movement developed an alternative anti-Socialist vision, which proved attractive to some Progressists. It combined authoritarianism with the incorporation of depoliticized trade unions, women's groups, and regionalists into the national community through corporatism. This strategy depended on the exploitation of ideas shared across the left–right boundary and of divisions among Socialists, feminists, and regionalists.

[4] Herman Lebovics, *The Alliance of Iron and Wheat in the Third French Republic, 1860–1914: Origins of the New Conservatism* (Baton Rouge, 1988), 184–92.

[5] *L'Éclair*, 8 October 1898; *L'Éclair (Midi)*, 1 September 1898.

The changing nature of Socialism facilitated the Nationalists' strategy. Increasing emphasis on Marxist internationalism and the factory proletariat, and presentation of the petty bourgeoisie as doomed vestiges of feudalism, undermined socially broader nationalist and populist socialisms. Socialist municipalities annoyed small traders by organizing cooperatives and alienated peasants by taxing the entry of agricultural products into the towns to pay for welfare schemes.[6] Nationalists took up these issues and idealized the petty bourgeoisie. The emergence in 1899 of the Jaunes, the Yellow Trade Union movement, demonstrated the existence of nationalist potential within the factory proletariat too. The first such union was founded at Le Creusot (Saône-et-Loire) on 30 October 1899 following an unsuccessful strike. It had around 4,500 members. A few weeks later Syndicat N° 2 was founded at Monceau-les-Mines. In 1901 Paul Lanoir, long active in national-Socialist and antisemitic circles in the eighteenth arrondissement, founded a Bourse du Travail Indépendant. In the following year the ex-Guesdist Pierre Biétry became leader of the Jaunes. He gave it a radical-nationalist imprint and founded a short-lived Fédération nationale des jaunes.[7]

The relationship between anti-feminism and the development of the women's movement is as complex as that between Socialism and anti-socialism. The first feminist congress, held in 1892, provoked much concern; the pejorative 'new woman', conflated with feminism, entered public discourse in 1896–1897. Anti-feminism became explicitly political only in Nationalism. Partly that was because a tiny number of women began to enter the professions, the core of the political class. The newspaper, *La Fronde*, produced entirely by female journalists and printers, appeared in 1897, and in 1900, Jeanne Chauvin, who wrote for *La Fronde*, was admitted to the Bar. Although these developments hardly disturbed the gender balance in the professions, they reinforced concern that sedentary professional employment undermined manliness, health, and, ultimately, civilization. Meanwhile, statistics published in 1897 intensified concern about the birth rate and provoked the foundation of the Alliance nationale pour l'accroissement de la population française. Pro-natalists attributed the falling birth rate to a crisis of gender roles, blaming men and/or women for the problem.[8] Catholic women also embraced anti-feminism, for female access to the professions implied that women and men were the same, and thus undermined Catholic women's claim to moralize the male world as mothers. To reconcile conflicting pressures, Nationalists combined exaggerated masculinism and misogyny with the organization of women's committees, the first of their kind in France, a strategy equivalent to its corporatist approach to the labour movement.

[6] Philip Nord, *Paris Shopkeepers and the Politics of Resentment* (Princeton, 1986), 424–33; Nancy Fitch, 'Mass culture, mass parliamentary politics, and modern antisemitism: the Dreyfus Affair in rural France', *American Historical Review* 97, no. 1 (February 1992), 55–95 at 70, 88–9; C. Stewart Doty, *From Cultural Rebellion to Counterrevolution: The Politics of Maurice Barrès* (Athens, 1976), 117–52.

[7] Edward J. Arnold, 'Counterrevolutionary themes and the working class in France', *French History* 13, no. 2 (1999), 99–133; Zeev Sternhell, *La Droite révolutionnaire (1885–1914). Les Origines françaises du fascisme* (Paris, 1978), 245–347.

[8] Mary Louise Roberts, *Disruptive Acts* (Chicago, 2002), 5–6; Christopher E. Forth, *The Dreyfus Affair and the Crisis of French Manhood* (Baltimore, 2004).

Regionalism represented a less often remarked upon dimension of the *fin-de-siècle* crisis. In the 1890s, it attracted Monarchists desirous of restoring their hegemony within provincial cultures as a route to national power.[9] Christian Democrats incorporated a populist defence of local languages into their attacks on the secularizing state. Conservative Republican erudites and artists promoted regional literature: typical was the Provençal poet, Mistral, founder in 1854 of the Félibrige. The regional revival also owed much to the self-assertiveness of students in the expanding provincial secondary schools and university faculties. The most gifted students went to Paris, and some combined literary avant-gardism with regionalism. They found their models in Barrès' *Déracinés* (1897), which recounted the disappointments of seven *lycéens* who had left the Lorraine for Paris.

In 1892, Charles Maurras and Fréderic Amouretti attempted to politicize the Félibrige and convert it to federalism. Subsequently Barrès and Maurras advocated regionalism in *la Cocarde*. Breton regionalism was political from the start, thanks to the weight of the Legitimist aristocracy and clergy, which ensured the pre-eminence of Bardic culture over avant-gardism. In 1898, the Legitimist Marquis Régis de l'Estourbeillon created the Union régionaliste bretonne (URB), from popular theatre groups. Closer to the radical student wing of Bretonism was Charles Le Goffic, a bourgeois Catholic who had met Barrès at the École normale supérieure.[10] The right never monopolized regionalism. Charles-Brun, founder in 1900 of the Fédération régionaliste française (FRF), was a Republican, but to promote unity, the FRF included Barrès and Estourbeillon in its patronage committee. Right-wing regionalism was simultaneously folded into the religious question. Consequently, as the Waldeck-Rousseau government revived anticlericalism, Catholics claimed that godless, materialist southern Republicans had taken control of the government. Nationalists endeavoured to recognize regional tensions and contain them within the national community through regionalized corporatist bodies.

The search for a hierarchical national community based on harmonious class, gender, and regional loyalties also reflected the desire for a France strong enough to compete in the 'Darwinist' international system. Attacks on the Army following exposure of the Henry forgeries coincided with the Anglo-French confrontation at Fashoda. The Progressist government's swift climbdown outraged Nationalists, but obscured the similarity of Nationalist and Progressists views of national power. Since Ferry, many Progressists expected struggle between autarkic national-capitalist economies.[11] France must be self-sufficient in industrial and agricultural goods, while securing political control over raw materials and markets through diplomacy and imperial conquest. Consequently, the Russian alliance was directed as much against Britain as Germany. This mercantilism required organic harmony within the nation and a strong birth rate to ensure the supply of workers, colonists, and soldiers. Nationalists accepted much of this and combined it with corporatism

[9] *Le Soleil*, 16 January 1899.

[10] Anne-Marie Thiesse, *Écrire la France* (Paris, 1991), 17–88; Julian Wright, *The Regionalist Movement in France 1890–1914* (Oxford, 2003).

[11] *Journal officiel. Chambre des députés*, 18 June 1891.

and a strong executive. There were differences among Nationalists. Déroulède sometimes rejected imperialism as a distraction from *revanche*, and he was relatively pro-English. Yet he was also tempted to use the returning Fashoda soldiers as the vehicle for a coup.[12] He too saw authoritarian nationalism as the precondition of military recovery.

Historiographical debate has revolved around the related questions of whether Nationalism was proto-fascist and/or conservative or revolutionary, modernizing or traditional. For different reasons Zeev Sternhell and Robert Soucy see Nationalism as proto-fascist. Sternhell detected proto-fascism in a synthesis of radical nationalism and non-Marxist Socialism, joining the extremes in a modernizing, revolutionary attack on the Republican and bourgeois mediocrity of the parliamentary Republic. For Soucy, in contrast, proto-fascism meant conservative defence by authoritarian means. René Rémond agreed with Soucy that Nationalism was conservative, but saw it as another metamorphosis of Bonapartism.[13]

There is truth in all these views. Nationalism owed much to Bonapartism; it contained the conservative impulses detected by Soucy, and we have seen that the extremes sometimes attempted to mobilize the people against the parliamentary centre. Yet Nationalism cannot be reduced to any of these elements. It was a contested notion, used as a weapon in political struggles. As for its revolutionary or conservative aspect, the debate is artificial, for those who argue for conservatism focus on the LPF, while those who see revolution focus on the LDP and Ligue antisémitique. What counted as 'revolutionary' or 'reactionary', 'traditional' or 'modern' depended on perspective and context. Preoccupation with classification obscures the specificity of Nationalism in its context, as well as the extent to which ideas, including antisemitism, crossed political boundaries.

I shall begin with problematization of the view that the Affair crystallized a confrontation of Republican science and Catholic obscurantism, for it illuminates the complex relationship and convergence between Progressism and Nationalism, particularly with its more moderate wing. Once again, to emphasize convergences is not to argue for an essential similarity. Rather, in the specific conditions of 1898–1899 common ground became important, without englobing all Progressists.

THE REVOLT AGAINST REASON

While the new term 'intellectual' was initially synonymous with 'Dreyfusard', the latter had no monopoly on educated opinion. Indeed, the LPF emerged from Madame de Loynes' literary salon. Lemaître, its leader, was a dramatist, Ferdinand Brunetière was a literary critic, Coppée was a poet, and Déroulède was a poet and

[12] Bertrand Joly, *Déroulède* (Paris, 1998), 222–5, 311.

[13] Sternhell, *La Droite révolutionnaire*, 15–32; Robert Soucy, *Fascism in France: The Case of Maurice Barrès* (Berkeley, 1972); René Rémond, *Les Droites en France*, fourth revised edition (Paris, 1982), 164–8; Michel Winock, *La Fièvre hexagonale. Les Grandes crises politiques 1871–1968* (Paris, 1986), 141–91.

playwright. Barrès was by then a significant author. Charles Maurras adopted a Bohemian lifestyle to sustain his position in the literary and political *avant-gardes*.[14]

Antidreyfusards were 'anti-intellectual' in so far as they were part of a 'rebellion against reason and positivism', which took several forms. First, some literary figures, including Paul Bourget, Brunetière, Lemaître, and Coppée, discovered Catholicism and became Antidreyfusards. Secondly, figures such as Henri Bergson claimed that scientific knowledge was provisional, while the monarchist, Denys Cochin, argued that in the natural sciences observation mattered less than imagination. In 1984–1985, Brunetière published a controversial article in which he argued that religion alone, not science, could provide moral guidance.[15] Thirdly, Le Bon, the race theorist Jules Soury, and others argued that non-rational forces—race, instinct, reflex, and contagion—determined human behaviour. Fourthly, some rejected the supposed retreat into art for art's sake of symbolists such as Wagner. They turned instead to Nietzsche, whom they saw as preaching engagement and regeneration rather than pessimism.[16] All these trends contradicted the Kantian view that morality was inherent in man's mind and accessible to scientific observation, and they rejected universalism in favour of national relativism and action.

Antidreyfusards were also anti-intellectual in that they attacked university academics in the emerging professional university disciplines in the name of the older generalist conception of the rounded man, the 'homme complet'. Brunetière and Barrès were especially negative. Many Moderate Republicans shared the right's preference for generalism, and so the division between Antidreyfusards and their opponents therefore ran *through* the ranks of the generalists. The 'positivist' claim that science underpinned morality was largely confined to the Radical and Socialist left, and even there it was not clearly distinguished from other forms of science.[17] Moderate Republicans shared with much of the right its idealization of the rounded, competent man, whose superiority lay in his practical experience and scientific understanding of the blind forces that drove the masses. Le Bon typified this kind of *savant*.[18] He is especially important because his sympathies lay on the margins of Progressism and Nationalism, and because use of crowd theory was not confined to a single political tendency.[19] Raymond Poincaré, the Moderate Republican, was an archetypal generalist, in that he combined rationalism with pantheism, and political with legal careers.

There was no clear distinction between positivism and its opponents either. Positivist social science was a complex doctrine. It assumed that society was an organism and thus argued by analogy as much as rational demonstration, and that

[14] Bruno Goyet, *Charles Maurras* (Paris, 2000), 192–3.

[15] H.W. Paul, *The Edge of Contingency: French Catholic Reaction to Change from Darwin to Duhem* (Gainsville, 1979), 66–7.

[16] Christopher E. Forth, 'Nietzsche, decadence and regeneration in France, 1891–95', *Journal of the History of Ideas* 54, no. 1 (1993), 97–117.

[17] Étienne Lamy, *La Femme de demain* (Paris, 1901), 43–6; Paul, *The Edge*, 66.

[18] Benoît Marpeau, *Gustave Le Bon. Parcours d'un intellectuel, 1841–1931* (Paris, 2000), 122–6; *L'Opinion*, 11 April 1908; Robert Nye, *The Origins of Crowd Psychology: Gustave Le Bon and the Crisis of Mass Democracy in the Third Republic* (London, 1975).

[19] Harris, *Dreyfus*, 158–61.

permitted the incorporation of prejudices about gender and race into their views of society. And since Catholics had long advanced an organicist critique of the Revolution, there was potential convergence between Republican science and counterrevolutionary thought too—as the wide influence of LePlay testified. Neither was there a necessary relationship between positivism and universalism. The positivist Taine stressed the instinctual, racial underpinnings of behaviour; interestingly, he was seen as an importer of German methods in the 1870s and by later generations as a defender of speculative thought against a new generation of specialized historians.

The Church's uncertain attitude to science further undermines the notion that a revolt against reason was co-terminus with opposition to the Republic. Certainly the hierarchy condemned Darwinism as a plot against religion and society.[20] Yet Catholics did not condemn science *per se*. They defined it differently and used it as a weapon in political struggles. Brunetière, in spite of his critique of science, did not abandon Darwinism, for he held that it contradicted Rousseau's optimism and confirmed the Church's doctrine of original sin.[21] Indeed, he helped to convert Social Darwinism from a progressive doctrine into a pessimistic, anti-egalitarian ideology of the right—while condemning the excesses of race theory. We saw in the previous chapter that Christian Democrats and Monarchists incorporated race science into their antisemitism and that integrist Catholics used the 'struggle for life' to legitimate intolerance of rival philosophies.[22] The Church's use of scientific expertise to validate miracles encouraged such amalgamations.[23]

The above considerations allow us to see that Nationalism emerged in the intersection of science and religion, Republicanism, conservatism, and the radical right. The different strands of Nationalism drew upon a common pool of ideas and deployed them in complex struggles among themselves and with the left. Moderate Nationalists and Progressists (Dreyfusard or Antidreyfusard), shared and disputed a vision of the 'competent' and 'experienced', which in the context of 1899 brought them together. Radical Nationalists accepted much of this too, but they defined their elite as much in terms of service to the nation as class superiority.

THE LIGUE DE LA PATRIE FRANÇAISE

In October 1898, three Parisian *lycée* professors, Louis Dausset, Henri Vaugeois, and Gabriel Syveton, launched a petition designed to demonstrate that not all intellectuals sympathized with the Dreyfusard Ligue des droits de l'homme. Hundreds of colleagues, along with Barrès, Coppée, and Lemaître, signed it. In the following

[20] Paul, *The Edge*, 64–108.

[21] H.W. Paul, 'The debate over the bankruptcy of science in 1895', *French Historical Studies* 5, no. 3 (spring 1968), 299–327; Jean-Marc Bernardini, *Le Darwinisme social en France. Fascination et rejet d'une idéologie* (Paris, 1997), 299–305.

[22] Abbé Bernard Gaudeau, 'Les Principes théologiques qui doivent régler les relations de l'Église avec la société civile en générale', in *Congrès national catholique de Reims* (Lille, 1897), 174–96.

[23] Ruth Harris, *Lourdes: Body and Spirit in the Secular Age* (London, 1999), 352–4.

January, on Barrès' initiative, the LPF was launched in the press, with an appeal signed by twenty-two members of the Academy and a bevy of professionals, writers, and artists. The LPF placed loyalty to France above the conflict between Dreyfusards and Antidreyfusards, but in fact recruited from the right and Progressists.[24] The first members included the Orleanist Ducs de Broglie, Haussonville, and Audiffret-Pasquier, along with Charles Maurras and de Mun. Also present were Progressists, notably Cavaignac and Louis de Marcère, author of the 1877 'Appeal of 363 Republican Deputies'. Many ordinary members came from the LDP, Justice-Égalité, and Union nationale.[25]

Inevitably there were conflicts. Coppée's campaign against President Loubet provoked the Republican Brunetière to leave. When Lemaître and Coppée reaffirmed their adhesion to the Republic, many Royalists departed. Lemaître, who soon emerged as the dominant figure, shared the Progressists' wish to settle the Affair quickly and re-establish the anti-Socialist alliance with Nationalist stiffening. Yet the LPF remained diverse; it did not cut ties with radical Nationalists; Barrès remained on its committee until October 1901.[26]

The elections of 1902 showed that the LPF was strongest in conservative areas where monarchism was weak, such as Lozère, the Rhône valley, Normandy, the Loire, and the Tarn.[27] In Paris, the Nationalist coalition, particularly the LPF, performed best in the wealthier central and western arrondissments, often in alliance with the right proper. But it was not wholly distinct from the radical leagues in their once-Boulangist and Bonapartist eastern strongholds. In Calvados, the collapse of Mélineism provoked a revival of radical Bonapartism, which fed into the LPF, and proved attractive to labourers, clerks, and small-towns artisans.[28] In the Mayenne the Bonapartist Rallié, the Comte d'Elva, backed the LPF, and used Socialist language.[29]

If the LPF was conservative, its elitism differed subtly from that of the Mélinistes, for it recruited from groups that, rightly or wrongly, charged the Republic with blocking their careers. Prominent were academics, lawyers, students of law and medicine, artists, writers, *lycée* professors, and members of the Institut and Académie française, the latter increasingly a refuge for conservative critics of university specialization. Recruits also included Catholic businessmen, such as Alfred Motte, Édouard Michelin, and the brothers Japy, along with a bevy of retired ambassadors and generals, some of whom had been removed for their political opinions. LPF lawyers and professors lived in a conservative provincial world, hostile to the

[24] André Siegfried, *Tableau politique de la France de l'ouest sous la Troisième République* (Paris, 1913), 493.

[25] Jean-Pierre Rioux, *Nationalisme et conservatisme. La Ligue de la patrie française, 1899–1904* (Paris, 1977), 7–20, 29.

[26] Jean-Pierre Rioux, *Nationalisme et conservatisme*, 14, 37.

[27] D.R. Watson, 'The nationalist movement in Paris 1900–1906', in David Shapiro (ed.), *The Right in France 1890–1919*, (London, 1962), 49–84; Rioux, *Nationalisme*, 55–8.

[28] Jean Quellien, *Bleus, blancs, rouges. Politique et élections dans le Calvados 1870–1939* (Caen, 1986), 166–81.

[29] Michel Denis, *L'Église et la République en Mayenne 1896–1906* (Paris, 1968), 134, 143.

École normale supérieure and the Sorbonne, which they saw as bastions of individualism and rationalism.[30] In the Paris Bar, the situation was somewhat different, for older lawyers were the most Antidreyfusard, while their younger colleagues more often embraced Dreyfusism.[31]

In the vein of collective psychology, the LPF placed the popular will at the heart of its discourse and charged the elite with embodying and interpreting it.[32] It evoked the instinctive nationalism of the mass, in which one could detect ancestral voices, traditions, and attachment to the native soil; it praised Taine's sense of race and Mistral's traditionalism.[33] Using socio-biological metaphors, Marcère explained that in troubled times anguish overtook the people as it did any living organism. While the people 'instinctively' understood the danger, it was reassuring to see 'the best minds... in perfect accord with popular instinct, without having looked for agreement'.[34] While the people were indentified with nature, the elite combined intuitive communication with the people with the possession of culture, enabling it to understand the national psychology both emotionally and scientifically.

The LPF's constitutional programme reflected this elitism, and introduced a major new theme into conservative politics. Coppée favoured a plebiscitary regime, but most preferred an American-style separation of powers and a president elected by two-degree suffrage. The LPF also advocated ministerial responsibility to the President and restriction of parliament's right to initiate spending.[35] This programme had precedents in Monarchism and Boulangism as well as foreign examples, and was inseparable from a desire to improve the quality of the elite. Coppée said that two thirds of deputies were distinguished only by 'the vulgarity of their physiognomy, their sloppy dress, arrogant speech and unkemptness'. Amongst them one could distinguish the 'course voice of the dialect speaker and former *faubourg* scum'.[36] This depiction paralleled Le Bon's view of the demagogue who never discarded the crowd mentality. The league sought the election of the 'capacities'—men of experience who had proved themselves in professional, academic, or cultural spheres.[37] A corporatist system would buttress their role.[38]

Corporatism was also part of a strategy designed to contain within the nation the aspirations that nourished Socialism. The league was strongly anti-Socialist, denouncing the multiplication of strikes and Millerand's presence in the government. Nationalism for Marcère was the antithesis of the Jacobinism and Socialism

[30] *Le Figaro*, 4 January 1899; Claude Digeon, *La Crise allemande de la pensée française (1870–1914)* (Paris, 1959), 319–488; René Rémond, 'Les Intellectuels et la politique', *Revue française de science politique* 9, no. 4 (December 1959), 860–80.

[31] Christophe Charle, 'Le Déclin de la République des avocats', in Pierre Birnbaum (ed.), *La France de l'Affaire Dreyfus* (Paris, 1994), 56–86.

[32] François Coppée and Jules Lemaître, *L'Œuvre de la patrie française* (Paris, 1899), 26.

[33] *Annales de la Patrie française*, 15 March 1900, 17–21 and 1900, no. 6, 161–2.

[34] *Annales de la Patrie française*, 1900, no. 6, 39–40 and 1900, no. 5, 129–31.

[35] *Annales de la Patrie française*, no. 1, 1900, 34–6; no. 12, 1900, 404–5, and 1 March 1901, 651–3.

[36] *Annales de la Patrie française*, 15 March 1901, 673–5 and no. 8, 1900, 236; Coppée and Lemaître, *L'Œuvre*, 17.

[37] *Annales de la Patrie française*, no. 11, 1900, 354–7 and 15 March 1901, 673–5.

[38] Rioux, *Nationalisme*, 45–6, 86–7, 90; Sternhell, *La Droite révolutionnaire*, 136.

that allegedly inspired government policy, including expropriation of the property of the congregations.[39] The league was divided on social issues. Cavaignac, unusually for a Progressist, advocated income tax. Other Nationalists preferred reforms similar to Progressist recipes—notably mutualism.[40] Nevertheless, Nationalism shaped social policy, for the League claimed that a strong France would guarantee prosperity and enable workers to realize their desires. Corporatism would teach Frenchmen 'to better know each other and learn to count upon each other', thus permitting the French soul to 'protect itself from unhealthy foreign influences'.[41] These influences included foreign labour. In Nancy and Rouen, the LPF's hostility to foreign workers and traders provoked conflict with Progressists.[42] Thus, the LPF attempted to integrate the proletariat into the nation by capturing the nationalist, reformist, and petty-bourgeois strands within Socialism. The LPF also backed the Jaunes, even though the pro-Jaune employer, Japy, sidestepped the issue of immigrant labour and substituted attacks on Jewish capital and Socialism.[43]

Similarly, the LPF attempted to incorporate the feminist aspirations into the nation, behind an aggressively masculinist leadership. It lauded military values and saw colonies as an arena for heroic struggle that would combat the degenerative effects of sedentary civilization, epitomized, allegedly, by the Dreyfusard intellectual.[44] Women would bear children, for the LPF was strongly natalist and was instrumental in shifting the blame for depopulation from men to women. Lemaître saw women who valued their figures more than childbearing as 'mere machines for selfish pleasure'.[45] Another writer saw feminism as Masonic and Jewish.[46] The eminent biologist, Edmond Perrier, endorsed the theory of 'telegony', according to which the trembling uterus destabilized the female brain.[47] The league was markedly more anti-feminist than the Progressists. Nationalist women endorsed the notion of separate spheres, and the League held family evenings to attract them.

Nevertheless, the LPF accorded women a role. They constituted 10–20 per cent of audiences at meetings, and the league boasted that it registered 'active members' on green cards and its many female recruits on violet cards.[48] Actually, women were 'active'. The league was founded partly on the initiative of Madame de Loynes at her salon.[49] The LPF inherited Catholic activism from Christian Democracy.

[39] *Annales de la Patrie française*, no. 17, 1 January 1901, 520.

[40] *Annales de la Patrie française*, 15 January 1901, 552–5; 1 September 1900, 16 June 1901; no. 6, 1900, 161–2; Mathius Bernard, *La Dérive des modérés. La Fédération républicaine du Rhône sous la Troisième République* (Paris, 1998), 101–6.

[41] L. de Contenson, 'Charité et solidarité' *Annales de la Patrie française*, 15 February 1901, 552–5.

[42] David M. Gordon, *Liberalism and Social Reform: Industrial Growth and Progressiste Politics in France, 1880–1914* (Westport, 1996), 144–8; Robert L. Fuller, 'Belle époque French nationalism: the example of Rouen', *French History* 13, no. 1 (1999), 26–47 at 35.

[43] Archives nationales Police générale (hearafter AN F^7) $F^7$12451, 15 March 1902; Arnold, 'Counterrevolutionary themes', 155.

[44] Forth, *The Dreyfus Affair*, 72–4

[45] *Annales de la Patrie française*, no. 12, 1900, 385–7.

[46] *Annales de la Patrie française*, no. 10, 1900, 332–3.

[47] Annelise Mauge, *L'Identité masculine en crise au tournant du siècle* (Paris, 1987), 24.

[48] *L'Éclair*, 16 February 1899.

[49] Pascal Ory, 'Le Salon', in Jean-François Sirinelli (ed.), *Histoire des droites en France*, ii. *Cultures* (Paris, 1993), 113–27.

Like Legitimist and Christian Democrat women, Nationalist women endeavoured to moralize a materialistic male society, and so their objectives differed from those of the leadership. Whereas the latter wished to unite Catholics and anticlericals in an anti-Socialist alliance, the Comité des dames spoke rather of a conflict between Christ and Satan, and concentrated on anti-Masonic, educational, and charitable activities. Women helped clericalize the LPF. After 1901, they cooperated with the new Catholic women's group, the Ligue des femmes françaises, which was linked in turn to Royalism. The formal creation of a Nationalist Comité des dames in January 1902 was probably intended to prevent members from deserting to Catholic groups. But later in the year, many women joined a group linked to the new Catholic party, Action libérale populaire (ALP), which had initially planned to work with Lemaître's league.[50] Unlike women, male activists were as likely to turn to Progressism as to the ALP as Nationalism declined.[51]

That reflected the greater anticlericalism of male Nationalists. Initially, the LPF leadership shared the Progressists' moderate anticlericalism. Lemaître wanted to replace declining Catholicism with a religion of the fatherland. Others saw the people as profoundly Catholic, yet opposed to clericalism. They favoured toleration pending the disappearance of organized religion, because it would unite Progressists and Ralliés within the nation. After all, Nationalists felt, Catholicism had helped make France, and meant something to women.[52] Some Ralliés accepted this strategy, for they saw the LPF as a means to obey the Pope's injunction to work with 'honest men' to defend Catholic liberties within the Republic. With time, clericalism gained ground. Coppée was openly Catholic; the UN and Justice-Égalité founded some LPF committees, especially in the Nord and Lyon.[53] In 1902, Lemaître's opposition to confessionalism provoked the departure of activists to the ALP, and in 1905 the ALP leader, Piou, allegedly ensured that the Catholic Republican, Marcère, succeeded Lemaître as president. Increasingly, the LPF focussed on anti-Masonism.[54] In 1906, the Nationalist deputy for Caen left the LPF because its members 'while claiming to be liberals are the worst of sectarians'.

Indeed, the Dreyfus crisis produced a new kind of Catholic nationalism. In 1900, following the dissolution of the Assumptionists, Général-Baron Raymond de La Rocque reorganized Justice-Égalité independently from *La Croix*, as the latter fell under the Rallié control. Royalist influence in Justice-Égalité grew as La Rocque declared that the committees would act constitutionally but include any anti-sectarian patriot. He promised that a campaign of lectures, beginning and ending with prayers, would demonstrate that France was essentially Catholic. Members would form compact groups publicly demonstrating their

[50] Magali Della Sudda, 'Une Activité politique féminine avant le droit de suffrage en France et en Italie', thèse de doctorat, EHESS Paris, 2007, 107–8.

[51] Rioux, *Nationalisme*, 73, 89, 107.

[52] Lemaître *L'Œuvre de la Patrie française*, 15–16, 17–19.

[53] ANPG F[7] 12 481, Sûreté générale report, 2 July 1900; Robert L. Fuller, 'Catholic women and the unmaking of French nationalism after the Dreyfus Affair', *European History Quarterly* 37, no. 2 (2007), 242–64.

[54] Rioux, *Nationalisme*, 48, 90–1.

Catholicism.[55] In March 1901, La Rocque, if *Le Siècle* is to be believed, opened a meeting by asking the audience to make the sign of the cross, by which one recognized the 'true French'. The meeting allegedly ended with cries of 'Vive Saint-Barthélémy'.[56] A circular stated that France's abandonment of her role as 'eldest daughter of the Church' had caused the rise of anti-militarism, strikes, and the expulsion of the religious orders.[57] Only in the Paris Municipal council and in the Parisian *L'Éclair* did Nationalist anticlericalism survive.[58]

Just as it converged with Catholic protest, the LPF shared much with radical Nationalism. Both denounced the government as the agent of an anti-national 'syndicate'.[59] The LPF was more legalist, but Syveton maintained that an illegitimate government should be overthrown illegally. Like the radical leagues, the LPF was anti-universalist, its very title a condemnation of the Ligue des droits de l'homme. One activist claimed that his studies at the Faculté de droit had revealed the bankruptcy of cosmopolitanism, individualism, and positivism. He endorsed Barrès' view that laws were valid only in national conditions and that parliamentarianism did not match the French character—a notion that actually owed as much to the positivists Taine and Le Bon as to the irrationalist Barrès.[60] The nation was an 'organism' possessed of interests, not a collection of individuals with rights. Since the national body was 'polluted, corrupt and rotten', it required the 'powerful depurative' medicine of Nationalism.[61] Nationalism also taught that love of the *petite patrie* preceded love for the *grande patrie*. Mistral joined the league, while Léon Daudet praised his father, Alphonse's, roots in the southern soil.[62]

The LPF was not immune from antisemitism. In the first number of the *Annales de la patrie française*, Lemaître remarked on the influence of Jews in the Waldeck-Rousseau government.[63] This antisemitism mixed biology, history, and culture. Thus, Jews and Freemasons promoted individualism and undermined religion; Jews, not capitalism, were responsible for the misery of the poor; they invaded the administration and professions, displacing the 'competent'. The pro-Jaune Japy wrote that 'The Socialist idea is a Semitic and Jewish idea; the Jaune idea is of Aryan and Indo-European superiority.'[64] Thanks to contact with the Jaunes, the influx of Catholics, and the need for electoral deals with the Ligue antisémitique, antisemitism became more marked with time, but never as extreme as that of the radical leagues. The LPF differed from the latter in refusing 'expulsions or burnings'; Jews could be dealt with by enforcing existing laws on speculation and by

[55] ANPG F[7] 12 481, Sûreté générale report 1 November 1900; *Le Siècle*, 5 January 1901.
[56] *Le Siècle*, 13 March 1901.
[57] 'L'Œuvre éléctorale' (November 1901), in ANPG F[7] 12 481.
[58] Rioux, *Nationalisme*, 100; Watson, 'The nationalist movement', 70, 76; Quellien, *Bleus, blancs, rouges*, 204.
[59] Lemaître, *L'Œuvre de la Patrie française*, 17, 20–1.
[60] Léon Fatoux, *Les Coulisses du Nationalisme* (Paris, 1903), 9–22.
[61] *Annales de la Patrie française*, 1901, 3, 4.
[62] *Annales de la Patrie française*, 15 March 1900, 17–21
[63] *Annales de la Patrie française*, 1 May 1900, 2, 20; Coppée and Lemaître, *L'Œuvre de la patrie française*, 24.
[64] Arnold, 'Counterrevolutionary themes', 117.

barring newly naturalized immigrants from the professions and administration. Only the grandchildren of immigrant Jews might become French.[65] Lemaître shared the antisemites' love of the 'race', but found certain of their judgements 'too summary'.[66] The LPF's Paris committees refused to support the antisemite Max Régis.[67] As in other matters, LPF members often resisted antisemitism, but their ideas were not entirely different from those of their radical allies.

Organizationally, the LPF was not entirely distinct from that of the radical leagues either. Its leaders were not interested in creating a mass party, and membership fell well short of the 40,000 it claimed. Many local committees were dominated by 'personalities', while the mass of 'non-subscribing' members merely attended meetings. Yet the organization's desire to reconcile contending parties and its organizational looseness opened it to rivals. Brunetière admitted that 'antisemites and the partisans of M. Déroulède will be welcomed by us'.[68] In Rouen, the LPF organized libraries, mutual aid, and professional sections. It was part of a broader network including Déroulèdistes and the Jeunesse nationaliste, which invented a quasi-Masonic system of pseudonyms and fought the left in the streets.[69]

THE RADICAL LEAGUES

Although Bertrand Joly shows that the radical leagues were not themselves a mass force, their links with the LPF ensured that they were influential. The LDP survived clandestinely before its revival in 1898.[70] At its apogee it counted at most 15,000–18,000 members, of whom at least two thirds were Parisian, and it could never mobilize more than a fraction of them on the streets. Rochefort's *L'Intransigent* and the nationalist wing of Blanquisme was a shadow of itself by 1899, while the Ligue antisémitique was a 'ghost organization', with at most 1,500 members.[71] Yet the antisemitic leagues and press played an important part in keeping antisemitism on the agenda. Déroulède saw his leaguers a 'leaven' in the mass, which he saw as only awaiting the signal to follow his lead. The radical leagues owed much to Boulangist organizations, which thought in terms of a 'movement of opinion' rather than a structured party—in that respect they differed from interwar movements, for whom number was all-important.

[65] *Annales de la Patrie française*, 15 February 1901; no. 15, 609–15; no. 8, 1900, 8–10; Coppé and Lemaître, *L'Œuvre de La Patrie française*, 24; Jeremy Jennings, 'Antisemitic discourse in Dreyfus-Affair France', in Edward J. Arnold (ed.), *The Development of the Radical Right in France: From Boulanger to Le Pen* (London, 2000), 16–32.

[66] *Annales de la Patrie française*, no. 12, 1900, 404–5.

[67] Rioux, *Nationalisme*, 77, 80.

[68] *Le Temps*, 3 January 1899, cited in Rioux, *Nationalisme*, 13.

[69] Rioux, *Nationalisme*, 52. 54, 75, 87; Fuller, 'Belle époque French nationalism', 33–4.

[70] Bertrand Joly, 'Les Antidreyfusards avant Dreyfus', *Revue d'histoire moderne et contemporaine* 39 (April–June 1992), 198–221; Peter Rutkoff, *Revanche and Revision: The Ligue des Patriotes and the Origins of the Radical Right in France 1882–1900* (Athens, 1981), 62–9.

[71] Joly, *Nationalistes*, 141–2, 276.

There were other continuities between the radical Nationalists and Boulangism, and that blurred the boundaries between left and right too. Radical Nationalists inherited Boulangists' populist ultranationalism, anti-parliamentarianism, idealization of the Army, hostility to foreign labour, and desire to incorporate workers into the nation. Since the left was not free from nationalism or antisemitism, the boundaries between it and the right remained unclear. In Bordeaux, antisemitism reinforced an alliance between Royalists and the left against Progressism.[72] In Draguignan (Var), in 1893, Joseph Jourdan, with the support of Progressists, Ralliés, and Socialists defeated Clemenceau. It was never clear whether Jourdan was a Radical or a right-winger practising the *politique du pire*. In 1893, he attacked Clemenceau as a Panamiste and for his links to Jews, and then, in 1898, Jourdan stood as an antisemite, but lost to a Socialist.[73] Some Socialists were also sympathetic to Nationalism; for instance the deputy and municipal councillor in Paris XV. In several Parisian constituencies Nationalists collected up to a third of Socialist votes on the second ballot, especially if confronting a Radical, and if the withdrawing Socialist had been a Blanquiste.[74] In Lyon, two Blanquiste deputies embraced Antidreyfusism, but were defeated in 1902.[75]

Radical nationalism was more than a re-edition of Boulangism. The internationalist, proletarian orientation of Socialism, coupled with the encounter between Boulangism and Christian Democracy, now ensured that left-wing recruits more clearly switched sides. At first, Boulangist deputies had voted largely with the left. Barrès attempted unsuccessfully to create an organized Socialist movement in Nancy, and then stood in bourgeois Neuilly in 1893 on a more moderate programme, before espousing an intellectualized Socialism as editor of *La Cocarde* in 1894–1896. In 1898, he still had the support of the Union socialiste, but had been excommunicated by its group in Paris.[76] Blanquistes became ever more nationalist and antisemitic and lost interest in social revolution, while retaining their antipathy to parliament and commitment to insurrection. In any case, by 1898 they were weak.[77]

Déroulède, meanwhile, had broken with the parliamentary Republic, calling on the people to recapture it from the neo-aristocracy of finance and sometimes Jews, and advocating direct action. The LDP borrowed increasingly from Barrès' romantic blood and soil nationalism and rejected the Dreyfusards' 'cosmopolitan intellectualism'. The people, he said, 'go straight to the point and rip away the veil of falsehood' while rootless intellectuals were lost in abstract reasoning.[78] Déroulède's

[72] Elisabeth Cazenave, 'L'Affaire Dreyfus et l'opinion bordelaise. Essai de methodologie', *Annales du Midi* 84, no. 107 (1972), 63–76.

[73] Jocelyne George, 'Provinciales. La France aux quatre coins', in *La France de l'Affaire Dreyfus*, 121–53, at 134–5.

[74] Watson, 'The nationalist movement', 69–70.

[75] Yves Lequin, *Les Ouvriers de la région lyonnaise (1848–1914)* 2 vols (Lyon, 1977), ii, 302–3; Fitch, 'Mass culture', 55–95.

[76] Doty, *From Cultural Rebellion*, 164–5.

[77] Sternhell, *La Droite révolutionnaire*, 127–8; Joly, 'Les Antidreyfusards', 212–14.

[78] Nord, *Shopkeeper Protest*, 381–92.

national-religious attacks on Jews were insufficient to win Guérin's approval, but few Jews would have considered him a friend. Many of his followers were more antisemitic than he was.[79]

If the radical leagues' hostility to parliamentarianism and international Socialism situated them on the right, they espoused a *radical* rightism. That was evident in their sociology and political culture. They were bourgeois who styled themselves in opposition to the bourgeoisie, identifying with the people while remaining distant from it. In Paris, they were 'boulevardiers', patrons of the Chat noir, writers like Gyp, dramatists like Déroulède, frustrated actors like Georges Berry, or dandies like Paul Bourget. They looked back to pre-Haussmann Paris, supposedly uncorrupted by commercialization and cosmopolitanism.[80] One radical, Lucien Millevoye, claimed that 'the street has a soul which the politicians do not have... the street is incorruptible'.[81] While radicals, like moderates, saw themselves as an elite, they stressed this oppositional culture and ideological purity more than their academic qualifications and class position. Déroulède told voters that his unwavering commitment to France was his only justification for seeking their votes.

Parisian shopkeepers also demonstrated a combination of conservatism and populism. They resented Progressism for its big business ties, support for free movement of labour and goods, failure to regulate department stores, and denunciation of shopkeeper profiteering.[82] The Nationalist Berry, along with Social Catholics, courted shopkeepers. He depicted department stores, deputies, Jewish artisans, and foreign competitors as ramifications of an anti-French conspiracy, and idealized the old Paris of narrow streets and small shops. In Tours, the 'Parti commercial et industriel français' admired Drumont, condemned parliament for neglecting economic issues in favour of anticlericalism, and denounced Socialism.[83]

The attitudes of the white-collar employees of the Paris Gas Company were equally paradoxical. Only a few sympathized with Socialists, who were more interested in manual workers, and they resented the Radical city council for refusal to grant them municipal employee status. Employees aspired to rise in the company hierarchy, yet their expectations were rarely met in practice. Nationalism appealed because it incorporated attacks on the monopolistic practices and authoritarian management of the gas company into denunciation of cosmopolitan capitalism. The gas workers' champion, Alexandre Patenne, was elected in 1900 as a 'socialiste patriote'.[84]

The slaughterhouses of La Villette were dominated by small entrepreneurs who worked alongside their employees. Both disliked the allegedly German and Jewish wholesalers, who moved into La Villette after 1890. Guérin inherited Morès' popularity amongst the butchers, who voted in 1900 and 1902 for national Socialists.

[79] Joly, *Déroulède*, 229–33.
[80] Nord, *Shopkeeper Protest*, 433–58.
[81] Rutkoff, *Revanche and Revision*, 79.
[82] Fuller, 'Belle époque French nationalism', 26–47.
[83] Nord, *Shopkeeper Protest*, 351–464; Fuller, 'Belle époque French nationalism', 42–5.
[84] Lenard R. Berlanstein, *Big Business and Industrial Conflict in Nineteenth-Century France* (Berkeley, 1991), 228–57.

These unskilled workers and their masters combined nationalism and dislike for 'les gros' with anti-socialism, for they found no place in the local Bourse du travail.[85]

Ideologically, Maurice Barrès most systematically articulated radical nationalism. He developed his ideas in opposition to LPF leaders, who in March 1899 had prevented him from giving a speech advocating 'integral nationalism'. Barrès held that since the French did not constitute a biological race, they were unable to define themselves in the 'struggle for life', unlike the Anglo-Saxons and Germans. That gave unscrupulous politicians the opportunity to create parties, each with their own priorities. The solution, Barrès wrote, was to resolve each question in relation to France. His definition of France was nearly as rigid as biological conceptions of the nation. He looked to a historical, 'flesh and blood' France rather than to 'metaphysical' abstractions. He rejected Bonapartism, royalism, and Catholicism as 'might have beens'. Nevertheless, since progress should be combined with tradition, the country must 'live with all her dead and place [itself] outside none of her experiences', for each, good or bad, was a fruit of the same tree. That meant endorsing the Revolution and Catholicism as the twin foundations of Nationalism: the Revolution had made possible the grouping of peoples with identical traditions and languages who affirmed themselves through hatred of neighbours.[86] Using the elite–mass distinction, Barrès urged the LPF to develop the country's latent nationalism. To do so it must rely on 'sentimental force' and on a 'less voluntary element', not on reason or the University culture of 'Man and Humanity'. National consciousness would emerge if individuals were rooted 'in the soil and the dead, in the soil of our dead'. Only then could the self (le moi) flourish.[87]

Practically, Barrès differed from moderate Nationalists in three respects. First, he had not given up the search for a new Boulanger and did not consider the LPF's programme of constitutional reform sufficient to regenerate France. In effect Barrès favoured charismatic rather than legal-rational government; a strong leader, arisen from the national consciousness, would express the latent nationalism of the mass.[88] Déroulède, whose coup Barrès backed, envisaged military intervention in politics, arrests, dissolution of parliament, re-establishment of universal suffrage, and direct election of the president. Although Déroulède's attempted coup was a fiasco, that should not disguise widespread acceptance among radical Nationalists and beyond that the Republic could not regenerate itself.

Second, Barrès incorporated decentralization and regionalism into a racist project designed to ensure that the heritage of the ancestors and the characteristics of 'our forest, agricultural and winegrowing race' would be transmitted to the new generation. A person 'genuinely' rooted in their locality would inevitably be in accord with the destiny of the country, even if he could not express it. Regionalism was 'a way to react in common in all circumstances with men of the same formation'.[89]

[85] Nord, *Shopkeeper Protest*, 388–91.
[86] Maurice Barrès, *Contre les étrangers* (Paris, 1893).
[87] Maurice Barrès, *Scènes et doctrines du nationalisme* (Paris, 1902), 85–94.
[88] Barrès, *Scènes et doctrines*, 6, 99; Doty, *From Cultural Rebellion*, 186–7.
[89] Barrès, *Scènes et doctrines*, 96–8.

In 1902, this regionalism shaded into autonomism. He warned the government that anticlericalism infringed the liberty of Catholic regions, and would detach Brittany and the Lorraine from France.[90] Even Maurras refused to go so far: he rejected federalism for Breton, Basque, and Flemish-speaking areas.[91] Déroulède advocated cultivation of local patriotism, but rejected decentralization.[92] Nevertheless, he too sought to reconcile regional and national identities through authority.

Thirdly, Barrès advocated antisemitism and racism. It is not true that he believed Dreyfus to be guilty simply because of his race. Rather he believed that Dreyfus' Jewishness made him *capable* of treason and he trusted that the Army had proved his actual guilt. Barrès accepted that foreigners could become French—after all, his native Lorraine had been French for only a century. Yet he owed much to Soury's biological determinism and Social Darwinism. While Lemaître saw the peasant as 'tolerant and liberal', Barrès wrote that a visit to rural voters had taught him 'fear of the human beast such as he is underneath his civilized exterior'.[93] He claimed that the death of three-quarters of its population during the Revolutionary Wars and an influx of French peasants had Gallicized the originally German Lorraine. If assimilation of foreigners into the French race was theoretically possible, an apparently French family might still hear the voice of its German or English ancestors. Indeed, the more the foreigner adopted the airs of an 'honest man', the more he must be distrusted. Barrès proposed reforms of naturalization similar to those of the LPF, but wondered whether some Jews could ever be assimilated.[94] Racism was not an end in itself, even for Barrès. In the 1902 *législatives*, Barrès attacked his opponent, a member of the LPF who was backed by the Ligue antisémitique, for substituting 'death to Jews!' for serious reforms.[95] Not all radical Nationalists were antisemites. Déroulède denied that he was an anti-Semite and did not advocate discrimination, but he often sounded like one.

The radical leagues' antisemitism lost some of its Boulangist anti-capitalism, while Drumont's eclectic antisemitism became more influential. Increasingly, antisemites identified Jews with Marxism, hitherto a minor theme.[96] The Jaunes were particularly alive to this notion, a part of their strategy for incorporation of the proletariat into the nation. The radical leagues also accused the Jews of damaging the Church in order to weaken national sentiment. Antisemitism was connected to xenophobia too, for antisemites accused Jews of recruiting foreign labour. Barrès placed protection of French labour at the centre of his 'Nancy Programme' (1898), while the LDP and the Ligue antisémitique were strong in areas of East European Jewish immigration in Paris, where workers, shopkeepers, and the La

[90] Maurice Barrès, *Les Lézardes sur la maison* (Paris, 1904).
[91] Wright, *The Regionalist Movement*, 83.
[92] Joly, *Déroulède*, 210.
[93] Maurice Barrès, *Mes Cahiers*, 11 vols (Paris), i, 1929–1938, 11; Sternhell, *La Droite révolutionnaire*, 165 ff.
[94] Barrès, *Scènes et doctrines*, 94–6.
[95] Doty, *From Cultural Rebellion*, 169–73.
[96] *L'Éclair*, 8 October 1898.

Villette butchers competed with migrants for jobs and customers.[97] The Jaunes called for a tax on foreign labour and for compulsory employment of French workers.[98] Guérin set up a Société mutuelle du protection du travail national as a rival to the Bourse du travail, hoping to detach the working-class from 'cosmopolitan Marxism'.[99]

Antisemitism and xenophobia served an ideology of class collaboration within the nation, but did not rule out reforms for French workers. As Barrès put it, 'we are obliged to protect the more humble of our compatriots because we recognize in him the eminent dignity of being a Frenchman'.[100] He advocated a progressive income tax, an idea rejected outright by conservatives. The Jaunes argued that profit-sharing and cheap housing would give workers a stake in property and the nation. A united France would be better armed in the struggle between nations.[101]

Radical Nationalists were more systematically anti-feminist than they were anti-Socialist, but their attitude towards women was complex. They saw the family as an integral part of the nation and conceived of women as child bearers, while Barrès feared that *La Fronde* would usurp masculine roles.[102] The League des patriotes collaborated with the Union des femmes de France, a part of the Red Cross, led by Déroulède's cousin, but women were less evident at the meetings of the radical leagues than in those of the LPF.[103] However, radicals permitted the atypical Gyp to participate in the movement as an honorary man. Her salon attracted Barrès, Coppée, Julia Daudet, and Déroulède, and provided one of the few locations in which an educated woman could speak.[104] It is perhaps significant that Gyp's reputation was based on her fictional male *alter ego*, Bob—the archetypal boulevardier-duellist. Her fiction also subordinated gender differences to the Jewish–French opposition, thus turning to her advantage the radicals' definition of the elite in ideological terms. For male Nationalists, Gyp was an Amazon, an exception.

Indeed, radical Nationalists embraced a masculinist, not to say violent, ethos, which we may interpret as a response to feminism, to the 'effeminacy' of the 'degenerate' Dreyfusard elite, and to the left's use of violence. Nationalists saw Republican concessions to feminism as evidence of degenerate effeminacy in the elite, and so they denounced 'puny' intellectuals' who led Dreyfusardism. Radical Nationalists loved duelling and prided themselves on their readiness to wield the sword on behalf of the people. Whereas Progressists approved of duelling only in private matters where the state had no business, the eponymous hero of Déroulède's play, *La Mort de Hoche*, spurns the idea of duelling for a personal motive. A major theme of the play is that the people have conquered the right to defend their honour with the sword.[105]

[97] Rutkoff, *Revanche and Revision*, 116–18; Nord, *Shopkeeper Protest*, 372–81.
[98] Arnold, 'Counterrevolutionary themes', 115–16.
[99] Sternhell, *La Droite révolutionnaire*, 227–8.
[100] Doty, *From Cultural Rebellion*, 208.
[101] Arnold, 'Counterrevolutionary themes', 99–133.
[102] *Le Drapeau*, 13 July 1897; Forth, *The Dreyfus Affair*, 151.
[103] Joly, *Déroulède*, 81; Fuller, 'Women', 255.
[104] Willa Z. Silverman, *Gyp: The last of the Mirabeaus* (NewYork, 1995), 119.
[105] Paul Déroulède, *La Mort de Hoche* (Paris, 1897), 1–28.

Radical Nationalists also endorsed popular violence, from which the codes of the supposedly civilized duel were not wholly separate. Violence between apprentices, French and foreign workers, was not as elemental as contemporaries sometimes believed. Use of knives was considered treacherous and unmanly; force was usually depicted as defensive, especially to protect women, and as a necessary intervention of the people in questions where the government had failed. Violent clashes between the Jaunes and the Socialists most obviously fell into this category. The Jeunesse antisémite specialized in protection of meetings, while the Jaunes charged armed squads with defending members against the reds. Biétry accepted the necessity of spilling blood to save France. Pacifists would be dealt with mercilessly. During the Affair, the Ligue des patriots staged violent street demonstrations, notably on 25 October outside the Chamber, all presented as a means to restore order.[106]

Some radicals saw violence as a good in itself, countering the 'decadence' symbolized by the Dreyfusard intellectual. But violence had to be regulated, for the elite must structure the mass. A Nationalist priest wrote 'I love force. I would be lying if I said otherwise. But I love it as guardian of the law.' At the turn of the century, this ethos of force, related to idealization of the Army, was perhaps displacing the culture of the *café-concert*, from which radical Nationalism had emerged. Radical Nationalists were not alone in advocating 'physical culture' as a means to counter decadence, but one Nationalist advocate of sport criticized the weakness of intellectuals, dandies, young men who 'lie about in scrawny carcasses in *café-concerts*'.[107] In this respect, at least, radical Nationalism anticipated interwar extreme-right movements, especially if we remember that fascists rarely saw force as an end in itself either.

Radical Nationalism's radicalism lay in its anti-capitalism, advocacy of social reforms, appeal to the people, willingness to countenance popular violence, and denunciations of the old right. Yet it was also violently anti-Socialist, anti-parliamentarian, anti-feminist, and antisemitic. Moderates accused Barrès of seeking a new Boulangism, but saw radical Nationalism as less dangerous than the left. Monarchists too saw Nationalism as a means to revitalize their cause.

MONARCHISM AND THE RADICAL RIGHT

In January 1898, Buffet's replacement of Dufeuille improved the position of radical Royalists relative to parliamentarians. The Affair further advantaged radicals. In his San Remo Manifesto, issued just before Déroulède's coup, the pretender declared that he had 'formally decided to rely on the Army and the people'—for the latter, read Nationalist leagues and Jeunesse royaliste (JR)—not universal suffrage.[108] These developments prepared the way for Action française (AF).

[106] Rutkoff, *Revanche and Revision*, 143. [107] Forth, *The Dreyfus Affair*, 209, 220.
[108] *Le Moniteur universelle*, 18 February 1899; see also *L'Éclair (Midi)*, 1 September 1898.

The JR was at the forefront of radicalization. It created a network of committees, and in 1899 claimed 30,000 members in thirty-four departmental groups. The real number was far less, for many committees grouped a handful of aristocrats.[109] Yet the JR intended to create an elite party rather than a mass movement. The future Royalist deputy, the Marquis de Rosanbo, told the JR that its essential hierarchy and discipline depended on the 'idea', not the number of members or even their quality.[110] Linked to the JR was L'Œillet blanc, a tiny group that claimed to be the prince's bodyguard, which participated in the Auteuil attack on Loubet, and which anticipated the Commissaires de l'Action française.

Ideologically, radical Royalists were not homogenous. Some, like the Boulangists Mackau and Breteuil ten years earlier, hoped to reconcile the 'marvellously supple' traditional principle with modern institutions.[111] Others, discouraged by decades of electoral failure, rejected democracy. They held that the natural constitution of the country was monarchical and authoritarian, that the people could not therefore be sovereign, and consequently that parliamentary monarchists were merely auxiliaries of the enemies of France. Since Jews, Protestants, and Freemasons, a 'counter-elite', had diverted France from its true nature, the French no longer knew their king, and would need to be reconverted. Furthermore, the JR argued for a 'national monarchy', which would put the nation above even the person of the king; the Royalist movement would obey a 'system' rather than the person; it would be independent of the pretender, and thus use its liberty to proselytize the royal cause.[112] And since the 'real' psychology of the people was monarchical, it could appeal to the people against democracy.[113] The ideology of the JR and later AF is sometimes seen as an absolute rejection of modernity. In fact, like other conservative movements, it wished to reconcile its own rather contingent ideas of tradition and modernity—Rasanbo saw both rural depopulation and the poor performance of the telegraph system as signs of decadence. The JR blended the science of the day, notably crowd psychology, with Legitimist traditionalism and Orleanist rationalism.

Parliamentary monarchism had not died. Indeed, several prominent Royalists were Dreyfusards, probably including Denys Cochin, their most authoritative figure. Dufeuille, a Protestant, saw Drumont's *Libre parole* as a manifestation of 'civil and social war'. A writer in *Le Soleil* declared that Henry's 'coup de rasoir'[114] had convinced him of the need for an 'open' trial, whatever the outcome; he opposed a new Boulangism, yet held that the Republic had 'dirtied everything', and that 'If the Army does not kill the Republic, the Republic will kill the Army.' Indeed, it was better for France to risk revolution, hopefully non-violent, than to die a slow

[109] Joly, *Nationalistes*, 195.

[110] *La Gazette de France*, 16 February 1899.

[111] *La Gazette de France*, 4 January 1899.

[112] *La Gazette de France*, 11 February, 17 January 1899.

[113] *La Gazette de France*, 14–15 March 1898; Bertrand Joly, 'Le Parti royaliste et l'Affaire Dreyfus', *Revue historique* 269, no. 546 (1983), 311–64 at 338–9, 325–6; Denis, *Les Royalistes de la Mayenne*, 328–9; Joly, *Nationalistes*, 194–206.

[114] Henry used a razor for his forgery and to slit his own throat.

death. *Le Soleil* depicted Déroulède's coup as the folly of a poet, but detected 'nobility in those who refused to resign themselves'.[115] Dreyfusard or not, parliamentarian or not, monarchists rarely ruled out a coup in principle, for they were uncertain how the regime would collapse. Dufeuille told the pretender that the public would follow the first person who captured the public imagination, and sounded out military circles.[116] He too knew that monarchism needed Nationalist support.

The Royalist leadership placed some hopes in the LPF; allegedly some sections were largely Royalist. Relations were not easy, for some Royalists disliked the 'national Socialist' component of the disparate LPF, while Lemaître's unequivocal Republicanism made it difficult to profess Royalism openly. Royalists gained little from alliance with Nationalists in the 1900 *municipales*. Jules Auffray, Mackau's former right-hand man, won the Sorbonne district from a Socialist, but generally Nationalists refused to support avowed monarchists, and by the end of the year Monarchists had given up on the LPF.[117]

Royalists also joined the Ligue des patriotes, encouraged by Déroulède's talk of reconciliation of aristocracy and people. One Royalist wrote to Déroulède that 'order must be restored by whoever is able to do it... we [Royalists] no longer have the right to be difficult'.[118] They hoped to take advantage of Déroulède's coup and Buffet laid plans for a new administration. Yet Déroulède never abandoned his antipathy to monarchism. His opposition to the pretender's appearance in Paris contributed to General Pellieux's refusal to back the coup. The pretender soon ordered his followers out of the LDP.[119] Déroulède was more sympathetic to Bonapartists, who had often abandoned dynasticism. In 1901, he declared that Bonapartists were Republicans.[120]

Like Nationalists, Monarchists endeavoured to exploit divisions within the proletariat. In 1898–1899, they subsidized workers' unions and claimed to have provoked a building strike. In 1899, the pretender believed that a syndicalist leader was ready to bring several unions into the Royalist camp.[121] These efforts to win over the left failed, not least because many Royalists saw minor reforms as 'collectivist'. Instead they proposed measures such as the employment of older, less productive workers on lower wages as an alternative to retirement pensions. The Comte d'Haussonville, a Social Catholic, advocated partnership between state and Catholic charity, for only the latter could provide the necessary auxiliaries.[122]

115 *Le Soleil*, 7 September, 5 October 1898, 25 January 1899; 24 January, for text of the Appel à l'Union, signed by academics and journalists including Hervé, and 16 February 1899.

116 Callais, 'La Jeunesse royaliste', 566–70; Joly, 'Le Parti royaliste', 355–60.

117 Rioux, *Nationalisme*, 15, 63–4, 79; Joly, 'Le Parti royaliste', 359, 361.

118 Joly, *Déroulède*, 266.

119 Rutkoff, *Revanche and Revision*, 125–33; Joly, 'Le Parti royaliste', 345–6, 355–9; Joly, *Déroulède*, 217–18.

120 Bernard Ménager, 'Nationalists and bonapartists', in Robert Tombs (ed.), *Nationhood and Nationalism in France: From Boulangism to the Great War* (London, 1991), 136–46 at 138; Joly, *Déroulède*, 240.

121 Richard Griffiths, 'From nostalgia to pragmatism: French royalism and the Dreyfus watershed', in Nicholas Atkin and Frank Tallett (eds), *The Right in France* (London, 1997), 115–28.

122 *Le Moniteur universel*, 6 January 1899, 7 February 1900.

Royalists also saw antisemitism as a means to reach the mass. We have seen that in the 1890s rural monarchists increasingly had recourse to antisemitism, and that it was integral to the philosophy of the JR.[123] From mid 1898, Buffet generously subsidized the Ligue antisémitique, convinced that antisemitism would permit re-conquest of the people. In his San Remo manifesto, the pretender condemned racial war, but declared that it would be 'puerile' to deny the existence of a Jewish question, and promised to defend those with roots in the soil against the vagabond power of money.[124] While Royalists embraced antisemitism for political reasons, it became integral to their political culture, not least because, as Lur-Saluces explained to the pretender, while people once feared that antisemitism would provoke class struggle and religious war, the racial definition made it more palatable.[125] Antisemitism also reinforced Royalists' Manichean belief in conspiracies and their millenarian expectations of imminent crisis. More prosaically it expressed discontent at the exclusion of Catholics from political office. Antisemitism slotted into the Catholic sectarianism of towns in Bouches-du-Rhône, Aveyron, Gard, and Vaucluse. Orleanist's antisemitism could be extreme: one wrote that the idea of a 'Jewish Saint-Bartholomew's [massacre] had passed like a bolt of lightning through the minds of the French', and that if the Jews provoke a new war, 'the next day not a single Jew will be alive in France'.[126]

Action Française

The evolution of the still obscure AF confirmed the incorporation of part of Royalism into the radical right. Maurice Pujo and Henri Vaugeois founded AF in the spring of 1898 with the objective of injecting nationalist priorities into the coming election campaign. AF re-emerged during the winter of 1898–1899 in informal meetings at the Café de Flore of a group including Mistral, Cavaignac, and Barrès. The group helped found the LPF, and Lemaître joined the AF Comité de patronage. Having failed either to radicalize the LPF or to mimic the LDP, AF became a nationalist counterpart to the Dreyfusard *Revue Blanche* under Barrès' guidance. Then, in 1900, Maurras converted AF to Monarchism.[127] Vaugeois announced his conversion late 1901. Only in 1905–1906 did AF capture a wide following, but it is interesting from the present perspective because Maurras synthesized and modified broader tendencies in monarchism and indeed in French political culture—which he rejected less systematically than he thought.

[123] Callais, 'La Jeunesse royaliste', 569.

[124] Samuel Osgood, *French Royalism under the Third and Fourth Republics*, second revised edition (The Hague, 1970), 71–2.

[125] William D. Irvine, *The Boulanger Affair Reconsidered: Royalism, Boulangism and the Origins of the Radical Right* (Oxford, 1989), 173.

[126] Joseph Reinach, *Histoire de l'Affaire Dreyfus*, iii: *La Crise* (Paris, 1901–11), 441–2.

[127] Eugen Weber, *Action Française: Royalism and Reaction in Twentieth-Century France* (Stanford, 1962), 43.

Maurrassian ideology was as eclectic as that of the JR.[128] From Legitimism Maurras took the notion that the individual acquired meaning in the natural order of family, profession, region, nation, and state. From Bonapartists, he took statism. From Catholic conservatism he took authority, dogmatism, and tradition. With thinkers from Bonald to Barrès, Maurras agreed that abstract universalism undermined the natural order, and as a creature of his time, he attributed the spread of universalism to cosmopolitan, Jewish, Protestant, and Masonic enemies of France.

Furthermore, Maurras shared the pseudo-scientific, racist, historical, gendered, and elitist ideas espoused in different forms by the 'generalists', the *hommes complets* of the political class more widely. His method was similar to that taught in the École libre des sciences politiques—Maurras admired Taine, one of its founders. The École prepared students to govern in the light of knowledge of the unique character of the nation, acquired through scientific study of its history, psychology, and laws. Maurras assumed the conventional elite–mass distinction, and sought a proper balance between tradition and progress. His specific contribution was the claim that order, monarchy, and Church rather than democracy defined the nation. We must therefore qualify the view that Maurrassianism corrupted Republicanism.

As a positivist, Maurras held that examination of 'natural' social facts and political history permitted the discovery of laws that would guide policy—that was his famous 'organizing empiricism'. These laws were specific to nations, so government in accordance with them was as necessary as was literature written in the national idiom. Indeed, Maurras held that French aesthetic and legal principles were superior because they derived from the authority principle of the Graeco-Roman legal tradition, the hierarchical organization of the Church, and the clarity of the national language. Having understood the principle of orderliness, a man's judgement would be sound in aesthetics and politics. Maurras (like Lemaître) condemned experimentalism in art and literature. *Mutatis mutandis* good government depended upon order. Departure from tradition caused 'decadence'—evident in anti-militarism, democracy, parliamentarianism, philo-Semitism, immigration, and the low birth rate.

For Maurras, the king was the head of the national body, and so restoration was a rational necessity rather than a sentimental act. On this point Maurras echoed the JR and Orleanists.[129] Hereditary rule also provided the state with memory, reason, will, and continuity. Buffet explained that since the monarchy was the central nervous system of the national body, it necessarily responded forcefully to any threat, and once restored it would avenge the country's wounds through a 'necessary repression'.[130] Only the monarchy was strong enough to deal with the Jewish question, implement administrative and corporative decentralization, and reconcile capital and labour without destroying the integrity of the nation.

The counterpart to restoration would be elimination of democratic institutions. Elections merely gave the people the opportunity to display their selfishness.

[128] Weber, *Action Française*, 25–6. [129] Callais, 'La Jeunesse royaliste', 563–4.
[130] Charles Maurras, *L'Enquête sur la monarchie* (Paris, 1910, first published 1900), 12–14.

Maurras ascribed to the people a desire to be governed strongly. For Buffet, France was 'poignarde'—it desired government by the fist.[131] Mass behaviour was determined by instinct; the people, like women, children, and 'primitive' peoples, gained knowledge through feeling, symbols, and repetition. Buffet explained that whereas parliamentarians uselessly explained their actions to the people and inevitably engaged in low deceit and ambiguity, the monarchy would simply display its standard.[132] The people could not be ruled through debate, only through manly frankness. One Royalist wrote 'The crowd is a woman; she is contemptuous of he who does not rape her.'[133] Collective psychology was as influential among neo-Royalists as it was among Republicans.

Yet Maurras did not believe it possible to govern against the people. He favoured corporatist 'representation' of regional and professional interests rather than popular sovereignty. Representatives would participate in decision-making as special—and therefore inferior—interests. That was another point on which the JR had anticipated Maurras. A corporatist parliament would monitor the executive. Likewise, Maurras did not entirely reject individual liberty. In the polemics over the *faux Henry*, Maurras accepted that an individual should not be unjustly condemned. The sin of the Dreyfusards was rather to question the state's right to decide matters of justice. Maurras proclaimed the principle of reaction, but more accurately he wished to contain representation and individual rights within an authoritarian, hierarchical nation.

Bonapartism

Bonapartism was too weak to play an autonomous part in the Nationalist movement. Prince Victor had little faith in his chances of reigning, refused to take sides in the Dreyfus Affair, and condemned antisemitism.[134] He had only 2,000 organized sympathizers, divided between the loyal Comités plébiscitaires and Cassagnac's disloyal Comités impérialistes. Both groups condemned Victor's inaction. The latter had little choice but to authorize membership in the LDP, and Bonapartists, including Le Provost de Launay and Georges Thiébaud, occupied senior positions in it.[135] Bonapartists (and royalists) were also prominent in its only important provincial section, in Marseille,[136] while in Normandy they preferred the Déroulèdistes in the disparate Nationalist coalition.[137] Bonapartists' ideological influence in the leagues was important too, notably in their constitutional schemes. Also, Bonapartist deputies had espoused antisemitism in the 1890s. The Prince was no more successful in preventing his followers from crying 'A bas les juifs!' than was Déroulède. Deputy Lasies, director of *Le Petit Caporal* and member of the Ligue

131 Maurras, *L'Enquête sur la monarchie*, 12–14.
132 Maurras, *L'Enquête sur la monarchie*, 14–16.
133 *Le Triboulet*, 26 June 1898, cited in Joly, 'Le Parti royaliste', 314.
134 Ménager, 'Nationalists and Bonapartists', 140; Joly, *Nationalistes*, 242–6.
135 Ménager, 'Nationalists and Bonapartists', 136–46.
136 Ménager, 'Nationalists and Bonapartists', 136–7.
137 Fuller, 'Belle époque French nationalism', 38–9; Quellien, *Bleus, blancs, rouges*, 173–84, 204.

antisémitique, argued that rural interests could be protected only by ridding France of the Jewish parliamentarian bourgeoisie.[138] From late 1898, *Le Petit caporal* openly called for a coup, and reassured readers that since Déroulède had revived plebiscitary ideas, Bonapartists would not be excluded from the new regime. Yet Déroulède's view of the plebiscite was different to that of the Bonapartists; for the former it meant election of the president for a determinate mandate, while for Bonapartists it meant the election at least of a dictator and at most a dynasty. Victor opposed Déroulède's coup, and after 1901 relations between Déroulède and the official Bonapartist movements deteriorated.[139]

CONCLUSION

Nationalism emerged from a complex crisis, involving powerful interests' resentment at their exclusion from political, administrative, and judicial power, real or perceived, at a time of threat from Socialism, feminism, anticlericalism, and regionalism. As the Méline coalition broke up, Nationalists endeavoured to remake the elite and contain social conflict through propagation of a religion of the *patrie*, corporatism, and reinforcement of the executive. They thus hoped to contain legitimate divisions within the nation. Yet Nationalism's real and perceived subversiveness permitted Waldeck-Rousseau to claim the conservative label and thus repress the leagues. Subsequently, the Progressists, and especially the Rallié ALP, proved better placed to pursue the right's agenda. The ALP channelled religious, regionalist, and female activism into an anti-Socialist and nationalist, but legalistic, movement.

The arrest of the plotters in Déroulède's coup, the dissolution of the LDP, and the dispersal of its cadres, gravely weakened the radical right. When in June 1899 the government attempted to arrest Guérin and dissolve his league, activists retreated to 'Fort Chabrol', but after forty days they gave in. Revelation of the shady manoeuvres of the royalists and arrest of Buffet and Lur-Saluces, who joined Déroulède in the High Court, further reduced the public stock of royalism. The JR lost its central administration and was integrated into the parent organization. Parliamentary royalism recovered ground, while the success of Maurras' *Enquete sur la monarchie* in 1901 kept the radical flame alive.

Neither radical Nationalists nor the royalists could compete with the LPF in the allocation of the best constituencies in the 1902 elections. Déroulède, exiled in Saint-Sébastien, impotently railed against Lemaître's preference for the conservative alliance. The rise of religious tensions also divided the LPF. In the end, around fifty Nationalist deputies were elected alongside Monarchists, Mélinists, and Ralliés. As the LPF declined after 1902, supporters turned to Progressism or the ALP. Lemaître abruptly embraced the plebiscite and later joined AF. The *Annales de la Patrie française* developed an anti-Progressist hue.[140] The Nationalist parliamentary group disappeared in 1910 when deputies could no longer belong to multiple groups.

138 Fitch, 'Mass culture', 77.

139 Ménager, 'Nationalists and bonapartists', 140; Joly, *Déroulède*, 240–2.

140 Fuller, 'Belle époque French nationalism', 28, 33, 39–40, 47.

The Jaunes lasted a little better. In December 1902, Biétry formed the Parti socialiste national in the hope of taking over from the defeated leagues. It survived only until November 1903, but the Jaunes reached a high point in 1906 with the election of Biétry and Duporque to the Chamber. By then, the Jaunes might have counted 100,000 members, but they too declined thereafter.[141]

Nationalism should be taken seriously, however ephemeral, and however few activists it had. It briefly set the agenda in the *fin-de-siècle* crisis, notably through the press. A substantial minority of electors were prepared to vote for anti-Republican parties or for men who demanded a profound reform of Republican institutions. Secondly, the idea of an illegal change of regime was endorsed by many royalists and Justice-Égalité. Cavaignac favoured Déroulède's coup in principle, and a few Progressists, including Deschanel, may also have done so. Elements in the Army, Paris police, and judiciary were not against a coup.[142] The LPF was less positive, but did not roundly condemn the notion either, and a few pro-LPF editorialists in *l'Éclair* claimed that the real master in France was not those who had elected Loubet to the presidency, but 'public opinion'.[143] However ridiculous its outcome, Déroulède's coup demonstrated the depth of political conflict. It did not fail because conservatives were profoundly democratic, for it did not need mass support. Rather, Nationalists, Monarchists, and the Army proved unable to act together.

Nationalism left a complex legacy. It permanently marked the diverse rural monarchist tradition in the west and south with antisemitism. It prefigured the leagues of the interwar years and even fascism. Barrès' 1898 Nancy Programme and his 1903 campaign in the fourth arrondissement of Paris seem especially proto-fascist.[144] But as Stuart Doty argues, whilst many of the constituent elements of fascism existed in *fin-de-siècle* France, they were rarely united in a single movement at a particular moment. There were also discontinuities. Above all, radical Nationalists made the Army rather than a mass party the vehicle of their hopes. Déroulède declared that while the population must go into the streets, a general must lead them. His constitutional schemes were as close to the US system as to dictatorship, and he left some room for individual liberty, even if his allies had different ideas.[145] We have seen too that Nationalism evoked much sympathy among Progressists. Of course, conservatives would often support fascism, but in the 1900s, the Progressists and ALP captured the LPF's programme.

[141] Arnold, 'Counterrevolutionary themes', 107–8.
[142] Barrès, *Mes Cahiers*, vol. 2, 92; Joly, *Déroulède*, 286–94.
[143] *L'Éclair*, 20, 28 February 1899.
[144] Doty, *From Cultural Rebellion*, 260.
[145] Joly, *Déroulède*, 209–11, 309–10.

6

Party Formation (1898–1906)

> Politics cannot be pursued against the feelings, or even the prejudices of the majority of a people.
>
> Frédéric Clément, 28 February 1906

The Dreyfus Affair was a founding moment for parliamentary conservatism. The Progressists split for and against Waldeck-Rousseau's government of Republican defence. The advanced wing joined the Radicals and Socialists in the new Bloc des gauches (I shall refer to this group as the 'centre'). The anti-ministerials kept the name 'Progressist' and joined the right in opposition. The Bloc des gauches triumphed in the 1902 elections, thus inaugurating the 'Radical Republic'. Yet no 'Bloc des droites' opposed the majority. The opposition comprised 127 Progressists, forty-three Nationalists, thirty-five Action libérale, and forty-three Monarchists and 'conservateurs'. The Progressists rejected the label 'right' as Monarchist, and maintained that they were true to Republican principles that the left had abandoned. The Action libérale populaire (ALP) distinguished itself from Monarchism too, but the absence in its title of 'Republican' reflected the Ralliés' rightwards shift. On both sides, the generation of 1900 remained influential into the 1930s, not least because organized parties crystallized within the fault-lines of the period.[1] Although they never succeeded in structuring conservative political life, parties became markers of important social, religious, and constitutional differences among conservatives and in relation to the left.

Parties emerged simultaneously on left and right. The Parti républicain radical et radical-socialiste was founded on 23 June 1901, while four months later the Dreyfusard wing of the Progressists formed the Alliance républicaine démocratique (ARD). In 1902, the Socialists consolidated as two major parties, which in 1905 merged as the Section française de l'internationale ouvrière (SFIO). On the right, the Ralliés set the pace. A few days before formation of the Radical-Socialist Party, Piou and de Mun had formed the Action libérale (AL) parliamentary group, which after the 1902 elections became the ALP. By 1905, the ALP claimed no less than 200,000 members in over sixty departmental committees.[2] Anti-government

[1] Jean-Luc Pinol, '1919–1958. Le Temps des droites?', in Jean-François Sirinelli (ed.), *Histoire des droites en France*, i. *Politiques* (Paris, 1992), 291–398 at 296–9.

[2] Benjamin F. Martin, 'The creation of the Action Libérale Populaire: an example of party formation in Third Republican France', *French Historical Studies* 9, no. 4 (Fall 1976), 660–89 at 675, 679, 680, 683; Gaetano Quagliariello, 'L'Action libérale populaire et l'illusion du parti politique (1901–1906)', in Claire Andrieu, Gilles Le Béguec, and Danielle Tartakowski (eds), *Associations et champ politique. La Loi de 1901à l'épreuve du siècle* (Paris, 2001), 245–64.

Progressists did not organize until November 1903, when they created the Fédération républicaine (FR). Weakened by repression, Monarchists remained apart from the organizational fashion. Later in the decade Action française (AF) provided a little cohesion; for now, many Monarchists joined the ALP.

Some historians see the formation of parties as a stage on the inevitable journey from notable politics to permanent, modern, national organizations with mass memberships to which leaders were answerable. For Raymond Huard, party formation demonstrated 'a more precise understanding of the necessities of universal suffrage'.[3] Similarly, Pierre Rosanvallon maintains that party formation expressed belated acceptance of pluralism and rejection of the Revolutionary view that the electorate was a sum of individuals possessed of a single will, in which opposition was illegitimate and anti-national.[4]

Even if we suspend disbelief in the recourse to a modernization narrative, we may doubt the linear progression from notables to parties. Right-wingers had never been able to rely for election on status or patronage alone. The distinction between notability and professionalism was complex, as was that between party formation and democratization of activism. Indeed, the 1900s witnessed the apogee and decline in the ALP of the extra-parliamentary Catholic populist politics that successively contributed to Legitimism, Christian Democracy, and Nationalism. After 1906, Orleanist and moderate Republican efforts to channel participation into legal forms triumphed, and with it an elitist politics of a new sort. These developments did not necessarily entail acceptance of pluralism, for many conservatives continued to assume an organic national community. Neither did they mean that voters chose candidates merely for who they were or for the services that they offered.

Conservative leaders understood parties in historically specific ways and used them for particular purposes. They certainly *believed* them to be necessary, but collective psychology taught that parties should preserve the leadership of an elite with privileged insight into a unitary national character. Rival parties were not legitimate contenders for power, but vehicles through which 'demagogues' exploited passions and materialism—the dark side of the mass. Party formation was also part of a struggle for position at a time of classificatory flux—the ARD's founders unsuccessfully attempted to pre-empt the launch of the Radical-Socialist Party. Indeed, party formation was an intrinsic part of the struggle between Antidreyfusards and Dreyfusards, as it mutated into one between clericals and anticlericals, without displacing class conflict.

PARTIES, RELIGION, AND SOCIAL CONFLICT

The 1901 Associations Law was both a weapon in the battle against the Church and a legal framework for the formation of parties that institutionalized the

[3] Raymond Huard, *La Naissance du parti politique en France* (Paris, 1996), 88.

[4] Pierre Rosanvallon, *Le Peuple introuvable* (Paris, 1998), 225–330.

anticlerical–clerical struggle. The Law allowed any group of citizens to form an association, while obliging religious orders to seek individual parliamentary authorization, for they allegedly owed allegiance to a foreign power. Following Radical-Socialist gains in 1902, Émile Combes' new government refused to authorize the orders, closed 12,000 religious schools, and severed diplomatic contact with the Vatican. In November 1901, Piou had already called for a mass organization of Catholics under the 1901 Law, drawn from all regions and classes, to defend Catholic rights.[5] In the Rhône, opposition to Combes and then to a 'Préfet de combat' also provoked the formation of several new Progressist committees, for the first time active outside electoral periods.[6] In 1905, Combes' successors disestablished the Church, and Catholic resistance climaxed in the Inventories Crisis of 1906.

Business interests also shaped party organization. The Dreyfus Affair coincided with significant industrial unrest and revolutionary rhetoric, while the Socialist presence in the Waldeck-Rousseau government compounded fears for property. Many conservatives believed that minor state intervention led inevitably to collectivism and that strikes threatened the very existence of property. Even when bosses made concessions, which they could afford to do in these years of rising profits, they were too jealous of their authority to negotiate with unions.[7] Consequently, employers reinforced their anti-strike organizations. Already in the 1890s, the Association de l'industrie et de l'agriculture française and the Comité républicain du commerce, de l'industrie et de l'agriculture (CRCI, later the Comité Mascuraud) had played a political role.[8] Now the Waldeck-Rousseau government's willingness to mediate labour disputes politicized employers' associations.[9]

Yet the Dreyfus Affair divided employers. The CRCI fell under Radical and centre influence. In response, conservatives founded the Union du commerce et de l'industrie pour la défense sociale and the Comité national républicain du commerce et de l'industrie (both 1899) and the Fédération des industriels et des commerçants français (1903), which was close to the FR. The Progressist André Lebon was able to devote himself to the latter because as Minister of Colonies he had been held responsible for the harshness of Dreyfus' prison conditions, provoking his Protestant electors to abandon him in 1902. Ideological and economic questions were as inseparable as ever.[10]

[5] *Bulletin de l'Action libérale*, November 1901.

[6] Mathias Bernard, *La Dérive des modérés. La Fédération républicaine du Rhône sous la Troisième République* (Paris, 1998), 118, 195–200.

[7] Peter N. Stearns, 'Against the strike threat: employer policy towards labour agitation in France, 1900–1914', *Journal of Modern History* 40, no. 4 (December 1968), 474–500.

[8] *La République française*, 19 November 1903; Mathias Bernard, 'La Diffusion incomplète d'un modèle partisan. Les Progressistes et la Fédération républicaine (1903–1914)', in François Roth (ed.), *Les Modérés dans la vie politique française (1870–1965)* (Nancy, 2000), 139–54; Joël Dubos, 'Organisation des réseaux modérés sous la IIIe République. André Lebon, un homme à l'intersection des cercles du pouvoir', in Roth (ed.), *Les Modérés dans la vie politique française*, 299–315 at 306, 309–10.

[9] Stearns, 'Against the strike threat', 489–500; Philip Nord, 'Social defence and conservative regeneration: the national revival, 1900–14', in Robert Tombs (ed.), *Nationhood and Nationalism in France: From Boulangism to the Great War* (London, 1991), 210–28 at 211–15.

[10] Dubos, 'Organisation des réseaux', 313.

Class, religion, and party also converged in the question of access to employment. Waldeck-Rousseau immediately closed the timid opening to moderate Catholics that had begun under Méline and initiated new purges of the judiciary and Army. He declared that a functionary with a 'reactionary' wife must be 'triply devoted' to the Republic.[11] The Radical victory of 1902 intensified secularization and politicization of the administration, schools, and hospitals. I shall discuss the issue further in the following chapter. For the moment, suffice it to note that conservatives perceived the Radical Republic as the triumph of mediocrity over competence. Parties were meant to counter this 'degeneration'.[12]

Yet the parties struggled to reconcile conflicting objectives. Politically, both the ALP and Progressists still wished to unite Catholics and Republicans in an anti-Socialist alliance. To preserve that possibility, ALP leaders defended religion and property in the name of liberalism, thus opening it to criticism from those in its own ranks who saw it as insufficiently Catholic and/or too socially conservative. Catholic women's groups, Social Catholics, Christian Democrats, Nationalists, and Monarchists all challenged the ALP's liberal strategy from different directions. In principle, the Progressists were open to the ALP's liberalism, but mixed messages confused them. In the tradition of Moderate Republicanism, Progressists tried to convince (male) voters that they were legally equal citizens rather than members of a class or religion. From that perspective, the ALP looked potentially illiberal in religious and social matters, preaching clerical and state intervention in social life. Moreover, the very intensity of anti-socialism potentially reinforced religious conflict, for Catholics and *laïques* advanced potentially incompatible solutions to social problems. Many liberal Catholics saw revolution as the logical outcome of religious hatred, and regarded assaults on the congregations as encouraging workers to attack employers.[13] Others looked to Social Catholicism and/or charity and education to solve the social question, while many in the Fédération espoused the liberal view that only increased productivity could improve the workers' lot. As for the centre, it combined anticlericalism and social reformism. Since the latter was, until 1906, part of the Bloc des gauches, I shall leave full discussion of it until Chapter 7. However, since the following section takes a longer-term view of party structures before 1914, I shall include the centre in it.

PARTY STRUCTURES

The Fédération and ARD represented the institutionalization of the Moderate Republican, parliamentary model, in which the elites endeavoured to channel

[11] Maurice Larkin, *Religion, Politics and Preferment in France since 1890* (Cambridge, 1995), 75–87, 91; Christophe Voilliot, *Le Candidature officiel. Une Pratique d'état de la Restauration à la Troisième République* (Paris, 2005), 235–41.

[12] Bernard, *La Dérive*, 119–20.

[13] *La République française*, 3 July and 28 September 1900.

social conflict into elections and parliament, a model shaped also by the assumption of an opposition between the rational elite and the irrational mass. Both parties presented simple programmes to the electorate, in tune with mass psychology, but expected that in parliament party discipline would be limited to general principles; deputies would decide practical issues on their merits, through reasoned debate, without recourse to ideology. The Russian political scientist, Moisey Ostrogorsky, who had studied at the École libre des sciences politiques, systematized this view in his *La démocratie et l'organisation des partis politiques* (1903). He argued that since parties prevented the emergence of an elite of brains and character, they should be 'abolished' inside parliament. Charles de Benoist of the FR, a teacher at the École, combined Ostrogorsky's and Le Bon's thinking. He claimed that in parties, the mass was 'drilled, agitated, stirred up', and that 'sparks, vibration, and trembling' would pass through it. Parties, he said, influenced the mass through 'images, which even the illiterate could read, to produce exaltation and faith', and they relied on fanatics who used the fist against adversaries. Parties were responsible for the 'industrial production of opinion'. Professional politicians would dominate them; a fraction would interpose itself between the deputy and his electors, and undermine liberty in parliament.[14]

This negativity did not prevent Benoist from going on to lead the Fédération, for he saw parties of a certain type as compatible with liberty—although in practice, his ideas were indeed hard to reconcile. Thus, the two wings of Progressism called themselves 'Alliance' and 'Fédération' rather than 'party' because looser organization would preserve elite autonomy and re-unite Republicans.[15] The parties' central organizations were weak. Aynard reported that the Fédération's future depended on how much time President Motte and Secretary-General Frédéric Clément could spare for it.[16] Both parties distinguished between members effectively in terms of social class. In the Alliance, those paying 100 francs per year were departmental delegates by right and had the power to designate arrondissement leaders. Delegates at annual assemblies listened to speeches and unanimously voted motions. Progressists feared that committees with open membership would permit Radicals—'professional politicians'—to exploit the state on behalf of local interests and 'occult forces'. Neither party recruited all centrists or Progressists; neither had much authority over their own deputies, who joined different groups in parliament; often the two parties endorsed non-members as candidates. Many deputies belonged to both Fédération and Alliance. This looseness enabled rival, better-organized groups to participate in the two parties. The Alliance overlapped with the Radical-Socialist Party; its Gironde committee claimed 6,000 members and was of semi-Radical proclivities. The Fédération drew on Nationalist and Catholic

[14] Charles de Benoist, 'Comment on capte le suffrage et le pouvoir', *Revue des Deux Mondes* 21 (15 June 1904), 885–916 at 895–9; *Correspondance d'Union républicaine*, 17 September 1908.

[15] *L'Alliance républicaine démocratique*, 13 December 1903.

[16] Archives nationales 563 AP 27 Fonds Ribot (hereafter ANFR, carton no.), Aynard to Ribot, 25 November 1903.

activists in Lyon, Le Havre, Rouen, Evreux, Nantes, and Chateau-Thierry, the latter group having 800 members.[17] The FR shaded into the ALP on its right.

The ALP combined elitist parliamentarianism with incorporation of Catholics into a structured party based on the parish, women's, charitable, and professional groups—it boasted regularly of the affiliation of committees (rather than of individuals). It did not impose discipline in parliament, except tacitly in matters important to the Church. The party thereby attempted to reconcile the Pope's instructions to ally with Moderate Republicans with his call for the unity of the faithful. Piou declared that the ALP programme would 'move the crowds',[18] but he did not expect the crowd to control the party. ALP leaders possessed social status, investment by the Pope and Church hierarchy, copious funds, and a powerful party press, and yet we shall see that they proved unable to control the Catholic movement.

All three parties recruited leaders from the privileged. As a 'party of government', the Alliance included several senior civil servants and 'establishment' intellectuals, mostly Dreyfusards, including some Jews and Protestants. Many Alliance leaders followed the classic route into politics through the Paris Law Faculty and Bar (which had been strongly Dreyfusard) and increasingly the École libre des sciences politiques, supplemented with service in ministerial cabinets. Typical were Léon Bérard and Maurice Colrat, both former secretaries of the Conference du stage of the Paris Bar. Both joined the Fédération on its formation but found the ARD more congenial. The liberal professions dominated the Alliance's parliamentary representation, while in its Conseil supérieur, businessmen, landowners, and academics were more visible. In 1911, at least twenty Alliance deputies sat on the boards of limited companies, while many Alliance lawyers worked for big business, including future President of the Republic, Paul Doumer, who was involved with the Comité des forges and the Compagnie générale d'électricité.[19]

Progressists initially recruited from the same circles. Intellectuals were well represented, including François Charmes, who from 1907 was director of the *Revue des Deux Mondes*, and the writer and École des sciences politiques professor, Anatole Leroy-Beaulieu. Barboux and Clément represented respectively the established and coming generation of the Paris Bar.[20] Particularly in the person of Louis Marin, such people continued to lead the Fédération into the 1930s. Yet thanks to

[17] Jean Vavasseur-Desperriers, 'Cultures, structures, stratégie d'une organisation de la droite parlementaire entre les deux guerres. La Fédération républicaine de 1919 à 1940', thèse de doctorat, Lille III, 1999, 71–5; Raymond Huard, 'Aboutissements préparés et cristallisations imprévues. La Formation des partis', in Pierre Birnbaum (ed.), *La France de l'Affaire Dreyfus* (Paris, 1994), 87–119; Donald G. Wileman, 'L'Alliance républicaine démocratique: the dead centre of French politics, 1901–1947', PhD thesis, York University, Toronto, 1988, 8–21; Rosemonde Sanson, *L'Alliance républicaine démocratique. Une Formation du centre (1901–1920)* (Rennes, 2003), 121; Bernard, *La Dérive*, 224.

[18] *Bulletin de l'Action libérale*, November 1901.

[19] Gilles Le Béguec, 'Un Grand parlementaire modéré', *Revue du Pau et du Béarn* 18 (1991), 305–24; Huard, 'Aboutissements', 87–119; David M. Gordon, *Liberalism and Social Reform: Industrial Growth and Progressiste Politics in France, 1880–1914* (Westport, 1996), 157–60; Mattei Dogan, 'Les Filières de la carrière politique en France', *Revue française de sociologie* 8, no. 4 (1967), 468–92; Sanson, *L'Alliance*, 59–63, 111–12.

[20] Nord, 'Social defence', 211–28; Bernard, 'La Diffusion incomplète', 145–6.

eviction from the governing majority, Progressist representation in the academic, legal, and administrative elite declined somewhat. The Progressists increasingly attracted the Catholic and ultra-liberal business interests of Lyon, the Nord, Seine-Inférieure, and Gironde. Aynard (Lyon) and Waddington (Rouen) were presidents of Chambers of Commerce. In Lyon, business leaders and Progressists met in organizations opposing income tax, notably a regional affiliate of Jules Roche's Ligue des contribuables.[21] Family traditions brought some big businessmen to the Fédération: in the Meurthe-et-Moselle, François de Wendel's Legitimist background tied him to the Progressists via Nationalism, while the self-made manager, Camille Cavallier, preferred the centre.

Eugène Motte, first president of the Fédération, approached provincial grand bourgeois to lead party groups, rather than the local businessmen and lawyers who had formed the first Fédération committees.[22] Yet provincial professionals, officers, and landowners became more prominent in the Fédération—the sort of people who had formed the backbone of Nationalism and Monarchism—and there was some broadening of the social base. In the cities, former Nationalist cadres often staffed committees and wrote for newspapers. In the Lozère, lawyers and doctors progressively displaced landowners; the former sanctioned peasant custom, including primogeniture, while doctors became the confidants of the peasantry. Both were more present among the population than absentee landowners were.[23] In Mayenne, nobles gave way to tenant farmers, the clergy, and to networks for the distribution of the *Courrier du Maine*.[24]

ALP leaders were similar to these Fédération neophytes. Landowners and ex-officers were numerous. A few great capitalists, including Eugène Schneider, and much of the Catholic minority of Nord business also joined. Titled and wealthy bourgeois women dominated the governing body of the ALP's ally, the Ligue patriotique des françaises (LPDF). Catholic professors, such as Jean Guiraud at the Besançon Faculty and Henri Groussau at the Catholic University of Lille, played a prominent role. In the Rhône, the ALP was led by lawyers of the old robe families, teachers at the Lyon Catholic Law Faculty, and Beaujolais winegrowers, often involved in agricultural syndicalism. Yet neither the status of its leaders nor its numerical importance translated into electoral victories in that department—to the surprise only of those who assume that electoral success requires a particular type of organization.[25]

Wealth and status permitted conservative parliamentarians some autonomy, but that did not mean that they were elected for reputation and patronage rather than for their ideas. Money certainly mattered. In his 1898 campaign against Jaurès,

[21] Bernard, *La Dérive*, 111–12. [22] Bernard, *La Dérive*, 123.

[23] Yves Pourcher, *Les Maîtres de granit. Les Notables de Lozère du XVIII siècle à nos jours* (Paris, 1987), 218–21, 258.

[24] Denis, *Les Royalistes*, 476–7.

[25] Malcolm Anderson, 'The right and the social question in parliament', in David Shapiro (ed.), *The Right in France, 1890–1919: Three Studies* (Cambridge, 1962), 85–134 at 90–1; Martin, 'The creation', 675; Michel Denis, *Les Royalistes de la Mayenne et le monde moderne (XIXe–XXe siècles)* (Le Mans, 1977), 490–1; Bernard, *La Dérive*, 108.

Solages spent 19,585 francs, and even then wanted the Prefect's neutrality.[26] In 1910, the administration found that no Republican possessed sufficient funds to stand against Mackau. Candidates with economic and cultural capital sometimes rejected party support altogether: in 1889, the Marquis de Vogüé refused Mackau's patronage because 'my candidacy has an entirely local and personal character. If I succeed, it will be through my relations.'[27] In 1905 an Ille-et-Vilaine deputy advised Louis Marin, then standing for the first time in the Lorraine, to emulate his own practice of visiting all the 'important electors of left and right', for it was 'insipid' to rely on a local agent or a committee. Yet Marin's counsellor also admitted that he canvassed for support from the presidents of parliamentary groups, while Marin carefully negotiated the wording of a denunciation of Freemasonry in his electoral programme with the local ALP.[28] Vogüé's anti-party stance did not really mean rejection of ideology, but of Boulangism. Indeed, candidates' need to negotiate and transcend divisions within the ideologically divided conservative electorate explains their relative autonomy as well as 'personal position' does.

The spiralling cost of elections, provoked by competition with rivals and the administration, constrained conservative candidates. They often had to beg or borrow money, and that compromised their independence. We have seen that business groups played an important role in funding campaigns, both of individuals and parties. The Ligue de la patrie française (LPF) and ALP particularly benefited, the latter also from the Church; in the 1902 elections, the Church spent between one and two million francs.[29] The ALP had sufficient funds to influence elections well after it declined as a party. Furthermore, notables had long recruited paid and/or volunteer agents and distributors of propaganda, as well as relying on intermediaries, such as village mayors. With time, these networks acquired authority of their own. The ALP relied on the clergy, women's groups, parishes, and Social Catholics for activists, and we shall see that their agendas often undermined those of the elites. Also, candidates sometimes needed the approval of assemblies of notables in the countryside or of plenary meetings of committees in the towns. The outcome was frequently decided in advance, but even then those who decided assumed limits that they could not cross.

Likewise, conservative leaders both attempted to shape and anticipate the electorate's choices and reactions—as Clément said, they could not govern 'against the people'. In conformity with the principles of collective psychology, they believed that the mass responded to material reward and simple ideas. Therefore, candidates had to render services. In 1887, Breteuil described the needs of universal suffrage as 'boring' but unavoidable: he had to deal with the *curé* who wanted to repair his bell tower, the proprietor who wanted a loan for a field, and the father who wanted

[26] Rolande Trempé, 'Une Campagne électorale étudiée d'après les archives privées', *Actes du 82e Congrès national des sociétés savantes, Bordeaux 1957* (1958), 471–90, 481–3.

[27] Éric Phélippeau, *L'Invention de l'homme politique moderne. De Mackau, l'Orne et la République* (Paris, 2002), 285.

[28] AN 317 221 Fonds Marin (hereafter, ANFLM, carton/dossier no.), Lefas to Marin, 7 September 1905; ANFLM 164, dossier 1905.

[29] Martin, 'The creation', 666–7, 673.

leave for his conscript son.[30] In 1894, the Prefect of the Orne complained that Mackau hypocritically attacked the administration while claiming credit for obtaining subsidies for his constituents.[31] Catholics used the Sociétés de St Vincent-de-Paul as unpaid agents for the right, while wives and daughters played an important part in the distribution of 'political charity'.[32] Control of Comices agricoles was essential for the distribution of prizes and subsidies, even if conservatives were not as free as Republicans were to expound their politics in prize-giving ceremonies.[33] In 1889, Solages pressured the workers of Decazeville to vote for him, and in 1898 he spent half his electoral budget on alcohol, including 'cinquante verres de Chartreuse vraie ou anisette Marie-Brizard', at forty centimes each for the electors of Larroque. At another village, his agent paid twenty francs for a band. A priest lamented that 'the argument of the bottle has now passed into our electoral habits, and for electors almost everywhere it is the condition, the *sine qua non*, of a favourable vote'.[34]

Since the Republicans often invalidated elections in which there was evidence of pressure on voters, conservatives had to devise other ways of reaching the 'mass'. Following the 1884 law on professional associations, a group of Rallié and Monarchist landowners in the Beaujolais created what would become one of the most powerful agricultural unions, the Union du sud-est (USE). The USE competed with the Republican administration to pose as protector of the peasantry at a time when phylloxera had destroyed vines and subsequently when overproduction caused a price collapse. The USE preached class collaboration against the harmful doctrines of Socialists, Radicals, and Christian Democrats. Landowners obliged workers and sharecroppers to join an organization that by 1914 had over 120,000 members in ten departments. The Société des agriculteurs de France (rue d'Athènes) provided a national link for conservative agrarians, Monarchist or Rallié.[35]

Conservatives also endeavoured to win votes through the repetition of simple themes, propagated through speeches, press, and posters; they aimed to awaken the Moderate Republican, Monarchist, or Catholic 'instincts' of the people through dissemination of resonate themes. Candidates therefore had to 'know' the crowd. In 1889, the Comité des douze rejected a candidate because he was 'too dry and abrupt, [and] he does not know how to speak to the crowds'.[36] André Maginot, elected in 1910, allegedly possessed 'a strong and *resonant* voice; one of those warm voices that please crowds'.[37] Piou urged the ALP to adopt a social programme that 'corresponds to interests that move the crowd'.[38]

[30] Henri de Breteuil, *La Haute société. Journal secret, 1886–1889* (Paris, 1979), 14 August 1887.

[31] Phélippeau, *L'Invention*, 146–74.

[32] Philippe Secondy, *La Persistance du Midi blanc* (Perpignan, 2006), 163.

[33] Phélippeau, *L'Invention*, 52, 55–6, 146–62.

[34] Trempé, 'Une Campagne', 481–3, 486.

[35] Gilbert Garrier, 'L'Union du Sud-Est des syndicats agricoles avant 1914', *Le Mouvement social* 67 (1969), 17–38; Pierre Barral, *Les Agrariens français de Méline à Pisani* (Paris, 1968), 128–39; Suzanne Berger, *Peasants against Politics: Rural Organization in Brittany* (Cambridge, MA, 1972).

[36] Phélippeau, *L'Invention*, 298.

[37] Marc Sorlot, *André Maginot (1877–1932). L'Homme politique et sa légende* (Metz, 1995), 180.

[38] *Bulletin de l'action libérale*, November 1901.

We should not take the principles of collective psychology literally, for although elitist parties dominated after 1906, it did not follow that ordinary conservatives actually were manipulable. One cannot say whether the targets of tracts or recipients of aid would have voted for the candidate anyway, or were simply taking advantage of largesse. Anyway, the elites disseminated conflicting messages and had conflicting objectives. In 1898, Solages found that the commercial priorities of the mine managers and the watchfulness of the unions prevented him from influencing workers.[39] While right-wing agrarians accused state schoolteachers of encouraging peasants to leave the land, the ARD advocated using teachers and civil servants to undermine *chatelaines*' and priests' hold over the peasantry.[40] The latter urged peasants either to create alternatives to 'reactionary' unions, or to join them *en masse* and dominate them.[41]

Collective psychology sometimes legitimated challenges from outside the elite. Social Catholics set about creating their own elites, allegedly better equipped than the 'selfish bourgeoisie' to provide the mass with moral guidance. Likewise, Catholic women endeavoured to create a female elite, thus contradicting the identification of the crowd with femininity. The influence of these groups was strongest in the ALP. Conservatives' conviction that they understood the national psychology also imposed limits upon them. Candidates had to participate in a culture that constrained and even challenged them. Political meetings were not only a means to transmit messages. Often packed, they provided an opportunity for raucous entertainment, the mocking of one's betters, and for debate on questions from relations with Italy and the likelihood of revolution to the state of the local roads. Electors were more familiar with their deputies than contemporaries are, possibly better informed, and better placed to challenge them face-to-face.

Candidates were rarely exempt from the requirements of the campaign. The ALP was rooted in popular religiosity. In the Mende constituency in Lozère, the party's victorious candidate passed through triumphal arches dressed with flowers and laughed at goats decorated with the symbols of freemasonry. He shook hands and drank all that was offered, distributed tobacco, and sat down to banquets to which all adult men were invited. A local ALP leader charged the Fédération's Pierre de Chambrun in neighbouring Marjevols with restricting himself to home visits in order to avoid noisy demonstrations that might upset Prefecture; in fact, the absence of campaign owed more to the fact that Chambrun was the only candidate.[42] Take also the Flandins. Ernest, a Progressist elected in the Avallonais (Yonne) in 1898, and his centrist son, Pierre-Etienne, elected in 1914, were the scions of a once Orleanist dynasty of the district, enriched by the purchase of *biens nationaux*. Pierre-Etienne conducted his profession as a Parisian business lawyer alongside his mandate. As a *roturier*, he was both similar to his electors and the possessor of competence acquired through

[39] Trempé, 'Une Campagne', 481–3, 486.
[40] *L'Alliance républicaine démocratique*, 17 March 1903.
[41] *Correspondance agricole et politique*, 14 December 1900.
[42] Emmanuelle de Las Cases, *Éphémérides: Journal inédit d'E. de Las Cases* (Montpellier, 1992), 2 and 22 April 1906, 63.

his own efforts. The Flandins participated in the egalitarian, anticlerical culture of the Avallonais, answering questions at meetings that some might have considered impertinent.[43] In the Rhône, Progressists relied on invited meetings and banquets for village mayors and notables. However, they could not afford to ignore the views of their voters, whose pressure forced them to take a harder line against the Inventories.[44]

The Progressist Pierre Leroy-Beaulieu's successful campaign for election in Montpellier-Ouest in 1906 epitomizes the complexities of conservative organization, for it combined notability and professionalism, party labels and independence, local and national connections, elite and popular culture. The candidate was the son of the liberal economist and Rallié, Paul Leroy-Beaulieu, and as a Polytechnicien, teacher at the École des sciences politiques and contributor to the *Revue des deux mondes*, Pierre was part of the same academic elite. He combined national notoriety with local roots; campaign literature described him as a Polytechnicien and a winegrower. He joined the Progressist group in parliament, and, like his father, he probably belonged to the Fédération. He also used the labels 'républicain indépendant' and 'conservateur', thereby appealing to Ralliés and even the Monarchist *l'Éclair*. Although not a party man, Pierre admired 'American' electoral techniques. An independent committee, backed by the Association catholique de la Jeunesse française (ACJF) and young Royalists, ran his campaign, hiring men to distribute ballots.[45] Leroy-Beaulieu also emphasized his roots in the popular Catholicism of a region in which anti-Protestant sentiment was strong, thus contributing to the clericalization of the Fédération and compromising its desire for a broad conservative alliance. His knowledge of *patois* underlined his connection with the mass. Other conservatives shared that advantage, for many had learned *patois* from servants. The former Secrétaire de stage and École libre des sciences politiques professor, Léon Bérard, first elected for the Alliance in 1910, shifted effortlessly from Béarnaise to French (the sign of competence), and studded his campaign speeches with Latin quotations.[46]

While the ALP, FR, and ARD all assumed the elite–mass distinction, they harnessed it to different projects. They defined the elite in their own way and disagreed, as Clément put it, on what 'governing with the people' meant. To mobilize the mass, they combined notable, professional, and party politics, and enunciated simple programmes, relayed through the local press, word of mouth, posters, and meetings. Only the ALP aspired to build a mass party, as it endeavoured to reconcile elite leadership and parliamentarianism with popular Catholicism. Yet the 'mass' possessed ideas of its own, which ultimately undermined the ALP. The loosely organized FR and ARD proved more durable.

[43] Marc Abélès, *Jours tranquilles en '89. Ethnologie politique d'un département français* (Paris, 1989), 61–92; Pourcher, *Les Maîtres*, 228–33.

[44] Bernard, *La Dérive*, 117.

[45] Philippe Secondy, 'Pierre Leroy-Beaulieu. Un Importateur des méthodes électorales américaines en France', *Revue historique* 107, no. 634 (2005), 309–41.

[46] Gilles Le Béguec, 'Un Grand parlementaire modéré', *Revue du Pau et du Béarn* 18 (1991), 305–24.

THE PROGRESSISTS

There is no clear reason why individual Progressists chose to support or oppose Waldeck-Rousseau's government of Republican defence. Those who backed it had usually approved of Méline in the past; few had criticized Méline's religious policy—the Dreyfusard, Jonnart, had even proposed modification of school laws—and none had an axe to grind with the Army.[47] True, some future Waldeckistes had wanted to include the Radicals in the majority, but that had been Méline's wish too.[48] Jonnart may have surrendered to Radical pressure in his constituency, but Waldeck-Rousseau did not.[49] Indeed, the latter had campaigned for a disciplined Progressist party behind Méline alongside Jean-Honoré Audiffred, who chose opposition in 1899. The clearest difference is that Protestant and Jewish Progressists largely became Dreyfusards. We have seen that André Lebon's Protestant voters punished him for his part in the Affair, and the Protestant director of the École des sciences politiques temporarily excluded him from teaching.[50]

On whatever basis Progressists chose, it created new markers. Dreyfusism reinforced the centre's identification with the lay Republic and softened its anti-socialism.[51] In May 1899, Poincaré declared that he could not accept 'as a programme simply resistance to Socialism. You [Méline] have around you—in spite of yourself no doubt—people with whom I could never associate... Instead of letting you be head of a party, they want to make you prisoner of a reactionary coalition.'[52] As Dreyfusism turned into anticlericalism, initial choices were revised. Paul Deschanel was privately Antidreyfusard and may have been sympathetic to Déroulède's coup, but his *laïcité* attracted him to the centre.[53] On the other side, the exacerbation of anticlericalism propelled the quasi-Dreyfusard Aynard from the Alliance to the Fédération.

Those who remained with Méline endeavoured to reconstitute the anti-Socialist alliance. They therefore dismissed the Affair as a 'fait divers', or argued that the separation of powers forbade politicization of judicial matters.[54] They sought to overcome religious differences through toleration in the hope of reunifying the Progressists and attracting ALP. In practice, this strategy split the Progressists into pro-centre and pro-right wings, the latter increasingly influential.

Whereas those Progressists who backed Waldeck stressed the common sense of the Socialist mainstream and claimed to moderate the Bloc des gauches, the

[47] Jean Vavasseur-Desperriers, *République et liberté. Charles Jonnart, une conscience républicaine* (Lille, 1996), 83.

[48] Paul Deschanel, *Comité national républicain du commerce et de l'industrie* (Paris, 1898); Judith Stone, *The Search for Social Peace* (Albany, 1985), 70; Martin E. Schmidt, *Alexandre Ribot: Odyssey of a Liberal in the Third Republic* (The Hague, 1974), 73–5.

[49] Pierre Sorlin, *Waldeck-Rousseau* (Paris, 1966), 73–80.

[50] Dubos, 'Organisation des réseaux modérés', 306.

[51] Michel Winock, 'Le Mythe fondateur. L'Affaire Dreyfus', in Serge Berstein and Odile Rudelle (eds), *Le Modèle républicain* (Paris, 1992), 131–45.

[52] Cited in Alexander Sedgwick, *The Ralliement in French Politics 1890–1898* (Cambridge, MA, 1965), 150–1; *L'Alliance républicaine démocratique*, 28 March 1902.

[53] Thierry Billard, *Paul Deschanel* (Paris, 1991), 128–31.

[54] Schmidt, *Alexandre Ribot*, 80–4; Claude Ferry, 'Un Républicain modéré face à l'Affaire. Charles Ferry, député des Vosges', in *Les Modérés*, 101–7.

Mélinists saw Socialism as a bloc, with Radicalism in its thrall.[55] Méline evoked the spectacle of red flag, collectivism, revolutionary strikes, and Millerand's alleged complicity in them. He saw Socialist Dreyfusism as a cover for anti-militarism.[56] To counter Socialism, he advocated state encouragement of mutualism under employers' control, which the ultra-liberal Aynard opposed.[57] Jules Roche campaigned obsessively against income tax. Benoist argued that proportional representation and charity would resolve the social question.[58]

Prioritization of anti-socialism obliged Progressists to minimize the danger from the right. For Méline, Monarchism lacked serious electoral support. He recognized that individual Monarchists refused to accept the inevitable triumph of democracy, but most had renounced intransigent opposition, and would vote with Republicans 'when they defend the permanent interests of the country'. Yet, he warned, if the government persecuted Catholics and permitted the Socialist threat to grow, Monarchists would be forced into opposition.[59] Some Progressists, including the aforementioned Pierre Leroy-Beaulieu, sympathized with Monarchism.[60]

Progressists also had some affinities with Nationalism. Méline's *République française* was quite favourable to the Ligue de la patrie française. Louis Marin had been a Boulangist as a law student in Paris, had worked with Barrès in Nancy, and had lectured on 'national psychology' at the École libre des sciences politiques.[61] In Lyon and Paris, young Nationalists provided lower-level activists for revived Progressist organizations and later the Fédération. In Rouen, Progressists rubbed shoulders with Nationalists in Progressist committees, employers' organizations, and a mutualist society for white-collar workers.[62]

In effect, Progressism developed the nationalist potential within Opportunism. Jules Ferry had advocated imperial self-sufficiency, and in the 1890s Méline had aimed to strengthen France socially, militarily, demographically, and economically for struggle in a hostile world. In 1903, a Progressist complained that the French government treated employers as enemies at a time when foreign governments 'crushed foreign competitors'.[63] Doubtless Marin was sympathetic to an elector who wrote to him to advocate a nationalist education based on the 'new tendencies in the social sciences and studies of the psychology of peoples and their conditions of existence', rather than on that of 'those simple traditionalists who defend patriotism maladroitly'.[64] Another activist evoked 'the ties of blood that unite us in spite of everything'.[65] Progressists urged the country to rally around the Army, while

[55] *La République française*, 11 November 1903.

[56] *La République française*, 6 July 1900; Jules Méline, 'Les Partis dans la République', *Revue politique et parlementaire* 23, no. 67 (1900), 5–16.

[57] Édouard Aynard, *Discours prononcés à la Chambre des députés de 1893 à 1913* (Paris, 1920).

[58] *La République française*, 28 September 1900; Anderson, 'The Right and the Social Question', 96–8.

[59] Méline, 'Les Partis dans la République', 13–16.

[60] Secondy, *La Persistance*, 192.

[61] Herman Lebovics, *True France: The Wars over Cultural Identity 1900–1945* (Ithaca, 1992), 17–20.

[62] Bernard, *La Dérive*, 101–6, 136–9.

[63] *La République française*, 9–10 November 1903.

[64] ANFLM, 64, Unknown to Ducrocq, 26 August 1905.

[65] *Le Courrier de l'Oise*, 15 October 1905.

Méline saw Nationalism as a legitimate response to the Socialist plot against the nation. Nationalism was nothing more than 'the protest of French feeling in the face of the international coalition born in the Affair'.[66]

Not all Progressists were so enamoured of Nationalism. In 1902, Méline failed to convince Progressists to join an electoral alliance with the Nationalists. In 1903, Nancy Progressists refused to work with them.[67] Aynard was especially equivocal. He felt that Fédération leader Motte was 'in the thrall of Nationalism', yet ceded nothing to Nationalists in his own depiction of 'the slow decomposition of all the moral and political forces of our country' and its incurable 'cancer'. He felt that the 'abasement' of the judiciary and Army was such that the country could not resist an internal crisis or a foreign attack. In 1905, Aynard hired some of the best local Nationalist journalists to work for a new Progressist organ.[68]

Progressists opposed antisemitism in the name of toleration, but antisemitism was not unknown in the party. For instance, Méline's evocation of an 'international' coalition of Dreyfusards evoked antisemitic resonances.[69] In the 1898 elections, Progressists even used antisemitism to attack fellow Progressists.[70] In a 1905 by-election, *Le Petit Antijuif* urged its readers to support Marin because he 'considers that Jews, in relation to their numbers, possess an enormously disproportionate governmental influence'.[71] The charge was exaggerated, but in Marin's 1905 novel, *Le triomphe du vice*, a Jewish moneylender stood for corruption through money.[72] Although Marin saw the ALP's attacks on Freemasons as 'excessive', other Progressists saw them behind the Waldeck-Rousseau administration.[73] This antisemitic and anti-Masonic sub-current implied that the government was a conspiracy against the people, a view that qualifies the alleged acceptance of pluralism in the new political parties.

The Progressists' religious policy was equally contradictory. In the Opportunist tradition, they saw secularism as the guarantee of toleration. They held that religious orders could not teach in the name of the state, and indeed that the state should not endorse 'backward' ideas. That policy persuaded the Centre gauche Union libérale, which had initially held aloof from the Mélinists because of their proximity to the Nationalists, to join the Fédération.[74] Yet this liberalism also caused the Fédération to reject the anti-religious views of some Radicals, who demanded a state monopoly on teaching. Progressists regarded the treatment of

[66] *La République française*, 15 and 16 February 1898, 3, 5, 6 July 1900; Ferry, 'Un Républicain modéré', 103.

[67] Gordon, *Liberalism*, 140–4.

[68] ANFR, Aynard to Ribot, 2 and 11 August 1903; Guy Laperrière, *La Séparation à Lyon: 1904–1908. Étude d'opinion publique* (Lyon, 1973), 90–1.

[69] Ferry, 'Un Républicain modéré', 102–3.

[70] Nancy Fitch, 'Mass culture, mass parliamentary politics, and modern antisemitism: the Dreyfus Affair in rural France', *American Historical Review* 97, no. 1 (February 1992), 55–95 at 66.

[71] ANLM, 164, draft newspaper article, undated.

[72] Louis Marin, *Le Triomphe du vice, étude réaliste et sociale* (Paris, 1905).

[73] ANLM, 164, Marin to leader of ALP in Meurthe-et-Moselle, 13 September 1905; *La République française*, 10 September 1900.

[74] Gilles Le Béguec, 'Le Bâtonnier Barboux (1834–1910)', in *Barreau, politique et culture à la Belle Époque* (Limoges, 1993), 5–27 at 21–3.

the Catholic orders and the terms of the Separation as attacks on liberty, and as a sign that the Bloc des gauches had 'replaced the institutions of free peoples with the brutal force of number'.[75] They condemned the 'sham neutrality' of irreligious, Socialist teachers.[76]

The evolution of the Fédération was evident in its changing electoral geography. It began as a largely eastern and northern party, with outposts in a few Breton and western regions of 'blue Catholicism', where the Republic had triumphed by distancing itself from anticlericalism: in Mayenne, the Progressiste senator Duboys-Fresnay campaigned against 'iniquitous' laws in alliance with Monarchists.[77] By 1914, the Fédération was also making inroads into rural Brittany, the west and southern fringe of the Massif Central (see Map 2). In the Catholic districts of Lyon, Lille, and Bordeaux the Fédération profited from the return to the Church of the 1900s, for it affected the wealthy bourgeoisie particularly. In the richest canton of Rouen two thirds of children in secondary education were in Catholic schools, while priests were increasingly of bourgeois origin.[78] In the Rhône,

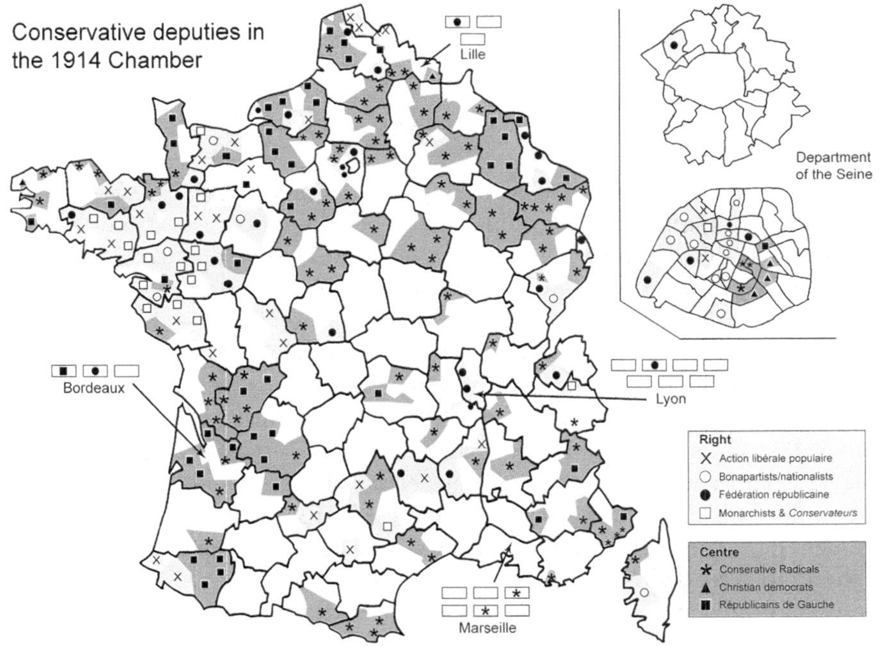

Map 2

[75] *La République française*, 4 July 1903.

[76] *Journal officiel. Chambre des députés*, 7 March 1904; *Le Courrier de l'Oise*, 15 October 1905.

[77] Michel Denis, *L'Eglise et la République en Mayenne 1896–1906* (Paris, 1968), 132–4; Caroline Ford, *Creating the Nation in Provincial France: Religion and Political Identity in Brittany* (Princeton, 1993), 135–72.

[78] Robert L. Fuller, 'Belle époque French nationalism: the example of Rouen', *French History* 13, no. 1 (1999), 40–1.

Aynard's denunciation of Jacobins and Masons won the sympathy of Nationalists and the ALP, at the price of weakening the *laïque* element within the Fédération. Most Progressist deputies in the Rhône initially took a moderate line on the Separation, but ultimately voted against it.[79] Similarly, Motte in Roubaix had shunned Social Catholics in the 1890s, but later developed ties with Colrat's pro-Catholic Confédération des groupes commerciaux et industriels.[80] In Meurthe-et-Moselle, Marin relied on the support of Catholic fraternities, which included both Progressists and ALP members—some of the latter allegedly spread the rumour that Marin was a Freemason and revolutionary Socialist.[81]

Compromises with Monarchists and Catholics provoked several crises. Duboys-Fresnay's collaboration with Monarchists split the Mayenne Comité républicain. In 1904, following the fall of Combes, several Fédération deputies who were tired of systematic opposition backed the succeeding ministry, presided by the old Opportunist, Rouvier. In March 1905, they formed a new group, named Union républicaine in reference to Gambetta's old formation.[82] Nevertheless, the Fédération's legalist disapproval of the Separation, coupled with its coolness towards demonstrations against the Inventories, allowed it to compete for Catholic support with the ALP.

THE ALP

In 1902, the weakening of rivals enabled the parliamentary Ralliés, led by Piou and de Mun, to capture the leadership of the Catholic movement. Lamy and the remainder of his Politique nouvelle joined the ALP. The Pope had condemned Christian Democracy, and only the Breton *Ouest-Éclair* still openly espoused its ideals. Some Christian Democrats, including Lemire and Charles-Brun, accepted *laïcité* and gravitated towards the centre. Conservative Christian Democrats, including the Union nationale as a body, moved into the ALP, as did Abbé Gayraud.[83] Following the dissolution of the Assumptionists, the Vatican ordered the ALP businessman, Paul Féron-Vrau, to take over *La Croix*. Whole sections of the LPF joined the ALP: the moderate Nationalist Ferdinand Brunetière bolstered the parliamentary strategy, while Elva, the ALP's founder in the Mayenne, brought more anti-parliamentarian Nationalists with him.[84] Repression and faction fighting undermined Monarchism as a rival to the ALP. Many Monarchists and partisans of the now extinct Congrès nationaux catholiques joined the new party,

[79] Bernard, *La Dérive*, 114, 133, 185–93.

[80] Gordon, *Liberalism and Social Reform*, 64–6.

[81] ANFLM, 164, Unknown to Marin, 7 and 10 September 1905.

[82] Gilles Le Béguec, 'Les Deux scissions du groupe progressiste (1905–1911)', *Revue du Nord* 89, 370 (2007), 363–75; Bernard, *La Dérive*, 227; Vavasseur-Desperriers, 'Cultures, structures, stratégie', 81–91.

[83] Jean-Marie Mayeur, 'Congrès nationaux de la démocratie chrétienne', *Revue d'histoire moderne et contemporaine* 9 (July–September 1962), 171–206; Jean-Marie Mayeur, *L'Abbé Lemire. Un Prêtre démocrate 1853–1928* (Paris, 1968), 258, 236–9; Christian Ponson, *Les Catholiques lyonnais et la Chronique sociale* (Lyon, 1979), 64–73; Philip Nord, *Paris Shopkeepers and the Politics of Resentment* (Princeton, 1986), 467.

[84] Denis, *L'Église*, 135.

including Charles Thellier de Poncheville, who sat in the ALP ruling council.[85] In Lyon, the ALP marked the return to politics of Legitimists, often with familiar names, and the arrival of a new generation.[86]

Piou's and de Mun's hegemony among Catholics revived the possibility of unity with the Progressists, and to that end, they emphasized toleration.[87] On that ground they also distanced themselves from the antisemitism of the Antidreydusards. Certainly, antisemitism was present in the ALP. De Mun sometimes identified Jews with capitalism; indeed, his antisemitism grew along with his enthusiasm for protecting workers from capitalist excess. A minor theme in the 1880s, it disappeared during the conservative 1890s, only to reappear during the Affair, when de Mun denounced the 'syndicate' and made one of the largest donations to the Henry monument fund.[88] De Mun was nevertheless contemptuous of Drumont's work, and antisemitism quickly retreated in the Catholic mainstream after 1901, as its political usefulness declined. Instead denunciation of a Masonic conspiracy against France became central to ALP propaganda, and underlined the difficulty of alliance with the Progressists.

The ALP's absorption of Christian Democrats, Nationalists, and crypto-Monarchists reduced scope for compromise with Moderate Republicans. Anyway, Méline wished to make any deal conditional upon the unlikely prospect of centre participation, and so proposed only a loose electoral agreement for 1902. The ALP continued to preach toleration, in the hope that Republicans would later change their mind, but willy-nilly, it took on a clerical, nationalist, and populist hue. That was made clear in November 1902 at Lille: with the assembled clergy on the platform behind him, Piou declared that when 'France acquires its "popular association", the reign of the sectarians [Freemasons, anticlericals] will be over'.[89]

Piou also announced his intention to use social reforms such as Sunday rest, retirement pensions, and a corporatist system of unions to conquer the masses. De Mun and he hoped that reaffirmation of *Rerum novarum* would arm the ALP against Papal disfavour, for the accession of Pius X in 1903 potentially put the Ralliement in doubt.[90] Reformism provided some common ground with Progressists. As we saw in the previous chapter, Ralliés, including de Mun, worked with Progressists and centrists in the Musée sociale and the networks around it.[91] In 1903, Las Cases wrote privately of his respect for Jean Monestier, a Radical deputy in the Aveyron: 'a ferocious arriviste, a Polytechnicien delighted with his technical superiority', yet 'admirable for his philanthropy', especially on behalf of country

[85] Martin, 'The creation', 660–89; Quagliariello, 'L'Action libérale populaire', 245–64.

[86] Bernard, *La Dérive*, 107.

[87] *Bulletin de l'Action libérale*, November 1901.

[88] Paul Duclos, 'Catholiques et juifs autour de l'Affair Dreyfus', *Revue d'histoire de l'Église de France* 64, no. 172 (1978), 39–53; Benjamin Martin, *Albert de Mun: Paladin of the Republic* (Chapel Hill, 1978), 116–17, 129–34.

[89] *Bulletin de l'action libérale*, November 1901; Martin, 'The creation', 660–89.

[90] Martin, 'The creation', 678.

[91] Janet Horne, *A Social Laboratory for Modern France: The Musée Social and the Rise of the Welfare State* (Chicago, 2002), 121–3; Christian Topalov, 'Les "Réformateurs et leurs réseaux". Enjeu d'un objet de recherche', in *Laboratoires du nouveau siècle. La Nébuleuse réformatrice et ses réseaux en France, 1880–1914* (Paris, 1999), 11–58.

medicine.[92] That ALP reformism was relatively moderate (and vaguely defined) also facilitated collaboration. With the eclipse of Christian Democracy, de Mun felt reformism to be safer. In 1904, he expressed his pleasure that his social doctrine, free from Christian Democrat 'distortions', had received Papal approval. He particularly disapproved of Naudet and Lemire's 'harmful' doctrines.[93] Nevertheless, the ALP was too advanced for most Progressists, even for those involved in the Musée sociale; Aynard was a long-standing critic of de Mun. In Calais, the ALP relied on professionals working through charities such as Notre Dame de Travail and the Liberté d'enseignement, which anticlerical, liberal, and Progressist tulle manufacturers distrusted.[94]

Moreover, there were tensions concerning social reform within the ALP. Social Catholicism was a diverse phenomenon, sometimes secular, sometimes integrist, ranging from conservative paternalism to proto-social democracy. It included trade unions, agricultural cooperatives and unions, organizations for assistance to the aged, and many more. In the 1900s, the radical wing expanded and its reflection deepened. The Semaines sociales and the Groupes d'études sociales provided an education in social issues for bourgeois Catholic youth, while Marc Sangnier's Sillon sought to reach workers in their own milieu. For Lemire's friend, Abbé Dabry, 'going to the people' meant participation in the world as it was rather than through a Catholic party—he thus anticipated the ethos of interwar Catholic Action.[95] Meanwhile, young women set up 'Settlements' in working-class districts and the first nursing school. Some Social Catholics denounced the indifference of liberals to the plight of the people, and increasingly they advocated state intervention to improve social conditions and fight Socialism. Henri Bazire, the new leader of the ACJF, worried about compromise with 'reactionaries', while Lemire was still more antipathetic to them.[96] In Mayenne, clerical pretention to control agricultural union funds particularly alarmed nobles: 'To be everyone's man, the priest must not be dependent upon anyone', said the local ALP leader.[97]

In effect, the ALP provided an organizational and ideological space within which Catholics with different agendas could operate. Particularly important for the history of the ALP was that it inherited Catholic women's action from nationalism.[98] Women came to the ALP via the Ligue des femmes françaises (LFF), founded in Lyon in the previous year.[99] The LFF initially backed the ALP, but in 1902 its Parisian Committee founded the LPDF, under the Baronne de Brigode, linked to both the ALP and La Patrie française, leaving Royalists in control of the LFF. After the

92 Las Cases, *Éphémérides*, 33–9, 17 October 1903.

93 Charles Molette, *L'Action catholique de la jeunesse française, 1886–1907. Une Prise de conscience du laïcat catholique* (Paris: Colin, 1968), 468–70.

94 Bernard Fauquet, 'La Section calaisienne de l'Action libérale populaire', *Revue du Nord* 56, no. 221 (1974), 207–9.

95 Molette, *L'Association catholique*, 290, 292.

96 Molette, *L'Association catholique*, 287–91; Mayeur, *Lemire*, 301, 314.

97 Denis, *L'Eglise et la République*, 135–7; Denis, *Les Royalistes*, 494–5.

98 James McMillan, 'Women and Social Catholicism in late nineteenth- and early twentieth-century France', in W.J. Sheils and Diana Wood (eds), *Women in the Church* (Oxford, 1990), 467–80.

99 ANPG $F^7$13 215, Report of August 1902; *Libre Parole*, 16 November 1902.

elections, the LPDF formalized its links to the ALP, and membership reached around 400,000 by 1910. At the height of the anti-secularization campaign, ALP speakers attracted as many as 2,000 women to meetings. Ordinary activists were drawn especially from the commercial classes and private school teachers, resident in cities and in smaller Catholic towns.[100]

Both ALP and LPDF were religiously and socially conservative, patriarchal, and anti-feminist. An important role in the formation of the LPDF was played by the Filles du Cœur de Marie, a small group of upper-class women, who discretely pursued a religious vocation without wearing clerical dress, while remaining strictly loyal to the Vatican. These characteristics made these women ideal agents for the Church's strategy of using Republican laws to defend itself.[101] Politically, LPDF leaders were often the wives of male politicians. One woman claimed that her speeches were merely the 'work of a phonograph'—she mouthed ideas elaborated by men—apparently, she agreed that women (like crowds) acted through imitation.[102] A male journalist reported that since women alone could not resolve the 'complex' issues of the day, the LPDF had allied with the ALP.[103] Some ALP politicians were 'not against' female suffrage, but positive support was rare, and even rarer in the LPDF.[104] Yet Piou urged women to abandon resignation for organized struggle, and he predicted that several would fall on the field of battle.[105]

In practice, LPDF women, at least its leaders, were able to carve independent activist careers. The discretion of the Filles du Coeur de Marie allowed them to engage in the world without 'masculinizing' themselves.[106] The LPDF also relied on 'dizainières', often middle-class women, who organized local groups of ten.[107] The league created a caste of female activists, who travelled alone on league business, spoke in public, and modelled themselves on the virginal Jeanne d'Arc—for Catholic women marriage was not the only route to fulfilment, even if married. LPDF activists contested the identification of (bourgeois) women with the mass, and defined themselves as an elite, invested with the task of transmitting religious and national ideas to children, reconciling the classes through charity, and inspiring men to action on behalf of Church and nation, thus moralizing the male world of politics. They combined Catholic natural law doctrine, collective psychology, and domesticity to legitimate women's ability to structure the social organism. In quasi-Maurrassian terms, a tract claimed that women possessed an innate sense of taste and order, a delicacy of mind and heart, and a love of the clear, clean, and nicely tidied.[108]

[100] Magali Della Sudda, 'Une Activité politique féminine avant le droit de suffrage en France et en Italie', thèse de doctorat, EHESS Paris, 2007; Bruno Dumons, *Les Dames de la Ligue des femmes françaises* (Paris, 2006), 84–94.

[101] Della Sudda, 'Une Activité', 64–73.

[102] Magali della Sudda, '"Servir Dieu et patrie". La Ligue patriotique des françaises, une activité politique féminine de masse avant le droit de suffrage', DEA, EHESS Paris, 2002, 56.

[103] *Libre Parole*, 16 November 1902.

[104] *Bulletin de l'action libérale*, 11 December 1901.

[105] Jacques Piou, *Les Femmes chrétiennes* (Paris, 1903).

[106] Della Sudda, 'Une Activité', 105–6. [107] Della Sudda, 'Une Activité', 97–8.

[108] Della Sudda, 'Servir Dieu et patrie', 63–4.

Female religiosity alienated Republicans, as countless references to 'fanaticism' in police reports testify. In 1909, conservatives' own fears that female activism undermined clerical and family authority would surface when a young social activist sued her Catholic mother for having forcibly interned her in a mental institution, allegedly to extract her from the influence of the 'heretical', sexually dangerous nun who had founded the Settlement movement. The father, a general, with the support of a priest, hired the lawyer who had defended Zola during the Dreyfus Affair to plead that the Settlement illegally reconstituted a dissolved congregation.[109] Medical reports cited in the trial recycled the usual prejudices about women's tendency towards 'fetishization' (like the crowd).[110] Such fears explain why ALP leaders sought to subordinate women's action to anti-socialism. Senator Las Cases praised the greater willingness of women to display their faith in public, yet held that their 'impressionability' meant that they could not make reason prevail in politics; women's social action should not therefore be politicized.[111] While women conceived themselves as an elite, male leaders saw their religiosity as a sign that they were insufficiently detached from mass unreason.

Women's goals were indeed different, for they often prioritized the Catholic struggle over alliance with the Progressists. They did not do so because they were naturally more religious than men were, but because Catholicism was the condition of their engagement in the world, and secularization threatened the identities of bourgeois and aristocratic women as the moralizers of society. For these reasons, some leaders denied that the LPDF was 'inféodé à l'ALP'. For the Baronnes de Brigode and Reille, the two organizations were 'friends and allies'. The pro-Royalist minority in the league, especially strong in Brittany, reinforced the tendency to prioritize Catholic unity. Royalists saw fighting Freemasons in social services and schools as more important than doing so through elections, and condemned electoral action as unfeminine. Whereas the ALP was open to non-Catholics but not Royalists, the LPDF included Royalists but excluded non-Catholics.[112] Reille wrote 'We have never wanted to found a political league—only a league of religious and social defence. We are neither Ralliés, nor Bonapartists, nor Royalists. We are convinced Catholics, who have decided to unite in the whole of France to defend our liberties [and] contribute our zeal to making a Christian France.'[113] Through rural and urban *oeuvres* the league would touch the hearts of the people by rendering services; it would bring men together and return the people to the Church 'on

[109] Brigitte Bouquet, 'L'Œuvre sociale', in Dominique Dessertine et al. (eds), *Les Centres sociaux 1880–1990* (Lille, 2004), 29–36.

[110] *Le Figaro*, 7 April 1909.

[111] Las Cases, *Éphémérides*, 17 October 1903, 43; Emmanuel de Las Cases, *Le Féminisme d'après l'école socialiste et d'après l'école de la paix sociale* (Paris, 1901).

[112] Della Sudda, 'Une Activité', 120–5.

[113] *La Patrie*, 8 May 1904.

the terrain of the constitution' (explicitly not the Republic).[114] The LPDF opposed the rival LFF only because it entailed Royalist *leadership* of the Catholic movement.

Republicans worried about 'surreptitious' female influence, fearing that electors were more willing to listen to seemingly apolitical women than to notorious reactionaries, and the religious division in many bourgeois households intensified their fear.[115] The LPDF press made much of the slap administered to Combes' Minister of Education by his pious wife. The LPDF thus reinforced the confessionalism of the ALP and created tensions among Catholics. Confessionalism opened the ALP to Monarchists, who sought to turn it into a Catholic party that would operate on the terrain of the constitution without endorsing the Republic.

The Inventories Crisis

The 1906 Inventories crisis brought quarrels among conservatives to a head. It trapped the ALP between fear of losing control of the Catholic movement to Monarchists through excessive moderation and of alienating Republicans through too strident resistance. The ALP therefore depicted the protest as popular defence of liberty and praised demonstrators for combining firmness with self-restraint—they were a structured crowd. De Mun advised believers to make government agents pass though a 'calm population, master of itself'. He toured Brittany urging both sides to lay down their weapons, insisting that national organization alone could defend Catholics effectively.[116] Generally, bishops backed the ALP's caution.[117]

Since the Inventories outraged a spectrum of opinion well beyond those who normally voted for conservatives, the ALP's line was potentially appealing. Certainly, areas of liberal Catholicism, such as Normandy, were relatively quiet. Disturbances were more numerous in Brittany, the southern fringe of the Massif Central, and parts of the east and north-east. The greatest demonstrations happened in areas of pilgrimage, while in the Lozère, conflict with Protestants stimulated opposition to the Inventories.[118] Sometimes a maximalist interpretation of the Papal encyclical of 11 February 1906 condemning the Separation encouraged resistance. Yet the correlation between integrism, anti-Republicanism, and resistance was imperfect. Republicans joined the resistance in regions where religion was part of the fabric of village identity—as one Haute-Loire peasant put it, 'Vous n'emporterez pas notre sainte'. In Finistère, where religious practice was more widespread than right-wing voting, even Radical municipalities backed the demand for authorization of the Filles du Saint-Ésprit.[119]

114 *La Croix*, 19 September 1902; Della Sudda, 'Une Activité'.

115 *L'Alliance démocratique*, March–April 1902.

116 Molette, *L'Association catholique*, 293.

117 Jean Quellien, *Bleus, blancs, rouges. Politique et élections dans le Calvados 1870–1939* (Caen, 1986), 210–16.

118 Pourcher, *Les Maîtres*, 216.

119 Jean-Marie Mayeur, 'Géographie de la résistance aux inventaires', *Annales ÉSC* 21, no. 6 (1966), 1259–71.

Consequently, the ALP had to reckon with the Progressists' pretention to defend Catholics on the terrain of toleration. The latter were rather better qualified to do so as Republicans, and they avoided the 'fanatical' demonstrations of women and young people.[120] We have seen that the Progressists had become increasingly pro-Catholic, and Paul Beauregard of the Fédération even shared a platform with Denys Cochin. Lyon Progressists originally condemned resistance to the Inventories, but hardened their line under pressure from their own militants and the ALP, without endorsing intransigent Catholicism. Their firm but legal defence of Catholics kept those tempted by the ALP within then fold.[121]

The ALP could not prevent radical groups from taking the lead either. Sometimes, resistance developed a regionalist dimension. In 1902, Barrès warned that anticlericalism, which he equated with the excessive influence of the Midi in parliament, might fracture the French state. He claimed that the government was breaking the contract linking the Lorraine to France, under which the province was entitled to defence against Germany and respect for local customs and religion. He cited a Breton language journal to the effect that 'the threats addressed by the French to the Bretons make our blood boil in our veins. Some are ready to become insurgents, like in the old days.'[122] Indeed, in Finistère, the resistance mobilized whole communities, across political divisions, as the culmination of a struggle against the state. The government's efforts to ensure that the catechism was taught in French rather than Breton intensified regionalist resistance, for there was no correlation between Breton-speaking and conservatism.

The ACJF, although allied to the ALP, often went beyond ALP instructions, sometimes because young royalists had joined it following the dissolution of their movement in 1899.[123] The leaders of resistance in southern towns and Paris included young members of AF, which was making its first forays into the streets. In Montpellier, Royalists instigated resistance; outside the Église Saint-Denis crowds singing hymns and anti-religious songs confronted each other; in Versailles, Bernard de Vesins struck the Prefect with a chair.[124] In the Calvados Bocage, resistance precipitated revival of Jules Delafosse's Catholic Bonapartist populism in the 1906 elections.[125] On 27 June 1903, the 'mothers of Paris', led by Mme Piou and Comtesse de Mun, marched in protest, and in the Inventories crisis many LPDF women were arrested.

The agitation weakened the ALP. Already in 1904, the Pope renewed support for the ALP only privately. With some success, Monarchists used the protests to convert the ALP into a Catholic party. In 1906, the ALP fended off an attempt by Keller and Cochin to form a Comité catholique including all Catholics regardless of political views, but conceded that the ALP could not succeed electorally without allies on the right.[126] In Rouen, the ALP included Royalists and invited Cochin to

120 *L'Alliance démocratique*, 4 February 1906. 121 Bernard, *La Dérive*, 114, 133, 185–93.

122 Maurice Barrès, *Les Lézardes sur la maison* (Paris, 1904), 15–16.

123 Molette, *L'Association catholique*, 293; Secondy, *La Persistance*, 170.

124 Secondy, *La Persistance*, 167; Mayeur, 'Géographie de la résistance', 1269; Michael Sutton, *Nationalism, Catholicism, Positivism: The Politics of Charles Maurras and French Catholicism, 1890–1914* (Cambridge, 1982), 94.

125 Quellien, *Bleus, blancs, rouges*, 212. 126 Martin, 'The creation', 675–7.

speak.[127] Piou admitted that it was legitimate for Monarchists to join, since the coming elections concerned religion rather than the form of the regime.[128] Complex struggles within the LPDF gradually ended formal links with the ALP.[129] Moderate Catholics found it difficult to maintain their independence. When *L'Ouest-Éclair* supported Progressist candidates, it provoked abuse from the right and risked accusations of 'modernism'. The newspaper advised Catholics to 'try' the Separation, but ultimately had to back monarchist and intransigent candidates.[130]

The ALP also had to contend with Interior Minister Clemenceau's tactics, which underlined once more the problematic relationship between the right and conservatism. To prevent the ALP from depicting the Radicals as anti-religious warriors, he halted the Inventories. He also exploited the knowledge that the ALP had donated a small sum to the CGT, to reveal a black and red 'conspiracy' to foment disturbances on 1 May 1906.[131] Whether Clemenceau actually believed in the conspiracy is hard to say. The right, from the Progressists to the Monarchists, ridiculed it. Yet it contained a degree of plausibility, for the right often resorted to the *politique du pire*, and the very fact that Clemenceau felt it to be worth publicizing shows that some conservatives believed the ALP to be revolutionary. The centre, indeed, was quite prepared to believe in a black and red alliance. The elections of 1906 were a disappointment for the ALP, demonstrating its inability to profit from the Inventories crisis. It won 64 seats—fourteen fewer than in 1902.

CONCLUSION

The defeat and decline of the ALP meant that until the mid 1920s, there was no conservative mass movement. For two decades, elections would be organized by looser groupings of powerful men, in which the rump ALP, Alliance, and Fédération were merely one part of broader networks. The vicissitudes of the parties suggests that the organizational wave of the early 1900s was not a functional response to democratization, and that mass-member parties were not intrinsically more effective than elite groupings: in the Rhône, the 40,000 strong ALP consistently deferred to the smaller Fédération at election time.[132] Party formation was a product of contingencies: the reworking of political identities in the wake of the Ralliement and Dreyfus Affair, employers' self-defence in a tense social climate, and resistance to secularization and republicanization of the administration, education, and social services, particularly on the part of women. Certainly, the conviction that parties were 'necessary' was important, but it was a 'constructed' belief, related

[127] Fuller, 'Belle époque French nationalism', 36.

[128] Piou, *Les Femmes chrétiennes.*

[129] Della Sudda, 'Une Activité', 116–17.

[130] Henri de Cadore, '*L'Ouest-Éclair* et les deux Ralliements (1899–1930): Contribution à l'intégration des Catholiques de l'Ouest dans la République', in Michel Lagrée, Patrick Harismendy, and Michel Denis (eds), *L'Ouest-Éclair: Naissance et essor d'un grand quotidien régional* (Rennes, 2001), 55–78.

[131] Martin, 'The creation', 685–7.

[132] Bernard, *La Dérive*, 224.

to the principles of collective psychology, organicism, and evolutionary science, applied in a particular context. Consequently, parties were torn between practical acceptance of the need for compromise with other parties and the belief that the electorate was a 'crowd', possessed of a single mind, the irrational volatility of which rendered it vulnerable to demagogic manipulation—parties did not always see rivals as legitimate contenders for power. Context explained the decline of the parties too: the withdrawal of Papal support from the ALP, the depoliticization of Social Catholicism and female activism, and the defeat of 1906.

Notwithstanding, the parties had a lasting impact on conservative politics. They provided a set of markers for religious and constitutional questions. Like Leroy-Beaulieu in the Hérault, candidates subtly blended references to different groups in an effort to win a majority. The need for a wide electorate contrasted with the entrenchment of divisions, especially after 1906: as the centre became more conservative, the gap between secularists and Catholics ran *through* conservatism and complicated efforts to unite the opposition.

The relative decline of parties did not mean that conservatives retreated into atavistic individualism, for parties had been only one part of a broader movement to 'organize' the social and political body. After 1906, the emphasis shifted to other methods, notably business representation and electoral and constitutional reform. Furthermore, the relative effacement of the parties initiated a long period of conservative hegemony, which would climax in the nationalist revival of 1912–1914 and above all in the election of the Bloc national in 1919.

7

Organization (1906–1914)

> The deputy Merlou's pretentiously curled moustache suggested the provincial beau and his uncomfortable frockcoat seemed to recall the fruitless efforts of a departmental under-clerk to acquire an inaccessible elegance.
>
> André Gaucher, *Son Excellence Monsieur Merlou* (1906)

Gaucher's satirical portrait of the fictional deputy Merlou epitomizes snooty conservative resentment of the apparently immovable 'Radical Republic'. In the pre-war years, the right reached its lowest ebb in the Third Republic. Even including the Progressists, it won only 136 and 128 seats in the elections of 1910 and 1914 respectively. Yet the centre's break with the Bloc des gauches opened new possibilities and familiar dilemmas. The story of the next fifteen years was the making of a centre-dominated conservative alliance, the weakening of the extremes, and the hegemony of informal party structures. This alignment rested on the fusion of parliamentarianism with a movement for 'organization', which meant partnership between business and the state, regionalization, and proportional representation (PR), all expected to counter the 'mediocrity' of the Radical Republic and subsequently to ensure that the competent ran the war effort. Organization also involved the use of social science to integrate workers and women into the nation and to improve the quality and quantity of the population at a time of working-class and feminist agitation and international tension. Depoliticization of Social Catholic and Catholic women's organizations, and incorporation of feminism and the 'middle classes' into the organizational movement, contained challenges from non-elite conservatives. Organization became a 'common sense', but it was not unreflecting, for it meant different things to its advocates, and it failed to achieve all its objectives.

Realignment happened against the background of tension. The years 1906–1911 witnessed major industrial action, often syndicalist inspired, climaxing in the transport strikes of October 1910. Most worryingly, state employees participated in strikes. June 1907 witnessed a huge winegrowers' rebellion in the Midi, with a strong regionalist dimension. The formation in 1909 of the Union française pour le suffrage des femmes boosted the campaign for universal suffrage. The Moroccan crises of 1906 and 1911 and the Balkan wars of 1912–1913 raised the possibility of European conflagration.

Danger had never been sufficient to unite conservatives, but the refusal after 1905 of the Socialist Section française de l'internationale ouvrière (SFIO) to back 'bourgeois' governments forced the Radical-Socialists to look to the centre.

The Clemenceau government of October 1906 to July 1909 did not entirely break with the left, for it advocated progressive income tax, introduced retirement pensions, nationalized the western railways, and made modest concessions to feminists. Nevertheless, conservatives admired Clemenceau's strong-arm methods against strikers, winegrowers, and minor feminist demonstrations.[1] The right viewed the succeeding Briand administration (July 1909 to February 1911) still more positively, for it continued to repress the Confédération générale du travail (CGT), reduced religious tension, and endorsed PR and regionalism. After a brief Caillaux interlude, Raymond Poincaré's 'national government' (January 1912 to January 1913) confirmed the dominance of the centre. His successor, Louis Barthou, was also moderately conservative, but the last peacetime government, that of Doumergue, revealed that tensions between centre and right persisted. These cracks helped to sustain Action française (AF), which now monopolized the extreme right. The neo-Royalists pursued potentially incompatible strategies, wooing both conservatives with a Catholic, authoritarian version of organization while making overtures to revolutionary syndicalists, who advanced schemes for proletarian self-organization.

From a historiographical perspective, the disposition of forces supports both the Marxist view that centre, right, and extreme right were fundamentally united against Socialism and Zeev Sternhell's contention that left- and right-wing extremists merged in opposition to the moderate Republic, for alignments were shifting and contested.[2] However, circumstances ensured the predominance of the tendency towards centre-led unity among elitist conservatives, culminating in the victory of the Bloc national in 1919. The conditions were the transcendence of parties through the movement for organization and the weakening of non-elite conservatism.

THE EFFACEMENT OF THE PARTIES

Defeat in 1906 undermined the ALP. Pius X did not abandon Piou's party, for he endorsed good government within the Republic, meaning cooperation of Catholics with Moderate Republicans. Yet he also urged 'all men of goodwill to [stand on] ground clearly Catholic and religious', meaning unity including Monarchists. And since the Separation ended the State's say in episcopal appointments, Royalist influence in the hierarchy grew, while the condemnation of 'modernism' in 1907–1908 put the Action libérale populaire (ALP) on the defensive. The party vainly protested that it was liberal only in pragmatic acceptance of reality, and did not relegate Catholicism to private opinion.[3]

[1] Judith Stone, *The Search for Social Peace: Reform Legislation in France 1890–1914* (Albany, 1985), 82, 88–98.

[2] Zeev Sternhell, *Ni droite, ni gauche. L'Idéologie fasciste en France* (Paris, 1983); Herman Lebovics, *The Alliance of Iron and Wheat in the Third French Republic, 1860–1914. Origins of the New Conservatism* (Baton Rouge, 1988).

[3] Benjamin Martin, *Albert de Mun: Paladin of the Republic* (Chapel Hill, 1978), 222–6; Archives nationales, Fonds Rochefoucauld, 142 AP 14 (hereafter ANFXR, carton/dossier no.), dossier 1, note of 1 October 1913; Piou to Rochefoucauld, undated? December 1913.

Gradually, Pope Pius turned away from party politics altogether. In 1905, he endorsed 'Popular Unions' as they operated in Italy. They aimed to return Christ to the family, school, and society; they were led by laics, and relatively independent from the hierarchy, especially in social matters. Thus were laid the foundations of what would become 'Catholic Action'. In 1912, the Church formalized men's Parish Unions, which operated within the Republic without endorsing it, and were open to Catholics of any political persuasion. Meanwhile the Association catholique de la jeunesse française (ACJF) and the Ligue patriotique des françaises (LPDF) distanced themselves from the ALP. The LPDF ceased from 1907 to collect funds for Piou's party, and in 1913 removed 'ALP' from its title. Catholic women were now to focus on apostleship, 'outside politics'—which actually meant that the LPDF became more open to Royalists.[4] The ALP remained the Church's representative in parliament, but was no longer the exclusive vehicle of lay Catholicism. In June 1911, only 400 delegates attended its congress. The weakened party retained seats in Upper Brittany and contiguous areas of the west and Normandy, as well as in the northeast and south of the massif Central, but became more elitist (see Map 2, p. 141).

The ALP's decline allowed Christian Democrats to re-assert their independence, but they remained weak. In 1911, moderate Sillonistes in Brittany, with *L'Ouest-Éclair*'s support, founded the Fédérations des democrats, which defended the Church and sought to re-Catholicize the mass through social action, corporatism, and defence of Breton.[5] Fear of tainting themselves with modernism restrained them, and they faced a united front of the ALP, Monarchists, Office central agricultural unions, and the clerical-controlled Union des Catholiques. Condemnation of Sillon in 1910 (for openness to Protestantism and preaching class war) was especially problematic for *L'Ouest-Éclair*, for its editor, Henri Teitgen, was a member. Breton bishops forbade priests to subscribe to the Christian Democrat daily, and ordered Abbé Trochu to leave it. Even when *L'Ouest-Éclair* endorsed Progressists, it provoked a storm from the right and risked provoking their defeat.[6]

The Fédération républicaine (FR) and Alliance démocratique (ARD) failed to fulfil their founders' hopes. Neither united all sympathetic deputies and both had to reckon with rival organizations. The electoral defeat in 1906 of president Motte and secretary-general Clément undermined the Fédération. Joseph Thierry, president from 1906, improved the Fédération's reach in the provinces, notably inaugurating annual conferences. However, in 1911 faction fighting caused cancellation of the congress. The Alliance meanwhile attempted to reinforce its autonomy. In 1909, to differentiate itself from the Radical-Socialists, it elaborated a programme, and in

[4] Magali Della Sudda, 'Une Activité politique féminine avant le droit de suffrage en France et en Italie', thèse de doctorat, EHESS Paris, 2007, 116–19.

[5] Caroline Ford, *Creating the Nation in Provincial France. Religion and Political Identity in Brittany* (Princeton, 1993), 188–90; Henri de Cadore, '*L'Ouest-Éclair* et les deux Ralliements (1899–1930): Contribution à l'intégration des Catholiques de l'Ouest dans la République', in Michel Lagrée, Patrick Harismendy, and Michel Denis (eds), *L'Ouest-Éclair: Naissance et essor d'un grand quotidien régional* (Rennes, 2001), 55–78 at 59–60.

[6] Cadore, '*L'Ouest-Éclair*', 55–78.

March 1910, it announced its transformation into the Parti républicain démocrate (PRD), in the expectation that PR would strengthen parties.[7] However, the PRD still held that parties should ensure that voters rose above village quarrels, without imposing Socialist-style 'collectivism' in parliament. Discipline was harmful because it allowed parties rather than deputies to make the law, and contradicted the Republican principle of 'free examination and the right to be mistaken'.[8] Anyway, the failure of PR meant that the PRD was stillborn. In 1910, the Alliance's attempt to form a party group in parliament failed.

Notwithstanding, the loosely structured Fédération and Alliance were well suited to the informal networks of the organizational movement, even if there were tensions over the precise role of parties. As part of the organizational trend, parties included extra-parliamentary competences—notably business—in their governing bodies. Paul Forsans, president of the Unions des interest économiques (UIE), one of the most important para-political business organizations, was a member of the Alliance.[9] Maurice Colrat's Association de défense des classes moyennes (ADCM), founded in 1908, provided a crucial link between parties, as did Jules Roche's Ligue des contribuables (LC). A spokesman for the ADCM claimed that Marx was mistaken to describe the economy as a substructure—it was everything.[10] Yet it proved impossible to dispense altogether with parties or ideologies. We shall see that some Alliance and Fédération activists resented business groups' displacement of parties, especially where the primacy of the economic appeared to legitimate alliance with doubtful Republicans. As Broglie had discovered in 1873, economic, political, and religious issues were inseparable. Nevertheless, on balance the organizational movement facilitated informal conservative unity.[11] In that light, I shall explore the rightwards turn of the Antidreyfusard centre.

THE CONVERGENCE OF THE CENTRE AND RIGHT

The centre's position in the Dreyfusard majority had always been uncertain. It was uncomfortable with Combes and abandoned the government over the Affaire des fiches, but supported the Separation. In August 1907, with Clemenceau in power, the Alliance proposed an anti-Socialist 'Bloc républicain démocrate', including, it said, Radicals, but not Radical-Socialists, and those Progressists who accepted *laïcité*. Radical-Socialist attacks on the 'Alliance dit démocratique' doomed the proposal.[12] After Clemenceau's fall, centre backing for PR set it against the Radicals,

[7] Rosemonde Sanson, *L'Alliance républicaine démocratique. Une Formation du centre (1901–1920)* (Rennes, 2003), 211–13.

[8] *L'Alliance démocratique*, 2 January, 22 June, 7 September 1913.

[9] *L'Alliance démocratique*, 29 February 1911.

[10] *Le Siècle*, 17 November 1909.

[11] Gilles Le Béguec and Jacques Prévotat, '1898–1919: L'Éveil de la modernité politique', in Jean-François Sirinelli (ed.), *Histoire des droites en France*, i: *Politique* (Paris, 1993), 213–87; Malcolm Anderson, 'The Right and the social question in parliament', in David Shapiro (ed.), *The Right in France, 1890–1919: Three Studies* (Cambridge, 1962), 85–134.

[12] Sanson, *L'Alliance*, 163–76, that is, 'the supposedly democratic alliance'.

who preferred *scrutin d'arrondissement*. Indeed, the Alliance saw PR as a means to liberate itself from electoral deals with Radicals. The Alliance did not envisage national cooperation with the Progressists either—in the 1910 campaign, it declared 'they have their policy; we have ours'.[13] Yet locally, broad conservative alliances appeared; in 1909 Clemenceau was re-elected senator of the Var with right-wing support, and the Radical federation witnessed an influx of conservatives.[14] In Calvados, Poincaré's Labour Minister, Henry Chéron, endeavoured to unite Republicans from the Radicals to the Progressists.[15]

Meanwhile, the centre began to occupy Progressist political space, provoking resistance within its own ranks. It competed with the Fédération in areas of *laïque* conservative Republicanism, notably western Paris and the east (see Map 2, p. 141). It absorbed Progressists who disliked the increasingly right-wing stance of their party—notably, in 1913, their former leader, Thierry. The future left-wing Présidents du conseil, Caillaux and Paul Painlevé, left the Alliance, while the conservative Poincaré became more prominent. In 1913, the pro-Radical Gironde federation also departed, protesting at the influence of 'enemies of our institutions', while the parliamentary Gauche démocratique denied links with the Alliance. In 1913, some local committees eliminated pro-Radical elements, while party secretary Charles Pallu de la Barrière welcomed 'those who do not yet accept the Republic'.[16] A few Nationalists joined. One of them, Henri Galli, former president of the Ligue des patriotes and Paris Municipal Councillor, received the Légion d'honneur for supporting Poincaré's presidential bid. Galli was not entirely out of place in the centre, for he was anticlerical and doubted Dreyfus' guilt. 'Outdated' issues remained pertinent.[17]

The centre's hostility to alleged Radical-Socialist subversion of the administration, Army, and education was crucial to its rapprochement with the right.[18] The 'Radical Republic' threatened a whole political culture, for right and centre agreed that government should be in the hands of the 'competent', a quality that they believed to derive from 'experience' in business, the professions, the arts, or the academe. Experience taught distrust of dogma and enabled treatment of political issues on their merits, in relation to the national interest. In contrast, Radicals allegedly entered politics because they had failed in their careers. They were lawyers without clients and doctors without patients at best, and under-vets at worst. The Radical Republic institutionalized the rule of provincial nobodies like the fictional Merlou. Professional politicians, lacking experience of life, were intrinsically mediocre.

13 Sanson, *L'Alliance*, 187–8.

14 Jocelyne George, 'Une Politique fin de siècle. Les Reclassements politiques après l'adoption de la République. Le Cas du Var', *Cahiers d'histoire de l'institut de recherches marxistes* 33 (1988), 30–40.

15 Jean Quellien, *Bleus, blancs, rouges. Politique et élections dans le Calvados 1870–1939* (Caen, 1986), 178–84, 191.

16 Sanson, *L'Alliance*, 215–21, 260, 370, 391.

17 Philip Nord, *Paris Shopkeepers and the Politics of Resentment* (Princeton, 1986), 468.

18 Maurice Larkin, *Religion, Politics and Preferment in France since 1890* (Cambridge, 1995), 75–87, 91; Christophe Voilliot, *Le Candidature officiel. Une Pratique d'état de la Restauration à la Troisième République* (Paris, 2005), 235–41.

Gilles Le Béguec has demonstrated that these criticisms were misplaced. The Republic was not really dominated by under-vets; on the contrary, the elite of the Parisian Medical Faculties and Bar and its Conférence du stage, and increasingly the École libre des sciences politiques, figured strongly in both the moderate left and moderate conservative leaderships. The number of École graduates and professors in parliament increased markedly in 1910, and they included leading conservatives from Paul Deschanel to Charles de Benoist.[19] Criticism of deputies was rather a matter of political positioning, for competence was in the eye of the beholder and everyone was somebody else's mediocrity. Attacks on the quality of deputies spread across the political spectrum. Although each group saw quality differently, the tendency towards unity predominated.

Beginning with Catholics and Monarchists, new purges of the judiciary, Army, and administration, coupled with secularization, reinforced long-standing frustration. In 1900, the Rallié Eugène Melchior de Vogüé, disappointed at his brief experience of parliament, published his parliamentary caricature, *Les morts qui parlent*. In 1907, the closure of his Jesuit school obliged Charles de Gaulle to prepare in Belgium for the St Cyr military academy. In a different register, the administration reduced the subsidy for Mackau's Comice agricole from 1,200 francs in 1894 to 100 in 1913, claiming that it was a vehicle for men 'hostile to Republican institutions'.[20] Mackau then sat with the ALP, for which denunciation of Masonic corruption was daily fare.[21]

Progressists too complained of Masonic influence, while Clément saw it as 'scandalous' that men who contribute to the life, activity, and the wealth of society are deprived, thanks to their opinions, of the right to discuss their interests, and lamented that provincial barristers, although equal to Parisians, were unable to get into the Chamber.[22] From 1906, Lyon Progressists fought a pro-Radical Prefect who had promised to ensure that 'rural democracy would march in step with that of the cities'. According to Aynard, the Prefect paid more attention to excessive ringing of Church bells than to revolutionary conspiracies.[23] In 1907, the Fédération set up a national body to defend local government against administrative misdeeds.[24]

Crucially, the centre too resented Radical 'clientelism'. Under the Bloc, some Alliance deputies had unashamedly called for administrative support in elections, while party president Carnot opposed it.[25] As the Nationalist threat subsided, the

[19] Gilles Le Béguec, 'L'Entrée au Palais-Bourbon: Les Filières privilégiées d'accès à la fonction parlementaire 1919–1939', thèse pour le doctorat d'état, Paris X Nanterre, 1989, 86–8, 95–9, 158–74, 681–8; Gilles Le Béguec, 'Le Bâtonnier Barboux (1834–1910)', in *Barreau, politique et culture à la Belle époque* (Limoges, 1993), 5–27; Herman Lebovics, *True France: The Wars over Cultural Identity 1900–1945* (Ithaca, 1992) 12–28.

[20] Éric Phélippeau, *L'Invention de l'homme politique moderne: De Mackau, l'Orne et la République* (Paris, 2002), 157.

[21] Emmanuel de Las Cases, *Éphémérides. Journal inédit d'E. de Las Cases* (Montpellier, 1992), 49–49, 4 September 1904.

[22] *La République française*, 28 August 1908; *Le Proportionaliste*, July 1909.

[23] *La République française*, 25 January 1906; *Journal des débats*, 27 April 1908; Bernard, *La Dérive*, 195–201.

[24] Bernard, *La Dérive*, 198.

[25] *L'Alliance démocratique*, 13, 17 March 1903.

centre became more inclined to denounce the exclusion of the 'competent', and so it abandoned Combes over the Affair des fiches. Poincaré criticized the 'stifling' Palais Bourbon and proved his roundedness by combining legal and parliamentary careers.[26] Briand attacked 'corrupt' *scrutin d'arrondissement*, and by 1914 centrist resentment of administrative discrimination was general.[27] In that year, Robert de Jouvenel, on the fringe of the centre and Radicals, authored the classic condemnation of parliamentary morals, *La République des camarades*.

Right and centre also converged in defence of intellectual generalism, which supposedly complemented experience. Conservatives considered knowledge of the classics (dispensed only in paying *lycées*) to be essential for civil servants and engineers. Therefore, the reduction in 1902 of the classical element of the Baccalauréat outraged politicians and business alike. In 1910, the president of Comité des forges regretted that the decline of Latin compromised Polytechniciens' ability to express technical ideas clearly.[28] Generalism also meant the application of the natural sciences, especially biology, to politics and society, and thus suspicion of the new specialized university disciplines.

Generalism brought together two intellectual generations. In the elder, Gustave Le Bon attacked university scientists for their alleged refusal to generalize from biology to sociology (actually, Durkheim often did so). Le Bon held that evolutionary biology and race revealed the workings of society. The younger generation was represented by pragmatists, such as Georges Sorel, who wrote to Le Bon that 'the French are hallucinated by university oracles and recyclers of Durkheimian pap'.[29] Where Le Bon had argued that the leader would use 'will' to dominate the crowd, the second generation took from Bergson a cult of youth, action, and faith, while defending Taine's generalism against specialism in sociology and history. There were disputes between and within generations. For instance, pragmatists rejected Le Bon's ultra-deterministic conviction that social reform was useless.[30]

Generalism crossed political boundaries. The *Écho de Paris* took the lead on the nationalist and pro-Catholic right.[31] Closer to AF were Gabriel Tarde and Henri Massis' 'enquiries' (under the pseudonym Agathon), *L'Ésprit de la nouvelle Sorbonne* (1911) and *Les Jeuenes gens d'aujourd'hui* (1912). Agathon asked, 'How could one doubt that science needs cultivated minds which have learned to think, to deduct carefully, and not to collect dates and facts?'[32] Charles de Gaulle, aged twenty-two in 1912, shared the themes of the enquiry; a reader of Barrès and Bergson, he saw

[26] *L'Écho de Paris*, 12 April 1912.

[27] *L'Alliance démocratique*, 6 April 1913.

[28] *Le Figaro*, 1 December 1910; André Chervel, 'Les Études littéraires dans la formation polytechnicienne', in Bruno Belhoste et al. (eds), *La Formation polytechnicienne 1794–1994* (Paris, 1994), 121–39 at 135–6.

[29] Robert Nye, 'Two paths to a psychology of action: Gustave Le Bon and Georges Sorel', *Journal of Modern History* 45, no. 3 (September 1973), 411–38 at 414.

[30] *L'Opinion*, 9 July 1910.

[31] *L'Écho de Paris*, 14 January 1910.

[32] *L'Opinion*, 27 August 1910.

himself as part of the elite, and envisaged war without fear.[33] Whereas de Gaulle had joined the Army, Massis and Tarde emerged from a milieu of cultivated amateurs, who moved between Bergson's courses at the College de France, fashionable cafés in Saint-Germain, the Ballet Russes, *salles d'armes*, the visitors' gallery at the Palais Bourbon, and the offices of *L'Écho de Paris* and *L'Opinion*.[34] The latter review had been founded in 1908 by the centrist Paul Doumer with the backing of figures in big business and the Musée sociale, and its aim was to reconcile the elites with democracy. In 1910, without abandoning its initial objective, it was taken over by Colrat, a pure product of Republican elite and a protégé of Poincaré. Although *L'Opinion*'s circulation never rose above 2,000, it was a major forum for the exchange of ideas.[35]

The prospect of war also brought conservatives together, for the SFIO had been founded on an internationalist programme and since the Dreyfus Affair the Radical-Socialist Party's left wing also distrusted 'militarism'. The Anglophobic Nationalist and Catholic right disliked the Franco-British Entente cordiale of 1904, but German attempts to undermine it in the Moroccan crises of 1906 and 1911 forced re-evaluation. Faced with German re-armament, Poincaré's government proposed extending military service to three years, which the Socialists and most Radicals opposed. The three-year campaign underpinned the 'nationalist revival' of the immediate pre-war years, personified in Poincaré's election as Président de la République in 1913. Preparation for war was a major impetus behind the organizational movement.

Thus, long-standing affinities among conservative politicians, academics, and business became relevant as Socialists and Radicals split in a tense social and international context. Common commitment of parties, social policy networks, and business groups to 'organization' cemented the new alignment. Organization was attractive because it proposed 'scientific' answers to the problems described above: it institutionalized the authority of the competent in a hierarchical society, proposed an answer to Socialism, and armed the nation for international struggle.

PR was essential to this strategy. Gilles Le Béguec rightly argues that conservatives saw it as a means to secure the hegemony of the 'competent'. Less convincing is Pierre Rosanvallon's claim that PR replaced the 'counterrevolutionary' notion of professional and/or family suffrage with a 'democracy of opinion', not least because he assumes a traditional/modern dichotomy.[36] I shall relate PR to its cultural and social context: the broader organizational movement and collective psychology. Organizationalists conceived the nation as an organic entity possessed of a single mentality, yet disagreed on the nature of the elite and the role of the state and Church.

[33] Alain Larcan, 'Boutroux, Bergson, Barrès', in *Charles de Gaulle. La Jeunesse et la guerre, 1890–1920. Colloque international, Lille, 5–6 novembre 1999* (Paris, 2001), 95–118.

[34] Raymond Isay, 'Une Revue politique et littéraire sous la Troisième République: *L'Opinion* (1908–1914)', *Revue des traveaux de l'Académie des sciences morales et politiques* 113, no. 1 (1960), 24–39.

[35] Isay, 'Une Revue politique', 24–39; Le Béguec, 'L'Entrée', 196–8.

[36] Pierre Rosanvallon, *Le Peuple introuvable* (Paris, 1998), 161–75; Le Béguec, 'L'Entrée', 179–245; Philip G. Nord, 'Social defence and conservative regeneration: the national revival, 1900–14', in Robert Tombs (ed.), *Nationhood and Nationalism in France: From Boulangism to the Great War* (London, 1991), 211–28.

ORGANIZATION

The notion that the social and political body should be 'organized' was not new. The hierarchical dimension of organization owed much to Monarchist belief that society needed a 'thinking head', while Frédéric LePlay's eclectic social science gave empirical underpinning to the old preoccupation with rooting the individual in the profession, family, and region. Nationalism brought institutional reform to organization. Collective psychology was equally important: the elite, the brain, should 'organize' the activity of the amorphous mass. Le Bon was as popular with politicians as with business and academic organizers: the engineer-manager Émile Cheysson, the management scientist Henri Fayol, and the car-maker Louis Renault all read him.

In the 1900s, the displacement of Darwinism by Lamarckianism in social science permitted the reconciliation of social cooperation with hierarchy and the leadership of an elite, the latter invested with countering degeneration in the social body. Darwinism lost its attraction for moderate conservatives because Socialists harnessed it to class conflict and the far right used it to attack democracy and legitimate aristocracy. Social Catholics condemned Darwinism for endorsing blind struggle between individuals.[37] In the Lamarckian alternative, the nature of the elite and the mass and the balance between them were contested. Radical-Socialist Solidarists wanted the state to ensure that each organ worked harmoniously for the social body, including trade unions. Centrists and Progressists placed greater emphasis on organic hierarchy and bourgeois leadership, and largely opposed independence for unions, even if some favoured limited state intervention in social matters. The Moderate Republican view shaded into the paternalism of conservative Social Catholicism. Thanks to the decline of popular conservatism, elitist conservatism dominated the organizational movement in the centre and even more the right.

The Organization of the Interests

The notion of the organization of the interests owed much to the development of large-scale capitalism. The last years of peace witnessed considerable economic growth, largely accounted for by big chemical and especially metallurgical firms. The Lorraine became a major centre of steel-making, characterized by semi-monopolistic cooperation between vertically integrated businesses, linked in the Comité des forges, which had been reorganized by Robert Pinot in 1907. Steel firms were run by industrial dynasties like the Wendels and salaried engineers like Camille Cavallier at Pont-à-Mousson. Big business still co-existed with small and medium firms, even in new sectors such as motor vehicle manufacture. In 1900, nearly 60 per cent of people lived in rural communes, the bulk of them on family farms. Diversity nurtured rival economic visions, and it was not inevitable that capitalist concentration should have produced 'organized capitalism'. However, the popularity of organicism ensured that it did.

[37] Jean-Marc Bernardini, *Le Darwinisme social en France. Fascination et rejet d'une idéologie* (Paris, 1997), 321–42, 357–60, 364–5.

Business functionaries, engineers, and managers took the lead. They identified with employers, but maintained that they were better equipped to see the general economic and social picture. In 1897, Cheysson, manager at Creusot, published 'Le rôle social de l'ingénieur', modelled on Lyautey's famous 'Le rôle social de l'officier' (1891). For Cheysson, the engineer, like the officer, was an expert, schooled in the methods of social science, able to secure the devotion of workers to the firm.[38] Business leaders came from the same nurseries as the political elite. Henry de Peyerimhoff of the Comité des houillères and the previously mentioned André Lebon both passed through the École libre.[39] The best lawyers had long worked for corporations. Joseph-Barthélemy remarked ironically that business denounced parliamentarians' 'incompetence', but chose 'personalities from outside their profession, endowed with a broad general culture' to represent it.[40]

Although he was not widely known before the Great War, Henri Fayol, director-general of the mining and metallurgy firm, Commentry-Fourchamboult et Decazeville, was especially important. He was the product, systematizer, and popularizer of pre-existing ideas as much as the inventor of management science. Fayol argued that productivity depended on unity of command and clear lines of communication to the executing organs. In effect, he applied a monarchical model to the factory, updated with Le Bon's idea of the *chef* as 'organizer' of the shapeless crowd.[41] Typically of business organizers, Fayol contrasted managerial effectiveness with deputies' demagogic nullity.[42] As Minister of Public Works and then of War, Alexandre Millerand applied Fayolist methods in the administration, and appointed the organizer, General Lyautey, as Resident-General in Morocco.[43] The latter, like Fayol, bridged military and managerial circles, as well as belonging to the Académie française. His Legitimism did not prevent him from cultivating relations with Millerand.[44]

The ideas and practices described above may be labelled 'organized liberalism'. Like Méline, organizers assumed that national power required an 'organic' balance between industry and agriculture, a neo-mercantilist policy of imperial preference, and 'conquest' of foreign markets. Thus, in international affairs, Darwinism persisted. Pinot claimed that the French state was less sympathetic to business than the German or American, and urged the government to promote national

[38] Yves Cohen, 'Les Polytechniciens dans le discours sur le commandement (1891–1940)', in *La France des X*, 157–68; Emmanuel de Las Cases, *Des Autorités sociales dans une démocratie et du rôle de l'ingénieur* (Avranches, 1903).

[39] Le Béguec, 'L'Entrée', 268–70; Nord, 'Social defence', 211–12; Gilles Le Béguec, 'Prélude à un syndicalisme bourgeois, l'association de défense des classes moyennes (1907–1939)', *Vingtième siècle* 37, no. 1 (January–March 1993), 93–104 at 97.

[40] Joseph-Barthélemy, *Le Problème de la compétence dans la démocratie* (Paris, 1918), 64.

[41] Yves Cohen, 'Fayol, un instituteur de l'ordre industriel', *Entreprises et histoire* 34 (2003), 29–67 at 47–8.

[42] *Les Études fiscales et sociales*, 15 April 1908.

[43] Marjorie M. Farrar, 'Politics versus patriotism: Alexandre Millerand as French Minister of War', *French Historical Studies* 11, no. 4 (Fall 1980), 577–609; Cohen, 'Fayol', 29–67; Stéphane Rials, *Administration et organisation. De L'Organisation de la bataille à la bataille de l'organisation dans l'administration française* (Paris, 1977), 158–60.

[44] Bruno Goyet, *Un Rôle en politique: Henri d'Orléans, Comte de Paris* (Paris, 2001), 158.

economic development.[45] The state should help create industrial investment banks and prospect for foreign markets. Domestically, harmony was more important than struggle. Business would join cartels, which would limit the 'anarchy' of the market and receive legal power to manage infrastructure, thus increasing exports and facilitating troop movements.[46] In the longer term, employer organizations would deal directly with a reinforced executive; in the meantime, they lobbied parliament and sponsored candidates. A few businessmen and centre politicians backed collective negotiation with labour unions, usually conditional upon restrictions on strikes, but they disagreed on whether or not contracts should be legally enforceable.[47]

Organization was intended both as an *alternative* to state control and as a means to discipline the profession. That posed a dilemma, for organization implied coercion of firms that did not accept the majority view (the sub-text was often that smaller firms were inefficient). Some liberals were therefore suspicious of organization. Aynard continued to fly the liberal flag in the Fédération, while the presence in the Alliance of the orthodox economist, Yves Guyot, confirmed the importance of liberalism in the centre. In 1906–1908, debates about the nationalization of the Western Railway revealed that many conservatives rejected Minister of Public Works Barthou's contention that a model company would inspire organizational efforts in private business.[48] These tensions intensified during the War, provoking a post-war reaction against organization. For now, organizers were largely united and enjoyed broad legitimacy.

Indeed, organizers presented themselves as part of the 'classes moyennes' movement, which was also endorsed by all parties from the Alliance to the ALP.[49] As president of the ADCM, Maurice Colrat depicted his constituency as the middle term in a hierarchical society, essential to the 'good organization of the social body', characterized by individual work and accumulation of property over generations. He included in the middle class 'the large and small bourgeoisie, meaning men of trade and industry'; he thus excluded financiers, but included industrial capitalists and *rentiers*. That middle-class ideology was compatible with conservative and big business leadership and with the social role of the engineer was confirmed by Colrat's ascription to the middle class of characteristics elsewhere attributed to the elite—realism, common sense, and independence. He also used 'middle class' and 'bourgeoisie' interchangeably. Unsurprisingly, the Comité de forges and Comité

[45] Richard Kuisel, *Capitalism and the State* (Cambridge, 1981), 20–6; Nord, 'Social defence', 212–13.

[46] Jean-Marc Moine, *Les Barons de fer* (Nancy, 1989), 193–200; H.D. Peiter, 'Institutions and attitudes: the consolidation of the business community in bourgeois France 1880–1914', *Journal of Social History* 9, no. 4 (1976), 510–25; Nord, 'Social defence', 212–15; Kuisel, *Capitalism and the State*, 24.

[47] Sanson, *L'Alliance*, 229–330.

[48] John F. Godfrey, *Capitalism at War: Industrial Policy and Bureaucracy in France, 1914–1918* (Leamington Spa, 1987), 33–4.

[49] Sanson, *L'Alliance*, 184–5; *Correspondance d'Union républicaine*, 12, 17 November, 10 December 1908, 17 June 1910.

des houillères endorsed the ADCM's 1910 election charter.[50] Again, there was opposition to this aspect of organizationalism: Aynard, in the name of the legal equality of individuals, publicly distanced himself from Colrat's use of the term 'middle *class*'.[51]

For its part, small business was more willing than in the past to accept big business and conservative leadership (or at least those who did not back the Radicals were). The once turbulent Parisian shopkeeper organizations now affiliated to another of Colrat's groups, the Fédération des groupes commerciaux et industriels, which was close to the centre, but open to Catholics and linked to the ALP. Shopkeepers began to see themselves as part of the 'classes moyennes' rather than the people. Small commerce disliked Socialist efforts to municipalize butchers and bakers, and opposed de Mun's campaign against night-work.[52] It also approved the ADCM's defence of apprenticeship, with its emphasis on using French traditions to inspire innovation. Given that big capitalism sought to profit from the French reputation for taste and refinement, quality was a unifying theme.[53]

Small business was not entirely subordinate to large, and had its own ideas about organization. The shopkeeper movement embraced 'associationism', which meant purchasing cooperatives and credit unions.[54] Social Catholics, often quite radical, played a part in the middle-class movement, especially following the international congresses of the petite bourgeoisie in Belgium in 1899 and 1901. Furthermore, big business secured its leadership at the cost of attacking department stores.[55] Nevertheless, for now, big business dominated organizational movement in the economic sphere.

During the War, organizers would combine Fayoliste economic organization with anti-parliamentarianism. Before then, they focussed more on improving the 'quality' of parliamentarians, their responsiveness to business, and thus their attentiveness to the national interest. That meant detaching deputies from 'outdated' political parties. In practical terms, business organizations sought to increase the representation of the competent in parliament: Colrat promised to help businessmen to stand for election and advocated a professional senate, while the Fédération's *Correspondance d'Union républicaine* began to promote his ADCM.[56] Secondly, business campaigned on specific issues. The ADCM and Roche's Ligue des contribuables opposed income tax, while in 1910 the UIE was formed to prevent nationalization of the liquor and insurance industries. These campaigns united

[50] *Les Études fiscales et sociales*, 15 September 1908, 15 November 1908, July 1909; *Correspondance d'Union républicaine*, 10 December 1908; Gilles Le Béguec, 'Le Moment de l'alerte fiscale. La Ligue des contribuables (1899–1914)', in Pierre Guillaume (ed.), *Regards sur les classes moyennes XIXe-XXe siècles* (Talence, 1995), 147–63.

[51] *Les Études fiscales et sociales*, 10 July 1910.

[52] Benjamin F. Martin, 'The creation of the Action Libérale Populaire: an example of party formation in Third Republican France', *French Historical Studies* 9, no. 4 (Fall 1976), 660–89 at 679; Sanson, *L'Alliance*, 300.

[53] Nord, 'Social defence', 217.

[54] Nord, *Paris Shopkeepers*, 465–77.

[55] *Les Études fiscales et sociales*, July 1909.

[56] *L'Opinion*, 9 March 1912; *Le Réveil économique*, 2 and 13 April 1913.

conservatives of all stripes. Thirdly, business intervened directly in elections. In 1908, a journalist attributed conservative successes in the Paris municipal elections to the willingness of professional and middle-class associations to intervene 'independently of any political committee'.[57] Finally, business backed proportional representation, which the Progressist Désiré Ferry described as a means for 'economic syndicates' in a decentralized France to replace electoral committees.[58]

The Organization of Universal Suffrage

The introduction of PR in Belgium in 1896 encouraged reflection in France. The first conservative movement to prioritize PR was La Patrie Française, as part of its advocacy of constitutional reform.[59] Then, in 1902, the left won a large majority of seats with a small majority of votes, provoking the formation of the Ligue pour la représentation proportionnelle, led by Georges Picot. After 1906, the decline of Nationalism made institutional reform respectable again for Republicans, while the SFIO's desire to separate itself from the Radicals converted it to PR. From 1907, Jaurès and Benoist campaigned jointly for PR, in the conviction that parliament would never reform itself.[60]

For Pierre Rosanvallon, PR would strengthen parties and ensure that all voters were represented without forcing them into the categories of professional suffrage, as other schemes for organizing universal suffrage did. Certainly, advocates of PR invoked fairness and argued that it would favour parties. Yet the desire to represent the competences and root the individual in the region and family was also important. Allegedly, PR would encourage the 'best' to stand for election at the head of party lists, without having to involve themselves in base politics, whereas the smallness of arrondissment constituencies supposedly favoured clientelism and demagogy.[61] Progressists held that PR would create parties that were characterized by 'elevated ideas', which alone were capable of cleansing pestilential arrondissment ponds (rotten boroughs).[62] The centre agreed that *scrutin d'arrondissement* lowered the quality of parliamentarians. Moreover, it saw society as a hierarchical agglomeration of 'interests', not as a collection of free individuals.[63] Poincaré saw PR as a means of re-establishing contact between parliament and the 'real world',[64] while Deschanel held that it would give deputies a national perspective appropriate to the telephone age.[65]

[57] *Les Études fiscales et sociales*, 15 June 1908.
[58] *Correspondance d'Union républicaine*, 25 November 1909.
[59] François Coppée and Jules Lemaître, *L'Œuvre de la Patrie française* (Paris, 1899), 7.
[60] *Discours de Charles Benoist, Ferdinand Buisson et Jean Jaurès en faveur de la R.P* (Paris, 1910).
[61] Le Béguec, 'L'Entrée', 207–16.
[62] *La République française*, 6 November 1908, 25 January 1911; *Correspondance d'Union républicaine*, 12 November 1908, 17 June 1909, 19 April 1910.
[63] Gaston Cagniard, *Politique nationale* (Paris, 1914), 236–42; *L'Alliance républicaine démocratique*, 6 April 1913, 28 January, 16 December 1909.
[64] Raymond Poincaré, *Questions et figures politiques* (Paris, 1907), 498–504; *Le Proportionaliste*, October 1909; J.F.V. Keiger, *Raymond Poincaré* (Cambridge, 1997), 120–4; *Revue de Paris*, 1 April 1910, 847–71 at 848.
[65] Paul Deschanel, *L'Organisation de la démocratie* (Paris, 1910), Speech of 21 October 1909.

In October 1909, at Périgueux, Président du conseil Briand denounced *scrutin d'arrondissement*.[66] On 8 November, the Chamber, by a large majority, including seventy-five Radicals, endorsed PR. Briand was horrified, and made reversal of the vote a question of confidence. Several centrist and Radicals changed their votes. PR came up for discussion again in January 1912. Once again, the Président du conseil, this time Poincaré, resisted a measure that he endorsed in principle. The bill that the Chamber eventually approved on 10 July 1912 represented a compromise between PR and the majority principle. Nevertheless, on 18 March 1913, Clemenceau and Combes persuaded the Senate to reject it.

Radical-Socialist defence of acquired positions was crucial to the failure of PR, but cleavages within and between the right and the centre were significant too. One problem was that Progressists, and even more the ALP, coupled PR with a wider institutional reform. For Rosanvallon, Benoist's espousal of PR signified his abandonment of professional suffrage.[67] In fact, Benoist saw it as a step towards regionalized professional suffrage, double votes, aptitude tests for voters, and reinforcement of the executive.[68] Jules Roche, editor of *La République française*, echoed many of these demands,[69] which shaded into anti-parliamentarianism, which had been demonstrated for the first time in Progressist criticism of the raising of the salaries of deputies in 1906.[70] Most Centrists opposed these schemes for constitutional revision, doubtless worried that some Royalists endorsed PR and that a Progressist journalist hoped that PR would destroy the Alliance.[71] André Siegfried saw direct election of the president as a danger to parliament.[72] André Maginot, a young Républicain de gauche, argued that *scrutin d'arrondissement* permitted the emergence of talents, whereas under PR the need to please party committees would encourage mediocrity. Poincaré thought constitutional reform unnecessary: the president merely had to exercise 'will'.[73]

Equally problematic was that PR could not be detached from regionalism. Many 'PR backers' advocated regional lists, seeing them as large enough to break clientelism, but small enough to root democracy in 'real' life. In the 1910 legislature, over 400 deputies supported regionalism, mostly of the right and centre. This apparent consensus owed much to the efforts of the president of the Fédération régionaliste française (FRF), Charles-Brun, to overcome divisions between centrists and leftists who wanted 'rational' regions, and right-wingers who wished to revive the old provinces. Personally, Charles-Brun, a member of the Alliance démocratique, was influenced by Christian Democracy and Proudhon's democratic federalism. Yet he

[66] Julian Wright, 'Social reform, state reform, and Aristide Briand's moment of hope in France, 1909–1910', *French Historical Studies* 28, no. 1 (Spring 2005), 31–67.

[67] Rosanvallon, *Le Peuple*, 170.

[68] *Le Proportionaliste*, July 1909; Gilles Le Béguec, 'Charles Benoist ou les métamorphoses de l'esprit modéré', *Contrepoint* 22–3 (December 1976), 71–95.

[69] *La République française*, 9, 20, 26 May 1911.

[70] *La République française*, 25–9 November 1906.

[71] *Correspondance d'Union républicaine*, 31 October 1911.

[72] *L'Alliance républicaine démocratique*, 2 February 1913.

[73] Marc Sorlot, *André Maginot (1877–1932). L'Homme politique et sa légende* (Metz, 1995), 36.

insisted that regionalism needed both modernizers and 'sentimentalist' admirers of the past, for contact with the 'necessities' of the soil and the dead allowed the individual to flourish.[74]

Charles-Brun (like some historians) glossed over the regionalist tensions of the period. Above all, the Midi winegrowers' rebellion of 1907 possessed a regionalist component. In Languedoc, left and right both blamed the overproduction crisis on fraudulent sugaring of wine, consequent upon the low tax on beet sugar, attributed to the political influence of northern beet growers. The right in the south enthusiastically equated the rebellion with nationalist movements in Ireland and Catalonia, while some Royalists saw an opportunity to overthrow the regime.[75] The Socialist mayor of Narbonne, a Félibrige, evoked the resistance of medieval Albigensians to 'northern barons'.[76]

The Midi rebellion simultaneously reinforced anti-southern prejudice. Already, Catholics blamed southern Freemasons for attacking eastern and northern Catholicism, and now conservatives generally began to equate parliamentary mediocrity with southern overrepresentation in parliament. Southerners, they maintained, were racially inclined to empty verbiage and materialism. Incapable of sustained work, they could not succeed in the professions, and so they turned to politics. Conservatives identified northern France with hard work and honesty, and accused southerners of living off northern taxes—and thus of supporting an income tax. In March 1911, Colrat devoted a special issue of *L'Opinion* to the 'southern question'. It provoked contributions from a panoply of writers, scientists, and politicians, from Barrès to Deschanel, almost all of whom endorsed the stereotype. Le Bon opined: 'We are in the age of the crowd, and thus of agitators. To be a good agitator, it is necessary to speak well and think little. Southern politicians possess this quality in a high degree and so will govern until the debacle.' A doctor at the Institut Pasteur likened southern brains to 'poorly equipped telephone exchanges'. Deschanel and others saw the remedy in PR.[77]

In Brittany, meanwhile, secularization and accompanying attacks on the Breton language radicalized regionalism. The aristocracy had long used regionalism in the hope of recapturing the state through resurrection of the ancient provinces. In 1909, the Marquis de l'Estourbeillon, a pro-Royalist ALP member and leader of the conservative Union régionaliste bretonne, demanded for the first time the teaching of Breton in public schools. He did so in response to pressure from radical students, who in 1911 formed the autonomist Fédération régionaliste bretonne (FRB) and the Parti nationaliste bretonne (PNB). Neither made much progress, but Christian Democrats embraced a regionalism that was mid-way between the regionalist nationalism of the right and the separatism of the PNB.[78]

[74] Julian Wright, *The Regionalist Movement in France 1890–1914* (Oxford, 2003), 80–6, 127, 142.

[75] *L'Éclair* (Midi) 11 June 1907; Philippe Secondy, *La Persistance du Midi blanc* (Perpignan, 2006), 161–4.

[76] René Merle, 'Autour de la crise viticole de 1907 dans le Var: Conscience "Méridionale" et Langue d'Oc', *Provence historique* 47, no. 188 (April–May 1997), 317–37; Jean Sagnes, *Le Midi rouge, mythe et réalité. Études d'histoire occitane* (Paris, 1982), 215–57.

[77] *L'Opinion*, 18, 25 March 1911.

[78] Ford, *Creating the Nation*, 138.

Although few regionalists questioned the integrity of France (in principle), these developments alarmed the centre. Clemenceau turned against regionalism. Poincaré held that rational economic activity required understanding of the locality in which it operated, but he did not favour resurrection of the provinces and maintained that suppression of regional 'dialects' permitted the emergence of national literature structured by Francophone 'clarté'.[79] Whereas Catholic conservatives and many Progressists saw the state as creating both region and nation, and envisaged homogenous, self-contained regions, the centre was suspicious of regionalization 'from above'. Charles-Brun believed that regionalism would emerge organically, through practical cooperation in economic, cultural, and administrative fields, which were not necessarily geographically co-terminus. These tensions put the FRF on the defensive. Pressed by Louis Marin, Charles-Brun endorsed Briand's regionalist initiatives of 1910, which were close to his own conceptions, but did little to ensure that they came to fruition. Charles Le Goffic, the Breton writer, opposed these proposals because they chopped up of what remained of the old provinces.[80] In 1914, the Independent Socialist, Jean Hennessy, founded a rival Ligue pour la régionalisation, which advocated rational economic regions as part of a social-democratic programme, an anathema to the right.

Along with regionalism, PR was linked to debates concerning women's suffrage. The centre saw votes for women as an essential part of the organization of universal suffrage, for it rooted the individual in the family. And according to the logic of the representation of interests, women's competence in family matters would strengthen natalism in parliament. Mainstream feminists, often close to the centre, largely agreed. They began to portray childbirth as an equivalent to military service, and argued that the vote was necessary to secure social legislation.[81] A few Catholic women, including Marie Maugeret and the Duchesse d'Uzès, approved this view. The latter served briefly as vice-president of the largely secular UFSF, suggesting the possibility of a 'union sacrée suffragiste'.[82] Yet suffragism failed thanks to Catholic opposition and tensions in the organizational project.

The historiographical view that Catholics favoured female suffrage in the hope that women would vote for them is largely a myth. The Pope opposed the suffrage, and consequently the ALP did so too. The Catholic Theodore Joran won a prize from the Académie française for his 'reasoned' refutation of feminism, which he saw as the product of Jewish and Protestant subversion.[83] The LPDF opposed the vote because it aimed to moralize society through the assertion of family values,

[79] Raymond Poincaré, *L'Idée de la patrie* (Paris, 1910), 14–16.

[80] Wright, *The Regionalist Movement*, 140, 184–9.

[81] M.H. Darrow, 'French volunteer nursing and the myth of experience in World War I', *American Historical Review* 101, no. 4 (February 1996), 81–106; James McMillan, '"A civilisation without sexes?" The Great War and gender relations in France', in Gail Braybon (ed.), *Evidence, History and the Great War: A Reassessment* (Oxford, 2003), 135–53 at 145; Steven C. Hause and Anne R. Kenney, *Women's Suffrage and Social Politics in the French Third Republic* (Princeton, 1984), 97.

[82] Hause and Kenney, *Women's Suffrage*, 132–68.

[83] Florence Rochefort, 'L'Antiféminisme. Une Rhétorique réactionnaire?', in Christine Bard (ed.), *Un Siècle d'antiféminisme* (Paris, 1999), 133–47.

and so felt that voting would corrupt women.[84] The Progressists, who included well-known partisans of the suffrage such as Louis Marin, often used the language of individual rights and justice to support the cause.[85] However, most Progressists were lukewarm. In July 1912, only 117 deputies supported a suffragist amendment to a PR bill. Even 'suffragists', such as Poincaré, voted against. In fact, female suffrage potentially contradicted organization, for it threatened the hierarchy of organs in the social body.

Moreover, natalist priorities could justify confinement of women to the home as easily as it could the vote. In 1911, at the ARD congress, a Dr Roussy, at Barthou's request, read a report evoking the deleterious effects of paid work upon women's reproductive capacities. He argued that domesticity must be 'organized' hierarchically and organically, for the family was the 'cell' of the social edifice. That required education in domestic science and child-raising, and choice of mates in accordance with scientific, psychological, and anatomical criteria. These measures would prevent degeneration and the occupation of France by the more fertile Germans, for the law of mechanics dictated the migration of a greater towards a lesser force.[86] National power mattered more than women's rights. Although the centre's support for feminism was highly qualified, mainstream feminism did not break with the centre. Lack of alternative outlets and the expectation that 'progress' worked in their favour, ensured that they did not challenge the dominance of the male conservative elite.

PR failed because it was inseparable from regional, religious, constitutional, class, and family issues. Anyway, the Chamber's votes for PR had been votes of principle, which owed much to confusion between genuine PR and a more limited 'representation of minorities', and to avoidance of the regional question. To scupper PR, Briand argued that it would benefit only the 'better-organized' enemies of the Republic; only when parties had been formed and the question of regionalism resolved could PR be implemented.[87] In 1912, when the Chamber once more accepted PR in principle, opposition from ARD committees helped scupper it.[88] PR is less important for its actual achievements than for renewing ties between centre and Progressists. In the Chamber, it had passed with a majority that included all the right and much of the centre, and thus illustrated the shifting balance of power.

Organizing Society

In the case of social reform, Catholic–secular cooperation was strong, while disagreements concerning the role of the state cut through both sides. Non-elite conservatives were influential, but could not challenge the elite politically. We have seen that the Musée social laid the groundwork for collaboration between Catholics and lay conservatives in the 1890s, which continued in the following decade.

[84] Hause and Kenney, *Women's Suffrage*, 166–8; Della Sudda, 'Servir Dieu et patrie', 155–60.
[85] *Correspondance d'Union républicaine*, 13 December 1910.
[86] B. Roussy, *L'Éducation domestique de la femme et rénovation sociale* (Paris, 1914).
[87] *Journal officiel. Chambre des députés*, 8 November 1909, 2512.
[88] Sanson, *L'Alliance*, 358–9.

Several proponents of business organization were Catholic conservatives from that milieu, who were used to cooperating with Republicans—Cheysson and Pinot among others.[89]

Conservative reformers wished to resolve the social question scientifically, achieve organic unity, improve the quality and quantity of the population, and thus strengthen the nation under elite leadership. Implicitly Lamarckian, they held that evolution depended on the ability of the active elite to counteract the tendency towards degeneration in the social organism, evidenced in the vulnerability of the population to alcoholism, tuberculosis, syphilis, and the low birth rate. The prospect of war intensified conservative fear of decadence. Jacques de Lannessan of the Alliance was not alone in thinking that unless it adopted the principle of preservation, France would soon be a 'race of bandits and alcoholics'.[90] The Progressist social scientist, Édouard Demolins, and the Alliance Deputy, Henry Chéron, did not oppose retirement pensions in practice but noted that they encouraged reproduction of the 'social waste'.[91]

Demographic worries reinforced Catholic–Republican cooperation. In 1911, pro-natalists and Catholic familialists formed a common parliamentary group, while Catholic conservatives began to join the hitherto *laïque* Alliance nationale pour l'accroissement de la population française (ANPAPF). Within the ANPAPF, the Catholic Progressist Fernand Boverat campaigned for national and religious education as the solution to the population problem. He combined Catholic notions of women's destiny with scientific arguments about the biological necessity of childbirth and was among the first to blame women rather than men for *dénatalité*. In Lyon, August Isaac, who would in future lead the FR, encouraged Progressists to embrace familialism and pro-natalism.[92]

Conflicts concerning state intervention divided reformers. Orthodox liberals believed that private initiative could organize society.[93] On the important issue of retirement pensions they wanted a scheme organized by mutualist societies, and condemned compulsion as 'Socialist and German'. The liberal Progressist Roche held that legislation could resolve neither demographic nor social problems; only moral education could change behaviour. He also condemned income tax, and favoured tax cuts to encourage the 'laborious classes'. Liberals insisted that expansion of production would ultimately defuse the class struggle. In the meantime, coordination of anti-strike action was an important function of business organization.[94] Renault felt that the class struggle would last as long as workers remained uneducated;

[89] Janet Horne, *A Social Laboratory for Modern France: The Musée Social and the Rise of the Welfare State* (Chicago, 2002), 165–82.

[90] *L'Alliance républicaine démocratique*, August 1907.

[91] *L'Alliance républicaine démocratique*, 2 January 1913.

[92] Cheryl Koos, 'Engendering reaction: the politics of pronatalism and the family in France, 1919–1944', PhD dissertation, University of Southern California, 1996, 22–8; Richard Tomlinson, 'The politics of *dénatalité* during the French Third Republic 1890–1940', PhD dissertation, University of Cambridge, 1983, 53–5; Bernard, *La dérive*, 214.

[93] *Correspondance d'Union républicaine*, 16 April 1908.

[94] Edward Shorter and Charles Tilly, *Strikes in France, 1830–1968* (London, 1974), 34.

until then, force was the only option.[95] In contrast, conservative Social Catholics advocated limited state support for paternalist reform and corporatism, while advanced Social Catholics advocated independent workers' unions and compulsory reforms.

Significantly, some Social Catholics began to work through centre groups—Lemire was the best known—and opened up to secular social science and state intervention. In the 1890s, the Christian Democrats' aggressive confessionalism and racism had prevented collaboration with Republicans. Now, depoliticization of Social Catholicism created new possibilities. Social Catholics regarded themselves as technicians possessed of competence, whose objective was to create material circumstances in which spiritual life could flourish. Consequently, the ACJF, Chronique sociale, and Sillon combined lay social science with Catholic objectives. The Catholic Charles-Brun, who joined the Alliance démocratique, held that democracy derived not from the abstract equality of individuals, but from recognition of 'social facts' that issued from the 'thread of history'.[96] The laicization and professionalization of Catholic social work after the Separation also brought social science into the women's movement. Social Catholics and Centrists from de Mun and the crypto-Royalist Hyacinthe Gailhard-Bancel to centrists such as Jules Siegfried and Barthou had come to agree with the left that compulsory pensions were necessary.[97]

Some Centrists saw Social Catholicism as dangerous. *Le Temps* regarded the 'anarchist' doctrines of the Semaines sociales as a sign that the Church aimed to 'flatter the people in order to re-conquer it'. Worse, seconding CGT demands risked worsening social conflict. The FR sometimes praised Social Catholics, but one journalist described Lemire as 'a Gallican among Catholics and a Frenchman of Germany'.[98]

These conflicts did not break up the emergent conservative alignment—indeed, the pension law passed nearly unanimously, for it eventually combined limited state support with compulsion and mutualism. Depoliticization ensured that Social Catholicism could not easily challenge the leadership of the right. In practice, Social Catholics, both conservative and progressive, accepted centre leadership.

THE RIGHT AND THE EXTREME RIGHT

The strength of centre-dominated conservatism weakened the extreme right. However, some of the latter's themes chimed with divisions among parliamentary conservatives, especially social and religious. In the late 1900s, conservative Catholics had to choose

[95] Aimée Moutet, 'Les Origines du système de Taylor en France. Le Point de vue patronal (1907–1914)', *Le Mouvement social* 93 (October–December 1975), 15–50 at 35, 40–1.

[96] Bernard, *La Dérive*, 216; Wright, *The Regionalist Movement*, 205–6; Yves Palau, 'Des Catholiques et de la politique. Les Transformations doctrinales du catholicisme social 1900–1930', *Revue française d'histoire des idées politiques* 4 (1996), 317–44.

[97] *La République française*, 7 August 1908; *Correspondance d'Union républicaine*, 29 March 1910; Louis Barthou, *La Politique de prévoyance sociale* (Paris, 1913), 231; Stone, *The Search*, 122; Horne, *A Social Laboratory*, 208–23; Sanson, *L'Alliance*, 317–21.

[98] *Le Temps* 10 August, 5 January 1910; Martin, *Albert de Mun*, 203–13, 238, 274–7; *Correspondance d'Union républicaine*, 20 February 1908, 16 December 1909.

between potentially sterile opposition and support for governments in which they could not participate and whose solutions to the social question often seemed worse than the problem. Moreover, the centre's anticlericalism hardly softened as it moved rightwards, and so most ALP deputies refused to follow de Mun in backing Poincaré's government because it reaffirmed the lay laws. In March 1912, Poincaré famously declared himself separated from the Progressist Benoist by the religious question. In the ensuing controversy, de Mun acknowledged the cleavage, but suggested that he and Poincaré shared nationalism.[99] Poincaré responded that Catholics were part of the nation, but since toleration made religion a private matter, opponents of the Separation were intolerant and, implicitly, not 'national'.[100] Only after Poincaré condemned anti-militarist and anti-religious teachers' unions did the ALP begin to praise his nationalism. Yet in a private letter de Mun confirmed to Poincaré that they understood pacification differently. For the relatively flexible Xavier de La Rochefoucauld, secretary-general of the ALP, Poincaré could not understand that while the Pope was the sovereign in a complete hierarchical society, Catholics could accept lay schools if Catholics could teach in them and if the state funded Catholic schools. Piou retorted that while Rochefoucauld was correct in principle, his ideal of liberty was not shared in Catholic universities and even less in monastic cells.[101]

Meanwhile, Nationalists, hard-line Catholics, and even Monarchists began to join the Fédération.[102] In the 1910 elections, the Fédération supported Barrès and Millevoye in Paris.[103] Following their subsequent failure to form an autonomous group in parliament, more Nationalists joined the Fédération. Some soon left, but the Nationalist Maurice Spronck became a regular contributor to *La République française*. In 1910, François de Wendel, a Lorraine steel magnate of Nationalist and Legitimist background, joined the Fédération. This influx marked the party. It condemned AF outrages while refusing to exaggerate them, and appealed to Catholics to abandon Royalism, while criticizing the lay laws in the name of liberalism.[104] There was no mistaking the Catholicization of the Fédération. In Roubaix, Motte was defeated in 1906 and 1912 because anticlerical small shopkeepers deserted to the SFIO.[105] In the Rhône, Aynard still defended *laïcité*, but took a leading role in 'non-clerical' associations of fathers' of families that promoted Catholic schools.[106]

Some Fédération activists resisted this evolution towards Catholics and Nationalists, which the emphasis on the primacy of 'economics' in the organizational movement seemed to favour. In Lyon, some activists fought the ALP in the name of Clemenceau; in the Beaujolais, the Progressist Villefranche bourgeoisie preferred

[99] *L'Écho de Paris*, 11 March 1912. [100] *L'Écho de Paris*, 12 March 1912.

[101] ANFXR, 14/1, 1 October 1913, Piou to Rochefoucauld, 8 October 1913.

[102] Bernard, *La Dérive*, 200.

[103] Bernard, 'La Diffusion incomplète', 152–3; Vavasseur-Desperriers, 'Associations politiques', 131–5.

[104] Gordon, *Liberalism*, 144–8, 161–2; *Correspondance d'Union républicaine*, 31 December 1908, 25 February, 9 September 1909, 28 October 1909.

[105] Gordon, *Liberalism*, 64–6, 73–5.

[106] Édouard Aynard, *Discours prononcés à la Chambre des députés de 1893 à 1913* (Paris, 1920), 24 June 1910, 247–69.

rural Radicals to Catholic landowners.[107] Nationally, Joseph Thierry urged acceptance of Briand's 'appeasement' policy, and in November 1910 asked his party to accept the lay laws. In March 1911, thirty deputies joined his revived Union républicaine in parliament, which, he claimed, represented Progressism better than the forty-five strong Groupe Progressiste. Related to Thierry's political grievances were tensions around the organizational project. Thierry disliked the increasing influence among Progressists of Roche's *La République française*, with its strategy of linking right and centre through business groups.[108] Thus, when Clément urged the Fédération to head a crusade against anticlericalism, Jacques Quantin, close to Roche, retorted that the 'interested parties'—i.e. business—should defend themselves, rather than follow 'outdated organizations fit only to resume adventures that have never attracted a following'.[109] Quantin was active in one business group, the ADCM.

In this struggle, Thierry was the loser. The parties had been decisively weakened, and many of his fellow dissidents in the FR were more conservative than him: the right-wing Benoist drafted the Union républicaine's programme. Thierry left the Fédération in December 1911 and later joined the Alliance; in the 1914 Chamber, with some of his allies, he joined a centre group, the Gauche démocratique. Other rebels rejoined the Progressists. From 1914, Benoist's presidency firmly anchored the Fédération on the right. He advocated far-reaching constitutional reform.[110]

The increasingly reactionary stance of the ALP did not discourage those Progressists who advocated alliance with it. Piou moved closer to Royalists and in 1910 addressed a Royalist meeting in Bordeaux. De Mun hesitated between backing centre governments for their nationalism and his suspicion that whichever Republican governed, Freemasonry would really rule. Auguste Cavalier, increasingly prominent in the ALP, embraced xenophobic nationalism and denounced excessive naturalizations, Freemasons, and Jews. Denys Cochin and others returned to Royalism and attempted to create a Catholic party, while La Rochefoucauld vainly fought for alliance with Republicans.[111]

Meanwhile, an unexpected Bonapartist revival linked the parliamentary and extreme rights, and in the coming decades, Bonapartists would contribute significantly to debates on political organization. Younger Bonapartists around Paul Cassagnac junior, Le Provost de Launay, and the Marquis de Dion, integrated Bonapartism into a broader authoritarian, plebiscitary conservatism, without entirely breaking with their pretender. The new generation also included Pierre Taittinger, future leader of the Jeunesses patriotes (JP), then of the Jeunesses plébiscitaires. After 1903, the reconstituted Appel au peuple imposed itself against the

[107] Bernard, *La Dérive*, 226–38.

[108] Gilles Le Béguec, 'Les Deux scissions du groupe progressiste (1905–1911)', *Revue du Nord* 89, no. 370 (2007), 363–75; Jean Vavasseur-Desperriers, 'Cultures, structures, stratégie d'une organisation de la droite parlementaire entre les deux guerres. La Fédération républicaine de 1919 à 1940', thèse de doctorat, Lille III, 1999, 84–91.

[109] *Correspondance d'Union républicaine*, 7 March 1911.

[110] *Correspondance d'Union républicaine*, 15 November 1910, 4 April 1911; Vavasseur-Desperriers, 'Cultures, structures, stratégie', 89–90.

[111] Martin, *Albert de Mun*, 218–22, 238–40.

pro-dynastic *L'Autorité* and the Comité politique plebiscitaire. The Bonapartists were more open to electoralism than the AF, which they often fought in the streets. They cooperated with the increasingly moderate Ligue des patriotes, while Déroulède moved closer still to Bonapartists. The latter won seats on the Paris Municipal Council, and, in 1914, they claimed twenty-one deputies, although Taittinger narrowly lost in still-Bonapartist Cognac, where he had stood on a plebiscitary, free-trade platform and backed the Three-Year Law.[112]

Action Française

AF too backed the Three-Year Law, but was also a refuge for those most intransigently opposed to the Republic. Like its Royalist precursors, AF hesitated between alliance with moderates around issues such as the Three-Year Law, a *coup d'état*, preservation of the ideal pending the inevitable disintegration of the regime, hastening collapse through the *politique du pire*, and/or alliance with the extreme left.

Religious tension offered hope of attracting Catholics. In the Inventories Crisis, the hitherto marginal AF proved to hard-line Catholics that it was the Church's firmest defender. Subsequently, AF took an extreme position in a campaign against anti-religious school textbooks, and used the Pope's insistence on Catholic unity to infiltrate bodies such as the Associations de pères de famille. Maurras' atheism hardly mattered to Catholics. After all, many of his lieutenants were believers, and members were unaware that in 1913 the Pope secretly condemned some of Maurras' works.[113] Furthermore, the Vatican's declining enthusiasm for the ALP encouraged Royalists, as did the appointment of Monarchists to the episcopate, made possible by the Separation. At least three Cardinals sympathized with AF—Sévin of Lyon, Cabrières of Montpellier, and Andrieu of Bordeaux. The loss of state funding for the clergy made parishes more reliant upon rich, often Royalist, parishioners.

AF's Catholic strategy attracted Legitimists. For the Mayenne nobility, AF became the sole means of affirming Royalism at a time when so many Orleanists and some Legitimists had rallied to the Republic. Landowning nobles dominated the league, which in Mayenne included few bourgeois, let alone workers. They were more faithful to Legitimism than to Maurrassianism, rejecting individualism, freedom of conscience, and popular sovereignty because authority came from God. They preferred the Œuvre des cercles to the Camelots du Roi.[114] Wherever AF prospered, from the Beaujolais, via Montpellier, to Loire-Inférieure, Legitimist women were involved. The first AF section in the west was formed at Saint-Brieuc following a lecture by the duchesse de MacMahon to the Oeuvre de Notre-Dame de France. Women's groups affiliated to the LFF, which benefited from transfers from

[112] Jean Philippet, 'Le Temps des ligues. Pierre Taittinger et les Jeunesses patriotes', thèse de doctorat, IEP Paris, 2000, 105–11.

[113] Jacques Prévotat, *Les Catholiques et l'Action française. Histoire d'une condemnation* (Paris, 2001), 144–61.

[114] Michel Denis, *Les Royalistes de la Mayenne et le monde moderne (XIXe–XXe siècles)* (Le Mans, 1977), 513–18.

the Rallié LPDF.[115] The *mondaine* Jeunes filles royalistes eschewed Republican café politics but were among the most active groups. AF also recruited from the Catholic bourgeoisie, notably the legal and medical professions of Montpellier. The Société des jurisconsultes catholiques was an AF stronghold. Nobles sought to extend their influence through involvement in Catholic oeuvres, agricultural unions, and the regionalist movement.

AF placed particular emphasis on spreading its ideas in elite circles, but the notion that AF insidiously 'corrupted' Republicanism requires qualification, for AF also shared much with Republicans, and presented an alternative organizational project. As Paul Bourget put it, AF would 'take science [heredity, race, and selection] from the Revolutionaries', and show that it endorsed aristocracy and tradition. Bourget agreed with the Montpellier Royalist physician, Joseph Grasset, that society was an organism, but that only tradition could provide morality—in other words, Catholicism underpinned organic hierarchy. Bourget preferred 'male, aristocratic, hierarchical' Catholicism to 'sentimental feminine, bourgeois' religion, and yet idealized the semi-noble *rentier* bourgeoisie.[116] In effect, AF redefined organization: instead of the slogan 'PR in the organized region' it proposed 'the profession represented in the organized region'. AF maintained that the collaboration of provinces and nationalities created France.

Appropriation of Republican intellectual and political culture risked undermining the integrity of AF doctrine. Maurras attempted to ward off the danger by enforcing purity within the movement, while allowing flexibility to fellow-travellers. Thus, in 1906, the Institut d'Action française opened, along with the publishing house, the *Nouvelle librairie nationale*. Prominent intellectuals joined AF, including Léon Daudet in 1905 and Jules Lemaître in 1908. The daily *L'Action française* (1908) was a platform for Maurras and Daudet, while the fellow-travelling *Revue critique* (1908) defended neo-classicism against romanticism. Yet influences did not go in one direction. AF had no monopoly on literary neo-classicism, also advocated by the *Nouvelle revue française* (1909) and the independent Socialist, Joseph Paul-Boncour. Bourget was closer to his eclectic literary friends than to the Camelots.[117] Moderate Republicans did not uncritically assimilate AF ideas. A Progressist journalist admitted to reading *L'Action française* for its style and out of respect for those who broke bones in adventures instead of fattening themselves on politics, but dismissed rule by 'fossilized' aristocrats.[118] Politically, AF wavered between defensive purity, alliance with the left, and participation in a centre-led nationalist coalition.

In theory, discipline preserved AF from contamination in such enterprises. For AF politics were the terrain of disciplined minorities, who would capture the state

[115] Bruno Dumons, *Les Dames de la Ligue des femmes françaises (1901–1914)* (Paris, 2006).

[116] Philippe Secondy, 'La "Science traditionaliste" du docteur Joseph Grasset. Une Légitimité intellectuelle pour l'Action française', in Sylvain Crépon (ed.), *Sciences sociales au prisme de l'extrême droite* (Paris, 2008), 133–58; Yehoshua Mathias, 'Paul Bourget. Écrivain engagé', *Vingtieme siècle* 45, no. 1 (1995), 14–29 at 15–16.

[117] Mathias, 'Paul Bourget', 18.

[118] *La République française*, 4 April, 30 May 1910.

through a coup. The purpose of the Ligue d'Action française, created in 1906, was merely to raise funds for the *Revue d'Action française*, while the Camelots du Roi, founded in 1908 and led by Maurice Pujo, hawked it in the streets. Nevertheless, the Camelots were very active. Within a year, there were sixty-five sections in the country, and 600 members in Paris. They recruited largely from students, but included some petty bourgeois. In the Gard and Hérault, AF membership was somewhat more popular. The Camelots were at the forefront of AF demonstrations, usually on highly charged occasions, such as the twelfth anniversary of Dreyfus' degradation in 1907 and the Panthéonization of Zola in 1908. AF also demonstrated against 'anti-national' professors in the Latin Quarter.[119]

In fact, AF tried to reach the mass through an updated version of the *politique du pire*, and that too created exchanges with Republicanism and even Socialism. Historiographical attention has focussed especially on advances to syndicalists—the left-wing trade union movement that advocated trade-union Socialism and opposed parliamentary action. Initially, AF had participated in the general enthusiasm for the Jaunes, but from 1908 it abandoned them for syndicalism. The Camelots were particularly enthusiastic, protecting Léon Daudet as he preached antisemitism in working-class districts. *L'Action française* reported strikes sympathetically, while Georges Valois, a former anarcho-syndicalist who had joined AF in 1906, courted syndicalist intellectuals. He informed workers that their enemy was not the bourgeoisie, but Maurras' 'confederated estates': Jews, Protestants, Freemasons, and foreigners. More originally, Valois argued that a monarch would confine the bourgeoisie to its productive vocation and allow unions to seek better conditions for workers. Valois was indebted to Georges Sorel's conviction that fear of syndicalism would revive combativeness in the bourgeoisie. He also shared Sorel's debt to Le Bon's idea of the active elite. Similarly, a Montpellier Royalist urged formation of an elite resembling the crusading military orders, for since Republican power depended on the 'grip of their doctrines on the mass', Royalists must use identical methods.[120] As for Sorel, in 1908–1909 he was abandoning syndicalist class struggle for nationalism, of which AF might be a vehicle. He approved restoration in principle, but doubted its practicality. Valois' most striking success was the conversion of Sorel's disciple, Édouard Berth, with whom he founded a social study group, the Cercle Proudhon in 1912.[121]

In 1910–1911, the syndicalist strategy appeared to be working, especially in the controversy surrounding claims that Jewish funders had obliged *Humanité* to betray the 1910 rail strike. In 1911, AF joined forces with Gustave Hervé's *Guerre sociale* to force cancellation of Henri Bernstein's 'Jewish' play, 'Après moi'. In the wake of that success, some workers, as well as the leader of the CGT electrical

[119] Eugen Weber, *Action française: Royalism and Reaction in Twentieth-Century France* (Stanford, 1962), 50–6.

[120] Secondy, *La Persistence*, 174–9.

[121] Allen Douglas, *From Fascism to Libertarian Communism: Georges Valois against the Third Republic* (Berkeley, 1992), 19–33; Michael B. Loughlin, 'Gustave Hervé's transition from socialism to national socialism. Another example of French fascism', *Journal of Contemporary History* 36, no. 1 (2001), 5–39; Paul Mazgaj, *The Action française and Revolutionary Syndicalism* (Chapel Hill, 1979).

union, participated in an anti-Masonic and antisemitic rally. However, AF contacts did not extend beyond a minority of syndicalist leaders who shared its liking for the *politique du pire*. Most workers rejected monarchy and did not distinguish Jewish from gentile employers. Moreover, from 1912, industrial strife declined and public attention turned to international affairs. AF began to see strikes as a national danger, and they supported the Three-Year Law, which syndicalists opposed.[122]

Nevertheless, AF's syndicalist strategy was important. First, it set radical against conservative Royalists. In October 1910, AF condemned the 'Jewish sword' of the generals who put down the railway strike. The horrified pretender withdrew support from AF, while the Marquis La Tour du Pin, a representative of dynastic monarchism within AF, opposed Valois' Cercle Proudhon project. In April 1911, the pretender won a pyrrhic victory. In return for Maurras' submission, he wound up Royalist committees and appointed regional delegates sympathetic to AF. Orleanists refused to serve, although a few liberal Monarchists, notably Cochin, remained in parliament. AF continued the syndicalist strategy, and Maurras backed Valois against La Tour du Pin in the Cercle Proudhon dispute. From the ephemeral Cercle emerged ideas that some have seen as pre-fascist.[123]

Secondly, the syndicalist strategy compromised AF's alternative organizational project. On the one hand, Maurras preferred hierarchical corporatism, close to that of Gailhard-Bancel and de Mun. He also distrusted neo-Royalist syndicalists for their admiration of Sorelian pragmatism, which offended his taste for order and threatened to alienate Catholics. Maurras backed Valois only because he thought that syndicalism might bring the regime down. On the other hand, Valois espoused a syndicalist form of organization. He may have been influenced by the evolution of the CGT, in which, after 1910, Alphonse Merrheim and Francis Delaisi argued that workers could not rely simply on decentralized unions and élan; they must imitate the complex centralized organization of the modern factory. Delaisi, in particular, combined preoccupation with factory management with anti-parliamentarianism, antisemitism, and hostility to reformist Socialism, themes that would become important to Valois. Both Maurrassian corporatism and Valoisian syndicalism contradicted the mainstream organizational programme.[124]

Thirdly, right–left alliances were far from unusual; a Fédération journalist commented, 'the method lacks originality as much as novelty', while another claimed that Catholics hated Radicals so much that they routinely voted for Socialists against them.[125] Boulangism and then the 'Pacte de Bordeaux' in the 1890s were particularly striking examples of the meeting of extremes. More recently, the Midi rebellion inaugurated cooperation of Royalists and Socialists against Radical Freemasonry.[126] Again, in 1910, Socialists and Progressists agreed mutual withdrawal in favour of proportionalists, a policy that the Alliance hardly appreciated.[127]

[122] Mazgaj, *Action française*, 128–72.
[123] Sternhell, *Ni droite*, 172–4.
[124] Weber, *Action française*, 55–61.
[125] *Correspondance d'Union républicaine*, 17 September 1908, 31 October 1911.
[126] Sagnes, *Le Midi rouge*, 252–5.
[127] Sanson, *L'Alliance*, 188; Bernard, *La Dérive*, 203.

Meanwhile, de Mun hesitated between backing centre governments' nationalism and the belief that Christian fraternity and dissemination of Christian morality in the schools was a more effective answer to working-class unrest than force. Increasingly radical, he blamed strikes on selfish employers, endorsed independent unions, and accepted the right of civil servants to strike.[128] The Vatican hinted that de Mun's social policy was modernist. Conservative Catholics and Moderate Republicans agreed that de Mun was as bad as the Socialists were.[129]

Moderates feared a clerical–syndicalist alliance, real and imaginary. The Fédération evoked the memory of aristocratic recruitment of ruffians to assault the bourgeoisie and make a white revolution.[130] The Alliance claimed that 'the extremes touch, and that produces a black anarchy that has nothing to learn from the other red anarchy'. The 1907 rebellion confirmed Alliance fears, for (using Le Bon's concepts), 'the parties of reaction and revolution wanted to profit from the popular exaltation they had provoked in order to fish in troubled waters'.[131] This does not mean that there was an 'essential' unity of the extremes against a well-entrenched Republican consensus. There were multiple possibilities and circumstances determined whether the affinities developed into actual alliances. AF's Catholic strategy confirmed the extent of tensions within the conservative alliance, while the syndicalist opening expressed frustrations at the strength of parliamentary conservatism. Yet the Three-Year Law confirmed the predominance of the centre–right alliance.

ORGANIZING THE NATION

In the last two years of peace, Poincaré epitomized the 'national revival' that crowned the conservative organizational strategy. His relative effacement since 1895 and his distance from the Dreyfus Affair lent him an independent air, while his apparent preference for the Bar over the Chamber gave him generalist credentials. The fact that a serving Président du conseil, whose belief in the need for a stronger executive was well known, should have stood for the Présidence de la République contradicted the expectation that the position was purely ceremonial. Poincaré negotiated secretly with the right to secure his victory.[132]

Just before he became président, Poincaré announced the three-year military service bill. The *Trois ans* brought together several themes of the organizational movement: nationalism, Social Darwinism, military strength, and pro-natalism. Its advocates held that in the age of democracy clashes of massive armies would settle wars. A Progressist deputy and member of the ANPAPF told parliament that since all Europeans were of the same race, 'force is proportional to number. It is simple and certain.' During the 1914 election campaign, the ANPAPF distributed 1.5 million tracts, linking population and military issues.[133] Also, the

[128] *L'Écho de Paris*, 11 January, 8 March 1910.
[129] *Le Temps* 10 August, 5 January 1910; Martin, *Albert de Mun*, 203–13, 238, 274–7.
[130] *Correspondance d'Union républicaine*, 17 September 1908.
[131] *L'Alliance démocratique*, 3 February 1907, 23 June 1907.
[132] Martin, *Albert de Mun*, 258–60.
[133] Tomlinson, 'The disappearance of France', 48, 62.

doctrine of attack emphasized the instilment of morale in the troops and thus required longer service. Following Le Bon, officers wished to harness the élan and initiative of the 'crowd-troop' to the offensive, while organizing it through repetitive drill. The officer, like the statesman, required both distance from his men and understanding of their psychology. The attack was more than a military tactic: it was an organizational strategy and the antidote to degeneration.[134]

There were differences in the emergent nationalist alignment. Symbolically, Poincaré defined his nationalism in a speech to the Ligue de l'enseignement, a pillar of *laïcité*. The nation, he explained, was a scientific fact, a 'perfectly determined organism', observable in psychology, for human beings instinctively loved the soil in which they were rooted and understood that their territory was part of a whole. Although all nations were racially diverse in origin, 'a long existence in common, the influence of the soil and the climate and identical morals ultimately created in the human type distinct, and perfectly recognisable categories', which were as meaningful as the German's division between brachycephals and dolichocephals. The monarchy had developed national feeling, but the Revolution ended the confusion between nation and the monarch. Poincaré's evocation of monarchy and blood and soil reached out to the right and to Nationalists.[135]

Poincaré differed from the right in the characteristics he ascribed to the French. He saw the country as naturally universalist; it promoted liberty, justice, and solidarity in the world. Just as love of one's family taught love of the nation, so love of the nation taught love of humanity. Poincaré added that Republican schools would educate children in patriotism and universalism; otherwise, patriotism would become chauvinism.[136] Vigorous defence of French interests was compatible with international cooperation. Indeed, many centrists, while rejecting unconditional pacifism, approved the movement around the Senator Paul d'Estournelles de Constant for international arbitration, economic cooperation, and European unity. Similarly, Charles-Brun defended regionalism as a manifestation of the brotherhood of peoples.[137] Subsequently, Socialist internationalism and the need for allies on the right caused the centre's faith in international cooperation to decline, but its nationalism was never identical to that of the right.

Compare Poincaré's thinking with that of the ALP. The latter was in one sense inclusive; Secretary-General La Rochefoucauld argued that religious liberty would 'seal forever the reconciliation of all Frenchmen'.[138] Yet more than in the early 1900s, de Mun saw patriotism as fundamentally Catholic.[139] France was the eldest daughter of the Church and only religion could teach the spirit of self-sacrifice on

[134] Benoît Marpeau, *Gustave Le Bon. Parcours d'un intellectuel, 1841–1931* (Paris, 2000), 271–302; Gerd Khrumreich, *Armaments and Politics in France on the Eve of the First World War* (Oxford, 1985); Jean-Jacques Becker, 'Les "Trois ans" et les débuts de la première guerre mondiale', *Guerres mondiales et conflits contemporains* 37, no. 145 (January 1987), 145, 7–26.

[135] Poincaré, *L'Idée de la patrie*, 5–13.

[136] Poincaré, *L'Idée de la patrie*, 7–8, 19–21.

[137] Sanson, *L'Alliance*, 377–8; Wright, *The Regionalist Movement*, 95.

[138] ANFXLR 14/1, note of 23 June 1913.

[139] *La Croix*, 5 February 1908.

which patriotism depended. Catholics must lead France to new patriotism, which would give the Church new influence. For de Mun, Catholic schools would teach children to give France 'their strength, their labour, their blood if necessary, and the example of their lives'; the ALP, not to speak of the Progressists, tirelessly denounced anti-patriotic state school teachers. De Mun rejected Poincaré's humanism. War was an instrument of divine justice that would punish and regenerate decadent France. He hoped that it would come sooner rather than later.[140] A few days before war began, the ex-Nationalist, now Progressist, Admiral Bienaimé claimed that humanity could not exist as a pacific entity.[141]

This belief in the regenerative potential of war was part of a broader interest in physical culture, an ideal rooted in the classical tradition of the healthy mind in the healthy body, and thus in the generalist ethos of conservatism. Agathon's *Les jeunes gens d'aujourd'hui* (1914) stressed the importance of sport for virility and claimed that modern youth read *L'Auto*, not the *Revue des deux mondes*. In 1911, Paul Leroy Beaulieu worried that too much mothering undermined manhood. Such thinking converged with syndicalist intellectuals' belief in bourgeois regeneration through violence, and thus with Bergsonism.[142] It also possessed an anti-parliamentarian potential. Colonel Driant (ALP) wrote 'The capital question is unity of command. Deliberation is the action of several, a thing of peacetime; action is another matter, and this other thing is a fact of wartime, the fact of a single man.'[143] Driant did not explicitly generalize from the military to the political, but during the War many conservatives would do so.

CONCLUSION

The story of the Fédération des gauches (FDG) confirmed the centre's pre-eminence, the parties' weakness, and tensions among conservatives. Briand, Millerand, and Barthou announced the FDG on 26 December 1913. They intended to rally a coalition around the themes of Poincaré's coalition—toleration and *laïcité*, PR, and the Three-Year Law. The creation of this new centre group underlined the problems of the Alliance. Two years previously, an admittedly unsympathetic Progressist had claimed that it would 'not have trouble dying, since it already plays the part of the suicide by persuasion'.[144] Since a considerable number of its parliamentarians backed the FDG, the Alliance had to endorse the new organization.[145]

[140] Martin, *Albert de Mun*, 214–17, 277.

[141] *Libre Parole*, 13 July 1914, 1 August 1914.

[142] Christopher E. Forth, *The Dreyfus Affair and the Crisis of French Manhood* (Baltimore, 2004), 230–1.

[143] Daniel David, 'Le Lieutenant-colonel Driant', *Revue historique des armées* 160 (1985), 84–95 at 90.

[144] *Correspondance d'Union républicaine*, 31 October 1911.

[145] Sanson, *L'Alliance*, 399–401.

The FDG's equation of Republicanism with *laïcité* excluded most Progressists.[146] Notwithstanding, de Mun and Piou hoped to include Catholics in it. They tried to persuade the Vatican that a struggle on the religious terrain would fail and that conservative divisions meant that victory would be sterile. De Mun warned that even the population of Catholic regions disliked clerical involvement in elections and that Royalism was so unpopular that few deputies dared openly express their views.[147] Yet in December 1913, the Royalist Colonel Keller announced a Catholic electoral committee, under the patronage of the Archbishop of Lyon. The Vatican advised both alliance with moderates and first-ballot support for any Catholic candidate, whatever their politics.[148] Not surprisingly, the FDG rejected ALP overtures. Religion remained a marker between the right and centre.

Although in 1914 nationalism united the right and centre, its electoral advantages were debatable. In the Rhône, conservative candidates avoided mention of the unpopular *Trois ans*. Nationally, the left won a majority and the *troisannistes* lost fifty seats, but there was a majority in favour of the law.[149] We have already noted the poor shape of the right proper, compensated by the resolute conservatism of the centre, and the development of informal ties between conservative politicians, business, social, and academic institutions, and by common commitment to organization and nationalism. Organizationalism, which would be modified by the experience of war, was henceforth central to conservative politics. The concomitant expansion of the centre vote in 1914 and the decline of Alliance seats underline the importance of informal ties through the organizational movement.

Indeed, Poincaré's determination to be a strong president was a product of organizational thinking, and it influenced the outcome of the ministerial crisis that followed the elections. He pressed for a centre ministry under the moderate Progressist Alexandre Ribot, and considered dissolution. Yet the centre would only accept Progressist and ALP support if counterbalanced by Radical ministers, while the latter would not accept Catholic participation. The left saw Poincaré's intervention as a deliberate affront to universal suffrage, and the Chamber rejected Ribot.[150] Yet the Chamber accepted the Independent Socialist René Viviani, whose declaration was similar to Ribot's. Viviani won the right's abstention by agreeing not to repeal the *Trois ans* and gained the left's goodwill by promising income tax—a proposal that had gained ground in the centre. The Socialists and ALP were excluded from a majority in which the axis had shifted back to the moderate left. Yet elitist centre politicians represented a credible conservative alternative to the left, and in the course of the Great War they would abandon their reticence regarding the ALP and become the core of a genuine conservative coalition.

[146] Martin, *Albert de Mun*, 282–6.

[147] ANFXLR 14/1, Piou to La Rochefoucauld, 6 April 1913; de Mun to Rampolla, 17 December 1913.

[148] ANFXLR 14/1, Rochefoucauld to Pacelli, 19 February 1914.

[149] Bernard, *La Dérive*, 210–11; Jean-Jacques Becker, *1914: Comment les Français sont entrés dans la guerre* (Paris, 1977), 20–52; Anderson, 'The right and the social question', 129–30.

[150] Becker, *1914*, 81–2.

8

The Union Sacrée (1914–1918)

> We accept without protest the humiliation that there are no more parties just as the justification for our own shines through.
>
> Louis Latapie, 20 December 1914

As German armies crossed the frontier, President Poincaré declared that 'nothing would break the sacred union [Union sacrée] of the French people'. Centre, right, and extreme right all rallied to René Viviani's government of the moderate left. On 2 August, *L'Alliance démocratique* announced that it would forget party politics and back national defence, while the Progressists lauded the patriotism of *instituteurs* and priests.[1] De Mun evoked the 'sacred vengeance that the prophets of Israel taught to God's people',[2] while *Action française* removed the usual Antidreyfusard slogan from its front page, and Maurras declared that the War had caused the *pays réel* to displace the *pays légal*. In 1916, Maurice Barrès published *Les Diverses familles spirituelles de la France*, celebrating the contribution to the War effort of 'all moral forces'—including Judaism.[3]

During the War, conservatives backed governments in which they were poorly represented—expansion of the government's base on 26 August had already suggested that national unity extended further left than right. Nevertheless, to win conservative support, Interior Minister Louis Malvy suspended school closures and allowed exiled religious orders to return. The government also resisted Radical and Socialist demands for parliamentary oversight of the War effort, and left conduct of the War to the 'competent'—War Minister Alexandre Millerand and Commander-in-Chief Joseph Joffre. Furthermore, conservatives had long viewed Viviani's successor (from October 1916), Aristide Briand, favourably. The latter improved his credit by increasing Progressist representation and adding Denys Cochin to the government, the first Monarchist to hold office since 1877. Briand's heir, Alexandre Ribot (from March 1917), a moderate, secular Progressist, was the most right-wing Président du conseil since Méline.

In 1917, in the midst of military and social crisis, the axis of the Union sacrée shifted decisively to the centre and right. Failure to break the stalemate on the Western Front had discredited successive governments; military disaster at the Chemin des Dames in the spring provoked mutinies in the Army as public faith in victory ebbed. Some Radicals, led by Joseph Caillaux, echoed Socialist demands for a

[1] *La République française*, 13 March 1915. [2] *L'Écho de Paris*, 8 August 1914.
[3] Maurice Barrès, *Les Diverses familles spirituelles de la France* (Paris, 1917), 1–2.

negotiated peace, while unrest among workers in the war industries grew. On 16 November, conservatives overthrew the short-lived Paul Painlevé administration—the sole occasion during the War when the Chamber disavowed a government. Although headed by the Radical, Georges Clemenceau, the succeeding administration was frankly conservative. The Socialists and some Radicals went into opposition.

That historians have barely researched the history of conservatism in the Great War has not prevented them from reading great significance into the Union sacrée. Some argue that the War 'modernized' the right; these historians accept contemporary conservative assertions that 'real' social, economic, and international questions had consigned 'anachronistic' religious and constitutional quarrels to the past.[4] Others claim that while the War made some businessmen, intellectuals, and statesmen aware of the dysfunctions of the Republic, politicians of left and right, equally stuck in outdated quarrels, blocked reform.[5] Jean-Jacques Becker's interpretation is the most nuanced: he argues that left and right initially embraced the Union sacrée without abandoning their old squabbles, but the length of the War permitted conflict to re-emerge, and eventually enabled conservatives to appropriate the national idea. However, Becker adds, ordinary people, even strikers and mutineers, remained united behind the war effort. He thus rejoins the familiar idea that the attachment of politicians, including conservatives, to atavistic quarrels isolated them from the 'real world'.[6] Becker rightly argues that conservative acceptance of the Union sacrée did not entail abandonment of anti-socialism, but he underestimates the depth of conflict within France and its impact on politics.

As Becker suggests, conservatives backed the Union sacrée conditionally. The long-enduring illusion that the next offensive would end the war encouraged them to see it as a 'temporary' truce. Anyway, it was difficult to express opposition, for in the first months of fighting, parliament was in recess, newspapers rarely appeared, censorship restricted dissent, and many parliamentarians were mobilized. Locally, conservative parties suspended their activities. In the Rhône, Fédération républicaine activists turned to the administration of their communes and war work. Seven of the fourteen Progressists on the Lyon city council went to fight.[7] The Fédération relied on elderly journalists such as Louis Latapie and mobilized deputies such as Georges Bonnefous to put across its views.

Soon, anti-socialism revived, even more strongly because it was folded into conservatives' views of Germany. Conservatives wholeheartedly embraced, perhaps more than the soldiers, what historians call the 'culture of war'—the belief that France was fighting for civilization against a barbaric racial enemy with which

[4] Michel Winock, *La Fièvre hexagonale. Les Grandes crises politiques 1871–1968* (Paris, 1986), 198–201.

[5] Richard F. Kuisel, *Capitalism and the State in Modern France* (Cambridge, 1981), 31–58.

[6] Jean-Jacques Becker, 'L'Union sacrée… L'Exception qui confirme la règle', *Vingtième siècle* 5, no. 1 (January–March 1985), 111–22; Jean-Jacques Becker, *Les Français dans la Grande Guerre* (Paris, 1983).

[7] Mathias Bernard, *La Dérive des modéré. La Fédération républicaine du Rhône sous la Troisième République* (Paris, 1998), 241–3.

compromise was impossible.[8] This binary opposition jostled with the conviction that Germanic degeneracy had entered France through the left, and so conservatives became convinced that Socialist 'illusions' had reappeared in the 'pro-German' movement for a negotiated peace. They also feared that Socialist demands for industrial mobilization masked their desire for the collectivization of industry—which they saw as a manifestation of their primitive Germanic fetishization of the state. Conservatives regarded the left's campaign for parliamentary inspection of the front as a means to install a Jacobin and Socialist parliamentary dictatorship.

In conformity with their elitist conception of organization, conservatives preferred to leave conduct of the war effort to business, the High Command, and War Ministry—the 'competent'. The War therefore reinforced and pushed rightwards the pre-1914 coalescence of an elitist, bourgeois, male conservatism, henceforth accentuated by the near silence of parties and the increasing importance to conservatives of hierarchical Fayolist managerialism, now coupled with Taylorism, familialism, and schemes for reform of the state and parliament. Conservatives embraced a programme designed to restore the predominance of the male elite in an organic hierarchy in family and economy, improve the quality and quantity of the population, counter degeneration, and defeat Socialism. In the 1917 crisis, conservatives accepted the necessity of total war only on condition that the Socialists quit the Union sacrée.

Thus, left–right polarization was not merely a surface phenomenon. It was entangled with deep divisions in French society. While, as Becker rightly argues, the overwhelming majority of French people wanted to win the War, many were also convinced that 'others' were not doing their bit. According to preference, workers, peasants, unmarried women, soldiers' wives, the rich, Catholics, Socialists, southerners, or northerners were 'embusqués'; that is, they avoided service at the front, and were enjoying themselves or profiting from the War while others suffered. The *chasse aux embusqués* both united the country and generated mutual suspicion, conspiracy, and rumour, inseparable from class, religious, and political conflicts.

A millenarian interpretation of the conflict, in which victory was expected to bring the definitive triumph of the Republic, Church, or Socialism, further embittered conflict. In an atmosphere of spy fever, each identified domestic enemies with foreign powers: Germans, Bolsheviks, or the Papacy. The elites were no less gullible than the masses were. The High Command encouraged local authorities to remove Maggi-Kub posters because they supposedly served as signposts for the invaders.[9] The usually level-headed centrist, Abel Ferry, saw the 'indecent and cynical' conversation of the

[8] Stéphane Audoin-Rouzeau, Annette Becker, and Leonard V. Smith, *France and the Great War* (Cambridge, 2003), 138–45; Annette Becker and Stéphane Audoin-Rouzeau, *14–18, retrouver la guerre* (Paris, 2000); Antoine Prost, 'La Guerre de 1914 n'est pas perdue', *Le Mouvement social* 199, no. 2 (2002), 95–102; Antoine Prost, 'Les Limites de la brutalisation: Tuer sur le front occidental, 1914–1918', *Vingtième siècle* 81, no. 1 (2004), 5–20.

[9] François Bouloc, 'L'Union sacrée des aveyronnais', *Annales du Midi* 112, no. 232 (2000), 447–62 at 452; Eugen Weber, *Action française: Royalism and Reaction in Twentieth-Century France* (Stanford, 1962), 91–2.

alleged spy, Bolo Pasha, as a sign of general corruption.[10] In this atmosphere, conservatives could not completely set aside religious or constitutional questions. Common commitment to victory co-existed with differences concerning both the means to win and the meaning of winning. The very belief of each side that the War *should* have reconciled classes and religions both overcame and intensified conflict, for nobody agreed on the terms of the settlement.

Powerful impulses to conservative unity co-existed with division, and context determined which prevailed. Some tensions persisted, notably concerning religion, but other matters brought right and centre together. They gradually overcame their differences concerning the organization of the war effort, the role of parliament, international relations, and the place of the Socialists in the Union sacrée. In 1917, right and centre came to agree that Socialist presence in the government risked turning effective organization of the war effort into full-scale collectivism. As before 1914, unity under centre leadership predominated, and the centre shifted further right, but Clemenceau's immense credit with public opinion was necessary to cement the majority.

ORGANIZATION

Before 1914, conservative organizationalism largely involved reinforcing contact between big business and parliament, and ensuring that the formless mass did not overwhelm competent and enlightened leadership. With the mobilization of enormous numbers of soldiers and the production of untold quantities of war material, organizationalism shifted from parliament to the military-economic field. Factories were militarized and the front was industrialized. 'Experts' played a greater role in policy formulation, notably at the Army's Grand Quartier Genéral (GQG). Fayolist hierarchies, Taylorist efficiency, and the élan of the attack became integral to organizational thinking and conservatives would apply these notions to parliament.

Before 1914, Fayolism interested a few centre politicians. Now, with the publication of *Administration Industrielle et Générale* (1916), Fayol himself became influential.[11] His system emphasized unity of command, leadership, the visionary qualities of the *chef*, and clear lines of communication. Mixing his metaphors, a journalist who spent the War in the GQG wrote that if 'the machine' was to function correctly, all organs had to be 'absolutely dependent' upon the command system.[12] Fayol himself echoed all the familiar criticisms of parliamentary talking, incompetence, and clientelism. There was little room in his schema for autonomous workers' organizations.

[10] Abel Ferry, *Les Carnets secrets d'Abel Ferry (1914–1918)* (Paris, 1957), 17 October 1917, 196–7.

[11] I disagree on this point with Charles S. Maier, 'Between Taylorism and technocracy: European ideologies and the vision of productivity in the 1920s', *Journal of Contemporary History* 5, no. 2 (1970), 27–61.

[12] Stéphane Rials, *Administration et organisation. De L'Organisation de la bataille à la bataille de l'organisation dans l'administration française* (Paris, 1977), 60–3.

The introduction of F.W. Taylor's methods of rationalized labour into the war industries reinforced these tendencies. Fayol criticized Taylor for giving too much power to engineers and thus dividing authority.[13] Actually, both envisaged a hierarchical separation of knowledge from execution within the industrial 'organism'—Henry Le Chatelier, a Catholic conservative and leading advocate of Taylorism, viewed the workers as an amorphous mass, requiring organization.[14] Like Fayolism, Taylorism straddled the military and economic domains. One observer wrote that 'German drill has imposed on the Army a sort of Taylor system: we know that this system rests on a minute division of labour, specialization, training of all workers, and constant surveillance of the accomplished task'.[15] These ideas began to influence constitutional schemes, undermining older ideas about careful parliamentary debate.

Military tactics also influenced organizationalism. Conservatives largely remained faithful to the doctrine of attack—that is to rapidity and massive force. Huge casualties caused them to insist on 'economy' in the use of military manpower through organization and Taylorization, but only to ensure that attacks were effective.[16] On the eve of Nivelle's disastrous offensive, *L'Alliance démocratique* condemned the war of attrition as a product of the 'law of least effort'.[17] Critics of the High Command emphasized preparation, avoidance of waste, leadership, and rapidity—all notions that were compatible with management science and transferable to politics.

Conservative organizers attempted to balance hierarchy with liberty, as demonstrated in Jean Labadié's 'enquiry' of 1916, conducted in response to German claims to be fighting for the organization of European society. In answer to the question 'is Germany the country of organization?' all the conservative contributors, from Carnot of the Alliance to Maurras, agreed that the French were too individualist. For Maurice Colrat, they had forgotten that nation and state were 'organisms' that had 'reasons to live'. However, he continued, the Union sacrée proved that France possessed an 'instinct and genius' for organization. The Germans, as an inferior race fetishized organization, and thus instituted despotism. The French reconciled order and liberty, and, as Colrat put it, laws for them were disciplines generative of liberty, not shackles.[18] True, Benoist, president of the Fédération républicaine, denied that society was an organism or a machine—he revealed a growing openness to Maurrasian thought—and preferred 'Latin individualism' to inhuman Germanic organization. Yet he too warned against 'excessive individualism' and argued that the French could reconcile liberty and authority because they submitted to a democratic government.[19]

[13] Henri Fayol, *Administration industrielle et générale (prévoyance, organisation, commandement, coordination, contrôle)* (Paris, 1917).
[14] Michel Letté, *Henry Le Chatelier* (Rennes, 2004), 214–16.
[15] *L'Opinion*, 28 October 1916. [16] *L'Opinion*, 28 October 1916.
[17] *L'Alliance démocratique*, 4 March 1917.
[18] Jean Labadié, *L'Allemagne a-t-elle le secret de l'organisation?* (Paris, 1916), ix–xx.
[19] Labadié, *L'Allemagne*, 4–9; *La République française*, 23 September 1918.

Conservatives saw organization of the war economy as necessary, but condemned excessive regulation as 'Germanic' and 'Socialist', and so inclusion of the Socialists in the government was problematic for them. In the first months, the War Ministry devolved power to the High Command and business, especially the Comité des forges. This arrangement was compatible with pre-war schemes for organization, which were designed to avoid state control over industry.[20] Then, from May 1915, the Socialist Albert Thomas took over responsibility for arms production. He built huge state-owned, Taylorized factories, and introduced factory delegates and compulsory arbitration of labour disputes, in the hope of educating a working-class elite that would manage the economy in partnership with the state and organized business.[21] Meanwhile, the pro-Radical centrist, Étienne Clémentel, Minister of Commerce from October 1915, organized the distribution of raw materials. He owed more than Thomas to the Fayolist view that organization of production, rather than wage rises, would assuage working-class discontent. Yet he also saw the state as playing a key role within an economy armed, though rationalization and standardization, for the post-war economic struggle against Germany.[22] In the 1917 crisis, Clémentel paid tribute to the French love of independence, but expected 'total submission to the discipline of the nation'.[23] These developments raised conservative fears that the Union sacrée was a cover for statism and Socialism, while differences among conservatives complicated matters. Centrists and Social Catholics were more willing to accept temporary state involvement in the war economy, and sympathized with certain of Thomas' measures, and even more with Clémentel's schemes. Other conservatives attempted to reconcile organization of the War effort with liberalism.

Many centrists saw state partnership with private initiative as necessary in an age of democratic war and international struggle. They assumed that military war would become economic war, and that France must arm itself for the peace.[24] Doubtless many agreed with Labadié, who argued that modernity no longer meant increasing 'pleasure-wealth' (richesse-jouissance) but the development of 'power-wealth' (richesse-puissance). Through tax incentives, the state must favour capital goods production; in the medium term, imports would decline and 'cosmopolitan finance' would lose its grip on the national economy. Labadié concluded that a 'powerful government must preside over this evolution, imposing sacrifice on the rich and discipline on the workers'.[25] From 1915, the Alliance démocratique demanded industrial mobilization and rationing. In 1918, the president of the Alliance's Industry Committee held that although most regulations would disappear after the War, the state would retain the role of regulator.[26]

[20] Rials, *Administration*, 76–80; Godfrey, *Capitalism at War*, 33–4, 50.

[21] Martin Fine, 'The movement for capital-labor collaboration in France, 1914–1936', PhD dissertation, Wisconsin, 1971, 16–50; Kuisel, *Capitalism*, 31–7, 48–50.

[22] Kuisel, *Capitalism*, 48–50; Godfrey, *French Capitalism*, 70–9, 97.

[23] Godfrey, *French Capitalism*, 97.

[24] *L'Opinion*, 19 March 1917.

[25] *L'Opinion*, 3, 10, 24 June 1916.

[26] *L'Alliance démocratique*, 3 May 1917, 11 July 1915, 24 June 1917, 27 Janaury 1918, 24 March 1918; Victor Boret, *La Bataille économique de demain* (Paris, 1917), 17–33.

The centre was closely linked to business, which had traditionally been part of the Alliance leadership. On resuming activity in October 1916, the party consulted business, notably Forsans of the Union des intérêts économiques (UIE), on the best means of winning the post-war economic battle.[27] Louis Loucheur, the archetypal businessman-technocrat, favoured the centre. He made millions from shell production; his factories sometimes built with government advances. In December 1916, he became undersecretary in Thomas' armaments ministry, and chose collaborators from his own École Polytechnique. Among them were the young Ernest Mercier, Raoul Dautry, and Auguste Detœuf, who, after the War, would all play significant roles in conservative politics. Now they linked military preoccupations with Taylorism and Fayolism.[28]

Historians sometimes depict Polytechniciens as outsiders, unusually conscious of French backwardness.[29] Polytechniciens were indeed open to the wartime discourse of efficiency and rapidity, for their school prided itself that its pupils could solve problems more quickly than anyone else could. They also expected the state to second private initiative.[30] However, Polytechniciens were not marginal, having provided many of France's generals, businessmen, and engineers. They shared the secular-scientific ethos of the regime, even if, like Le Chatelier, they were Catholics. Polytechniciens embraced the generalism of the political mainstream: proficiency in fencing still counted in favour of applicants to the Polytechnique, while Le Chatelier claimed that he had profited from his scientific education only because he was able to express himself agreeably. The Polytechnique defined science widely. The positivism of its former professor, Auguste Comte, still marked it, according to which laws regulated society in the same way that they did natural phenomena, and in our period Le Bon, Spencer, and Darwin still counted.[31] Polytechniciens were also influenced by Lyautey's writings, especially as adapted to the role of the engineer by Émile Cheysson.[32] Dautry admired Sorel and Bergson for their activism in the service of a mystique.[33]

If Polytechniciens were part of broader conservative culture, they placed too much emphasis on the state for orthodox liberals, even if the latter did not reject organization *per se*. Liberals were influential among parliamentary Monarchists,

[27] *L'Alliance démocratique*, 20 October 1918; Rosemonde Sanson, *L'Alliance républicaine démocratique. Une Formation du centre (1901–1920)* (Rennes, 2003), 438–9.

[28] Louis Loucheur, *Carnets secrets 1908–1932* (Brussels, 1962); Stephen Carls, *Louis Loucheur* (Baton Rouge, 1993), 3–110; Godfrey, *French Capitalism*, 192–9; Richard Kuisel, *Ernest Mercier: French Technocrat* (Berkeley, 1967), 1–20; Kuisel, *Capitalism*, 38–9; Richard Kuisel, 'Auguste Detœuf, conscience of French industry', *International Review of Social History* 20 (1975), 150–74; Remi Baudouï, *Raoul Dautry 1880–1951: Le Technocrate de la république* (Paris, 1992), 45–54.

[29] Le Béguec, 'L'Entrée', 646–52; Carls, *Louis Loucheur*, 23–32; Fabienne Bock, *Un Parlementarisme de guerre* (Paris, 2002), 109–19.

[30] Jean Dhombres, 'L'Image "scientiste" de l'École polytechnique', in Bruno Belhoste et al. (eds), *La Formation polytechnicienne 1794–1994* (Paris, 1994), 281–96 at 292–3.

[31] Letté, *Henry Le Chatelier*, 31–2, 214–15; Dhombres, 'L'Image "scientiste"'; André Chervel, 'Les Études littéraires dans la formation polytechnicienne', in *La Formation polytechnicienne*, 121–39.

[32] Yves Cohen, 'Les Polytechniciens dans le discours sur le commandement (1891–1940)', in Bruno Belhoste et al. (eds), *La France des X: Deux siècles d'histoire* (Paris, 1995), 157–68 at 162.

[33] John M. Sherwood, 'Rationalization and railway workers in France. Raoul Dautry and the Chemins de fer de l'État, 1928–1937', *Journal of Contemporary History* 15, no. 3 (1980), 443–74 at 444–5.

Progressists, parts of the centre, and in *Le Temps* and the *Revue des Deux Mondes*. The Alliance was divided between liberals such as Forsans and advocates of regulation, such as Augustin Baudouin, president of the Alliance's Comité républicain des enterprises.[34] Throughout the War, liberals attacked price controls, war-profit taxes, requisition of the merchant fleet, and income tax.[35] It was hard for liberals to deny the need to organize the war effort, because the term covered both specific management methods and the general notion of doing things efficiently. Liberals therefore advocated an alternative version of organization, combining racial struggle, Taylorism, and Fayolism with a greater emphasis on consumption industries, individualism, and French taste. Progressists such as Roche argued that the scope of government must be limited so that the gifted could innovate, for organization must 'develop the virtues of our race, which are not those of the Teuton, but of the Gaulois'.[36] Liberals nevertheless concurred that struggle between economic blocs would continue after the War. Consequently, they urged the government to ensure that consumer industries were well-positoned for this battle.[37] In the first month of War, *Le Temps* urged the government to encourage resumption of non-war-related business activity.[38] Liberals were also committed to efficiency and rapidity in the political and economic spheres.[39] Some believed that there was no shortage of goods, only disorganization. From 1916, the pro- Action libérale populaire (ALP) *Libre Parole* published a weekly rubric showing that the administration was responsible for waste. Liberals also accepted the need for a massive increase in arms production and the organization of transport, while *Le Temps* condemned the state's 'incapacity to accelerate'.[40]

Liberals presented these ideas as an alternative to state intervention, but differences were blurred in practice. They held that businessmen must be left to run their businesses, and the military must be allowed to make war, but they expected the state to guarantee their ability to do so.[41] The Progressist Latapie argued that the French honoured competence and science as much as the Germans, but lacked a government willing to treat industry as a friend. He appealed for legislation more favourable to large corporations and for banks to support industry.[42] Latapie described the recently created Office de ravitaillement de la Seine as an excellent model, for although it included a few civil servants and had only a consultative role, it was headed by an 'experienced administrator' and incorporated representatives of business, cooperatives, and farming, who would 'direct' and 'organize' supply.[43] Denais (ALP) called for mobilization of all men aged eighteen to forty-eight, regulated by

[34] Rosemunde Sanson, *L'Alliance républicaine démocratique centre*, 426–7.

[35] *Le Temps*, 26 October 1914 (price controls), 1 July 1916 (profit tax), 13 July 1916 (merchant fleet), 12 December 1916 (income tax); *La République française*, 29 March 1915, 1 April 1917 (price control), 13 March 1916 (income tax), 30 July 1916 (rents), 10 May 1918 (luxury tax); *Libre parole*, 17 March 1916 (rents), 2 April 1916 (income tax). Godfrey, *French Capitalism*, 147–8.

[36] *La République française*, 10 April 1916, 9 October 1916, 27 May 1918.

[37] *La République française*, 21 December 1916.

[38] *Le Temps*, 27 August 1914.

[39] *Le Temps*, 28 August 1914, 16 December 1916.

[40] *La République française*, 25 April 1915; *Le Temps*, 11 December 1916.

[41] *Le Temps*, 27 May 1918.

[42] *Le Temps*, 7 November 1915.

[43] *Le Temps*, 22 June 1917.

local commissions composed of representatives of business and the Army (not the state).[44] Like interventionists, liberals actually envisaged harmony between individualism and order, but conceived the relationship differently.

No conservative favoured unadulterated individualism or state planning. All preferred the Fayolist model, for it allowed liberty to the competent. And since Fayolism always entailed coercion in practice, competing groups tended to cast as 'Socialist' and/or 'Germanic' those interventions that they opposed—again, anti-socialism and intra-conservative conflict were inseparable. Initially, centrists hoped that Socialists' participation in the government would tame them, while the right was more sceptical. In 1917, both centre and right came to agree that intensified organization of the War effort was unavoidable, while simultaneously attributing 'excessive regulation' to Socialist influence. Latapie spoke for many when he wrote that Socialists, particularly Thomas, had used the Union sacrée as a pretext to abolish liberty of trade and provoke 'total ruin and anarchy'.[45] By 1917, the centre agreed that organization of the country for war required exclusion of the Socialists from the government.

THE CULTURE OF WAR AND ANTI-SOCIALISM

The application of anti-German feeling to domestic enemies also brought right and centre together. To understand why, we must begin with the researches of Stéphane Audoin-Rouzeau, Annette Becker, Leonard Smith, and others, who argue that the trauma of war caused atavistic, quasi-religious hatreds to surface in the collective psyche, causing soldiers to kill willingly for their countries. They add that the conviction that one's country was fighting a defensive battle for civilization against barbarism, and that the enemy was racially predisposed to atrocity, turned war into a religious crusade.[46] As Antoine Prost argues, this interpretation wrongly assumes a uniform national psyche (and unwittingly borrows from collective psychology).[47]

Centre and right undeniably embraced the 'culture of war', with its struggle of good and evil, Darwinism and racism. However, that they did so (usually) without experiencing battle directly suggests that ahistorical psychological mechanisms, dubious even when applied to combatants, were less important than the inscription of pre-existing cultures in new conditions, and their use for specific purposes. Conservatives applied the culture of war to domestic politics, expelling the left from the national community because they were allegedly allies of the Germans and shared their racial defects. However, right and centre appropriated these ideas differently, according to their attitudes to religion and the state.

[44] *Le Temps*, 31 May, 13 September 1916.

[45] *Le Temps*, 3 August 1915; Godfrey, *French Capitalism*, 58.

[46] Audoin-Rouzeau, Becker, and Smith, *France and the Great War*, 138–45; Becker and Audoin-Rouzeau, *14–18*.

[47] Prost, 'Les Limites', 5–20; 'La Guerre de 1914', 95–102.

All conservatives understood the War in the light of collective psychology. A contributor to *L'Opinion* argued that democracy created gigantic conscript armies—'vast, blind organisms, in which formidable hatred burned'. War was more violent, and yet it was nobler because it pursued the ideal.[48] To these beliefs, conservatives added the mercantilist view of inevitable struggle between nations, according to which gains by one country entailed losses for another. They had treated pre-war diplomatic crises as manifestations of the German desire for resources for their expanding population.[49] When war broke out, they regarded it as an extension of the same struggle between racially defined nations, in which victory depended on the quantity, quality, and unity of the population. In the 1900s, Colonel Driant, the ALP deputy, wrote popular fiction depicting the yellow and black perils. On the outbreak of war, he regretted having caricatured the British in his *La Guerre fatale* (1902), and so converted the Germans into the racial enemy. The anecdote indicates that racial categories were both common sense, in that everybody 'knew' that there was a hierarchy, and 'available discourses', to be used and manipulated, taking on different meanings in different contexts, for the racial hierarchy varied according to purpose.[50]

Conservatives identified France with civilization and Germany with barbarism, and saw the difference racially, even if biological ideas were rejected in theory as 'Germanic'. *Le Temps* contrasted the 'hereditary' destiny of France to defend civilization with the 'formidable machine for murder, arson, and devastation' that was Germany.[51] The Progressist Ribot agreed that the War confronted the spirit of liberty of modern societies with the spirit of domination of societies still enslaved by military despotism.[52] In August 1914, de Mun claimed that the Kaiser might invoke heaven, 'but the blood of murdered children cried out against him'. France was fighting for its souls and laws.[53] Barthou regarded German soldiers as 'specimens of a lesser breed', and urged his compatriots to hate Germans with all the intensity ensured by our claims against them.[54] Latapie held that since the Germans comprised a single race, all classes were identical, and their government, as credulous as the people, stupidly deluded itself on the ease of victory.[55] Similarly, while rejecting Darwinism as 'Germanic', conservatives endorsed it implicitly or explicitly. André Tardieu stated that the French 'are struggling for their existence' against 'aggressor peoples that have not hesitated to trouble the life of Europe and to cause civilization to retreat'.[56] Barrès praised Clemenceau's view that nations

[48] *L'Opinion*, 23 January 1915.

[49] *L'Alliance démocratique*, 2 January 1913.

[50] Daniel David, 'Le Lieutenant-colonel Driant', *Revue historique des armées* 160 (1985), 84–95 at 90–3.

[51] *L'Alliance démocratique*, 9 May 1915; 24 June 1917; *Le Temps*, 31 August 1914.

[52] Dr Alexandre Ribot, *Journal d'Alexandre Ribot et correpondances inédites, 1914–1922* (Paris, 1936), 52–3.

[53] *L'Écho de Paris*, 8 August 1914.

[54] Robert J. Young, *Power and Pleasure: Louis Barthou and the Third French Republic* (Montreal, 1991), 137; *L'Alliance démocratique*, 13 June 10 October 1915.

[55] *La République française*, 4 March 1917.

[56] Archives nationales 324 AP 26, Fonds Tardieu (hereafter ANFT, carton/file no.): Speech of 17 August 1916, 'L'Effort de L'Italie'; *L'Alliance démocratique*, 7 March, 20 June 1915.

must permanently engage in an 'effort for life'.[57] The Bonapartist Engerand claimed that Germany had understood that mastery of the modern world depended on conquering markets.[58]

Initially, conservatives integrated these beliefs into contrasting views of international relations, but they converged in the 1917 crisis. The right was most hostile to Germany. Progressists all wanted dismemberment of Germany, but were divided between those who envisaged the survival of the Catholic Habsburg Empire, and those who preferred a Europe of free peoples and nation states.[59] They also claimed to fight for the 'soil of France' rather than 'international arbitration and a united states of the world'.[60] The Catholic René Bazin advocated 'Christian fraternity, starting with our brothers and with those who are in danger' to the religion of humanity.[61] The right was little inclined to distinguish good Germans from bad, for as a journalist put it, 'there are not two Germanys; there is only the same Germany that France has had to master for centuries'.[62] Maurras rejected the 'nationalities principle' on the grounds of the inequality of races. For him, the only possible universalism was Latin and Catholic, under French hegemony. Civilization depended on the dismemberment of Germany.[63] The Right rejected universalism. For Denais (ALP), reason and moral authorities were useless—'only force can protect us against force'.[64] Bazin preferred 'Christian fraternity, starting with our brothers and with those who are in danger' to the religion of humanity.[65]

The centre initially distinguished good from bad Germans. It held that a democratic Germany might be able to live peacefully in the community of nation states, and thus saw the War as a struggle of democratic peoples against German imperialism.[66] In 1916–1917 there were some signs of openness to a negotiated peace, before revival of a hard line in late 1917.[67] The centre still supported the proposed League of Nations, but held that it must possess a military force capable of dealing with a resurgent Germany.[68] In 1918, Louis Barthou spoke of visiting a punishment 'implacable, inexorable without pity...on the bandit kings', and called for disappearance of all German influence from the Rhine frontier.[69] The centre never abandoned its commitment to the Europe of peoples, but came to see Germany as unfit to participate in it; consequently, its views converged with those of the right.

[57] *L'Écho de Paris*, 8 September, 1916, 20 November 1917.

[58] *L'Écho de Paris*, 23 February 1918; *Libre parole*, 2 August, 5 September 1914.

[59] *La République française*, 19 April 1916.

[60] *La République française*, 3 February 1915.

[61] *L'Écho de Paris*, 26 August 1917.

[62] *L'Écho de Paris*, 23 October 1916, 16 February 1918.

[63] Weber, *Action française*, 98; Jacques Prévotat, *Les Catholiques et l'Action française. Histoire d'une condemnation* (Paris, 2001), 198.

[64] *La République française*, 19 October 1915; 2 April 1918.

[65] *L'Écho de Paris*, 26 August 1917.

[66] *L'Alliance démocratique*, 21 February 1915; Stéphane Audoin-Rouzeau, '"Bourrage de crane" et information en France en 1914–1918', in Stéphane Audoin-Rouzeau and Jean-Jacques Becker (eds), *Les Sociétés européenes et la guerre de 1914–1918* (Paris, 1990), 163–74.

[67] Keiger, *Raymond Poincaré*, 195–6; Young, *Power and Pleasure*, 139, corrects Jean-Jacques Becker, 'Louis Barthou devant la guerre de 1914–1918', in Michel Papy (ed.), *Barthou, un homme un époque* (Pau, 1986), 153–65.

[68] Boret, *La bataille*, 18; *L'Opinion*, 24 February 1917.

[69] *L'Alliance démocratique*, 24 June, 19 August 1917, 22 September 1918; Young, *Power and Pleasure*, 138.

Michael Jeismann's view that as the War progressed, the press evoked humanity only to justify penning up the barbarians on their reservations, applies to both right and centre.[70]

Importantly, conservatives did not draw an absolute distinction between France and Germany (just as elite and mass were not absolutely opposed). Germanic defects were latent within France, as decades of worries about 'Germanic' Socialism and 'degeneration' confirmed. Now, the culture of war made available a discourse of national enemies and friends that could be applied to Socialists. In 1914, conservatives enthused at left-wing participation in the Union sacrée, yet gloated that Socialism had bowed to the reality of national struggle. De Mun wrote of the recovery of the Socialists from their 'pacifist illusion'.[71] The Alliance secretary-general, Charles Pallu de La Barrière, crowed that the Socialist 'dream of universal brotherhood would momentarily vanish in the face of the immediate necessity for unity'.[72] Initially, the centre hoped that keeping the Socialists within the government would neutralize them, but that did not imply tenderness towards the left. The centrist Deschanel was privately furious to see in power those he blamed for France's lack of preparation.[73] Loucheur, in constrast, opined 'that the presence of a few of these *embusqués* [the Confédération générale du travail (CGT)] has allowed us to avoid many hiccups with the workers'.[74] Consequently, when the military situation became difficult, it was easy to blame the Socialists. The strikes of 1917, against the background of revolution in Russia, exacerbated conservative fears. A private letter expected the poor to burn the furniture of the rich to keep warm; another urged a relative to shut his business and flee from revolutionary Paris to the countryside.[75] The view that the Socialists were using the Union sacrée as a cover for revolution was often repeated, especially by the right, as was the charge that they were in the pay of the 'barbaric' Germans. The spy scandals of 1917 would unite anti-Germanism and anti-socialism.[76] Had France been defeated, a 'stab in the back' myth was available.

Meanwhile, the human cost of the War reinforced conservative fears of degeneration. Conservatives initially saw war as regenerative: there was little difference on this score between Barrès, who wrote that it had dragged France out of the 'cesspool', and the Alliance deputy, Paul Reynaud, whose heart beat joyously at the prospect of national regeneration.[77] Soon, concern surfaced that war had destroyed the best elements of the population. Barthou wondered whether 'in order to survive France has not sacrificed the very sources of its life'.[78] A Catholic journalist accused anticlericals wanting 'our clergy [to be] annihilated by Boche

[70] Michael Jeismann, *La Patrie de l'ennemi* (Paris, 1997), 312–16.

[71] *L'Écho de Paris*, 3 August 1914.

[72] *L'Alliance démocratique*, 2 August 1914; *Le Temps*, 8 August 1916; *La République française*, 31 March 1915; *L'Écho de Paris*, 12 March 1918.

[73] Thierry Billard, *Paul Deschanel* (Paris, 1991), 202.

[74] Loucheur, *Carnets secrets*, 22–7, 38; Godfrey, *French Capitalism*, 196–7.

[75] Becker, *Les français*, 185.

[76] *La République française*, 2 and 11 September 1917.

[77] *L'Écho de Paris*, 29 August 1914; Thibault Tellier, *Paul Reynaud. Un Indépendant en politique* (Paris, 2005), 52.

[78] Becker, 'Louis Barthou', 158–60.

machine guns'.[79] In 1916, even the gung-ho Barrès called for economical use of men through the industrialization of warfare.[80]

The War also aggravated natalist worries. In November 1914 a note emanating from the GQG, probably authored by Tardieu, stated that the birth rate had been a casualty of the struggle of the 'nation armée'.[81] Similar views were expressed across the political spectrum, and in January 1918, Jules Siegfried, Alliance deputy and *doyen d'age* of the Chamber, made protection of the quality and quantity of the population a major theme of his speech opening the new session—conventionally a time for emphasizing agreement.[82] Meanwhile, Catholics increased their commitment to natalism. In 1915, the Catholic Progressists Louis Duval-Arnould and Auguste Isaac founded the Plus grande famille as a Catholic alternative to the ANPAPF.[83] There were still tensions between Catholics and secular pro-natalists concerning birth out of wedlock and state intervention in family affairs. Nevertheless, conservatives agreed that large families had made the greatest military sacrifices. Fayolists added that large families were 'schools of organization' in which boys learned command.[84]

One of the most striking developments of the war years was that right and centre came to believe that the family vote would organize universal suffrage hierarchically and thus counter degeneration, neutralize feminist demands for the vote, and defeat Socialism. It is not surprising that the Catholic Bazin believed that proportional representation, plural votes for fathers of families, and municipal voting rights for women would create the moral climate necessary to raise the birth rate.[85] More intriguingly, Adolphe Carnot, president of the Alliance, converted to the family vote. The state, he wrote, owed a greater debt to a family than to an individual.[86] The family vote was gendered and misogynist and it confirmed the longer-term tendency towards an elitist, male, bourgeois conservatism. Yet during the War, it was rarely connected explicitly to anti-feminism. The conservative press was less likely to denounce women's independence than to praise their contribution to the war effort. The family vote's immediate political significance was that it contributed to conservative unity against the left, for it rooted the nation in families rather than Thomas' partnership of classes. A contributor to *L'Alliance démocratique* argued that the family vote would remove the syndicate of bachelors and Malthusians who ruled France, while the nationalist, Henri Clouard, saw it as part of the 'New Order of Qualities and Competence'.[87] Thus, the culture of war,

[79] *Libre Parole*, 22 November 1916.

[80] Michel Baumont, 'Maurice Barrès et les morts de la guerre', *L'Information historique* 31, no. 1 (1969), 30–5. See also René Humbert, *La République française*, 24 July 1915.

[81] ANFT, 26, 27 November 1914. Note de Service.

[82] *L'Alliance démocratique*, 13 January 1918.

[83] Richard Tomlinson, 'The politics of *dénatalité* during the French Third Republic 1890–1940', PhD dissertation, University of Cambridge, 1983, 120–2; Cheryl Koos, 'Engendering reaction: the politics of pronatalism and the family in France, 1919–1944', PhD dissertation, University of Southern California, 1996, 149–58; Yves Le Naour and Catherine Valenti, *La Famille doit voter. Le Suffrage familial contre le vote individuel* (Paris, 2005), 79–82.

[84] Rials, *Administration*, 98–101.

[85] *L'Écho de Paris*, 15 October 1916.

[86] *L'Alliance démocratique*, 9 May 1915. See also 18 June 1916, 8 April 1917, 15 July 1917.

[87] *L'Alliance démocratique*, 8 September 1918; *L'Opinion*, 18 November 1916.

with its demonization of Germany, was inseparable from fear of decadence in France, the desire to promote competence, and to eliminate the Socialists from the Union sacrée.

CIVIL–MILITARY RELATIONS

In this respect, the left's demand for the government and GQG to be accountable to parliament (which reconvened on 15 January 1915 and soon declared itself to be in permanent session) was crucially important. By December 1914, Joffre's GQG at Chantilly had acquired vast powers in the twenty-one departments of the 'zone des armées', extending into economic, diplomatic, and administrative matters. Initially, centre and right approved this arrangement, for they expected the War to be short, and Joffre's position owed much to the Fayolist-inspired decree of 1911, which restored unity of command in the Army. Moreover, the presence of centre politicians such as Tardieu at Chantilly confirmed that the three-year military service campaign had restored good relations between the Dreyfusard centre and the officer corps.[88] Fear mattered too, for rumours of a military coup lasted though the War.[89] The soldier-minister, Abel Ferry, reported that the government worried that if it criticized Millerand, 'the Army will detect a dark conspiracy. Parliamentarians are very unpopular. They are reproached for not being at the front.'[90] Neither the deaths of ten deputies on active service, including Colonel Driant and Ferry, nor Paul Doumer's loss of four of his five sons, dented the popular conviction that deputies were *embusqués*. Their unpopularity contrasted with Joffre's reputation as a military genius.

Failure to break the military stalemate confronted conservatives with a dilemma similar to that in the war economy—how to win the War without recourse to Socialist 'dictatorship'. In 1916, the huge casualties at Verdun seemed to justify the left's criticisms of the High Command. Socialists and Radicals looked to the Jacobin precedent of the nation in arms and called for parliamentary representatives to inspect the front. Significantly, some conservatives began to criticize the High Command too, and they combined with the left to force the government to hold secret sessions of parliament, in which deputies interrogated those responsible for the war effort. By 1917, as the military situation deteriorated, eviction of the Socialists from the Union sacrée, coupled with reduction of parliamentary power, became the condition of reasserting civil power over incompetent generals. In the process, analogies with management, the factory, productivity, and the attack began to displace the idea that legislation should be elaborated through

88 Gilles Le Béguec, 'L'Entrée au Palais-Bourbon. Les Filières privilégiées d'accès à la fonction parlementaire 1919–1939', doctorat d'état, Paris X Nanterre, 1989, 339; Bock, *Un Parlementarisme de guerre*, 66–7.

89 Paul Dutton, 'The Union sacrée and the French cabinet crisis of October 1915', *European Studies Review* 8, no. 4 (1978), 411–24 at 415; Ferry, *Carnets secrets*, September 1918, 240.

90 Ferry, *Les Carnets*, 29 June 1915, 81; Bock, *Un Parlementarisme de guerre*, 33–47, 95–119; Becker, *The Great War*, 96–7, 218.

debate.[91] Differences among conservatives remained significant, but in the specific context of 1917–1918, right and centre converged.

The right and extreme right barely wavered in support for the High Command, the authority of which they saw as rooted in sound organizational principles, guaranteeing the leadership of the competent. Action française (AF) claimed that war had ended democratic pretence: now experts, soldiers, and administrators governed the many; the days had gone when 'anyone could say anything on any subject in any circumstances'.[92] Piou agreed that 'war must be made by men of war' (to which a Socialist wit replied that 'a builder might have defended Verdun!').[93] In September 1916, at the height of the Verdun battle, *L'Écho de Paris* dismissed criticisms of the GQG as irrelevant.[94] Latapie claimed that if there was any inefficiency, political meddling was to blame.[95] Jules Roche held that the Chamber's Army Commission, however well intentioned, did not possess the necessary 'competence and experience'.[96] The right largely opposed secret sessions, which it interpreted as a weapon against the GQG. When parliamentary inspection became inevitable, the right sought to confine it to the rear and to ensure that parliamentary commissions elected inspectors, rather than the Chamber.[97] Louis Marin opposed the proposal for a powerful body of inspectors as 'inorganic' and 'unorganized'—it would divide authority.[98] The right called instead for 'virile' government in the present and for constitutional reform after the War.[99] Now, the Progressist Georges Bonnefous proposed that parliament temporarily delegate powers of inspection to a commission of forty deputies and forty senators, leaving parliament to meet weekly to register government decrees.[100] Many right-wing deputies were close to reactionary generals. They doubtless knew that, in 1915, General Castelnau had urged a horrified Poincaré to 'act like a king', and 'show the deputies the door'.[101]

The centre was less enamoured of the generals, but admired the 'democratic' Army, and wished to reconcile the rule of the competent with parliamentary sovereignty. From late 1915, a small group of centrist deputy-combatants, notably Tardieu, Maginot, and Ferry, took the lead in criticizing the generals. Initially, they echoed the left's Jacobinism, arguing that whereas in the past war had been monarchical, the peoples were the wellspring of the current conflict, and so the nation in

[91] Dutton, 'The Union sacrée', 411–24; Marjorie M. Farrar, 'Politics versus patriotism: Alexandre Millerand as French Minister of War', *French Historical Studies* 11, no. 4 (Fall 1980), 577–609.

[92] *L'Action française*, 24 April 1915, cited in Weber, *Action française*, 94.

[93] *Journal officiel. Chambre des députés* (hereafter JOCD), 18 July 1916, 1574–6; *Libre Parole*, 19, 27, 28 July 1916.

[94] *L'Écho de Paris*, 12 September, 6 October 1916.

[95] *La République française*, 22 September 1915, 20 January, 8 April 1916; *Libre parole*, 5 January 1916.

[96] *La République française*, 6 and 26 June 1915.

[97] *L'Écho de Paris*, 29 October 1916; *Libre parole*, 23 February 1916.

[98] JOCD, 18 July 1916, 1573; Bock, *Un Parlementarisme de guerre*, 185–95.

[99] *L'Écho de Paris*, 8 December 1916; *La République française*, 6 and 8 January, 29 July 1917.

[100] Bock, *Un Parlementarisme de guerre*, 262–3.

[101] Yves Gras, *Castelnau, ou l'art de commander, 1851–1944* (Paris, 1990), 230.

parliament must 'inspect' the war effort.[102] More typical of centrists was President of the Chamber, Paul Deschanel, who in 1917 scolded the GQG for intervening in diplomatic and social affairs, congratulated deputies for establishing an armaments programme, and urged the political system to be 'productive'.[103] Whereas the right, especially AF, endowed generals with the general competence needed for government, the centre did not; it saw military men as *specialist* competences who should merely advise the government.

Yet the centre's criticisms of parliamentary inefficiency pushed the centre closer to the anti-parliamentarianism of the right. The centre harnessed ambient ideas about rapidity, rationalization, and productivity to schemes for the organization of parliament. Jules Correard (penname Probus) took the lead. This director at the Finance Ministry and teacher at the École des sciences politiques denounced in *L'Opinion* 'the unorganized and mediocre tyranny of an assembly made to deliberate and not act', and looked to Fayolism and Taylorism to make it more efficient. He argued that the chief characteristic of competence was experience of the art of organization and command, in whatever field.[104] To render the legislature more efficient, the centre looked particularly to parliamentary commissions, which it saw as bastions of competence, for they recruited from deputies possessed of expertise and heard evidence from non-parliamentarians. In June 1917, a centre-inspired parliamentary report praised the commissions' remarkable work in calling the government to account, and suggested that the Chamber should rationalize its debates, while continuing to orientate the government and compensate for its shortcomings.[105]

Centrists also advocated strengthening of the executive, while rejecting constitutional reform. Georges Lachapelle insisted on the wide applicability of Fayol's hierarchical principles, and added that 'The art of getting oneself elected and the art of speaking have no relation with administrative science, with administrative capacity.'[106] Again following Fayol, Probus argued that ministers should see themselves not as heads of department who occasionally attended cabinet meetings, but as cabinet members collectively responsible for determining the direction of government action.[107] Ferry regarded even the president of the Army commission, General Pédoya, as a creature of the République des camarades'.[108]

Such attacks on Deputies may have encouraged the right to endorse centrist criticisms of the generals. By the end of the year, Monarchists such as the Marquis Baudry d'Asson, perhaps responding to Maurras' recent call for military dictatorship, had joined the critics. Driant denounced deficiencies in the defence of Verdun and admitted that 'that parliament and inspection by the Commissions is seriously important'.[109] Ybarnégaray dramatically returned from Chemin des Dames to

[102] JOCD, 20 July 1916, 1604–9; Ferry, *Les Carnets*, May 1916, 140 and April 1917, 174.

[103] Billard, *Paul Deschanel*, 199 ff; Tellier, *Paul Reynaud*, 57; *L'Opinion*, 20 January 1917.

[104] *L'Opinion*, 9 December 1916, 16 June and 13 October 1917.

[105] Bock, *Un Parlementarisme de guerre*, 267–72; Forcade, 'Censure, secret et opinion en France', 51.

[106] Georges Lachapelle, 'Les Idées de M. Henri Fayol', *Revue politique et parlementaire* 272 (1917), 100–11 at 107.

[107] *L'Opinion*, 23 December 1916.

[108] Ferry, *Les Carnets Secrets*, June 1916, 142.

[109] Bock, *Un Parlementarisme de guerre*, 181–4.

denounce General Nivelle's failings in a secret session.[110] Some conservatives admitted that secret sessions, if not abused, could be useful, if only as a means for the government to 'surgically remove' opposition.[111]

In November 1916, the opposition formed a parliamentary inter-group patronized by Clemenceau, the Action nationale, which the centre dominated. On 7 December 1916, 118 deputies voted for a Tardieu motion critical of the Briand government.[112] In response, Briand created a war cabinet, which seemingly realized the Fayolist ideal of unity of command and enhanced the role of the competent.[113] Millerand gave way to another organizer, General Lyautey (whose contempt for parliament quickly led to his downfall). Briand insisted that only the government could realize the necessary unity of military and industrial warfare.[114] Centre and right largely backed Briand's request in December 1916 for wide decree powers. Then, in the crisis of 1917, the implicit anti-parliamentarianism of the centre converged with the stronger views of the right. The *Écho de Paris* maintained that democratic war required sacrifice of democracy.[115] Yet the problem of how to prosecute the War more effectively without playing into the hands of Socialists remained. For the centre, the difficulty was double, for whilst it moved rightwards, it remained suspicious of Catholics and Monarchists.

THE RELIGIOUS QUESTION

There was a fundamental uncertainty in the widespread notion that the Union sacrée proved the triumph of patriotism over religious conflict, for both Catholics and *laïques* believed that their own views had won, and attacked each other for betraying the spirit of the Union sacrée. Catholics claimed that the War had exposed the iniquity of the lay laws, while Republicans countered that it had demonstrated their inviolability. Furthermore, religious conflict was inseparable from the dispute over the conduct of the War, for the left and centre (justifiably) doubted the Republicanism of Catholic Generals such as Castelnau and Lyautey.

Meanwhile, wartime expansion of the state, coupled with the mobilization of Catholic and *laïque* social organizations, spread the religious conflict to new areas and provoked as much competition as cooperation. Catholics, from the Progressists to AF, complained that the administration disregarded the Union sacrée, distributing material aid on 'political' grounds. 'We still live', Latapie wrote, in 'the regime of persecution'.[116] In Aveyron, Las Cases denounced state discrimination

[110] Ferry, *Les Carnets secrets*, 12 July 1917, 179.

[111] *La République française*, 29 November 1916; *L'Écho de Paris*, 3 July 1917.

[112] Georges and Édouard Bonnefous, *Histoire politique de la Troisième République*, ii. *La Grande guerre* (Paris, 1957), 203–6; Ferry, *Carnets secrets*, February 1917, 161–6; *Journal officiel. Chambre des députés*, 7 December 1916, 3564–5.

[113] *La République française*, 4 December 1915.

[114] Rials, *Administration*, 63–4.

[115] *L'Écho de Paris*, 28 July 1917.

[116] *La République française*, 13, 30, 31 March, 26 April 1915, 6 February 1916.

against orphans who attended Catholic schools.[117] Monseigneur Eyssautier of La Rochelle-Saintes set a good example of collaboration, but found it harder to persuade his flock to contribute to the works of the 'état spoliateur'.[118] Progressists accused the government of failing to call upon all competent people, regardless of 'party'.[119] The ALP too condemned administrative discrimination against Catholics and demanded revision of the lay laws and re-establishment of diplomatic relations with the Vatican.[120]

The anticlerical press spread a series of '*rumeurs infâmes*', questioning Catholics' patriotism, some of which the centre believed. It accused priests of having fomented war in order to provoke religious revival and of seeing the War as divine punishment for the sins of the French. Priests allegedly refused to serve at the front, while the 'Pape bochophile' intrigued with the enemy and Catholic charities proselytized, converted the wounded, and refused to treat non-Catholics.[121] *Le Temps* described the Catholic demand for the attendance of the President of the Republic at religious ceremonies as an 'inopportune' attack on *laïcité*. Subsequently, it condemned the Bishop of Rennes' claim that France deserved divine punishment because of its religious indifference and love of luxury.[122] No centrist envisaged modification of the lay laws. As the Alliance démocratique revived, most members stated their preference for a *laïque* party, free of 'clerical influences' in the arrondissments.[123]

The centre's commitment to *laïcité* was not necessarily exclusionary, however, and there were grounds for rapprochement with Catholics. In the logic of the culture of war, it emphasized the religion of the *patrie*. It was sympathetic to Bergson's notion that religion, whether true or not, provided 'energy' that could be used in war. The centre praised Christians, Muslims, and Jews for prioritizing the religion of the *patrie*, and for preaching against Teutonic barbarism.[124] In other words, the centre was open to Catholics so long as they accepted secularism, which of course, many did.

Joseph Denais warned that Catholics could not accept a religious peace dependent on the 'war card'.[125] For Catholics, whether liberal, integrist, Progressist, Rallié, or Monarchist, war had proven their patriotism and thus the iniquity of the lay laws. For Catholics, the Union sacrée demonstrated the Catholic foundations of the nation, a belief they cast in the millenarian language of the culture of war.

[117] Emmanuel de Las Cases, *Éphémérides. Journal inédit d'E. de Las Cases* (Montpellier, 1992), 13–14.

[118] Philippe Bon, 'L'Engagement des catholiques du diocèse de La Rochelle-Saintes dans le premier conflit mondial', *Guerres mondiales et conflits contemporains* 197 (2000), 73–82; Bernard, *La Dérive des modérés*, 243.

[119] *La République française*, 6 February 1916.

[120] *Libre parole*, 11 October 1914, 22 November 1916, 23 July 1916; *L'Écho de Paris*, 10 September, 15 October 1916, 19 August 1917.

[121] Jacques Fontana, *Les Catholiques français pendant la grande guerre* (Paris, 1990), 123–66; McMillan, 'French Catholics', 121–7.

[122] *Le Temps*, 29 September 1914.

[123] *L'Alliance démocratique*, 5 November 1916, 21 January 1917, 16 September 1917.

[124] *L'Alliance démocratique*, 10 March 1918.

[125] *Libre parole*, 20 February 1917.

Indeed, there was a grain of truth in the *rumeurs infâmes*. Eyssautier believed that the War had put an end to 'arriviste and forced irreligion', which destroyed morality and 'debased souls'.[126] Admiral Bienaimé thought that collective prayers at Notre Dâme directly influenced the outcome of the Marne battle.[127] A contributor to the ALP journal claimed that since Clovis had baptized the barbarians, France had become a 'work of flesh and blood, haloed with the supernatural'. France must safeguard civilization by defending the Papacy against Germanic, Protestant barbarism.[128] For Maurras, France was the guardian of European, Latin, and Catholic civilization, from which the Reformation had expelled Germany. He admitted that the Church saw France as deserving of punishment for having persecuted the Church, but claimed that it saw the Germans as more blameworthy for their pride, vulgar materialism, and decadent morals. AF defended the Church's right to proselytize and distribute medals and scapulars to the wounded.[129] In some localities, the War may have led to a revival of prophecies.[130] Only a few Progressists showed any scepticism. Latapie mocked the notion that the War was a divine punishment. Yet he advised struggle against those anticlericals who hoped to resume their activities after the War.[131]

The clerical–anticlerical conflict was integral to the 1917 crisis. By then, many Catholics were disappointed with the fruits of the Union sacrée. Benedict XV's peace initiative of August, launched as conservative attacks on the left intensified, further complicated matters. Most Catholics dismissed the proposal, and some echoed condemnation of the 'Pape boche', but Cochin took it seriously. He soon resigned from the government in disgust at the alleged demise of the Union sacrée, just as anticlerical sniping forced Admiral Lacaze out of the Navy Ministry.[132] Lyautey had resigned in December 1916, and Las Cases refused to join the Ribot administration because it would not re-establish relations with the Vatican.[133]

These developments revealed the continuing significance of both political divisions among Catholics and of the clerical–anticlerical conflict in French politics. In effect, an aspiration for national unity coexisted with ongoing struggle as a kind of depoliticized politics, embittered by each side's conviction, intensified by the culture of war, that their own principles were the foundation of disinterested patriotism and that their opponents' activities represented sectarian attacks on the Union sacrée. Religious conflict was also important in the revival of the conservative parties in the winter of 1916–1917.

[126] Bon, 'L'Engagement des catholiques; Bouloc, 'L'Union sacrée des aveyronnais', 447–62.
[127] *Libre parole*, 15 September 1914, 25 March, 1916.
[128] *Libre parole*, 28 April 1916, 17 July 1916. [129] Prévotat, *Les Catholiques*, 199.
[130] Bouloc, 'L'Union sacrée des aveyronnais', 452.
[131] *La République française*, 2 March 1917.
[132] Brigitte Waché, 'Un Parlementaire catholique dans la guerre', in Nadine-Josette Chaline (ed.), *Les Chrétiens dans la première guerre mondiale* (Paris, 1993), 47–66 at 61–3; Jean-Marie Mayeur, 'Les Catholiques français et Benoît XV en 1917', in *Les Chrétiens dans la première guerre mondiale*, 153–65; Adrien Dansette, *Histoire religieuse de la France contemporaine*, ii: *Sous la Troisième République* (Paris, 1951) 490–2.
[133] Las Cases, *Éphémérides*, 13–14.

THE REVIVAL OF PARTIES

In August 1916, *Le Temps* denounced the activities of the 'Socialist and Catholic parties', both of which it described as enemies of liberty, and asked, without naming it, what had become of the Alliance démocratique?[134] On 4 October, the Alliance's executive met for the first time in two years, perhaps encouraged by its pro-Radical Gironde federation, which had remained active.[135] Secretary-General Pallu maintained that parties could propagandize as long as they prioritized the national interest and did not act as parties—unlike the Socialists.[136] In the winter of 1916–1917, Alliance members rejected a proposal to suppress the Parti républicain démocrate (PRD), for that implied openness to the increasingly Catholic Fédération républicaine.

If we believe Engerand, even right-wing deputies deserted the Chamber when one of their colleagues got up to speak.[137] Yet there was some activity on the right too. On 26 November, the Fédération reaffirmed opposition to party politics and urged all citizens to collaborate with the government. Deputies would determine the broad outline of national remaking, but realization depended upon the Army.[138] Subsequently, the Fédération showed no sign of life at the national level, although in the Rhône, Laurent Bonnevay's attack on Briand's proposal for rule by decree lifted the taboo on opposition to the government there.[139] In late November, the ALP reassured its followers that inactivity and 'decimation' of the membership had not shaken the party. It reaffirmed faith in the Union sacrée, which it depicted as the triumph of the ALP programme.[140] In practice, the ALP merged into a heterogeneous group of right-wing Progressists, Nationalists, and Monarchists, around journals such as *Écho de Paris* and *Libre Parole* (where it shared space with Drumont). In December 1918, the effacement of the Fédération and ALP allowed Catholics and Nationalists to found a new inter-group, the Entente républicain démocratique. ALP party secretary, La Rochefoucauld, correctly assessed the mood of Catholics: he maintained that the War had made a 'liberal party a national necessity' but felt that the failure of Catholics to receive 'satisfaction' for their adhesion to the Union sacrée had caused many to conclude that Royalist critics of the Ralliement were right.[141]

Indeed, in 1916, the print run of *l'Action française* attained 156,000. Thanks to its enthusiastic support of the Union sacrée and its willingness to say publicly what others could not, the neo-Royalists recovered the support of some of those parliamentary Monarchists who had abandoned it in the 1910 crisis. Royalist rivals,

[134] *L'Alliance démocratique*, 27 August 1916; Sanson, *L'Alliance*, 439–40; *Le Temps*, 16 August, 19 September 1916.

[135] Sanson, *L'Alliance*, 437–48.

[136] *L'Alliance démocratique*, 22 October 1916; *L'Opinion*, 28 October 1916, also welcomed the revival of parties.

[137] *L'Écho de Paris*, 19 September 1917.

[138] *La République française*, 26 November 1916.

[139] Bernard, *La Dérive des modérés*, 243.

[140] Archives nationals, 142 AP 42, Fonds Xavier de Rochefoucauld (hereafter ANFXR, carton/file no.), note of 17 November 1916; *Libre Parole*, 27 November 1916.

[141] ANFXR, 42, Rochefoucauld to Pacelli, 10 October 1917; Rochefoucauld to Prévost 15, 21 March 1918 and undated, probably April or May 1918.

notably the *Soleil* group, disappeared. In 1917, Poincaré encouraged Daudet's campaign against spies, while the Rallié Gérard de Boury, who sat with the Gauche démocratique, claimed that the government's weakness had made AF attractive to him.[142] In the intellectual world, André Gide, Paul Valéry, Guillaume Apollinaire, and the Cubists all tried to invent a classicist national art, without slipping into Maurrasianism, but were frustrated by Maurras' negativity towards them.[143] In fact, as always, Maurras struggled to combine the purity of his ideal with expansion of AF influence. On 10 December 1916, he urged the installation of a dictator, preferably military. Somewhat inconsistently, he argued that since Germany was inherently militarist and anti-Catholic, victory for French culture would bring the Republic down.[144] In late 1917, AF rallied to Clemenceau, and played a significant part in the crisis that brought him to power.

THE RISE OF CLEMENCEAU

In late 1917, conservatives largely agreed that it would be possible to mobilize the economy for total war and recover control over the generals only if the Socialists and their Radical allies quit the Union sacrée. The problem was not simply that revolutionary Socialists' pacifism and labour militancy threatened victory. Paradoxically, reformist Socialist commitment to the War effort allegedly entailed the rule of the incompetent, softness towards 'embusqués' in the factories, and covert socialization of the means of production—all of which offended conservatives' conceptions of organization, not to speak of corrupting France with Germanic notions. Socialism must therefore be fought at the front, in the factories and in parliament. However, religious and constitutional issues remained so entangled with the crisis, that it was difficult to form a new majority in parliament. The centre had moved closer to the right, but religious and constitutional conflicts could not easily be separated from other issues. Clemenceau turned out to be the solution.

That Clemenceau, at the head of a conservative majority, should have stabilized the situation nobody could have foreseen in 1914. His one-time position on the far left of the Radical Party and his reputation as a breaker of ministries compromised his standing as a statesman. His tough anti-labour stance and backing for the *Trois ans* won some credit with conservatives, but during the War he forfeited some of that by ridiculing the religious revival as a conspiracy to inveigle crazed souls into Church.[145] His attacks on the High Command earned charges of defeatism, while his sarcasm and credulity concerning rumours about those whom he disliked made

[142] Weber, *Action Française*, 93, 110; Fred Kupferman, 'Le Rôle de Léon Daudet et de l'Action française dans le contre-offensive morale: 1915–1918', *Études maurrassiennes* 2 (1973), 121–44.
[143] Bruno Goyet, *Charles Maurras* (Paris, 2000), 195–6.
[144] Weber, *Action Française*, 89–112; Prévotat, *Les catholiques*, 198.
[145] D.R. Watson *Georges Clemenceau: A Political Biography* (London, 1974), 247; McMillan, 'French Catholics', 122.

him a host of enemies.[146] Deschanel still bore the mark of Clemenceau's sword; Poincaré and Clemenceau had fallen out during the 1913 presidential election. So why did Poincaré feel that he had to call upon him in November 1917?

Clemenceau's advantage was that his popularity overcame the impasse in parliament. Since 1914, he had condemned foreign labour, inadequate medical services, and the General Staff's wasting of soldiers' lives.[147] He relentlessly denounced *embusqués* and often visited the combat zone—to 'sniff the Boche'.[148] Clemenceau benefited from the fact that people both castigated politicians as shirkers and expected them to solve their problems.[149] As Ferry pointed out, junior officers and even generals invested their hopes for redress of grievances in parliament.[150] Clemenceau received a massive correspondence from soldiers and civilians, as did Poincaré.[151] Meanwhile Clemenceau's campaign against censorship established him as the champion of a populace kept in the dark by their leaders. He tapped into a vein of populism, which combined an egalitarian hatred of 'les gros' with an appeal to a strong leader. On presenting his ministry to the Chamber, Clemenceau claimed that 'an irresistible movement of opinion' had brought him to power.[152]

However popular Clemenceau was, we should not, as some historians do, see him as the embodiment of national unanimity (minus a tiny pacifist and revolutionary minority), imposed over the heads of politicians. Of course, hardly anybody wanted to leave the Germans in possession of invaded territory. Yet rightly or wrongly, many ordinary people *believed* that the government had lost the chance to negotiate peace, and many conservatives *believed* that France was close to revolution. Ferry was alarmed that while on parliamentary mission, frontline soldiers had surrounded him and said 'We don't give a toss about honour!', and 'You could have made peace. You didn't want to. The government will pay for that!'[153]

In fact, Clemenceau's government represented the victory of one part of the country over another. Clemenceau's condemnation of Thomas' handling of the arms industry, coupled implicitly with spy scandals, legitimated both eviction of Socialists from the majority and tacit acceptance of some of their policies. Although Clemenceau dismissed Léon Daudet's more extreme allegations—that Caillaux was complicit with the anarchist journal, *Bonnet rouge*, that Malvy's 'softness' towards pacifism derived from treason, and that he had sold the Nivelle plans to the enemy—the AF campaign effectively complemented Clemenceau's. Daudet's assertion that the same treasonable clique was behind the failure of the offensive, mutinies, industrial unrest, and pacifism provided conservatives with an excuse to fight Socialism and prosecute the War more effectively without offending the High Command.[154]

146 *L'Écho de Paris*, 18 December 1916; *Libre parole*, 5 January 1916.

147 For example, *L'Éclair du Midi*, 6 June 1917. 148 Duroselle, *Clemenceau*, 592–7.

149 Becker, *The Great War*, 42–3, 135–6, 219; Bock, *Un Parlementarisme de guerre*, 208–9.

150 Abel Ferry, *La Guerre vue d'en bas et d'en haut (lettres, notes, discours et rapports)* (Paris, 1920), 52–7.

151 Jean-Baptiste Duroselle, *Clemenceau* (Paris, 1988), 608; Leonard V. Smith, 'Remobilizing the citizen-soldier through the mutinies of 1917', in John Horne (ed.), *State, Society and Mobilization in Europe during the First World War* (Cambridge, 1997), 144–59; Farrar, 'Politics versus patriotism', 594.

152 Georges Clemenceau, *Discours de guerre* (Paris, 1934), 165. Duroselle, *Clemenceau*, 629.

153 Ferry, *Les Carnets*, April 1918, 230.

154 Weber, *Action française*, 102–7; Watson, *Georges Clemenceau*, 261.

Clemenceau's condemnation of Thomas' handling of the arms industry, coupled implicitly with spy scandals, legitimated both eviction of Socialists from the majority and tacit acceptance of some of their policies.

For the right, Latapie explicitly described proposals for civil requisition as necessary in principle, but 'dangerous', for vast powers would be given to Thomas, who had already demonstrated his incompetence, and who was the delegate of the Socialists rather than the representative of the nation. Latapie added, 'We would not have the same fears if the dictator was "non-political", chosen for his qualities as a leader or as an administrator, a loyal soldier, for example, or a senior magistrate, or a big businessman who had proved himself.'[155] In the Rhône Fédération républicaine a veritable culture of opposition developed, denouncing the Socialist dictatorship, Caillaux and Malvy's scheming, and the weakness of the government. Gradually, it rallied to Clemenceau.[156] The Progressist press accused the Ribot government of being too favourable to the Socialists.[157]

Crucially, the centre came to the same conclusion. Ferry, who began the War on good terms with moderate Socialists, endorsed Clemenceau's spy campaign. He wrote that 'We are going to peace through revolution', and believed that 'reverse selection had left France only with '*embusqués*, profiteers and traitors'.[158] Depiction of the Socialists as degenerate *embusqués* expelled them from the Union sacrée and legitimated strong government. Loucheur no longer believed that inclusion of Socialists in the cabinet neutralized them. In 1917, he helped engineer his own succession to Thomas as Armaments Minister in the Painlevé government, thereby ensuring a victory for Fayolist over social-democratic conceptions of organization.[159] Although the Painlevé government included no Socialists and promoted 'competences' in the persons of Loucheur and Claveille, it won few conservative votes. *La République française* asked when we would 'at last be delivered from Socialist tyranny?'[160] Soon, conservatives and Socialists combined to overthrow Painlevé. *L'Écho de Paris* appeared with the headline 'Liquidation du Bloc [des gauches]'.[161]

The right hoped that the new ministry would be open to them. Barrès wrote 'the time has come for the responsible men to express the will of conservative France'.[162] In the event, common anti-socialism did not overcome the religious or constitutional divide. Clemenceau's ministerial team comprised right-wing Radicals and centrists, including four members of the Alliance. Clemenceau told a confidante that as an 'old Jacobin' he would rather thump the right, but was prepared to accept its votes.[163] The need for Radical support and the relative assertiveness of the Alliance and the effacement of the Fédération and ALP constrained the right, once again, to support a

[155] *La République française*, 10 February 1917; *La Libre parole*, 1 June 1916.
[156] Bernard, *La Dérive des modérées*, 245.
[157] *La République française*, 24 May, 11 September 1917.
[158] Ferry, *Les Carnets*, June 1916, 142, 147; 12 July 1917, 178–85; 17 October 1917, 196–7.
[159] Loucheur, *Carnets secrets*, 22–7, 38; Godfrey, *French Capitalism*, 196–7.
[160] *La République française*, 12 September 1917; *L'Écho de Paris*, 19 September 1917.
[161] *L'Écho de Paris*, 17 and 20 November 1917.
[162] *L'Écho de Paris*, 19 October 1917.
[163] Bock, *Un Parlementarisme de guerre*, 290.

government in which Catholic representation had actually declined. Nevertheless, it did so enthusiastically, for the majority was clearly conservative.

CONCLUSION

Clemenceau resolved many, but not all, of the problems that confronted conservatives once it became clear that the War would be a long one. His government excluded the Socialists. It executed the minor players in the Bonnet rouge scandal, exiled Malvy, and imprisoned Caillaux. Ordinary people felt the weight of the law too. A Parisian court ruled that saying 'the damage is frightful' before a bomb-damaged Parisian house was defeatist.[164] In spite of promises to the contrary, Clemenceau increased censorship. There was no more discussion of the shape of post-war France.[165] While it may be an exaggeration to say that Clemenceau's government 'personified the brutalization of politics in France in 1917',[166] its actions are meaningful only in the context of the Manichean world view of the period, spy scares, and conviction that Socialists were agents of the 'Germanic' decadence and treason.

With the Socialists excluded from Union sacrée, it was safe to intensify the War effort. From the beginning, Clemenceau had demanded a 'government of steel', able to 'unite all French energies in a common movement of discipline'.[167] Under Clémentel and Loucheur, state control over the economy advanced. Notably, Clémentel established consortiums of businesses under state control for the allocation of raw materials. The government required state arsenals to adopt Taylorist methods and in June it created a Commission permanente de standardization.[168] An enormous regulatory bureaucracy developed, asking firms for information about production, stocks, and sales.

Clemenceau's government also applied organizational principles to government. The premier himself called for politics to be treated as a business, to ensure rapidity.[169] He brought the competent into government, naming four extra-parliamentary ministers. Institutionally, Clemenceau strengthened the Présidence du conseil, held fewer meetings of the Conseil des ministres, used relatively limited decree powers, and appointed Commissariats headed by parliamentarians directly responsible to him.[170] These measures helped Clemenceau to establish its primacy over the High Command, which deferred to his authority thanks to his pursuit of defeatists and protection of generals from political criticism.[171] The executive simultaneously asserted its authority over parliament, without reducing the latter

[164] Benjamin Martin, *France and the Après Guerre, 1918–1924* (Baton Rouge, 1999), 8.

[165] Watson *Georges Clemenceau*, 288; Forcade, 'Censure, secret et opinion', 47.

[166] Smith, Audoin-Rouzeau, and Becker, *France and the Great War*, 145.

[167] Duroselle, *Clemenceau*, 581–6.

[168] Godfrey, *French Capitalism*, 60–4.

[169] Rials, *Administration*, 81–2.

[170] Bock, *Un Parlementarisme de guerre*, 302–4.

[171] Françoise Navet-Bouron, 'La Censure de la presse en France en 1918', *Revue historique des armées* 3, (1998), 13–18; Guy Pedroncini, *Pétain, général en chef, 1917–1918* (Paris, 1997); Watson, *Clemenceau*, 293–325.

to a cipher—Clemenceau's campaign for parliamentary accountability had not been cynical. Parliament met even more frequently than in the past; Clemenceau attended and regularly faced confidence votes. Thus, Clemenceau implemented something like the ideal of organized parliamentarianism espoused by the centre, with a government that governed and yet respected parliament.[172]

Nonetheless, personal loyalty to Clemenceau was essential to the functioning of the government, and it depended on the conviction that he intuitively expressed the national will. To maintain his popularity, Clemenceau personally took charge of the *chasse aux embusqués* and continued his visits to the front. He claimed later that his speeches were directed not at parliament but at the country as a whole.[173] Clemenceau's power depended also on the belief that he represented the last rampart before Socialist revolution and/or military dictatorship. Indeed, Clemenceau's Jacobinism shaded into Bonapartist personal rule—perhaps the liberal, bellicose, parliamentary Bonapartism of Emile Ollivier. Of course, there were many differences too, but use of the term helps us to distinguish it from run-of-the-mill Republican governments and from dictatorship. More prosaically, the comparison reminds us that Clemenceau's position depended on a unique set of circumstances.

Indeed, unity was fragile, and the crisis provoked by the German offensive of spring 1918 exposed cracks. The liberal *La République française* criticized disorganization in the War economy and denounced the Chamber as a Soviet, while *L'Alliance démocratique* protested that regulation had not gone far enough, even in agriculture. Catholics complained privately that they had received no reward for their loyalty.[174] The War over, conservatives abandoned Clemenceau as soon as they could do so.

In the longer term, the major beneficiary of the Union sacrée was the centre. The War had disorganized the right. The Fédération was barely visible. The ALP, which had already been in difficulty in 1914, did not win the new Pope's confidence. AF attracted many Catholics, but its Royalism prevented it from winning mass support. That did not mean that Catholicism had ceased to be politically important, as the elections of 1919 would demonstrate, but that Catholics had no outlet. In contrast, the Alliance's inclusive strategy proved profitable. When the reversal of majorities became likely, Alliance activists decided that after all the PRD served no useful purpose. They now saw an alliance as better suited to forming a broad coalition extending to the Radicals and Ralliés; the Alliance should not become enmeshed in 'arrondissement struggles' between Republicans and clericals.[175] In November 1917, the Alliance buried the PRD. The Executive resumed regular meetings, discussed nationally important issues, and planned a daily newspaper.[176] This non-party orientation permitted the centre to play a key role in Clemenceau's administration.[177] The Alliance also became markedly more

[172] Bock, *Un Parlementarisme de guerre*, 275–82. [173] Watson, *Georges Clemenceau*, 280.
[174] ANFXR, 42, Rochefoucauld to Prévost, 15 March 1918.
[175] *L'Alliance démocratique*, 2 September, 16 September, 28 October 1917.
[176] *L'Alliance démocratique*, 2 December 19.
[177] Marc Sorlot, *André Maginot (1877–1932). L'Homme politique et sa légende* (Metz, 1995), 69–70; Sanson, *L'Alliance*, 45.

conservative. Pallu called for the reorganization of France as a 'national republic', while another activist suggested renaming the party the 'Alliance démocratique et nationale'.[178] Crucially, it was now prepared to ally with Ralliés, and it shared with the right the desire to regenerate France through pro-natalism and familialism. These rapprochements made possible the mutation of the Union sacrée into the Bloc national under centre leadership.

[178] *L'Alliance démocratique*, 2 September 1917, 22 September 1918; Sanson, *L'Alliance*, 426–7.

9

The Bloc National (1919–1924)

> There were times when France, singing the Marseillaise and the Chant du Départ, shook and broke absolute governments all over Europe. Today, in an upside-down Europe, France gives the example of order: the good sense, the historical sense, of this admirable people equals its bravery. It is without doubt a new order, transformed and changed, that reigns here—it is order.
>
> Denys Cochin, 2 December 1919

That an Orleanist, writing on the sixty-eighth anniversary of Louis-Napoléon's *coup d'état*, should have greeted thus the Bloc national's crushing victory in the elections of 16 November 1919 is a measure of the hopes it engendered. With 338 seats against 176 for the left, conservatives won their first victory for forty-three years, and the influence of the right within the coalition was far greater than in the conservative-inclined governments of the *Belle époque*. Monarchists and 'conservateurs' won twenty-nine seats, while the Entente républicaine démocratique (ERD), with 183 members, united Progressists, Nationalists, and the Action libérale populaire (ALP). The centre comprised three groups, of which the Républicains de gauche (61) and the Action républicaine et sociale (ARS) (46) had overcome their aversion to alliance with Catholics. As pro-Radicals, only the Gauche républicaine démocratique (96) preferred 'Concentration républicaine'. Several leagues, which campaigned for institutional reform in 'the spirit of 1919', also gravitated in the orbit of the Bloc. They included Démocratie nouvelle, the Association nationale pour l'organisation de la démocratie (ANOD), and Quatrième république (QR). They derived from the meeting of Fayolist organizers with centrist politicians, Bonapartists and Catholics seeking a way to act within the Republic, and veterans desirous of perpetuating the trench spirit.[1]

For Michel Winock, the Union sacrée created a united constitutional conservatism: 'the whole family of founders of the Republic—Opportunists, Republicans, Progressists—gave to the right the gift of their Republicanism'.[2] Winock's interpretation complements Antoine Prost's claim that French political culture differed from German in placing justice to individuals above *raison d'état*. Consequently, Prost argues, the veterans' desire to reconcile the French people did not entail

[1] Gilles Le Béguec, 'Le Parti', in Jean-François Sirinelli (ed.), *Histoire des droites en France*, ii: *Cultures*, (Paris, 1993), 13–59 at 48–9.

[2] Michel Winock, *La Fièvre hexagonale. Les Grandes crises politiques 1871–1968* (Paris, 1986), 198–201; H.W. Paul, *The Second Ralliement: The Rapprochement between Church and State in France in the Twentieth Century* (Washington, 1967).

elimination of domestic enemies, and so fascism did not develop in France.[3] Most recently, Nicolas Roussellier admits the contradictions of the Bloc, but argues that they were the condition of its willingness to compromise through debate. This flexibility permitted the Bloc to abandon intransigence for more realistic foreign policies. Yet, Roussellier argues, Socialist dogmatism undermined this realism, for the party presented potentially sensible international and domestic policies as party ideology, and refused the compromises on which parliamentarianism depended. Consequently, there was no counterweight to the 'outdated' liberal policies of the Bloc.[4] Each of these historians assumes an inevitable 'modernization' and implicitly sees the Bloc as part of a democracy that accepted legitimate disagreement.

Certainly, 1919–1920 represented the apogee of Republican conservatism, which endeavoured to channel popular politics into formal consultations, while leaving the elites in parliament to discuss issues on their merits, free from party dogma. From the late 1900s, this conservatism united Republicans and Ralliés with business, charitable, and intellectual networks, in a movement designed to 'organize' parliament's relations with the 'real world' and ensure the presence in it of the 'competent'. During the war, organizationalism shifted to the administration and economy, and emphasized action and rapidity and the directing role of the executive. Now, in reaction against Thomas' social democracy and the 'excesses' of Clemenceau's wartime regulation, a liberal version of organization developed, which became the programme of the Bloc. It rejected organizational schemes associated with Loucheur and Clémentel. Now organization meant employer authority, repression of unions, and the application of hierarchy to the administration, constitution, and family. It also meant 'production', in a context of Darwinian struggle between nations.

By 1924, most conservatives regarded the Bloc as a failure; right and centre were at loggerheads and most observers expected the left to win the coming elections. René Rémond's view that religion divided the Bloc partly explains these conflicts, especially given its entanglement with other aspects of the Bloc's programme.[5] The transfer into domestic politics of the culture of war, of which the unrealizable hopes of November 1919 were an intrinsic part, further raised the political stakes, not just between right and left. Although conservatives believed in parliamentary deliberation, the war culture encouraged them to suspect that their coalition partners were ideologues with whom one could not debate. As the Bloc split, rival organizational projects developed in the centre and right, each with complex relations to foreign movements.

[3] Antoine Prost, 'The impact of war on French and German political cultures', *Historical Journal* 37, no. 1 (1994), 209–17.

[4] Nicolas Roussellier, 'Phénomène de majorité et relation de majorité en régime parlementaire. Le Cas du Bloc national dans le premier après-guerre européen (1919–1924)', thèse de doctorat, IEP Paris, 1991; Nicolas Roussellier, *Le Parlement de l'éloquence. La Souveraineté de la délibération au lendemain de la Grande Guerre* (Paris, 1997).

[5] René Rémond, *Les Droites en France*, fourth revised edition (Paris, 1982), 187.

On the one hand, the right and extreme right, impressed by foreign dictatorships, developed a liberal and/or corporatist, Catholic organizationalism. It was designed to reconcile the classes, restore patriarchal authority, and improve productivity and the birth rate without state intervention. On the other hand, without necessarily abandoning Fayolism, Centrists and especially Christian Democrats moved closer to the Radical-Socialist version of organization, which entailed secularism and social reform in a European framework, with some state intervention. Both forms of organizationalism advocated the family vote, pro-natalism, and social and institutional reform, but conceived them differently. The very nature of the ruling class and its claim to competence, was at stake: each group claimed the general competence needed to govern, while relegating competitors to 'special competence', or denying their competence altogether. Meanwhile, disappointed right-wing activists began to criticize their leaders and restructure their organizations, opening the way for the revival of conservative activism in various forms.

THE POST-WAR CRISIS

In 1919–1920, social and political tension was high. Large tracts of the country had been devastated; nearly 1.3 million men were dead, and many more wounded. Major strike waves in the spring of 1919 and 1920, especially in the mines and railways, coinciding with the Soviet advance on Warsaw, convinced conservatives that Bolshevik revolution would spread to France. The impact of inflation on bourgeois savings exacerbated crisis. Elsewhere, such conditions favoured extremism. Given the tradition of radical rightism in France, the Clemenceau government's institution of the eight-hour day, proposed capital levy, and its failure to secure the left bank of the Rhine might have persuaded conservatives that the government was pro-Socialist and insufficiently national, and that they must defend themselves. In Italy, the Fascisti assumed the task of destroying socialism and liberalism and remaking the ruling class and the nation.[6] In France, right-wing extremism was weaker and conservatives largely accepted Bloc leadership.

As its Italian counterpart did, the French extreme right attracted some individuals who had started out on the left. The war convinced the ex-syndicalist, Gustave Hervé, that nation, not class, was the moving force in history, and like Mussolini, he retained the syndicalists' fascination with action. Yet in 1919, Hervé merely hoped that his Parti socialiste nationale would form the left wing of the Bloc.[7] Démocratie nouvelle also had something in common with the Fascisti. Its leader, Eugène Letailleur (pseudonym, Lysis), had previously worked on *L'Humanité*, Hervé's *Victoire*, and Clemenceau's *Homme libre*.[8] Initially moderate, by 1919 Démocratie nouvelle combined anti-communism with denunciation

[6] Andreas Wirsching, 'Political violence in France and Italy after 1918', *Journal of Modern European History* 1, no. 1 (2003), 60–79.

[7] Michael B. Loughlin, 'Gustave Hervé's transition from socialism to national socialism: another example of French fascism', *Journal of Contemporary History* 36, no, 1 (2001), 5–39.

[8] Olivier Dard, *Le Rendez-vous manqué des relèves des années 30* (Paris, 2002), 35–7.

of the bourgeoisie for allowing Communism to thrive. Lysis especially criticized the Alliance démocratique, for instance for refusing to have Jean Longuet shot, and saw the Union sacrée as 'a touching fraternity of all the politicians who exploit the state'.[9] The league also denounced the decadence evident in the fashion for stage nudity and insane dancing, and threatened that if the police did not intervene, then a group of Frenchmen would treat this corruption as it deserved.[10] In June 1919, Démocratie nouvelle created a Section combattante, dedicated to protection of meetings and the right to work. The Section would prove that 'Frenchmen who had vanquished the Boches would not be troubled by the Boches of the interior'.[11] Although Démocratie nouvelle never became a mass movement, it demonstrated that France could generate something similar to Fascism. However, its constitutional proposals were limited to strengthening the Presidency through election by an enlarged college; the president would still be accountable to parliament, and constrained by a supreme court.[12] *Le Temps* condemned Lysis for presenting reactionary Bonapartism as if it was new.[13] The Fédération was more favourable.[14]

Action française (AF) was stronger than Démocratie nouvelle, but it admired Clemenceau, Millerand, and Poincaré; Royalist officers helped administer Alsace-Lorraine, while Maurras thought as much about joining the Académie française as about overthrowing the Republic. In 1919, AF presented candidates for the first time. In the Hérault, the three deputies elected on the Union national list had long sought to integrate Royalism into a 'conservative' alliance and after the election denied belonging to AF—to local neo-Royalists' annoyance.[15]

The story of the Unions civiques confirms the hegemony of the parliamentary right. The Unions recruited an army of volunteers to break the Mayday 1920 strike. The first appeared in February in Lyon, during a railway strike, and quickly spread to the rest of France once the government had made them a public utility. They ran public services and helped the police keep order. Affiliated to the Unions were conservative groups from the Ligue des patriots to the Union national des combattants (UNC). In Lyon, Jacques Millevoye urged imitation of Italy and Spain 'through methodical application of the clarity that one finds in all institutions of the Latin Race'. As some Italian Fascists did, the Unions presented themselves as a 'bourgeois rebellion' against Socialist enemies of the country. Unlike the Fascists, they did not envisage an autonomous political role and were not anti-capitalist. They understood 'that they could not leave it wholly up to the state and its organs to defend the nation', but largely followed the authorities' orders. True, Italian Fascists often enjoyed official support, but the balance of power was different in France.[16]

[9] *Démocratie nouvelle*, 10 April 1919, 20 June, 26 and 30 September 1919.

[10] *Démocratie nouvelle*, 8 January 1919.

[11] *Démocratie nouvelle*, 20 June 1919.

[12] Lysis, *Ce que veut la Démocratie nouvelle* (Paris, 1919), 15–18.

[13] *Le Temps*, 26 August, 21 December 1919.

[14] *La République française*, 24 September 1919.

[15] Philippe Secondy, *La Persistance du Midi blanc* (Perpignan, 2006), 202–7.

[16] Théodore Aubert, *Une Forme de défense sociale. Les Unions civiques* (Paris, 1921); Maurice Moissonnier and André Boulmier, 'La Bourgeoisie lyonnaise aux origines de l'Union civique de 1920?', *Cahiers de l'histoire de l'institut de recherches Marxistes* 38, no. 4 (1980–1), 106–31.

One reason was that conservative veterans mostly backed the Bloc. In Italy and Germany, in contrast, war turned into civil war, thanks to the collapse of central authority, the outbreak of paramilitary wars on the Yugoslav and Polish borders. The veterans who fought these wars then turned their attention to the left, which in both Italy and Germany contained strong anti-war tendencies (in Britain, the veterans recruited to fight Irish Nationalists had no equivalent left-wing enemy). In France, failure to gain the left bank of the Rhine upset French conservatives, and some began to speak of a 'lost peace',[17] but there were no French minorities in the Rhineland for paramilitaries to defend. Moreover, French veterans returned home as conquering heroes; most French Socialists wanted victory.[18]

Certainly, conservative veterans wished to perpetuate the spirit of the front, but for the moment they saw the Bloc as the means to do that. Jean Binet-Valmer created the Ligue des chefs de section to regenerate France, and drew support from AF to the centre.[19] Of the two major veteran groups, the Union fédérale was close to the Radical-Socialists and centre. Its rival, the UNC, emerged from an initiative of the Church, senior officers, and business, and possessed 300,000 members in 1920. It was broadly favourable to the Catholic right, but also included Christian Democrats and centrists, such as Secretary-General Charles Bertrand (ARS).[20] In 1919, the two movements jointly urged voters to choose veterans rather than *embusqués*—in effect, the Bloc national. In some departments, veterans presented their own lists, but gained few votes. In the Chamber, the proportion of veterans among deputies increased from 25 per cent in Socialist Party (SFIO) to 55 per cent in the ERD. That did not justify conservative claims to represent exclusively the veterans (one newspaper produced a diagram showing that all the deputies killed in the war had been conservatives), but it underlined conservative veterans' allegiance to the Bloc.[21]

We should not exaggerate the Bloc's moderation, for it neutralized the extreme right by absorbing some of its themes. Veterans' readiness to claim a moral authority above that of politicians potentially challenged the principle of democratic debate and reduced room for compromise. Quatrième république was quite typical of a certain ambiguity in the Bloc. It enjoyed broad conservative support, ranging from Charles Bertrand of the centrist ARS and UNC to Binet-Valmer of the Ligue des chefs de section, and claimed that the veterans confusedly felt that 'the fate of France is still at stake and that it was their job, once again, to save the *patrie*'.[22]

17 *L'Alliance démocratique*, 27 April 1919.

18 Antoine Prost, *Les Anciens combattants et la société française 1914–1939*, 3 vols, i. *L'Histoire* (Paris, 1977), 33–46; Wirsching, 'Political violence', 69.

19 Prost, *Les Anciens combattants*, 1, 33–46; Robert Lynn Fuller, 'The dynamics of conservative politics in Upper Normandy, 1898–1928', PhD dissertation, University of Virginia, 1994, 530–1; Gilles Le Béguec, 'L'Entrée au Palais-Bourbon. Les Filières privilégiées d'accès à la fonction parlementaire 1919–1939', doctorat d'état, Paris X Nanterre, 1989, 353–6.

20 Le Béguec, 'L'Entrée', 357–9.

21 Prost, *Les anciens combattants*, i, 63–8; Roussellier, 'Phénomène de majorité', 143–54; *Le Nouvelliste de Bretagne*, 11 April 1924.

22 Le Béguec, 'L'Entrée', 299–301; *Petite Gironde*, 30 August 1919; *L'Intransigeant*, 16 January 1920.

The Bloc was quite authoritarian. Already Clemenceau had ruled by quasi-Bonapartist means, and the Bloc presented itself as his heir. Rightly or wrongly, conservatives believed that Clemenceau's popularity made him indispensable. An ALP journalist wrote that Clemenceau was the favourite of the peasant masses, and possessed a legend, 'like the little corporal'.[23] Since the resumption of war remained possible, Clemenceau alone could conduct negotiations at Versailles. Like Napoléon III, he mixed repression with concession, notably introducing the eight-hour day.[24] The future leader of the Jeunesses patriotes (JP), Pierre Taittinger, standing in Charente-inférieure, amalgamated Bonapartist and Clemenciste themes.[25] As premier, Millerand claimed Clemenceau's mantel; he arrested union leaders, sacked twenty thousand railway workers, and prosecuted the Confédération générale du travail (CGT), while promising social reform.

Furthermore, conservatives transferred the culture of war into anti-communism, identifying the Bolsheviks and Germans with barbarous Asia. During the war, conservatives' conviction that Thomas' moderate social democracy threatened the end of civilization had hardly suggested acceptance of pluralism. Now, Louis Latapie wrote that 'from the unfathomable depths of Russia, from the atavism of centuries of suffering ferment, a wave is breaking over Europe and threatens to swallow up the Latin conquest of Law and the benefits of civilization'.[26] Mathiot of the Alliance likened Communism to 'infection with the plague'.[27] The conviction that Communists manipulated the Socialists and Radicals cast the entire left as anti-French. Thus, the unity of the Bloc depended as much on repression and the language of civil war (readily used by the left too) as on commitment to democratic debate.

Notwithstanding, the extreme right was weak. Whereas years of power discredited Italian and German conservatives, their French counterparts had been out of office for forty years and so they captured the fear of Communism and millenarian expectations of regeneration that led to Fascism in Italy. When Jules Roche (Fédération républicaine (FR)) urged 'the friends of order' to 'take their place in the civic army' and 'save France from the interior enemy, which will enslave and ruin France to the point that it will signify death', he meant the Bloc, not a paramilitary force.[28]

These exaggerated hopes for the Bloc were bound to be disappointed—the harmony conservatives imagined was impossible and anyway they conceived regeneration differently. The *Le Temps* journalist who proclaimed that 'the objective is to remake France'[29] would not have endorsed an ALP colleague's estimate that the election was 'a salutary reaction of French instincts against all the distortions that twenty years of Jacobin domination have attempted to impose on the generous soul of the race and its Christian tradition'.[30] Extreme but contradictory expectations ultimately divided the right and centre.

[23] *Bulletin de l'ALP*, 1 February 1922; AN 317 AP 167, Fonds Louis Marin (hereafter ANFLM, carton/dossier no.), 'Situation électorale dans le département des Basses-Pyrénées'.

[24] D.R. Watson, *Georges Clemenceau: A Political Biography* (London, 1974), 381–2.

[25] Jean Philippet, 'Le Temps des ligues. Pierre Taittinger et les Jeunesses patriotes', Doctorat, IEP Paris, 2000, 129–32

[26] *La République française*, 27 September 1919.

[27] *L'Alliance démocratique*, 27 April 1919.

[28] *La République française*, 15 September 1919.

[29] *La Presse de Paris*, 19 November 1919.

[30] *Bulletin de l'ALP*, 11 December 1919.

THE ELECTIONS

Only hindsight allows us to see the seeds of the Bloc's break-up in November 1919. The elections represented the highpoint of the Moderate Republican electoral model, in which informal networks of parties and leagues, unaffiliated committees, newspapers, 'congrès républicains', bishops, and business groups, notably the Union des intérêts économiques (UIE) and Comité Mascuraud, chose candidates. The Bloc list in Ille-et-Vilaine brought together 'the best elements of the political elite of the region', reported the press.[31] As conservatives had hoped, the proportional element in the new electoral system reinforced elitism; the composition of lists reflected deals among the few as much as the views of the conservative electorate, a fact that contributed to the return of Royalists.

In these conditions, the flexible Alliance démocratique was admirably suited to direct affairs. In December 1918, Carnot confirmed that it would remain an alliance, linking all Republicans, rather than a party.[32] The Alliance faced little competition in this role, for the Fédération was slow to reorganize,[33] while the ALP barely revived. Socialist separatism further increased the Alliance's advantage, forcing the Radical-Socialists to choose between the Bloc and electoral suicide on autonomous lists.[34] The Alliance also benefited from a strong centrist presence in the ANOD and QR, which played a significant electoral role in Lyon, Bordeaux, and Lille.[35]

The Alliance was the lynchpin of two agreements, of which the contradictory nature would later emerge, but which now facilitated unity. The Bloc national, presided by Adolphe Carnot, existed only in Paris, although a Bas-Rhin list also used the title. It stretched from right-wing Radicals to the ALP and Nationalists, including Barrès, but faced an AF list on its right. Piou's woolly statement concerning the religious question sealed unity: 'the fact of the *laïcité* of the state must be reconciled with the rights and liberties of all citizens, whatever religion they confess'. The second accord, the Cartel républicain, in contrast, united the Alliance with the Radical-Socialists, while the Fédération figured as a supplementary signatory, 'guarantied' by the Alliance. The Cartel insisted upon 'the absolute *laïcité* of state and school as a safeguard for the absolute liberty of conscience'. Latapie saw 'former sectarians' behind the Cartel.[36]

Real electoral lists reflected the interleaving of social and religious issues. The Radicals joined the Alliance and sometimes the Fédération in fifty-four out of ninety-seven constituencies. Other lists united the Alliance and Fédération alone

[31] Jacqueline Sainclivier, *L'Ille-et-Vilaine 1918–1958. Vie politique et sociale* (Rennes, 1996), 78.

[32] *Alliance démocratique*, 26 October 1918; Rosemonde Sanson, *L'Alliance républicaine démocratique. Une Formation du centre (1901–1920)* (Rennes, 2003), 442–5.

[33] Bernard, *La Dérive des modérés*, 246–7.

[34] Roussellier, *Le Parlement*, 25–34; Sanson, *L'Alliance*, 460–71; C.S. Maier, *Recasting Bourgeois Europe: Stabilization in France, Germany and Italy after World War One* (Princeton, 1975), 27–61; Serge Berstein, *Histoire du Parti radical*, i. *La Recherché de l'age d'or* (Paris, 1980), 114–18; *La République démocratique*, 18 June 1922.

[35] Le Béguec, 'L'Entrée', 279–306.

[36] *La République française*, 25, 26 October 1919.

or extended to the ALP and even crypto-Royalists.[37] In departments where Socialism was important, conservatives usually achieved unity. Where Socialism was less threatening, especially in the West and Brittany, centre and right often confronted each other. Yet closer analysis reveals that religious and class conflict were entangled everywhere. In the Nord, where Socialism was strong, a centre list, led by Loucheur and Lemire, endorsed the lay laws and preached social reform. A rival, ALP-dominated list approved the Republic as a fact rather than a principle, called for liberty of teaching, and scolded those Catholics in other departments who accepted the lay laws in return for unity against Socialism.[38] The opposite applied in Mayenne, where Socialism was absent, and yet social questions were important. Conservatives refused to allow the neo-Royalist Bernard de Vesins to join their list, for he attacked Republicans, and demanded an end to discrimination against Catholics and recognition of the place of the land in the economy against the omnipotence of the factory worker. To the horror of Royalists, the conservative list included a Christian Democrat, who prioritized social reform.[39]

These tensions were not immediately evident in parliament, where centre and right united around Millerand. In his programmatic Bataclan speech of 7 November 1919, Millerand had presented a conservative interpretation of the Bloc. His leftist past and inclusion of Radicals in the government reassured the centre, while the right remembered his wartime defence of Joffre. The ERD initially complained of underrepresentation, but soon warmed to Millerand.[40] In September, following the sick Deschanel's resignation, centre and right secured Millerand's election as President of the Republic. In parliament, conservatives avoided overt displays of clericalism or anticlericalism. True, in January 1920, Clemenceau's defeat by Deschanel in the presidential election, thanks to Catholic votes, signalled problems to come. Yet in 1920 and 1923, many Catholics voted for motions endorsing the laws of the Republic in order to fend off Radical attempts to divide the majority.[41]

ORGANIZATION, ECONOMIC WAR, AND COMPETENCE

Millerand's government represented the triumph of Moderate Republicanism, united around the organizational project of the 1900s, as modified by the culture of war, the encounter with management science, and the post-war reaction against state intervention. Contrary to Stéphane Audoin-Rouzeau and Annette Becker's contention that peace saw the sublimation of the culture of war into equally millenarian pacifism,[42] this programme assumed the continuation of a Darwinist struggle against foreign enemies and their domestic allies.

[37] Roussellier, 'Phénomène de majorité', 65–84.
[38] Jean-Marie Mayeur, *L'Abbé Lemire. Un Prêtre démocrate 1853–1928* (Paris, 1968), 541–9.
[39] Michel Denis, *Les Royalistes de la Mayenne et le monde moderne (XIXe–XXe siècles)* (Le Mans, 1977), 519.
[40] *Discours de M. Millerand prononcé à Ba-ta-Clan* (Paris, 1919), 7–8.
[41] Roussellier, *Le Parlement*, 208–9.
[42] Annette Becker and Stéphane Audoin-Rouzeau, *14–18, retrouver la guerre* (Paris, 2000), 182–8.

For most conservatives Germany remained the enemy. They were mesmerized by its economic potential and superior birth rate, and believed that barbarism impelled it to seek world domination. France must defend itself by minimizing imports through industrial and agricultural self-sufficiency, and use political influence and military power to conquer foreign and imperial markets—the Congrès de l'outillage colonial of July 1922 signalled a new enthusiasm for empire.[43] Economic struggle also implied strict enforcement of the Versailles Treaty. Charles de Gaulle later remembered that he had returned from prisoner of war camp 'overflowing with a generalized sentiment of xenophobia', and convinced that it was time to 'make ourselves respected through judicious use of [our] armed force, now the best in the world'.[44] *La République française* cited Le Bon's *Le Déséquilibre du monde* (1923) as support for an anti-humanitarian view of international relations.[45] In the immediate post-war years, the centre did not fundamentally disagree. André De Fels (Alliance) gloomily concluded that given the chimerical nature of the League of Nations and the attitude of the British, France must concentrate on reconstruction, develop its colonies, and maximize its remaining economic and demographic strength.[46]

Conservatives (along with much of the left) saw 'production'—material, demographic, and industrial—as the key to victory in the struggle. Paul Jourdain (centre) held that 'Everything that makes the power of a nation—agriculture, industry, commerce, merchant navy, colonies, letters, sciences, arts, and lastly the Army and Navy—exists in direct relation to the population'.[47] At Bataclan, Millerand declared that 'Yesterday France had to vanquish or perish. Today it must produce or disappear'. He urged the mobilization of science to develop natural resources, improve productivity, and rebuild the devastated regions. Contradicting their alleged Malthusianism,[48] conservatives unanimously approved Loucheur's injunction to sing the 'hymn of production'—a cliché of the day. Meanwhile, in the new chamber, the proportion of deputies belonging to the pro-natalist and family intergroup doubled. It was presided by Castelnau, father of eleven children, of whom three had died in the war.[49] Isaac charged advocates of birth control with 'treason against the nation'.[50] Productivist principles could also be applied to the legislature. The Fédération programme enshrined its commitment to 'improve legislative productivity', while ANOD focussed particularly on that theme.[51]

[43] *La République démocratique*, 22 January 1922; *Action nationale républicaine*, 22 November 1923.
[44] Éric Roussel, *Charles de Gaulle* (Paris, 2002), 32.
[45] *La République française*, 3 March 1921; *Bulletin de la Fédération républicaine*, 30 September 1921; *Bulletin de l'ALP*, 1 September 1922; Jean-Noël Jeanneney, *François de Wendel en République. L'Argent et le pouvoir* (Paris, 1976), 120.
[46] Comte André de Fels, *Essai de politique expérimentale* (Paris, 1921), 302–6.
[47] *La République démocratique*, 6 January 1924.
[48] Richard Kuisel, *Capitalism and the State in Modern France* (Cambridge, 1981), 50, 59.
[49] Richard Tomlinson, 'The politics of dénatalité during the French Third Republic 1890–1940', PhD thesis, University of Cambridge, 1983, 334.
[50] Tomlinson, 'The politics', 139–52.
[51] *La Fédération républicaine*, January 1922.

Productivity depended on organization. Indeed, Bonnefous claimed that the Bloc's primary task was 'organization of the Republic in an organized society'.[52] In the immediate post-war years, Fayol sold 15,000 of his *Administration industrielle et générale*, and he advised the government on administrative reform. In June 1923, the first Conférence de l'organisation française met in the presence of thirteen ministers.[53] Millerand, who had long been interested in organization,[54] declared, 'I cannot conceive any other way of managing the state than by following the rules of a well-directed industrial enterprise', while Probus complained that the random improvisations of parliamentary discussion would make anyone with a sense of the practical realizations of private enterprise smile.[55]

Conservatives also presented the Bloc as the triumph of competence. Confirming the malleability of the notion, they applied term widely. First, many Bloc deputies owed their position to their role in the war effort.[56] Loucheur was one of several Polytechniciens elected in 1919 who came to parliament by that route. Secondly, landowners and aristocrats saw themselves as competences previously excluded from power by an unfair electoral system. An aristocratic agricultural unionist equated capitalists, technicians, and workers with landowners, tenants or sharecroppers, and labourers respectively, and charged the leisured class with 'watching over the especially delicate mechanisms of the corporative machine'.[57] In the same spirit, a Royalist newspaper emphasized the 'rapidity' of their candidate, both on foot and in his car.[58] Lawyers too presented themselves as competent: Joseph-Barthélemy, president of the ARS, urged the best lawyers to enter parliament, for they allegedly possessed the necessary 'general competence'.[59] Some deputies affected a new speaking style—General Castelnau made brief, acerbic interventions combining military expertise with the moral authority of the veteran; Loucheur made technical speeches. Their target might have been the rhetorical flourishes of the *Palais*, epitomized in Briand's speeches. Yet in his own way, Briand too wished to 'modernize' politics. Most conservatives actually agreed with Georges Bonnamour (QR) that 'We must end the separation of parliament and the elite, and bring together nation and parliament through the representation of interests and competences.'[60]

[52] *La République française*, 7 October 1919.

[53] Stéphane Rials, *Administration et organisation. De L'Organisation de la bataille à la bataille de l'organisation dans l'administration française* (Paris, 1977), 132–44.

[54] Rials, *Administration*, 158–64.

[55] Quoted in Rouchon-Mazerat, 'Idées directrices de la doctrine administrative', in Antonin and Léon Franchet (eds), *Pour former les hommes qu'il faut à la France de l'après guerre* (Paris, 1923), 21; Sanson, *L'Alliance*, 486–7; *Démocratie nouvelle*, 26 May 1919; *L'Intransigeant*, 16 January 1920.

[56] Nicholas Roussellier, 'Les avocats et la Chambre "blue horizon". Rhétorique et délibération', in Gilles Le Béguec, *Avocats et barraux en France—1910–1930* (Nancy, 1994), 119–26.

[57] David Bensoussan, *Combats pour une Bretagne catholique et rurale. Les Droites bretonnes dans l'entre-deux-guerres* (Paris, 2006), 279–82.

[58] Secondy, *La Persistence*, 204.

[59] Barthélemy, *Le Problème de la compétence dans la démocratie* (Paris, 1918), 62–5; Roussellier, 'Phénomène de majorité', 136–43; Rials, *Administration*, 98–113.

[60] *L'Éclair*, 4 November 1922; Roussellier, *Le Parlement*, 222–3.

'Realism' was another new term in the organizational lexicon, or rather an old term given greater emphasis. It was rooted in pragmatic liberal-conservative opposition to ideology, traceable back at to Le Bon's notion that the elite must elaborate realistic policies in the light of the national psychology. After the war, realists depicted themselves as 'new men', veterans and/or the young generation, even though many had long been politically active. Belief in the need to confront post-war 'realities' and 'facts', rather than engage in empty talk, was universal in post-war political discourse.[61] Of course, each group contrasted its own realism to opponents' dogmatism.

The Bloc integrated productivism, competence, and realism into a liberal version of the organizational project. During the war, liberals reluctantly accepted the war economy as a temporary evil, at least once the Socialists had been evicted from the government. By 1919, liberal orthodoxy predominated, for business actually experienced 'organized liberalism' in the war economy as 'Socialist coercion'. Economic controls were quickly dismantled, and those, like Loucheur and Clémentel, who saw organization of the international economy and domestic labour relations as a third way between individualism and Socialism were defeated.[62] Repression of the general strike of 21 July 1919 further reinforced liberals.[63] Millerand appointed the ultra-orthodox Isaac to the Ministry of Commerce and initiated legal proceedings against the CGT. *Le Temps* argued that the best way to defeat Germany in the economic war was to encourage competition in France.[64]

The Bloc's organizational project was liberal in so far as it freed business from state control, but was less so in other respects. It mobilized the resources of state and civil society to ensure that the CGT could not contest employer authority. It endeavoured to transfer the hierarchical Fayolist model to the state through reinforcement of the executive, and to the family and society via the family vote. The latter was crucially important, for in principle it united right and centre, and was meant to provide organic structure for the electorate, while resolving broader social and moral difficulties. In the event, each aspect of the Bloc's organizational strategy failed, for they were predicated on subordination of Germany, receipt of reparations, and transcendence of the religious question, and left open the role of the state.

REPARATIONS AND ORGANIZATION

At Bataclan, Millerand demanded strict enforcement of the Treaty in concert with Britain and the United States, for, like most conservatives, he had not forgotten

[61] *Bulletin de l'ALP*, 11 November, 11 December 1919; Barthélemy, *Le Problème*, 78–81.

[62] Kuisel, *Capitalism and the State*, 51–4.

[63] Kuisel, *Capitalism and the State*, 55–7; Martin Fine, 'The movement for capital-labour collaboration in France, 1914–1936', PhD dissertaiton, Wisconsin, 1971, 60–71; Georges Lefranc, *Les Organisations patronales en France du passé au présent* (Paris, 1976); Maier, *Recasting*, 78–85; Michel Launey, *La CFTC. Origines et développement 1919–1940* (Paris, 1986), 128–30.

[64] *Le Temps*, 3 December 1920.

German barbarism. We have seen that in 1919–1920, right and centre broadly agreed on foreign policy—the hard-liners, Poincaré and Tardieu, were centrists.[65] The centre differed only in seeking to use the League of Nations and the British alliance to prevent Germany from undermining the freedom of new European nation states, while Catholics were more favourable to restoration of the Habsburg Empire, and were more anti-British. From 1921, as Germany began to resist reparations, the Alliance pressed for occupation of the Rühr, and accused the left of taking bribes from Russia and Germany.[66]

In practice, enforcement conflicted with other conservative priorities and presented insuperable obstacles anyway. Weakening Germany potentially favoured Bolshevism. The alternative of payments in kind threatened French producers of those goods. Worse, Germany would have to export so much to earn the gold marks required for reparations that, as one conservative remarked, 'on the day that Germany has finished making payments, she will have become the economic master of the world'.[67] The centrist Paul Reynaud evoked deputies' stupefied discovery that 'the iron laws of political economy make no distinction between good or bad peoples', and that when transporting the riches of one country to another 'the state to which one gives is as troubled in its internal economy as that from which one takes'.[68] Reynaud's speech apparently struck at the heart of the Darwinist conception of international relations and thus at the whole edifice of the conservative organizational project, for it implied that international cooperation was better than struggle.

Yet Reynaud and other critics broke only partially with Darwinism. Rather, they began to develop a vision of a European political and economic bloc under French leadership, including Germany, but competing with the Anglo-Saxon, Soviet, and/or Asian blocs. At Versailles, Clemenceau, Clémentel, and Loucheur had endeavoured to perpetuate Allied cooperation through military guaranties and continuation of purchasing cartels. The Briand government of 1921, which included Loucheur as Minister for Liberated Regions, showed some sympathy for this approach, while simultaneously seeking to coerce Germany.[69] Some moderate Catholics also embraced Europeanism, heeding the Pope's insistence that charity should regulate international relations. Monseigneur Chapon of Nice urged his flock not to hold the German race responsible for individuals' crimes. In the spring of 1922, Marc Sangnier, elected on a Bloc list, accused Poincaré of discouraging moderate Germans—a Royalist heckler dared him to give his speech at Verdun. Few Catholics went so far as Sangnier. Yet in key votes, the ERD divided for and against Briand.

[65] *La République démocratique*, 1, 13 May 1922; Robert J. Young, *Power and Pleasure: Louis Barthou and the Third French Republic* (Montreal, 1991), 163–5.

[66] *La République démocratique*, 23 April, 17 December 1922, 11 February, 23 July, 14 October 1923.

[67] Camille Aynard, *L'Europe nouvelle*, 31 March 1923.

[68] Thibault Tellier, *Paul Reynaud. Un Indépendant en politique* (Paris, 2005), 81.

[69] Jules Laroche, *Au Quai d'Orsay avec Briand et Poincaré 1913–1926* (Paris, 1957), 151; Bernard Oudin, *Aristide Briand* (Paris, 2004), 413–16, 442–3; Roussellier, *Le Parlement*, 194–7.

The failure of reparations also undermined the Bloc's liberalism. Advocacy of state intervention had not entirely disappeared among conservatives. Even the Millerand government, to the annoyance of *Le Temps*, accepted 'controlled liberty' as it instituted a monopoly of petrol imports.[70] Loucheur's bid for economic cooperation converged with forgemasters' desire for access to Rühr coke, essential for smelting recovered Lorraine ore. The senator and steel magnate Gaston Japy saw agreement as the foundation of peace.[71] This strategy broke with liberals' consumption-oriented view of organization, in favour of the view that reconstruction and success in the international struggle depended on capital goods. Loucheur concluded that since reparations were impossible, reinforcement of income tax must substitute for it; he advocated international economic cooperation, including regulation of currencies by institutions that he called 'Socialist'.[72] In 1924, as the Franc fell, Poincaré had to raise taxes.

Nevertheless, firmness prevailed. In January 1922, Poincaré returned to power, and presented reparations as the fulfilment of the veterans' sacrifice. On 11 January 1923, he sent troops into the Rühr, to the applause of conservatives and many Radicals. The rhetoric of the culture of war revived. An Alliance spokesman described a Léon Blum speech in Hamburg as 'nothing more and nothing less than a denial of *la patrie*'.[73] An ALP journalist unwittingly exposed the Darwinist assumptions of foreign policy, claiming that it did not matter whether or not the occupation made a profit, for the real objective was to deprive Germany of the 'super-production' of the Rühr, without which it could not make war.[74] Centrists argued that France should ultimately evacuate the Rühr but convert the Rhineland into a 'productive guarantee'.[75]

In September 1923, Germany gave in, yet Poincaré could not exploit victory. Disintegration of Germany raised the prospect of Bolshevization, and Poincaré knew that American finance might be necessary to prop up the ailing Franc. Consequently, on 17 May he accepted the Dawes Report, which imposed concessions on France. He saved his majority only by attacking the left. Foreign policy had become a major source of intra-conservative conflict. On the one hand, the right saw any reduction in reparations as failure to claim the fruits of victory, for which it blamed domestic enemies. On the other hand, the centre used its commitment to the British Alliance and League of Nations as a stepping stone to an alternative policy, involving organization of the economy in a European framework, closer to that of the Radical-Socialists. Religious conflict reinforced these divisions.

70 *Le Temps*, 3 December 1920.

71 Maier, *Recasting*, 199–202, 406–7; *La République française*, 13 July 1922.

72 Maier, *Recasting*, 274–5.

73 *La République démocratique*, 8 July, 7 October 1923; *Action nationale républicaine*, 22 November 1923; *Le Nouvelliste de Bretagne*, 7 April 1924.

74 *Bulletin de l'ALP*, 1 February, 1 June 1923.

75 *L'Europe nouvelle*, 3 March 1923; *La République démocratique*, 8 July, 7 October 1923.

RELIGION

Conservatives certainly wanted to set the religious question aside. Bonnefous asked whether they should quarrel over fiscal, constitutional, or school laws at a time when 'the essential question is to know if tomorrow, thanks to the barbarians who threaten us, France, and even a human society worthy of the name will still exist'.[76] Yet aspiration did not mean realization. Charles Chaumet, prominent in the left of the Alliance, saw Piou's formula on *laïcité* as 'meaningless without elucidation of the conditions on which this reconciliation depends'.[77] Piou refused union at the price of 'forgetting the past'.[78] For the centre, the war proved the solidity of the *laïque* Republic: Chaumet asked conservatives 'not to revive past quarrels by undermining conquests that must now be considered definitive'.[79] At the other end of the majority, Salvetti claimed that since the Union sacrée won the war, not the sects, Republicans must reform the lay laws.[80] Because religious questions were supposedly no longer controversial, teachers in Breton public schools began to wear religious dress.[81] Religious struggle was woven into the fabric of French life, and in some respects, recent developments intensified it.

The interwar years witnessed the formation of a plethora of associations within lay and Catholic networks. Wartime organization, increased leisure thanks to the eight-hour law, and new strategies on the part of the Church, all stimulated membership of associations. The religious divide was bridgeable, yet there were competing Catholic and *laïque* organizations among engineers, parents of schoolchildren, the women's and trade union movements, and business and veterans' groups. The question of whether or not village war memorials should feature crosses reactivated religious disputes.[82] Extension of the *secular* state during the war complicated these conflicts. For instance, the Catholic engineers' union, USIC, opposed its *laïque* rival's view that the state should validate engineers' qualifications.[83]

Catholics still experienced discrimination, notably in the *corps préfectoral* and upper ranks of the Interior and Education Ministries. Clemenceau's refusal to make Castelnau a marshal provoked noisy Catholic resentment. Catholics only obtained token presence in Bloc governments, and those who did serve, such as Léon Bérard,

[76] *La République française*, 7 October 1919.

[77] *La République démocratique*, 1, 15 October 1922; *Le Temps*, 3 December 1920; *Le Petit Journal*, 10 October 1923; Paul, *The Second Ralliement*, 97–8; Raymond Poincaré, 'Preface', in Ferdinand Buisson, *La Foi laïque. Extraits de discours et d'écrits (1878–1911)*, third edition (Paris, 1918), vii–x.

[78] Archives nationales, 142 AP 14, Fonds Rochefoucauld (hereafter ANFXR, carton/dossier no.), Piou to Rochefoucauld, 1 October 1919.

[79] *L'Alliance républicaine démocratique*, 20 July 1919, 13 February 1921, 20 March 1921. See also Charles Dumont's speech, *Lycée Henri IV, Distribution solennelle des prix* (Paris, 1920), 2–4.

[80] *Bulletin de l'Action libérale populaire*, 15 August 1919.

[81] Caroline Ford, *Creating the Nation in Provincial France: Religion and Political Identity in Brittany* (Princeton, 1993), 162–3.

[82] Maurice Gobillon, 'Châtelains et conseil municipal à Fossé', in Maurice Agulhon et al. (eds), *Les Maires en France du Consulat à nos jours* (Paris, 1986), 367–74; Hervé Joly (ed.), *Auguste Isaac. Journal d'un notable lyonnais, 1906–1933* (Lyon, 30 October 1921), 356.

[83] Jean-Louis Robert, 'Les Syndicats d'ingénieurs et de techniciens et la protection du titre d'ingénieur (1919–1934)', in André Grelon (ed.), *Les Ingénieurs de la crise. Titre et profession entre les deux guerres* (Paris, 1986), 141–57.

endorsed the lay laws unreservedly. Meanwhile, there was an influx of women into the lower ranks of the administration, some embracing Catholic Action's emphasis on visible faith. The anticlerical CGT *fonctionnaires* and teachers' unions used Freemasons as watchdogs.[84] The left's campaign for application of the lay laws to Alsace-Lorraine and for unification of primary and secondary education (the *école unique*) also kept the religious question alive.

There were countless complaints about Prefects' 'Combist spirit', and some took discrimination personally.[85] The antisemitic Monarchist, Xavier Vallat, evoked the harassment of his Catholic *instituteur* father.[86] The fiercely Republican Fédération leader, Auguste Isaac, asked why France could not be more like Britain or Switzerland, where a man's 'religious practice does not harm his career'.[87] We may gauge far-right bitterness from Jules Delahaye's chillingly prescient speech in a Senate debate concerning access to military schools:

> Gentlemen. There is an amendment that I have not proposed, but which in the future I might present.... 'No one should be admitted to the examination for the École polytechnique unless they can demonstrate that they are French, and of French descent for three generations'. These criteria will ensure that we do not find in our country's best schools undesirables preparing future war.... However, if I propose this amendment today..., you will say that it is contrary to the laws of hospitality. Therefore, it is perhaps not yet time to propose it. However, a day will come when I shall put it before you: it will be at a time when you have seen the attacks of the enemy multiply, with the help of the undesirables, without French blood in their veins, who occupy strategic posts.[88]

More moderately, the Fédération saw constitutional reform as a means to defend Catholic liberties, and revision of the lay laws figured in its programme. In December 1921, 120 Independents and ERD members voted in favour of state funding for Catholic Schools. The debate also revealed Catholic divisions, for to avoid fomenting religious hatred Isaac advised abstention.[89]

In the centre, Chaumet, Loucheur, and Albert Mamelet, secretary-general of the Alliance, were especially anticlerical. The latter urged Catholics to confine their preference for theocracy to their hearts where transcendent principles have no influence over action. Catholics did not, he admitted, need to embrace the absurd view that the lay laws were intangible, but they must promise not to touch them.

[84] Maurice Larkin, *Religion, Politics and Preferment in France since 1890* (Cambridge, 1995), 158–68.

[85] *Action nationale républicaine*, 3 May 1923; *Bulletin de l'ALP*, 15 May 1924; *Documentation catholique*, 9 (1923), 1144–6; *Le Nouvelliste de Bretagne*, 26 September, 1 October 1920.

[86] Laurent Joly, *Xavier Vallat. Du Nationalisme chrétien à l'antisémitisme de l'État* (Paris, 2001), 105–6.

[87] *Journal des Débâts*, 16 December 1923; Paul Féron-Vrau, *Après la guerre* (Paris, 1919), 16–17.

[88] Patrick Cabanel, 'La République contre les catholiques', in Marc-Olivier Baruch and Vincent Duclert (eds), *Les Serviteurs de l'état. Une Histoire politique de l'administration française* (Paris, 2000), 169–82. For Delahaye's speech, see *Journal officiel, Sénat*, 3 June 1919, 867.

[89] *La République française*, 25 October 1919; *Bulletin de la Fédération républicaine*, 31 January 1921; Fuller, 'The Dynamics', 525; Paul, *The Second Ralliement*, 87–90; Mayeur, *Lemire*, 567–71.

In 1918, Poincaré reaffirmed *laïcité* in a preface to a book of Ferdinand Buisson's speeches.[90] Isaac saw Poincaré as 'fundamentally hostile to the Catholic religion'.[91]

The Bloc's concessions to Catholics were largely compatible with the centre's long-held belief that liberal enforcement of the lay laws guarantied religious peace—indeed, the Alliance defended concessions in those terms.[92] Millerand allowed religious orders unofficially to return, but opposed legislative authorization, and broke his promise to grant orders the right to teach.[93] The centre backed the re-establishment of diplomatic relations with the Vatican for pragmatic reasons, and because the exchange of ambassadors confirmed the Pope's recognition of the Separation and helped to settle the question of the *associations cultuelles*. Again, little actually changed, for the law had long been applied liberally.[94]

As in the days of Méline, Catholics supported Republican governments in the hope of revision of the lay laws, while Republicans insisted that concessions were impossible. Meanwhile, on the fringes of the majority and in the towns and villages, religious conflict continued. In the elections of 1924, as in 1898, extremists gained on both sides. Religious struggle also compromised the Bloc's legislative programme, reinforcing the gap between the Catholic, often corporatist and authoritarian right and the democratic organizationalism of the centre. The Bloc's social programme confirmed these developments.

THE FAMILY VOTE, PRO-NATALISM, AND SOCIAL INSURANCE

At the heart of the Bloc's organizational programme was an organicist, patriarchal, sometimes explicitly Fayolist, conception of the family, designed also to stabilize the social and political order. It rested firstly upon the family allowance schemes that from 1919 employers in the metallurgical industries had introduced as a means to separate married fathers from single workers, moralize the workforce, and encourage the birth rate (for employers saw immigrant labour as second rate).[95] Now, natalists and social reformers lobbied for wider application of family allowances, as well as a system of 'social insurance', also presented as a pro-natalist measure, remedy for labour discontent, and an encouragement to productivity through elimination of sickness.

Secondly, whereas during the war conservatives had rarely attacked women for 'selfishness', they now exaggerated changes in their status and used the independent women, the *garçonne* (laddish woman), to signify a crisis in family, nation, and state.

[90] *La République démocratique*, 1, 15 October 1922; *Le Temps*, 3 December 1920; *Le Petit Journal*, 10 October 1923; Paul, *The Second Ralliement*, 97–8; Poincaré, 'Preface', vii–x.

[91] *Isaac*, 1 January 1921, 353, 20 April 1922, 364.

[92] *L'Alliance républicaine démocratique*, 1 October 1922, 12 August 1923.

[93] *La Nation*, 25 November 1925.

[94] *Le Temps*, 3 December 1920; *L'Alliance républicaine démocratique*, 1 October 1922, 12 August 1923.

[95] Susan Pedersen, *Family, Dependence, and the Origins of the Welfare State: Britain and France, 1914–1945* (Cambridge, 1995).

Thus, a conservative doctor denounced the *garçonne* and asked what would become of the family and birth rate when the wife was out visiting the sick or pleading in court?[96] Georges Noblemaire (ARS), wrote that in parliament the 'honest women' of the Bloc had not been sufficiently visible, whereas the *garçonne*, 'or any other bitch [garce] from a novel or real life, all equally revolting, the future women ambassadors and ministers of tomorrow, made one hundred times as much noise'.[97] In September 1919, the first Congrès de la natalité staged a Union sacrée, with *laïque* natalist, Berthillon, the Catholic liberal, Isaac, and the Catholic familialist, Maire, all in attendance. Conservatives largely saw familialism and natalism as complementary, for few accepted the left's tolerance of birth outside marriage. The Millerand government created a Conseil supérieure de la natalité, in which sat politicians and 'experts' from the ANPAPF.

The family vote, which involved allowing fathers, and perhaps mothers, to vote for children, brought these issues together and revealed tensions in the majority. The proposal seemingly united right and centre with the UNC, business groups, and the ANPAPF.[98] Its sponsor, Henry Roulleaux-Dugage (FR), presented the family vote as recompense for the sacrifice of large families in the war and as a pro-natalist measure. Like organizational theorists, he compared it to the multiple votes of shareholders and claimed that headship of large families represented an apprenticeship to government.[99] The family vote would restore the 'natural' order that the war had supposedly overturned and buttress male authority.[100]

So long as conservatives had been out of government, the fact that only private action was possible for them obscured divisions concerning social policy. Even then, conservatives disagreed about the state's role in retirement pensions. Now, the prospect of state intervention revealed the inseparability of economic and religious questions. Mamelet attacked Catholics 'who claimed to be the only ones able to resist the revolutionary upsurge and yet who have never been able to do anything other than reinforce it with all the repulsion that their odious selfishness inspires'. Only sincere democrats could recapture the people.[101] Piou, in contrast, held that 'At the bottom of any social question is a religious question', for religion was the rampart of society.[102] Isaac agreed that 'only Catholicism is capable of pacifying anger and conciliating interests'.[103]

Religious differences, coupled with disagreement concerning female suffrage, helped undermine the family vote. In December 1923, the Chamber agreed that

[96] *La République française*, 7 October, 10 November 1922; Cheryl Koos, 'Engendering reaction: the politics of pronatalism and the family in France, 1919–1944', PhD dissertation, University of Southern California, 1996, 35–45.

[97] Georges Noblemaire, *Carnet de route au pays des parlementaires* (Paris, 1923), 16–19.

[98] Jean-Yves Le Naour and Catherine Valenti, *La Famille doit voter. Le Suffrage familial contre le vote individuel* (Paris, 2005), 89–90, 104–8.

[99] *Bulletin de la Fédération républicaine*, 31 January 1921; Le Naour and Valenti, *La Famille*, 89–90, 95–8, 99–101, 130–5; Rials, *Administration et organisation*, 98–101.

[100] Mary-Louise Roberts, *Civilization without Sexes: Reconstructing Gender in Postwar France, 1917–1927* (Chicago, 1994); Christine Bard, *Les Garçonnes. Modes et fantasmes des années folles* (Paris, 1998).

[101] *La République démocratique*, 1, 15 October 1922.

[102] *Bulletin de l'ALP*, 1 January 1922.

[103] *Isaac*, 344–5, 23 May 1920.

wives should vote for themselves and husbands for the children, only for the government to force a confidence vote, in which many centrists put loyalty to the government first.[104] In fact, centrist enthusiasm for the project had been declining since Catholics had rallied to it, following the Pope's endorsement of female suffrage. Whereas centrists used the family vote to reconcile pro-natalism with female suffrage and autonomy for women within a patriarchal society, many rightists preferred fathers alone to vote for wives and children. The latter incorporated the family vote into a corporatist, hierarchical Catholic vision. Their attempt to attach freedom of testament and modification of the lay laws to the family vote also alarmed centrists.[105]

Pro-natalism foundered on similar problems. Liberals opposed state regulation of the family—for Isaac, the family wage and living wage encouraged laziness. In addition, the centre opposed *Catholic* familialism, while conservative Catholics saw depopulation as a malady of soul, which only religion could remedy.[106] Isaac had to struggle hard to overcome episcopal opposition to Catholic attendance at the 1921 natalist congress, where they might discuss marriage with Protestants and non-believers.[107] Moreover, Catholic familialism was often anti-parliamentarian. The Ligue des droits de la famille, presided by Senator Joseph Massabuau (ALP), advocated liberty of testament, suppression of divorce, and transformation of parliament into a 'great council of the families of the nation'.[108] Isaac reported that the 1923 natalist conference accepted that reform must have a religious basis.[109] These tensions explain the mediocrity of legislative output. On 22 July 1923, the Chamber approved a weak Family Allowance Law. The majority agreed to act against 'Malthusian' propaganda and abortion, causing misery to women without affecting the birth rate.

The Social Insurance Bill introduced in 1921 was even more problematic, for it was the work of one of those Radical-Socialists, Daniel-Vincent, whom the right would rather not have seen in government. Once more, state involvement divided conservatives, as did the role of mutualist organizations, Catholic charities, and employers' initiatives.[110] Isaac was a liberal, who wished to leave everything to employers' charitable spirit. Other conservatives preferred corporatism; ninety-two of them signed Gailhard-Bancel's counter-bill, based on the conviction that modern social science demonstrated the need to reinsert individuals in the region and profession, from which the Revolution had removed them. The state would have no role in social insurance beyond loaning money.[111] This project was backed

[104] *La République démocratique*, 12 August 1923; Le Naour and Valenti, *La Famille*, 102–10.

[105] Mayeur, *Lemire*, 574–5; Le Naour and Valenti, *La Famille*, 99–100, 130–5.

[106] *La République démocratique*, 16 January 1921, 4 December 1921, 19 November 1922, 5 August 1923, 6 January 1924; *Le Temps*, 30 November 1921; *Isaac*, 2 October 1921, 355; *Nouvelliste de Bretagne*, 4 Janvier 1919.

[107] *Isaac*, 2 October 1921, 353–4.

[108] Le Naour and Valenti, *La Famille*, 80–1; Féron-Vrau, *Après la guerre*, 16–17.

[109] *Isaac*, 27–30 September 1923, 375.

[110] Paul V. Dutton, *Origins of the French Welfare State: The Struggle for Social Reform in France 1914–1947* (Cambridge, 2002), 19–37, 57–75.

[111] *Bulletin de l'ALP*, 1 March 1922.

by business and agricultural organizations, including the Comité des forges and Confédération générale de la production française (CGPF), for it would reduce the tax burden and allow benefits to be adjusted on a regional basis. Employer and Catholic opposition converged in the person of Eugène Mathon, pro-Royalist leader of conservative textile bosses in the Nord, who would promote the corporatist alternative to social insurance in the extreme right.[112]

The centre was more favourable to the bill (especially the Christian Democrats). The Catholic trade union, the Confédération française des travailleurs chrétiens (CFTC), founded in 1919, saw social insurance as a means to 'humanize' and pacify industrial relations through restoration of moral (Catholic) standards. The CFTC envisaged equal employer and worker management of social insurance through joint commissions, compulsion, and state control—an affront to conservative Fayolism.[113] The lay centre was less keen on state control or worker involvement than were the Christian Democrats, but opposed the right's corporatist alternative.[114] Just before dissolution, the Chamber unanimously passed a bill, only because essential questions remained unanswered, and the hurdle of the Senate remained. Poincaré declared, 'Have no illusions. The law will not be applicable for several years.'[115]

Conflicts over the Bloc's social programme widened the gap in the majority. The centre, especially the Christian Democrats, moved closer to the Radical-Socialists, while the right's corporatist proposals were part of a plan for remaking the regime. Disillusion set in especially quickly among pro-natalists, and the organized movement took on a reactionary hue. Whereas 64 per cent of the Entente and 76 per cent of Independents belonged to the parliamentary pro-natalist group, 44 per cent of centrists were members. Almost all its leaders were conservative Catholics. Some no longer believed that parliament could save the race. Louis Madelin, historian and future Fédération deputy, wanted to imitate Mussolini's appointment of a 'dictateur de la natalité'.[116]

INSTITUTIONAL REFORM

That brings us to institutional reform. At Bataclan Millerand argued that *scrutin d'arrondissement* encouraged clientelism, that proportional representation, regionalism, and reinforcement of the presidency would ensure the primacy of the national interest, and that partial professionalization of the Senate would reinforce representation of the competent.[117] The moment for reform seemed propitious because the

[112] Dutton, *Origins of the French Welfare State*, 34–5, 48–9.
[113] Dutton, *Origins of the French Welfare State*, 72–3.
[114] *Alliance républicaine démocratique*, 5 and 19 June 1921.
[115] Georges and Édouard Bonnefous, *Histoire politique de la Troisième république*, ii: *L'Après guerre* (Paris, 1968), 428, n. 1.
[116] Tomlinson, 'The politics of *dénatalité*', 123–35, 171–4; Koos, 'Engendering reaction', 35–45; *La Petite gironde*, 4 October 1923.
[117] *Discours de M. Millerand*, 9–11.

previously cautious Alliance now advocated measures similar to Millerand's, and endorsed the programmes of ANOD and Démocratie nouvelle.[118]

In practice, the Bloc barely touched the structures of the regime. Roussellier rightly argues that reform foundered because many deputies remained attached to the idea of careful deliberation. However, he neglects the universal discontent among conservatives with excessive speechmaking and the influence among them of military and industrial notions of rapidity, efficiency, and command. In fact, careful deliberation and efficiency were potentially compatible, for both were ambiguous concepts that depended on the eye of the beholder—only opponents were ever verbose.[119] Le Béguec's contention that there was a gap between the generation of 1919 and those who wished to return the 'old elites' to power, is more convincing.[120] His interpretation works if detached from the implicit tradition–modernity polarity: reform failed because divergent ideological and social agendas shaped competing programmes.

The centre and 1919 movement proposed surprisingly cautious reforms. Probus wanted the Conseil d'État and competences to take over the detailed discussion of laws leaving parliament to discuss general issues, but he put these measures off to an unspecified future. He prioritized reform of parliamentary procedure, so that the high-quality deputies already in parliament would have better tools, and laws would be well-drafted and voted rapidly. He nevertheless preserved the deliberative model, for he condemned long speeches as an obstacle to 'in-depth discussion' of laws.[121] Reconciling this apparent contradiction was the notion that parliament was a crowd, which alternated between routine, verbosity, and febrile activity, and which therefore required organization. Indeed, the December 1919 motion to reform the Chamber's regulations, presented by Charles Reibel (QR, ARS), explained that 'this Chamber should not imitate its predecessors, which sometimes hastily voted ill-conceived projects, designed to grant an apparent satisfaction to public opinion'.[122]

Quatrième république was more anti-parliamentarian than ANOD, claiming that politicians' 'camaraderie' undermined their sense of the public interest. QR members too were moderate in practice. André de Fels, later vice-president of the Alliance, presented himself as a 'realist', and argued that action must counter degeneration.[123] Yet he contended that seemingly useless words were necessary in a democracy and that patronage defended the individual against the state. His only concrete proposal was for the Président de la République to take responsibility for foreign affairs and use his power to dissolve the Chamber in the event that it overthrew the government on a secondary matter. Another QR member, Joseph-Barthélemy, president of the reforming ARS, was a little more adventurous. He used Darwinism

[118] *L'Alliance démocratique*, 8 December 1918.
[119] Roussellier, *Le Parlement*, 228–32, 235–8.
[120] Le Béguec, 'L'Entrée', 327–31.
[121] *L'Intransigeant*, 19 December 1919, 3 and 16 January 1920.
[122] *Journal officiel. Chambre des députés*, 19 December 1919, 5313.
[123] De Fels, *Essai*, 48–50, 61–3, 71–82, 118–19, 129–42, 166–89, 242–8; Le Béguec, 'L'Entrée', 136–43, 383–7.

and collective psychology to prove that the war had exposed the unfitness of parliament, but proposed only compulsory consultation of the Conseil d'État in the legislative process. He opposed direct technocratic rule as encouraging routine, and lauded the general competence of lawyers.[124]

Even the right included many who were cautious. Louis Marin was already establishing a reputation as an intransigent defender of parliament, and saw ANOD as 'interfering'.[125] Many Fédération activists still saw full-scale proportional representation as the best way to ensure that 'les meilleurs' entered parliament.[126] Moreover, they saw parliament as the site of 'general competences'. A Fédération journalist suggested that 'special competences' might occupy one third of seats in the Senate, but Bonnefous saw even that as conceding too much to special interests.[127] Further to the right, Denys Cochin opposed revision, for, pending restoration, parliamentary government was the surest guardian of liberty. He added that as a Catholic he had suffered from the majority, but even more from excessive zeal in applying the law.[128]

In contrast, the circle around Jules Roche, director of *La République française*, was anti-parliamentarian and sympathetic to Démocratie nouvelle.[129] It saw parliament as a Soviet that crushed liberties, turning citizens into mere numbers.[130] It demanded a constituent assembly, which would withdraw the right to propose spending legislation from parliament and create an executive endowed, in Fayolist terms, with stability and foresight. A guarantee of rights would ensure freedom of conscience, the right to own property, and to work.[131] Roche's views on the constitutional issue were close to those of the ALP. The latter reaffirmed its commitment to the Republic as the best means of defending conservative principles and praised it for having won the war, but it cared more for the liberty of the Church than of individuals: it demanded a new constitution recognizing the rights of God.[132] Senator Magallon, close to AF, distinguished the abstract constitution of the Republic from one based on the past, progress, tradition, order, religion, family, and *patrie*—this nation had a 'right to live'.[133]

Unlike the right, the centre and some Progressissts did not see constitutional reform as necessary to improve the quality and efficiency of parliament. They saw

[124] Joseph-Barthélemy, *Le Problème de la compétence*, 47, 62–7, 71–2, 110–11; Gilles Martinez, 'Joseph Barthélemy et la crise de la démocratie libérale', *Vingtième siècle* 59 (July–September 1998), 28–47.

[125] ANFLM, 168, Probus to Marin, 8 October 1922.

[126] ANFLM, 81, Conseil général, 14 November 1923; *La Fédération républicaine*, May 1922.

[127] *La Fédération républicaine*, January and February 1923.

[128] *Bulletin de l'ALP*, 15 September 1920.

[129] *La République française*, 24 September 1919.

[130] *La République française*, 26 October, 4, 7 November, 20 December 1919, 15 January 1920; Jules Roche, *Quand serons nous en république?* (Paris, 1918), 196.

[131] Roche, *Quand serons nous en république?*, 27, 73; *La République française*, 4 November 1919.

[132] Féron-Vrau, *Après la guerre*, 5–7; René Rémond, 'L'Évolution du journal "La Croix" et son rôle auprès de l'opinion catholique (1919–1939)', *Bulletin de la société d'histoire moderne* 12, no. 7 (1958), 3–11 at 5.

[133] Féron-Vrau, *Après la guerre*, 5–7; *Bulletin de l'ALP*, 15 July 1919, 1 September 1920, 1 January 1922, 1 September 1922, 15 May, 15 October 1923.

the question as bound up with religious and political matters. The Clemenciste QR member, Maurice Bokanowski, condemned 'a right in which, in spite of appearances, opposition to the Republic persists, and that is on the lookout for the opportunity to carry out a coup', and restore 'outdated privileges'.[134] Similarly, although his party stood for reform in principle, Mamelet opposed revision of the Chamber's regulations, because it would produce larger parliamentary groups and permit reactionaries to infiltrate the Republic.[135]

Regionalism complicated these disputes. After the war, Charles-Brun's efforts to unite the diverse regionalist movement became still more difficult. For many conservatives, especially in the centre, regionalism meant adaptation to the modern world. For Marin, it would reduce government spending through economies of scale in the automobile age—oddly for a man who refused to install a telephone in his house.[136] Many centrists and Progressists approved Clémentel's economic regions, created in 1919, but rejected his social democratic agenda—only Christian Democrats, perhaps including Charles-Brun, sympathized with that.

Meanwhile, linguistic and ethnic regionalism became more radical. In Alsace, Christian Democrats voiced Germanophone protests against discrimination. Breton regionalists used the notion of a war of peoples, enshrined in President Wilson's Fourteen Points, to defend minority rights. The Marquis de l'Estourbeillon (ALP), president of the Union régionaliste bretonne (URB), demanded inclusion of minority language rights in the peace treaty, declaring that 'Brittany truly forms within the French community a distinct nation and people'. Eight hundred politicians and clergy were among the 360,000 who signed a petition calling for application of the Covenant. Against Estourbeillon's wishes, sixteen Bloc Deputies endorsed the joint programme of the URB and autonomists.[137] The Breton right saw regionalism as part of a corporatist project, which, in conjunction with proportional representation, would bring the competences to power within historic geographical and ethnic units. The right insisted that an agricultural minister should be able to distinguish corn from maize, and increasingly landowners defined themselves as 'agriculteurs' or even 'paysans'.[138] That did not mean that an agricultural labourer could become minister of agriculture, but that a leisured, generalist elite with experience of business and agriculture must be represented in a corporatist body.[139] Specialists would make recommendations to a strong 'authority', representing the general interest.[140]

All this was too much even for some on the right. Given that conservatives had seen the recovery of Alsace-Lorraine as restoring the wholeness of the nation, discontent in Alsace was especially troublesome. Some attributed autonomism to a Socialist–German plot to destroy France, and some turned against regionalism

134 *La Petite Gironde*, 28 July, 30 August 1919.

135 *L'Alliance démocratique*, 7 December 1919.

136 Rials, *Administration et organisation*, 181.

137 Jack Reece, *Bretons Against France: Ethnic Minority Nationalism in Twentieth Century Brittany* (Chapel Hill, 1976), 69.

138 *Bulletin de l'ALP*, 1 February 1921, 15 August 1923.

139 Bensoussan, *Combats*, 279–82.

140 *Bulletin de l'ALP*, 1 February 1924.

altogether, perhaps including Barrès.[141] At the league of Nations, the centrist Henry de Jouvenel declared that 'to find minorities in France, they would have to be created in the imagination'.[142]

Given these differences, one understands why at Bataclan Millerand promised to tackle more pressing problems before constitutional revision, and reassured listeners that regionalization would not compromise the unity of the nation.[143] In practice, Millerand saw reform as a question of will: as President of the Republic, he later vowed to act as head of the majority and to take charge of foreign policy.[144] He intervened in foreign affairs, notably in January 1922, in the somewhat unconstitutional eviction of Briand from the Présidence du conseil. In October 1923, in a speech at Evreux, he implicitly appointed himself guarantor of the Bloc programme. Joseph-Barthélemy wrote that 'at last the country received from above the direction that it has been hoping for', but other centrists were more doubtful.[145] Président du conseil Poincaré saw Millerand's ambitions as illegitimate, and in fact Poincaré's strong foreign policy deprived Millerand of a pretext to interfere. Moreover, Poincaré reinforced the machinery of the Présidence du conseil (a Fayolist measure) and used his personal authority to rationalize parliamentary business.[146] Thus, the centre's preference for improving parliamentary efficiency without constitutional revision prevailed.

THE PARTIES

The outcome of the struggle between the two Presidents mirrored the victory of the centre over the right. In fact, no Bloc Président du conseil would break entirely with the Radicals, not even Millerand, and the ERD complained incessantly of underrepresentation. Following his election as President, Millerand signalled his intention to ensure continuity by calling upon the Alliance member Georges Leygues to head a ministry with the same personnel. The ERD would no longer tolerate underrepresentation, and soon overthrew Leygues, only to find that the succeeding ministries of Briand (from January 1920) and Poincaré (from January 1922) made few concessions to them either. In February 1924, Poincaré threatened to send his seconds to the ERD's Désiré Ferry, who had accused him of betraying his majority.[147] Relations between the Fédération and Alliance soured. While the right insisted that the real majority of November 1919 was primarily anti-communist and excluded the Radical-Socialists, the centre claimed in its pamphlet 'The lie of Bloc' that the Bloc national had never existed.

[141] *La République française*, 24 October 1919.

[142] Tara Zahra, 'The "minority problem" and national classification in the French and Czechoslovak borderlands', *Contemporary European History* 17, no. 2 (2008), 137–65 at 137.

[143] *Discours de M. Millerand*, 9–11.

[144] Marjorie M. Farrar, *Principled Pragmatist: The Political Career of Alexandre Millerand* (New York, 1991), 305–11.

[145] *La Petite gironde*, 23 October 1923.

[146] Roussellier, *Le Parlement*, 179–80, 201–3, 205–7, 233–4; Farrar, *Principled Pragmatist*, 335–8.

[147] ANFLM, 168, Minute, 8 February 1924.

Conservatives agreed only that the legislature had been fruitless. In January 1922, Mamelet urged parliament to avoid wordy outpourings and enact real reforms; six months later, he admitted that his appeal had gone unheeded.[148] The movement towards unity, evident since the 1900s, reversed, and parties began to revive, with the religious question as a frontier between them: for Isaac, the Fédération's unwillingness to interfere with private beliefs divided it from the Alliance.[149] On the right and among Christian Democrats there developed challenges to the elitist networks that had dominated since the 1900s.

The Alliance was divided between advocates of formal agreement with the Radical-Socialist Party itself (Concentration) and those who wanted to attract Radical-Socialist voters into a centre-led coalition with the right on the model of the Bloc (Union nationale). On 28–29 June 1920, the pro-Radical Jonnart replaced Carnot as president of the Alliance and the party adopted a compromise between the two options. The Alliance became the Parti républicain démocratique et social (PRDS), with a *laïque* programme; it aimed to split the Radical-Socialists and unite 'democratic Republicans', while excluding partisans of class struggle and reaction. The Comité Mascuraud and *Le Temps* backed the PRDS, while numerous businessmen, including the president of the Paris Chamber of Commerce, joined its Comité directeur.[150] In the Drôme the PRDS and Radicals concluded an agreement, but nationally, the PRDS attracted only a few dissident Radicals.[151]

In 1923, after Jonnart resigned, a compromise candidate, Antoine Ratier, replaced him, and disputes continued. In August 1923, Chaumet, now president of the Comité Mascuraud, attacked the 'camouflaged Republicans' of the ERD for their hostility to the lay laws, and called for alliance with the Radical-Socialists, an appeal he repeated in November in Poincaré's presence. Tardieu condemned Chaumet's excommunication of the right and Poincaré's failure to dissipate confusion. Although most centrists still preferred to entice the Radical rank-and-file into the PRDS rather than ally with the party itself,[152] the Alliance effectively broke with the Bloc.[153] Briand and Loucheur made overtures to the left, advocating European economic cooperation, perhaps including Germany, social reform, and *défense laïque*.

Meanwhile, the right reorganized. The first initiatives came from above. In April 1922, the ERD, part of the ARS, the Fédération, and a few nationalists, formed the Action nationale républicaine (ANR). François Arago doubled as president of the ERD and ANR. The new group aimed to bridge the clerical–anticlerical divide (on its terms) and connect with 'the country' (i.e. the non-parliamentary elites), where the true majority allegedly lay. To achieve the latter objective, it relied on the Ligue

148 *La République démocratique*, 8 January; 23 July 1922.
149 *Bulletin de la Fédération républicaine*, November 1922.
150 Sanson, *L'Alliance républicaine démocratique*, 478–81; *La République démocratique*, 21 July 1921.
151 *La République démocratique*, 2 December 1921.
152 *La République démocratique*, 18 August 1923; *L'Écho national*, 18, 21 November 1923; *La République française*, 3 August 1923.
153 *La République démocratique*, 20 March 1921, 18 June 1922.

Civique, Hervé's PSN, QR, and ANOD.[154] The ANR failed because the Alliance opposed it, while the Fédération resented it as a rival, and the leagues were moribund.[155] Arago's implication in a tax scandal weakened the ARS; its newspaper fell under the sway of the future fascist Hubert Bourgin, secretary of the Ligue Civique.

In the event, the Fédération captured leadership of the right. Reorganization began in 1921, when its president, Senator Victor Milliard, asked sympathetic deputies to join. It continued from November 1922 under Isaac, by which time the party claimed 100 deputies, and a 'considerable number' of committees.[156] Initially, elitist organizational methods persisted. Milliard castigated the party spirit, and insisted upon the primacy of 'deliberative assemblies'. For him, contact between parliament and people meant connection with 'les compétences'.[157] Isaac struggled against members who believed that 'parties have had their day like leprosy, the plague, and cholera', thanks to 'the progress of public health [that] protects us against their microbes'.[158] He privately regretted taking on the presidency of 'a party without consistency', comprised of 'people who are losing confidence in their own re-election'.[159]

Yet disillusion with the Bloc mobilized ordinary right-wing activists. In March 1922, the unaffiliated conservative committees of the Seine announced a 'great popular party' under the auspices of QR. Their leader complained that he had 'had enough' of parliamentarians' repeated betrayal of activists, and called for a 'powerful organization', with a clear programme, statutes, and discipline. Quatrième république proved unequal to the task of organizing such a party, and worse, refused to break with the Radical-Socialists. Therefore, in January 1923, the committee joined the Fédération—while asserting its autonomy.[160] In Lyon, former Nationalists reorganized the Fédération and privileged attacks on the Radicals over support for the government.[161]

In January 1924, a few young men resolved to revitalize the moribund Ligue des patriotes (LDP) through the creation of the Jeunesses patriotes (JP).[162] Their president was Pierre Taittinger, whom we have met as a Bonapartist dedicated to the incorporation of his movement into the right, and who now belonged to the Fédération. At the launch of the JP, Taittinger implicitly attacked the Bloc, calling for 'a complete, radical, revolutionary transformation of our methods; we waste our time in endless discussion... We need men with souls of bronze, not diplomats of the heart.'[163] The JP blended Fascism with Bonapartism, without breaking with the parliamentary right.

[154] ANFXR, 14, Rochefoucauld and Arago speeches, 13 June 1922; Jean Vavasseur-Desperriers, 'Les Tentatives de regroupement des droites dans les années trente', *Annales de Bretagne* 109, no. 3 (2002), 61–77.

[155] ANFLM, 81, Conseil général, 14 November 1923.

[156] *La Fédération républicaine*, July 1922.

[157] *Bulletin de la Fédération républicaine*, January 1921; *La Fédération républicaine*, November 1922.

[158] *La République française*, 30 October 1922.

[159] *Isaac*, 20 April 1922, 364.

[160] ANFLM 81, PV of Fédération républicaine de la Seine, especially 10 March and 10 April 1922 and 20 January 1923.

[161] Bernard, *La Dérive*, 262–4.

[162] Philippet, 'Le Temps des ligues', 41–157.

[163] *Quatrième République*, 2 April 1924, quoted in Philippet, 'Le Temps des ligues', 155.

Simultaneously, AF recovered its combativeness, especially with the arrival in power of its old enemy, Briand: Daudet demanded that this 'agent of Anglo-German Jewry' appear before the High Court. Poincaré's return temporarily appeased AF, yet on 22 January 1923 an anarchist assassinated the veteran Marius Plateau, secretary-general of the League, thus provoking a series of confrontations with the left. Maurras claimed that government inaction justified violence, and demanded postponement of the 1924 elections. This agitation exacerbated the crisis within the majority. In parliament, twenty pro-Royalist and fourteen ERD deputies voted against a motion criticizing AF, while many more abstained and others voted in favour.[164] In the same period, AF's Georges Valois campaigned for a new Estates General. He took up the unrealized causes of the Bloc, including privatization of monopolies, spending cuts, and rationalization of public services. He presented an organizationalist alternative to the CGT's campaign for a national economic council, maintaining that only a king could realize the project. The Estates campaign achieved some success in business—another index of disillusion with the Bloc.[165]

Daudet explicitly likened AF to Fascism, which he saw as a legitimate reaction against Jewry, Bolshevism, and Germany. He insisted that AF was ready, like Mussolini, to take power by force and to carry out a purge even more extensive than that of the Fascists. That did not mean that the two movements were identical, for neither was homogeneous. Both contained tensions between elitism and populism, corporatist devolution and statist centralization, order and violence. On the one hand, Daudet was closest to the hierarchical, statist, and monarchist Fascism, that which saw itself as a 'bourgeois' reaction. In the Mayenne, aristocratic leaguers criticized Daudet's interventions in the Chamber, and no Camelot group existed before 1926.[166] On the other hand, Valois' Estates General movement possessed, via Sorel, affinities with the corporatist wing of Fascism, which also advocated organization and competence.[167]

The ALP, Ligue civique, and, to some extent, the Fédération, were also impressed by Primo de Rivera's Spanish dictatorship and Italian Fascism. In *La Liberté*, Camille Aymard campaigned for a leader who would express popular discontent with politicians. For another journalist, Mussolini symbolized the movement for efficiency and rapidity. He admired Mussolini's 'slow, dry, manner of speaking, his hard eyes, short, measured, sentences, stripped of ornaments'—the antithesis of the 'loquacious lawyer'.[168] Catholics praised Mussolini for restoring religion in schools and for making it the basis of the struggle against depopulation, Muscovite barbarism, and demoralization. Without explicitly endorsing paramilitarism,

[164] Eugen Weber, *Action Française: Royalism and Reaction in Twentieth-Century France* (Stanford, 1962), 160–70.

[165] Allen Douglas, *From Fascism to Libertarian Communism: Georges Valois against the Third Republic* (Berkeley, 1993), 53–64.

[166] Denis, *Les Royalistes*, 512–18; Weber, *Action Française*, 132–5.

[167] Weber, *Action française*, 155–9; Joel Blatt, 'Relatives and rivals: the responses of Action française to Italian fascism, 1919–1926', *European Studies Review* 11, no. 3 (1981), 263–92.

[168] *La République française*, 12 October 1922. See also *L'Indépendent* (cantons of Pont-a-Mousson, Nomeny and Thiaucourt), 13 September 1923.

conservatives lauded the destruction of Socialism.[169] Mussolini's French admirers interpreted Fascism in their own, divergent ways, and did not necessarily believe that it was appropriate to France, but it offered new possibilities and chimed with some French traditions.

Right-wing extremism was not the only response to the failure of the Bloc. Loucheur and Briand led part of the centre towards the Radical-Socialists, while attempting to give the latter's organizational project a conservative inflexion. Meanwhile, Christian Democracy began to coalesce in the centre, in the form of the Fédérations des républicains-démocrates of the Seine, Finistère, and Nord. They promised religious pacification through *laïcité*, regionalism, and social insurance. Christian Democracy was strongest among the urban white-collar classes and tenant farmers in Brittany, but also enjoyed elite support. In Mayenne, the deputy César Chabrun, scion of a Royalist family, attacked AF and the left; he claimed that property entailed duties in human and divine law, backed public-sector unions, and declared himself a 'Catholique convaincu et républicain laïque'.[170] Attempts to unite the Christian Democrats in the Ligue nationale de la démocratie failed because Marc Sangnier found the Fédérations des democrats too conservative. In 1922–1923, the Républicains démocrats, CFTC, and ACJF, united in the Bureau d'Action Civique, situated in the centre.[171] Some bishops condemned Christian Democracy for dividing Catholics.[172]

CONCLUSION

The perceived failure of the Bloc ended the convergence of Republican and Catholic conservatives that had been developing since the 1900s. Initially, Millerand symbolized unity, advancing a programme of economic liberalism, anti-communism, and application of Fayolism to family and society, as part of a struggle to arm France in the economic war against Germany. However, even Millerand preferred to exclude Catholics from the government rather than risk confrontation with the Senate, and hedged his programme with qualifications. The majority could not agree on the role of the state, while its refusal to make religion an explicit issue contrasted with the persistence of religious conflict in the country and its imbrication in social, economic, and institutional questions. These problems in turn compromised the Bloc's organizational project. The Bloc initially united around a liberal version of organization, but subsequently it divided between the right's corporatist, Catholic authoritarian project and the

169 *Bulletin de l'ALP*, 1 January, 15 April, 1 August, 15 October 1923; *Action nationale républicaine*, 3 May 1923.

170 Denis, *Les Royalistes de la Mayenne*, 522–7.

171 Jean-Claude Delbreil, *Centrisme et démocratie chrétienne en France. Le Parti démocrate populaire des origines au M.R.P* (Paris, 1990), 16–22.

172 *Le Nouvelliste de Bretagne*, 3, 4 April 1924; Henri de Cadore, '*L'Ouest-Éclair* et les deux ralliements (1899–1930). Contribution à l'intégration des Catholiques de l'Ouest dans la République', in Michel Lagrée, Patrick Harismendy, and Michel Denis (eds), *L'Ouest-Éclair. Naissance et essor d'un grand quotidien régionale* (Rennes, 2001), 55–78; Ford, *Creating the Nation.* 197–207.

centre's preference for the Radical-Socialists' schemes for the organization of capitalism in a European framework.

In 1924, only Poincaré's prestige remained to conservatives. He avoided close alignment with any tendency and made vague speeches at the Alliance and Fédération congresses. In the elections, both right and centre used his name to cover their squabbles. In some departments, Catholics presented lists demanding state aid to Catholic schools, while the Assembly of Cardinals and Archbishops ordered believers to vote for lists that condemned the lay laws. The *Croix du Nord* denounced Lemire's presence on Loucheur's list, while discontent among *fonctionnaires* and conservative hostility to a textile strike ensured that Loucheur lost votes to Socialists and Catholics.[173] Ordinary activists complained. In Meurthe-et-Moselle, the administration pressed Marin to form a single list, but his supporters refused to be taken for 'flunkies'. They opposed the inclusion of the Alliance, which they accused of undermining the Fédération in the Prefecture, press, cooperatives, and Comices agricoles, of weakening France through 'amiability towards our adversaries', 'sterilizing' the work of the Chambers, attacking the Entente, and 'resuscitating outdated quarrels'.[174] Radicals abandoned the Bloc completely. A dissident Radical organization, sponsored by the UIE, won little support and only in the Var did a Radical figure on a Bloc list.[175] In the Allier, where in 1919 conservatives united behind right-wing Radicals, two lists now confronted each other, permitting the Socialists to win four out of five seats.[176] Nationally, the left benefited from the electoral system, winning 266 seats, compared to 229 for the former majority.

[173] Mayeur, *Lemire*, 584–94; *La Nation*, 13 December 1926.

[174] ANFLM 168, dossier élections 1924.

[175] Berstein, *Histoire du Parti radical*, I, 376–89.

[176] Jean-François Viple, *Sociologie politique de l'Allier. La Vie politique et les élections sous la Troisième République* (Paris, 1967), 226–30.

10

The Revival of Activism (1924–1926)

> There exists now in France an army of young, ardent, disciplined, disinterested citizens. This army is organized in the formations of the great national leagues. They offer a solid political framework for the government of tomorrow.
>
> Pierre Taittinger, 1926

The brief period in office of the Cartel des gauches was a turning point in the history of conservatism. The re-emergence of anti-parliamentary leagues struck contemporaries (and historians) most forcefully, but was only part of a revival of activism across the conservative spectrum. This mobilization owed much to fear. The new left-wing majority recognized the USSR, amnestied the 'traitors', Caillaux and Malvy, and threatened a capital levy to finance social insurance and fill the hole in French finances that the failure of reparations had created. Catholics were alarmed by the Cartel's threats to extend the lay laws to Alsace-Lorraine, dissolve unauthorized religious orders, suppress the Vatican Embassy, and oblige civil servants to attend public schools. Nationalists objected to Briand's policy of reconciliation with Germany, which culminated in the Locarno Accords of 1925–1926. August Isaac, as leader of the Fédération, argued that the rise of communism made conservative unity essential. He offered the choice between defending a centuries-old society and endangering 'everything hitherto considered essential to human society—property, family, inheritance, respect for conscience, and individual liberty'.[1] Yet hostility to the Cartel was inseparable from conflict among conservatives, and the mobilization took diverse forms.

At first, Catholics led the anti-Cartel movement. In June and July 1924, they organized monster meetings in Alsace to protest against its religious policy, notably in Strasbourg, where 40,000 people, including all the parliamentarians of the Bas-Rhin, heard the deputy and veteran, Abbé Bergey, thunder against Édouard Herriot's government. The priest attracted large audiences in his native southwest too, and was instrumental in spreading the movement across France. On 18 February 1925, General Castelnau (beaten in the 1924 elections) united parish protest groups in the Fédération nationale catholique (FNC), which soon claimed two million members.

The general was a key figure in the opposition. On 13 November 1924, as president of the Ligue des patriotes (LDP), he warned that a 'faction bribed by foreigners' was

[1] *La Fédération républicaine*, December 1924.

preparing a 'vast revolutionary plot' under the cover of the coming transfer of Jaurès' ashes to the Panthéon.[2] The day after the ceremony, the league endorsed its youth wing, the Jeunesses patriotes (JP), as a 'fighting instrument'. The JP held its first public rally in March 1925, and it expanded rapidly from April, after three members died at the hands of the Communists at the rue Damrémont. In October 1925, it absorbed a smaller league, Antoine Rédier's Légion, founded a few weeks before the elections, and, by mid 1926, the JP may have had 65,000 members.

In February 1925, Georges Valois of Action française (AF) launched a newspaper, *Le Nouveau siècle*, and some weeks later, he established the Légions pour la politique de la victoire. The parent league initially supported the venture as another front organization, but after Valois transformed it into the Faisceau in November 1925, relations deteriorated. The next month, a neo-Royalist attack on a meeting of Faisceau students confirmed the breach. The Faisceau also became a mass movement, with up to 60,000 members.[3]

Meanwhile, Alexandre Millerand was looking for a political outlet. The victorious Cartel had punished his partisan support for the Bloc national by forcing him to resign the Presidency of the Republic, and he failed to negotiate a safe seat in parliament.[4] On 14 November 1924, he formed the Ligue républicaine nationale (LRN), in a bid to unite the conservative parties and to create a mass organizaion. A week later, he became vice-president of the LDP, doubtless recalling that in 1899 he had joined a government committed to its suppression. The LRN held several huge public meetings, at which the JP and nationalist students maintained order.[5]

In 1925, Louis Marin re-founded the Fédération républicaine (FR). Rank-and-file disquiet at deputies' behaviour had been evident since 1922, and now the right's parliamentary representation was diminished and discredited. The parliamentary Union républicaine démocratique (URD), successor to the Entente républicaine démocratique (ERD), had only 104 members. François Arago was permanently shamed by financial scandal. In June 1925, the defeated and sick Auguste Isaac resigned as Fédération President, reflecting that the situation of France was worse at the end of his political career than at the start.[6] He failed to ensure his succession by a liberal Progressist, and instead Marin anchored the Fédération on the nationalist right. Marin's ally in Lyon, Victor Perret, declared that it was time to call upon activists, the true servants of the people, rather than notables. In the winter of 1925–1926, Marin and the new party secretary, Jean Guiter, toured the provinces, provoking the formation of committees.[7]

[2] Jean Philippet, 'Le Temps des ligues. Pierre Taittinger et les Jeunesses patriotes', thèse de doctorat, IEP Paris, 2000, 53–4.

[3] Sternhell, *Ni droite, ni gauche* (Paris, 1983), 117.

[4] Philippet, 'Le Temps des ligues', 50–1.

[5] Robert Soucy, *French Fascism: The First Wave* (New Haven, 1986), 50, 53–4, 55; *Le Canigole*, 23 January 1926.

[6] Mathias Bernard, *La Dérive des modérés. La Fédération républicaine du Rhône sous la Troisième République* (Paris, 1998), 272.

[7] Archives nationales 317 AP 81, Fonds Marin, (hereafter ANFLM, carton/dossier no.), Comité directeur and Conseil général, 14–15 November 1925; ANFLM, 73, Guiter to Marin, 3 March 1926.

Henri de Kerillis' Républicains nationaux embodied an alternative way of reorganizing conservatism, on a firmly Republican basis, situated politically at the junction of the Fédération and the centre. In March 1926, Kerillis, who was a member of the Fédération, stood in Paris II on a joint ticket with Paul Reynaud of the Alliance. He attributed their defeat to bourgeois pusillanimity and to conflicts between Royalists, fascists, Catholics, veterans, and others in his own camp. He urged conservatives to rally around the label, 'Républicains nationaux', and to create a common propaganda and campaigning service.[8]

The Alliance démocratique was largely immune from the revival of activism, but the centre more broadly was not, for gradual repositioning in the centre-right coincided with reconfiguration of the Catholic electorate. The most visible sign was the emergence of the Parti démocrate populaire (PDP), which held its founding congress on 15–16 November 1924. Under the Bloc, it had proved impossible to unite Christian Democrats of left and right. Now, in the midst of crisis, the PDP crystallized in the centre-right, bringing together the Fédérations de democrats, Social Catholic groups, activists from the Confédération française des travailleurs chrétiens (CFTC), Catholic intellectuals, and regionalists—all but one member of the fourteen-strong PDP group were from Brittany, Alsace, or the Béarn. Locally, the PDP emerged from ongoing struggles against the right, but the new group was initially among the sternest opponents of the Cartel, and some observers positioned it on the extreme right.[9] Less visibly, the 1920s extended the attraction of a part of the Catholic electorate to the secular centre, notably in areas of 'blue Catholicism'. In ways that historians have yet to untangle, these two developments eventually softened the anticlericalism of the centre, and made possible cooperation between Social Catholics and conservative reformers.

Historians have been less interested in this multidimensional revival of activism than in debating the fascism or otherwise of the JP and Faisceau. Yet the assumption that the leagues were part of a broader anti-Cartel movement is implicit on both sides of the fascism controversy. On the one hand, Robert Soucy argues that out of fear of the Cartel many conservatives rejected parliamentarianism for authoritarianism, without abandoning their conservative social principles, and that for him amounted to fascism. Indeed, French conservatives admired Italian Fascism, which, for Soucy, was also an authoritarian, reactionary movement, using paramilitary violence to crush the left.[10] On the other hand, Pierre Milza agrees that the leagues represented a reaction against the Cartel, but contends that the radical, totalitarian dimension of fascism was absent in France because the crisis there was less serious than in Italy or Germany. Consequently, the JP was merely an appendage of the parliamentary right, which at most aped the conservative features of Italian Fascism. Similarly, in the Faisceau, Fascism was meaningful only for Valois and his circle; the bulk of members were conventionally conservative.[11]

[8] *L'Écho de Paris*, 23 April 1926; Bernard, *La Dérive*, 316–17.

[9] Jean-Claude Delbreil, *Centrisme et démocratie chrétienne en France. Le Parti démocrate populaire des origines au M.R.P* (Paris, 1990), 11–35.

[10] Soucy, *French Fascism*, 21–4.

[11] Pierre Milza, *Fascisme français, passé et présent* (Paris, 1986), 109–13.

There is no need to rehearse again the difficulties of the 'categorical' approach. Suffice it to say that the desire to measure political movements against abstract definitions obscures the complexity of relations between the leagues, their conservative competitors, and with their left-wing enemies, as well as the extent of disputes within the leagues themselves. As both Soucy and Milza insist, the leagues were linked ideologically and personally to parliamentary conservatism; they owed much to hostility to the Cartel, but they also expressed activists' unhappiness at their leaders' 'betrayal', and reflected religious, regional, class, and gender conflicts among conservatives. The leagues also attracted a few ex-leftists, and in principle nothing ruled out more extensive transfers, even if in the context of 1924–1926, links between the leagues and the parliamentary right were more important. Nonetheless, the leagues endeavoured to defeat the left by incorporating some of its themes into an authoritarian, corporatist, national movement. Conventional conservatives were attracted by the leagues' anti-socialism, but alarmed by this implicit dialogue with the left.

Indeed, the categorical approach also obscures the complexity of the left–right relationship. Anti-Cartel feeling did not always provoke conservative unity, and anti-parliamentarianism was not the only response. One reason for historiographical neglect of this issue is that the Cartel's policies have been reduced to anachronistic anticlericalism, utopian internationalism, and empty class rhetoric.[12] In fact, the Cartel elaborated a social-democratic, European version of the organizational project, to which the corporatism of the leagues may be seen as a response. Furthermore, some centrists, notably Louis Loucheur and Aristide Briand, were not systematically hostile to this project, even if they attempted to give it a more Fayolist slant. Their parliamentary strategy converged with the gradual softening of the PDP's view of the Cartel. Meanwhile, Kerillis' Républicains nationaux attempted to capture the Cartel's social reformism for a united parliamentary party modelled on the British Conservative Party. These centre initiatives, rather than the authoritarian organizationalism of the leagues, would be the beneficiaries of the Cartel's collapse.

RANK-AND-FILE MOBILIZATION IN CONTEXT

In contradictory ways, the revival of activism mobilized disgruntled regionalists, white-collar workers, peasants, and women, and it affected the centre, especially the PDP, as much as the right. First, take regionalism. The Cartel's desire to extend lay legislation to Alsace-Lorraine was part of a broader campaign to reinforce national unity, notably through promotion of the French language. In July 1925, Education Minister Anatole de Monzie declared that 'in the interests of the unity of France, the Breton language must disappear'. Regionalist outrage complicated conservative leaders' responses to the Cartel, for they struggled to reconcile regionalism and

[12] Jean-Noël Jeanneney, *Leçon d'histoire pour une gauche au pouvoir. La Faillite du Cartel 1924–1926* (Paris, 1977).

nationalism. In Alsace, the major pro-French conservative party, the Union patriotique républicaine (UPR), was allied to the FR, and was backed by the francophone business and landowning elite, Catholic hierarchy, and FNC. Fearful of autonomism, the UPR and FNC endeavoured to present the Cartel's policies as an attack on French Catholics as a whole, while denouncing the affront to Alsatian liberties. That did not assuage the discontent of German-speaking Catholic white-collar unions, which largely favoured the pro-PDP and autonomist wing of the UPR. Abbé Haegy, the leader of the regionalists, attacked both 'bourgeois gentlemen' and Socialism, and called himself a 'Catholique d'abord', who did not love France because it was 'an atheist land, a Freemason state'. Alarmed, some Alsatian French speakers turned to the AF, JP, and Faisceau as a means to reconcile defence of Catholic rights and national unity.[13] In Brittany, advanced regionalists saluted not only the Alsatian autonomists, but the anti-colonial rebellion of Abdul Krim in Morocco. Meanwhile, right-wing Breton Catholics, on the margins between the FR and AF, promoted ethnic difference to justify their claim to primacy within the region, and in the Alsatian crisis proclaimed their solidarity with the 'Bretons of the East'. These conservatives did not defend the language as enthusiastically as they did the rights of the Church or agricultural organizations. That left an opening for the PDP, which was largely a party of regionalists.[14]

The PDP also profited from the emergence of independent peasant unionism. Landowner control over peasants had always been problematic, even where peasants voted for the right. Landowners were divided politically and preached conflicting messages, while priests did not necessarily back them. The war further encouraged peasant independence. Peasants benefited from high prices, while inflation reduced debts and rents and permitted consolidation of holdings. Sometimes prosperity encouraged conservatism, sometimes independence. Service in the trenches may also have widened peasant horizons, and new peasant movements claimed that the war had revealed peasants' bravery and their importance in the nation. In response, conservative agricultural unions, notably the Office central in Finistère and the Union du sud-est, created communal syndicates and began to valorize the term 'paysan'.[15] This strategy sometimes inadvertently reinforced the peasant elite, while in regions where the aristocracy was too sensitive to its preeminence to accept communal syndicates, it potentially left space for more radical peasant movements.[16]

The most important peasant unions were the Syndicats bretons de Cultivateurs-cultivants, founded in 1920 by Abbé Mancel with the support of *L'Ouest-Éclair*,

[13] Christian Baechler, *Le Parti catholique Alsacien. Du Reichsland à la République jacobine* (Paris, 1982), 239–327, 353–9; Samuel Goodfellow, *Between the Swastika and the Cross of Lorraine: Fascisms in Interwar Alsace* (DeKalb, 1999), 28–41, 89.

[14] Yves Guiomar, 'Régionalisme, fédéralisme et minorités nationales en France entre 1919 et 1939', *Mouvement social* 70, no. 1 (1970), 89–108; Campbell Hudson Meadwell, '"Brittany Always": ethnic collective action in Brittany during the Third Republic', PhD dissertation, Duke University, 1988, 338–63; David Bensoussan, *Combats pour une Bretagne catholique et rurale. Les Droites bretonnes dans l'entre-deux-guerres* (Paris, 2006), 78–9.

[15] Pierre Barral, *Les Agrariens français de Méline à Pisani* (Paris, 1968), 198–202.

[16] Bensoussan, *Combats*, 274–6.

and the PDP. The latter took up many of their demands. In Vannes in 1928, deputy Ernest Pezet denounced the 'feudal' practice of rent in kind, endorsed by his Royalist opponent.[17] The emergence of the Cultivateurs-cultivants also reflected the attachment of some Catholic peasants to the secular centre, for the Cultivateurs-cultivants originated in Ille-et-Vilaine, an area of blue Catholicism in which conservative syndicalism was weak, and advanced later in Republican Léon. The Cultivateurs-cultivants demanded an end to payment of rent in kind, compensation for improvements made by tenants, and were not afraid to express their demands in market squares. They appropriated the conservative doctrine of 'competence' to claim that only peasants could represent peasants—not landowners and even less town dwellers. Relatively prosperous farmers ran the unions and, in 1926, they created a political wing, the Ligue des paysans de l'ouest, for 'peasants alone'.[18]

Thirdly, Catholic and other independent unions had expanded greatly since 1918, especially among white-collar workers. The leaders of the new CFTC were close to the PDP, but many members backed the lay centre or right. Unaffiliated Catholic unions were still more right-wing, and some of their members supported the leagues. Independent unions dreamed of class collaboration, but resented employers' refusal to treat their 'collaborators' fairly, accusing them of denying them promotion opportunities, and hiring female competitors. Conservative white-collar workers also backed social insurance. The anticlerical CGT and the Communist Confédération générale du travail unitaire (CGTU) condemned Catholic unions as 'bosses' creations, but the conservative Isaac felt that the CFTC shared the Socialist 'misconception that the boss is always rich' and did not understand how hard it was for the bourgeoisie to find good servants.[19] In the Nord, the CFTC struggled against the Catholic employers group, the Consortium du Textil of Désiré Ley and Eugène Mathon. In 1923, Mathon asked the Vatican to condemn the CFTC as 'Socialist'. The CFTC retorted that Ley, an Alsatian, was a German agent.[20]

Fourthly, bourgeois women returned to political activism. After the war, lack of dowries and the shortage of marriage partners obliged a growing number of bourgeois women to work. That introduced a new figure into the discourse of the right—the single, working woman. She enabled the upholders of the traditional view of women's place to negotiate changes in women's position more generally, by conceptualizing independence, even for married women, as 'exceptional'.[21] Many single women turned to nursing and social work, which had developed further thanks to the growth of employers' family allowance schemes. The small but growing band of female professionals provided leaders for women's groups. Meanwhile, the largest Catholic women's group, the Ligue patriotique des françaises (LPDF),

[17] Bensoussan, *Combats*, 154.

[18] Bensoussan, *Combats*, 283–290.

[19] *La Voix sociale*, 29 July 1922.

[20] Michel Launey, *La CFTC, origines et développement, 1919–1940* (Paris, 1986), 21–107; Kevin Passmore, *From Liberalism to Fascism: The Right in a French Province* (Cambridge, 1997), 82–8.

[21] Mary-Louise Roberts, *Civilization Without Sexes: Reconstructing Gender in Postwar France, 1917–1927* (Chicago, 1994), 11.

converted to suffragism, and that too intensified dilemmas for conservatives, among whom fears of the breakdown of the traditional family were great. The PDP, JP, and Faisceau all possessed women's sections, and even the Fédération nourished links with female social activists.

Lastly, politicization and division of the veterans stimulated conservative reorganization. In 1923, the foundation of the Fédération nationale des combattants républicains (FNCR) was one sign of that—the new organization was close to the emergent Cartel and denounced the nationalism and clericalism of the Union nationale des combattants (UNC). Meanwhile, the Union fédérale (UF) made contact with German veterans and was hesitant towards the Rühr occupation. In the UNC, Jean Goy took the lead in the anti-Cartel agitation, while the influence of the moderate Humbert Isaac declined.[22] The JP's and Faisceau's claim to speak for the veterans therefore represented an attempt to undermine their fellow combatants' sympathy for the Cartel. The transfer of the culture of war onto Communism provided a weapon in this struggle, but via the sense of 'never again' this culture also fed the movement for reconciliation with Germany and social reform within France. These differences widened the gap between centre and right that had opened under the Bloc, and the emergence of the leagues was a major sign of polarization.

THE LEAGUES

Although the leagues had no monopoly on anti-Cartel feeling, the conviction that conservative deputies had betrayed the nation through their compromises with the left and the Germans was an important part of their appeal and identity. Complex religious, class, regional, and gender antagonisms among conservatives reinforced these tensions. In this context, the leagues created new movements from diverse traditions, including collective psychology and organizationalism, as they were modified by total war, the 1919 reform movement, and reflection upon dictatorial regimes in Italy and Spain. The leagues were all the more open to European ideologies because French thinkers had contributed to them. Mussolini's cult of action and pragmatism reworked the collective psychology of Sorel, Le Bon, Vilfredo Pareto, and Scipio Sighele, before re-appropriaiton in France.

Elitism and Populism

The leagues' populism did not overturn class and gender hierarchies, but it did more than place them on a new footing. Moreover, the leagues conceived the relationship between hierarchy and populism differently. The FNC and LRN were largely elitist but contained populist elements; the reverse applied to the JP and Faisceau, while AF was somewhere between. There were also multiple links between the leagues; many people belonged to more than one organization.

[22] Antoine Prost, *Les Anciens combattants et la société française 1914–1939*, i. *L'Histoire* (Paris, 1977), 89–90.

The FNC and LRN identified the nation and people with the established authorities. Castelnau was influential in the Army, Church, and press (through his editorials in the *Écho de Paris*). As president of the Ligue des patriotes, he exercised influence in the JP, and he dined regularly with Marin and Wendel of the Fédération.[23] The FNC and LRN appealed to competence, by which they meant reinforcement of business, Army, Church, and administrative hierarchies at the expense of arriviste parliamentarians. Millerand, a former Secrétaire de stage of the Paris Bar, and Castelnau, the Catholic general, were pure representatives of the Republican and Catholic elites respectively. The historian Émile Bourgeois claimed that the LRN's originality lay in having recruited 'non-parliamentary competences' to its committee, and thus to have made contact with 'opinion', which alone could guide us to our goal.[24]

The LRN nevertheless contained a populist sub-current. A retired vice-admiral told Millerand that he was a 'traditionalist' who had the weakness to believe that youthful idealism would save the country. He continued, 'I have become a revolutionary to the point of accepting your Evreux programme' (which others might not have seen in the same light).[25] The league was also linked to the extreme right, particularly to the JP, which it used to guard its meetings. Some members were worried by extremism. A banker approved Millerand's speech at Luna Park, but disliked the security guards' 'extreme youth', 'doubtful manner', and 'too obvious carrying of the "special club"'. Bourgeois reproached Millerand for reliance upon 'discordant elements in parliament', such as Vallat.[26]

As for the JP and Faisceau leaders, they were largely bourgeois, but owed their position as much to their roles in party organizations and their status as veterans. Hubert Bourgin of the Faisceau attended the Law Faculty and the École normale supérieure, but had been a Socialist and Dreyfusard before war service awakened his nationalism. Taittinger was more typical of the ordinary activists of the right. From a déclassé bourgeois family, he began work at seventeen as a clerk, and thanks to family relations and a good marriage, he succeeded in business. He started the war as a sergeant, and ended as a captain. Valois was the orphaned son of a butcher, educated in a technical college, and he too served in the trenches.

The populism of the JP and Faisceau derived from a combination of actual social inferiority and from the invention of popular credentials as an act of political positioning, in proportions difficult to determine. Socially, both leagues recruited from the student offspring of the elites, the professions, and from clerks, artisans, shopkeepers, merchants, and the like—many of them veterans.[27] Some activists adopted what they saw as working-class manners, mixing Parisian argot with the conversation of the Left Bank in order to differentiate themselves from

[23] Soucy, *French Fascism*, 50.

[24] AN 470 AP, Fonds Millerand (hereafter ANFAM, carton/dossier no.), 88, Bourgeois to Millerand, 18 November 1924.

[25] ANFAM, Bourgeois to Millerand, 10 December 1924.

[26] ANFAM, Bourgeois to Millerand, 15, 18 November 1924, 23 April 1925.

[27] Philippet, 'Le Temps des ligues', 685–706.

the 'bourgeois' right.[28] The aforementioned banker regretted that JP members at Luna Park were 'smoking, spitting, and laughing' during the speeches.[29]

The leagues' claim to represent the veterans enabled them, in different ways, to reconcile populism with social hierarchy, for service in the trenches implied both equality in danger and command. Castelnau evoked the nation's debt to the dead, but claimed privately that the real artisans of victory were not ordinary *poilus*, but the educated youth that led the troops and organized production in the war industries.[30] Castelnau's view reflected the great preoccupation in the interwar Army with command, epitomized in Lieutenant-Colonel de Gaulle's insistence that 'without a master, the mass is vulnerable to the effects of its turbulence'.[31] The numerous ex-officers in the leagues also brought with them their wartime fascination with the manipulation of masses of men by road and rail.

In contrast, veteran status permitted the humbler military chaplain, Bergey, to promote a more populist agenda in the FNC. In the Gironde, he relied on a security service, the Volontaires de l'Abbé Bergey, 'beefy chaps from the Mériadeck district', personally loyal to his person rather than his programme, 'probably on a secret, atavistic basis', the police opined.[32] Nationally, Bergey organized veteran clerics in the Prêtres anciens combattants and the Droits du religieux ancien combattant. He claimed to have learned in his Republican *école primaire* that insurrection against unjust laws was a sacred duty. He was not alone in applying the language of war to politics. The Jesuit Paul Doncœur said that as soldiers of Verdun, Catholics knew how to defend ground, and did not fear *embusqué* politicians. He wanted the JP to ignore bans on its demonstrations.[33] Castelnau agreed, but felt that as FNC leader he could not say so publicly.[34]

The Faisceau and JP also interpreted the lessons of war in a more populist manner. They called for a governing elite drawn from the veterans, and saw military service as more important than class in recruitment of this elite. For Valois, the future dictator would not be the product of a 'class or a caste'. Another activist described the dictator as a 'living synthesis' of the whole nation, possessing the virtues of the peasant, worker, and bourgeois.[35] For Taittinger, the fallen had left a painful and sacred testament to their surviving comrades: 'France'. However, out of tiredness and timidity, the survivors delivered the country to politicians, who allowed Germany to recover, forgot the veterans' suffering, amnestied deserters, and allowed the country to slide into anarchy. The veterans should have insisted on

[28] Soucy, *French Fascism*, 49–50.

[29] ANFAM, 88, Bénistant to Millerand, 15 November 1924.

[30] *Auguste Isaac. Journal d'un notable lyonnais, 1906–1933*, ed. Hervé Joly (Lyon, 2002), 341, 19 October 1919.

[31] Charles de Gaulle, *Le fil de l'épée* (Paris, 1972, first published 1932), 183.

[32] Abbé Benjamin Bordachar, *Un Grand orateur, l'abbé Bergey, député de la Gironde* (Paris, 1963), 147–8.

[33] Corinne Bonafoux-Verrax, *À La Droite de Dieu. La Fédération nationale catholique 1924–1944* (Paris, 2004), 25–6, 35, 38.

[34] Soucy, *French Fascism*, 57–60.

[35] Maurice de Barral, *Le Faisceau* (Paris, 1926), 18; Georges Valois, *La Révolution nationale* (Paris, 1924), 181.

their right and duty to govern the country.[36] These criticisms were directed as much at the mainstream veterans movement and conservative politicians as at the Cartel. Some younger members of the leagues regarded politics as a substitute for fighting in a war that they were too young to have experienced.[37] In power, the Faisceau promised to make the veterans, along with representatives of the family, soil, and intelligence, responsible for government.

Yet if the leagues identified the elite with the veterans, that did not make them revolutionaries in a Marxist sense. For Valois, the equality of the trenches did not invalidate hierarchies that were 'useful to the country'.[38] That logic permitted him to advocate a strong capitalism, agriculture, and patriarchal family. He did not contest the existence of the bourgeoisie, only the transfer of materialism into politics; once the bourgeoisie was eliminated from government, it would return to its original vocation, for war had taught it the 'realities of production'.[39] Taittinger frequently castigated the 'stupid and flat bourgeoisie' for not understanding the lessons of the war, yet praised the 'classes moyennes', to whom he ascribed somewhat bourgeois characteristics.[40] As for the workers, they would be integrated into the nation as a class; hierarchies would not be abolished.

Above all, the JP and Faisceau attempted to contain social conflict by absorbing class struggle within a mobilized national community. Both the JP and Faisceau recruited many white-collar workers and possessed dedicated organizations in the bank and insurance sectors. Both leagues opposed strikes, but in the summer of 1925 backed a bank-workers' stoppage; Valois hoped that unionized bank workers could defeat international capitalism.[41] In the Bonapartist tradition, Taittinger looked to a benevolent, authoritarian state to win over workers and white-collar workers. In the spirit of the age, he claimed that high production in industry and agriculture and the provision of cheap, standardized, but aesthetically pleasing housing would remove the causes of Socialism.[42] The JP's demand for obligatory social insurance was controversial among conservatives at the time.[43] In the syndicalist tradition, Valois placed less emphasis upon the state than the JP did, and more upon self-governing corporations of workers and employers.

The leagues adopted a parallel stance towards women. The JP and Faisceau embraced a masculine style of politics, partly to position themselves as 'radical' and partly in response to the supposed disturbance of gender relations during the war. Antoine Rédier contrasted the veterans' virility and physical strength with parliamentary

36 Taittinger, *Les Cahiers de la jeune France* (Paris, 1926), 77–80.

37 *Le Drapeau*, 25 June 1924, quoted in Philippet, 'Le Temps des ligues', 52.

38 *Le Nouveau siècle*, 1, 25, 26, 27 January 1926.

39 *Le Nouveau siècle*, 3 September 1925; Valois, *La Révolution nationale*, 175; Barral, *Le Faisceau*, 1–12.

40 *La Liberté*, 3 January 1926.

41 Soucy, *French Fascism*, 75–6; Philippet, *Le Temps* 2, 697–700; Robert Lynn Fuller, 'The dynamics of conservative politics in Upper Normandy, 1898–1928', PhD dissertation, University of Virginia, 1994, 555–8; Allen Douglas, *From Fascism to Libertarian Communism: Georges Valois against the Third Republic* (Berkeley, 1992), 81–2, 119.

42 Taittinger, *Les Cahiers*, 33–7, 42–5.

43 ANPG $F^7$13232, 'Notre Doctrine'.

effeminacy; he urged the veterans to rule French society as masters and eliminate the Socialist demagogues who had corrupted the masses.[44] The JP and Faisceau also attracted some familialists and pro-natalists, who were disappointed with the Bloc. For instance, Duval-Arnould of the ANPAPF, without leaving the Fédération, joined the JP. Rédier, who sat on the council of La plus grand famille, urged men to father children to perpetuate their own blood, and proposed replacing parliament with an assembly of heads of family.[45] Valois too envisaged a constitutional role for fathers, and advanced typical views concerning the relationship between national power and the quality and quantity of the population.[46] All of this implied domesticity for women.

Yet the JP created the first women's section in a conservative movement since the LPDF had broken with the ALP, while Valois encouraged women to join a parallel organization, the Faisceau civique, along with non-combatant older men. This openness was a response to pressure from right-wing professional women and to the conversion of the Church to suffragism. The JP women's section president, Marie-Thérèse Moreau, was a lawyer and activist in the Catholic suffrage organization, the Union nationale pour le vote des femmes (UNVF). She devoted much of her time to speaking tours for the JP and lived as an independent woman. Female activism also derived from women's charitable work, which had expanded and professionalized during and after the war. Within the leagues, female activism was gendered. For Taittinger, women must remain the 'smiling queens of the home', and not become 'amazones or pétroleuses'.[47] Moreau, however, saw no contradiction between political activism, anti-feminism, and familialism. Her definition of the nation as a family justified female action in society and reconfigured the opposition between public and private.[48] The leagues aspired to contain gender conflicts within an authoritarian movement, just as they did class struggle.

Similarly, the leagues advocated regionalism within an authoritarian nation. The JP and Faisceau appealed to the Francophone middle classes of Colmar and Mulhouse, who both opposed the Cartel's religious policy and sought to defend their labour-market advantages against Germanophones. AF may have had over 2,000 members in Alsace, making it one of its most important provincial sections.[49] Meanwhile, some Alsatian-speaking peasants began to turn to the pro-autonomist Bauernbund, which sought to create an alternative to established farming organizations.[50]

[44] Roberts, *Civilization without Sexes*.

[45] Richard Tomlinson, 'The politics of dénatalité during the French Third Republic 1890–1940', PhD thesis, University of Cambridge, 1983, 179–83; Cheryl Koos, 'Engendering reaction: the politics of pronatalism and the family in France, 1919–1944', PhD dissertation, University of Southern California, 1996; 162–72; Cheryl Koos, 'Fascism, fatherhood, and the family in interwar France: the case of Antoine Rédier and the Légion', *Journal of Family History* 24, no. 3 (1999), 317–29.

[46] *Le Nouveau siècle*, 24 January 1926.

[47] Taittinger, *Les Cahiers*, 29–32; *Le Nouveau siècle*, 14 February 1925.

[48] *La Liberté*, 18 March 1925; Cheryl Koos and Daniella Sarnoff, 'France', in Kevin Passmore (ed.), *Women, Gender and the Extreme Right in Europe (1919–1945)* (Manchester, 2002), 168–88 at 176–9.

[49] Goodfellow, *Between the Swastika and the Cross of Lorraine*, 28–41, 89; Baechler, *Le Parti catholique alsacien*, 353–9.

[50] Baechler, *Le Parti catholique alsacien*, 239–327.

Thus, the leagues were a complex mixture of populism and elitism. There were also significant political differences within and between them, and they adopted contrasting stances on economic and religious questions. Only the Faisceau was entirely opposed to parliamentary conservatism, but all the leagues, in different degrees, contained authoritarian elements, and all were influenced by wider European developments. Monarchism remained influential, while Republicans in the extreme right had an elastic notion of Republicanism.

The Fédération Nationale Catholique

The FNC was not just an improvised response to the Cartel, but also to rising religious tensions under the Bloc and to changing strategies on the part of the Church. From 1906, Pius X distanced himself from the Action libérale populaire (ALP) and sought to unite Catholics outside political parties. From 1910, diocesan unions emerged, grouping believers for what would become 'Catholic Action'. Disrupted by the War, they were reconstituted from 1922; in 1923, there was already talk of uniting them in a national federation. The FNC was part of this strategy of re-Christianization through 'action civique'.

Paradoxically, apoliticism strengthened the Catholic right, including monarchism, for commitment to the Republic was not a condition of membership in the FNC. Indeed, the FNC resembled the 'Catholic party', operating on the terrain of the Republic without endorsing it, that monarchists had long wanted. Like Castelnau, the leaders of the FNC were largely intransigent Ralliés with some sympathy for Monarchism. Hyacinthe Gailhard-Bancel and Henri Groussau, respectively president and vice-president of the Independents, had been in the conservative wing of the ALP. The FNC chaplain, Père Janvier, was close to AF, while Royalists were common in departmental federations. Most FNC leaders were mature men, for whom Combism was a recent memory, but the FNC also included a new generation represented by Bergey, Vallat, and Philippe Henriot, who conceded nothing in the strength of their convictions.[51]

Likewise, the FNC's programme positioned it on the margins of Monarchism and the ALP. It saw politics as a combat between good and evil, with Freemasons incarnating the latter, and advocated unity of all Catholics against atheist materialism. It campaigned for revision of the lay laws, religious teaching in public schools, restoration of the family, corporatism, and strengthening the executive. In Brittany, the pro-Royalist right saw the FNC's campaign as a means to repeal the lay laws and to domesticate the Christian Democrats and even the FR. It interpreted Catholic defence widely, monitoring discrimination in the villages. Christian Democrats were not absent from the FNC, especially in areas of 'blue Catholicism', but relations between the PDP and FNC were equivocal.[52]

The immense success of the FNC confirmed that religion was an integral part of political culture, still able to mobilize millions of men and women, and

[51] Bonafoux-Verrax, *À La Droite de Dieu*, 39–42, 94–129, 252–3.

[52] Bensoussan, *Combats*, 93–5.

provide leverage for conservative, sometimes anti-Republican Catholics. Furthermore, FNC activities helped to sustain anticlericalism; municipalities refused the FNC the right to parade, while railway companies declined to provide special trains.[53] The Church recognized that in the local elections of 1925 the left made its greatest gains in localities in which FNC demonstrations had been most successful.

The Ligue Républicaine Nationale

The LRN could not reconcile its authoritarian tendencies with the aspiration to unite parliamentary conservatives. It shared some characteristics with Bonapartism: Millerand intended to capitalize upon his personal status as one of the architects of victory, unjustly evicted from power by conspiring politicians. His popularity in some quarters was immense—a reserve Lieutenant wrote him a five-page homage in verse.[54] The LRN announced itself in the press with an 'Appeal to the Nation', recalling the Bonapartist 'Appeal to the People'.

Millerand's popularity persuaded the leaders of the Alliance and Fédération to sit on the LRN's Comité directeur. Right-wing figures in the centre, such as Maginot, regarded the LRN relatively positively, for it saw it as a bridge to the moderate elements of the Catholic right. The Alliance left had less sympathy with the LRN's nationalism and with its desire to become a super-party with direct membership.[55] Likewise, the Fédération endorsed the LRN's call for unity against Communism, but refused subordination to the league. Isaac had unspecified doubts about the LRN programme and admitted that some did not trust Millerand because of his past.[56] Millerand's secularism was doubtless one problem, for the Bishop of Nantes condemned his backing for the lay laws—an 'instrument for the persecution of Catholics' that was 'contrary to the rights of God'. On 11 March, the Assembly of Cardinals and Archbishops reported papal advice that a Catholic could not logically belong simultaneously to the FNC, which fought the lay laws, and to the LRN, which included them in its programme. Isaac and Marin, who were hostile to the Declaration's integrism, had to distance themselves from the LRN.[57] Religion continued to divide conservatives.

These issues prevented the LRN from uniting conservative parties. In the winter of 1925–1926, a number of LRN committees deserted to the Fédération.[58] On the streets, the LRN could not compete with the JP or Faisceau, and did not wish to. However, the LRN, particularly through Maginot, did help to link the right of the Alliance with the moderate wing of the Fédération, thus paving the way for the

[53] Bonafoux-Verrax, *À La Droite de Dieu*, 36.

[54] ANFAM, 88, Bunel to Millerand, 4 December 1924.

[55] *L'Avenir*, 7 November 1924; Jean Vavasseur-Desperriers, 'Les Tentatives de regroupement des droites dans les années 30', *Annales de Bretagne* 109 (2002), 61–77 at 64–5.

[56] *La Fédération républicaine*, December 1924; ANFLM, 81, Minutes, FR de la Seine, 23 May 1927.

[57] Bonafoux-Verrax, *À La Droite de Dieu*', 252–3; Bensoussan, *Combats*, 98–102; *Isaac*, 380–92, 23 March 1925.

[58] *La Nation*, 10 November 1925; ANFLM 73, Guiter to Marin, 3 March 1926.

conservative hegemony of 1926–1932. In April 1926, the LRN and JP provided the backbone of Paul Reynaud and Henri de Kerillis' joint campaign in the Paris by-election.

Action Française

The fortunes of AF were mixed. Its parliamentary strategy failed to bear fruit. Daudet tried to persuade conservatives that AF saw a coup only as a last resort and appealed for a strong government including Herriot. Yet however much conservatives admired Maurras' nationalism and Daudet's attacks on the left, they were aware of the electorate's hostility to Royalism. In 1924, AF lost the seats it had won through alliance with the right, including Daudet's in Paris. In June 1925, the latter's defeat by a moderate Catholic in a senatorial election in Maine-et-Loire confirmed AF's limited appeal to mainstream conservatives.[59] Simultaneously with the collapse of AF's electoral adventure, Maurras failed to secure election to the Académie française.

More positively, neo-Royalist influence in the episcopate and FNC remained strong, while electoral bastions in the Loire-Inférieure, the Vendée, and Flanders just held out. Initially, AF profited from the fear provoked by the Cartel's victory, and joined other leagues in skirmishing with Communists in the streets. When the police tried to enforce the law banning the carrying of firearms, Maurras claimed that to do so was a duty and threatened the Interior Minister. In the spring of 1925, neo-Royalists were conspicuous in a campaign against the nomination of the pro-Radical Georges Scelle to a chair in the Faculté de droit. In 1926, in the final crisis of the Cartel, the circulation of *L'Action française* rose substantially.[60]

Nevertheless, the Cartel years marked the beginning of the end for AF. For the first time, it faced intruders in its political space. Christian Democracy challenged it in the countryside, while the JP ate into student support, and reorganization of the Fédération provided bourgeois leaders for the nationalist right in western strongholds. In 1922–1923, AF had attempted to appropriate the prestigious fascist label, but had to abandon it once Valois adopted it. AF had reached an impasse before the Papal condemnation.

The Jeunesses Patriotes

At the JP's inaugural meeting, the Bonapartist Henri Provost, the Royalist Henri Simon, and the Republican Henri Soulier, son of the Fédération deputy, promised to put France ahead of their personal preferences.[61] Too close an identification with a single tradition would have been divisive, just as use of the fascist label might have been. From a historical perspective, to categorize the JP as 'fascist' or

[59] Eugen Weber, *Action française: Royalism and Reaction in Twentieth-Century France* (Stanford, 1962), 150–3.

[60] Weber, *Action française*, 162–3.

[61] *Le Drapeau*, 20 April 1924.

not fascist would be to ignore its specificity and its diversity as well as its complex relationships with other movements, including Mussolini's. The JP copied Italian Fascism and acted as militia for the parliamentary right, but was reducible to neither.

Taittinger rarely identified the JP with Fascism, especially after the Faisceau appropriated the label, but his members admired aspects of Mussolini's movement, and not just its conservative elements. Taittinger refused to adopt the 'axe or the fasces of the old Roman lictors as their badge'—even though JP shock troops were organized in 'centuries', wore a uniform of blue raincoats and berets, and used the fascist salute. Indeed, the JP expressed few reservations about what they saw in Italy, and some members were positively sympathetic. Camille Aymard, director of *la Liberté*, in which Taittinger wrote, claimed that Fascism meant rejection of useless words, impotence, and parliamentary waste. Our principles, he said, are 'brutal like life'.[62] Taittinger claimed that the JP did not want reaction, but 'action, simply action, only action, immediate action'. He called for a government of energetic young men.[63]

Taittinger's Bonapartism was another ingredient in the JP brew. Several Bonapartists joined him in the JP, including Prince Joachim Murat. However, it makes little sense to reduce Bonapartism to a nineteenth-century essence. On the one hand, Bonapartism and Fascism both evoked the model of the Roman dictatorship. On the other, Tattinger's election in Paris in 1924 as Barrès' successor and his engagement in the LDP confirmed the success of his campaign to integrate Bonapartism into the broader nationalist right.

Bonapartist engagement in the eclectic 1919 movement further modified it. Taittinger led a large section in Saintes of one 1919 group, the Ligue des chefs de section, which endeavoured to mobilize the veterans for constitutional reform. The League's leader, Binet-Valmer later joined the JP. Taittinger was one of several Bonapartist participants in Quatrième république, and he sat in the chamber with the Action Républicaine et sociale, in which QR members were prominent. The JP gave a Bonapartist inflection to the 1919 movement's plans. Thus, whereas many conservatives saw cuts in the administration as part of constitutional reform, Taittinger held that the administration guarantied order in the nation. He reasoned that in return for higher wages, *fonctionnaires* would rationalize and 'industrialize' the administration, from the tax department to primary school—this programme represented an amalgam of Bonapartism with Fayolism and the 'syndicalist' programme of the CGT *fonctionnaires* leader, Georges Mer.[64] Taittinger's Bonapartism was also evident in his view that the Army was the 'sole source of national recovery'.[65] Somewhat confusedly, he preferred the British or Roman parliament to the French model (in which he sat), which he dismissed as a 'feudalism of the mediocre'. Taittinger's advocacy of election of the President of the Republic by a

62 *Le National*, 17 January 1926; *La Liberté*, 2 April 1925, 21 and 31 May 1926.
63 Taittinger, *Les Cahiers*, 87–9.
64 Taittinger, *Les Cahiers*, 46–9, 56–60.
65 Taittinger, *Les Cahiers*, 56–60.

college of economic, family, and other associations departed from Bonapartist direct election, and indeed from the idea of some Fascists that the leader would 'emerge' naturally from the people.[66] The JP's plans for constitutional reform were part of its version of organizationalism. In the Bonapartist tradition, it envisaged the representation of the 'competences' through professionalization of the Senate, recruitment of ministers from outside parliament, and preparation of legislation by the Council of State.

Bonapartist technocracy complemented the 1919 movement's interest in industrial efficiency, and connected with the organizational movement's concern with national self-sufficiency. Taittinger advocated standardized mass production to incorporate the workers into the nation. He reconciled this strategy with 'French' traditions, lauding artisan work as 'finesse allied to a taste for order'. He described the Art Déco exhibition of 1925 as a celebration of the 'order and harmony' that represented the 'true face of France'.[67] Harmony also entailed strengthening agriculture through consolidation of holdings, social insurance, and electrification, all of which would encourage a return to the land.

The JP also owed a debt to the Catholic and Royalist right. Taittinger's wife was from a Legitimist family, some members of which preferred the JP to the 'Orleanist' AF. That did not prevent AF members from joining the JP. The FNC and the ALP aided the league financially and doubtless most ordinary members were Catholics.[68] Taittinger sometimes spoke at FNC meetings.[69] He demanded religious teaching in public schools and complained of administrative discrimination against Catholics.[70] This 'liberalism' earned the JP the support of some Protestants, including the Souliers.

Pastor Soulier, the father, was one of many JP members who also belonged to the FR, on the General Council of which Taittinger sat. That the Fédération felt the need for the support of the paramilitary JP is revealing of its fears. Yet there was also suspicion between the two movements. Georges Peissel, deputy of the Rhône, pressed the Fédération's General Council to dissociate itself from the JP. Although Marin's relations with Taittinger were strained, he refused to forbid party members to join, but said that 'the greatest caution is necessary'. He was more suspicious of Rédier's Légion because of its links with AF, yet admitted that the Fédération had friends there too.[71] Links between the Fédération and JP were significant, but the latter was not simply a militia for the former.

The JP also resembled those Italian Fascists who presented themselves as youthful and vigorous defenders of the bourgeoisie.[72] Describing a confrontation with Communists in the Salle Japy, Taittinger praised the 'miraculous' refusal of the

[66] Taittinger, *Les Cahiers*, 81–3.
[67] *La Liberté*, 2 January 1925; Taittinger, *Les Cahiers*, 38.
[68] Soucy, *French Fascism*, 30, 51–2; ANFXR, 14, 15 February 1933, Taittinger to La Rochefoucauld.
[69] Taittinger, *Les Cahiers*, 26–8; *La Liberté*, 9 February 1925.
[70] Taittinger, *Les Cahiers*, 26–8; *La Liberté*, 2 March 1926.
[71] ANFLM, 81, Fonds Marin, minutes, Conseil général, 24 October, 14 November 1925.
[72] *La Liberté*, 6 January 1925.

bourgeois to be gutted by Communists and lauded their having inflicted a good thrashing on their attackers.[73] The league claimed that its primary purpose was to re-establish order in the event of a Communist coup.[74] It made elaborate plans to oppose a Communist revolution, and in 1925 they began to carry out practice mobilizations at short notice.[75] The Faisceau and the Croix de feu would subsequently imitate this method, borrowed from Italian Fascism. JP members often carried firearms and sometimes used them.

JP members clashed frequently with the Communists. On 8 February, Communists shot dead two JP members. On 23 April, they shot four more in the rue Damrémont, including one student each from Sciences Po, the École des beaux-arts, and the Polytechnique. Among those involved in the fighting was the young Jean-Louis Tixier-Vignancour, a member of the AF, who would subsequently join the Alliance démocratique.[76] Aware that some conservatives opposed violence, Taittinger claimed in the Chamber to have discouraged his followers from seeking revenge, since France was a country of justice. He also incriminated 'men who were not even French, including Kabyles and Annamites'. If their deeds did not lead to the scaffold, 'it will be up to citizens to defend themselves', in which case, 'you [the deputies] would be taken hostage and it would be you who would be the first to be executed'.[77] The JP, he added, would obey the leader, and rapidly carry out the necessary cleansing of political personnel.[78] It is not easy to reconcile such pronouncements with the parliamentary right's vision of reform.

Castelnau described Taittinger as 'astride the two camps of the right, the fascist and the non-fascist, between which, thanks to good relations with both, he serves on occasion as a link, although he possesses little sympathy for Monsieur Valois'.[79] This assessment is valid, so long as we do not view fascism as a homogeneous movement and are aware of its complex relationship with other traditions. In January 1926, Taittinger claimed that the Ligue des patriotes' reliance on speechifying and commemoration would lose it members to AF and the Faisceau, and proposed to defy a government ban on a march to the Arc de Triomphe. That was enough to cause an irreparable breach with the parent league.[80] Taittinger set up his own newspaper, *Le National*, and drew up a detailed programme. His new course had much to do with the rivalry of the Faisceau, which had recently split from AF—one whole JP century had joined Valois.[81] In December 1925, Rédier was expelled from the JP; he and many of his followers joined the Faisceau.[82]

[73] *La Liberté*, 3 January 1925.
[74] *La Liberté*, 3, 5 January 1925; *L'Écho de Paris*, 5, 12 January 1925.
[75] Soucy, *French Fascism*, 44–7; *La Liberté*, 17 April 1925.
[76] Soucy, *French Fascism*, 55–6.
[77] Philippet, 'Le Temps des ligues', 217–25.
[78] Taittinger, *Les Cahiers*, 87–9.
[79] Soucy, *French Fascism*, 57–9.
[80] Philippet, 'Le Temps des ligues', 266–71.
[81] *Bulletin du Comité régional de Provence des Jeunesses patriotes*, 17 November 1926.
[82] Soucy, *French Fascism*, 37.

The Faisceau

Unlike the JP, the Faisceau assumed the fascist label. Valois sought to build a mass movement dedicated to the conquest of power, if necessary, violently. The Faisceau des combattants wore a dark blue uniform and participated in military-style mobilizations accompanied by the rhetoric of D-Day. It held mass meetings, with grandiose *mise en scène*. On 21 February at Verdun and 27 June 1926 at Reims, around 8,000–10,000 Faisceau assembled. Like Italian Fascists, the Faisceau endeavoured to reconcile legitimate conflicts of interest through a mobilized, mass, authoritarian movement, a model for the future fascist state. That said, Valois saw fascism as an international force that took different forms in different countries. He understood Fascism in particular ways, and assimilated it into French traditions. Just because it used the word, the movement was not fascist in an essential sense.[83]

Valois' debt to AF was evident in the conviction that Fascism emanated from orderly, hierarchical Mediterranean Graeco-Roman classicism, and was antipathetic to Nordic liberalism and communistic Germanism and Slavism.[84] He spoke of conflict between 'sedentary' European civilization and the 'nomadic' hordes of the east—*Nouveau siècle* ran a column entitled 'The open and hidden manoeuvres of the horde', by which he meant Communism. Valois believed that Western liberalism sapped military values and hierarchy, and rendered it vulnerable to invasion. Dictatorial fascism would defend the nation against Communist horde and international plutocracy and ensure that all classes contributed to the well-being of the nation, rather than fight each other.

The Faisceau were also indebted to the 1919 movement and to organizationalism more generally. In March 1920, Valois had launched the Confédération de l'intelligence et de la production française (CIPF) in the hope of persuading workers and employers to recognize their common interest as 'producers'. In 1922, he broadened this movement through the États généraux de la production française. In the Gironde, the Faisceau inherited the 800 members of Démocratie nouvelle, many of whom also belonged to the UNC.[85]

Some historians argue that within the Faisceau there was a conflict between the 'modernizer' Valois and the 'traditionalist' Eugène Mathon.[86] The two did indeed come into conflict, and they used the terms in question. However, tradition and modernity were historical constructions, used for specific purposes. Valois was typical of conservatives in advocating the rule of competence, and equally predictable in using the term as a weapon: he saw Loucheur, for others the epitome of technocracy, as a 'profiteer', 'lacking entirely in competence', and 'without credit in the world of serious production and finance'.[87] Furthermore, Valois and Mathon

[83] *Le Nouveau siècle*, 28 January 1926.

[84] Joel Blatt, 'Relatives and rivals: the responses of Action française to Italian fascism, 1919–1926', *European Studies Review European Studies Review* 11, no. 3 (1981), 263–92.

[85] Sylvain Trussardi, 'Faisceau, Croix de feu, PSF. Trois mouvements girondins du milieu des années 1920 à la fin des années 1930', *Parlements*, special issue (2005), 55–64.

[86] Douglas, *From Fascism*, 82–8; Kalman, 'Vers un ordre nouveau', and Sternhell, *Ni droite, ni gauche*', 108.

[87] *Le Nouveau siècle*, 30 December 1925.

agreed that tradition and modernity must be reconciled. Valois celebrated the age of the machine, admired Le Corbusier's modernist urban planning, and yet called for reconstruction of basic social forms that liberal individualism had destroyed.[88] The veterans would build a new house including all the old traditions, the eternal and historic principles that had permitted victory.[89] Typically again, Valois espoused a nationalist economics in which a balance between industry and agriculture, tradition and modernity, were essential.[90] Mathon, the alleged traditionalist, embraced rationalization and used corporatist organization among employers to enforce standard wage rates and force the inefficient out of business. He was vice-president of Étienne Fougère's organizationalist Association nationale d'expansion économique (ANEE), which may have funded the Faisceau. Ernest Mercier's Redressement français may also have contributed funds.[91] Another Faisceau journalist, Hubert Bourgin, argued that the peasantry preserved France from a British-style overproduction crisis and that peasant virtues of work, savings, and foresight permitted controlled progress.[92]

Conflict within the Faisceau revolved around the definitions of tradition and modernity, and more particularly around the familiar matter of the role of the state in the organized economy and the related issue of attitudes to Communism. Valois advocated a degree of state control that went beyond what was acceptable to those who advocated a partnership of capitalism and the state, to corporatists like Mathon, let alone to liberals. Valois held that although Communism wrongly suppressed private initiative, like Fascism it realized unity of command in the state, which, as a Fayolist, he could not but approve.[93] He invested a strong leader with responsibility for determining the general interest, and denied that technical competences could rule directly. Assemblies of heads of family and producers could be effective only if 'disciplined, co-ordinated and balanced by an authority that depends on none of them', even if the state should not encroach on the liberty of 'chefs' in lower levels of the corporatist system.[94] Valois gave the state the task of planning the relationship between economic sectors of the economy.[95] He did not back privatization of monopolies unconditionally—a touchstone of economic orthodoxy for the right.[96] Worse, he denounced not just anonymous finance, but targeted Standard Oil, the pro-Cartel banker, Horace Finaly, and the solidly conservative head of the Comité des forges, Robert Pinot.[97] Disputes within the Faisceau concerning the relationship between the state and corporations mirrored those within Italian Fascism.[98]

[88] *Le Nouveau siècle*, 26 January, 1, 3 April 1926; Mark Antliff, 'La Cité française: Georges Valois, Le Corbusier and fascist theories of urbanism', in Matthew Affron and Mark Antliff (eds), *Fascist Visions* (Princeton, 1997), 134–70.

[89] *Le Nouveau siècle*, 1 January, 2 February 1926.

[90] Valois, *La Révolution nationale*, 175–6.

[91] Douglas, *From Fascism*, 52–3.

[92] Hubert Bourgin, *Les Pierres de la maison* (Paris, 1926), 104–5.

[93] *Le Nouveau siècle*, 3 December 1925.

[94] Barral, *Le Faisceau*, 18; Le *Nouveau siècle* 20 August, 3 December 1925, 6 March 1926.

[95] Valois, *La Révolution nationale*, 175–6.

[96] Barral, *Le Faisceau*, 20.

[97] *Le Nouveau siècle*, 20 August 1925.

[98] Kalman, 'Vers un ordre nouveau', 30–62.

Valois' efforts to integrate the proletariat into the nation represented another cause of disagreement with Mathon. Valois claimed that the materialist bourgeoisie had expelled the proletariat from the nation; to reincorporate it, he evoked the principles of social justice as laid out by La Tour du Pin. He advocated humanization of labour in a national community: the nation would make the law in the factory. More practically, he endorsed, in principle, the eight-hour day.[99] These policies attracted a few Communists, notably, in November 1925, the mayor of Périgueux, Marcel Delagrange. The result was meagre in relation to the effort deployed, for the left offered more, and Valois' modernist utopia was unappealingly Spartan, for he possessed a Catholic uneasiness about enjoyment.[100] Notwithstanding, Mathon and Ley were alarmed. The textile manufacturers, who had previously failed to enrol the CFTC in their cause, wanted Valois to create company unions and an anti-communist spy network.[101] In August 1925, Valois' qualified backing for the bank strike widened the breach, while another Faisceau leader, Marcel Bucard, clashed with the Comité des forges of the Loire over the eight-hour day.[102] Maurras saw Valois' attacks on the bourgeoisie as foolhardy, given it constituted nine-tenths of the population; for him, Jews, Protestants, and Freemasons were more to blame for social problems than the bourgeoisie was.

The Faisceau's relationship with parliamentary conservatism was equally complex. On the one hand, Valois condemned the Bloc for having reduced veteran-deputies to servants of the *embusqués*.[103] Bucard, a future admirer of Nazism, entered politics as a protégé of André Tardieu, but accused Tardieu of using him to attract the veteran vote.[104] Valois denounced democracy and was prepared to destroy parliament and if necessary parliamentarians.[105] He accepted atrocity as an inevitable part of modern life, and, as a Sorelian pragmatist, argued that political systems should be judged by their ends, not their means.[106] Such pronouncements help to explain why Castelnau saw the Faisceau as 'too fascist'. Millerand refused an invitation to attend the Faisceau's Reims meeting because 'I do not work for dictatorship and if it is established, I shall submit to it, nothing more'. In *Écho de Paris*, Kerillis attacked fascism.[107] On the other hand, *L'Éclair* saw the emergence of the Faisceau as evidence that 'the bourgeoisie have stopped being resigned sheep, exposing their throats to the knife of the Bolshevik killer'.[108]

99 *Le Nouveau siècle*, 27 August, 17 September 1925; Valois, *La Révolution nationale*, 178.

100 *Le Nouveau siècle*, 26 January, 6 March, 8 May 1926; Soucy, *French Fascism*, 168–9.

101 Douglas, *From Fascism*, 251–2; *Le Nouveau siècle*, 1 January 1926; Soucy, *French Fascism*, 114, 118–19.

102 Douglas, *From Fascism*, 117.

103 *Le Nouveau siècle*, 20 August 1925.

104 Arnaud Jacomet, 'Les chefs du francisme. Marcel Bucard et Paul Guiraud', *Revue d'histoire de la deuxième guerre mondiale* 97 (January 1975), 45–66.

105 *Le Nouveau siècle*, 20 August 1925, 7 February 1926.

106 *Le Nouveau siècle*, 3 December 1925.

107 Soucy, *French Fascism*, 176; Douglas, *From Fascism*, 133.

108 *L'Éclair*, 17 November 1925, quoted in Soucy, *French Fascism*, 96.

Many conservatives saw the Faisceau as a lesser evil and it attracted business finance; many members were resentful, radicalized conservatives.

CONSERVATIVES AND THE COLLAPSE OF THE CARTEL

The agony of the Cartel in the summer of 1926 took place against the background of financial crisis and extra-parliamentary mobilization. Small traders began to refuse their tax assessments. At Reims, on 27 June, the Faisceau held a massive rally, demanding defence of the Franc and a 'national revolution'. The JP also attended, and the combined leagues, allowing for overlapping membership, now had over 100,000 members. Valois told his leaguers that they would soon inherit power. Meanwhile, the UNC mobilized in defence of the Franc and against the Mellon-Béranger accords on US war debts. On 11 July, 20,000 veterans demonstrated their opposition to ratification. The knowledge that the UF had been meeting German veterans further inflamed tempers.[109] On 26 July, as Herriot presented his government, thousands demonstrated outside the Chamber. The leagues and the UNC possessed considerable sympathy among the right in the Chamber.

While the mobilization of extreme right may have helped to frighten the Cartel from power, the right found itself on the margins of the Union nationale coalition under Poincaré that succeeded it. The right and extreme right were disappointed with an outcome that, they believed, they had enabled. In fact, if anything, the centre's hostility to the left had softened by 1926, and the extremists proved unable to dominate the agenda.

The Fédération Républicaine

Jean-Noël Jeanneney dismantles the myth that François de Wendel used his dual position as deputy and member of the Council of Regents of the Bank of France to single-handedly engineer the collapse of the Cartel.[110] He shows that his nationalism often isolated him from other industrialists and that economic and political matters divided business. However, Wendel had significant leverage. On 30 March, the Council of Regents, faced with Wendel's threatened resignation, agreed that the practice of fudging the Bank's accounts must end, thus forcing Herriot out of office.[111] Of course, Radical economic failures and parliament's opposition to Herriot's proposal for a capital tax also undermined the government, and Jeanneney

[109] Trussardi, 'Faisceau', 56; Prost, *Les Anciens combattants*, i, 95–107; *L'Écho de Paris*, 27 November 1925.

[110] Jean-Noël Jeanneney, *François de Wendel en République. L'Argent et le pouvoir* (Paris, 1976), 179–318.

[111] Jeanneney, *François de Wendel*, 87–107.

rightly shows that Wendel proved unable to exploit his victory. The reasons are worth re-examining, for they reveal the depths of divisions among conservatives.

Wendel, Marin, and the Fédération's right-wing espoused a combination of nationalism and liberal orthodoxy that set them against both the Fédération left and the centre, and in practice aggravated rank-and-file discontent. The right wanted protection of property, indirect taxes, spending cuts, privatization, protection of bondholders, and revaluation of the currency. They also advocated a strong line on reparations and war debts, for these measures would permit tax cuts and avoid the 'servitude' of a US loan. Wendel hoped that Herriot's successor, Paul Painlevé, and his Finance Minister, Joseph Caillaux, would implement this policy. He persuaded the Fédération—and PDP—to back Painlevé as lesser evil, his case helped by Socialist victories in the May 1925 municipal elections. Wendel encouraged the Bank to grant the government funds on condition that it launched a domestic loan—the right's favoured solution to the financial crisis because it avoided income tax rises, and effectively rewarded the wealthy for funding the government.[112]

A backlash from ordinary conservatives ensured the failure of this strategy, for they denounced the party's backing for the ministry and refused to subscribe to the loan. In that sense, the *mur d'argent* was real.[113] One deputy reported that in the Eure, small savers would not subscribe to a loan associated with the traitor, Caillaux.[114] Indeed, it was from this point that the JP expanded. In a letter to party secretary Guiter, the Marquis des Roys announced his backing for 'another league', while another member accused the Fédération of being afraid to apply its programme and of prefacing all its speeches with '"Respectful of legality..." when it is necessary to reform and restrict universal suffrage'. He added that dictatorship was 'regrettable' but that without it France was lost.[115] Rank-and-file opposition scuppered Wendel's political strategy and deprived the right of its alternative, the domestic loan. Subsequently, in response to Taittinger's claim that 'criticism [of the government] is insufficient', Marin declared that he did not want to risk unpopularity, so would merely denounce inflation, taxation, and consolidation.[116]

Meanwhile, Marin and Wendel's nationalism provoked opposition from Fédération moderates. In November 1925, Marin told party leaders that the Locarno agreement was 'pure madness. Everything has been abandoned.'[117] Wendel feared that Briand, who came to power in November 1925, would use the ANEE, Comité des houillères, and Nuncio, all Locarnistes, to pressure Fédération deputies. This nationalism provoked a wave of resignations.[118] In early 1926, Laurent Bonnevay left the Fédération, citing Marin's hostility to Locarno, his desire for a disciplined

[112] Jeanneney, *François de Wendel*, 242–50.
[113] Jeanneney, *François de Wendel*, 260.
[114] ANFLM, 73, Crises de la Fédération, Delacroix Petit to Guiter, 9 July 1925; ANFLM, 81, Comité directeur and Conseil général 14–15 November.
[115] ANFLM, 73, Crises de la Fédération, des Roys to Guiter, 7 December 1925; Ferraux to Guiter, 25 November 1925.
[116] ANFLM, 81, Comité directeur and Conseil général, 23, 25 October, 14 November 1925.
[117] ANFLM, 81, Comité directeur, 14 November 1925.
[118] ANFLM, 73, Villard to Guiter, 31 October 1925.

party, and his alleged sympathy for AF and the Faisceau.[119] Part of the Fédération was sympathetic to the Locarno policy, and that helped ensure that the centre, rather than the right, benefited from the collapse of the Cartel.

THE CENTRE AND THE CARTEL

Soon after the elections, the influential pro-Alliance démocratique journalist Émile Buré wrote that thanks to fear of Germany and Communism, a well-organized opposition might split the Cartel, even if for the moment the victors were 'drunk with success'.[120] Flandin announced that 'our goal is the triumph of a policy of Republican Concentration'.[121] The forty-three members of the Gauche républicaine démocratique and thirty-eight Républicains de gauche largely opposed the Cartel for the moment, and the PDP, outraged at its religious policies, did so even more systematically. Yet the forty-one members of the Gauche radicale behind Loucheur backed the government. The right and extreme right denounced this refusal of systematic opposition, and put it down to desire for ministerial office. There was more to it than that.

In so far as historians have paid attention to the centre's attraction to the Cartel, they attribute it to refusal of two-party politics and to an 'anachronistic' anticlericalism, shared with the Cartel.[122] Certainly, the religious question mattered. Loucheur's anticlericalism was widely shared, and the emergence of the FNC intensified it. *La Petite Gironde* compared the lay laws to bodily laws that regulate health.[123] Mamelet, secretary-general of the Alliance-Parti républicain démocrate et social (PRDS), accepted that the war had integrated Catholics into the Republic, but rejected state funding of Catholic schools as an attack on the fundamental laws of the Republic. He promised only to apply the lay laws in their true spirit and to defend the Vatican embassy. He accused the FNC of provoking anticlericalism and condemned the 'vieux parti conservateur' for its 'periodic effervescences that obscure its political sense'. Only non-sectarian, *laïque* Republicanism could attract the masses.[124] Catholic supporters of the lay centre took a similar line. Lemire reaffirmed the distinction between anticlericalism and *laïcité*: he charged conservative Catholics with confusing the *école unique* (merging of state and private secondary education) with a state monopoly on teaching, and with denaturing Herriot's views on Alsace-Lorraine.[125]

Anticlericalism was not however an anachronistic relic. It was inseparable from commitment to reform. Loucheur claimed that the Gauche radicale differed from 'the modérés' in its commitment to social reform and *laïcité*, and both attracted

[119] Passmore, *From Liberalism*, 138.
[120] *L'Éclair de l'Est*, 22 May 1924.
[121] Georges Suarez, *Peu d'hommes, trop d'idées* (Paris, 1928), 49.
[122] Jean-Marie Mayeur, *La Vie politique dans la Troisième République* (Paris, 1984), 599.
[123] *La Petite Gironde*, 2 October 1925.
[124] *La République démocratique*, 9, 30 November 1924.
[125] Jean-Marie Mayeur, *L'Abbé Lemire. Un Prêtre démocrate 1853–1928* (Paris, 1968), 595–9.

him to the Cartel.[126] For instance, '*école unique*' possessed an anticlerical dimension, but was also intended to improve the quality of the elite, and was part of the Cartel's social-democratic, internationalist version of the organizational project. The project also involved the creation of a Conseil nationale économique (CNE), designed to allow organized interests a voice in policy and to improve the efficiency of the administration, and was linked to economic collaboration in Europe, an integral part of the rapprochement with Germany.

In 1924–1925, much in the Cartel's programme attracted Loucheur, Clémentel, and Briand, who had opposed the Bloc's liberal organizationalism and nationalism in the name of partnership between state and business in a European framework.[127] Defeated under the Bloc, they turned leftwards. They attempted to give the Cartel's social project a more Fayolist dimension, and to ensure that reconciliation with Germany did not mean abandonment of strong defence. The business lobby, Redressement français, founded in December 1925 by the Polytechnicien Ernest Mercier, embraced similar ideas, and operated on the margins of Radicalism and the centre.

Loucheur played an important part in the Cartel, serving twice as minister. He was ready to collaborate with the Socialists on specific issues.[128] He advocated raising income tax, abandonment of the revaluation of the Franc to its 1914 value, moderation of reparations, and stimulation of exports.[129] Under Painlevé, he worked with the Socialists on a modified version of the tax on capital; while serving as Briand's Finance Minister, he remarked privately that his proposals provoked 'fury in industrial and banking circles, general outcry'.[130] Actually, Loucheur did not abandon Fayolist commitment to primacy of the employer in the organized economy. He envisaged organization of industry into cartels producing standardized goods, in collaboration with the state in a European framework. Together with allies in the Gauche radicale, he had attempted to create a business friendly alternative to the Cartel's Conseil national économique.[131] Thus, Loucheur provided a bridge from Radicalism to the centre.

Most centrists were more committed than Loucheur was to fiscal orthodoxy, and, like the Fédération, demanded spending cuts, privatizations, and increased indirect taxes.[132] In practice, they were more flexible than the Fédération. Some proposed automatic repayment of the short-term debt by the Bank of France—the so-called 'plafond unique'; Poincaré eventually implemented this inflationary

126 Suarez, *Peu d'hommes*, 78–83.

127 Gilles Le Béguec, 'L'Entrée au Palais-Bourbon: Les Filières privilégiées d'accès à la fonction parlementaire 1919–1939', doctorat d'état, Paris X Nanterre, 1989, 307–16.

128 Suarez, *Peu d'hommes*, 78–83; Mayeur, *Lemire*, 595.

129 Jeanneney, *François de Wendel*, 243.

130 Stephen D. Carls, *Louis Loucheur and the Shaping of Modern France* (Baton Rouge, 1993), 237–59; Louis Loucheur, *Carnets secrets 1908–1932* (Brussels, 1962), 151–7.

131 Georges Dubost, 'Le Conseil national économique, ses origines, son institution et son organisation, son œuvre, son avenir', thèse de droit, Université de Paris, 1929, 68–9; Pierre-Georges Lambert, *La Représentation des intérêts professionnels* (Paris, 1929), 36–8; Alain Chatriot, *La Démocratie sociale à la française, L'expérience du Conseil national économique* (Paris, 2003), 34–6.

132 *La République démocratique*, 18 December 1925.

measure. The centre also accepted printing money 'for the needs of commerce', implicitly rejected revaluation of the Franc, and was less concerned with the defence of small savers than was the Fédération.

The centre gradually accepted Briand's foreign policy. It had distrusted Herriot's lyricism,[133] but abstained in the vote on the ratification of Locarno, while the PDP largely voted for it. Pacification looked safer under Briand, who combined idealism with pragmatism. Maginot described Briand's speech in favour of Locarno as the best he had heard in all his years as a deputy. Maginot did not want to prevent the olive branch from growing, but to prevent 'moral disarmament' a firm defence policy must accompany Locarno (perhaps the equivalent of the Fayolist principle).[134] The centre saw European unity as a means to defend French and European civilization against the United States, Bolshevism, anti-colonial movements, and the 'east'. The *Petite Gironde* opined that whereas the League of Nations ignored the inequality of races, the United States of Europe would protect civilization against the invasion of eastern peoples.[135]

Redressement français encapsulated the contradictory strands of the centre. It brought together the Saint-Simonianism, Taylorism, Fayolism, and anti-parliamentarianism of the Polytechnique with the democratic progressivism of Mercier's Protestant family. Redressement claimed to be 'above politics', called for the competent to displace professional politicians and demanded a firm authority, inspired by a 'realistic organizationalism [sic]'. Redressement attracted business leaders such as René Duchemin of the Confédération générale de la production française (CGPF) and Jacques Bardoux, director of the Comité des Forges' in-house journal. Redressement's connections with the centre politicians such as Maurice Petsche and André de Fels soon became apparent. In the spirit of the centre, it promised to neither overthrow the regime nor return to an 'outdated' one.[136] Another centrist sympathizer, Reynaud, saw Mercier's attacks on politicians as excessive. He countered that parties were rooted in the real life of the provinces, and cited the Fédération in the Rhône as exemplary. Reynaud advocated rationalization and organization of politics, through measures ranging from electronic voting in parliament to standardization of political propaganda. Mercier conceded that he had misjudged the parties; Redressement became an important collector of electoral funds, and its antiparliamentary sub-current retreated.[137]

Redressement also contained tensions between liberals and their opponents. De Fels represented the former. He argued that Redressement would end the isolation of the 'real' social authorities, the producers, from government and recover the initiative from professional politicians, thus reducing the role of the state in the economy. He proposed devolution of social insurance to individual factories, an

[133] *La République démocratique*, 9 November 1924; John Keiger, *Raymond Poincaré* (Cambridge, 1997), 315–17.

[134] Marc Sorlot, *André Maginot (1877–1932). L'Homme politique et sa légende* (Metz, 1995), 167.

[135] *La Petite gironde*, 12 October 1925.

[136] 'Le Redressement français', in *Les Documents politiques, diplomatiques et financiers* 7, no. 11 (1926); Richard Kuisel, *Ernest Mercier: French Technocrat* (Berkeley, 1967), 45–63.

[137] Olivier Dard, *Le Rendez-vous manqué des relèves des années 30* (Paris, 2002), 45.

alternative to 'collectivist' measures.[138] In spite of later denials, Mercier probably approved Fels' vision.[139] Redressement's first pamphlets certainly opposed inflation and included other orthodox measures. Yet the programme also included tax rises to pay for expenditure on social insurance and housing. In foreign policy, Redressement demanded security based on ententes between nations and a technologically advanced Army.[140] In August 1926, de Fels left Redressement, as it moved in a direction more compatible with the Cartel's organizationalism, thus helping to secure the centre's domination of the Union nationale.

In April 1925, after Herriot's fall, conservatives hoped to split the majority by supporting his successors. Wendel's backing for Caillaux and Painlevé had failed to achieve that objective, and the right henceforth called for a national union government, while the leagues increased their agitation. Yet the centre and Fédération moderates backed Briand's Concentration government (November 1925 to 17 July 1926) to the end, resisting calls for Union nationale. Loucheur and Colrat even joined the abortive Herriot government that succeeded it. The evolution of the PDP was also significant. Initially, the pre-eminence of the religious question positioned it among the most determined opponents of the Cartel. Yet once Herriot had fallen, the desire to split the Cartel and to differentiate itself from the right allowed its more advanced social and international programme to come to the fore.[141]

In the event, Concentration proved impossible, but that did not prevent the victory of the centre. As the Franc plummeted, retail prices rose hourly, and the Bank threatened to close its counters, it became clear that only under a Union nationale government would savers renew their bonds and subscribe to loans. In that respect, rank-and-file conservative discontent, of which the leagues were one manifestation, coupled with the intransigence of the right, played a part in the fall of the Cartel.

One reason for the centre's ultimate victory was that it won the battle to define expertise. Back in May, the Briand government asked a Committee of Experts to find a solution to the financial crisis. The Committee included no Regent of the Bank of France, and was weighted towards pro-centre business.[142] While its report, delivered on 4 July, stressed small savers' interest in monetary stability, a favourite theme of the right, its practical recommendations included abandonment of revaluation of the currency, stabilization through the 'plafond unique', and an American loan secured in return for ratification of the Mellon-Béranger Accords. Recovery was thus predicated upon international pacification and economic growth in an 'organized' European economy. Caillaux described the plan to Wendel as a step towards a United States of Europe, constructed in opposition to the Anglo-Saxons.[143] Caillaux proved unable to win the majority he needed to implement the report, yet it survived him, for it was difficult to criticize 'expertise'. Poincaré's government made it the basis of its

138 André de Fels, 'Redressement Français', *Revue de Paris*, 1 May 1926, 5–17.
139 *Le Figaro*, 7, 8, 17, 18 November 1927.
140 'Le Redressement français'; Kuisel, *Ernest Mercier*, 45–63.
141 Delbreil, *Centrisme*, 139–60.
142 Jeanneney, *François de Wendel*, 299.
143 Jeanneney, *François de Wendel*, 306.

financial and international policy for the coming years. Even Valois accepted the report, subject to reservations on the US loan.[144]

The centre accepted that there was no alternative to the Union nationale. Loucheur lost control of the Gauche radicale to the conservative Raoul Péret. The centrist Petsche persuaded 230 deputies to sign a manifesto calling for a 'government of public safety', led by men able to harness 'all French energies and wills', which would implement the 'objective' experts' report, perhaps with unspecified modifications. The signatories formed an 'Intergroupe républicain de salut public', including all groups from the Gauche radicale to the URD.[145] The intergroup appealed to Radicals to join as individuals. Parliamentary arithmetic meant that the Radicals could not be ignored, but only divisions among conservatives explained why the centre of gravity of the new government was on its left. Marin alone represented the Fédération, while his nemesis, Briand, remained at Foreign Affairs. The Faisceau endorsed Poincaré's financial measures, yet declared them insufficient and proclaimed its readiness to head a government of public safety.[146] Kerillis wrote of the government: 'Let's speak frankly: it's disappointing.'[147] Maurras predicted—with some foresight—that Poincaré would carry out his opponents' policies.

As Poincaré stabilized the situation, the leagues declined. In January 1927, following his failure to gain re-election to the Senate, Millerand resigned as president of the LRN. Although he returned to the Senate at the end of the year, he never again played a significant political role. In the Faisceau, Philippe Barrès and the eastern legions pressed Valois not to be too harsh on Poincaré, their fellow Lorrainer, while others accused Valois of being too soft. Valois began to 'republicanize' his movement. Before the end of the year, *Nouveau siècle* abandoned daily publication. The right wing of the JP declined too, but the league survived because it backed Kerillis' more moderate strategy and became integral to the conservative hegemony of the following years. The weakened right, increasingly anti-parliamentarian and nationalist, coalesced around Marin's wing of the Fédération.

The events of 1924–1926 cast doubt upon Pierre Milza's claim that the leagues represented a route for conservatives' integration into the Republic, and that leaving aside the few 'demagogues' who attempted to exploit it, their anti-parliamentarianism was a proto-Gaullist means to 'modernize' the Republic.[148] In fact, there were marked anti-democratic tendencies in both the leagues and the parliamentary right. Mathias Bernard's view that the leagues renewed the cadres and practices of the parliamentary right at the price of initiating the logic that led to Vichy is closer to the mark.[149] For the right and extreme right, the

[144] *Nouveau siècle* 21 July 1926; *L'Écho de Paris*, 20 July 1926.

[145] *L'Écho de Paris*, 22, 25 July 1926.

[146] *Le Nouveau siècle*, 6 July 1926.

[147] *L'Écho de Paris*, 24 July 1926.

[148] Jeanneney, *Leçon d'histoire*; Michel Winock, *La Fièvre hexagonale. Les Grandes crises politiques 1871–1968* (Paris, 1986), 198–201; H.W. Paul, *The Second Ralliement: The Rapprochement between Church and State in France in the Twentieth Century* (Washington, 1967).

[149] Mathias Bernard, *La Guerre des droites. Droite et extrême droite en France de l'affaire Dreyfus à nos jours* (Paris, 2007), 60–94.

disappointments of the Bloc, coupled with anger at the centre's response to the Cartel and its hegemony in government from 1926 to 1932, contributed to frustration with the Republic. Yet nothing was decided. The Cartel also made possible a new reformist, democratic conservative alignment, led by the centre, and based on a reworking of the Radicals' programme of economic organization within reconciled Europe.

11

Apogee and Crisis (1928–1932)

> We've seen that neither the Union des intérêts économiques, the Alliance démocratique, nor the Fédération républicaine have wanted to let the Radicals monopolize 'realism'. The three party congresses that have just taken place engaged in a veritable abuse of the word 'realist'. And as the spirit of competition prevails, everyone claims to be more realist than the other.
>
> Jean Luchaire, 20 December 1927

If the dream of a united, reformist, Republican conservative majority ever came close to realization, it was in the six years following the defeat of the Cartel. In the elections of April 1928, conservatives won an overall majority (twelve *conservateurs*, 131 largely Fédération members in the Union républicaine démocratique (URD), 165 centrists, and eighteen members of the Parti démocrate populaire (PDP)). In November 1928, the Radicals left the government, leaving conservatives in sole charge for only the second time in the history of the Republic. The centre dominated the majority—in 1929, two of their number, André Tardieu and Pierre Laval, succeeded the sick Poincaré as Président du conseil—but won support on both wings. True, the Radicals intensely disliked Tardieu in particular, but that did not prevent them from collaborating with the majority on specific issues. To the right, much of the Fédération républicaine (FR) also backed centre governments, partly thanks to the efforts to bring them together of Henri de Kerillis' Centre de propaganda des républicains nationaux (CPRN). Moreover, Kerillis enrolled the bulk of the Jeunesses patriotes (JP) in his movement, moderating it at a time when Papal condemnation of Action française (AF) had weakened neo-Royalism. Circumstances outside parliament favoured moderation too. The economic situation was good, for the Wall Street Crash of October 1929 did not immediately affect France; on the contrary, prosperity produced budget surpluses and gold flowed into the Bank of France. Following Locarno, international tension declined and reconciliation with Germany seemed possible. The conservative governments of 1926–1932 proved far more fruitful legislatively than the Bloc had been. They stabilized the Franc, established a welfare system, and introduced free secondary education.

Some historians see the Tardieu governments of 1929–1931 as an abortive attempt to modernize French society, heroic failures that foundered on the reef of narrow political priorities and ignorance of post-war realities.[1] Tardieu had indeed

[1] Richard Kuisel, *Capitalism and the State in Modern France: Renovation and Economic Management in the Twentieth Century* (Cambridge, 1981), 90–2; François Monnet, *Refaire la république. André Tardieu, une dérive réactionnaire, 1876–1945* (Paris, 1993), 169–70.

long patronized organizationalist groups, presiding over the 1927 Congrès de l'organisation and the 1929 Congrès du travail, products of the fusion of Taylorist and Fayolist organizations.[2] In fact, Tardieu was representative of wider conservative reformism. The governments of 1926–1932 remade the Cartel's 'realist' organizational project in Fayolist form, without completely abandoning the left's social-democracy.

Indeed, the late 1920s represented the high-point of the cross-party appeal of organizationalism, in all its complexity, encapsulated in the Exposition international des arts industriels et décoratifs of 1925. The exhibition's funding had been approved under the Bloc, which presented it as a means for France to compete in the international struggle for artistic and commercial domination. To that end, 'Art déco' combined artisan and colonial motifs with straight lines and modern industrial material; in effect, it commercialized and rationalized tradition.[3] One exhibit, Le Corbusier's Plan Voisin to reconstruct Paris and create 'machines for living in', combined rationalism with organic, functional hierarchy. The architect contended that standardized, cheap housing would reinforce family life and assuage proletarian discontent—housing would be a major priority of conservative governments.[4] The eclectic appeal of organizationalism was also symbolized by the publication in 1929 of the Confédération générale du travail (CGT) activist Hyacinthe Dubreuil's immensely successful *Standards*, prefaced by the Catholic conservative Henry Le Chatelier. All areas of human life were deemed open to organization, from the factory to housework, career choice to city planning, national defence, to political parties.

Electoral defeat in 1932, economic crisis, and the revival of German nationalism undermined reformist conservatism. Hindsight reveals that even before 1932, there were cracks in the majority. Whereas after 1910, moderates had neutralized the extreme right, they did so only partially in the late 1920s; worse, the greater legislative output of the period provoked a right-wing reaction. Preoccupied with the Radicals' political antagonism to Tardieu, historians have not seen how much the reforms of 1926–1932 owed to their organizational project.[5] The Radical deputy who interrupted Tardieu's ministerial declaration with the cry 'It's the Radical programme!' exaggerated only a little. Tardieu, like the rest of the centre, aimed to undermine Radicalism by incorporating its electorate into a reformist conservative party. His extravagant promises to the Radicals and the key roles in successive governments of the pro-Radicals Briand and Loucheur contrasted with token gestures to the Fédération.

Annoyed, the nationalist right developed a thoroughgoing attack on government policy, which merged with that of the so-called 'non-conformiste' intellectuals: young bourgeois frustrated at the scarcity of openings in academe and politics

[2] Monnet, *Refaire*, 93–4.

[3] Simon Dell, 'The consumer and the making of the "Exposition internationale des arts décoratifs et industriels modernes", 1907–1925', *Journal of Design History* 12, no. 4 (1999), 311–25.

[4] Jean-Louis Cohen, *Le Corbusier* (New York, 2005), 28–9.

[5] Monique Clague, 'Vision and myopia in the new politics of André Tardieu', *French Historical Studies* 8, no. 1 (Spring 1973), 105–28; Kuisel, *Capitalism*, 91–2.

at a time when the number of qualified individuals was growing.[6] This disparate group mixed Catholic traditionalism, crowd theory, and anti-Americanism with efforts to capture organizationalism and the movement for competence. It included the Jeune droite, a group of intellectuals who had broken with Maurras, if not with Maurrasianism, and who replaced the master's primacy of politics with primacy of the spiritual. Robert Aron and Arnaud Dandieu, in *Le Cancer américain* (1932), rooted anti-organizationalism in nationalism, Catholicism, and the defence of spiritual values against American materialism.[7] Others were more open to secular society. For instance, the ubiquitous *non-conformiste* writer Daniel-Rops feared that mechanization might endanger the life of the mind, but urged the elite of youth to 'adhere passionately to their century', and 'take control of the movement' for mechanization.[8] Daniel-Rops provided an intellectual bridge to centre figures, such as the Republican doctor-novelist Georges Duhamel, who denounced American materialism in *Scènes de la vie future* (1929).

More frequently, *non-conformisme* resonated with the wider political, social, and religious grievances of the right. The latter opposed government spending especially on welfare; it defended individual initiative, and valued quality over mass production. It counterpoised French hegemony in Europe and imperial autarky to the government's European policy. The right's programme appealed explicitly to small savers, small business, and peasants, but also won the support of conservative big business. It barely contained the discontent of peasant and small business groups, which attacked conservative leaders for having backed the Social Insurance Law of 1928–1930. Catholic discontent extended the audience of the right-wing opposition, for the integration of Christian Democrats and Social Catholics into the centre-led majority incensed conservative Catholics.

Anti-communism both united conservatives and envenomed the disputes between them: André François-Poncet complained that it was hard to steer a course between Flandin's desire to fight the Cartel from the left, and the inflexible Fédération.[9] Those who detected a mortal danger to France found ample confirmation in the anti-militarism and violence of the Communist Party in these years. In Rouen, the level of electoral violence was especially high in 1928; in the rural Yonne, Flandin's ironic comments on freedom of opinion in the USSR provoked cries of 'Kill him' and 'Go f...yourself' from the audience.[10] Poincaré's Radical Interior Minister, Albert Sarraut, famously declared, 'Le Communisme, voilà l'ennemi'. His successor, Tardieu, was even more active in hunting down Communists, in collaboration

[6] Laurent Kestel, 'De La Conversion en politique. Genèse et institutionnalisation du Parti populaire français, 1936–1940', thèse de doctorat, Paris I, 2006, 104–54, 219.

[7] Olivier Dard, *Le Rendez-vous manqué des relèves des années 30* (Paris, 2002), 114–15, 125; Jean-Pierre Loubet Del Bayle, *Les Non-conformistes des années 30* (Paris, 1969), 487–9.

[8] Daniel-Rops, 'La Jeunesse et l'ère de la machinisme', *Revue des deux mondes*, February 1928, 106–28.

[9] Archives nationales, 317 AP 73, Fonds Marin (hereafter ANFLM, carton/dossier no.), François-Poncet to Soulier, 21 March 1928.

[10] Robert Lynn Fuller, 'The dynamics of conservative politics in Upper Normandy, 1898–1928', PhD dissertation, University of Virginia, 1994, 574–81; Marc Abélès, *Jours tranquilles en '89. Ethnologie politique d'un département français* (Paris, 1989), 84.

with Prefect of Police Jean Chiappe. As Président du conseil, Tardieu retained the post of Interior Minister, thus signalling the seriousness with which he took the danger. Anti-communism was linked to anti-socialism. Georges Bidault, close to the PDP, wrote that for conservatives, Socialism represents 'pure barbarism, bloody revolution, and all the furies of the horde'.[11]

PARTY ORGANIZATION

Interwar initiatives in party organization confirmed the strength of conservative unity and its limits, as rival groups endeavoured both to rival Communist organizations and remake conservatism in their own image. Conservatives now showed greater interest than Le Bon had in actual techniques of mass mobilization, from advertising to the cinema, and combined them with Fayolist organization and Taylorist rationalization. While dictatorships provided some inspiration for new initiatives, admiration for British conservatives and developments in the French advertising industry were equally important. Reorganization expressed both the desire of conservative parliamentarians and their allies to reinforce their position and the new assertiveness of the rank and file, evident since the decomposition of the Bloc.

In different ways, the creation of Kerillis' CPRN and reorganization of the Fédération, as well as the Alliance républicaine démocratique (ARD)'s winding up of the Parti républicain démocrate et social (PRDS), all expressed the conviction that the modern politician must direct 'the crowd', protect it from communist demagogues, and shape broad currents of opinion. Organizational innovation was compatible with existing ideas about the autonomy of deputies in parliament. In that respect, Auguste Mamelet's reasoning is revealing, since as secretary-general of the Alliance, he passed for a party man. He argued that parties must crystallize the choices of universal suffrage (a crowd) around a few simple ideas. Yet in parliament, the elite should rise to the national interest and collaborate with opponents where necessary.[12] Kerillis did not dissent. He saw parties as 'necessary in the age of the masses', but rejected the parliamentary 'caporalism' of the Socialists (SFIO).[13] Ostrogorsky would not have differed.

Sociologically, the conservative elites showed some continuity. The Alliance was still led by the flower of the Parisian Bar—those who had learned oratory in the Conférence Molé-Tocqueville and served as secretaries of the Conférence du stage.[14] The Alliance still deserved its reputation as a party of big business, with the qualification that it recruited from the *laïque* tradition—as reflected in the election

[11] *Politique*, 15 January 1928; *La République démocratique*, 3 July 1927; *Le Petit Démocrate*, 30 June 1929.

[12] *La République démocratique*, 20 March 1927.

[13] Henri de Kerillis and Raymond Cartier, *Faisons le point* (Paris, 1931), 138–9.

[14] *La République démocratique*, 20 March 1927; Gilles Le Béguec, 'Les Circuits de la formation politique', in Serge Berstein and Pierre Milza (eds), *Axes et méthodes de formation du personnel politique* (Paris, 1998), 311.

of centre deputies in the relatively non-practising east and south of France (see Map 3, p. 267). The École libre des sciences politiques remained important. The institution had hardly changed, except perhaps in so far as it became more right-wing. Its teaching corps included laissez-faire liberals, such as the economist Charles Colson, while in its Conseil d'administration sat military and business organizers, such as the Royalist Lyautey and the pro-Fédération businessman de Peyerimhoff. Tardieu, Flandin, and Reynaud, the great rivals for the leadership of the centre in the final decade of the regime, had all attended the École as teachers or students. A Belleville worker claimed that his candidature had been rejected because he was not an 'eminent personality'.[15]

Many Fédération leaders issued from the same circles as Alliance leaders. Bonnefous, Lasteyrie, Marin, and Guiter were all linked to the École des sciences politiques. Heavy industry, especially Catholics such as François and Guy de Wendel, Amidieu du Clos, and Jean Plichon, was also well represented. The Fédération differed from the Alliance in that it also recruited from aristocratic landowners and provincial Catholic notables, including the lawyers Jean Ybarnégaray and Vallat (although the latter later joined the Paris Bar). In fact, while lawyers were prominent in the leadership of all parties, the average lawyer now backed the Fédération. Doctors played an increasingly significant role too, especially with the expansion of rural social services.[16] In the west, aristocrats continued to dominate the anti-Republican right, and many sat with the URD (see Map 3).

The renewal of methods of political mobilization increased the influence of professional politicians, but they did displace notables, in so far as the two categories were distinct. The most significant new initiative was Kerillis' CPRN, which linked the Fédération's moderate wing with Reynaud and Maginot on the right of the Alliance.[17] Kerillis achieved some success: Fédération deputies, including some of his bitterest opponents, praised his methods. The propaganda delegates of the Alliance, Reynaud and René Montillot, were also sympathetic to the CPRN, as was Maginot.[18] Kerillis also aimed to undermine the financial power of Ernest Billiet's Union des intérêts économiques (UIE), which he saw as too favourable to Concentration républicaine.[19]

Kerillis had imbibed organizationalism at the Ministry of Armaments in 1917–1918, and saw the British Conservative Party (which he and Reynaud visited frequently) as a model. The British Conservatives supposedly owed their broad appeal to their moderate reformism and to their organization 'according to a veritable science'.[20] However, the CPRN did not slavishly imitate the Tories.

[15] Rosemonde Sanson, *L'Alliance républicaine démocratique. Une Formation du centre (1901–1920)* (Rennes, 2003), 491.

[16] Gilles Le Béguec, *La République des avocats* (Paris, 2003), 141–7; W.D. Irvine, *French Conservatism in Crisis: The Republican Federation of France* (Baton Rouge, 1979), 18–23.

[17] The hitherto vaguely named group used 'CPRN' from November 1930.

[18] ANFLM, 81 Comité directeur de la Seine, 2 March, 20 July 1927; ANFLM, 73 Baudoin to Guiter, 24 June 1927; *L'Écho de Paris*, 9 July 1931; François Audigier, 'Les Modérés face au Front Populaire. Les Ambiguïtés de l'Alliance démocratique', *Annales de l'Est* 47, no. 2 (1997), 321–49.

[19] Archives de la préfecture de la police (hereafter APP), BA 2011, rapport août 1927.

[20] *L'Écho de Paris*, 16, 11 June, 9 July 1926.

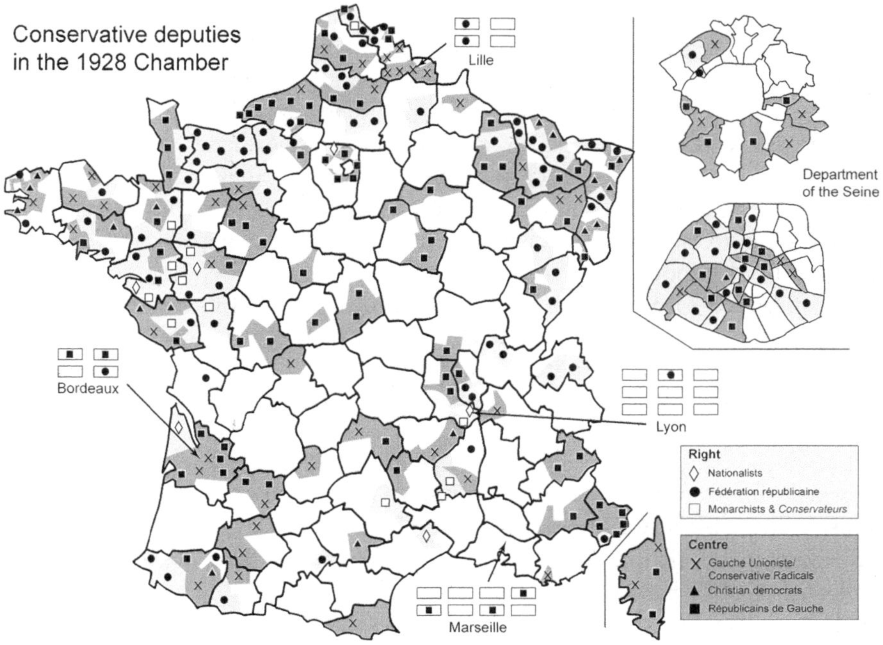

Map 3

It preferred to coordinate existing parties by providing them with services. It created a Parisian and three provincial sections, funded by yearly appeals to the public. Fayolism and Taylorism were evident in the allocation of specific tasks to activists and in avoidance of waste through concentration on undecided voters.[21] Taylorism inspired mass production of standardized tracts, posters, and speeches in an attempt to unite Conservatives around the lowest common denominator: anti-communism. The CPRN was best known for its striking anti-communist posters, the first of which showed a communist casually spitting on the tomb of the Unknown Soldier.

In accordance with collective psychology, the CPRN aimed to implant simple themes in the group mind through repetition of 'obvious facts', rather than through academic explanations. Kerillis used the methods of the advertising industry, which also espoused the principles of collective psychology. Advertisers were then moving away from text-based posters (themselves based on Le Bon's principles) towards arresting images, often using the 'science' of 'facial-types', and brief slogans, designed to act on the unconscious through repetition.[22] And whereas conservatives traditionally learned parliamentary debating in the Conférence Molé-Tocqueville and preferred private electoral meetings, the CPRN's École d'orateurs

[21] APP BA 2011, undated circular, ?1927.

[22] *L'Écho de Paris*, 4 June 1925; Sarah Howard, 'The advertising industry and alcohol in interwar France', *Historical Journal* 51, no. 2 (2008), 421–55.

taught young bourgeois, often recruited from the finalists of the Ligue des droits du religieux ancien combattant (DRAC)'s annual speaking competition, to address crowds, deal with hecklers, and intervene in opponents' meetings.[23]

The CPRN endeavoured to combine elite leadership with the mobilization of activists. A friendly journalist deplored 'Monsieur and Madame', so concerned to go driving on Sundays and teach their children English that they do not realize that they are 'engaged in an underhand, very ugly war [that] we fight with electors, votes, committees, posters, pamphlets, tracts, and newspapers; indeed with books'.[24] Kerillis mocked the 'artificial' congresses of the Fédération, where delegates applauded speeches and voted the motions placed before them by crafty activists; he ridiculed Marin's devoted Lieutenants as 'sous-marins' [submariners, and a play on *sous-officiers*/non-commissioned officers (NCOs)]. He demanded democratization of the Fédération, so that voters would not dismiss it as Wendel's creature.[25]

In fact, the CPRN never developed a democratic structure. For activists it relied informally on women's and student groups, while priests were the best collectors of funds.[26] The CPRN was also linked to the Ligue républicaine nationale (LRN), and especially the JP. Kerillis rejected the latter's fascist and dictatorial proclivities, for he believed the French to be firmly attached to liberty.[27] He was encouraged by the JP's moderate turn; the league abandoned its initial hostility to Poincaré, and nevertheless substantially increased its membership, if not to the 350,000 that it claimed. Taittinger declared that the JP would 'modernize the parliamentary regime' and ensure that a strong president was assisted by competent men, if necessary non-parliamentarians. He urged leaguers to back the CPRN. There was much overlap in membership, and the JP provided a considerable proportion of the CPRN's distributors of its fliers and billposters.[28]

If the CPRN helped to cement the reformist conservative alliance, it did not monopolize it. Tardieu advocated a strong governing majority and benefited from the efforts of the CPRN, which produced dramatic posters for the 1932 election that presented him as leader of the majority. Yet Tardieu contributed little to party organization himself. He rejoined the Alliance in 1930 as vice-president, but played no public role in it. Like his mentor, Clemenceau, he envisaged a personal relationship with the majority; he made frequent use of confidence in parliament and refused to deal with the parliamentary groups. He directly addressed the electorate, making so many radio broadcasts that the left parodied him as 'l'homme au micro entre les dents'.[29] His 'prosperity policy' was intended not only to appeal to the material instincts of the mass, but to create for it a mobilizing myth (or 'mystique'), a 'grande projet mobilisateur'.[30] Mercier

[23] Le Béguec, 'Les Circuits', 303–18. [24] *L'Écho de Paris*, 8 May 1925.

[25] *L'Écho de Paris*, 23 May, 4, 9 July 1931.

[26] Archives nationales. Police générale F^7 1327, 17 February 1927.

[27] *L'Écho de Paris*, 26 May, 4 June 1925, 29 April 1926.

[28] Jean Philippet, 'Le Temps des ligues. Pierre Taittinger et les Jeunesses patriotes', thèse de doctorat, IEP Paris, 2000, 299–330.

[29] Monnet, *Refaire*, 123–8, 172. [30] Monnet, *Refaire*, 166.

saw prosperity similarly, and argued that through education, the press, cinema, and radio, the 'neocapitalist' elite could direct the mass.[31]

As for the Alliance démocratique, it was untouched by the organizational movement of the period. Indeed, in November 1926, the PRDS dissolved itself, realizing that Radicals would not join it. The Alliance returned to its original objective of linking Republicans of different parties. Centrist deputies remained largely independent of the Alliance, and sought to attract a spectrum of voters through enunciation of broad Republican principles and—like all parties—the provision of favours. In 1928, Maginot's electoral campaign trumpeted 'the multiple services that he still renders with the same alacrity to all those who address themselves to him'.[32]

In contrast to the Alliance, the PDP claimed that its strength came from popular activists, a pretension hitherto only seen in left-wing parties. The PDP saw parties as part of the organic structure of democracy, a counterpart to its corporatist vision, and therefore included a woman's and other sectional groups, and modelled the party structure on that of the Socialists. The party developed a lively network of sections, and like the Alliance, but unlike the right, it was quite open about debate and disagreement within them. None of that meant that the PDP had abandoned crowd theory. Pezet argued that 'insofar as parties defend the interests of [social] categories, they correspond to an organic and biological necessity. However, as in human economy, politics requires a regulator, something that fulfils the function of a brain and a nervous system.'[33]

We saw in the previous chapter that the Fédération initiated a major organizational drive in 1925–1926. While elite leadership was integral to this reorganization, it owed much to the discontent of rank-and-file activists. In Lyon, under Victor Perret, the FR developed a network of committees, student and workers' groups, social centres, a *boules* federation, and a housing charity.[34] Important Fédération groups also emerged in Rouen and Bordeaux, led by Marin's allies, Jean Baudouin and Philippe Henriot respectively. Chafing at the hegemony of moderate conservatives in parliament, Marin appealed over their heads to activists and thence, he believed, to the nation. He expressed pleasure at the departure from the Fédération of 'unreliable' Deputies, while Perret condemned parliamentarians' excessive influence in the party and accused the press of taking bribes from the government and big business. Perret wished to remake the party without the 'bourgeosie en place'.[35] He held that reflexes and mystiques motivated the masses, who knew little of politics and regarded issues morally or self-interestedly. Firm leadership would wrest the people from the grasp of the *mauvais bergers*.[36]

The Fédération's structure reflected this desire to mobilize the people from above. Party organizers were bound to Marin by a personal loyalty: Isaac wrote that

[31] Ernest Mercier, 'Réflexions sur l'élite', *Revue des deux mondes*, February 1928, 882–95.

[32] Sorlot, *André Maginot. L'Homme politique et sa légende* (1877–1932) (Metz, 1995), 188.

[33] *Le Petit démocrate*, 29 September 1929; *L'Avenir*, 21 January 1931.

[34] ANFLM, 80, Guiter to Marin, 11 January 1933.

[35] ANFLM, 73, Minutes of Conseil national, 28 December 1928.

[36] *La Nation*, 2 January 1932, 9 January 1932; translation: bad shepherds.

'Perret's idolatry of Marin makes one smile'.[37] Indeed, Perret's belief in his leader's unfailing foresight reflected a mixture of Fayolism and Mussolinian omniscience. A Lyon activist claimed that 'personalities disappear in an organism in which everyone contributes his share of effort, without thinking of any result other than defeat of the revolution'.[38] In Lyon, the Fédération contented itself with lectures to tame workers in its Cercle ouvrier, charity, and the encadrement of the leisure of the members of parish men's unions—notably through *boules* tournaments.

Fédération organization was incomplete and did not displace notables. In Lyon, even pro-Fédération deputies kept their distance from Perret, for election depended on broader appeal. There were few permanent committees in Lyon's rural hinterland.[39] After 1928, most Breton conservatives sat in the URD, without involving themselves in the organized Fédération. In so far as the latter existed in Brittany, it was the work of the urban Catholic bourgeoisie of towns such as Nantes; in Quimper, the organized Fédération was close to the PDP.[40] Usually, the Catholic right preferred to use charity, agricultural unions, and local office to secure the notoriety necessary for election. In Maine-et-Loire, the Catholic *cercles* on which the right relied were largely recreational.[41] Comices agricoles remained highly politicized: in July 1936, that of Nancy witnessed a fight between Communists, led by the mayor and *instituteur*, and nationalists.[42]

Monarchism too depended on the interleaving of political, religious, and social networks. In Paris, it was no longer a political force, but survived as a marker of cultural distinction for the aristocrats and upper bourgeoisie of the Faubourgs Sainte-Antoine and Saint-Germain. This elite society was nevertheless connected to the wider world. Salons served as a reminder of the centrality of the court, while opening aristocratic circles to activists such as Maurras. They also offered the possibility of converting conservative politicians, such as Marin, Reynaud, Taittinger, and even the peasant activist Dorgères, who could not resist attending them. Women, such as the duchesse de Guise and Queen Amélie of Portugal, played a central part in salons, as they did in the Dames and Jeunes filles royalistes and Catholic women's movement. Men in these circles were also close to the religious hierarchy—no less than sixty per cent of the 224 invitees to the reception of the new Papal Nuncio in 1926 had signed the visitors' book at the residence of the heir to the throne, and most of the rest were diplomats and clerics.[43]

37 ANFLM, 73, Isaac to Guiter, 19 April 1930.

38 *Union républicaine du Rhône*, 30 September 1934, cited in Mathias Bernard, *La Dérive des modérés. La Fédération républicaine du Rhône sous la Troisième République* (Paris, 1998), 278–308, 308.

39 Passmore, *From Liberalism*, 147–9; Bernard, *La Dérive*, 278–308; Fuller, 'The dynamics', 525–30.

40 David Bensoussan, *Combats pour une Bretagne catholique et rurale. Les Droites bretonnes dans l'entre-deux-guerres* (Paris, 2006), 147–61, 370–4.

41 Jean-Luc Marais, *Les Sociétés d'hommes. Histoire d'une sociabilité du 18e siècle à nos jours* (Vauchrétienne, 1986), 139–46; Passmore, *From Liberalism*, 155–6.

42 *La Nation*, 25 July 1936. See also ANFLM, 83, 'Préfets et les fonctionnaires en général contre la Fédération'.

43 Bruno Goyet, *Un Rôle en politique. Henri d'Orléans, Comte de Paris* (Paris, 2001), 90–111.

Some Parisian aristocrats possessed summer residences in the Monarchist electoral bastions in the contiguous departments of Morbihan, Maine-et-Loire, Vendée, and Loire-Inférieure (see Map 3, p. 267). In the latter, a powerful Comité des droites invested candidates. The wealth of the aristocracy and the absence of industrial development (except in Nantes) meant that landowners faced less competition for leadership than elsewhere, and did not face the rivalry of wealthy tenants that had undermined aristocratic Royalism in the Mayenne. Nobles constituted 41 per cent of Loire-Inférieure *conseillers généraux* in the interwar years; they were omnipresent in charitable works and Comices agricoles. Antagonism towards Protestants in Nantes, coupled with memories of the Revolution, created cross-class unity, while the high birth rate ensured that demand for tenancies exceeded supply, enabling landowners to award them to the politically reliable and to threaten the recalcitrant with eviction. The lower clergy also backed the aristocracy.[44]

The organizational initiatives of the late 1920s reinforced the role of professional politicians, notably through the creation of the CPRN, without abandoning the principles of collective psychology or eliminating notables, who remained influential in all parts of the conservative spectrum. The CPRN played a significant part in bringing together the conservative majority of 1926–1931. Yet the majority's axis was further to the left than the highly anti-Radical Kerillis would have preferred, and the loosely organized Alliance démocratique may have played a greater role in the majority than the CPRN. On the right, the CPRN faced Marin's blend of party and notable politics. There was also opposition to the CPRN within the JP. One leaguer accused Taittinger of favouring a new Bloc national, and another claimed that CPRN campaigns were better suited to selling chocolate than to political action. JP students, among whom Maurrassian influence was strong, were especially turbulent. Their leader, Pighetti de Rivasso, opposed Taittinger's moderation, but when Pighetti resigned in 1930, few followed him out of the league. Taittinger was careful not to merge his league completely into the CPRN.[45]

THE MAJORITY

For now, the centre dominated. It developed close ties with Catholics, and yet did not exclude the Radicals from legislative work, permitting broad convergence around the organizational project. Certainly, disputes continued within the Alliance about the relationship with the Radicals, but only Reynaud (allied to Kerillis) envisaged a complete break with them. In 1927 Chaumet, on the left of the Alliance, proposed a formal electoral agreement between the Radicals and the Alliance, while Tardieu, on its right, urged the Radicals and Alliance to unite in a 'new party' anchored in the centre-right.[46] In the election campaign of 1928, Poincaré

[44] Bensoussan, *Combats*, 171–98.

[45] ANFLM, 73, 'Un Groupe de JP', 19 April 1930; *L'Alerte*, August 1929; Philippet, 'Le Temps', 352–70.

[46] Berstein, *Histoire du Parti radical*, ii. *Crise du radicalisme* (Paris, 1982), 39–41.

held joint meetings with the Radicals. Afterwards, Mamelet echoed François-Poncet's call for a 'broad centre', linked to Radicals and to Marin.[47]

In November 1928, the departure of the Radicals from the government threatened to push it to the right—Mamelet interpreted their exit that way, so he resigned as secretary-general of the Alliance. Yet no such evolution developed. At the Alliance's 1929 Dijon congress, a 'party of order' motion prevailed and helped prepare the way for Tardieu, who nevertheless appealed for the Radicals to join the majority. In 1930, the Alliance congress endorsed the government as one of 'Concentration', even though the Radicals were in opposition. Frustrated at the Alliance's refusal to accept a right-wing alliance, Reynaud gave up his attempts to reform it.[48] In 1931, agreement with the Radical Party itself briefly seemed possible; negotiators agreed even that the SFIO should participate in the majority. The Socialists refused, and anyway Flandin would not accept their participation.[49]

Influential business groups worked to keep the government in the centre. Resisting Kerillis' attempt to undermine it, the UIE continued to favour alliance with the Radicals. Redressement français favoured Tardieu in particular, seeing him as a 'technician', possessed of a veteran's energy and realism, while Tardieu supposedly consulted Mercier on the constitution of his second ministry. Having been criticized by Reynaud and Mamelet, Mercier attenuated his antipathy to political parties; he was firmly *laïque* and he preferred Concentration to Union nationale.[50] Mamelet claimed that Redressement's policies were those for which the Alliance had fought for twenty-five years.[51]

Informal links with Radicals were strong. Tardieu secretly funded the conservative wing of the Jeunes Turcs, a reformist think tank within the Radical Party, which Caillaux also patronized, and which saw Concentration as a means to implement the 'ordered economy'. Close to the Jeunes Turcs were the Jeunes équipes, a loose group of intellectuals, politicians, and journalists, led by Luchaire, which brought Radicals together with some centrists. Maurice Petsche, illustrated the interpenetration of intellectual, business, and political networks. This Polytechnicien and teacher at the École libre des sciences politiques served as a junior minister in the governments of Poincaré, Tardieu, and Laval and was linked to the Jeunes turcs, Redressement, and Loucheur.[52]

Openness to the Radicals did not prevent the centre from cooperating with Catholics. The latter had often supported centre governments as a lesser evil, but now there was genuine convergence, facilitated by the 'Second Ralliement'. The conflict of the mid 1920s had been a draw: the Radicals failed to extend the lay laws to Alsace-Lorraine, while the Vatican noted the counterproductiveness of the

[47] *La République démocratique*, 15 July 1928.

[48] Sanson, *L'Alliance*, 493; Mayeur, *Lemire*, 600; *L'Avenir*, 14 December 1926.

[49] *L'Avenir*, 16, 21, 24 January, 4 February 1931; Pierre-Étienne Flandin, 'Après la chute du cabinet Tardieu', *Revue de Paris* 38, 15 January 1931, 430–7; Berstein, *Histoire*, ii, 169–70.

[50] Jean-Noël Jeanneney, *François de Wendel en République. L'Argent et le pouvoir* (Paris, 1976), 374–6.

[51] *La République démocratique*, 20 March 1927.

[52] My analysis differs from Dard, *Le Rendez-vous manqué*, 51–6 and 78–82.

Fédération nationale catholique (FNC)'s demonstrations. In 1926 came the condemnation of AF. Significantly, in 1927 the anticlerical Mamelet endorsed the right of religious orders to teach—after all, he said, Communists could do so. The equally anticlerical *Le Temps* also backed pacification.[53] Tardieu, was on good terms with the clergy, and was less anticlerical than Poincaré. The desire for pacification reached into the Fédération. Georges Pernot, leader of the party's left wing, refused to renew conservatives' past faults; he criticized those on the Fédération right 'whose intransigence had harmed them in the past, and who were depriving themselves once again of the influence that they ought to have on the destiny of the country'.[54] A 'groupe de catholiques' warned Marin that intransigence threatened to bring back the Cartel, with the *école unique*, expulsion of the Congregations, and religious war.[55]

For Marin, Pernot and Kerillis were victims of 'gauchite' (leftitis)—a sickness provoked by the desire for a ministerial portfolio. Actually, ideological affinities with the centre also mattered. Kerillis advocated British-style conservative reformism and embraced Social Catholicism in an attempt to attract Radical and working-class voters to a democratic conservative party. Pernot represented a Social Catholic, pro-PDP tendency within the Fédération, and served in the Tardieu and Laval governments—along with Champetier de Ribes of the PDP.[56]

As for the PDP, it rejected the conservative Catholic strategy of re-Christianization through capture of the state—re-Christianization by *coup d'état*, as one of them put it.[57] It also refused first-wave Christian Democrats' desire for a counter-society. Rather, the PDP saw participation in society as it existed as the precondition of evangelization. The theologian Maurice Blondel urged Social Catholics to examine social problems as they presented themselves, in the light of Catholic doctrine, and resolve them legislatively. That permitted cooperation with non-Catholics at various levels, from participation in government to discussion with the pro-Radical syndicalists around Georges Mer of the CGT civil-service union.[58] This strategy received a boost in 1929 when the Vatican rejected Mathon and Ley's demand for condemnation of the CFTC's 'Socialism', all the more so as in its response the Papacy approved alliances with Socialist unions for specific purposes.[59] Electorally, the integration of moderate Catholic reformism into the centre reflected the latter's growing presence in the bastions of the Catholic right (see Map 3, p. 267).

The PDP continued to battle with Catholic conservatives, and now found that the Vatican increasingly took its side. Prior to the 1928 elections, the Vatican politely ignored La Rochefoucauld's lobbying for reinstatement of the Action libérale populaire (ALP) as the official Catholic party now that AF had been condemned. Instead, a Vatican circular described the PDP as the heir of the ALP, and

[53] *La République démocratique*, 25 September, 27 November 1927; *Le Temps*, 27–28 January 1931.

[54] ANFLM, 73, Isaac to Guiter, 19 April 1930; ANFLM, 74, Pernot to Guiter, 14 September 1929.

[55] ANFLM, 73, 'Un Groupe de Catholiques' to Marin, 15 November 1929.

[56] *Le Petit démocrate*, 10 November 1929.

[57] *La Croix*, 1 August 1929.

[58] Delbreil, *Centrisme*, 223.

[59] Delbreil, *Centrisme*, 152–3.

claimed that the FNC's intransigence compromised the Catholic cause.[60] In 1928, the Vatican forced the Royalist Archbishop Charost of Rennes to remove Eugène Delahaye from the *Nouvelliste de Bretagne*, *L'Ouest-Éclair*'s great rival, while in 1929 Bishop Mignen of Montpellier forbade Catholics to read *L'Éclair*. *La Croix* became more favourable to the PDP, although the conservative Jean Guiraud continued to write for it.[61] From 1932, the publication of *L'Aube* gave Christian Democrats a sympathetic daily.

If religious pacification underpinned the conservative coalition, decades of religious conflict left their mark. Social Catholics did not forget that they were Catholics. Indeed, whereas previous generations had adopted an apolitical and technical stance to facilitate working with Republicans, the PDP proclaimed its desire to suffuse the Republic with Catholic values.[62] It saw Catholicism as essential to social reform because it moderated pursuit of self-interest, rooted individuals in society, and enabled class collaboration. Christian Democrats criticized AF precisely for separating religious and political realms, and for neglecting the divine in man's nature. By the same token, the PDP academic, Marcel Prélot, criticized Radical syndicalists for materialism and for neglecting the family and the region.[63] The PDP embraced rationalization and productivism, but in the name of Catholic respect for the person warned that 'standardization of individuals' was 'incompatible with the genius of our race'.[64] The PDP participated in the 1927 campaign for reform of the 1901 laws, opposed the establishment of free secondary education, and was the first party to propose that private schools should receive state funding in return for administrative inspection.

There were therefore barriers to formal alliance between Catholic and lay reformers. In 1930, debates around the formation of a 'centre party' showed how entrenched positions were on the religious question—Mamelet accused the PDP's Cornilleau of hiding a desire for proselytization.[65] For the PDP, electoral cooperation with the Radicals was even more unlikely. In principle, the PDP favoured a 'Concentration', alignment, for it saw the politics of two Blocs as an encouragement to class and religious conflict.[66] In practice, it would only accept Radical integration into a centre-dominated conservative majority.[67] Indeed, it associated Radical demands to hold the 'levers of power' in a Concentration government with discrimination against Catholics, which they resented as much as any believer. Anyway, the Church opposed cooperation with 'atheists', and even Christian Democrat voters were attached

[60] Arch.Segr.Vat., A.E.S., Francia, an.1927–1928, Pos. 666PO, Fasc.225. Memoriale circa le elezioni di Francia. N°2751/27, rubr. Francia 666, Memoriale circa le elezioni in Francia, 10 ott.1927, date istruzioni a nunz 8 X 1927. Thanks to Magali Della Sudda for this reference. AN, Fonds Tardieu 142 AP 14, various letters, 1928–30.

[61] René Rémond, 'L'Évolution du journal *La Croix* et son rôle auprès de l'opinion catholique (1919–1939)', *Bulletin de la société d'histoire moderne* 12, no. 7 (1958), 3–11 at 8–9.

[62] Yves Palau, 'Étude des fondements théoriques du catholicisme républicain dans la France de l'entre-deux-guerres', *Mil neuf cent* 13 (1995), 46–66; Yves Palau, 'Des Catholiques et de la politique. Les Transformations doctrinales du catholicisme social 1900–1930', *Revue française d'histoire des idées politiques* 4 (1996), 317–44.

[63] Delbreil, *Centrisme*, 223.

[64] *Politique*, 15 April 1928.

[65] *Le Petit démocrate*, 2 February 1930.

[66] *Le Petit démocrate*, 29 September 1929.

[67] Delbreil, *Centrisme*, 166–7, 178–9, 211–14.

to Catholic unity.[68] In 1928, the Vatican backed Abbé Trochu's eviction from *L'Ouest-Éclair*, a punishment for having backed the entry into a short-lived government presided by the Freemason Chautemps of a Radical whom the paper had endorsed in the elections.[69] None of these difficulties prevented the PDP from participating in a majority that implemented much of the Radicals' reformist programme.

Conservative Reformism

Complex debate between the components of the majority shaped its legislative output: if the Fayolism of the centre dominated, PDP and Radical social democracy were important too. The Fédération right and its crypto-monarchist allies were less influential, but more so than orthodox liberals, who were still present in both centre and right.

Foreign policy most united the coalition. Briand participated in the Poincaré, Tardieu, and Laval governments, and these years saw the apogee of pacifism and of the movement for reconciliation with Germany. Even the nationalist wing of the veterans movement, the Union nationale des combattants (UNC), largely embraced Briandism. There was an element of idealism in this enthusiasm for peace, especially among the Alsatian supporters of the PDP. Yet conservatives generally combined Briandism with a hard-headed Darwinist view of international relations that contrasted with the pacifism of the left. They tempered reconciliation with firmness on defence—the equivalent, perhaps, of Fayolism in domestic policy. Under Tardieu, Maginot's presence at the Defence Ministry symbolized this combination of persuasion and dissuasion. The Maginot fortifications represented a rationalized, mechanized solution to the problem of the defence at a time of declining birth rate; they were built by André Borie, a well-known centrist organizer. Maginot told the Chamber that 'The efforts of M. Briand, far from contradicting mine, are complementary.'[70]

August Isaac's views reveal the mixed motives behind foreign policy. He pessimistically asked what alternative there was to peace, given that France was abandoned by her allies, that it had too rapidly demobilized, that the 'country wants to hear nothing of war, or military effort', and that youth had been lost to anti-militarist teachers. More optimistically, he saw reconciliation with Germany and international cooperation as the policy of 'modern times'. He spoke of the 'reciprocal penetration of young generations', which he expected to 'teach them to settle together the economic questions that cause confrontations between peoples'. Marin and Poincaré, he added, did not understand that a new war would precipitate the triumph of Bolshevism and the end of civilization.[71]

[68] Bensousan, *Combats*, 331.

[69] Henri de Cadore, '*L'Ouest-Éclair* et les deux Ralliements (1899–1930). Contribution à l'intégration des Catholiques de l'Ouest dans la République', in Michel Lagrée, Patrick Harismendy, and Michel Denis (eds), *L'Ouest-Éclair. Naissance et essor d'un grand quotidien régional* (Rennes, 2001), 55–78 at 77–8.

[70] Sorlot, *Maginot*, 201–5.

[71] ANFLM, 73, Isaac to Guiter, 19 April 1930 and 74, Guiter to Marin, 7 September 1929; *Auguste Isaac. Journal d'un notable lyonnais, 1906–1933*, ed. Hervé Joly, (Lyon, 2002), 2 September 1930, 515.

Reconciliation with Germany was part of a European vision. In 1929, Briand presented his Memorandum on European unity to the powers. The PDP demanded a European federation to resist Bolshevism, allegedly more dangerous even than war.[72] European unity was also directed against the United States. In 1927, the pro-centre journalist Lucien Romier recounted European–American rivalry in *Qui sera le maître, Europe ou Amérique?*, while another pro-centrist journalist imagined an intercontinental war.[73] European unity was inseparable from struggle between continental blocs.

European unity implied 'organization' of the international economy. Both Loucheur of the centre and Cornilleau of the PDP advocated Europe-wide industrial ententes and rationalization.[74] In his ministerial declaration, Tardieu argued that 'arbitration, economic ententes, intellectual penetration, [and] European co-operation remain our objectives'. He also advocated something like the future European Common Agricultural Policy.[75] Europeanism was compatible with reinforcement of the Empire. The colonies would provide France with raw materials and an outlet for industrial goods, a policy that for Flandin had 'many advantages from the point of view of national defence'.[76]

Domestically, organization implied harnessing all parts of the social organism to the national interest. For Romier, governmental stability, a 'general plan of action', and rationalization of urban living space and transport would permit France to compete internationally, for France, unlike new nations, did not have 'men to waste' and relied on efficiency.[77] André François-Poncet, Redressement member and Minister of the National Economy under Tardieu, argued that the latter's plan to invest in national re-tooling encompassed 'race, public health, and education', and urged the government to defend agriculture as essential to social 'balance'.[78] Centrists sought to modernize agriculture, thus providing markets for French goods. In 1930, as farm prices fell, the government intervened in the wheat, wine, and grain markets, and introduced import quotas. In 1931, as Laval's agricultural minister, Tardieu discouraged overproduction in the beet, wheat, and wine markets, perhaps the most striking example of state involvement in the economy before 1936.[79]

This interventionism was part of a broader rethinking of the role of the state. The Jeunes équipes, Redressement, and mainstream politicians such as Maginot all advocated reinforcement of the state and the representation of the interests as a

[72] *Le Petit démocrate*, 28 July 1929, 16 November 1930; *Politique*, 15 December 1928; Delbreil, *Centrisme*, 259–72.

[73] *L'Avenir*, 26 April 1930.

[74] Louis Loucheur, *Carnets secrets 1908–1932* (Brussels 1962), 160–2; *Le Petit démocrate*, 16 November 1930, 28 July 1929; *Politique*, 15 December 1928.

[75] André Tardieu, *L'Épreuve du pouvoir* (Paris, 1931), 25–34.

[76] *La République démocratique*, 20 March, 27 November 1927.

[77] Lucien Romier, *Idées très simples pour les français. Le Redressement français* (Paris, 1928) 64–75.

[78] *Journal officiel. Chambre des députés* (hereafter JOCD), 8 July 1930, 2993, cited in Monnet, *Refaire la République*, 161.

[79] Pierre Barral, *Les Agrariens français de Méline à Pisani* (Paris, 1968), 118–227; Monnet, *Refaire*, 149–50.

means to render the regime more 'productive'. That did not (in principle) mean state control: rather, Tardieu advocated organization of the 'inevitable' relationship between state and big business in a period of competitive international trade. Inspired by Fayolist notions of unity of command, he reinforced the Présidence du conseil, created a Ministry of the National Economy, and a united Defence Ministry. To Taylorize the government, Tardieu multiplied the number of specialized under-secretariats. In his ministerial declaration he described the Conseil national économique (CNE) as 'in substance and tendency an appeal to the competences and enlightened', and was the first Président du conseil to solicit its advice.[80] Tardieu ignored business demands for increased representation in the CNE, which remained much as the Cartel had created it.

Furthermore, the conservative majority's institutional reforms accorded with Radical notions of Republicanism. Millerand's misadventure and Poincaré's success had restored conservative faith in the regime. Maginot ruled out constitutional reform, while Poincaré stamped on minor manifestations of anti-parliamentarianism, calling Flandin to task for a casual suggestion that parliamentary wheels 'turned slowly'.[81] Proportional representation now seemed impossible and even dangerous, thanks to the Cartel's victory. For the elections of 1928, parliament restored *scrutin d'arrondissement*, and the following legislature approved single round voting, in the hope of cementing the majority, only for the Senate to reject the measure.[82]

Proportional representation remained entangled with the problem of regionalism, but now conservatives of all shades were against it. In May 1928, the prosecution of Alsatian autonomists, including two newly elected deputies, raised fears for national unity. The newly created Breton Nationalist Party sympathized with the Alsatians and preached international federalism. Fearful of autonomism, the Breton right increasingly stressed the integration of Bretons into the nation via the *petite patrie*, while AF was extremely hostile to the autonomists. Within the PDP, relations between Alsatian deputies and the rest of the party became tense. In 1929, parliament, in the name of the defence of its rights, reversed the timid concessions to regionalists that Poincaré had made in 1926.[83]

Economic and social reform also commanded wide assent. Again, it would secure 'organic' harmony and hierarchy within the nation: for the PDP, Tardieu was 'the man of a total Locarno, internal and external'.[84] In fact, Tardieu had no monopoly on reform. By stabilizing the Franc at 20 per cent of its pre-war value in 1928, Poincaré had laid the foundations of Tardieu's 'politique de prospérité'. Sympathetic as he was to *rentiers*, Poincaré listened to business and CGT warnings that a dramatic rise in the Franc would harm exports, reduce wages, and increase

[80] Alain Chatriot, *La Démocratie sociale à la française* (Paris, 2003), 127–31.

[81] *Politique*, 15 May 1928; 'Organisation politique et administrative. La Réforme parlementaire', *Cahiers du Redressement français* 25 (Paris, 1927); Sorlot, *André Maginot*, 182, 184; *La République démocratique*, 20 March 1927.

[82] John M. Sherwood, *Georges Mandel and the Third Republic* (Stanford, 1970), 118 ff.

[83] Bensoussan, *Combats*, 229–33.

[84] *Le Petit démocrate*, 10 November 1929.

unemployment. Poincaré's government had ensured passage of Loucheur's Housing Law and the first Social Insurance Law, and anticipated Tardieu's plan for infrastructural improvement. Poincaré rationalized spending on schools, roads, rural electrification, military equipment, and technical education as a temporary breach of orthodoxy that would be compensated by future increases in tax revenue.[85] Meanwhile, Kerillis urged conservatives to take the initiative in social reform and encourage private industry to bring prosperity through modernization and reorganization of production.[86] Social Catholics in the Fédération, such as Peissel and Pernot, played a major part in discussion of reforms.[87] Laval's governments continued reform, notably passing a Family Allowance Law.

Inevitably, there were differences within the majority concerning social reform. The centre was largely Fayolist. With the exception of Petsche, it rejected the syndicalism of the Jeunes équipes and Christian Democrats'.[88] Certainly, Tardieu had once suggested that the reformist CGT represented a counterrevolutionary army. Yet he opposed civil servants' right to strike and in a preface to a book by Petsche praised him more for his provocation than for his actual conclusions. Valois, now on a journey to the left, accused Tardieu of denaturing syndicalism.[89] Tardieu urged the elite to provide the authority and guidance that the mass craved. Mercier concurred that the 'neocapitalist' elite could direct the mass, so long as it addressed social problems. Otherwise, Communists would feed on the oversensitivity and predilection for abstraction in the French character.[90] In a polemic with Cornilleau, Mamelet made clear the limits of his reformism. He wanted tax cuts to stimulate production and entrepreneurship and claimed that 'the proselytism of [Cornilleau's] religious soul' had caused him to 'too easily absolve Marxist demagogy'.[91]

Indeed, much as the PDP admired Tardieu, it condemned his social conservatism.[92] And although Christian Democrats appealed to the social conscience of the bourgeoisie, they advocated a middle way between individualism and collectivism in a system of regional collective bargaining under state supervision. Unlike Fayolists, they believed that each class could generate its own elite; strikes arose from real problems, not 'the passing effervescence of brains overexcited by agitators', as the right thought they did. Therefore, workers and employers could resolve social issues together—without ceasing to be workers or employers. Cornilleau rejected class struggle, but recognized that social groups had differing interests and lauded syndicalism as a form of socialization of production.[93]

[85] John Keiger, *Raymond Poincaré* (Cambridge, 1996), 324–34; Jeanneney, *L'argent*, 321–54; Pierre Saly, 'Poincaré keynésien', in Patrick Fridenson and André Straus (eds), *Le Capitalisme français, 19–20ᵉ siècle. Blocages et dynamisme d'une croissance* (Paris, 1987), 33–45.

[86] *L'Écho de Paris*, 29 April, 17 June 1926.

[87] Passmore, *From Liberalism*, 138–9.

[88] Olivier Dard, 'Maurice Petsche, itinéraire, réseaux, valeurs', in François Roth (ed.), *Les Modérés dans la vie politique française (1870–1965)* (Nancy, 2000), 397–417.

[89] Maurice Petsche and Jacques Donge, *Signe positif. À La Recherche des temps nouveaux*, Preface by André Tardieu (Paris, 1928); Monnet, *Refaire la République*, 158–9.

[90] Mercier, 'Reflexions', 882–95.

[91] *L'Avenir*, 2 January 1930.

[92] *Politique*, 15 January 1930.

[93] *Le Petit démocrate*, 2 February 1930.

The legislation of 1926–1932 reflected compromises between the Fayolism of the centre and the social democracy of the Radicals and PDP. Certainly, Tardieu's re-tooling plan suffered from Radical suspicion, not unfounded, that it was designed to strip them of their voters.[94] Loucheur's Housing Law of 1928 most reflected the centre's views. In the late 1920s, Le Corbusier adapted his architecture to Redressement's austere rationalism; he advocated the use of modern building techniques to enable workers to have a proper family life, and render them more productive biologically and economically. He named his standard dwelling, the 'maison Loucheur'.[95] Radical and PDP influence was greatest in the Social Insurance Law, voted in 1930, which retained the principles of obligation, state oversight, and trade union involvement, while pleasing the centre with its concessions to mutualism.[96] Radicals and Christian Democrats also approved Labour Minister Laval's attempts to arbitrate the Roubaix textile strikes of 1929–1930, which concerned the payment of Social Insurance contributions.[97] The gradual introduction of free secondary education from 1930 represented the most significant concessions to the Radicals, and outraged Catholics including the PDP. Even the right approved the Family Allowance Law of 1932, for pro-natalism trumped opposition to compulsion and state involvement. Yet it had no sympathy for the rest of the programme.

THE RIGHT AND THE EXTREME RIGHT

In the late 1920s, the main fault-line among conservatives ran through the Fédération. In parliament, Marin's opponents accused him of leading his party as a sniper on the right wing, and predicted that he would soon be 'le seul Marin à bord'. In fact, he was not entirely isolated. On international issues he could count on ten to fifteen Fédération deputies, the dozen 'marquises' of the Independents, and the half dozen nationalist followers of Mandel and Franklin-Bouillon. Major newspapers backed him, including Wendel's *Les Débats*, *L'Éclair*, and *Le Figaro*, not to mention *L'Action française*. On domestic issues, Marin's support was wider: in April 1930, fifty-nine URD deputies voted for Vallat's corporatist alternative to the Social Insurance Law, along with thirteen Independents. Liberals in the centre, notably Ernest Billiet of the UIE, *Le Temps*, and many businessmen, also endorsed the alternative. The right was best supported in votes on the lay laws and free secondary education.

The Fédération right became the lynchpin of right-wing nationalism. Paradoxically, the condemnation of AF brought the Fédération right closer to Royalism. Charles de Benoist, the Fédération's former president, rallied to Royalism and

[94] Tardieu, *L'épreuve*, 25–34; Monnet, *Refaire la République*, 140–51, 160–1.

[95] *Le Petit journal*, 24 December 1923.

[96] Paul V. Dutton, *Origins of the French Welfare State: The Struggle for Social Reform in France 1914–1947* (Cambridge, 2002), 97–107. Eighty per cent of workers joined Mutualist Caisses.

[97] Michel Launay, 'Le Syndicalisme chrétien dans un grand conflit de travail', *Mouvement Social* 73 (October–December 1970), 39–78; *Politique*, 15 January 1930.

became tutor to the Comte de Paris.[98] Marin shared a platform with Jean-Pierre Maxence of the Maurrassian Jeune droite at a meeting protesting against ratification of the Mellon-Béranger Accords.[99] As business and peasant opposition to Social Insurance grew, radicalization of the right was underway well before the depression affected France. Historiographically, the conviction that the condemnation of AF buried the religious and constitutional questions has obscured these developments.

The Condemnation

In September 1926, Cardinal-Archbishop Andrieu of Bordeaux declared that AF doctrines were incompatible with Catholicism. On September 17 and again on 20 December, Pius XI confirmed the condemnation; Maurras responded with his 'non possumus' ('we cannot'), denying the Pope's temporal authority. In March 1927, the Vatican announced sanctions against readers of *L'Action française*, and in 1928 they were effectively excommunicated.[100] The condemnation dealt a severe blow to AF, and strengthened the moderate coalition, for unlike in 1892, the Vatican acted against refractory clerics. It reconfigured, but did not destroy, the extreme right.

On the eve of condemnation, a dozen prelates explicitly supported AF, while another fifty were relatively favourable. Forty-three were hostile to AF.[101] Royalists were influential in the Legitimist aristocracy, newspapers such as the *Nouvelliste de Bretagne* and *L'Éclair du Midi*, agricultural unions, the Association catholique de la Jeunesse française (ACJF), Ligue patriotique des françaises (LPDF), and especially the FNC.[102] Neo-Royalists fronts, such as the Cercle Fustel de Coullanges, attracted a broader constituency of sympathetic critics of the Republic, including Colonel Charles de Gaulle, whose lectures were disrupted by left-wing students.[103] Yet by the early 1930s, recalcitrant bishops had given way to prelates prepared to assert the authority of the Church. A bishop from outside Brittany succeeded Charost at Rennes, and in 1932 the clergy in Brittany and the Midi blanc largely obeyed orders not to support Royalist candidates, who suffered accordingly.[104] The circulation of *L'Action française* fell by over 40 per cent by 1928 and the league lost over half its members.[105]

The condemnation harmed AF, but did not fatally wound the anti-Republican right. First, Royalists exploited Pius' refusal to denounce Monarchism *per se*—he had condemned Maurras for encroaching on the Church's right to decide moral

[98] Bruno Goyet, *Charles Maurras* (Paris, 2000), 34. [99] Dard, *Le Rendez-vous manqué*, 148.

[100] Eugen Weber, *Action française: Royalism and Reaction in Twentieth-Century France* (Stanford, 1962), 219–55; Jacques Prévotat, *Les Catholiques et l'Action française. Histoire d'une condamnation* (Paris, 2001), 298–522.

[101] Prévotat, *Les Catholiques*, 395.

[102] Bensoussan, *Combats*, 103–13.

[103] Éric Roussel, *Charles de Gaulle* (Paris, 2002), 43–4.

[104] Bensoussan, *Combats*, 379–82; Philippe Secondy, *La Persistance du Midi blanc* (Perpignan, 2006), 152–60.

[105] Weber, *Action française*, 242; Bensoussan, *Combats*, 154.

issues.[106] Catholics, from the Pope's champion, Monseigneur Rémond, to Léon Merklen, the new editor of *La Croix*, insisted that while believers collectively had to accept the regime 'inwardly', individuals could follow the dictates of their consciences so long as they did not harm the public good or religion.[107] Consequently, anti-Republicans, including Monarchists, could participate in Catholic organizations if they renounced AF.[108] The Pope condemned that interpretation of his intentions, but set a poor example by negotiating with Mussolini.

Royalists also took advantage of the Pope's insistence on unity of the faithful, and on Castelnau's claim that the FNC's 'above politics' status made members' choices a matter of conscience.[109] The FNC remained the most significant lay Catholic organization, attracting thousands to its congresses.[110] In the 1928 elections, its diocesan unions played a crucial role in the choice of candidates. Castelnau estimated that 278 deputies accepted its minimum programme.[111] In the 1932 election, the FNC's role was not nationally coordinated, but still locally important. In Meurthe-et-Moselle, for instance, it joined with AF to support the Fédération's Warren.[112] Through the FNC, Royalists intensified their condemnation of the lay laws and thus embarrassed the PDP.[113] Cornilleau lamented that the pretext of defending religious liberties forced the PDP to ally with those who 'did not share their political, social, or even their religious convictions'.[114]

Secondly, Royalists found alternative political outlets. In Loire-Inférieure, La Ferronnays formed a *cercle* for those who had left AF, while Jean Le Cour Grandmaison was the best-known Royalist to join the Fédération—to Isaac's annoyance. Several Fédération politicians were among those who signed the visitors' book at the home of the heir to the throne.[115] In 1928, Eugène Delahaye, after eviction from the *Nouvelliste de Bretagne*, founded *La Province*, and in March 1930 created the Alliance nationale de l'Ouest (ANO) to fight 'laicism, revolution and demagogy, even supposedly Christian', while avoiding the question of the regime. It won some support from the Fédération in Rennes, and Delahaye urged Marin to endorse the ANO, but Warren, closer to the ALP, counselled against. The Church also condemned the ANO.[116] In the Hérault, hostility to the condemnation united neo- and traditional Royalists, and found considerable support in the Confréries des pénitents and Catholic women's groups. Royalists attacked the Bishop for his ignorance of 'antidemocratic' southern religion and

[106] Monseigneur Rémond, *Ce qu'il faut répondre aux objections de l'Action française* (Paris, 1927), 10; Prévotat, *Les Catholiques*, 402–4, 419.

[107] *La Croix*, 15 April 1928; Rémond, *Ce qu'il faut répondre*, 18.

[108] Rémond, *Ce qu'il faut répondre*, 6, 26; Bensoussan, *Combats*, 129.

[109] Delbreil, *Centrisme*, 176; Bensoussan, *Combats*, 137.

[110] Nadine-Josette Chaline, *Des Catholiques normands sous la Troisième République* (Roanne, 1985), 182–3.

[111] Corinne Bonafoux-Verrax, *À La Droite de Dieu. La Fédération nationale catholique 1924–1944* (Paris, 2004), 233–44; Bensoussan, 'Le Réveil des catholiques bretons', 75.

[112] Delbreil, 'Le Démocrates chrétiens', 430–1, 435–7.

[113] Rémond, 'L'évolution', 3–11 at 9–10.

[114] *Le Petit Démocrate*, 29 September 1929; *La Croix*, 1 August 1929.

[115] ANFLM, 73, Isaac to Guiter, 19 April 1930; Goyet, *Un Rôle en politique*, 106–7.

[116] Bensoussan, *Combats*, 367–8, 372.

endorsed Provençal regionalism; Breton Royalists hesitated to do likewise for fear of encouraging the independence movement.[117]

Thirdly, a new generation of Maurrassians detached counter-revolutionary ideology from Royalism. In May 1924, a group of Maurrassian students, including Jean de Fabrègues and Jean-Pierre Maxence, patronized initially by Jacques Maritain, founded the *Gazette française*, marked by Thomism, anti-modernism, and idealization of medieval spiritualism. The condemnation dispersed these groups. Some refused to submit. Others embraced Maurrassianism without Maurras. From 1930, Maxence edited the established *Revue Française*, while Fabrègues founded *Réaction* (1930). Contributors to these reviews included Robert Brasillach, Thierry Maulnier, Maurice Bardèche, and others who would become notorious. The cluster of reviews constituting the Jeune Droite attacked modernism, productivism, materialism, and Americanism in the name of tradition, Catholicism, and nation. In his *La Défense de l'Occident* (1927), Henri Massis denounced the 'techniciens soi-disant réalistes'.[118] These themes resonated in the nationalist right more generally, including the Fédération right, and the precise direction of influence is unclear.

The Fédération Right

In 1931, Kerillis informed Lyautey that the Fédération was divided between 'men of order who were prepared to govern' and 'the spiritual heirs of the vanquished parties and those who were intoxicated with Maurrasianism'.[119] Marin's past was impeccably Republican, but the charge that he possessed an 'opposition mentality' had some validity. In July 1926, he joined the government as Minister of Pensions, allegedly telling Poincaré that he alone sufficed to represent the right.[120] He found himself imprisoned in a secondary ministry. He fumed at Briand's presence in the government, the execution without ratification of the Mellon-Béranger debts accords, and the return of *scrutin d'arrondissement*. That some Fédération activists accused him of endorsing these policies by remaining in the government did not improve Marin's humour. In fact, *La Nation*, the party journal, effectively under Marin's control, vented his reservations. Warren claimed that Poincaré, once again brought to power by a 'great movement', had showed 'great timidity', leaving the levers of command in the hands of the Cartel.[121]

In November 1928, Poincaré sacked Marin, leaving him free to attack the government. In November 1929, Marin voted with the left to overthrow Briand. Angry Fédération members complained that only Socialist refusal to participate had prevented the formation of a Cartel government. Lacking an alternative, Marin voted

[117] Secondy, *Le Midi blanc*, 153.

[118] Del Bayle, *Les Non-conformistes*, 11–70; Dard, *Le Rendez-vous manqué*, 95–130 (Massis quotation, 110).

[119] Goyet, *Un Rôle en politique*, 106–7.

[120] ANFLM, 75, Soulier to Guiter, 2 October 1929.

[121] *La Nation*, 1, 22 October 1927; ANFLM, 75, for example, Vavasseur to Guiter, 26 February 1927, Robert to Guiter, 10 March 1927; ANFLM, 75, Soulier to Guiter, 26 October 1928.

in favour of the succeeding Tardieu administration, even though it was similar in composition and included Briand. Subsequently, Marin's clashes with the government provoked several deputies to resign from the URD and many members to leave the party.[122] In July 1931, Marin botched an attempt to expel Kerillis from the Fédération, in a stormy meeting, reported in embarrassing detail in *L'Écho de Paris*.[123] In November, the Fédération congress resolved that in the next legislature all members must belong to a single parliamentary group. That would precipitate the departure of Pernot and his followers after the 1932 election.

The Fédération right attacked successive governments in the name of liberal orthodoxy and nationalism. It condemned the Social Insurance Law as 'statist, Marxist and under the rod of Léon Jouhaux's CGT'. Tardieu's agricultural laws were 'impregnated' with Marxism, while free secondary education was a 'pure example' of statism, and the re-tooling plan was collectivist.[124] Tax reductions were better, since they encouraged private initiative.[125] Only the Family Allowance Law met with approval.[126]

Marin especially opposed Briand's foreign policy. He condemned the memorandum on Europe as a 'mortal illusion'.[127] The Fédération preferred a 'United States of France', by which it meant consolidation of the Empire. The Fédération envisaged French domination of Europe, guaranteed by alliances with the eastern powers.[128] France needed neither the 'experts' of 1926 and 1928, nor the support of Britain or the United States. It must have faith in its own people, not in vague ideals or in German good faith, for defeat had aggravated the Germans' innate faults.[129] The foreign affairs rubric in *La Nation* was entitled 'La France lutte pour son existence'.

There was also something new in the right's discourse: a critique of 'productivism' and 'rationalization' in the name of the spiritualism more usually associated with the *non-conformistes*. In 1927, François Coty in *Le Figaro* attacked Redressement français' claim that 'the old methods have had their day'. He countered that 'experience and tradition are the best guides that can direct the hesitating journey of humanity and its sad guides'. Coty condemned schools in which 'morality has no sanction, the family is outdated, and work on the land is slavery'. He attacked the influence of Freemasons in Redressement, and denounced the visit of the German Jew, Dr Hirschaeur, to 'initiate us into the marvels of rationalization'.[130] Two years later, as Tardieu presented his ministry, *La Croix* warned of the import of American manners through the cinema and feared that English brutality would triumph over French finesse in rugby and boxing.[131]

The Fédération still sometimes defended liberalism in the language of organization, but increasingly it attacked its materialist implications. Marin had no time

[122] ANFLM, 73, Guiter to Marin, 18 November 1929; Perret to Marin, 23 December 1929; JOCD, 28 March 1930.

[123] *L'Écho de Paris*, 9 July 1931.

[124] *La Nation*, 3 May, 7 June, 2 August 1930.

[125] *La Nation*, 14 June 1930.

[126] *La Nation*, 27 February 1932.

[127] *La Nation*, 24 May 1930.

[128] *La Nation*, 4, 25 January 1930.

[129] Camille Blaisot, *La Nation*, 4 January 1930; Marin, 6 September 1930.

[130] *Le Figaro*, 18 November 1927.

[131] *La Croix*, 13 November 1929.

for the 'conjuror', Loucheur, and maintained that 'money does not enrich the kingdom; rather it is the spirit directing labour that does so'. He added that we need quality as well as quantity.[132] Defending his indiscipline before his URD colleagues, Marin mixed positivism, Maurrassianism, and Bergsonism. He took pride in the 'traditional instincts of life', imbibed in his family; they were not a 'Cartesian provisional', but a 'force'. Yet he did not attack progress in principle. Rather, new problems could be resolved using existing principles. He accepted the need for empirical testing, but argued that 'experience' had proved certain principles beyond question.[133]

The Fédération actually condemned a mythical notion of production at all costs, and presented an alternative version. One journalist claimed that while everyone agreed that national power depended on productivity, readers should not be duped by rationalization. Standardization could reduce costs, but France must 'adapt to the rapid progress of modern technology without sacrificing its originality'. That meant reinforcing small property through reform of the inheritance laws and mechanization of agriculture.[134] Likewise, Warren saw the 1931 colonial exposition as a 'manifestation of the productive power of the overseas French', and claimed that prosperity depended on abundant production.[135] Désiré Ferry claimed that the 'organization of the frontier', the Maginot line, represented 'a truly modern spirit, furnished with the most perfected mechanization'.[136]

Like the centre, the Fédération right saw agriculture as essential to national power, but saw rural prosperity as dependent upon moral reform and the removal of 'Combists' from the administration as well as upon mechanization. The Fédération accused all governments since Méline of neglecting agriculture, or rather of not applying the Fédération's programme: reduced taxes on agriculture, protection of the rural family, and consultation of agricultural organizations in parliament.[137] This ruralism owed much to the growing influence in the Fédération of Catholic landowners. Nationally, this was the golden age of the agricultural unions affiliated to the rue d'Athènes, including the Union du Sud-est and the Office Central in Finistère.[138] The unions sought to isolate the peasantry from the secular state and to combat collectivism by providing services to the peasantry. 'Moral reform' meant 'organization' of the rural family through reform of the inheritance laws, cheap credit, and cooperatives, implemented by the 'organized profession'.[139] Landowners did not see ruralism as incompatible with residence in Paris; they hardly contested capitalism and lamented the fact that French agricultural production had fallen behind that of its competitors.[140] Their regionalist, corporatist schemes were meant to recover national power for the right.

The Fédération also allied with conservative Catholics. The latter were bloodied, but unbowed. In 1930, André Siegfried (sympathetic to *laïque* moderate Republicanism) could still write that 'There is no commune, however tiny, in which the

[132] *La Nation*, 2 August 1930. [133] ANFLM, 73, 15 November 1929.
[134] *La Nation*, 18 February 1928. [135] *La Nation*, 8, 22 February 1930.
[136] Sorlot, *André Maginot*, 212–14. [137] *La Nation*, 14 June 1930.
[138] Barral, *Les Agrariens français*, 209–12; Passmore, *From Liberalism*, 107–10.
[139] Bensoussan, *Combats*, 171–200, 217. [140] *La Nation*, 14 June 1930.

Church does not gather together and organize resistance; and wherever there is a chateau, a bourgeois dynasty, in short a self-conscious social aristocracy, this resistance finds support.'[141] In Brittany, some priests still refused the sacraments to parents who sent their children to the École publique. As late as 1939, Marin told the Nuncio that Poincaré's declaration that left and right were divided by the 'chasm' of the religious question still held good.[142] Marin exaggerated, because many Catholics supported the centre and even the left. His claim was a political intervention, designed to persuade the Papacy to abandon the PDP. Yet this strategy also revealed the extent of conservative Catholic resentment of *laïcité* and of administrative discrimination. The disappearance of the ALP brought conservative Catholics into the Fédération. Back in 1925, La Rochefoucauld suggested to Isaac that the Fédération should absorb the ALP's remnants.[143] Four years later, Guiraud reminded Catholics that the Pope opposed a Catholic party but he was pleased that the URD included many Catholic deputies—he ignored the PDP.[144] Several Fédération leaders had belonged to the ALP, including Joseph Denais (deputy for Paris), who as late as 1935 wished to revive it.[145] Through Paul Féron-Vrau's Presse régionale, conservative Ralliés influenced important regional dailies such as *Le Nouvelliste de Bretagne, La Liberté du Sud-est*, and *L'Éclair de l'Est*.[146] In Lyon, the commercial success of the Catholic conservative *Nouvelliste* prevented moderate conservatives from creating a daily. In the same city, Piou's Ligue des droits de la nation brought ALP and Fédération activists together, despite Rochefoucauld's efforts to dissuade Marin from patronizing the league.[147] The Fédération also inherited the ALP's roots in the men and women's parish groups especially after the eviction of AF supporters from them.[148]

Marin (sometimes wrongly described as an agnostic) claimed that the war had resolved the religious question and made anticlericalism an old 'routine'. Yet, like Maurras, he saw anticlericalism as the antithesis of the 'traditions' which have made our country. The Fédération demanded reform of the lay laws and condemned the *école unique* as an attack on the Catholic education.[149] It saw religion as integral to social order and anticlericalism as another manifestation of Marxist materialism (and *vice versa*). Each week in *La Nation*, Jean Le Mee reported the misdeeds of *instituteurs*, portraying them as enemies of property and religion. The Fédération complained that 'Combistes' in the administration harassed Catholics, and that Tardieu's re-tooling plan entailed favouritism.[150]

141 André Siegfried, *Tableau des partis en France* (Paris, 1930), 179.

142 ANFLM, 119, Marin to Valeri, 19 February 1937.

143 *Isaac*, 394, 24 March 1925.

144 *La Croix*, 20 November 1929.

145 AN, 142 AP 15, Fonds Rochefoucauld (hereafter ANFXR, carton/dossier no.), 19 April 1935, Chollet to La Rochefoucauld.

146 ANFXR, 14, Daussonville to Rochefoucauld, 27 September 1926. The Presse régionale possessed the majority of shares in the *Nouvelliste de Bretagne*.

147 ANFXR, 14, Dossier Lyon.

148 Passmore, *From Liberalism*, 140–62; Marais, *Les Sociétés d'hommes*, 139–46; Jean-Luc Marais, 'La Défense de l'Anjou chrétien', in François Lebrun (ed.), *Le Diocèse d'Angers* (Paris, 1981), 235–61.

149 *La Nation*, 15 February 1930, 21 January 1932.

150 *La Nation*, 2 October 1926, 14 June 1930.

The appearance of the PDP reinforced the place of conservative Catholicism in the Fédération. Borrowing from the reactionary (ex-ALP) polemist Auguste Cavallier,[151] the Fédération condemned the PDP's 'demagogic' social policies and charged that 'their Briandist zeal has led the PDs [pédés] to adhere enthusiastically to pan-Europe'. The Fédération posed as the guardian of theological orthodoxy and accused the PDP of representing a 'perilous and criminal dissidence among Catholic troops'.[152] In Brittany, these accusations had some purchase, for the PDP's hostility to the FNC alienated potentially sympathetic local *élus*.[153] Throughout the period, the Fédération struggled to reconcile its ambition to monopolize Catholic discontent, which entailed assumption of the fundamentally Catholic nature of the country, with desire for alliance with the *laïque* Alliance, usually justified using the necessity of toleration.[154] Religion subverted the majority as a whole. In July 1930, Tardieu's majority split on a seemingly banal motion praising Jules Ferry as the founder of modern education. Tardieu had attempted to prevent controversy by combining celebration of Ferry with a coded attack on anticlerical excess. That did not prevent him from presenting himself to the anticlerical Senate as Ferry's heir. URD members spoke of an 'anniversary of mourning'.[155] In 1935, Tardieu wrote that the parties of the right 'are composed, more or less equally, of tenants of the Catholic tradition and of the French Revolution. This division is at the origin of their misfortunes.'[156] That was true, but the enactment of a Social Insurance Law—partly inspired by Social Catholicism—posed even greater problems for conservatives.

PEASANT AND SMALL-BUSINESS MOBILIZATION

Parliament approved the Social Insurance Law in 1928 on condition that it was corrected in a new law, taking account of the criticisms of mutualist associations, employers, and, above all, agriculture. Peasants and small business resented having to pay contributions for their own employees, including family members, especially given that to benefit from the Law themselves they had to pay higher optional premiums. As the economic crisis began, big business also turned against the Law. The Corrective Law of 1930 did not assuage discontent.

The resulting agitation, especially in the countryside, embarrassed Social Catholics, from the PDP to the conservative agricultural Unions, for in different ways they all saw the Law as a step towards the organization of rural society. The PDP accepted some conservative criticisms, while defending the Law against those who used agricultural grievances to undermine it. The PDP's allies, the Cultivateurs-cultivants, were

151 *L'Intérêt français*, 30 June 1934.
152 *La Nation*, 30 January 1932. In *La Nation*, 6 September 1930.
153 Bensousan, *Combats*, 331.
154 Kevin Passmore, 'Catholicism and nationalism: the Fédération républicaine, 1927–1939', in *Catholicism and Politics in Twentieth-Century France* (Liverpool, 1999), 47–72.
155 Clague, 'Vision and myopia', 124–6; Tardieu, *L'éprueve*, 247–50.
156 André Tardieu, *Sur la pente* (Paris, 1935), xxxvi.

particularly affected. They were already retreating thanks to the Church's opposition, and because conservative agricultural unions reinforced their communal presence and made concessions on rents—in spite of criticism from some landowners who opposed compromise with 'rural Socialism'.[157] The Social Insurance Law further weakened the Cultivateurs-cultivants, because the *abbés démocrates* favoured it, while peasant activists did not.[158] Significantly, in 1930, a genuine peasant won a by-election in the Côtes-du-Nord, as a 'cultivateur républicain et démocrate', but did not sit with the PDP.[159]

Conservatives were not well placed to capture peasant discontent. Initially, conservative agrarian organizations opposed the Law because the principle of national inter-professional solidarity seemingly threatened their regional, exclusively agricultural structures. Many preferred Vallat's corporatist, regionalist counter-project. Yet agrarians, along with the FNC, saw the revised 1930 law as a lesser evil, and even as a first step towards genuine corporatism. They pressed peasants to join their own mutual societies rather than *laïque* rivals.[160] Most peasants refused, for they rejected the law itself.

Radicalization of the Parti agraire et paysan français (PAPF) was one sign of this discontent. This party had been founded in 1927 by Gabriel Fleurent, pseudonym Fleurent-Agricola, a former teacher. He celebrated peasant civilization and attacked industrial society and civil servants; he sought to create an Eastern European style peasant party, and demanded that a peasant corporation organize the profession. At first, the PAPF was politically eclectic, but gradually it moved to the right, finally eliminating its Republican faction in 1936.[161]

Henri Dorgères, who led peasant resistance to Social Insurance in Brittany and Normandy, was instrumental in the transformation of the PAPF. He proved a gifted journalist and market-place speaker.[162] He urged peasants not to join *mutuelles* and to go 10,000–15,000 strong to their *chef-lieu* and demand abrogation.[163] He formed the first Comité de défense paysan in January 1929. He soon claimed that 40,000 peasants in Brittany, Normandy, and the west had signed a petition against obligation, and in February 1930, 10,000 peasants attended a meeting at Rennes. Dorgères accused the agricultural unions and the FNC of 'treason'.[164] Initially, he favoured regionalization of the Law, but peasant pressure pushed him towards abolition.[165]

157 Bensoussan, *Combats*, 290–313.

158 *Politique*, 15 January 1930; Delbreil, *Centrisme*, 242–52; Bensoussan, *Combats*, 406–15.

159 Bensoussan, *Combats*, 154.

160 Bensoussan, *Combats*, 406–9.

161 Robert O. Paxton, *French Peasant Fascism: Henry Dorgères' Greenshirts and the Crises of French Agriculture* (Oxford, 1997), 37–8; Thierry Hohl, 'Le Parti agraire et paysan français. Une Tentative agrairienne en Côte-d'Or', *Annales de Bourgogne* 49 (1988), 49, 140–50; Denis, *Les Royalistes de la Mayenne*, 522–3.

162 Bensoussan, *Combats*, 409–24; Pascal Ory, 'Le Dorgèrisme. Institution et discours d'une colère paysanne', *Revue d'histoire moderne et contemporaine* 22 (1975), 168–90.

163 *Progrès agricole de l'Ouest*, 7 October 1928.

164 *Progrès agricole de l'Ouest*, 11 May 1930.

165 *Progrès agricole de l'Ouest*, 4, 11 May 1930.

Concessions did not end peasant discontent because it derived from the old conviction that the government and administration favoured towns, workers, and big business. Thus, while the PAPF and Défense paysan were to the right of the Cultivateurs-cultivants, they reworked its radical, anti-bourgeois strand, and activists of the Cultivateurs-cultivants joined Défense paysan. Dorgères denounced Social Insurance as an instrument of the bureaucracy, arguing that *fonctionnaires* earned most and worked least, while peasants earned least and worked most.[166] He attacked the Tardieu government as 'affairist' and condemned Loucheur, one of the architects of Social Insurance, as the personification of big business.[167] Dorgères subjected the grain trader Louis Louis-Dreyfus to antisemitic attacks.[168] He also adopted the Cultivateurs-cultivants demands for tenancy reform. The peasant movement turned the doctrine of competence to its advantage, claiming that only peasants could determine agricultural policy. In 1928 at Vire, a 'peasant candidate' claimed that neither his conservative nor Socialist rivals, respectively a lawyer and professor, could represent an agricultural constituency. In 1932, all candidates in Calvados stressed their agricultural links. Peasant activism took on a special colour in Haut-Rhin, where the Bauernbund defended both economic interests and Alsatian-German culture.[169]

In spite of its populism, the peasant mobilization won approval from conservatives. Agricola helped found the sugar-beet association while Dorgères was linked to Monseigneur Charost and AF. Delahaye's *Province* backed Dorgères, as did the president of the Morbihan Chambre d'agriculture. Hervé Budes de Guébriant, president of the Breton Office central, was torn between desire to remain close to the peasantry and Social Catholic sympathy for Social Insurance.[170] Ultimately, conservatives chose what one aristocrat called the 'demagogic terrain'. In the 1932 election campaign, Breton and Norman agrarian leaders attended Dorgères' mass meetings, notably Jacques Le Roy Ladurie, president of the Union des syndicats agricoles du Calvados.[171]

Also present were delegates of the Fédération des contribuables (FC, Taxpayers Federation), founded in 1928 by the business accountant André Large with the support of François Coty and Auguste Cavallier. The FC won the backing of major agricultural and business associations, and constituted groups in several cities. Initially, the FC was politically eclectic; it excluded one of its founders because he was too far to the right. However, it soon became clear that the FC's attacks on taxation and Social Insurance and its desire to form a middle-class counterpart to the CGT constituted a right-wing challenge to conservative organizationalism. The FC saw itself as 'a thoughtful elite, capable of influencing the electoral mass through instruction'. In 1930, it joined Dorgères in a Front unique contre les assurances

166 *Progrès agricole de l'Ouest*, 13 April 1930.

167 *Progrès agricole de l'Ouest*, 16 November, 14 December 1930.

168 *Progrès agricole de l'Ouest*, 28 December 1930.

169 Jean Quellien, *Bleus, blancs, rouges. Politique et élections dans le Calvados 1870–1939* (Caen, 1986), 340; Samuel Goodfellow, *Between the Swastika and the Cross of Lorraine: Fascisms in Interwar Alsace* (DeKalb, 1999), 86–102.

170 Bensoussan, *Combats*, 412–17.

171 Bensoussan, *Combats*, 423–4.

sociales, and in 1930–1931, it advocated a tax strike.[172] The FC issued from tensions paralleling those in the countryside, for many big firms initially favoured obligation because their own private insurance schemes gave small business a cost advantage. Employers' leaders attempted to defuse tension by urging application of the letter of law and refusal of wage increases to cover employee contributions. As the economic crisis intensified, business hostility to the law grew, facilitating the creation of broad alliance against it.[173]

CONCLUSION

The onset of economic crisis and the revival of German nationalism undermined conservative reformism, and strengthened right and left opposition to it. In May 1931, Briand's failure to win the Presidency of the Republic demonstrated the decline of his position. Tardieu secretly worked against him, while the nationalist Georges Mandel did so openly. On 20 June 1931, Hoover's moratorium on reparations and debts revealed the seriousness of the international situation. Since the government staked its future on prosperity and European cooperation, it was not well placed to fight the elections of 1932. Tardieu faced opposition from both left and right. While the left attacked Tardieu as a reactionary, Wendel attributed conservatives' defeat to its 'stupid' policy of pro-Radical Concentration.[174]

Historians have rightly stressed Radical opposition to the conservative governments of 1926–1932. In fact, the story was more complex. Certainly, the Radicals opposed the government in principle and often in practice, rightly detecting an attempt to incorporate their electorate into a conservative coalition. Yet the majority's strategy also permitted Radicals to shape legislation and help anchor the coalition in the centre. In the elections, notwithstanding, the Radicals attacked Tardieu as a pro-Catholic reactionary, and their charges resonated in the centre. For instance, the *Dépêche de Brest* initially backed Tardieu, but in 1932 declared that 'the saviour operates outside our frontiers'.[175]

Indeed, in Brittany, the election took the usual form of a conflict between the lay and Catholic blocs, thus revealing that religion continued to divide. A Catholic journalist complained that one only had to shout 'down with reaction', and the crowd, 'as if obeying an instinctive impulse, forgets all professional, social and religious considerations and votes with élan against the white, the Chouan'.[176] The PDP rejected Marin's offer of a pact except in constituencies where there was a clear Cartel danger, thus intensifying conflict between the Fédération and Christian Democrats. The PDP was usually too Catholic for the left and won seats only where it represented the right.[177] However, joint action with the left was possible:

[172] William A. Hoisington Jr, *Jacques Lemaigre-Dubreuil de Paris à Casablanca* (Paris, 2009), 19–26; Dutton, *Origins*, 108.

[173] Dutton, *Origins*, 107–11.

[174] Jeannney, *François de Wendel*, 481.

[175] Bensoussan, *Combats*, 377.

[176] Bensoussan, *Combats*, 377.

[177] Fuller, 'The dynamics', 525–30, 588; Bensoussan, *Combats*, 374–7; Delbreil, *Centrisme*, 224–5, 231–4; Monnet, *Refaire*, 170–1.

in Meurthe-et-Moselle, the Fédération's Warren, backed by the Bishop and the FNC, fell to a candidate jointly supported by the PDP, Jeune république, and Radicals.[178] Warren was just one of the Fédération deputies whose defeat could be attributed partly to Marin's attacks on the government.

The centre held up well in the elections. Yet radicalization of the extreme right was the counterpart of the successes of conservative reformism. Opposition to Social Insurance radicalized ordinary conservatives and obliged the Fédération, like conservative agrarians, to incorporate peasant demands into its programme. The Fédération generally used leaguers to keep order at meetings, both in the cities and countryside.[179] The JP and AF incorporated regionalization of Social Insurance into their corporatist schemes and the Croix de feu would do likewise. Even Kerillis and Pernot saw the JP as a paramilitary rampart against revolution. Tardieu secretly funded the Croix de feu. The outline of the crisis of the 1930s was already visible: a dual fracture between conservatives and the left, and between the right and the centre.

[178] Jean-Claude Delbreil, 'Les Démocrates-chrétiens en Lorraine dans l'entre-deux-guerres', *Les Cahiers lorrains* 4 (1987), 419–47; Fuller, 'The dynamics', 565–7.

[179] Quellien, *Bleus*, 304.

12

Fascism in France? (1934–1940)

> A national mystique is not at all particular to Italy, to Germany, to Russia. It has not been invented in recent years. It has been numbed in France by the false appearances of the victory, by the folly of the 'hymn to production' etc. [Now] the French people awaken. They rally around a mystique that is doubtless national, but in a friendly, balanced, ordered spirit, in conformity with healthy French tradition.
>
> François de La Rocque, 27 October 1935

On 6 February 1934, several tens of thousands of sympathizers of Action française (AF), the Jeunesses patriotes (JP), the Parisian group of the Union nationale des combattants (UNC), and the Fédération des contribuables (FC), along with Communist veterans, converged on the Place de la Concorde, while on the Left Bank, outside the Chamber of Deputies, the Croix de feu demonstrated separately. They were protesting against the installation of a government under the Radical-Socialist Édouard Daladier. They accused Daladier of sacking the anti-communist Paris Prefect of Police, Jean Chiappe, in order to secure left-wing support for his new government; they also charged his Radical-Socialist predecessor, Camille Chautemps, with covering up a financial fraud orchestrated by Alexandre Stavisky. The most determined demonstrators attempted to force their way across the Pont de la Concorde and into the Chamber. In the ensuing riots, fourteen demonstrators and one policeman died. The next day, Daladier tendered his resignation, frightened by the reluctance of the judiciary and forces of order to defend him. His party switched its support to a Union nationale government under the elderly ex-President Gaston Doumergue, which promised to reform the constitution and restore economic confidence.

In 1926, the return of the Union nationale had inaugurated six years of moderate conservative government; now, bitter polarization followed the reversal of majorities. Fearful that fascism was spreading to France, Communists, Socialists, and Radicals united in what became known as the 'Popular Front'. For them, the embodiment of fascism was the Croix de feu. It had been founded in November 1927 by François Coty in an effort to bolster the nationalist wing of the veterans movement at a time of great enthusiasm for Briand. At first, the league was open only to decorated veterans. From August 1931, under the leadership of Lieutenant-Colonel François de La Rocque, it widened its horizons. It demonstrated in favour of Tardieu and Laval, and helped disrupt a meeting of the Congrès international du désarmement. In the course of 1929–32, the league added a youth section, the Fils et filles des

Croix de feu, and the Dispos, a security service with Paul Chopine at its head. The movement also mobilized non-combatants and women in the Regroupement national, while the Volontaires nationaux (VN) formed in 1933 were open to men too young to have served in the trenches. Although the Croix de feu played an ambiguous part in the 6 February riots, it was the major beneficiary, growing from around 60,000 in February 1934 to perhaps half a million in June 1936.[1]

Historians have focussed largely on the question of 'fascism', especially in relation to the 6 February riots and to the Croix de feu. Rather than rehearse again the limitations of the 'classificatory approach', suffice it to recall René Rémond's view that fascism was essentially a 'revolutionary ideology'. Since, he continues, the conservative Doumergue's arrival in power defused the 6 February crisis, and since the Croix de feu too was conservative, neither can have been fascist.[2] Robert Soucy uses the same method to reach an opposite conclusion. He concurs that the leagues were conservative, but because he sees fascism as conservative, the leagues become fascist.[3] Even if we could agree on a definition, it would explain only the degree to which a movement conformed to it, for elements not included in the definition shaped the actual history of the leagues. Anyway, the leagues, like all parties, were internally diverse. Consequently, they possessed affinities with other political movements, and not only parliamentary conservatives.

These considerations do not mean that the question of fascism is irrelevant. We may identify similarities and/or differences between the leagues and Fascism and Nazism, so long as we remember that the leagues cannot be reduced to those characteristics. We may also explore the leagues' use or refusal of the fascist label. We have seen that Valois' appropriation of the term had caused AF and the JP to avoid it.[4] And we may explore the leagues' positioning in conservative political culture, remembering that it was never isolated from international developments.

In particular, the leagues represented one form of Europe-wide interest in mobilization of the crowd through repetition of images in mass meetings and propaganda. In France, new methods were used to promote a 'mystique'—a keyword of the decade. In late 1935, a *Petite Gironde* journalist defined a mystique as 'the fashionable term commonly used, doubtless to express the feeling that our post-war and rising generations lack an ideal that can enflame their hearts and exalt the highest virtues of our race'. A mystique bonded the elite and the crowd without undermining hierarchy. The journalist asked politicians of both left and right what a 'mystique' meant for them, thus indicating its contested nature.[5]

[1] Sean Kennedy, *Reconciling France against Democracy: The Croix de feu and the Parti Social Français 1927–1945* (Montreal, 2007), 17–44.

[2] René Rémond, *Les Droites en France*, fourth revised edition (Paris, 1982), 206–8.

[3] Robert Soucy, *French Fascism: The Second Wave* (Newhaven, 1995).

[4] Michel Dobry (ed.), *Le Mythe de l'allergie française au fascisme* (Paris, 2003).

[5] *La Petite Gironde*, 23 October 1935; Mark Meyers, 'Feminizing fascist men: crowd psychology, gender, and sexuality in French antifascism, 1929–1945', *French Historical Studies* 29, no. 1 (Winter 2006), 109–42.

I shall also position the extreme right in the context of conservative understandings of crisis. Often, historians casually assume that the emergence of the extreme right was a response to 'obvious' problems: economic crisis, the rise of Communism, the German threat, and parliamentary instability. Some go further, arguing that there was an 'objective' crisis of the Republic, to which the solutions were therefore technical rather than ideological. For Michel Winock, the rioters of 6 February recognized 'a real deficiency of parliamentary institutions in France', even if the emotion provoked by the riots permitted the unscrupulous to 'install in the collective psychology [sic] the demonology of civil war' inherited from past divisions.[6] In reality, it is not self-evident that resolution of the economic crisis required constitutional reform, or that the turnover of governments harmed the national interest. Not all conservatives agreed that it did.

In fact, the definition of a set of events as a 'crisis'—especially of a particular *kind* of crisis—is ideological and political. Conservatives had formulated their critique of the Republic well before the Republic established itself, even if their criticisms subsequently evolved. It was rooted in dubious beliefs, including collective psychology, with its gendered, racial, and class baggage, and a quasi-monarchist notion of authority refracted through crowd theory, management science, and more. Only if we relate conservatives' understandings of crisis to their beliefs and purposes can we understand why they saw strengthening of the executive, representation of the interests, and restriction of the role of professional politicians as so important, and why reform ultimately failed.

I shall argue that the leagues emerged from four developments. First, historians have correctly emphasized polarization between right and left, and we have seen that since 1918 the language of civil war was available for use in domestic politics. From 1934, the resurgence of Communism reinforced conservatives' conviction that the left as a whole was part of a diabolical conspiracy originating in Moscow. Secondly, relations among conservatives deteriorated, for they never agreed whether to fight Communism through reform or repression, religion or secularism. Thirdly, the perceived failure of the Bloc alienated ordinary conservatives from their deputies. In the late 1920s, revamped parliamentary conservatism absorbed this mobilization, but, from 1932, it once again escaped their control. Peasant, small-business, regionalist, white-collar, and women's groups were prominent in this anti-parliamentary movement, directed against both the left and the established right. Lastly, the economic crisis precipitated a struggle between a multiplicity of interest groups (towns and cities, importers and exporters, large and small business, and many more), which rendered coherent formulation policy difficult. In a political culture marked by readiness to use the language of conspiracy and civil war and in which parliamentary weakness had long been denounced, these conflicts encouraged recourse to coercion, from decree laws, through institutional reform and corporatism, to dictatorship, and violence in the streets.

[6] Michel Winock, *La Fièvre hexagonale. Les Grandes crises politiques 1871–1968* (Paris, 1986), 193–238.

That said, neither the 6 February riots nor the leagues were the inevitable outcome of conservative political culture. In the late 1920s, the centre had dominated and the right had been marginalized, and in the right circumstances, that alignment might have persisted. Nevertheless, moderate conservative hegemony radicalized the right, as the 1932 elections demonstrated. With 169 deputies out of 280, the centre increased its strength relative to the right, but the latter became more extreme. Thirty-three deputies joined the Independents; forty-four sat with Marin's Fédération, while only eighteen joined Pernot's pro-centre Groupe républicain social, itself less moderate than in the past.

After 1932, circumstances favoured the right. The resurgence of German nationalism made Marin's hostility to Briandism more appealing, while the economic crisis seemed to vindicate his critique of productivism. Business and agricultural hostility to Social Insurance intensified, and the Fédération, now with centre support, demanded its regionalization. As the centre's democratic reformism collapsed, it moved closer to the right, and some individuals would embrace the extreme right; few centre deputies disapproved of the riots of 6 February. The Doumergue government was the expression of this new climate.

The centre did not entirely capitulate to the right; it helped ensure Doumergue's failure, and in 1935 Flandin formed a Concentration government. He attempted to adapt conservatism to 'new realities', in effect producing a centrist, authoritarian version of the organizational project. He succeeded only in antagonizing the right and leagues and intensifying rank-and-file discontent. The Croix de feu was the major beneficiary of the successive failures of centre and right. The league combined attacks on state intervention in the economy with schemes for an authoritarian 'organization of the profession', through which it mobilized groups that considered themselves—rightly or wrongly—unrepresented in parliamentary conservatism.

LE 6 FÉVRIER

For centre and right, the Stavisky scandal confirmed longstanding criticisms of the parliamentary system, fears concerning France's international position, and the immediate problem of the economic crisis. The alleged cover-up of the affair symbolized professional politicians' manipulation of the system for gain, especially through interference in the judiciary. For Kerillis, 'the Stavisky scandal is essentially one... of the lawyer who does not plead, who does not wear the robe, but who, all powerful, circulates in ministerial offices, profits from influence, paralyses justice and thence the administrative machinery'.[7] An *Alliance démocratique* editorialist claimed that Daladier headed a government without significant personalities, rather than one of 'worthy and respected men in whom the country could have confidence'.[8] The right emphasized Chautemps' Masonic connections.

[7] *L'Écho de Paris*, 20 January 1934.
[8] *L'Alliance démocratique*, 7 February 1934.

Secondly, conservatives believed that professional politicians' corruption was linked to state interference in private matters, epitomized by Social Insurance—and to the resistance of government workers to spending cuts. *Les Débats* claimed that since France had outlawed individual initiative, Stavisky could use the whole edifice of state regulation.[9] Not surprisingly, the Fédération des Contribuables (FC) participated in the 6 February riots, for it had been in the forefront of agitation against Social Insurance. In November 1932, the FC, with a number of business organizations, Défense paysan, the UNC, and JP agreed upon a partial tax strike (in which the Croix de feu also participated). On 19 March 1933, their campaign culminated in demonstrations for tax and spending cuts, which were especially successful in provincial towns and in western areas where Défense paysan was influential. The FC's president, André Large, predicted that H-Hour would soon arrive and called for a 'national revolution'. Its Alsatian branch added that the Protocols of the Elders of Zion proved the Jews' desire for world domination. Parisian business affiliates were more moderate.[10]

Thirdly, Stavisky's status as a naturalized Ukrainian Jew connected deputies' 'unpatriotic' refusal to make cuts to an international anti-French conspiracy. In 1933, the arrival in France of some 25,000 German Jews increased antisemitism, even if it was explicit only in AF and Défense paysan. Antisemitism was implicit in a more widespread xenophobia. In line with mercantilist thinking, conservatives (and the left) saw protection of French labour and markets as an 'obvious' solution to economic difficulties, and accused refugees—frequently Jewish—of using the crisis to set up businesses in France. Medical and law students and doctors and lawyers demanded restrictions on foreigners and the recently naturalized. Xavier Vallat proposed the creation of prisons on the frontiers and the expulsion of foreigners who had committed crimes.[11] Stavisky evoked fears that France might be absorbed by its more fertile, productive, and strongly governed neighbours, and perhaps fall victim to Communism, the latest manifestation of Asiatic barbarism. *Les Débats* claimed that the Stavisky scandal revealed parliamentarians' submission to internationalism and feeble response to German infiltration.[12]

The breadth of conservative approval of the riots is as striking as the absence of condemnation of 'excesses'. Indeed, for most conservatives the riots revealed the positive potential of the crowd: *Le Figaro* differentiated between 'demonstrators singing the *Marseillaise*' and 'gangs screaming the *Internationale*'.[13] *Les Débats* claimed

[9] *Journal des débats*, 6 January 1934.

[10] William A. Hoisington Jr, *Jacques Lemaigre-Dubreuil de Paris à Casablanca* (Paris, 2009), 28–38; Samuel Goodfellow, *Between the Swastika and the Cross of Lorraine: Fascisms in Interwar Alsace* (DeKalb, 1999), 120–2; 451 AP 81, Fonds La Rocque (hereafter ANFLR, carton/dossier no.), 22 May 1933.

[11] Gérard Noiriel, *Les Origines républicaines de Vichy* (Paris, 1999), 141–9: Ralph Schor, *L'Opinion française et les étrangers* (Paris, 1985), 597–612; Ralph Schor, *Histoire de l'immigration en France* (Paris, 1996), 130–1; Mary Dewhurst Lewis, *The Boundaries of the Republic. Migrant Rights and the Limits of Universalism in France, 1918–1940* (Stanford, 2007).

[12] *Journal des débats*, 11, 23, 31 January 1934; Jean Guiraud, *La Croix*, 30 January 1934.

[13] *Le Figaro*, 8 February 1934. My emphasis.

that the government had used troops against peaceful veterans and lauded those who had fought so disinterestedly.[14] Moreover, identification of 'Staviskites' with professional politicians and the demagogy of the left as a whole endorsed 'defensive' violence against an anti-national, criminal government, especially as the sacking of the anti-communist Chiappe seemingly proved the government's revolutionary intentions.[15] *Les Débats* compared present moral corruption with that of the Directory prior to Bonaparte's coup and expected that the 'honest and hardworking' country would soon demand the application of the scalpel.[16] Already in 1932, Wendel saw dictatorship as the only alternative to inflation. He admired Mussolini and believed Maurras to be right except about the monarchy.[17] Jean Guiraud in *La Croix* of 9 February invoked the 'right of insurrection' against a tyrannical government.

Le Temps, bastion of conservative Republicanism, hardly differed. Initially, it refused to identify individual criminals with the regime. Then it admitted the existence of a moral crisis and argued that a 'party' had covered up the wrongdoings of a few guilty men. On 3 February, *Le Temps* reviewed Tardieu's recently published *L'Heure de la décision* positively and commented that only public opinion, enlightened by the Stavisky Affair, could reform the regime. On 6 February, it evoked the divorce between parliament and the people, Socialist tutelage of the government, and failure in the economic and international domains. Afterwards, *Le Temps* blamed the riots on the government.[18] The Alliance denounced the corrupt 'république staviskienne' and the influence of Socialists in the Daladier government. It attributed Daladier's fall to his defiance of public opinion—represented by 'unarmed veterans'.[19] Thus, support for the riots spread across the conservative spectrum. Police reports in Paris and Lyon also emphasized the unusual sympathy of the watching crowd for the demonstrators.[20]

The leagues expliclity attacked parliament, but were not wholly detached from parliamentary conservatism. *L'Action française* played an appreciable role in turning a judicial matter into a crisis of the regime, and made no secret of its desire to overthrow the Republic, even if privately Maurras was doubtful. Solidarité française counted only 1,500 demonstrators, but they were among the most violent. The JP was closest to the parliamentary right, thanks to its links with the Fédération and presence in the nationalist majority in the Paris municipal council. Yet in a tract handed out on the Place de la Concorde, the JP called for a 'national revolution'. Separation between the 5,000 UNC demonstrators and the leagues broke down in the confusion; the UNC's claim that that Staviskites dominated the government was an implicit invitation to rebellion.[21]

14 *Journal des débats*, 9 February 1934.
15 *Journal des débats*, 23, 31 January 1934.
16 *Journal des débats*, 5, 13 January, 6 February 1934.
17 Jean-Noël Jeanneney, *François de Wendel en République. L'Argent et le pouvoir* (Paris, 1976), 485.
18 *Le Temps*, 6, 9 February 1934.
19 *L'Alliance démocratique*, 10 January, 7 February 1934.
20 Serge Berstein, *Le Six février 1934* (Paris, 1975), 104–5.
21 Berstein, *Le Six février*, 120; Chris Millington, *From Victory to Vichy. Veterans in Interwar France* (Manchester, 2011), 52–75.

Hardest to read was the behaviour of the Croix de feu. The league demonstrated alone on the left bank of the Seine, and broke through some police barriers. It could perhaps have entered the Chamber, but chose not to do so. Caution owed nothing to sympathy for the regime. In previous months, the league had denounced foreign and financial dangers and parliamentary corruption, and called for renewal of the elite with veteran blood. It threatened that if government resisted reform, then 'our vibrant, organized mass will know how to impose it'. La Rocque was most concerned with maintaining the movement's independence, and felt that the Croix de feu was not yet ready to act alone. He did not deny the possibility of overthrow of the government, only that the time was not right.[22] Some Croix de feu and UNC demonstrators participated in the fighting on the right bank, breaking through several barriers guarding the Elysée.[23]

THE CRISIS OF CONSERVATISM

In the aftermath of the riots, parliamentary conservatives and the leagues, with some reservations, coalesced around right's position concerning deflation and constitutional reform. The Alliance welcomed Doumergue as 'the only worthy and respected man'; *Le Figaro* was disappointed that he did not form an extra-parliamentary ministry of technicians, which 'the Parisian crowd would have approved', while La Rocque saw the new government as a dressing on a gangrenous wound.[24] Contrary to Rémond's view, Doumergue's accession did not calm the situation.

The failure of successive governments to realize the promise of 6 February widened conservative divisions and seemingly vindicated La Rocque, for he was more reserved towards the government than were the JP and its allies. Initially, Doumergue followed the right's programme: cooperation with the leagues, institutional reform, and deflation. Then, Flandin abandoned deflation and constitutional (but not institutional) reform, distanced himself from the leagues, and endeavoured to arm democracy for the struggle against dictatorships by organizing the relationship between business and the state. In May 1935, Laval's more right-wing administration used Flandin's revamped administrative methods to introduce a 'super-deflation'. None of these governments countered the Popular Front or restored prosperity; rather, they alienated ordinary conservatives. Politics shifted to the streets.

Doumergue: The Failure of the Right

Doumergue's government represented a synthesis of the parliamentary and extra-parliamentary groups that had brought it into being. The Président du conseil saw his administration as a re-edition of Poincaré's Union nationale, and, as in 1926,

22 *Le Flambeau* 1 March 1934; ANFLR, 81, circulars of 21 January to 5 February 1934.

23 Millington, *From Victory to Vichy*, 25–75.

24 *L'Alliance démocratique*, 7 February 1934; *Le Figaro*, 9 February 1934; *Le Flambeau*, 1 February 1934.

the centre dominated, while Radicals retained key posts and the right possessed only secondary ministries. Yet the government also expressed an authoritarian mood. The presence of Georges Rivollet, secretary-general of the Cartel des Combattants, at the Ministry of Pensions acknowledged the government's debt to the rioters. *Le Figaro* warned that 'the nation' would closely watch the government.[25] Doumergue was the first non-parliamentary Président du conseil in the history of the Third Republic; in June 1940, Maréchal Pétain, now Defence Minister, would become the second.

The latter's presence was especially significant, for occasionally he had been mentioned as a possible dictator or president, notably in the veteran press. As Lyautey put it, Pétain's presence 'covered the Army, Croix de feu and veterans'.[26] In 1935, an unscientific newspaper poll would put Pétain at the head of a list of potential dictators. In fact, the cautious Pétain did not actively aspire to the role. Lyautey did, and on 7 February he volunteered to take the head of the veterans if Daladier did not resign.[27] Later in 1934, other officers conspired with Vallat and a number of Fédération deputies, but Pétain demanded their removal from the Army. The Royalist press cited Weygand as a potential dictator.[28]

Recourse to authority was also evident in the use of decree powers to overcome parliamentary resistance to deflation.[29] The decrees cut *fonctionnaires*' wages by 10 per cent and veterans' pensions by 3 per cent.[30] In accordance with liberal orthodoxy, the government aimed to reduce taxes and interest rates (by reducing government borrowing), and thus cut costs for industry. Inevitably, the decrees alienated the left, but conservatives faced discontent too. Joseph-Barthelémy for the centre and Gustave Guerin for the Fédération both complained that they encouraged taxpayers to inform on each other. Guérin added that the decrees increased the tax burden. On 21 December 1934, the Fédération deposed a motion inviting the government to modify them.[31]

In any case, conservatives saw the decrees as a stopgap, for only constitutional reform could ensure the primacy of national over sectional interests in parliament. The right had long advocated dissolution and reform, but the centre historically sought institutional without constitutional reform. Now, key centrists changed their minds. Paul Reynaud advocated immediate dissolution, proportional representation, and revision. The Alliance reaffirmed its commitment to the family vote and proportional representation, and added the right of dissolution for the Président de la République, the withdrawal of spending initiative from the Chamber,

25 *Le Figaro*, 9 February 1934.

26 *Un Lyautey inconnu. Correspondance et journal inédits 1874–1934*, ed. André Le Révérend (Paris, 1979), 339, 11 Febraury 1934.

27 *Un Lyautey inconnu*, 344–9, 11 February 1934.

28 Jacques Nobécourt, *Le colonel de La Rocque (1885–1946), ou les pièges du nationalisme chrétien* (Paris, 1997), 273–8; Millington, *From Victory*, 61–5; Marc Ferro, *Pétain* (Paris, 1987), 8–11, 118–21.

29 Julian Jackson, *The Politics of Depression in France* (Cambridge, 1985), 88–92.

30 Jackson, *The Politics of Depression*, 81–92.

31 *Le Temps*, 25 December 1935; *La Nation*, 5 January 1935.

and the 'representation of collective forces in the state'.[32] Cross-party initiatives became possible. Deputy Jacques Bardoux of the Fédération formed the Comité technique pour la réforme de l'État, which mostly attracted jurists of the centre.

There were extra-parliamentary initiatives too. At the end of June, left and right came together in the États généraux de la jeunesse, but only a negative unity emerged. More successful was the Plan du 9 Juillet, elaborated by a group of Neo-Socialists, dissident Radicals, Croix de feu, JP, and Polytechniciens, among whom Jean Coutrot was pre-eminent. The Plan's interventionist economic proposals were contentious, but its proposed constitutional reform—reinforcement of the Présidence du conseil, reduction of parliament's right to initiate spending, and strengthening of the Conseil national économique (CNE)—were more banal. The Plan revealed that some centrist and left-wing organizers had re-evaluated their options. They advocated a transitional government whose nature they could not foresee, and some of them ended up on the extreme right.[33] In the veterans movement, the Republican Union fédérale (UF) endorsed the constitutional reform long advocated by the UNC. The UF promised that if the government did not undertake constitutional reform or purge Staviskites by 8 July, the veterans themselves would take the helm, and the UNC backed the threat. Yet as the deadline arrived, doubts surfaced in both camps. The UNC feared toppling the government, while many in the UF turned against reform.[34]

Indeed, the 6 February consensus soon disappeared, as the Radicals, and, more importantly from our perspective, the centre, opposed the right's version of constitutional reform. It did not help that Tardieu set the tone. In 1932, he had concluded that parliament could not reform itself, engaged in a quasi-Bonapartist appeal to the 'depths of the nation' and advocated use of the referendum. In fact, this was an 'Orléano-Bonapartisme', for Tardieu railed against unions, demanded a 'statut des fonctionnaires', and condemned government intervention in the economy.[35] He preferred the upper-class lecture circuit to 'vain' demonstrations, arguing that only political and moral action could master the crisis.[36] He resisted appeals to join Chiappe, Mercier, and Kerillis in a league. Tardieu's campaign found favour only with the right. Yet Marin and Wendel had little time for him, still blaming him for undermining the Fédération in the previous legislature.[37] Flandin too was suspicious of Tardieu, condemning in July his efforts to revive the Stavisky Affair.

Equally worrying for the centre was that the right demanded a veritable constitution to replace the 'botched' 1875 laws. The right's anti-parliamentarianism shaded into frank hostility to democracy. It saw the pursuit of 'staviskites' as a means to purge the regime and definitively weaken Radicalism. Denunciations of

[32] *L'Alliance démocratique*, 9 May 1934.

[33] François Monnet, *Refaire la République. André Tardieu, une dérive réactionnaire, 1876–1945* (Paris, 1993), 311–12.

[34] Monnet, *Refaire*, 316–17; Millington, *From Victory*, 83–103.

[35] Nicholas Roussellier, 'André Tardieu et la crise du constitutionalisme libéral (1933–1934)', *Vingtième siècle* 21 (January–March 1989), 57–70; Monnet, *Refaire*, 307–64.

[36] André Tardieu, *Sur la pente* (Paris, 1935), xxiv.

[37] Monnet, *Refaire*, 255–7; Jeanneney, *François de Wendel*, 481–3.

the 'rule of number' were legion, as were tirades against immorality and decadence. For Bardoux, the obsession with number and uniformity was responsible for overproduction and the economic crisis, and the swamping of the elite by the mass.[38] Others saw constitutional reform as a means to protect Catholic liberties,[39] or to a roll-back of the reforms of 1926–1932, especially Social Insurance. For the agrarian wing of the Fédération, constitutional reform and corporatism went together: the Breton agrarian Hervé de Guébriant regretted that the Republic entrusted vital interests to hazardous elections and accorded the same rights to the unmarried, lazy, ignorant, and degenerate as to the father, the educated, the philanthropist, and the man charged with responsibilities by his peers. For others, corporatism was a 'mystique', capable of mobilizing the peasantry in an age in which only the mass counted.[40]

On 4 October, Doumergue outlined his plan for revision, and submitted a definitive version to the Council of Ministers on 2 November. His proposals equipped the Président du conseil with the power of dissolution, strengthened the independence of the judiciary, and gave the CNE the right to initiate legislation. *A statut des fonctionnaires* abolished their right to strike.[41] The Radicals rejected these proposals. They opposed stripping the Senate of its right to veto dissolution and above all would not accept a reform that was intended to facilitate deflation; their alternative proposals involved moderate state intervention and social democracy.[42]

In the centre, few quarrelled with Doumergue's view that in the modern world the final decision must be taken by the head of government in the light of his 'culture and human and historical experience' on the advice of 'technicians', or that classical education must be restored.[43] Yet the conversion of prominent figures to actual constitutional reform masked others' suspicion. The Alliance rejected both the Radicals' 'corporatist' (actually social-democratic) schemes, and those who desired a 'grandiose upheaval', threatening 'who knows what dictatorship'.[44] As Alliance deputy Pierre Duchesne-Fournet put it, 'We must envisage reform with courage and firmness; that is all the more difficult because those who criticize the Republic most bitterly are the first to propagate disorder and abuses.'[45] At its Arras congress on 3 November, the Alliance charged de Fels—an opponent of reform—with presenting the report on constitutional reform, but did not publish it in the party press, claiming that his opinions were 'personal'! The manner in which Doumergue went about reform provoked centrists to oppose him. In a radio speech, he

[38] Jacques Bardoux, *Le Drame français. Refaire l'état ou subir la force* (Paris, 1935).

[39] Archives nationales, 317 AP 74, Fonds Louis Marin (hereafter ANFLM, carton/dossier no.), Boulenger to Marin, 1 June 1934.

[40] David Bensoussan, *Combats pour une Bretagne catholique et rurale. Les Droites bretonnes dans l'entre-deux-guerres* (Paris, 2006), 471–5.

[41] Monnet, *Refaire*, 333; Georges and Édouard Bonnefous, *Histoire politique de la Troisième République*, vii. *La Course vers l'abime* (Paris, 1967), 240–3.

[42] Jackson, *The Politics of Depression*, 90–1.

[43] *Journal des Débats*, 9 February 1934.

[44] *L'Alliance démocratique*, 24, 31 October.

[45] Jean Quellien, *Bleus, blancs, rouges. Politique et élections dans le Calvados 1870–1939* (Caen, 1986), 305.

threatened dissolution, and then in parliament demanded the vote of temporary taxes—signs that he was preparing for executive rule. Herriot felt able to resign from the cabinet and precipitate Doumergue's fall because he knew that Flandin was ready to form a Concentration government.

Flandin: Towards Centrist Authoritarianism

Flandin became president of the Alliance démocratique in 1933, Tardieu having refused the position, doubtless realizing the extent of resistance to his right-wing strategy. For the first time, an Alliance leader possessed real authority in parliament, and he was well placed to impose his concentration line. Flandin declared his desire to keep his distance from the Fédération, 'in which dominates the concern to preserve the existing social order, even its excesses and abuses'.[46] In alliance with moderate Radicals, Flandin sought to arm democracy in the struggle against dictatorships. He used collective psychology to advocate organization of democracy and provide it with a mystique. He passed legislation permitting the dissolution of the leagues, thus earning their enmity.

Flandin, like Kerillis, claimed to be inspired by British Conservatism, and he revived the Alliance. Membership increased to around 20,000 in fifteen departmental and three regional federations, in Paris, the Loire, and the Gironde. Reflecting the spirit of the times, the Alliance created a youth group, the Jeunesse républicaine française, and a women's section, the Ligue de la femme française. Nevertheless, the Alliance did not become a structured mass party. Its electoral programme remained general; members sometimes confronted each other in elections and parliamentary indiscipline was endemic. The party was unashamedly elitist: one member asked 'what could be done with a committee with too numerous members, rendered nervous by the simple effect of number, [they are] centres of permanent agitation, in which rivalries would soon appear? What we need is to create cells in which the members will be usefully chosen.'[47]

There was also a new accent: the Alliance press lauded 'notre chef', Flandin, for his foresight, character, and personification of the party's principles, in a manner that recalled both the personality cult and Fayolist managerialism. Flandin expected the elite to create a 'movement of opinion', or 'mystique'. He criticized Tardieu for ignoring the crowd, and the Popular Front and Croix de feu for generating a mystique that mobilized crowds but not an elite capable of converting faith into acts. Flandin's recommended mystique was economic, for he believed that political mystiques were anachronistic.[48]

He maintained that a sound economic mystique should underpin Concentration.[49] He found support in the proposal of the Radical former Jeune Turc, Émile Roche, for a 'Tiers Parti', based on a an 'économie dirigée'. Flandin also drew on

[46] *L'Alliance démocratique*, 17 June 1933.

[47] *L'Alliance démocratique*, 17 January 1936; François Audigier, *L'Anachronisme de l'Alliance démocratique (1933–37)*, *Vingtième siècle* 47 (July–September 1995), 147–57.

[48] *L'Alliance démocratique*, 18 Novembre 1935, 20 March 1936.

[49] *L'Alliance démocratique*, 18 November 1935.

the German Freiburg School of economics, for which the market did not naturally exist, but required state intervention to create it.[50] Paradoxically, he aimed to reduce state intervention in the economy through 'counter-interventions'. He warned also that further public spending reductions were impossible.[51]

To realize these counter-interventions, Flandin implemented institutional reforms designed to render the state more effective without constitutional reform. He wanted a 'strong but liberal state'.[52] His government organized the Présidence du conseil in accordance with Fayolist principles, endowing it with a secretariat located at the Hôtel Matignon. It reformed parliamentary regulations to give the majority greater power to regulate debates and eliminate 'abuses of the right to speak'. These measures would create a 'general staff' able to coordinate policy, if necessary through decree-laws, and improve parliamentary productivity.[53]

Organization would also regularize relations between big business and the state. Better informed policy would allow the calculation of profitability in the interests of the whole national economy, thus allowing targeting of government support.[54] More concretely, Minister of Commerce Marchandeau deposed a bill to make business cartels legally enforceable in sectors in which a majority of producers possessing a majority of equipment demanded it. Cartels would regulate prices and production, because it was 'wasteful to produce goods that lacked a market'. At the same time, the government sought to stimulate production through reduction of interest rates, to be achieved by financing government by issuing treasury bonds rather than competing with business in the open capital market.[55] Another plank of Flandin's counter-intervention was to abolish the minimum grain price, in the expectation that lowering bread prices would reduce wage pressure. That policy involved spending enormous sums to acquire excess grain.

Flandin failed on all fronts. The Marchandeau proposal provoked quarrels within business, everyone accusing the other of 'Malthusianism', and ultimately most businesses opposed the law.[56] The right either condemned it as another example of *étatisme* or proposed corporatist alternatives. Meanwhile, Wendel and the Regents sabotaged the 'inflationary' interest-rate plan.[57] An enraged Flandin attacked 'privileges that can only be tolerated in the obscurity of confused situations', thus earning the applause of the left, while Tardieu regretted 'hearing the vocabulary of the Front commun (of Socialists and Communists) in the mouth of

[50] Arnaud Chaumette, 'Sauver une France libérale. Pierre-Étienne Flandin entre stratégie centriste et attraction autoritaire', in Gilles Morin and Gilles Richard (eds), *Les Deux France du Front populaire. Chocs et contre-chocs* (Paris, 2008), 117–30 at 123.

[51] Pierre-Étienne Flandin, *Discours. Le Ministère Flandin (novembre 1934–mai 1935)* (Paris, 1935), 87, 151, 174.

[52] *L'Alliance démocratique*, 18 January 1934.

[53] Flandin, *Discours*, 61–7, 88–9, 92–4, 172–3; Nicholas Roussellier, 'Gouvernement et parlement dans l'entre-deux-guerres', in Marc-Olivier Baruch and Vincent Duclert (eds), *Serviteurs de l'état. Une Histoire politique de l'administration française, 1875–1945* (Paris, 2000), 109–26.

[54] Flandin, *Discours*, 27 November 1934, 45–55.

[55] Flandin, *Discours*, 179.

[56] Flandin, *Discours*, 153–67; Alain Chatriot, *La Démocratie sociale à la française* (Paris, 2003), 263–6.

[57] Jeanneney, *François de Wendel*, 308–23; *La Nation*, 16 March 1935.

a bourgeois'.[58] The abolition of the minimum wheat price made Flandin the most hated man in the countryside, and drove peasants towards Dorgères and the Croix de feu. The FC and Dorgèrists renewed calls for a tax strike, a proposal that *Le Journal des Débats* condemned as 'revolutionary'.[59] When in May 1935 the government sought decree powers to deal with a new financial crisis, many conservatives did not trust the 'socialisant' Flandin, and he fell on 31 May 1935.[60] However, his reform of the Présidence du conseil, designed to enable the competent to formulate and coordinate economic policy, proved useful to his successor.[61]

Laval: The Crisis of Parliamentary Conservatism

In reaction against Flandin's 'socialism', the succeeding Laval government turned back to the right and promised deflation, yet combined it with expensive efforts to organize the economy. Laval obtained decree powers not simply to make cuts, but to avoid devaluation, a brief he interpreted widely. Thanks to Flandin, experts, including the technocrat Raoul Dautry, the business journalist and former centre deputy Claude-Joseph Gignoux, and the civil servant Jacques Rueff, contributed to the decrees. Three batches of decrees increased taxes and imposed another 10 per cent cut in government spending, including interest on *rentes*, while raising support for agricultural prices and introducing measures promoting industrial organization, trade liberalization, and investment. These measures added sixty *milliards* to spending.

In principle, Laval's measures should have pleased business. They combined deflation with the consultation of 'experts', thus avoiding state control and compulsory corporatism.[62] Yet as had happened under Loucheur and Clémentel, organization appeared in practice to mean intervention.[63] Wendel saw reduction in payment of *rentes* as an attack on capital, while Perret denounced the role of irresponsible experts. An attempt to enforce cartels by decree provoked enormous controversy.[64] Anyway, deflation did not produce the expected recovery.

Ordinary conservative voters rarely contested the decrees in principle, and often denounced their softness. Yet they demanded exemption for themselves, usually in the 'national interest'.[65] The natalist Paul Haury cancelled his subscription to *La Nation* because two Fédération deputies had proposed a reduction in family allowances paid to *fonctionnaires*.[66] Another conservative demanded that *fonctionnaires*

[58] Flandin, *Discours*, 180; Tardieu, *Sur la pente*, xxiv–xxv.

[59] Robert O. Paxton, *French Peasant Fascism: Henry Dorgères' Greenshirts and the Crises of French Agriculture* (Oxford, 1997), 33–5; Hoisington, *Jacques Lemaigre-Dubreuil*, 43–4.

[60] Jackson, *The Politics of Depression*, 99–105.

[61] Roussellier, 'Gouvernement', 119–21.

[62] Alexandre Israël, *La Réforme de L'état devant les partis* (Paris, 1934), 63–7.

[63] Kevin Passmore, 'Business, corporatism and the crisis of the French Third Republic: the example of the silk industry in Lyon', *Historical Journal* 38, no. 4 (1995), 959–87; Jackson, *The Politics of Depression*, 105–11.

[64] Jeanneney, *François de Wendel*, 540–2; *La Nation*, 27 July 1935.

[65] *Le Temps*, 1–2 November 1935 and *La Nation*, 16 November 1935 denounced rumours of amendment of the decrees.

[66] ANFLM, 72, Maillard to Guiter, 25 July 1935.

who were veterans should be exempt from wage cuts. The falling wheat price radicalized the peasantry.[67] In spite of the huge proportion of tax income spent on them, farmers complained that their interests had been sacrificed to middlemen, export industries, workers, and *fonctionnaires*, a view apparently confirmed by the government's efforts to reduce consumer prices for meat and bread. Business replied in kind, condemning excessive agricultural protectionism.[68]

Authoritarianism

In the winter of 1935–1936, conservatives were in an impasse. The centre and right were at loggerheads over constitutional reform, deflation, and the leagues. Successive economic policies had failed. The decree laws provoked discontent among conservative electors and helped to cement the Popular Front. The Communists seemingly ruled the streets. Many conservatives concluded that the free market and liberal parliamentarianism were outdated. We have already noted the increasing use of decree laws. The turn to authoritarianism was manifest in other ways too.

In March 1936, René Dommange, Vallat, and Le Cour Grandmaison, deputies at the junction of AF and the Fédération, proposed to the Chamber a system of decentralized corporations, similar to the schemes of conservative agrarians and the Fédération nationale catholique (FNC). Self-regulation of the profession would overcome the anarchy of liberalism and ensure experts a say in policy formulation, while avoiding the statism of fascism or Socialism.[69] Corporatists were perhaps unaware that in Germany and Italy too some had presented corporatism as an alternative to state intervention. In fact, the belief that corporations could manage their own affairs depended implicitly on the establishment of an authoritarian state and the purging from the profession of 'antinational elements'.[70]

Authoritarianism was also evident in the right's collaboration with the leagues. We have already seen that many Fédération deputies belonged to the JP. Kerillis, who had previously attempted to steer the JP in a parliamentary direction, endorsed its re-discovered hard-line and now supported the Croix de feu too. Fewer Fédération deputies belonged to the latter, but they included Vallat, Henriot, and Ybarnégaray.[71] Support was higher among ordinary activists. In 1935, the Fédération mayor of Saint-Paul-de-Vence (Alpes Maritimes) led a 300-strong Fédération committee to the Croix de feu because Marin had allegedly pursued 'a policy of good wives'. He promised that the people would soon sweep career politicians away.[72]

[67] Jackson, *The Politics of Depression*, 101; *La Nation*, 26 January 1935.

[68] Kevin Passmore, *From Liberalism to Fascism: The Right in a French Province* (Cambridge, 1997), 182.

[69] *Action française* 5, 12 April 1936; Bensoussan, *Combats*, 470–88.

[70] Passmore, 'Business', 982–3; Benoussan, *Combats*, 474–88.

[71] ANFLM, Guiter to Marin, 23 August 1935; W.D. Irvine, *French Conservatism in Crisis: The Republican Federation of France* (Baton Rouge, 1979), 98–126.

[72] ANFLM, 72, Aubeuf to Guiter, 14 June 1935, and Guiter to Marin, 17 and 20 June, 5 July 1935.

Some Fédération deputies had reservations about the leagues: Deputy André Parmentier (wrongly) claimed to be the only democrat in the Fédération.[73] In Normandy, another deputy resigned from the parliamentary Union républicaine démocratique (URD) in protest at Marin's extremism and condemned the Croix de feu's anti-parliamentarianism; yet another complained that the league stirred up disorder.[74] Deputy Jacques Poitou-Duplessy argued that the levers of power were not in the streets, and that 'certain members' were wrong to advocate force because it provoked electoral abstention on the right. The leagues were a bulwark against Communism, he admitted, but were unreliable.[75]

The centre was more hostile to the leagues, but not exempt from authoritarianism. In November 1935, Deputy Maurice Ajam claimed that the leagues expressed the stay-at-home bourgeoisie's justifiable fear of the *banlieue rouge*.[76] The Alliance's youth group, founded in 1934, demonstrated certain ambiguities. It was meant to free the Alliance from dependence upon the JP to keep order at its meetings, and while most members were *laïque* Moderate Republicans, some demanded the cleansing of public morals. The Lyon group was founded by a former member of the JP; it called for the Alliance to reconcile the French 'above the old parties'.[77]

Other centrists were determined opponents of the leagues. Laurent Bonnevay chaired the enquiry into the events of 6 February, and became a hate figure on the far right for his condemnation of the leagues. In his Monts du Beaujolais constituency, Bonnevay joined the Confédération française des travailleurs chrétiens (CFTC) and the Parti démocrate populaire (PDP) in condemning wage cuts and described Perret as 'leader of the fascist politicians of the Rhône'.[78] Flandin, as Président du conseil, claimed that those who attacked the government's lack of energy were suffering from a 'neurosis of the baton'.[79] The Communists hoped to include centrists such as Flandin in the Popular Front, and in January 1936 he outraged many of his colleagues by joining the pro-Popular Front Sarraut government that succeeded Laval. The leagues were a product both of hostility to Communism and of the crisis of conservatism.

THE LEAGUES

On the eve of 6 February, the leagues jointly enrolled over 100,000 members, taking account of the overlap in membership between them. They enjoyed considerable sympathy in parliament, notably in the Fédération. They espoused radicalized anti-parliamentarianism and anti-communism, while seeking to regenerate or supplant the established political and social elite. They reworked collective psychology, through redefinition of the mystique.

[73] ANFLM, Guiter to Marin, 10 September 1935.
[74] Quellien, *Bleus*, 305–7.
[75] *La Nation*, 10 August 1935.
[76] *L'Alliance démocratique*, 1, 18 November 1935.
[77] Passmore, *From Liberalism*, 191.
[78] Passmore, *From Liberalism*, 191–3.
[79] *La Nation*, 14 September 1935.

Soon after 6 February, the JP, Solidarité française, and FC formed the Front national, under Lyautey's patronage. AF would not join a 'Republican' organization, but associated itself with the initiative. It left autonomy to individual leagues, while pooling their resources for meetings. In Brittany, Delahaye's Alliance Nationale de l'Ouest (ANO) lent its support to the Front, which took on some importance. Even there, it did not secure the backing of the Fédération or the Croix de feu.[80] In the end, the Front national did not prevent the decline of its constituent elements, perhaps thanks to too close association with the Doumergue government. In late 1935, in the hope of preserving the JP's parliamentary position, Taittinger proposed merging the Front national groups into the Croix de feu.[81] La Rocque rejected the proposal, aware that, along with Défense paysan, only his movement really counted.

DÉFENSE PAYSAN

By late 1935, Défense paysan was influential in Brittany, Normandy, Loir-et-Cher, and Eure-et-Loir.[82] In Alsace, Dorgères made contact with the Bauernbund, which attracted Catholic Alsatian-speaking peasant support; the movement attacked international capitalism and its political allies, while pursuing regionalist and familialist objectives.[83] Dorgères also allied with the conservative agrarian movement, of which he had hitherto been critical. In July 1933, Défense paysan joined with the Parti agraire and Union nationale des syndicats agricoles (UNSA) in the Front paysan, thus gaining access to the enormous resources of the agrarian unions. In the following month, the president of the Ille-et-Vilaine agricultural union reported that Dorgères had agreed to become his 'auxiliary'. In the summer of 1935, a representative of the Finistère Office central told an audience of Greenshirts that government was responsive only to 'strength and the dynamism of disciplined number'.[84] To cement the conservative alliance Dorgères abandoned his call for state support for agriculture and accepted corporatism. In Calvados, the UNSA leader Jacques Le Roy Ladurie and Dorgères, along with the Croix de feu, stirred up peasant antagonism to parliament; they profited from the once Bonapartist peasantry's distrust of tax collectors, which the tradition of semi-clandestine distillation of alcohol kept alive. In 1935, Dorgères joined the campaign to restore the so-called 'privilège des bouilleurs de cru', during which several hundred Calvados municipal councillors resigned and refused to organize new elections.[85]

[80] Bensoussan, *Combats*, 496–7.

[81] Jean Philippet, 'Le Temps des ligues. Pierre Taittinger et les Jeunesses patriotes', thèse de doctorat, IEP Paris, 2000, 2044–79.

[82] The following paragraphs rely upon Bensousan, *Combats*, 427–59.

[83] Christian Baechler, *Le Parti catholique Alsacien. du Reichsland à la République jacobine* (Paris, 1982), 629–32.

[84] Bensoussan, *Combats*, 431–2.

[85] Quellien, *Bleus*, 327–31.

Cooperation with conservatives did not make Dorgères their creature. On the one hand, agrarians turned to Dorgères because the condemnation of AF and defeat in the 1932 elections had weakened them. Agrarians had little choice but to back Dorgères' immensely popular resistance to forced land sales, although they sometimes tried to moderate them. On the other hand, Défense paysan had not entirely abandoned its radicalism. Activists of the progressive Cultivateurs-cultivants joined Défense paysan, and the emergent Jeunesse agricole chrétienne (JAC) may have contributed to it too. The Church opposed Dorgères, but Guébriant reassured the sceptical clergy that the Front paysan complemented the JAC's efforts to create an anti-communist peasant elite.[86] In fact, Dorgères spoke little of Guébriant's Christian social order. He sought to promote the peasants as a class, not to buttress notables. He called for a leader 'from the people', like Hitler or Mussolini, and in 1935 he envisaged a 'March on Paris'.[87]

Like Fascists in Italy, Dorgèrism combined extreme hostility to the left with antagonism to the liberal economic and political order and with ambiguous relations with conservatives. Without approaching the extremes of Nazism, the movement was antisemitic. Yet Dorgèrisme lacked a mass party, struggled to reach beyond the peasantry, and was organizationally dependent on conservative unions. By the winter of 1935–1936, it suffered from the rivalry of the Croix de feu.[88]

The Croix de Feu

The Croix de feu's seemingly equivocal behaviour on 6 February permitted it to claim that it held the fate of the nation in its hands and could choose its moment to act. Its combination of restraint, independence, and threatened insurrection held the key to its success. It promised an ordered society and strong state, able to arbitrate the conflicting interests that seemingly made government impossible. It also condemned established conservatism and the government, and insisted that honest people might legitimately take defence against Communism upon themselves. Thus, the league, like Fascism and Nazism, emerged partly from a radicalization of conservatism, from a sort of revolution in the name of order. It also shared with Fascism and Nazism extreme nationalism and militarism, the call for a moral revolution against decadence, and for the triumph of action over words, coupled with hostility to parliamentarianism, liberalism, Socialism, and Communism.

Yet given Fascism and Nazism were diverse and frequently changed their priorities, it is as easy to find differences as similarities. The Croix de feu was xenophobic, indeed, racist, but except in Algeria its antisemitism was insignificant compared to that of the Nazis or even AF. And whereas Hitler openly (if inconsistently) promised to abolish democracy when he won power, the Croix de feu claimed to be Republican and advocated temporary dictatorship. The Croix de feu more closely resembled Italian Fascism—more so than some historians have allowed.

86 Bensoussan, *Combats*, 435–55.
87 Bibliothèque nationale de France, Fonds Flandin, carton 65 (15 May 1935).
88 Bensoussan, *Combats*, 443–59.

Yet while the league stressed national unity and wished to defend the Empire, it did not prioritize social and political mobilization for expansionist war. Since these similarities and differences were incommensurate, it is impossible to say whether one or another was more essential.

We may more usefully ask how the Croix de feu saw matters. On the one hand, La Rocque regarded as 'interesting' the 'results' that Fascism and Nazism had achieved through participation in elections and meditated on the lessons to be learned.[89] Some members regarded themselves as fascist, notably in Montpellier, where Royalists had long admired Mussolini.[90] On the other hand, Croix de feu leaders denied affinities with Fascism and especially Nazism, and insisted on the league's Republicanism. La Rocque considered that Fascism meant the 'cult of the state, a sort of national religion', whereas the Croix de feu, he said, advocated service, organization, regulation, protection, and punishment.[91] Like other conservatives, he appears unaware of disputes among Fascists and Nazis concerning the role of the state in the corporatist system, or that corporatism had often been presented there too as an alternative to state control.

Notwithstanding, La Rocque avoided identification with Nazism because he viewed it as an extreme form of Pan-Germanism. Since Italy had been an ally, Fascism was less problematic. Yet as Pozzo di Borgo put it, the Croix de feu must avoid alienating the 'men from diverse tendencies and formations within our ranks'. It must 'avoid all the political categories that are currently in use, that is proclaim ourselves neither Bonapartist, Royalist, Republican or Fascist, and never pronounce these words that sow discord'.[92] Also, in keeping with the precepts of collective psychology, La Rocque believed that the elite could not govern against the Republican and national 'psychology' of the French people. And like earlier nationalist movements, La Rocque defined his movement in opposition to monarchism: he had good reason to do so because his brother was a Royalist.

In fact, the ideology and practice of the Croix de feu derived from a mixture of French and foreign precedents. The fascination with number and manoeuvre born of the war inspired the league's notorious paramilitary demonstrations. The FNC initiated the use of mass meetings. In 1919, Démocratie nouvelle created paramilitary groups recruited from veterans, but the JP and Faisceau were the first to develop significant paramilitary organizations, while Valois' H-Hour rhetoric and mobilizations anticipated La Rocque's. The structure of the Croix de feu also resembled that of the Faisceau, with its hierarchy of sub-groups organized around veterans, non-combatants, and women's groups. Indeed, in the Gironde, a group of veterans who had moved from the Faisceau to Hervé's Parti national révolutionnaire and to the UNC founded the Croix de feu section.[93] The Croix de feu's

[89] ANFLR, 193, 2 January 1936.

[90] Philippe Secondy, *La Persistance du Midi blanc. L'Hérault (1789–1962)* (Perpignan, 2006), 237–8.

[91] *La Petite gironde*, 27 October 1935.

[92] Didier Leschi, 'L'Étrange cas la Rocque', in *Le Mythe de l'allergie française au fascisme*, 155–94.

[93] Sylvain Trussardi, 'Faisceau, Croix de feu, PSF. Trois mouvements girondins du milieu des années 1920 à la fin des années 1930', *Parlements*, Special issue (2005), 55–64.

'manoeuvres', in which it drove in convoys to towns and enacted its ability to fight Communism, were copied from Italy, but were far less violent.

The inseparability of French and transnational currents is especially evident in the Croix de feu's desire to compete with the mass mobilization of the 'totalitarian' regimes through the promotion of the mystique Croix de feu. The dictatorships had reworked Le Bon's ideas, which had never been exclusively French anyway. Collective psychology was still less exclusively the monopoly of the extreme right. La Rocque often placed the Soviet Union in the same category as Fascist and Nazi dictatorships, seeing all three as characterized by subordination of the individual to the state. The Croix de feu would reawaken the French mystique, which La Rocque saw as characterized by 'amicability' and 'measure'.[94] Likewise, the league's social services would inculcate the social spirit that allegedly motivated Nazi and Communist elites.[95]

The Croix de feu used the notion of the 'mystique' to create what Le Bon (and some contemporary historians) saw as a 'political religion'. However, whereas Le Bon associated political religion with the Socialists, La Rocque related it to the positive potential of the crowd. He claimed that militarized hierarchy ensured the discipline and predominance of national sentiment in the mass. He evoked

> the awakening of the individual and collective conscience of the people through the flourishing of its essential wellsprings, spontaneously and through encouragement, in the protective, coordinating, and guiding framework of renovated and imposed national discipline.[96]

The league assigned sacred status to its objective, borrowed the paraphernalia of traditional religion, and subsumed Catholicism into the mystique.[97] La Rocque spoke of the Croix de feu as engaged in a 'crusade'.[98] Members were 'the faithful in the same faith'. He asked, 'Who will prevail against our patriotic faith, our incorruptible poverty, our enthusiastic discipline, our cult of the dead and our passionate gift to our children?'[99] La Rocque's writings had a biblical status, to be elucidated and commented upon. At monster meetings, the faithful communed with the charismatic leader, expressing their mystical bond with him by using the fascist salute, even though it was not officially a part of the league's rituals.[100] One should not dismiss as 'imitation' a gesture that expressed ritual solidarity with one's comrades and loyalty to the leader, towards whom one's arm was outstretched. A report on a rally commemorating the battle of the Marne recorded that after

[94] *La Petite gironde*, 27 October 1935.

[95] Laura Lee Downs, '"Nous plantions les trois couleurs". Action sociale féminine et recomposition des politiques de la droite française. Le cas du mouvement Croix de feu et du Parti social français, 1934–1960', *Revue d'histoire moderne et contemporaine* 58, no. 3 (2011), 118–62 at 120.

[96] François de La Rocque, *Service public* (Paris, 1934), 19.

[97] Emilio Gentile, 'The sacralization of politics: definitions, interpretations and reflections on the question of secular religion and totalitarianism', *Totalitarian Movements and Political Religions* 1, no. 1 (2000), 18–55.

[98] La Rocque, *Service public*, 22.

[99] La Rocque, *Service public*, 222, 269, 271.

[100] Jean-Paul Brunet, *Jacques Doriot, du communisme au fascism* (Paris, 1986), 203.

La Rocque's speech 'a human tide rushed towards the leader to cry out its faith, its tenderness, and its devotion'.[101] To propagate the mystique, La Rocque emphasized the repetition of a few 'master ideas': restoration of public morality, state authority, and the creation of a culture in which the interests of France would be paramount.[102] Party orators were instructed to avoid démonstrations savantes and end with a eulogy of La Rocque.[103]

Of course, we should not take Le Bon's categories literally. The 'crowd' did not really possess a collective mind, and neither did the reiteration of images dictate its behaviour. Members brought their own agendas to collective action, conscious and unconscious, and they understood the movement to which they belonged in diverse, often contradictory, ways.[104] The notions of elite, mass, and mystique were historical constructions, used in struggles between and within political movements. The Croix de feu appealed to groups that considered themselves unrepresented within parliamentary conservatism, even though some possessed considerable social and cultural power.

Take Catholicism. The league placed the mystique *Croix de feu* above religion, yet some leaguers assumed that this mystique was Catholic. They were encouraged to do so because the Church was less hostile to the Croix de feu than it had been to AF. It waited until July 1936 to warn Catholic Action to keep out of the leagues.[105] It hesitated because of dissent in the hierarchy and because the Croix de feu, unlike AF, did not presume to speak for the Church and claimed to be Republican. Moreover, some members endorsed the Church's demands for fair treatment; Vallat detected a fundamental similarity between the FNC and the Croix de feu, for both wanted 'bread, peace, and liberty'.[106] La Rocque explained to the Catholic newspaper *Sept* that although the league was 'outside' the religious sphere, it was compatible with his own faith.[107] The league press rarely mentioned religion, except to stress that Jews, Protestants, and Catholics were all welcome in the league.

The Croix de feu was also positioned in relation to struggles among Catholics. It attracted individuals involved in the nascent specialist Catholic Action movements, the Jeunesse ouvrière chrétienne (feminine), the Jeunesse agricole chrétienne (féminine), and the Jeunesse étudiante chrétienne, all of which were ambiguous concerning their goals. Politically, they ranged from sympathy for the left-wing Jeune république to the extreme right, while theologically they included integrists committed to living their faith publicly and others who were prepared to play down Catholicism in order to reach the workers and peasants in their 'milieu'. In the Rhône, the JAC chaplain reported 'a growing confusion' between the Croix de

[101] *Le Flambeau*, 5 October, 16 November 1935.

[102] La Rocque, *Service public*, 14–19; *Le Flambeau*, 1 April 1934; ANFLR 451, 5 February 1934.

[103] ANFLR, 81, 'Régulations pour un bureau de propagande'.

[104] Kevin Passmore, 'The gendered genealogy of political religions theory', *Gender & History* 20, no. 3 (2008), 644–68.

[105] Pierre Christophe, *1936, Les Catholiques et le Front populaire* (Paris, 1986), 121.

[106] *La Nation*, 2 May 1936.

[107] Kennedy, *Reconciling*, 61.

feu and Catholic Action.[108] Also present in the league was the young Catholic activist, François Mitterrand.[109] Catholic Action defined itself in opposition to 'superficial' conservative Catholicism, and thus reinforced the populism of the Croix de feu, even if figures such as Mitterrand were solidly bourgeois.

Reference to the veterans also shaped the mystique, expressing the primacy of the nation as well as the league's combination of elitism and populism. In an allegedly materialist age, the league 'remained in contact with all the martyrs of French passion', and revived the 'national mystique, rich with heroism, self-denial and vigour, that of the days of Joan of Arc, Fontenoy, Valmy, Montmirail, and Verdun'.[110] The appeal to the veterans evoked both national unity and war, with its apocalyptic, quasi-religious predictions of a conflict between civilization and its enemies. It also placed the Croix de feu above Republican legality, and invested it with the task of judging and perhaps punishing the legal government. Many UNC veterans belonged to the Croix de feu.[111]

The veteran mystique encapsulated too the combination of order and insurrection in the Croix de feu. La Rocque drew inspiration from his one-time superior, Maréchal Lyautey. In his 'Le rôle social de l'officier', Lyautey had argued that the officer had to instil morale in his troops, a task that required knowledge of their predispositions and of collective psychology. In the interwar years, the officer corps developed an ethos of self-sacrifice for the nation, inspired by its high mortality rate in the Great War—an ethos easily transferable to the Croix de feu. Simultaneously, the veteran mystique introduced a new criterion for fitness to govern, thus potentially threatening the political order: communion with the veterans mattered more than the traditional pathways into power. This new veteran elite was egalitarian in that it shared a community of courage, while the military ethos reiterated hierarchy. That is why the Croix de feu's youth groups placed so much emphasis on leadership and self-mastery through active learning.[112] The Croix de feu rarely used the idea of the 'new man', often deployed in Italy. Yet there were many similarities. A PDP journalist lamented the Croix de feu's cult of 'action for action's sake'.[113]

The Croix de feu's economic ideas were equally complex. La Rocque's understanding of the elite reworked the military-industrial Fayolist tradition; Lyautey had maintained that officers had to be technicians and masters of organization. Fayol's grandson, also a management specialist, was a member of the league. Using Fayolist vocabulary, La Rocque regretted that the state had not adapted its organisms of regulation and study, enlarged its field of vision, warned, and forearmed. He wanted coordination of economic organisms, the CNE having achieved

[108] Gayet, Georges. 'L'Union du sud-est des syndicats agricoles', Mémoire de maîtrise, Lyon II, 1972, 73–4.

[109] Passmore, *From Liberalism*, 242.

[110] La Rocque, *Service Public*, 28.

[111] Millington, *From Vichy*, 107–32.

[112] Laura Lee Downs, '"Each and every one of you must become a chef": toward a social politics of working-class childhood on the extreme right in 1930s France', *The Journal of Modern History* 81, no 1 (March 2009), 1–44.

[113] Bensoussan, *Combats*, 497.

nothing.[114] The Croix de feu sympathizer, Georges Lamirand, future Vichy youth minister and author of the *Le Rôle social de l'ingénieur* (prefaced by Lyautey), combined Catholicism with science: it was insufficient, he claimed, for the engineer to master science and mathematics. If he was to reconcile capital and labour, he must have a vocation and be a leader.[115]

These ideas were compatible with membership in the league of both advocates of technical progress and of the spiritualist critique of productivism that had gained ground in the early 1930s. Thus, La Rocque condemned the 'cancerous overproduction of inflationary periods', and Gaston Rageot, president of the Société des gens de lettres de France, advanced views close to those of the *non-conformistes.*[116] In contrast, an engineer described machines as the means for man to liberate himself from animal tasks and move towards his 'destiny'.[117] The league saw aviation as both technical achievement and a means to propagate heroism, notably through the cult of Jean Mermoz, who joined the movement in 1935.[118]

Mercier was the most famous, if not the most prominent, of the technocrats in the movement. The so-called 'Maréchaux' led the VN until the summer of 1935. They included the banker Bertrand de Maud'huy, who had participated in the Plan du 9 Juillet, Pierre Pucheu, the secretary of the Comptoir Sidérurgique, and the mining engineer, Robert Loustau, who had belonged to X-Crise and the *non-conformist* Ordre nouveau. The Maréchaux broke with La Rocque because he refused to elaborate a detailed programme, yet their own closely resembled that presented in La Rocque's *Service public.*[119] The departure of the Maréchaux did not eliminate technocracy from the league. In the Rhône, Marcel Canat de Chizy, former president of the Lyonnais branch of the Catholic engineers' union, Union sociale des ingénieurs catholiques (USIC), espoused a Social Catholic third-way ideology.[120] In the league's women's section, Catholic charity blended with scientific understandings of the social question couched in the language of productivism. Two of the three women who had drawn up Redressement français' *Cahier* on social policy joined the Croix de feu.[121]

Turning to social origins, the overwhelming majority of members were bourgeois—in Lyon, at least, the Croix de feu was more bourgeois than the Fédération.[122] Members included businessmen, doctors, lawyers, and white-collar workers, especially

[114] La Rocque, *Service public*, 39.

[115] *Le Flambeau*, 1 December 1933; Georges Lamirand, *Le Rôle social de l'ingénieur. Scènes de la vie d'usine* (Paris, 1932).

[116] La Rocque, *Service public*, 39; Samuel Kalmann, *The Extreme Right in Interwar France: The Faisceau and the Croix de Feu* (London, 2008), 263–6. Kennedy, *Reconciling*, 63.

[117] *Le Flambeau*, I January 1934.

[118] Kennedy, *Reconciling*, 110–12.

[119] Laurent Kestel, 'De La Conversion en politique, genèse et institutionnalisation du Parti populaire français (1936–1940)', thèse de doctorat, Paris I (2005), 244–7.

[120] Passmore, *From Liberalism*, 173–5.

[121] Marie Diémer, Mlle Bassot, and Yvon de Robien, *Les Centres sociaux. L'enseignement ménager*, Cahiers du Redressement Francais, no. 20 (Paris, 1927); Kevin Passmore, '"Planting the tricolor in the citadels of communism," Women's social service in the Croix de feu and Parti social français', *Journal of Modern History* 71, no. 4 (December 1999), 814–51 at 839; Downs, 'Nous plantions les trois couleurs', 136.

[122] Passmore, *From Liberalism*, 240–1; Kennedy, *Reconciling*, 89.

from the private sector, all of whom traditionally voted for the right. The league did not bite into the constituency of the left, and probably not that of the centre either; consequently, public employees, artisans, small shopkeepers, and workers were underrepresented.[123] From late 1935 the Croix de feu began to recruit the peasantry.

Bourgeois predominance was compatible with populism and hostility to established conservatives. The Croix de feu mystique allegedly permitted La Rocque to commune with the people in the way that conventional conservatives (and the left) could not. He claimed that in spite of his 'encumbering name', he had been a trooper during the war and so his 'new companions in struggle'—the Croix de feu—accepted his leadership.[124] As 'men of action and thought', the Croix de feu must resist the old right's efforts to annexe them.[125] La Rocque claimed that on the day of reckoning, the 'guardians who have been unfaithful to their charge' would be at the head of the list of guilty: 'Their disavowals, their turpitudes will be proclaimed and punished.'[126] He opposed the idea of a parliamentary Union nationale, for only mobilization of the people in the Croix de feu could unite France. The Croix de feu often associated politicians with capitalism, denouncing the grip of international finance on France.

Neither did bourgeois origin rule out a sense of marginality. In Lyon, the previously mentioned Canat de Chizy did not get on with his employer, the president of the Chamber of Commerce and wealthy silk manufacturer, Henry Morel-Journel. The latter's brother Jacques, who allegedly resented his exclusion from the family business, led the Croix de feu in the Beaujolais. The league also recruited from the Lyonnais engineering industry and silk weaving firms, both of which complained of silk merchants' dominance in the city. In 1935, Lyonnais small business presented a member of the Croix de feu as an opposition candidate to the Chamber of Commerce.[127]

The large female membership, perhaps 100,000, of the Croix de feu reinforced this bourgeois populism.[128] We have seen that the league espoused a military, masculine ethos, and it insisted that women were predestined for childbirth and the home. However, separate spheres doctrine had always been contradictory. Bourgeois women had long undertaken the task of overcoming class hatred through charitable work outside the home; Catholic women saw charity as a means to regenerate a corrupt, materialistic, male world, and that ambition survived in the Croix de feu. However, whereas in the days of the Action libérale populaire (ALP) women had intervened in the proletarian family primarily as Christians, they had since the mid 1920s done so through a range of political parties, from the PDP to the JP. Now they did so as technicians inspired by the Croix de feu mystique. Moreover, under the influence of Catholic Action, women saw themselves as an

[123] Bensoussan, *Combats*, 492–5.
[124] La Rocque, *Service public*, 26.
[125] *Le Flambeau*, 1 January, 12 October 1935.
[126] *Le Flambeau*, 1 January, 6 April, 12 October 1935.
[127] Passmore, *From Liberalism*, 173–5.
[128] Passmore, "Planting the tricolor in the citadels of communism".

'elite', thus appropriating the categories of collective psychology. La Rocque's recourse to women would eventually replace the narrowly political action of the parliamentary right with a social form of activism.[129]

Technical training reinforced these women's claim to elite status. Their leaders were the product of the interwar expansion of professional health and social professions, reinforced after 1930 by the Social Insurance Law. Croix de feu women claimed a scientific ability to overcome the proletarian family's hereditary dysfunction and to identify the genuinely deserving. Furthermore, they applied their claims to the movement itself. One of their leaders demanded that since the social services possessed vast quantities of information, they should be consulted on the 'morality' of male applicants for membership in the VN. In her view, some sections of the VN included so many individuals of deplorable background that respectable families avoided them.[130] La Rocque reminded male section leaders not to obstruct social work.

Peasant support for the Croix de feu resulted from the intersection of top-down and bottom-up initiatives, together with appropriation of the notions of elite and technical competence. In late 1935, the league launched a propaganda offensive in rural areas. It produced a relatively radical programme, calling for syndicates mixing peasants and agricultural workers, the renewal of agricultural unions through replacement of 'selfish' leaders by new cadres drawn from the Croix de feu, and for a tax on big proprietors to protect peasants from falling grain prices.[131] In the Rhône, where Dorgères was weak, the promotion of peasant elites in agricultural unions and Catholic Action contributed to the advance of the Croix de feu.[132] In the Côte d'Or, peasants rejected the Fédération and turned first to the Parti agraire and then the Croix de feu.[133] In Alsace, the Croix de feu made inroads into support for the Bauernbund.[134] The winegrowers of Saumur, marked by a Bonapartist tradition, mobilized behind the Croix de feu in opposition to the wine decrees of the conservative governments of 1935.[135] In Calvados, the Croix de feu joined the defence of the *bouilleurs de cru* and allowed its Dispos to protect meetings of the Front paysan. In the elections of 1936, candidates backed by the Croix de feu, agrarians, and Front paysan gained at the expense of the moderate right.[136] La Rocque was suspicious of Dorgères, but could not prevent members from cooperating with his movement.

In the capitalist farming areas of the Paris Basin and northeast, landowners traditionally dominated a mass of landless labourers, half of them immigrants, forcing

[129] Passmore, "Planting the tricolor in the citadels of communism", 820.

[130] ANFLR, 87, report of Mme Gouin, April 1936.

[131] *Le Flambeau*, 7 September 1935.

[132] Passmore, *From Liberalism*, 90–115, 241–2.

[133] Thierry Hohl, 'Le Parti agraire et paysan français. Une Tentative agrairienne en Côte-d'Or', *Annales de Bourgogne* 49 (1988), 140–50.

[134] Baechler, *Le Parti catholique*, 629–32; Goodfellow, *Between the Swastika and the Cross of Lorraine*, 88–101.

[135] Philippe Gabillard, 'Les Viticulteurs angevins et le mouvement Croix de feu-PSF', *Annales de Bretagne* 90, no. 3 (1983), 483–93.

[136] Quellien, *Bleus*, 327–31.

them to attend Church services and to vote with open ballots. Sometimes, labourers expressed resentment through Socialism and/or Dorgèrism, both of which demanded paid holidays and a minimum wage. The Croix de feu was more conservative, but pressurized large farmers into raising wages and limiting sackings by evoking the spectre of collectivization and memories of wartime unity. In the Oise, a Communist activist reported that two pro-Croix de feu farm labourers had applauded his speech because his programme was the same as that of the Croix de feu. When questioned, they 'understood' that low agricultural prices prevented their Croix de feu employer from paying higher wages, and so they fought 'capitalism', not him.[137]

The league's notorious paramilitary mobilizations also expressed the elitist and populist impulses within the league. From one perspective, they were defensive, for after 6 February the extreme right quickly lost its mastery of the streets, as anti-fascists disrupted the meetings of parliamentary conservatives and the leagues. The Doumergue government's alleged failure to defend freedom of assembly helped discredit him, and indeed his allies in the Front national. From the autumn of 1934, the Croix de feu adapted to these difficulties by holding secret mobilizations. Members were convoked individually at short notice by messages passed down through the league's hierarchy. Columns of motor vehicles converged on a point revealed in the course of the exercise. In September 1935, La Rocque claimed that 16,000 vehicles transported 80,000 people to a rally commemorating the Battle of the Marne. Other mobilizations ventured into proletarian districts, and some rehearsed the 'neutralization' of strategic points, such as town halls.[138] To fend off accusations of subversion, La Rocque endeavoured to present an image of disciplined force. The movement stressed that its demonstrations were not those of an amorphous mass, for an elite gave them structure and direction. They functioned as a sort of visual propaganda for a public only able to understand images. La Rocque often repeated Lyautey's injunction that one should show one's force in order to avoid having to use it. The Croix de feu promised to suppress Communism itself if the government shirked its duty.[139]

Indeed, La Rocque saw paramilitary display as essential to his bid for power. At the time of the 1934 Marne demonstration, a party circular warned that 'the third Battle of the Marne is near'.[140] That was just one example of the application of the apocalyptic language of war to domestic politics. Furthermore, La Rocque advocated a transitional period of non-parliamentary government, in which 'disorderly elements' would be eliminated and silence imposed on the 'obscure forces that claim to govern the country'.[141] He reassured his followers

[137] John Bulaitis, *Communism in Rural France: French Agricultural Workers and the Popular Front* (London, 2008), 61–88; ANFLR 451 AP 85, Ferte to Feraud, ? March/April 1936; Paxton, *French Peasant Fascism*, 49.

[138] Kevin Passmore, 'Boy-scouting for grown-ups? Paramilitarism in the Croix de feu and PSF', *French Historical Studies* 19, no. 2 (Fall 1995), 527–57.

[139] *Le Flambeau*, 25 November 1935.

[140] ANFLR, 81, circular, 1 September 1934.

[141] ANFLR, 5 February 1934; *Le Figaro*, 7 August 1935; Kennedy, *Reconciling*, 42–3; Passmore, 'Boy-scouting', 527–57.

that once the '"great cleansing" of the Republic (for we are Republicans)' had been achieved, then he and his followers would return to their jobs and families. He reassured readers that, 'to save the country from dictatorship I exercise over my men, with their accord, a veritable and conscious dictatorship'.[142] He demanded banning of the Communist Party, arrest of the leaders of the Popular Front, elimination of politics from local elections, and 'depoliticization' of the trade unions.[143]

In practice, the Croix de feu could not reconcile its desire to defend order with its claim to represent the nation better than the government did. Paul Chopine, a leader of the Dispos, who had resigned from the movement, accused La Rocque of both adventurism and excessive caution.[144] Some activists pressed for decisive action, and there were rumours of plots against La Rocque. Matters came to a head on 16 November 1935, when anti-fascists exchanged shots with Croix de feu activists surrounding in a meeting hall in Limoges. Pressure grew on Laval to dissolve the leagues. On 6 December, to avoid this eventuality, and to preserve the image of the league as a disciplined force, Ybarnégaray rose in the Chamber to offer mutual disarmament of leagues and anti-fascists, without accepting that the former bore arms. Rival leagues and some leaguers cried treason. In one section, the VN split from the Croix de feu.[145]

The Ybarnégaray pact prompted La Rocque to reorganize the league. Aware that the movement faced enormous hostility in proletarian districts, he decided that social work must precede or accompany political action, and so he created a Section féminine d'action sociale.[146] The Parti social français (PSF) developed further this strategy, but for the moment La Rocque also reaffirmed the hierarchical and authoritarian nature of the movement, and reassured members that apparent conformity to the 1901 Associations Law was less important than obedience to a 'higher truth'. He 'profoundly felt himself' to be a 'temporary instrument', invested with the task of bringing together and guiding the movement to its goal of reconciliation and order, the condition of all progress. He emphasized that the league's strength lay in 'our popular substance and the homogeneity of our mass', and denied that the movement would enter electoral politics.[147] La Rocque claimed that the very thought of seeking an elective mandate made his heart sink.[148] As a compromise, La Rocque discretely supported candidates who accepted the Croix de feu ethos, whether or not they belonged to the movement.[149]

142 *La Petite gironde*, 27 October 1935.
143 *Le Flambeau*, 25 November, 14 December 1935.
144 Paul Chopine, *Six ans chez les Croix de feu* (Paris, 1937).
145 Kennedy, *Reconciling*, 70–3, 95–6; Philippe Secondy, *La Persistance*, 257–8.
146 ANFLR, 129, undated circular, ? late 1935.
147 ANFLR, 193, circular of 2 January 1936.
148 ANFLR, 129, circular of 2 January 1936. *Le Flambeau*, 11 May 1935.
149 ANFLR, 91, undated.

CONCLUSION

The Croix de feu's intervention in the elections added to the cacophony of conservative voices. Joseph-Barthélemy complained that the leagues united the left, while their secret interventions and demands for blind obedience disorganized conservatives.[150] He may have been thinking of Jacques Arnoult, the league's Marseille president, who declared this the last time that voters would have to vote.[151] Fédération candidates, including Kerillis and Perret (the latter stood against Bonnevay), were the major beneficiaries of Croix de feu support, but La Rocque refused to back Louis Duval-Arnould, because he was 'too old'.[152] The Fédération approached the 1936 elections more united than in the past, if at the cost of concessions to the Croix de feu and peasant movement. Whereas in the Midi and Brittany, Dorgèrists usually allied with the Fédération, in the Paris Basin they caused it difficulties.

Relations between the Alliance and Fédération were execrable, thanks to Flandin's participation as Foreign Minister, along with four more centrists, in the Radical-led Sarraut government. The Alliance president protested that participation prevented the government from being one of the Popular Front. Yet his invocation of the Waldeck-Rousseau precedent and his endorsement of the Franco–Soviet Pact seemed to contradict that. In November 1935, the re-affiliation to the Alliance of the powerful, traditionally pro-Concentration Gironde federation had provided Flandin with the means to counter the more right-wing Parisian federation. For the right, and for many centre deputies, the Sarraut government was indeed a Popular Front administration. Kerillis campaigned against 'Flandin the traitor'.[153] Even *Le Temps* believed that Concentration was currently impossible. The former deputy, Charles Reibel, re-emerged from retirement to oppose Flandin. The Alliance Comité directeur negotiated a compromise, according to which the party manifesto, signed by Flandin, would describe the Popular Front as 'monstrous'.[154] The Alliance at first refused to participate in Kerillis' arbitration committee for Paris, but changed its mind thanks to opposition from its own candidates.

The PDP experienced similar difficulties. The party felt the competition of the leagues, but underwent a revival in Brittany, where the radicalization of the right and the greater sympathy of the clergy made it the only Republican Catholic party. Yet PDP deputies refused to back the Sarraut government, and were criticized by some activists for surrendering to the logic of block against block.[155] Support of the clergy was a mixed blessing, for many spoke of re-conquest and

[150] *La Petite gironde*, 8 May 1936.

[151] Kennedy, *Reconciling*, 99.

[152] Xavier Vallat, *Le nez de Cléopatre. Souvenirs d'un homme de droite* (Paris, 1957), 134–5; Passmore, *From Liberalism*, 191–3.

[153] François Audigier, 'Les Modérés face au Front Populaire. Les Ambiguïtés de l'Alliance démocratique', *Annales de l'Est* 47, no. 2 (1997), 321–49.

[154] *Le Temps*, 28 February 1928; *L'Alliance démocratique*, 8 March, 17 April 1936.

[155] Bensoussan, *Combats*, 498–9.

expressed admiration for the Salazar and Dollfuss regimes, while lamenting the absence of a Catholic party.[156]

The elections were marked by extreme polarization.[157] Spanish events seemed to confirm that Popular Frontism meant civil war; even *Le Temps* surrendered to the temptation of lurid propaganda. Conservatives, including Flandin, saw the Popular Front as an impossible alliance, and agreed that the Radicals would eventually leave it. Yet successive conservative governments had exhausted the options open to them. Now they defended deflation only half-heartedly, admitting the need for 'humanization'. La Rocque condemned deflation outright, especially its impact on 'small producers', and thus captured rank-and-file conservative discontent.[158] The league's combination of authoritarianism and populism promised to sweep away discredited parliamentary conservatism, defeat Communism, and reconcile 'legitimate' differences of interest within the organized profession, by ensuring the predominance of the national interest and eliminating anti-national elements. La Rocque also promised that his league was prepared for possible dissolution. Perhaps some members expected that in such an eventuality La Rocque would take power.

[156] Bensoussan, *Combats*, 499.
[157] Georges Dupeux, *Le Front populaire et les élections de 1936* (Paris, 1974), 113–17.
[158] *Le Flambeau*, 17 August, 28 December 1935, 1 February 1936.

13

Conservatives and the Popular Front (1936–1939)

> The problem of big bucks (salaries, profits, holidays etc) would be resolved very quickly if something could bring the opposing positions together morally. This something, it must be recognized that Fascism has found it, Hitlerism too. However, how can it be acceptable for social equilibrium to be paid for with the death of liberty?
>
> Charles de Gaulle to Paul Reynaud, 13 November 1937

When Léon Blum's Popular Front government took office on 4 June, a massive wave of strikes with factory occupations was underway. On 7–8 June, at Matignon, employers' and workers' representatives agreed improvements in wages and conditions. That did not prevent strikes from affecting virtually all the economy, including department stores and large farms. Huge demonstrations accompanied the strikes, often in city centres that rarely saw workers. Parliament enacted twenty-four important laws in less than twelve weeks—'hastily' said conservatives more used to criticizing parliamentary slowness. Measures included paid holidays, collective contracts, reform of the Banque de France, a Wheat Office (the Office du blé), nationalization of certain arms industries, raising the school leaving age, the forty-hour week without loss of pay (to be implemented from December), and dissolution of the leagues. By the end of 1938, majorities had once again reversed. The Radical Édouard Daladier headed a right-wing administration.

In 1966, Janine Bourdin and René Rémond argued that conservatives largely confined themselves to constitutional opposition to the Popular Front, even if they were too weak to play an important part in its defeat. In the country, they argue, the conservative press and leagues set limits on government action, notably concerning intervention in the Spanish Civil War, but there was no thought of repeating 6 February. Conservatives were content to rely on the Senate to moderate legislative excess and to await the inevitable departure of the Radicals from the coalition.[1] Recently, Jean-Paul Thomas has argued that the Parti social français (PSF), the successor of the Croix de feu, habituated the electorate of the extreme right to democratic politics.[2]

1 Janine Bourdin and René Rémond, 'Les Forces adverses', in *Léon Blum, chef de gouvernement* (Paris, 1967), 137–59.

2 Jean-Paul Thomas, 'Droite et rassemblement du PSF au RPF, 1936–1948. Hommes, réseaux, cultures. Rupture et continuité d'une histoire politique', thèse de doctorat, IEP Paris, 2002.

While most historians agree that Radical disillusion was crucial to the disaggregation of the Popular Front, some are less convinced that the conservative opposition was entirely democratic. First, William Irvine argued that the Fédération républicaine embraced authoritarianism and cooperated with the extreme right—so long as it did not compete with it electorally.[3] Secondly, Robert Soucy argued that the PSF was fascist, while Sean Kennedy saw it as an instance of anti-democratic Catholic authoritarianism.[4] Thirdly, Peter Larmour maintained that as the Radical Party abandoned the Popular Front, it became authoritarian, a view subsequently developed in Serge Berstein's history of the Party.[5] Fourthly, Gilles Le Béguec saw the use of decree laws by the Daladier government (1938–1940), as foreshadowing Vichy. Most recently, historians have explored the continuities and discontinuities between Republican and Vichy pro-natalist, family, and immigration policies.[6]

Conservatives were certainly weak. They hardly dared resist the June strikes. Wendel saw Matignon as absurd but inevitable, given the government's disrespect for property and the possibility of revolution.[7] In parliament, conservatives possessed around 220 seats, to the Popular Front's 385. The Alliance démocratique admitted that the elections represented a 'serious defeat' and that only 40 of the 135 candidates it had supported were elected.[8] Altogether, there were 83 centrists, while the Parti démocrate populaire (PDP) had been reduced to 12 seats. The right did better, with 110 deputies, and on 2 June, 75 Fédération deputies and 40 senators celebrated at Salle Wagram. At the end of the meeting, Taittinger, 'saluted by his numerous partisans', demanded a 'united national movement to sweep away the revolutionaries'.[9] Two weeks later, the government dissolved the leagues.

In fact, the leagues had been on the defensive since mid 1934. Rather than resist, Taittinger revived the Parti républicain, national et social (PRNS), originally formed in 1930, while Solidarité française became the Parti du faisceau français. Both were marginal. As for Action française (AF), the pretender's disavowal in 1936 represented a further blow, although most Royalists chose the league over the prince. AF's strength remained the newspaper, with a circulation of 72,000

[3] W.D. Irvine, *French Conservatism in Crisis: The Republican Federation of France* (Baton Rouge, 1979), 128–58.

[4] Robert Soucy, 'Fascism in France: problematizing the immunity thesis', in Brian Jenkins (ed.), *France in the Era of Fascism: Essays on the French Authoritarian Right* (Leamington Spa, 2005), 65–104; Sean Kennedy, *Reconciling France against Democracy: The Croix de feu and the Parti social français, 1927–1945* (Montreal, 2007), 130.

[5] Peter Larmour, *The French Radical Party in the 1930s* (Stanford, 1964), 197–253; Serge Berstein, *Histoire du Parti radical*, ii. *Crise du radicalisme* (Paris, 1980), 227–53.

[6] Gilles Le Béguec, 'L'Évolution de la politique gouvernementale et les problèmes institutionnels', in René Rémond and Janine Bourdin (eds), *Édouard Daladier, chef de gouvernement* (Paris, 1977), 55–64; Cheryl A. Koos, '"On les aura!": the gendered politics of abortion and the Alliance nationale contre la depopulation, 1938–1944', *Modern & Contemporary France* 7, no. 1 (1999), 21–33; Michael Marrus and Robert Paxton, *Vichy France and the Jews* (New York, 1981); Gérard Noiriel, *Les Origines républicaines de Vichy* (Paris, 1999).

[7] Jean-Noël Jeanneney, *François de Wendel en République. L'Argent et le pouvoir 1914–1940* (Paris, 1976), 560–1.

[8] Bibliothèque nationale de France (hereafter BNF), Fonds Flandin 89. 'Rapport sur la situation de l'Alliance démocratique', ? 1936.

[9] *La Nation*, 6 June 1936.

compared to 50,000 for *Figaro*. Locally, *cercles* such as Le Bouclier in Loire-Inférieure and Lugdunum in Lyon kept the flame burning. None of these movements could compete with the Parti populaire français (PPF) or the PSF.

Jacques Doriot's PPF was formed on 28 June 1936 at the 'rendez-vous de Saint-Denis', so-called because of its cross-party appeal to Saint-Denis Communists and ex-Croix de feu activists, including at least one whole section. In early 1937, the PPF claimed 120,000 members, but the real figure was much lower. The party's notorious role under the Occupation, together with fascination with the case of Communists who became fascists, may have caused historians to exaggerate its importance.

There is no denying the significance of the PSF, formed on 18 July 1936. Scholarly estimates of between 750,000 and 1.2 million members make it the largest party hitherto to have existed in France.[10] In 1935–1936, La Rocque reassured his followers that he would respond appropriately to dissolution, and doubtless many thought that he meant to resist. In the event he did not. In Lyon, the Croix de feu merely offloaded stocks of *Le Flambeau*. In Montpellier, where the Popular Front was weaker, leaguers demonstrated on the Place de la Comédie.[11] Perhaps La Rocque had privately resolved never to act; perhaps he envisaged resistance and backed down. We can only say that he faced a choice between illegality and submission, and that the size of the left's electoral victory, the scale of the strikes, and the left's domination of the streets, made the former option hazardous. With the formation of the PSF, La Rocque announced that the movement would win power legally, and unlike Hitler, he did not combine electoralism with denunciation of democracy. Yet the transition from league to party was troubled and gradual; there were continuities between league and party, and the PSF programme was similar to the PPF's. By 1938–1939, the PSF was more integrated into the Republic, but the Republic was more authoritarian.

I shall not depart from the orthodoxy that the reorientation of Radicalism decisively undermined the Popular Front. However, Conservatives were not entirely ineffective, and neither were they entirely democratic. The Daladier government owed much to the influence of the centre, in which authoritarianism had been developing since 1934. The right was less influential in parliament, but executive rule permitted it to shape some policies. Furthermore, the PSF played a part in the extra-parliamentary offensive against the Popular Front, even if it eventually profited Daladier. To understand this constellation of forces, we must remember that June 1936 weakened parliament and installed a form of social democracy.

THE CRISIS OF JUNE 1936

In June 1936, many conservatives saw the situation as revolutionary. Communist electoral gains, factory occupations, the seeming impotence of employers, and

[10] Jean-Paul Thomas, 'Les Effectifs du Parti Social Français', *Vingtième siècle* 62 (April–June 1999), 61–83; Kennedy, *Reconciling*, 200–1.

[11] Philippe Secondy, *La Persistance du Midi blanc* (Perpignan, 2006), 259.

passivity of the police all frightened them, for they understood events in the light of the Bolshevik Revolution refracted through the lens of collective psychology. Communists were a counter-elite, which exploited mass nervousness and materialism to prepare a 1917-style coup. Hitler's recent reoccupation of the Rhineland, coupled with the Communists' new bellicosity, revived the belief that war and revolution went together. The Christian Democrat L.-A. Pagès wrote that 'what the leaders of the majority want is the installation of Marxism, that abominable old German idea, and of a Judaic inhuman system'.[12] In September, *Je suis partout* warned that 'nationals' must prepare to meet a coup in two months. Wendel believed a coup to be possible, while Marin spoke of civil war. Two bishops advised priests to obtain passports and civilian clothing.[13]

The clerics in question certainly feared repetition of the anticlerical violence of the Spanish Civil War. Virtually all conservatives backed the Nationalists and used the Civil War to make veiled threats. *La Nation* held that Franco's coup was 'an indignant revolt arising from all classes against a government that has brought only disorder and anarchy instead of the reforms [it] promised'. It reported as 'a well-deserved lesson' predictions in the German press that Communist France could go the same way, and denied that Franco was a dictator: he wanted 'a Republic free from Marxist poison'.[14] Spanish events reinforced the already endemic recourse to the language of civil war.

Given that all adult male citizens had received military training, and that possession of firearms was widespread, civil war was thinkable. In November 1935, *Vu* had asked 'Si les français se battaient. Front national contre Front populaire?'. In the same month, a group of Camelots in the exclusive Sixteenth Arrondissement left the AF in protest at its inaction. Led by the Polytechnicien, career officer, and businessman Eugène Deloncle, they formed what became the Comité secret d'action révolutionnaire (CSAR), committed to violent overthrow of the Republic. Linked to it was the Union des Comités d'action défensive (UCAD) under Pozzo Di Borgo, of which the Cagoule (named after their hooded jackets) was the secret wing. The Cagoule planned a coup, and received backing from the Banque Worms and the pretender. Pétain watched but did not commit, while a member of his staff, Georges Loustaunau-Lacau, formed cells to report on Communist activity in the Army.[15]

On the streets, tension grew. On 5 July 1936, 105 police were injured in clashes with the PSF and other leagues at the Place de l'Etoile. In the Lyon suburb of Vaise, there were nightly skirmishes between Communists and the nationalists, mostly supporters of the PSF.[16] On 4 October, 15,000–40,000 PSF members

[12] *L'Ouest éclair*, 4 June 1936, quoted in David Bensoussan, *Combats pour une Bretagne catholique et rurale. Les Droites bretonnes dans l'entre-deux-guerres* (Paris, 2006), 504.

[13] *La Nation*, 5 September 1936; Pierre Christophe, *1936, Les Catholiques et le Front populaire* (Paris, 1986), 140–2; Jeanneney, *François de Wendel*, 565.

[14] *La Nation*, 1 August 1937.

[15] Gayle K. Brunelle and Annette Finley-Croswhite, *Murder in the Métro* (Baton Rouge, 2010), 99–122.

[16] *Lyon républicain* and *Le Nouvelliste*, 5 July 1936.

protested against a Communist rally at the Parc des Princes. There were 1,139 arrests, and a taxi driver reported having his car stoned by demonstrators saluting in the Roman style and chanting 'La France aux français'.[17] The PSF and Communists often used firearms.[18] In the autumn, the PSF resumed its motorized convoys.[19] Troubles culminated on 16 March 1937, when anti-fascists attacked a private PSF meeting at Clichy.

With hindsight, we know that neither right not left envisaged the violent seizure of power. In fact, the Spanish Civil War drew a line that neither side dared cross. A military rising was unlikely because officers were politically divided and thought their conscripts to be unreliable. Wendel expected nothing of the police, and thought that the Army would march only on the orders of Defence Minister Daladier, whom he urged conservatives to cultivate.[20] Indeed, in September 1937 the frustrated Cagoule blew up the employers' union headquarters in a vain attempt to provoke the impression of a Communist takeover, and justify a coup. In 1937, the PSF reduced its mobilizations. Meanwhile, Popular Front leaders urged workers to accept Matignon. In practice, June 1936 inaugurated a social democracy—in a climate of fear.

In 1936, the Third Republic scarcely resembled the caricature of parliamentary misrule that persists in some historiography. The Matignon Agreement and compulsory arbitration law of December 1936 ensured that organized interests negotiated social policy under the auspices of a reinforced Présidence du conseil, Labour Ministry, Conseil d'État, and Conseil Nationale Economique (CNE). Blum bolstered the Présidence du conseil's coordinating role by taking no ministry himself and creating an under-secretariat. Already in early 1936, the CNE had been given a legislative foundation;[21] now, accords for the implementation of the forty-hour week were negotiated there. Meanwhile, the renamed Confédération générale de la production française (CGPF) reorganized itself to represent employers in negotiations with the Confédération générale du travail (CGT).[22] Social democracy also provided new opportunities for female professionals, thanks to efforts to create a climate favourable for collaboration in the factories and to ensure that workers used their new leisure soberly. The appointment of Suzanne Lacore as Under-Secretary for Child Protection consecrated the importance of social work, while extending political and religious conflict over it.[23]

Conservatives had long opposed social-democratic left-wing versions of organizationalism. Now, weak in parliament and on the streets and absent from the factory floor, they developed novel means to fight the Popular Front. They promoted

[17] AN BB^{18} 30482, 5 January 1937, 2 April 1937; F^{2} 2761, report of 8 October 1936.

[18] AN F^{7} 14 817, 20 January 1937.

[19] Archives départementales du Rhône, 41m 236, 22 September 1936; AN, BB^{18} 30482, 9 October 1936, BB^{18} 30483, 20 January 1937; AN, F^{7} 14817, May 1937 on the Cher.

[20] Jeanneney, *François de Wendel*, 565.

[21] *Le Figaro*, 13 February 1936; Alain Chatriot, *La Démocratie sociale à la française* (Paris, 2003), 90–108.

[22] Ingo Kolboom, *La Revanche des patrons* (Paris, 1986), 111–334.

[23] *La Nation*, 7 November 1936; Siân Reynolds, *France Between the Wars: Gender and Politics* (London, 1996), 150–4.

ideological themes that resonated with conservative Radicals, exploited links with the reorganized employer movement, proposed authoritarian versions of organizationalism, and created rival unions that exploited fractures in the labour movement. These strategies sometimes united conservatives, and they opened more room for right-wing themes and provoked greater polarization. Few Conservatives showed the sympathy for the Popular Front that they had shown to the Cartel, and ultimately Radicals turned decisively against the Popular Front too. Yet the anti-Popular Front movement developed within pre-existing liberal and corporatist conceptions of economic organization, cross-cut by religious and social differences, and permitted intra-conservative conflict to continue.

As Jessica Wardhaugh demonstrates, opponents of the Popular Front alleged that the social legislation of 1936 had always figured in their programmes, and the claim must be taken seriously.[24] The PSF and PPF in particular, attempted to contain workers' legitimate' aspirations within the organized profession. At the same time, conservatives would accept only those reforms that were compatible with the 'national interest', as they defined them. They were especially hostile to the forty-hour week. To counter it, as well as to show the disruptive nature of strikes, they emphasized production.

A central theme of the counter-offensive was production, and as always, the use of such terms betrayed political agendas rather than deep psychological structures. With the onset of the depression, conservatives had abandoned post-war productivism for harmonization of production with market possibilities.[25] Now, hostility to labour disruption and the forty-hour week revived productivist rhetoric. Advocates of productivism, such as Paul Reynaud and his economic advisor, Alfred Sauvy, were prone to depict themselves as outsiders, but their ideas were widely shared, as was the notion that Popular Front reforms were 'Malthusian'. Henri de Peyerimhoff, head of the coal industry employers' group, defined 'Malthusian' as the 'voluntary mutilation of the nation's productive capacity'—he meant the forty-hour week.[26]

Hostility to Malthusianism connected production to pro-natalism. Rising unemployment had imposed discretion on pro-natalists, in spite of the resurgence of Germany. However, the belief that strikers in occupied factories were engaging in orgies intensified familialist hostility to pornography, and reinforced calls for restoration of the family. Some conservatives believed that Blum's inclusion of three women in his government would strengthen the maternal dimension of policy, but claims that Popular Front 'women's materialism' undermined the birth rate were more common.[27]

[24] Jessica Wardhaugh, *In Pursuit of the People: Political Culture in France, 1934–3* (Basingstoke, 2009), 94–102.

[25] Jackie Clarke, *France in the Age of Organization* (Leamington Spa, 2011); Patrick Fridenson, 'L'Idéologie des grands constructeurs dans l'entre-deux guerres', *Le Mouvement social* 81 (October–December, 1972), 52–68; Patrick Fridenson, 'Le Patronat français', in *La France et les français en 1938–9*, 139–57; Gérard Noiriel, *Longwy. Immigrés et prolétaires* (Paris, 1984), 225–305.

[26] *La Nation*, 7 November 1936.

[27] *L'Alliance démocratique*, 12–18 June 1936; *La Nation*, 13 June 1936.

Along with work and family, the opposition emphasized nation, and equated the Popular Front with outsiders, whom it identified with demagogues, who would ultimately be unable to control the crowd that they had set in motion.[28] *La Nation* claimed that Spanish refugees had given the southwest a sight of the 'hideous face of civil war and a foretaste of what happens to a country when it abandons itself to Communism, even hidden under the cover of a so-called Popular Front'.[29] Conservatives hoped thus to exploit ethnic rivalry among workers. Meanwhile, antisemitism intensified. Vallat's notorious antisemitic attack on Blum was quite typical of the Royalist-nationalist right, but particularly shocking because directed at the Président du conseil in the Chamber.[30] More unexpectedly, antisemitic attacks emanated from outside these circles. A Union nationale des combattants (UNC) journalist claimed that the men of the 'Jewish front' who had not fought in the war were ready to join the Communists in feeding on French blood.[31] Antisemitism was usually expressed more euphemistically, but it helped to credit the idea of a Judeo-Bolshevik conspiracy against the hard-working French.[32]

Finally, conservatives identified the nation with the 'classes moyennes'.[33] There was nothing new about the claim that the real casualty of Socialism was not big capital, but the *classes moyennes*. Since the 1900s, they had been the victims of income tax, stabilization, and Social Insurance; now their interests had been sacrificed to the CGT and perhaps the 'trusts'. For conservatives, classes moyennes ideology was promising because Radical opponents of the Popular Front had also taken it up. It was also adaptable to different conservative ideologies, but that was potentially divisive. For the right, the *classes moyennes* were the repository of individualism, financial good sense, and economic liberalism, the antithesis of collectivism; for the centre, they naturally favoured parliamentary Concentration.[34] The PSF incorporated the middle classes into the organized profession as a third force, able to reconcile capital and labour and structure the 'gregarious and unstable crowd'.[35] There was much disagreement on who belonged to the *classes moyennes*. Some included shopkeepers, small business, white-collar workers and technicians, engineers, managers, and the professions. Others defined them morally, thus including 'healthy' elements of the proletariat and big businessmen who treated their workers humanely. Also important was the notion of 'patrimony'. It potentially mobilized a broad constituency, linking personal management of a family firm to the possession of savings and an engineer's management of a family-sized department within a factory. Patrimony also entailed individual sacrifice for the family and nation. It excluded cosmopolitan capital and Communism, as well as 'rootless' civil servants.

[28] Wardhaugh, *In Pursuit of the People*, 108-9.
[29] *La Nation*, 7 November 1936.
[30] Bensoussan, *Combats*, 504.
[31] Chris Millington, *From Victory to Vichy: Veterans in Interwar France* (Manchester, 2012).
[32] Bourdin and Rémond, 'Les Forces advereses', 154–5.
[33] Luc Boltanski, 'Taxinomies sociales et luttes des classes. La Mobilisation de la classe moyenne et l'invention des cadres', *Actes de la recherche en sciences sociales* 29 (September 1979), 75–100.
[34] *L'Alliance démocratique*, 28 June 1936.
[35] *Le Flambeau*, 20 March 1937.

Classes moyennes ideology might also appeal to those who felt that their leaders had betrayed them, or that they were excluded from the nascent social democracy. Small and medium businessmen complained that they paid the price of strikes that were the fault of 'cosmopolitan' capital. In the summer of 1936, small-business organizations endeavoured to break the monopoly of the CGPF or to reform it from the inside.[36] Similarly, engineers faced threats to their authority from workers as well as to their material position, for they lacked collective contracts. They often felt let down by their employers, whom, they alleged, were also too distant from workers. Female social workers believed that their message of class harmony could have avoided class conflict, had 'selfish employers' been willing to listen to them. Conservative workers and white-collar workers felt that existing parties did not protect them from intimidation by strikers. The Confédération française des travailleurs chrétiens (CFTC), which had supported the strikes, found itself excluded from collective negotiations. Increasingly it seemed to the CFTC that defence of working-class interests required defeat of the CGT. Indeed, many new members joined the CFTC out of hostility to Communism. Finally, while the Wheat Office raised prices and reassured many peasants, others saw the government as exclusively devoted to the urban classes.

In spite of the anti-capitalist subtext of these grievances, big business attempted to instrumentalize them. In the CGPF, a new team used small business criticisms of the organization to reform it, while preserving big business hegemony. Business also promoted the 'cadres' (engineers/managers) movement; Lamirand advised employers on management and relations with workers. Business rejected engineers' claim to be a third force, preferring to depict them as 'collaborators' of the *patronat*. The CGPF and CGT both opposed representation of USIC in the Conseil supérieure du travail.[37]

While conservatives shared many themes, their stances were different. The Fédération and its nationalist and crypto-Royalist allies opposed the Popular Front from a liberal and/or corporatist perspective, and were close to the familial and natalist movement.[38] The PSF, more open to populism than the Fédération, attempted to recast working-class aspirations in its 'organized profession', while attracting many of those who felt excluded from the emergent social democracy. The PPF's programme was similar, but it did not succeed in finding a place in the political landscape. The centre and moderate Radicals were linked to the employers' movement and espoused a new anti-communist, liberal version of productivism and organization. Conservative Radicals, with centre support, won the struggle with orthodox liberals and corporatists to succeed the Popular Front. From 1938, Daladier's government broke decisively with social democracy, without embracing corporatism.

[36] Kolboom, *La Revanche*, 143–80.

[37] Le Chanoine Reviron, 'Notes sur les syndicats d'ingénieurs', *La Chronique sociale* (1937), 364–9; Ingo Kolboom, 'Patronat et cadres. La Contribution patronal à la formation du groupe des cadres', *Le Mouvement social* 12 (October–December 1982), 71–95; Marc Maurice, 'L'Évolution du travail et du syndicalisme chez les cadres', *Le Mouvement social* 61 (October–December 1967), 47–64.

[38] Richard Tomlinson, 'The politics of *dénatalité* during the French Third Republic 1890–1940', PhD dissertation, University of Cambridge, 1983, 228–42; Cheryl Koos, 'Engendering reaction: the politics of pronatalism and the family in France, 1919–1944', PhD dissertation, University of Southern California, 1996.

THE PPF

In the desperate summer of 1936, conservatives hoped that Doriot's PPF would reincorporate the proletariat into the nation through organization of the profession and acceptance of workers' legitimate grievances. Doriot's own trajectory apparently proved the viability of the programme. A decorated veteran, metal worker, and Communist activist, he became notorious in the 1920s for his brawling, anti-militarism, and anti-imperialism. After the 6 February riots, Doriot demanded anti-fascist unity, and in June the Communist Party expelled him, just as it embraced his strategy. Doriot remained in control of the party apparatus in Saint-Denis and was triumphantly re-elected in 1936.

At that time, Doriot still saw himself as part of the Popular Front. His growing anti-Communism might have led him to join the far left, with which he shared anti-militarism, and he did indeed make contact. However, joining the Trotskyists promised obscurity at a time when the Popular Front dominated the left. Since parliamentary conservatism was in crisis and the leagues had been dissolved, a new space seemed available. Doriot made contact with 'démissionnaires' from the Radicals and Croix de feu, who were also looking for new openings.[39] Perhaps on their advice, he created a party that would oppose existing parties. The ex-Radical Bertrand de Jouvenel evoked the reconciliation of the nationalist and Communist demonstrators of 6 and 9 February 1934 respectively.[40]

Initially, the PPF won significant communist support, notably in Saint-Denis and Marseille, where another dissident Communist, Simon Sabiani, joined the party. Doriot's Communist past was most evident in his conception of the party as disciplined and hierarchical, his tactical conceptions, and his denunciations of the bourgeoisie, if only for selfishness. With time, the PCF regained ground in Saint-Denis, while ex-Communists became relatively less important in the party except at leadership level.[41]

Literary figures, *non-conformistes*, and organizationalist intellectuals represented the second element in the PPF. The writer Drieu La Rochelle had defended 'art for art's sake' before flirting with the Radicals and Redressement français (despite denouncing 'mechanization'). Several 'Maréchaux', the Croix de feu dissidents, also joined the PPF, including Robert Loustau, along with Jean de Fabrègues of the Jeune droite. From the néo-Socialistes came Paul Marion and from the Radical-Socialists, Alfred Fabre-Luce. In 1937, some intellectuals joined the party leadership, and Jouvenel became editor of *L'Émancipation nationale*. The *Je suis partout* journalists Brasillach and Gaxotte supported the PPF from a distance. The party expected intellectuals to elaborate Doriot's ideas. Yet since Doriot had abandoned

[39] Jean-Paul, Brunet, *Jacques Doriot, du communisme au fascisme* (Paris, 1986); Jean-Paul Brunet, *Saint-Denis, ville rouge* (Paris, 1980); G.D. Allardyce, 'The political transition of Jacques Doriot', *Journal of Contemporary History* 1, no. 1 (1966), 56–74; Dieter Wolf, *Jacques Doriot, du communisme à la collaboration* (Paris, 1969).

[40] Laurent Kestel, 'L'Engagement de Bertrand de Jouvenel au PPF, 1936–1938. Intellectuel de parti et entrepreneur politique', *French Historical Studies* 30, no. 1 (2007), 105–25 at 116–18.

[41] Brunet, *Saint-Denis*, 404–5.

his old ideas and new ones had not occurred to him, intellectuals had some latitude. Doriot recycled their ideas in his *Refaire la France* (1938). They were not markedly different from those of the PSF. [42]

Loustau was representative of the intellectuals. He was an engineer and former member of Ordre nouveau, who harnessed organizationalism to *non-conformisme* and anti-communism. He followed the *non-conformistes* in attacking liberalism and Communism for undermining nation, family, and profession. As an engineer, he was especially concerned with restoring harmony in large enterprises, which 'finance' and Communism had destroyed. Citing Jean Coutrot and Hyacinthe Dubreuil, Loustau advocated mechanization and humanization of work. He spoke of the necessary responsibility of the employer in Fayolist terms, infusing his authority with fascistic leadership cult. He proposed a common welfare fund financed by a levy on profits on a regional and professional basis—a programme suspiciously like the regionalization of Social Insurance demanded by the right and PSF. As in the PSF's *profession organisée*, the elimination of Communism and the promotion of a national mystique would enable collaboration between workers, *cadres*, and employers' unions. Typical of organizers from the centre to the PSF, Loustau held that 'the state will not have a management role, but one of accountability and arbitration'. Reinforcement of state authority would nevertheless enable it to represent the general good, for Loustau restricted corporations to an advisory role. As an advocate of imperial autarky, he considered agriculture to be the 'foundation of our national economy' and 'the model of our social life since it accords best with the temperament of our people'.[43] Loustau's constitutional proposals were no more original: reinforcement of the executive, proportional representation, decentralization, and strengthening of the family. The most significant difference between the PPF and the PSF was that the former proposed use of the referendum, a device aligning it both with Bonapartism and Nazism.

Conservatives constituted the third element of the PPF. The right-wing press publicized the party while business financed it. Anti-communism ranked highly among business' motives for doing so, but given that business financed a range of parties, it is difficult to gauge its sympathy for the party's programme. All we can say is that both liberals who wished to destroy the labour movement and those who wished to incorporate it into a hierarchical, organized economy found something in the PPF. Representatives of the old right were rare in the higher reaches of the party and among its intellectuals, but were important locally. Albert Beugras, leader of the Rhône section, had not been politically active before 1936, but enjoyed reading *Je suis partout*.[44]

The balance between these groups varied. The possibility that the government would revoke him as mayor of Saint-Denis, coupled with consciousness of the greater success of the PSF, and the desire to exploit Radical discontent with the

[42] Kestel, 'L'Engagement', 105–25.

[43] Robert Loustau, *Un Ordre social français* (Paris, n.d); Wolf, *Jacques Doriot*, 295–311.

[44] Kevin Passmore, 'Class, gender and populism: the Parti populaire français in Lyon, 1936–1940', in Nicholas Atkin and Frank Tallett (eds), *The Right in France 1789–1997* (London, 1998), 184–214.

Popular Front, provoked Doriot to bid for conservative support. On 27 March 1937, he called for a 'Front de la liberté', to include all opponents of the Popular Front. Borrowing from the PCF strategy book, the Front would be independent of, but led by, the PPF. Unity of conservatives at the summit would entice the PSF and Radical base into the PPF. Doriot did not intend to be submerged by conservatives any more than the PCF wished to melt into the Popular Front. Yet he effectively endorsed the existence of two blocs, while the Front's respect for sitting deputies confirmed the hegemony of the parliamentary right. The PPF provided security for Fédération meetings and played a junior role in the 1937 local elections. The party also became involved in strike-breaking. In Lyon, a group of ex-Francistes left the PPF in protest at its moderate line, and warned of the uselessness of electoral victories.[45] The failure of the Front de la Liberté, coupled with Doriot's revocation as mayor of Saint-Denis and electoral defeat, radicalized and marginalized the PPF. Doriot visited Spain and later Lourdes, while the party campaigned for political status for the detained Cagoulards. Support for appeasement led to admiration for Nazism, if not endorsement in principle, while Drieu La Rochelle declared himself a fascist.[46] The Fédération warned activists against the PPF. By then, it was clear that the PPF had failed to win the proletariat, and so conservatives lost interest in it. Splits between pacifists and nationalists at the time of Munich all but destroyed the party. Well before then, the PSF was the only significant nationalist party.

THE PSF

While the formation of the PSF represented a significant break with the paramilitarism of the Croix de feu, change was slow. The aforementioned violence of 1936–1937 was not the product of the leadership's failure to impose its line, for La Rocque was inconsistent. In September, he informed local leaders that if the police were ineffective, then good citizens must help or replace them. He added that 'if the private property of our comrades is the victim of insults or violence on the part of Popular Front organizations, [you must] engage in demonstrations of the same type, but organized, against your aggressors or their representatives'. Indeed, the 'Marxist danger must provoke not fear, but a general upsurge'.[47] Subsequently, the PSF organized fewer motorized sorties. Violence survived largely in strike-breaking and electoral meetings, but no longer would paramilitary display justify the bid for power. The PSF began to emphasize that it would descend into the streets to support the police, not replace them. La Rocque urged members to avoid provocation.[48]

[45] Passmore, 'Class, gender and populism', 206–8.

[46] Philippe Burrin, *La Dérive fasciste. Doriot, Déat, Bergery* (Paris, 1986), 291–311.

[47] Archives nationales, 451 AP 116, Fonds La Rocque (herafter, ANFLR carton/dossier), 18 September 1936 (2); W.D Irvine, 'Fascism in France: the strange case of the Croix de feu', *Journal of Modern History* 63, no. 2 (June 1991), 159–88; Kennedy, *Reconciling*, 124.

[48] Kevin Passmore, 'Boy-scouting for grown-ups? Paramilitarism in the Croix de feu and PSF', *French Historical Studies* 19, no. 2 (Autumn 1995), 527–57 at 552–6; Kennedy, *Reconciling*, 148–9.

The government's institution on 5 April 1937 of proceedings against the PSF for reconstitution of a dissolved league discouraged violence. In any case, La Rocque had already concluded that the Popular Front must be defeated electorally, and placed much hope in local elections planned for November. He also felt that the Popular Front must be fought in the factories. Both electoral and industrial victory depended on social preparation. The party elaborated a three-pronged trade union, social, and political strategy in which, once again, the principles of collective psychology were important. The league sought to channel legitimate conflicts of interest into the organized profession, reconciling them through propagation of the 'mystique Croix de feu', and eliminating Communism and foreign influences. Elites in each group—women, peasants, engineer-managers, and workers—would embody and promote this mystique.

Whereas the Croix de feu endeavoured to win power by presenting an image of physical strength, the PSF sought to achieve the same objective through irresistible electoral force. In both league and party, that entailed propagation of the Croix de feu mystique through the repetition of simple ideas, the visual impact of large meetings, and satisfaction of the masses' material needs. As the sympathetic novelist Jacques de Lacretelle put it, La Rocque would appeal to the masses' good instincts, not their bad ones.[49] To that end, the PSF organized itself in sections corresponding to electoral constituencies rather than in military-style sectors of the Croix de feu, while the Dispos became the less threatening Équipes volantes de propagande (EVP). As director of the PSF Bureau politiques, Edmond Barrachin, formerly of the centre and Fédération, was the architect of the electoral strategy.[50] He aimed to capture the Radical electorate by redefining the centre ground in a more conservative and authoritarian manner. Indeed, the party remained hierarchical. Fayol's grandson Robert Désobliaux joined the Croix de feu and designed the PSF's top-down administrative system, which gave the party an organic structure, with La Rocque as the central reference.[51]

By extension, the PSF envisaged an authoritarian-corporatist reconfiguration of the Popular Front's social democracy. Capital and labour would be reconciled through depoliticization of the unions and propagation of the mystique. Just before dissolution, La Rocque created the Syndicats professionnels français (SPF). They recruited factory workers, senior personnel, white-collar, and shop-workers, and claimed one million members in 1939 and nearly 4,000 factory delegates. The real numbers were far lower, but the unions would play an important role in breaking strikes.[52] The SPF was founded on the principle that Communists—demagogues—directed workers' materialism against the rich, thus creating a cycle

[49] Kennedy, *Reconciling*, 148.

[50] Jean-Paul Thomas, 'Le Parti social français (PSF), obstacle à la radicalization des droites. Contribution historique à une réflexion sur les droites, la radicalité et les cultures politiques françaises', in Philippe Vervaecke (ed), *À Droite de la droite. Droites radicals en France et en Grande-Bretagne au XXe siècle* (Lille, 2012), 243–73 at 255–6.

[51] Jacques Nobécourt, *Le Colonel de La Rocque (1885–1946), ou les pièges du nationalisme chrétien* (Paris, 1997), 484–5. Alternative sources refer to Désaubliaux, Fayol's grandson-in-law.

[52] Philippe Machefer, 'Les Syndicats professionnels français', *Le Mouvement social* 119 (October–December 1982), 91–112 at 91–5; Bensoussan, *Combats*, 510–11, 513.

of agitation and disappointment. The SPF would work from the 'inside' (like Catholic Action); they would enlist those workers, the elite, whose moral qualities prevented them from joining the CGT, and ultimately win over the mass of disappointed workers. The SPF would be integrated into the *profession organisée*, perhaps alongside a purged CGT. The *profession organisée* would take responsibility for collective bargaining; membership of unions would be compulsory. The SPF would assume 'total charge' of its members, who would benefit from the care of PSF social services.[53]

Social work was essential to the PSF's bid to reconcile the classes and win power. The PSF Section feminine may have recruited 200,000–300,000 members, a substantial proportion of whom were involved in social work.[54] More than in the PSF, social action reached beyond the party, notably through Travail et Loisirs, which created social centres in proletarian suburbs. The movement was inspired by a combination of secularized Social Catholicism and Lyautey's method of colonial pacification and organization. As Laura Lee Downs points out, PSF social work slipped between pacification as reconciliation of the classes and the occupation of a colonized space. Possessed both of a vocation and technical expertise, social workers conceived of themselves as soldiers, operating on the frontier of the *banlieue*, engaged in a civilizing mission. They promoted a 'mystique' of nationalism and reconciliation in a hierarchical society. They placed a special emphasis on the formation of working-class elites, notably through their work with children. Whereas left-wing and Catholic *colonies de vacances* allowed for children's self-government, PSF *colonies* emphasized discipline and self-mastery and refused to accept 'weak' children. PSF social work was part of a broader conservative effort to break down the gap between the classes that had allegedly caused June 1936, and to 'organize' workers' leisure.[55]

From one perspective, this tripartite strategy represented an attempt to revise the June 1936 settlement in the interests of business. The PSF endorsed most of the employers' demands, including depoliticization of trade unions, reform of the forty-hour week, and regionalization of Social Insurance. The party received business funding; business was overrepresented among party members. Ideologically, La Rocque shared the Fayolism of the military-industrial elites. In Lyon, the deputy director of the local branch of the CGPF wrote a weekly column in the PSF press, and condemned big business intervention in politics only if it was 'occult'. Local shopkeeper activists, who had challenged big business in the Chamber of Commerce before 1936, now backed the counter-offensive.[56]

[53] ANFLR, 97, 'Note sur l'action syndicale', undated, ? June 1936; Passmore, *From Liberalism to Fascism: The Right in a French Province* (Cambridge, 1997), 273–4.

[54] Kennedy, *Reconciling*, 199.

[55] Laura Lee Downs, '"Nous plantions les trois couleurs". Action sociale féminine et recomposition des politiques de la droite française. Le Cas du mouvement Croix-de-feu et du Parti social français, 1934–1960', *Revue d'histoire moderne et contemporaine* 58, no. 3 (2011), 118–62 at 129–31; Kennedy, *Reconciling*, 211–12.

[56] Passmore, *From Liberalism*, 174–5, 201, 271–2.

Support for the employers' movement was nevertheless compatible with anti-capitalism, which was stronger in the PSF than in the Croix de feu. The PSF sought to fight the Popular Front on its own terrain, echoing its calls for social revolution to complete political revolution. Of course, the PSF's idea of revolution differed from that of the left. It attacked anonymous international capital rather than capitalism *per se*. Notwithstanding, anti-capitalism was meaningful in the context of the belief that big business colluded with the Popular Front to suppress the middle class and that its selfish liberal individualism had driven workers to Communism. Anti-capitalism was also a weapon deployed in the struggle between capitalists. In Lyon, industrialists opposed to the hegemony of the silk industry joined the PSF, as did Protestant wine traders and their workers in the quai des Chartrons district of Bordeaux, who had lost ground to Catholic business.[57]

PSF anti-capitalism also attracted managers and engineers who saw themselves as victims of Matignon, who situated themselves in opposition both to Communism and to the 'selfish employer'. They saw themselves as an elite in the sense that their intermediate position enabled them to know and discipline the working class.[58] Canat de Chizy, an engineer in a Lyonnais artificial fibre factory, promoted the *cadres* movement in the PSF press and created an SPF union. He saw the *cadres* as the core of the *classes moyennes* and claimed that competence was their defining characteristic; he advocated the division of large enterprises into departments run by engineers.[59] Luc Touron in *Le Flambeau de Bourgogne* invested managers with overseeing a dynamic economy while preserving order.[60] Lawyers and doctors saw PSF corporatism as a means to eliminate foreign competition. Doctors, moreover, had long demanded a legal order, not least to protect them from the 'statism' of Social Insurance. Doctors in the prestigious Montpellier Medical Faculty believed themselves to have lost their social status and came from a milieu in which Royalism and admiration for Mussolini were both strong.[61]

The transition from league to party had mixed consequences for women in the movement, but for them too anti-capitalism mattered. On the one hand, conservative fears that June 1936 had undermined the gender hierarchy, together with increased emphasis on the traditionally male fields of electoral politics and labour relations, potentially marginalized women in the PSF. Most women joined a new body, Action civique, designed to prepare them for the vote. Male activists were largely indifferent or hostile towards Action civique and its members were often limited to routine tasks such as folding newspapers. Anyway, the PSF's endorsement of female suffrage was weak, tempered by the family vote and initial restriction to municipalities.[62] Other women joined Action social, which dealt with social work within the party, or engaged in professionalized social work with Travail et

[57] Sylvain Trussardi, 'Faisceau, Croix de feu, PSF. Trois mouvements girondins du milieu des années 1920 à la fin des années 1930', *Parlements*, Special issue (2005), 55–64.

[58] Downs, 'Each and every one', 22.

[59] Passmore, *From Liberalism*, 271–3, 281–3.

[60] Kennedy, *Reconciling*, 175.

[61] Secondy, *La Persistence*, 298–301.

[62] Kennedy, *Reconciling*, 206–7.

Loisirs in proletarian suburbs. Even this field was more closely controlled than in the past, for the Travail et Loisirs patronage committee was made up of male businessmen and doctors. In 1939, there were fears that graduates of a proposed school for male social workers would take top jobs.

On the other hand, male encroachments made women more sensitive to their separateness. They emphasized their professionalism to claim equality with doctors and used the feminine discourse of vocation to resist male intrusion into social work. Anti-capitalism was meaningful to these women, in that they saw themselves as humanizing industrial relations through the exercise of their vocation and propagation of the *mystique Croix de feu*. The Section feminine set out to create 'leaders'.[63]

Anti-capitalism also attracted peasants. Since late 1935, the Croix de feu had expanded in the countryside in tandem with Défense paysan, even though La Rocque and Dorgères both forbade collaboration. There were was much double membership. In the Creuse, the PSF initially backed Défense paysan, but gradually gained the upper hand. In Brittany, the PSF recruited peasants in communes where Défense paysan had been strong, often provoking the hostility of the Dorgèristes and their conservative allies.[64] Fearful of losing out to the PSF, Dorgères began to distance himself from notables. Of course, the populism of the PSF and Dorgèristes was strongly anti-communist, as their role in the 1936 strikes had proven. That did not rule out affinities with the left. For instance, the PSF and Dorgèristes opposed modifications of the Office du blé in the name of small growers. And while conservative agricultural unions approved a proposal to extend family allowances to agriculture in order to ensure that they played a role in administering it, Défense paysan and the PSF refused to accept the measure unless the state paid the contributions of labourers working for relatives.[65]

Finally, the PSF attracted some workers. Communists claimed that workers joined the SPF in the hope of getting employment.[66] Perhaps some did, but there had always been conservative workers, and there were reasons, rational in their own terms, why they might turn to the far right in the mid 1930s. They included anger at intimidation, real or perceived, in Communist-dominated areas and the complex ethnic structure of the workforce. At Longwy, where a minority of the population was French, employers exploited ethnic divisions in the workforce. The mayor and Fédération deputy, Pierre Amadieu du Clos, had told the Chamber in 1930 that France did not suffer from an unemployment crisis, but of foreign invasion.[67] The SPF's exclusion of non-French workers tapped into such conflicts, and folded into conservative identification of Communism with foreigners.

[63] Kevin Passmore, '"Planting the tricolor in the citadels of communism": women's social service in the Croix de feu and Parti social français', *Journal of Modern History* 71, no. 4 (December 1999), 814–51 at 838–40.

[64] Kennedy, *Reconciling*, 197; Bensoussan, *Combats*, 453–4, 602 n. 106, 512.

[65] Bensoussan, *Combats*, 465–8.

[66] Kennedy, *Reconciling*, 195–6.

[67] Noiriel, *Longwy*, 264–8, 282–4.

As agents of a foreign power, the Communists were the chief obstacles to propagation of the Croix de feu mystique of reconciliation. That legitimated strike-breaking in the name of class harmony. In the capitalist farming areas of the Paris Basin and northeast, Défense paysan and the PSF held large meetings, while the SPF bussed in strike-breakers; one PSF supervisor sacked a worker for singing the 'Internationale' in the fields.[68] Yet like Fascist unions in Italy, the SPF could not afford to ignore workers' demands entirely. In Lyon, the SPF was less systematically opposed to the forty-hour week than were employers or the PSF.[69]

The PSF's conservative populism may also be seen in its combination of Catholicism with fidelity to the Revolution. The overwhelming majority of PSF supporters were recruited from the Catholic right, underlining once again the importance of the religious division. Indeed, use of Social Catholicism to build the party's electoral programme, along with the prominence of the Spanish question, made the PSF more explicitly Catholic. It ceased the Croix de feu's practice of holding ecumenical services. La Rocque told *Sept* that the PSF programme exactly matched pontifical precepts, and spoke repeatedly of the defence of Christian civilization, a cause for which he hoped that Franco would be victorious. A cleric in Saint-Brieuc urged Catholics to join the PSF to prevent churches being destroyed as they had been in Spain.[70] Female activists in Loire-Inférieure saw their action as inspired by de Mun and Harmel.[71]

Such claims do not in themselves position the PSF; after all, de Mun and Harmel had espoused conflicting social philosophies. The PSF represented an authoritarian and populist version of Social Catholicism. It amalgamated a secularized version of the methods of Catholic Action, notably the creation of elites in the 'milieu', with identification with the Revolution. La Rocque regarded commemorations of the fall of the Bastille and of Jeanne d'Arc as equally important. The insignia of the EVP featured a reproduction of Rude's Marseillaise. The titles of PSF newspapers in the Rhône and the Vendée referred to the Volunteers of 1792. We shall see that this populism contributed to the deterioration of relations between the PSF and the Fédération.

For the moment, I shall conclude by asking whether the PSF prepared the extreme right for democracy, as Thomas argues it did. Given that Republicanism was a contested ideology with no fixed meaning, there is no simple answer. Four points are relevant. First, PSF efforts in 1938–1939 to woo Radical politicians and voters proved little, for every party of left and right did the same. What mattered were the *terms* of the appeal. On the one hand, Barrachin urged the PSF to play down its paramilitarism in order to reassure Radicals. On the other, he believed that the decomposition of Radicalism would open its electorate to what he called

[68] John Bulaitis, *Communism in Rural France: French Agricultural Workers and the Popular Front* (London, 2008), 116, 120–2, 128; Robert O. Paxton, *French Peasant Fascism: Henry Dorgères' Greenshirts and the Crises of French Agriculture* (Oxford, 1997), 24; Machefer, 'Les Syndicats professionnels', 91–112.

[69] Passmore, *From Liberalism*, 284–95.

[70] Kennedy, *Reconciling*, 154.

[71] Bensoussan, *Combats*, 515.

a synthesis of Barrèsian nationalism, Péguy's mysticism, and syndicalism.[72] Secondly, the PSF rejected the Radicals' conception of parliamentary Republicanism in favour of a nationalist tradition that favoured strengthening of the executive. The PSF's admiration for the Austrian and Portuguese dictatorships and for Franco, along with La Rocque's insistence that he would never stand for election, suggested that the PSF leaned towards authoritarianism, as did his insistence that reconciliation meant not an alliance of parties, but unity in the country.[73] Thirdly, like conservatives in general, the PSF defined Republicanism as freedom of assembly, speech, and work—hence Doriot's use of 'liberty' as a rallying point. By this means, the right attempted to capture the defence of Republican freedoms from the Popular Front. This stance was not intrinsically pro- or anti-Republican, for Republicans too debated the relative value of individual and collective rights. Finally, we may also ask how far the PSF accepted the principle of competition among parties with opposed views. It dropped the Croix de feu's talk of purges and did not speak of putting an end to elections, but anti-communism remained extreme and the PSF never hid its desire for depoliticization of the CGT. Indeed, the PSF's role in breaking strikes and its promotion of *classes moyennes* ideology helped consolidate the Daladier government, which gave Republicanism an unprecedentedly authoritarian meaning, and won broad conservative support.

THE FÉDÉRATION RÉPUBLICAINE

The elections of 1936 confirmed that the Fédération had overcome the crisis of 1928–1932, for it increased its parliamentary representation and Marin's position was largely uncontested. Twenty dissidents joined Pernot's Républicains indépendants et d'action sociale, but the Fédération's divisions concerning social and foreign policy declined. Instead the elections revealed new cleavages. The Fédération had been obliged to compromise with the peasant movement and eight deputies joined an agrarian group. Many deputies had benefited from Croix de feu support, and in July eight deputies, mostly from the Fédération, joined the PSF group.

In December 1936, Guiter urged Marin to consider whether the PSF was friendly or hostile, given that whole sections were joining the new party.[74] Actually, Marin had already condemned the PSF in *La Nation*.[75] In March 1937, the Fédération, along with the JP and AF, welcomed Doriot's Front de la liberté, for it reaffirmed the (alleged) principle that sitting conservative deputies would not be challenged. Privately Marin did not wish the Front de la liberté to become a 'super-party', and he was reluctant to be seen together with Doriot or even Taittinger. Guiter stalled on Front meetings, except where local party groups wanted them.

[72] Kennedy, *Reconciling*, 150–1. [73] *Le Flambeau*, 24 April 1937.

[74] Archives nationales, 317 AP 72, Fonds Marin (herafter, ANFLM carton/dossier), Guiter to Marin, 7 December 1936; Alicot to Guiter, 20 March 1937; Irvine, *French Conservatism*, 136–7.

[75] *La Nation*, 26 September 1936.

In Brittany, Royalist and Fédération notables were often hostile to Doriot, even though they saw the Front as a means to broaden their appeal.[76]

In revenge for La Rocque's refusal to join the Front, his enemies exposed his links to Tardieu in 1929–1930, while *Action française* attacked his military record. In the winter of 1937–1938, La Rocque pursued his critics in the courts. That did not prevent the PSF, PPF, Fédération, and some centrists presenting single candidates in most constituencies in the November 1937 local elections. Perhaps because the PSF and PPF overestimated their working-class support, they stood largely in left-wing constituencies. The PPF did very badly, while the PSF won only a handful of seats, overwhelmingly in conservative areas. The PSF announced that it would henceforth present its own candidates everywhere. In practice, it remained flexible, but there were many conflicts. Most spectacularly, in October 1938, Charles Vallin defeated a Fédération candidate in Paris IX.[77] In the winter of 1937–1938, PSF activists disrupted meetings of their critics, Taittinger, Vallat, and Henriot.[78] These disputes show that it is far from clear whether the PSF or the Front de la liberté was the more moderate, since the latter especially was diverse.

Fédération antipathy to the PSF had much to do with the latter's electoral ambitions, for relations with the Croix de feu had been better. To delegitimize the PSF, the Fédération claimed that its programme was identical to that of the Fédération—just as it had once claimed that the centre's programme was.[79] Wendel complained that 'if we believe [La Rocque], his troops seek action, and (that's a good one), they are more to the left than ours!! His programme too! (allegedly because it includes paid holidays: it's childish!)'. Wendel saw the PSF only as a useful paramilitary recourse.[80]

Certainly, both parties shared belief in property, family, nation, and religion and used the categories of collective psychology. Privately, Guiter and Marin were less categorical about the PSF programme, for they accused the PSF of adding unspecified 'demagogic' elements.[81] In fact, there were important differences between the Fédération and PSF, which may be obscured when historians use the vague categories on which abstract definitions of fascism depend. Cooperation was possible, but the PSF challenged the Fédération—and its nationalist and Royalist allies—ideologically, organizationally, and socially.

There was some agreement on the question of corporatism. The PSF stood for compulsory corporatism, and in the 1930s some agrarian supporters of the Fédération, especially those involved in the agrarian Union nationale des syndicats agricoles (UNSA) did so too. Victor Perret also advocated compulsory membership as a means to prevent domination by big business and to preserve the supply of skilled labour in his luxury silk business. Yet the Fédération's corporatism was equivocal.

[76] Bensoussan, *Combats*, 518–19; ANFLM 72, 17, 20 December 1937, 9 February 1938, 15 January 1939.

[77] Kennedy, *Reconciling*, 135–8, 164–72; Passmore, *From Liberalism*, 291–2.

[78] Passmore, 'Boy-scouting', 555–6; Kennedy, *Reconciling*, 140; Irvine, *French Conservatism*, 154.

[79] *La Nation*, 26 September 1936.

[80] Jeanneney, *François de Wendel*, 568.

[81] ANFLM, 72, Conseil national, 4 November 1936.

The most enthusiastic advocate of agrarian corporatism, Senator Guérin, turned to the PSF, perhaps because Dorgèristes pressed him in his constituency.[82] Even in Perret's Lyon, sympathy for orthodox liberalism was as strong as corporatism.[83]

Indeed, the Fédération espoused a liberalism with which the PSF had no sympathy. In response to Matignon, the Fédération stressed the freedom of labour;[84] it attacked the Office du blé as 'economic dictatorship', while the economic page in *La Nation* was entitled 'The sovietization of the French economy'.[85] As always, the Fédération agitated for a balanced budget, protection of savings, tax cuts, reform of Social insurance, and a return to the gold standard. Marin saw individual initiative as the core of the thousand-year-old French tradition, conserved especially in the countryside and the petty bourgeoisie, the source of the elite and the origin of progress.[86]

This 'liberal traditionalism' did not necessarily dictate anti-industrialism. The Fédération's economic spokesman, Pierre Rossillion, idealized small and medium firms' quality production; Perret campaigned for the preservation of the family workshop, but envisaged the transformation of shopkeepers (whom he saw as profiteers) into the agents of big companies.[87] *La Nation* carried a weekly 'Chronique de l'automobile', in which one could read that 'in the car industry one best observes this law of constant search for progress that is the essential characteristic of modern times'.[88]

The Fédération attacked the PSF in the name of liberty. Pro-Fédération landowners in the Beaujolais denounced the PSF's regimentation of thousands in service of a mystique, in total subservience to a leader. They warned that 'fetishization', evident in the display of monster portraits of La Rocque, would lead to excess and foment Communism.[89] A Loire-Inférieure activist denounced the 'Roquolatorie [sic] and demagogy of the PSF', while *La Province* claimed that one could 'admire a man without being hypnotized by him', and for Henriot the PSF's 'freely consented discipline' undermined 'intellectual independence'.[90] Marin counterpoised parliamentary discussion by independent, generalist men, imbued with the national interest, to the PSF's demagogic manipulation of the mass. He explained that while parties were essential, there should be cross-party agreement on fundamentals, for divisions would ruin the country. He rejected the PSF's very claim to be a party: it was a 'single-issue' movement, lacking a programme of government.[91] The Fédération and Royalists in areas such as Brittany used the categories of collective psychology to depict the PSF as demagogic manipulators of crowds. Rightly or wrongly, they saw the PSF as 'totalitarian'.

Socially too the PSF challenged the Fédération, as we saw in Lyon and Bordeaux. The Fédération's parliamentary group relied increasingly on Norman, Breton, and western landowners, often pro-Royalist, many with a military background, who

[82] *La Nation*, 23 May 1936.
[83] Passmore, *From Liberalism*, 171–2.
[84] *La Nation*, 13 June 1936.
[85] *La Nation*, 13 June, 11 July 1936.
[86] *La Nation*, 8 January 1938.
[87] Passmore, *From Liberalism*, 202–3.
[88] *La Nation*, 25 June 1938.
[89] Passmore, *Form Liberalism*, 294.
[90] Bensoussan, *Combats*, 520; *La Province*, 17 July 1937; *La Nation*, 8 May 1937 (and 15 August 1936).
[91] *La Nation*, 19, 26 September 1936.

ruled though local government, agricultural unions, and alliance with conservative clerics. This rapprochement with rural conservatives provoked some complaints, for often Federation activists represented an urban rival to them. The Fédération leader in Ille-et-Vilaine complained to Marin of the party's backing for the Royalist Alliance Nationale de l'Ouest (ANO).[92] Nonetheless, the Fédération and AF were increasingly close.[93] Anyway, Royalism had been absorbed into a broad nationalist coalition. In 1937, *La Province*'s 1,700 readers voted for their preferred 'chef national'. They chose Henriot, followed by Marin, Vallat, La Rocque (not yet discredited by refusal to join the Front de la Liberté), and Doriot. Maurras was sixteenth, Pétain nineteenth, and the pretender thirty-seventh.[94]

Since the 1900s, conservative landowners had faced challenges from Social Catholics, Christian Democrats, Cultivateurs-cultivants, Dorgèristes, and the organized wing of the Fédération. Now the PSF succeeded in federating peasants and bourgeois behind an authoritarian version of the Christian Democrats' third-way ideology. Moreover, as a mass party, the PSF was sufficiently wealthy to undermine landowner influence.[95] In Loire-Inférieure, pro-Fédération Royalist landowners, including deputies La Ferronnays and Juigné, had joined the Croix de feu in the hope of buttressing their influence. Without entirely cutting ties with the party, most refused to join the PSF parliamentary group. There were fewer retired senior officers in the PSF than in the Croix de feu. Weygand and Pétain refused to back La Rocque in his quarrel with Tardieu.[96] In 1938, Guiter advised Marin to back a 'Royaliste de tradition' in Roche-sur-Yonne (Vendée) against a PSF candidate. He pressed Marin to persuade the Royalist that he should sit in the Fédération's parliamentary group, since it included the Le Cour Grandmaison, while Mandel presided over the Independents. The PSF failed to convince the mayors to back a PSF candidate instead, but local PSF leaders persuaded 2,500 members to vote blank. Barrachin declared that notables would no longer be permitted to fix elections.[97] In the Rhône, a PSF candidate for the Conseil général accused his Fédération opponent, a retired career officer, of crushing the humble peasantry and of not being a genuine *poilu*.[98]

Religion reinforced the conflict between the Fédération and PSF, for it remained an important structurant of political conflict. Marin, we have seen, endorsed Poincaré's declaration that left and right were divided by the 'chasm' of the religious question,[99] while in 1936 the Fédération in the Rhône admitted its inability to cross the clerical–anticlerical divide.[100] Both Fédération and PSF claimed Catholic inspiration. Yet the PSF owed more to a form of Social Catholicism long opposed to

92 ANFLM, 72, Alicot to Guiter, 15 February 1937.
93 Bensoussan, *Combats*, 524–5; Bruno Goyet, *Henri d'Orléans, Comte de Paris* (Paris, 2001), 106–7.
94 *La Province*, 3 April 1937.
95 ANFLM, 72, Guiter to Marin 15 February 1937, Alicot report.
96 Nobécourt, *Le colonel de La Rocque*, 581–98.
97 ANFLM, 72 Taittinger to Guiter, 15 February 1938, Guiter to Marin, 25 February 1938.
98 Passmore, *From Liberalism*, 267–8.
99 ANFLM, 119, Marin to Valeri, 19 February 1937.
100 *L'Union républicaine du Rhône*, 21 June 1936; Passmore, *From Liberalism*, 96–7.

'reaction', which it subsumed into the Croix de feu mystique. The Fédération's Catholicism was more conservative. In Montpellier, crypto-Royalists, led by doctors, were unenthusiastic towards the PSF, which recruited outside the constituency of white Royalism.[101] Marin regarded the Popular Front as a conspiracy of Freemasons and teaching unions, another episode in the clerical–anticlerical struggle.[102] In 1936, his appeal to voters claimed that on one side stood the Fédération, which included the great mass of believers, whom no other party defended, while on the other was the 'comrade's Republic', controlled by Freemasons, whose mission was to undermine religion and nation.[103] Moreover, the expropriation of Church property in 1905 set a precedent for the occupation of factories in June 1936.[104] For Marin, the murder of priests, monks, and nuns, rape, pillage, violation of tombs, and the crucifixion of skeletons in the Spanish war exposed Communism's true nature. He linked these crimes to the burning of a convent at Vénissieux in the Lyonnais *banlieue*.[105]

These complaints confirm once again that many Catholics still saw themselves as victims of discrimination that excluded the competent from power. Le Mee continued his weekly denunciations of administrative favouritism in *La Nation*.[106] Mixing anti-Masonism and antisemitism, he described Education Minister Jean Zay as 'the strange grand-master whom the sadistic fantasist Léon Blum has given to French education', and accused him of plotting to exclude graduates of private schools from public employment.[107] Marin claimed that just as Waldeck-Rousseau and Combes 'installed the system of electoral conquest that became the *république des camarades*', Blum had replaced the competences with the servile.[108] The Fédération believed that the bookish culture of 'primaires', their lack of contact with 'reality', opened them to Marxist utopias; it opposed the raising of the school-leaving age.[109]

In sum, the Fédération and the once-Royalist right sought to defend the business, military, agrarian, and ecclesiastical hierarchies through a combination of conservative Catholicism, corporatism, liberalism, and anti-communism. Some Fédération activists saw the PSF's challenge as 'fascist' or 'totalitarian', but stretched the meaning of Republicanism pretty far themselves. The Fédération's Le Cour Grandmaison was notoriously Royalist, while Perret pursued the Action libérale populaire (ALP) project of confessionalizing the Republic and Marin remained faithful to elitist parliamentarianism. The nature of the dispute between the two sides thus problematizes historiographical attempts to claim that the PSF habituated the extreme right to democracy, notably in areas such as Brittany, where Royalism had been strong. Indeed, one might say that the intra-conservative disputes in Brittany prefigured those within the Vichy regime.[110] Whatever the case, the Fédération and PSF

101 Secondy, *Le Midi blanc*, 261.
102 *La Nation*, 2 May 1936.
103 *La Nation*, 18, 25 April and 29 August 1936.
104 *La Nation*, 20 June 1936.
105 *La Nation*, 13 February 1937.
106 *La Nation*, 18 April 1936, 14 November 1936, 5 December 1936, 26 December 1936, 6 May 1939.
107 *La Nation*, 27 June 1936, 13 March 1937.
108 *La Nation*, 2 May 1936, 25 June 1938.
109 *La Nation*, 23, 30 May 1936.
110 Thomas, 'Le Parti social français', 184.

contributed to the authoritarian mood from which the Daladier government emerged. The Fédération supported Daladier in parliament while complaining, as always, of marginalization.

THE CENTRE

In spite of—or because of—the extreme polarization of 1936, the centre was initially more committed to enticing the Radicals into a Concentration majority than ever. The Alliance promised to support sensible reforms, reminded Blum that reform depended upon order, and appealed for honest application of Matignon.[111] Although Flandin's ambiguity towards the Popular Front probably contributed to the centre's defeat, he was unchallenged as leader. Tardieu had withdrawn from parliament. His dauphin, Paul Reynaud, marginalized himself by backing the Franco–Soviet Pact and devaluation. As an admirer of the British model, Reynaud described opposition as 'public service'.[112] Flandin attempted to unite the centre, anti-Popular Front Radicals, and the PDP in a single group, but Marin helped ensure the failure of the scheme. Flandin did succeed in forming an official Alliance group, its forty-four members allegedly representing the 'great majority' of Alliance deputies.[113] At the November 1936 Alliance congress, pro-Concentration Girondins once again triumphed over pro-right Parisians. The Alliance repeatedly expressed preference for a government in the spirit of Waldeck-Rousseau—a direct affront to Marin, who saw Belle époque anticlericalism as a portent of the Popular Front. The PDP too showed some sympathy for Popular Front reforms, thanks to the participation (with reservations) of the CFTC and Catholic Action activists in the strike movement.

Some centrists were quite favourable to the government's social-democratic project, endorsing collective contracts, arbitration, and profit sharing. One activist suggested that since profits of limited companies were produced collectively, they should be shared between capital and labour. Another proposed renaming the party the 'Alliance républicain travailliste'. In debates concerning compulsory arbitration, the Alliance claimed inspiration from the Neo-Socialists Montagnon and Déat, and was prepared to accept requisition of the factory should employers or workers disobey judgements. Another activist saw insistence upon the illegality of the CGT as 'puerile'.[114] Yet the Alliance overwhelmingly voted with the opposition, rarely keeping its promise of flexibility.[115] There was no repeat of its behaviour in 1924–1926.

111 *L'Alliance démocratique*, 12–18 June 1936.

112 *L'Alliance démocratique*, 26 June 1936; BNF Fonds Flandin, 89. 'Rapport sur la situation de l'Alliance démocratique'; François Audigier, 'Les Modérés face au Front Populaire. Les Ambiguïtés de l'Alliance démocratique', *Annales de l'Est* 47, no. 2 (1997), 321–49; Thibaud Tellier, *Paul Reynaud* (Paris, 2005); 334–8; Pierre-Étienne Flandin, *Paix et liberté (L'Alliance démocratique à l'action)* (Paris, 1938).

113 *L'Alliance démocratique*, 26 June 1936.

114 *L'Alliance démocratique*, 4 December 1936.

115 Audigier, 'Les Modérés', 338–43.

In fact, the Alliance rejected social democracy. It condemned mass politics in the name of crowd psychology, preferring elitist parliamentarianism, Fayolist organizationalism, and sometimes authority. A journalist depicted Communism as a product of the age of the 'mass'; it was a mystique, a 'periodic eruptive phenomenon, a morbid state originating in Asia'. In the right circumstances, the French people would sing the Marseillaise, so a government representing the whole nation must 'purge France of foreign mystiques'. The writer claimed that only a parliamentary government could do that.[116] Another journalist saw 'the politics of vélodromes and street demonstrations as contrary to the maintenance of the Republic'.[117] In response to a conference delegate who urged the centre to form a single 'faisceau' against the extreme left and 'fascist' extreme right, André Terrasse, head of propaganda, countered that small groups of 'perfectly educated men were more effective than mass meetings'. In the latter, men behaved like 'flocks of geese', whereas in groups of no more than three hundred one could train men to engage with the arguments of opponents. Senator Caillier declared that if the government did not protect liberty he would exercise the Republican right to resist oppression himself. He rejected totalitarianism, but favoured temporary dictatorship.[118]

Flandin's anti-communism was accompanied by strong backing for appeasement and a degree of sympathy for Fascism and Nazism. Having previously been a partisan of the Soviet alliance, he came to see German and Italian expansionism as a natural consequence of high birth rates and urged France to ensure that German energy was directed towards Central Europe rather than the Mediterranean. He advocated imperial autarky and the economic organization of Europe.[119] Flandin presided over the Franco lobby in parliament and saw the Spanish coup as a legitimate response to a fraudulent government. His opponent in foreign affairs, Caillier, was equally unprepared to join a crusade for Communism in Spain.[120] The Spanish War connected international Communism to a foreign threat within France, for as a speaker at the Alliance's October 1936 conference put it, 'this country has become the dumping ground for all the undesirable foreigners who attempt here the revolution that they failed to foment in their own countries'.[121]

Centrists were ambivalent towards the PSF and PPF. One journalist reproved their demagogic anti-capitalism but regarded them as a sign of the health of democracy. Another claimed that Republicans would not follow La Rocque onto the 'fascist terrain', but wished Doriot success in his anti-communist campaign.[122] Subsequently, common hostility to the Front de la Liberté brought the Alliance and PSF closer. One activist claimed that La Rocque's opposition to the policy of

[116] *L'Alliance démocratique*, 15–26 September 1936.

[117] *L'Alliance démocratique*, 20 November 1936, 9 April 1937.

[118] *L'Alliance démocratique*, 4 December 1936.

[119] *L'Alliance démocratique*, 13 March 1938.

[120] *L'Alliance démocratique*, 9 January, 3 December 1937; Arnaud Chomette, 'Sauver une France libérale. Pierre-Étienne Flandin entre stratégie centriste et attraction totalitaire', in Gilles Morin and Gilles Richard (eds), *Les Deux France du Front populaire* (Paris, 2008), 119–25 at 121.

[121] *L'Alliance démocratique*, 20 October, 4 December 1936.

[122] *L'Alliance démocratique*, 5 July 1936.

two blocs had earned him a certificate of Republicanism and anti-fascism.[123] deputy Paul Creyssel of the Radicaux independents joined the PSF, while the PSF's agricultural expert, Jacques de Nadaillhac, had been an Alliance deputy. In the Ariège, the PSF, Fédération, and Radicaux indépendents shared a newspaper. By late 1937, even the pro-Concentration Gironde federation saw the PSF and PPF as allies, criticizing only their electoral ambitions.[124] In a municipal by-election at Arcachon (Gironde) in 1938, an old Alliance fief, André de Fels, headed a centre-PSF list.[125] Whether these developments prove the growing moderation of the PSF and PPF or the growing extremism of the Alliance is an open question.

The centre was close to the increasingly hard-line *patronat*. Wendel's withdrawal from the CGPF illustrated the relative decline in it of Catholic, conservative forgemasters. Gignoux, the new head of the organization, had been a centre deputy, while Louis Germain-Martin, head of the CGPF's new propaganda branch, the Comité de prévoyance et d'action social, had been a centrist minister. These figures were also connected to anti-Popular Front Radicals, notably to Émile Roche, who played an important part in forming the Daladier majority.[126] There were important ideological affinities between the centre and the *patronat*. Both rejected liberal individualism and preferred Fayolist hierarchy to social-democratic equality of interest groups. Étienne Fougère, the Alliance's economic expert, called for 'methodical organization' linking employers and workers' unions, disciplining their members while respecting individual initiatives. He opposed the left's allegedly tumultuous organization of labour relations, designed to regenerate universal suffrage, and opposed the CGT's monopoly on representation of workers.[127] Fougère had worked for decades through the Association nationale d'expansion économique (ANEE) to bring business and the administration together. Flandin's views on foreign policy converged with those of Detœuf's *Nouveaux cahiers*, which advocated peace through economic ententes, the removal of European trade barriers, and arms limitation.[128]

With the entry of Alliance members into the Daladier government, Concentration seemed to have been realized. Yet this was Concentration of a new kind.[129] In January 1937, an Alliance member had urged the formation of a new centre alliance: unlike the old Union nationale, it would be national and social, prioritizing the birth rate, improvement of the race, and education. He called for an elite characterized by intellectual, moral, affective, and material independence—virtues

[123] *L'Alliance démocratique*, 11 June 1937.

[124] ANFLM, 72, Remaury to Guiter, 28 November 1936; Thomas, 'Le Parti social français', 256.

[125] Trussardi, 'Faisceau, Croix de feu, PSF', 59; Passmore, *From Liberalism*, 190–1.

[126] Kolboom, *La Revanche*, 291.

[127] *L'Alliance démocratique*, 13 December 1936.

[128] Richard Kuisel, 'Auguste Detœuf, conscience of French industry', *International Review of Social History* 20 (April 1975), 150–74.

[129] Chomette, 'Sauver une France libérale', 117–25.

possessed by the few—to denounce the lies of the two blocs.[130] That would prove to be a fair description of the Daladier government.

THE DALADIER GOVERNMENT

The story of 1936 to 1938 was of gradual detachment of the Radicals from the Popular Front and of the difficult search for an alternative. In June 1937, the Radical Camille Chautemps took over leadership of the Popular Front. He tried to save the social-democratic project by organizing it through the 'Statut modern du travail', but failed because the CGT and CGPF, the latter backed by conservatives, opposed restrictions on their freedom of action. In January 1938, as the international situation deteriorated, Blum attempted to entice Reynaud into a government of national unity, including the PCF leader Thorez, that would resist Hitler. He failed because Reynaud made participation conditional on the inclusion of Marin, who was unacceptable to the left. Following the Anschluss, Blum again appealed for unity, this time from Thorez to Marin. Reynaud and Kerillis endorsed the proposal, but most conservatives, Flandin at their head, categorically opposed participation.[131] A traditional Union nationale government was equally impractical because the overwhelmingly pro-Popular Front Radicals would not accept Marin without balance on their left. Concentration was impossible because its chief centrist advocate, Flandin, was too pro-Appeasement. After a brief Blum interlude, on 13 April 1938, Daladier formed a Radical-led government.

Initially, the Daladier government's orientation was unclear, for it included partisans and opponents of the forty-hour week, and pro-and anti-appeasers. Daladier both retained credibility with the left, and put himself at the head of the anti-Popular Front movement among ordinary Radicals. In March 1937, the Radicals created the Confédération générale des syndicats des classes moyennes (CGSCM) as a counterweight to the CGT and CGPF. This abandonment of the claim to represent the people represented a shift to the right.[132] Meanwhile, frankly authoritarian tendencies emerged in the Jeunes radicaux, while at the party's December 1936 Biarritz congress, pro- and anti-Popular Front factions demonstrated with fascist and Communist salutes. The pro-Radical veterans' organization, the Union fédérale, participated in a campaign for the formation of a 'government of public safety', while the UNC circulated petitions calling upon President Lebrun to invite honest men to form a government.[133] The government's recourse to decree laws partially answered this demand for authority. In by-elections, the Radicals began to win seats against the Socialists thanks to the transfer of conservative votes.

[130] *L'Alliance démocratique*, 9 January 1937.

[131] Berstein, *Histoire*, ii, 525–8, 535–6; Tellier, *Paul Reynaud*, 392–400. The deputies favourable to Reynaud were Mandel, Jacquinot, Laniel, and Kerillis.

[132] Berstein, *Histoire, ii*, 460–3, 491–3; Kolboom, *La Revanche*, 131–8.

[133] Millington, *From Victory to Vichy*, 197–8.

Gradually, the Daladier government's shifted rightwards. The Munich crisis cemented an anti-communist alliance, for appeasers agreed that the fundamental international conflict was not between democracy and fascism, but between Communists and anti-communists. Flandin covered the walls of Paris with a poster denouncing the Communist war party and afterwards sent a congratulatory telegram to Hitler. In the PSF, only Deputy Paul Creyssel joined the extreme pacifists. La Rocque remained anti-German, but his anti-communism ultimately propelled him into the peace party. He spoke of defending 'Christian civilization' against both 'Asiatic Communism' and 'Teutonism'.[134] While Henriot was the leading appeaser in the Fédération, Marin denounced both Communist and fascist totalitarianism, but even he agreed in the crisis that the Communists intended to launch revolution in the midst of defeat and declared that France could fight only when order was restored and education purged of Zay's unpatriotic policies.[135]

Anti-communism in international policy did not necessarily translate into an anti-labour domestic policy, for the appeasers' denial of the German threat contradicted the claim that strikes weakened the nation's defences. Indeed, Flandin argued that prioritization of military over domestic spending would favour Bolshevism.[136] Furthermore, the government was divided between partisans of an 'économie dirigée' including exchange controls, and its opponents. Yet on 1 November, Reynaud's appointment as Finance Minister signalled defeat not only for social democracy, but for corporatism and the PSF's 'profession organisée'. Reynaud re-established employer authority, justified by the need to prioritize arms production.[137] His decrees of November instituted budgetary cuts, taxes rises, and all but abolished the forty-hour week. The government embraced a more orthodox liberalism, designed to free the labour market and cheapen credit by reducing state borrowing. However, the decrees also formed part of a unitary economic policy. Increased funding for the Centre national de recherche de scientifique and the creation of an Institut de conjoncture improved the government's foresight, as Fayolists would have put it.[138]

Furthermore, executive rule built upon Flandin's 1935 organization of the Présidence du conseil. The March 1939 decree powers were virtually limitless, and almost impossible for parliament to amend.[139] Reynaud evoked the Roman precedent, according to which a Republican government temporarily delegated its power to the executive in times of crisis. In July 1939, the government prorogued parliament for two years. The pretext was the dangerous international situation, but it also reflected the desire to see through Reynaud's three-year recovery plan. Just as Reynaud announced his first measures, Tixier-Vignancourt had argued that without prorogation, the left would unite in 1940 against the decree laws as it had in 1936.[140]

[134] Kennedy, *Reconciling*, 155; *Le Petit journal*, 29 September 1938.
[135] *La Nation*, 24 September, 1, 8 October 1938.
[136] *L'Alliance démocratique*, 2 December 1938.
[137] Tellier, *Paul Reynaud*, 490–1.
[138] 'Les décrets de novembre', *Centre polytechnicien d'études économiques* 53 (January 1939), 32–6.
[139] Le Béguec, 'L'Évolution', 55–64.
[140] *L'Alliance démocratique*, 2 December 1938, 28 July, 4 August 1939.

Daladier called upon experts to advise the executive—administrators, Inspecteurs de finances, Polytechniciens, and bankers—many of whom would subsequently serve the Vichy government. One of the most influential was Reynaud's Director of Cabinet, the Polytechnicien and enemy of Malthusianism, Alfred Sauvy. Some of Daladier's experts came from the Polytechnique think tank *X-Crise* (since 1933 the Centre polytechnicien d'études économiques (CPEE)), which advocated scientific economics and improved statistical services. The experts displaced the CNE, which was not consulted on the November decrees. The latter had been weakened by a decree introducing representatives of the veterans and *classes moyennes* into it. Unintentionally, veterans and the *classes moyennes* movements reinforced big business influence.[141]

Conservatives also contributed to the defeat of the general strike of 30 November, called by the CGT in protest against the decrees. The strike was the culmination of a remarkable mobilization in November, as the CGT and PSF held monster meetings. The latter's showing at the 11 November parade was its most impressive of the whole period. Along with troops and police, the SPF and sometimes the CFTC helped to break the strike. Since 1937, on the large north-eastern farms, as the employers took the offensive, the SPF profited from the racism of French workers. Unemployed labourers demonstrated against immigrants rather than against their employers.[142] After the strikes, the government's removal of immigrants' right to vote for factory delegates may have favoured the SPF. In Marseille, where ethnic competition was intense, SPF and PPF unions made gains.[143] A decree of 12 November 1938 increased the range of offences for which foreigners could be deported, a provision of which the police made ample use.[144] In May 1938, the Daladier government announced the first camps for 'undesirables', a measure first proposed by Vallat.[145] In April 1939, even the Alliance denounced 'wogs dedicated to doing us harm'.[146]

The defeat of Communism in domestic and international politics broke the Popular Front and largely overcame conservative reservations towards Daladier. The Radicals' changing attitude towards *laïcité* encouraged rapprochement, for the government sought Papal backing for peace, while anticlericalism appeared to be an obstacle to reaching the *classes moyennes*. In June 1939, several Radicals signed a petition in favour of the abrogation of the lay laws, although most of their colleagues refused.[147] On 29 October, Marin reported a 'productive' meeting with Daladier. In December, for the first time, the Fédération approved the government's decree powers, while continuing to resent its absence from the government. La Rocque alternated between approval of Daladier and annoyance at the powerlessness of the PSF.

141 Chatriot, *La Démocratie sociale*, 323–6.
142 Bulaitis, 'Le Communisme', 217–19, 276–81, 283–7.
143 Antoine Olivesi, 'Marseille et le sud-est', in *Édouard Daladier*, 169–80.
144 Noiriel, *Les Origines*, 144–6. 145 Noiriel, *Les Origines*, 138–41.
146 *L'Alliance démocratique*, 31 March, 7 April 1939.
147 Berstein, *Histoire*, ii, 584–6.

Nevertheless, the marginalization of parliament had provided openings for experts close to the Fédération and even the PSF, especially in natalist and family policy. In June 1936, pro-natalism had returned to the agenda, for conservatives saw the strikes as the product of a crisis in the family and as a threat to gender hierarchy. Moreover, since appeasers had claimed that French decadence, reflected in the low birth rate, made war impossible, pro-natalist measures seemed urgent. The experts of the ANPAPF, including the Fédération's Duval-Arnould, the ex-Fédération member Pernot, and the conservative Boverat (along with Sauvy) played an important part in formulating the Code de la Famille of 1939. The right did not entirely get its way, for the Code did not include the family vote, but its influence was stronger in population policy than anywhere else.[148]

The Daladier government's re-establishment of employer authority, its combination of executive rule, anti-communism, religious pacification, and pro-natalism consolidated a conservative coalition that stretched further right than any since 1873. The continuities with Vichy are obvious, but there were also discontinuities, which, moreover, reveal conservative reservations towards Daladier. These would prove important, for they help to explain the alignment that underlay the Vichy regime.

First, the Daladier coalition stood in a complex relation to the antisemitism that marked the last years of the Republic, especially following Munich, for the right charged Jews with seeking war. The prominence of Mandel, Zay, and Blum among the anti-appeasers provided an ideal focus for these prejudices—the first two would pay with their lives under Vichy. In the winter, the arrival of refugees fleeing *Kristallnacht* further exacerbated antisemitism. The PSF felt compelled, in the interests of the profession and the country, to publish an enquiry into the number of Jews in the Medical Faculty. The party condemned Nazi biological racism, while complaining that too many foreign Jews had been naturalized.[149] In 1938, antisemitism attained the Radical Party, notably through the pen of L.A. Gaboriaud, director of *L'Ère nouvelle*.[150] We should not exaggerate the extent of antisemitism. One Fédération journalist described Nazi antisemitism as 'sometimes sadistic and always barbarous'.[151] The Daladier government included anti-racists such as Marc Rucart and introduced no discriminatory measures against Jews, foreign or French. In 1939, a decree outlawed the incitement of racial and religious hatred. Vichy quickly annulled it.

Secondly, foreign policy remained divisive, for the appeaser Bonnet and anti-appeaser Reynaud were both in the cabinet. The former continued to seek alliance with dictatorial Italy, Spain, and Germany. On 6 December, he signed a non-aggression pact with Ribbentrop, neglecting to invite Jewish ministers to the reception. Conservatives applauded these moves, but increasingly contested appeasement. The defeat of the general strike rendered Communism less dangerous. Italian claims on Nice, Savoy, and Corsica (December 1938), Hitler's invasion of the rump Czech state (15 March 1939), and Mussolini's invasion of Albania (April

148 Koos, 'Engendering reaction', 173–200.
149 Kennedy, *Reconciling*, 190–1.
150 Berstein, *Histoire*, 586–9.
151 *La Nation*, 2 July 1938.

1939) further hardened conservative resolve. Yet Wendel, and especially Kerillis, were among the tiny few who advocated the Soviet alliance. La Rocque accepted only economic accords with Russia, which he depicted as the Asiatic enemy of Christian civilization, equal in dangerousness to Germany.[152]

Flandin's appeasement campaign provoked trouble in the Alliance. In protest against his telegram congratulating Hitler for his role at Munich, Reynaud, along with the presidents of the Seine and Gironde federations, resigned from the party. Reibel saw Flandin's poster as an 'inadmissible' attempt to undermine mobilization. Flandin was more popular among activists. He toured the federations, harvesting endorsements. The Flandiniste Georges Portmann took over the Gironde federation, which moved closer to the PSF. In November, Flandin was re-elected president with a huge majority, while Reibel lost his Comité directeur seat.[153] After Hitler's invasion of the Czech state, Flandin claimed 'not to find it scandalous, especially after the example of the Spanish revolution, that certain French people, in their conscience, and without ever wanting to make the choice, prefer fascism to Bolshevism', even if the question ought not to be posed in those terms.[154] His party adopted a stronger line and some of those who had resigned after Munich returned.[155]

When war broke out, conservatives overwhelmingly supported the war effort, but were uncertain who the chief enemy was. There was no repeat of the reconciliation of extremes of August 1914. The Nazi–Soviet Pact confirmed conservative fears. In the weeks before the German invasion of France, many conservatives were as preoccupied with fighting the Soviet Union as Germany. Flandin urged France to treat Soviet aggression against Finland as it had the Nazi attack on Poland.[156] Reynaud's civil servant, the future Vichy minister Yves Bouthillier, held back war production. Many were equivocal towards Britain. When defeat came, hard-core appeasers rallied easily to Vichy, and found the stab-in-the-back myth conveniently to hand.

[152] Kennedy, *Reconciling*, 185–6.

[153] *L'Alliance démocratique*, 28 October 1938; Trussardi, 'Faisceau', 59; Tellier, *Paul Reynaud*, 435–7.

[154] *L'Alliance démocratique*, 31 March 1939.

[155] Rosemunde Sanson, 'L'Alliance démocratique', in *Édouard Daladier*, 338.

[156] *L'Alliance démocratique*, 29 March, 20 December 1939.

14

From Republic to Vichy (1940–1944)

> The new order cannot in any way mean a return, even disguised, to the errors that cost us so dearly; neither can we see in it a sort of 'Moral Order' or a revenge for the events of 1936. The new order cannot be a servile imitation of foreign experiments; some of them have a meaning and beauty, but each people must conceive a regime adapted to its climate and genius.
>
> Philippe Pétain, 11 October 1940

On 12 June 1940, as the German armies crossed the Somme-Aisne line and advanced towards Paris and beyond, the Council of Ministers met for the second time that day at the thirteenth-century Chateau de Cangé on the Loire. The Président du conseil was Paul Reynaud, who had led the conservative riposte to the Popular Front, opposed Appeasement, and played a major part in organizing the country for war. Already at the earlier meeting, commander-in-chief General Weygand had challenged Reynaud to negotiate an armistice. Now Weygand claimed that the Communists had seized power in Paris, but a telephone call to the Paris Prefect of Police quickly exposed this mendacious attempt to exploit fears that Reynaud certainly shared. Unabashed, Weygand condemned the 'cowardice' of the government for leaving Paris.

Doubtless, the Ministers expected as much from Weygand, a known enemy of the Republic. He opposed exiling the government to the Empire because it could not incarnate the nation as a monarchy would have done. Marshal Pétain's intervention was more surprising. Reynaud had brought this reputedly Republican soldier, the living symbol of resistance at Verdun in the Great War, into the cabinet to stiffen resolve. Yet Pétain sided with Weygand. In a prepared statement he ruled out the possibility that France might fight on from the colonies, insisted that the country's 'natural defenders' must remain on French soil, and 'accept the suffering that will be imposed on the fatherland and its children'. He added that 'the French renaissance will be the fruit of this suffering'. Five days later, at Bordeaux, Reynaud told the Council—probably wrongly—that partisans of resistance were now in a minority, and so he must resign. Pétain became Président du conseil and subsequently 'Head of the French State'. Seventy years of Republican rule ended, and few of even the most staunchly Republican conservatives mourned its passing.

Only seven of them were among the eighty parliamentarians who on 10 July 1940 refused to accord full powers to Pétain. Paul Simon and Pierre Trémintin belonged to the Parti démocrate populaire (PDP), Laurent Bonnevay and Joseph Lecacheux sat with the centre, and Lionel de Moustiers with the Pernot Group. In the Senate, the PDP's Champetier de Ribes and the Independent Pierre de Chambrun, close to the Christian Democrats, also voted against. No monarchist, member of the Fédération républicaine (FR), or of the Parti social français (PSF) voted no, but two Fédération members, Joseph Denais and Bernard de La Groudière, were among the five conservatives who were excluded from the vote for having departed on the *Massilia* in the hope of continuing the war from North Africa. Admittedly, Denais wrote that he was in North Africa unwillingly, and only because Marin had told him to go.[1] The other conservative passengers were the Independent Georges Mandel, Senator Tony-Révillon of the Gauche démocratique, and the Alsatian Alexandre Wiltzer. Aware that membership of the war party endangered him, Henri de Kerillis did not attend the vote; neither did Reynaud, sick and soon to be arrested. Louis Marin, an opponent of the armistice, voted in favour of constitutional revision on 9 July, but refused to take part in the vote the following day.[2]

Historians rightly emphasize conservatives' central role in the Vichy regime.[3] For Olivier Wieviorka, their 'abdication' in July 1940 underlined 'the limits of their attachment to the Republic', and he adds that the rare conservative opponents of full powers came largely from the centre, especially the Christian Democrats.[4] His verdict is more convincing than René Rémond's contention—yet another recycling of collective psychology—that the trauma of defeat caused the resurfacing of an atavistic desire for protection by the natural authorities, the heirs of Legitimism.[5] Yet Wieviorka's interpretation too relies on hindsight: had Gamelin not overestimated the defensive qualities of the Ardennes, the extent of conservative anti-Republicanism might have remained unknown.

Vichy was not the necessary outcome of Third Republican conservatism. While the response to defeat of conservatives as a body is not surprising, individual choices were unpredictable. Once again, conservatives confronted circumstances for which nothing had prepared them: for or against Boulanger and the Ralliement; for or against Dreyfus; for or against de Gaulle in 1940—and again in 1958. Pre-1940 attitudes did not always serve as a guide: among centrist opponents of full powers, Bonnevay was the Popular Front's greatest friend, while Lecacheux was among its bitterest enemies. Furthermore, the majority of Radicals and Socialists voted for full powers and some of them served the Vichy regime.

[1] Jean Vavasseur-Desperriers, 'Cultures, structures, stratégies d'une organisation de la droite parlementaire entre les deux guerres. La Fédération républicaine de 1919 à 1940', thèse d'état, Lille III, 1999, 566.

[2] Jean Sagnes, 'Le Refus républicain: Les Quatre-vingts parlementaires qui dirent "non" à Vichy le 10 juillet 1940', *Revue d'histoire moderne et contemporaine* 38 (October–December 1991), 555–89; Olivier Wieviorka, *Les Orphelins de la république. Destinées des députés et des sénateurs français, 1940–1945* (Paris, 2001).

[3] Robert O. Paxton, *Vichy France: Old Guard and New Order, 1940–1944* (New York, 1972); Gérard Noiriel, *Les Origines républicaines de Vichy* (Paris, 1999); Mathias Bernard, *La Guerre des droites. Droite et extrême droite en France de l'affaire Dreyfus à nos jours* (Paris, 2007), 25–101.

[4] Wieviorka, *Les Orphelins*, 133.

[5] René Rémond, *Les Droites en France*, fourth revised edition (Paris, 1982), 234–5.

If anti-Republicanism had never died, it had waxed and waned according to circumstances. The Great War had channelled conservatism into exaggerated hopes for the Bloc; the return of the leagues in 1924–1936 was followed by absorption into the centre-led mainstream. The 1930s witnessed the emergence of new forms of authoritarianism, and the Daladier governments of 1938–1940 stretched the meaning of Republicanism quite far. However, there were counter-tendencies and nothing guaranteed permanency. As in each previous reconfiguration of conservatism, multiple groups came together at Vichy and discovered or invented affinities of which they might not previously have been aware.

This is not the occasion to explore in detail the history of Vichy, but to use it to review some of the themes of this book. Since Rémond wrote his classic study, historians have been preoccupied with classification. They see political movements as falling into a number of irreducible, incompatible categories, and debate the belonging of new movements. I have argued firstly that the subjects of this book participated in a common political culture (which extended beyond French territory and included parts of the left). They used the principles of collective psychology to divide the world into elites, demagogues, and masses, and resorted to the notions of tradition and modernity to structure their ideas and actions and to remake the world. Each conservative group defined these categories using inherited-but-contested traditions, including Rémond's, some of which were borrowed from outside the political sphere. Consequently, tendencies towards unity and division were present in all periods, and which prevailed depended on context.

The historiographical consensus that Vichy was an 'authoritarian conservative dictatorship', distinguished from totalitarian movements by the relative freedom of the traditional authorities (Church, business, landowners, administration) and absence of mass mobilization, makes it an excellent case study for the limits of the categorical approach. For one thing, the consensus is incomplete: Robert Paxton argued that since fascism and conservatism had much in common, Vichy qualified as fascist.[6] As usual, there is evidence to support both views. Advocates of the authoritarianism interpretation emphasize that Vichy claimed inspiration from the Salazar regime in Portugal, with which it shared Catholicism, nationalism, hierarchy, order, corporatism, anti-communism, and more. Yet if Pétain owned a copy of Salazar's speeches, he publically repudiated the notion of a 'new Moral Order'. He claimed that the French 'New Order'—a more contemporary expression—could not be a 'servile imitation of foreign experiments', even if 'certain of them have their meaning and beauty'. After meeting Hitler at Montoire, he spoke of collaboration within the New Order in Europe.[7] Indeed, many of the characteristics that Vichy shared with Salazar's New State were also present in Nazism and Fascism (especially given that the elements of the definitions are vague). True, Vichy did not display the same desire for a mobilized national community that marked the Nazi regime, yet the aspiration was not absent from France, while in Germany and

[6] Paxton, *Vichy*, 232–3.

[7] Speeches of 10 and 30 October 1940, in *Actes et écrits, Philippe Pétain*, ed. Jacques Isorni (Paris, 1974), 470–1, 549–60.

especially Italy, much latitude remained for the Church, Army, and monarchy. Moreover, Vichy was marked by an antisemitic racism that was largely absent from Portugal. In effect, categorization of Vichy with the Portuguese regime depends on arbitrarily designating totalitarianism as definitional and antisemitism as a secondary variation.

In fact, Vichy was a complex patchwork of shifting interests and ideologies,[8] and it reflected upon German as much as Portuguese precedents, among others—of both left and right. Categorization obscures the diverse reasons for which people embraced Vichy, their different degrees of commitment, their various appreciations of what it stood for, not to mention their understandings and misunderstandings of foreign ideologies. It also masks the shifting and contested ways in which contemporaries conceived and used political labels, combined them with others, and manoeuvred for advantage. There were differences between Vichy and foreign regimes, but they were the product of intended and unintended actions of groups with different agendas, differentially endowed with power, which drew on transnational ideologies, in particular contexts—not of the working out of a pre-given essence.

Notwithstanding the limits of the classificatory method, we may examine the power of particular groups at Vichy and the evolving relationship between them. The Army, Church, and administration (although divided) dominated the regime, especially in its early stages, because they retained greater ability to act institutionally amidst the chaos of June 1940. Military service and capture dispersed the cadres of the leagues, who were younger than those of the parliamentary right, and therefore more often mobilized. Repression and the Nazi–Soviet Pact weakened the Communists. In the dramatic conditions of the summer of 1940, as democracy became the scapegoat for defeat, the future—modernity—seemed to lie with dictatorship. Vichy reinforced the executive rule of the late Republic, with its experts and administrators, and gave new power to military, business, and agricultural interests. Politically, the new climate brought together conservative Republicans, who had hitherto claimed to want reform rather than overthrow of the Republic, with the extreme right—Catholics, nationalists, monarchists, and leaguers—who thus ended their long exclusion from national power. The regime advanced new, authoritarian versions of the organizational project, designed to restore the state and regenerate society through incorporation of regional, class, and gender differences into a hierarchical, harmonious organic community, accompanied by elimination of racial and national enemies. Hostility to the Republic and to Communism, together with the conviction that German hegemony in Europe was a fact in the medium term at least, also united this coalition, even if different factions understood these issues in different ways.

Although the established authorities dominated Vichy, we cannot reduce it to their story. First, religion, class, and gender divided the elites, and they disagreed on the role of the state in society, economy, and family. Secondly, ideology and practice was a product of dialogue and struggles among conservatives and against

[8] Julian Jackson, *France: The Dark Years 1940–1944* (Oxford, 2001), 142–7.

its enemies. Vichy was never a pure expression of any ideology, and it changed over time. Under Darlan in 1941, those committed to mass mobilization became more influential. Thirdly, conflict among Vichy conservatives often echoed right–left conflicts, and thus created affinities with the left. Under Vichy, anti-communism, pacifism, and the desire to pursue syndicalist projects in new conditions attracted a significant minority of the left. Finally, recent historiography has problematized the relationship between Vichy, collaboration, and resistance.[9]

THE VICHY COALITION

Recourse to the familiar categories of collective psychology both underpinned Vichy elitism and shaped struggle within the regime. To conservatives, the *Exode*, the massive flight of refugees ahead of the German Army, represented the disintegration of the crowd without its natural guides. In her *Exode* novel, *Suite française*, Irène Némirovsky, who had written for *Gringoire*, depicted Parisian refugees as a bestial and ruthless herd. Pétain evoked 'a people thrown far from their homes, their fields and their trades, reduced to the condition of nomads'. He saw the *Exode* as justification for the sacking of mayors who had fled with the population and for restoration of the natural frameworks of profession, family, and nation in a 'strong state'.[10] Pétain declared that the 'time of elites' had arrived, and envisaged power flowing downwards through subordinates at each level.[11] He and his circle envisaged a sort of devolved authoritarianism reliant upon the Army, Church, and administration. The pro-Vichy right-winger, Jean Fernand-Laurent, declared that the masses were only 'an instrument aware or unaware, good or bad, depending on who is leading them'.[12] Vichy represented another attempt to secure the pre-eminence of the elites and organize the formless mass.

There were certainly affinities between Vichy and Moral Order, but we have seen that neither regime was pure. Each was a product of diverse sources and of dialogue with opponents. Under Moral Order, monarchist factions had responded in different ways to the democracy that they opposed in principle. Likewise, Vichy kept many of the trappings of the Republic, and, as Noiriel argued, it claimed to serve the people better than the Republic had.[13] Close examination reveals the 'monoglottic' nature of Pétain's speeches, to use Bakhtin's term. For instance, the notion of the elites was as ambiguous as that of hierarchy. In the Army, Pétain had apparently learned both that one man must transmit orders to lower levels through obedient subordinates and that the latter should be *chefs* in their own right.[14]

[9] Jackson, *France*, 1–20.

[10] *Revue universelle*, 1 January 1941, in *Actes*, 479–81.

[11] *Gringoire*, 14 November 1940, in *Actes*, 482–3; 'Tout à refaire', *Gringoire*, 14 November 1940, in *Actes*, 482–3.

[12] Cited in W.D. Irvine, *French Conservatism in Crisis: The Republican Federation of France* (Baton Rouge, 1979), 211.

[13] Noiriel, *Les Origines*, 57–8.

[14] *Gringoire*, 14 November 1940.

His speeches drew on Fayolism as much as Maurrassianism, while the voice of the advanced wing of Social Catholicism may be heard in the notion that 'in every order, we shall endeavour to create elites, and with no other consideration apart from their capacities and merits, we shall grant them the power of command'.[15] Peasant and proletarian elites remained 'elites in their place', but that did not eliminate quarrels concerning their rights, the nature of their morality, religious or lay, or their relationship to the state.

The very expression, 'National Revolution', was potentially dangerous, and Pétain largely avoided it. It was not just 'another name for counterrevolution', as Rémond has it, for again both 'national' and 'revolution' were Republican in origin. The National Revolution could mean the assertion of the national interest over Marxist, liberal, and Jewish cosmopolitanism, but it also involved compromise with the national enemy and perhaps elimination of the failed ruling class. Vichy contained powerful drives towards unity among conservatives, without removing class, religious, and gender conflicts among them. In different measure, each of the conservative tendencies, along with the left, was represented at Vichy. Let us take each in turn.

Vichy appealed particularly to the descendants of monarchism, the disparate group that had absorbed nationalism and antisemitism in the previous decades. These were the *conservateurs* reduced to a few seats in Brittany, the west, and Midi, but strong in the officer corps and Church. Action Française (AF) intellectuals were prominent in the regime, especially in Pétain's entourage. They included Henri Massis, who wrote some of Pétain's speeches, and Raphël Alibert, the regime's first Minister of Justice. In Montpellier, the doctors and lawyers who led the Catholic far right took power, dominating the Légion des combattants (Vichy's veterans' organization). Some of them were unconditional supporters of Pétain; some were openly pro-Hitler, while others rejected Nazism for what they took to be the lessons of Salazar and Mussolini. Unusually for the leaders of the Légion, they were on good terms with the local Milice.[16] Elsewhere, noble landowners were influential in the Peasant Corporation. Yet the agrarianism of 1940 was the outcome of struggle and compromise between landowners, Christian Democrats, Dorgèristes, and the PSF, and conflict continued under Vichy.

If Pétain was not simply a new MacMahon, neither was he the first soldier to whom conservatives had turned, and nor would he be the last. While the Army as a body never moved against the regime, a troubling number of generals had wanted it to. Legitimists toyed with using General Ducrot to compel restoration, and in the aftermath of the Republican victory of 1877, the fleeting premiership of General Rochebouët had witnessed further plotting.[17] De Mun opposed a coup, but subsequently joined the Orleanists in backing General Boulanger. In 1899,

[15] Pétain, Radio broadcast, 11 July 1940, *Actes*, 455–6.

[16] Philippe Secondy, *La Persistence du Midi blanc. L'Hérault (1789–1962)* (Perpignan, 2006), 267–308.

[17] Philippe Levillain, *Albert de Mun. Catholicisme français et catholicisme romain du syllabus au ralliement* (Rome, 1983), 516–19, 685–6; Xavier Boniface, 'Le Loyalisme républicain de l'armée dans la crise du seize mai 1877', in Jean-Marc Guislin (ed.), *Seize-Mai revisité* (Lille, 2009), 89–93.

many nationalists, Royalists, and even some Moderate Republicans backed Déroulède's attempted military coup in principle, if not practice. During the Great War, the possibility of a coup terrified politicians: in 1915, General Castelnau urged the horrified Poincaré to 'act like a king' and 'show the deputies the door';[18] in September 1918, Clemenceau, well qualified in the subject, worried about the Boulangist atmosphere around General Mangin. In the 1920s, Lyautey saw himself as a potential dictator, while in the 1930s the Cagoule tried to rally military support. Ironically, Pétain had a reputation as a Republican general, prompting even the left-wing Radical Pierre Cot to pronounce his name in 1935. Pétain was actually more legalist than democratic, and in 1940 saw himself as the legal head of state (as did his rival, General de Gaulle). Nevertheless, Pétain's Republican reputation won support beyond the regime's hereditary enemies.

Although parliamentary conservatives were suspect and largely eliminated from the government in successive reshuffles, they too defined themselves as elites. The Fédération ceased political activity at the national level in 1940, but continued to publish newspapers and hold informal meetings locally. The Fédération right was especially prominent in support for Vichy. In Lyon, Victor Perret declared that the Republic had been 'eliminated by the very debacle that it had caused'.[19] Xavier Vallat served as Commissar for Jewish Affairs. In 1943, German pressure secured Philippe Henriot's appointment as Secretary of State for Information.[20] Marin initially adopted an *attentiste* position, but did not oppose the entry of his colleagues into the government, if only to have an eye in the regime.

Meanwhile, as Minister of Foreign Affairs and deputy to Pétain in the winter of 1940–1941, Flandin endeavoured to reinforce the centre's role in the regime. In February 1941, he created the Conseil national, a consultative body, which included seventy-eight parliamentarians out of 188 members. Its purpose was to bring together politicians and the competences. Among the centrist members were André François-Poncet and André Siegfried; alongside them were the physicist Maurice de Broglie, Doriot, and La Rocque.[21] Flandin named Joseph-Barthélemy Minister of Justice, a position he held until 1943. Flandin's Alliance ally, Georges Portmann, succeeded Jean-Louis Tixier-Vignancour, also of the Alliance, as Secrétaire-général à l'Information. Centrists were also numerous in the Légion.[22] The involvement of centrists in Vichy reminds us that since 1935, many of them had become convinced that rule by decree should be normalized, and had endorsed Flandin's pacifism and his accommodating estimate of Hitler.

The leagues played a secondary, but significant, role at Vichy. Attempts to form a single party failed in first months of the regime, for the parties could not agree amongst themselves, while Pétain distrusted parties of any kind. Marcel Déat's

[18] Yves Gras, *Castelnau, ou l'art de commander, 1851–1944* (Paris, 1990), 230.

[19] Cited in Irvine, *French Conservatism*, 211.

[20] Wieviorka, *Les Orphelins*, 250–2; Bernard, *La Guerre des droites*, 95–101.

[21] Michèle Cointet, *Le Conseil national de Vichy. Vie politique et réforme de l'état en régime autoritaire* (Paris, 1989).

[22] Jean-Paul Cointet, *La Légion française des combattants. La Tentation du fascisme* (Paris, 1995), 306–16, 323.

Rassemblement National populaire sided with the Germans and Laval in the hope of winning power, but had little influence before 1944. Doriot was loyal to Pétain, and from 1943, the Parti populaire française (PPF) fought the Resistance. The PSF embraced the National Revolution, while manoeuvring to use a crisis following Pétain's expected early demise to take power itself.[23] Although the PSF's radicalism had been attenuated since 1937, its desire to integrate sectional groups into a mobilized national community persisted. It still claimed to represent an elite of veterans and youth that was better qualified to represent France than the established authorities. La Rocque attacked the power of the 'trusts' in the Vichy regime and claimed that his movement would carry out the National Revolution more effectively. Such pretensions explain why Prefects often overlooked PSF activists in appointments to municipal councils and dismissed them as 'sectarian'.[24]

Leaguers were more prominent in the regime as individuals. Pétain's entourage included Roger de Saivre of the Jeunesses patriotes (JP), while Taittinger presided over the Paris Municipal Council. League influence was greatest under Darlan, when Paul Marion, Pierre Pucheu, and other PPF members occupied ministerial office. This group did not share Pétain's view that the military-managerial model resolved the problem of the elite–mass relationship. In 1941–1942 as Darlan's Secretary for Propaganda, Marion advocated the supremacy of the State and the mobilization of the people through propaganda. Marion, an ex-Communist who had passed through *non-conformiste* circles, argued that in the Russian, Italian, German, and Spanish revolutions, 'Each *chef* knew how to give the people the essential, a design, a mission'. He advocated a single party and the unification of youth groups, and tried to infiltrate the Légion. The Church, Prefects, and Pétain's military and civil cabinets ensured Marion's failure. Yet his opponents did not achieve their aims either. For instance, Vichy did not succeed in creating a corporatist or regionalist state.[25]

The support for Vichy of Socialists such as Charles Spinasse and Paul Faure and of trade unionists such as René Belin, Minister of Labour from the beginning of the regime until July 1942, reminds us that the cooperation between left and right was not unprecedented in Third Republican politics. True, contacts between moderate conservatives and the extreme right had been more frequent, but that was an effect of context rather than of an essential affinity, not least because neither side was homogenous. Conflicts *among* conservatives often paralleled those *between* left and right, and that created multiple affinities. Catholic trade unions had long debated their relationship to the Confédération général du travail (CGT), while Catholic women's groups enjoyed a complex relationship with the feminist movement—which included many conservative women anyway.

Historically, relations between conservatives and the left had taken many forms. Bonapartists and Boulangists had allied with the extreme left against the Republic,

[23] Sean Kennedy, *Reconciling France Against Democracy* (Montreal, 2007), 233–50.

[24] Passmore, *From Liberalism to Fascism: The Right in a French Province* (Cambridge, 1997), 306–8.

[25] Denis Peschanski, 'Vichy au singulier, Vichy au pluriel. Une Tentative avortée d'encadrement de la société (1941–1942)', *Annales ESC* 43, no. 3 (1988), 639–61.

while during the Dreyfus Affair many Progressists had joined the left in defending it. In the 1920s, part of the centre had backed the Cartel des Gauches' version of the organizational project, if not for the same reasons. Before the war, René Belin and his *Syndicats* faction of the CGT had opposed the Communists' bellicism and confrontational approach to industrial relations, to which he counterpoised 'constructive syndicalism'. Under Vichy, Belin's circle advocated a syndicalist version of authoritarian organizationalism.

Vichy also gave power to experts, whose role had grown since the 1920s, as the use of decree laws increased, especially under Daladier. The Inspector of Finance, Yves Bouthillier, who helped draw up Daladier's decrees, served as Finance Minister under Vichy. Demographers from the Alliance nationale took over natalist policy, as Daladier's Haut comité de la population became the Fondation française pour l'étude des problèmes humaines, headed by Nobel Prize winner Alexis Carrel.[26] Big business functionaries and activists dominated the significantly named Organization Committees, which ran the war economy at the expense of smaller competitors. Georges Lamirand, as Youth Minister under Laval, Flandin, and Darlan, brought the ideas of Lyautey, Fayol, and Social Catholics to Vichy. The role of experts was consecrated in the new constitution, drawn up by a commission of the Conseil national, under Joseph-Barthélemy's presidency. The constitution invested legislative power in the head of state, while giving a consultative role to two assemblies, one named by the head of state, the other elected by regional assemblies. The constitution was never implemented, and in practice experts were most prominent in the ministries, notably the so-called 'synarchy' of the Darlan government, including the engineer-managers Pucheu and Lehideux, the journalist Jacques Benoist-Méchin, the Polytechnicien Jean Bichelonne, and Bouthillier.

Vichy experts had imbibed the general culture and science dispensed by private foundations, medical and law faculties, and the École des sciences politiques. The latter, as Philip Nord says, was 'more than ever an antechamber to power'; its professionalization in the 1930s had not entailed abandonment of the commonplaces of collective psychology.[27] Students and teachers of the École des Roches, founded in 1899 by Édouard Demolins to form French elites, were also influential at Vichy. The school used the English public school method to train the whole person, including the body, without neglecting the Baccalaureate, rather than following the cramming methods allegedly used in state schools. One admirer of the École was Jérôme Carcopino, Education Minister under Darlan. Carcopino, an academic, had met Pétain at the 'déjeuner Hervieu' in the 1930s, another habitué of which was Léon Bérard, whose fruitless campaign to restore classical learning under the Bloc national had brought him close to the Maurrassians of the Cercle Foustel de Coulanges. As Education Minister, Carcopino removed many of his predecessor's concessions to the Church, but unpicked the democratic reforms of secondary education that had begun under Tardieu, and made concessions to the Latin lobby.[28]

[26] Andrés Reggiani, 'Procreating France', *French Historical Studies* 19, no. 1 (Spring 1996), 725–54.
[27] Philip Nord, *France's New Deal* (Princeton, 2010), 89.
[28] Stéphanie Corcy-Debray, 'Jérôme Carcopino, du triomphe à la roche Tarpéienne', *Vingtième siècle* 58 (April–June 1998), 70–82.

Carcopino thus demonstrated that Vichy had not resolved the religious question. Developments in the last decade of the Republic pointed in multiple directions. Without abandoning secularism, the anticlericalism of the centre had been attenuated, notably as it began to accept that religious orders should have the right to teach. There were many moderate Catholics in the ranks of the centre, yet their disappointment that suspicion of them had not disappeared may explain the support for Vichy of centrists such as Bérard. Religious animosity had also declined somewhat on the extreme right, for the Croix de feu was less clerical than AF or even the JP—but the PSF was more Catholic than the Croix de feu. As for the Catholic right, now strongest in the Fédération, it may have been shrinking, but it had not become more moderate on religious matters. Resentment of discrimination remained as strong as ever; it saw the Popular Front as another manifestation of Godlessness, and attributed the defeat to divine punishment. One bishop claimed that the real disaster came in 1936, not 1940.[29] Thanks to the centre's abandonment of democracy and the strength of Catholics in the Army and natalist movement, the Catholic right was able to play a considerable role at Vichy. The Church won major concessions in education, before Carcopino partially overturned them. The continued divisiveness of the religious question was underlined by Dumoulin de Labarthèthe's claim that Darlan had described his new ministerial team as 'better than the sacristy virgins who surround you [Dumoulin]; no generals, no seminarists, but young chaps who've lost their virginity, who will come to an understanding with the Fritzes and make sure we're cooked in the right pot'.[30]

TRADITION AND MODERNITY

Conflicts within the Vichy coalition cannot be reduced to a clash between tradition and modernity. In the Third Republic, conservatives defined these terms (and related terms, such as 'progress') in historically specific, often contingent ways, for specific purposes. Like collective psychology, the categories of traditional and modern persisted because they could justify almost anything. Conservatives of radically different disposition assumed that progress depended on secure traditions, and that modernity entailed the channelling of traditional ideals into constructive action through the discipline of reason. For instance, Georges Valois based his political action on the need to reconcile traditional constancy with modern evolution, and thus to protect humankind against the progressively cooling globe.[31] Jean Crussol of the Alliance démocratique advocated female suffrage because his party 'accepted modern evolutions while retaining traditions'.[32]

[29] Jackson, *Vichy*, 269.

[30] Cited in Peschanski, 'Vichy au singulier', 639–61 at 640.

[31] Allen Douglas, *From Fascism to Libertarian Communism: Georges Valois against the Third Republic* (Berkeley, 1992), 16–17.

[32] *L'Alliance démocratique*, 11 October 1935.

Understandings of tradition and progress varied according to circumstances, often rapidly, and were constructed from diverse materials. In the 1890s, Méline harnessed the idea of France as a peasant nation to military and economic struggle against Germany and Britain. During the Great War and in the 1920s, all parties prioritized production; from military tactics and Taylorism they took the idea of rapidity and speed, and from Fayol they took hierarchical organization. During the depression, conservatives condemned excessive production; some espoused the anti-materialist, anti-American discourse sometimes wrongly associated exclusively with the marginal Jeune droite. In 1936–1937, the institution of the forty-hour week, coupled with the renewed danger of war, caused conservatives to rediscover the necessity of production, and to transfer the term 'Malthusian' from demography to economics. Under Vichy, partisans of industrialism confronted those who wished for a 'return to the land'. However, we have seen that the Taylorism and Fayolism advocated by the industrializers was inseparable from organicist social science, pro-natalism, and belief in the family, land, and national character. As for the traditionalists, they drew on the same social sciences, and saw technological improvement as a way to save the small farm. The resulting quarrels concerned the very props of the regime: travail, famille, patrie.

TRAVAIL

Disagreements on the role of the state in the economy had cut through the conservative factions in the Third Republic. Broadly, they were divided between orthodox liberals, partisans of organization of the relationship between big business and the state, social democrats (especially Christian Democrats), and the authoritarian syndicalists and corporatists of the extreme right. In the economic sphere, Vichy gave control over the economy to a partnership of big business and the state. The creation of Organization Committees and a powerful Ministry of Industrial Production permitted big business and the state to allocate resources, fix prices, and close plants. The ensemble resembled the organization of the economy in the Great War in the period of Loucheur's supremacy, as well as displaying similarities to the abortive Marchandeau Law of 1935. It matched the conceptions of centrist organizers most closely, adapted to the authoritarian climate.

Belin saw the Charte du Travail of October 1941 as a counterweight to excessive business influence, giving rights to autonomous syndicates within the national community. However, he faced opposition from Pétain's civil cabinet, which sought to restrict the autonomy of workers' unions. Vichy rehearsed again arguments that once set de Mun against the Christian Democrats, and which had also exercised Italian Fascists. The result satisfied the corporatists more than the syndicalists. The latter, drawn from the CGT, Confédération française des travailleurs chrétiens (CFTC), and Syndicats professionnels française (SPF), attempted to give life to Vichy's syndicates, but they were divided between those who linked syndicalism to collaboration with employers and those who were more concerned to defend immediate working-class interests.[33]

FAMILLE

Women had played a considerable role in the right's successive reorganizations: they were essential to the Catholic popular politics of the 1870s and 1880s, to Christian Democracy in the 1890s, and subsequently to Nationalism and the Action libérale populaire (ALP). In each, women's refusal to downplay religion—the condition of their influence—undermined male leaders' efforts to build an anti-Socialist alliance across the religious divide. From 1906, Papal policies, coupled with conservatives' changing conceptions of organization, ensured that Catholic women turned away from direct political involvement. From the mid 1920s, they returned to activism through the leagues, thanks to the politicization of professionalized social work and secularization of the Catholic notion of vocation. They reworked the principles of crowd theory and domesticity to cast themselves as an elite invested with the task of moralizing and ordering corrupt, male bourgeois society.

Vichy allowed fewer openings for women. Its leaders saw the National Revolution as a virile reaction against the feminine vices of the Republic. Pétain was the epitome of patriarchal values, under whose authority the masses would re-learn the feminine virtue of self-sacrifice for the nation. The restoration of 'natural' female characteristics became one of the regime's priorities. The fight against depopulation, carried over from the Daladier period, became even more familialist thanks to the influence of Catholics such as Paul Haury, who headed the cabinet of the Secretary of State for the Family. Vichy's draft constitution declared the family to be the basic unit of society. Divorce was restricted (except in the case of mixed marriages involving Jews); women were barred from certain jobs and abortion was made a 'crime against society'. There was no equivalent of the PSF's efforts to mobilize women within a mass party.[34] Yet Vichy family policies were not without tensions. Vichy made some concessions to feminism, while constraining women within conventional spheres. Appointed municipal councils in the cities were to include a woman in the position of social delegate, while two women were named—as pro-natalist and familialist 'experts'—to the Conseil national. As always, women pushed against the boundaries of their allotted sphere. PSF women continued to provide social services, now with the involvement of some men, to seek protection for social professions through Vichy's corporatist system, and to develop their social conception of politics. In the absence of men, women now constituted a considerable proportion of its activists. One PSF member condemned the party's 'petticoating'.[35]

[33] Jean-Pierre Le Crom, *Syndicats, nous voilà!* (Paris, 1995).

[34] Francine Muel-Dreyfus, *Vichy et l'éternel féminin* (Paris, 1996).

[35] Jacques Nobécourt, *Le colonel de La Rocque (1885–1946), ou les pièges du nationalisme chrétien* (Paris, 1997), 1089, n. 54; Laura Lee Downs, '"Nous plantions les trois couleurs". Action sociale féminine et recomposition des politiques de la droite française. Le Cas du mouvement Croix-de-feu et du Parti social français, 1934–1960', *Revue d'histoire moderne et contemporaine* 58 (July–September 2011), 143–50.

PATRIE

The third element of the triptych was the most problematic, even though everybody at Vichy, including the most devoted advocates of collaboration, viewed themselves as patriotic. German hegemony in Europe, the division of France into occupied and unoccupied zones, and the arrival in power of advocates of the old provinces called the integrity of the territory into question, and anyway conservatives had never agreed what the national interest was. Certainly, most thought in terms of a Darwinist zero-sum struggle between self-sufficient blocs. That idea had been as compatible with reliance on Empire as with Europeanism, Christian or democratic. It had informed Appeasement, and now it underpinned views of the French place in the German New Order in Europe. As always, success in international struggle depended on the unity, quantity, and quality of the population, a preoccupation that now assumed frankly racist and discriminatory tones.

While since Boulangism the Right had been open to bellicose nationalism, that did not rule out internationalism and ultimately collaboration. An element of aristocratic cosmopolitanism and Catholic internationalism also persisted—some aristocratic conservatives had belonged to Europeanist peace organizations in the 1920s. Further to the right, in the 1920s some anti-German nationalists advocated the resurrection of the Catholic Habsburg Monarchy, while in the 1930s the defence of Western civilization against Communism fed into Appeasement. Under Vichy, the majority of the right advocated collaboration, but their reasons for doing so varied. Pétain and some in his circle struggled to defend French sovereignty, win concessions that would improve the lives of the population, and secure a favourable peace treaty. This pragmatic collaboration was hard to separate from ideological collaboration: in the circumstances, the similarities that existed between Nazi and Vichy ideologies were bound to be privileged, and the desire to please the Nazis was a slippery slope. Henriot, for instance, accepted the permanence of Nazi domination in Europe and envisaged French participation in the New Order.

Other conservatives rejected collaboration, but approved of the National Revolution. Maurras was the best known of those, though his views were most evident in his silences. Weygand was more direct. He saw the National Revolution as an equivalent of the Prussian reform that had prepared the way for revenge upon Napoléon. The FR in the Rhône simply avoided the issue of European cooperation.[36] La Rocque was more equivocal. He initially approved collaboration in principle, and recognized some similarities between the PSF and Nazism, but insisted on the protection of French interests. In the course of 1942, he turned against collaboration, while regretting privately that the Germans had not taken the opportunity for collaboration between equals. Like others on the right, he doubted that the National Revolution could be implemented under Nazi rule.[37]

The most grandiose collaborationist schemes came from the extreme right. Explicit sympathy with Nazism had been rare in 1940, although many conservatives had

[36] Irvine, *French Conservatism*, 215–17.
[37] Kennedy, *Reconciling*, 233–50.

admired aspects of the regime. In new circumstances, collaborators adapted the old notion of struggle between European, Bolshevik, and Anglo-American blocs. Darlan imagined that France, as a naval and colonial power, could protect the maritime flank of the German bloc. As in the interwar years, the European New Order was founded on economic cooperation, and under Darlan ministers attempted to integrate the French economy into the European. The Polytechnicien Jean Bichelonne, Secretary-General and later Minister of Industrial Production, combined economic planning with collaboration.[38]

Conflicts around regionalism continued under Vichy. Rightly, historians have argued that commitment in principle to regionalism contrasted with fear of compromising the national community in practice. We have seen that conflict between largely right-wing advocates of the old provinces and politically eclectic partisans of a rational regionalism also mattered. Monarchists and their heirs saw resurrection of the old provinces, along with corporatism, as a means to protect themselves against secularization and democratization and to recover national power. Christian Democrats regarded regionalism and defence of minority languages as part of a social-democratic project, while the centre advocated rational regions designed to reflect new technological and economic realities (which might not be geographically co-terminous). Regional antagonisms reached a peak in the early 1900s, when largely northern conservatives denounced southern anticlericalism, and Midi winegrowers blamed northern beet-growers for falling prices. In the interwar years, the growth of Alsatian and Breton autonomism caused many conservatives to draw back from regionalism, but tensions persisted.

In the autumn of 1940, Pétain lauded Provençale culture and advocated a regional constitution. While Charles-Brun lobbied the government, the Marquis de l'Estourbeillon, leader of the Union régionaliste bretonne, petitioned for the restoration of the province of Brittany, with an assembly and compulsory employment of Breton-speaking functionaries. Meanwhile, the pro-German Parti National Breton proclaimed a National Council and started a newspaper that reached 8,000 readers. Some Alsatian autonomists embraced Nazism. The government made limited concessions concerning language teaching in schools, but did little more than celebrate regional cultures. Vichy's desire to defend French sovereignty ruled out anything else, and in any case, Pétain and his advisors cared as much for the military-Fayolist chain of command, administrative efficiency, and the 'dynamic' economic role of the big cities as for resurrection of the 'static' historic provinces. Under the guidance of the government, the Conseil national elaborated a constitution that conceded little to 'sentimental regionalists'. In April 1941, the institution of Regional Prefects detached Nantes from Brittany, alarming advocates of the old provinces.[39]

The other side of national unity was exclusion of 'enemies'. At one time, apologists presented Vichy's Jewish Statutes as a German imposition. Now, the centrality

[38] Marc Ferro, *Pétain* (Paris, 1987), 289–329.

[39] Pétain, Speech of 20 October 1941, in *Actes*; Pierre Barral, 'Idéal et pratique du régionalisme dans le régime de Vichy', *Revue française de science politique* 24, no. 5 (1974), 911–39 at 915–16.

of antisemitism to Vichy is well established. The Jew was the antithesis of the National Revolution. The Jew's materialism inspired Communism and set workers against employers. The Jew lacked roots in the land, and the Jew's individualism dissolved the family. Overcoming decadence required expulsion of the Jew from the national body. Antisemitism was also vital to Vichy's reforms. The peasant corporation would eliminate the 'Jewish middlemen' that peasant activists from the first Christian Democracy to Dorgères had condemned. The Ministry of Industrial Production saw Aryanization of the economy as an excuse for concentration and rationalization, and struggled for control of the process with the ideologues of the Commissariat aux affaires juives.[40] Concern to preserve national sovereignty and win a favourable peace encouraged a competitive radicalization of antisemitic measures, and deeply implicated Vichy in the implementation of the Final Solution.[41]

The question of the relationship between Vichy antisemitism and the different threads of conservatism has been less well explored, and is obscured completely in interpretations that regard France in 1940 as universally antisemitic.[42] In the late 1930s, centre and even Radical politicians had espoused antisemitism, especially the apologists of Appeasement. This antisemitism of the centre—which should not be exaggerated—was part of a broader xenophobia—centrists were less hostile to French Jews. Yet, as Gérard Noiriel argues, the first antisemitic measures of Vichy stemmed from an escalation of Republican measures against immigrants and refugees, via the Republic's invention of a mediating category between French and foreigner: the recently naturalized citizen. Also, the efforts of the professions to exclude foreign-born colleagues permitted amalgamation of foreign and French Jews, because many of the foreigners in question were Jewish. Consequently, jurists, police, and civil servants who had previously served the Republic implemented Vichy's measures. For Noiriel, the Alliance member, Joseph-Barthélemy, Vichy's justice minister, epitomized this transition.[43]

The right and extreme right had before 1940 espoused a more extreme racism, demanding revision of naturalizations and internment of refugees. In 1940, their accession to power therefore brought something new to public policy: the longstanding obsession with the enemy within. Antisemitism had been daily fare in *L'Action française* and in regional nationalist organs such as the Breton *La Province*. For the right and extreme right, the Jew symbolized everything that it condemned—*laïcité*, Republicanism, Communism, individualism, and materialism. Resentment of discrimination against Catholics also sustained this antisemitism, and was linked to anti-Masonic prejudice. Jules Delahaye's disturbing promise of 1919 made that clear, while Vichy's publication of lists of Masons in the *Journal officiel* was a belated response to the Affair des fiches. The FR's Henriot spread antisemitic views on the radio, and Vallat became Commissaire for Jewish Affairs. Again, we must

[40] Henry Rousso, 'L'Aryanisation économique. Vichy, l'Occupation et la spoliation des Juifs', *Yod* 15–16 (1982), 51–80 at 62–6.

[41] Laurent Joly, *Vichy dans la 'solution finale'* (Paris, 2006).

[42] Michael Marrus and Robert Paxton, *Vichy France and the Jews* (New York, 1981).

[43] Noiriel, *Les Origines*, 105–8, 149–60.

not exaggerate. The equally right-wing Lyon branch of the Fédération largely ignored Henriot and Vallat, and showed hardly any antisemitism. The local deputy Pierre Burgeot was particularly opposed to persecution of Jews.[44] Had it not been for Nazi pressure, Vichy would probably have stopped at the exclusion of Jews from the professions and state apparatus.

Indeed, it is impossible to separate Vichy from the transnational context. The trend since Paxton published his work to insist on the Vichy's Frenchness is a mirror version of that which once insisted on France's uniquely democratic past.[45] The assumption of national uniqueness compounds the problem of the classificatory method, which also assumes that each country represents a self-contained 'case', with its own history, which can be compared to other cases using categories that are abstract and universal. Michel Espagne points out that comparing national cases forces scholars to deduce national differences, even where historical actors did not privilege them.[46] Actually, actors in the Vichy regime were situated within multiple relations differentially endowed with power: a fractured territory, an economic space dominated by the German state, a universal Catholic Church, regional languages, an empire, and transnational intellectual exchanges, not to mention their families and professional networks.

We should therefore ask how historical actors perceived 'foreign' ideologies—which often owed much to French thinkers—and what they appropriated from them. This research remains to be done, but a hint comes from Gaston Bergery's declaration of 10 July, signed by ninety-seven deputies including several from the centre, right, and PSF. It spoke of a universal movement towards 'a national form of socialism', which took radically different forms in different countries, from the New Deal to Stalinism. The declaration urged collaboration, participation in the European economy, and authoritarianism, and claimed that France would 'draw from its substance a regime that would be compatible with those in all continental Europe, but also with its own genius'.[47] Vichy appropriated and re-appropriated ideas from a multiplicity of sources, Nazism included.

Third Republican politicians had long been preoccupied with the German superiority in organization. Broadly speaking, conservatives assumed that France was characterized by a harmonious balance of order and individual liberty. America and Britain, in contrast, were too individualistic, while Germany was too regimented. Yet since France incorporated characteristics associated with foreign countries, conservatives feared the enemy within: Socialists were thought to be the agents of Germany, while American cinema threatened to import American materialism into France. Since conservatives also saw present-day France as decadent compared to stronger countries, they were also prone to admire foreign characteristics, which they also saw as French virtues. That was why, under the Occupation,

[44] Irvine, *French Conservatism*, 213.

[45] Serge Berstein, 'Pour en finir avec un dialogue des sourds', *Vingtieme siècle* 27, no. 3 (2007), 243–6.

[46] Michel Espagne, 'Sur les limites du comparatisme en histoire culturelle', *Genèses. Sciences sociales et histoire* 17 (1994), 112–21.

[47] Philippe Burrin, *La Dérive fasciste. Doriot, Déat, Bergery* (Paris, 1986), 333–4.

collaborators thought that contact with virile Germany would regenerate feminized France and yet make France more true to itself.[48]

In the course of 1943–1944, conservatives increasingly regretted alignment with Germany, and many joined the Resistance. Anyway, they had never been absent from the Resistance, and in its early stages dissidents, such as the military men Charles de Gaulle and Henri Frenay, played defining parts. Later, the passage from Vichy to the Resistance was eased, once again, by the affinities that may be found between any two ideologies, and by the creative use that protagonists made of these connections. The Resistance was as critical of the Third Republic as was Vichy, and many partisans of the latter shared the Resistance's hostility to Germany. Indeed, the Resistance was sometimes less antipathetic to Pétain than it was to the Germans: Frenay was the best-known example, but initially de Gaulle condemned Vichy's collaborationism more than the objectives of the National Revolution. La Rocque, whose anti-Germanism became increasingly obvious, was deported in March 1943, while his Lieutenants, Edmund Barrachin and Charles Vallin, joined de Gaulle. Eventually, Marin rallied to de Gaulle too. More frequently, conservatives turned to General Giraud's pro-Vichy Resistance, as did François Mitterrand. Others joined Ceux de la Libération, which had been founded by a PSF sympathizer, or the Organisation civile et militaire, which also provided a home for Vichy experts. At the Liberation, the conservative presence within the Resistance helped de Gaulle to prioritize re-establishment of the Republican state over more radical projects.

Nonetheless, de Gaulle could not prevent the balance of power from shifting, and he did not wish to do so. He established his leadership over the Resistance at the price of compromise with the Socialists and Communists. Consequently, in 1945, the dissonance between the terms 'conservative' and 'right' with which I began this book remained unresolved. Furthermore, the old conservative parties were discredited and most of their parliamentarians were barred from elected office for having voted full powers to Pétain. Only the Christian Democrats emerged from the Occupation with any credit. Members of the PDP had played a significant role in the Resistance, and so they were able to profit from this latest rebellion of the conservative electorate against its leaders. The centre of gravity of Christian Democracy too had shifted, as the new Mouvement républicain populaire positioned itself on the moderate, social-democratic left. Conservatives might have feared that they would never again be in power. By 1951, they were back in government.

THE LONG VIEW?

It is conventional to end a book such as this with a look forward, and to ask what the legacy of our subject is for contemporaries. However, one of my major contentions is, precisely, that no single thread—such as 'modernization'—allows us to make sense of the history of conservative politics under the Third Republic and

[48] Jackson, *France*, 328.

Vichy or to project trends into the future. Rather, I have argued that contested and constructed traditions were constantly recombined and remade in new contexts. What is more, I have argued that there is a complex interchange between some historians' beliefs about the necessary 'modernization' of the political parties, and indeed of the French political system, and the political strategies of the conservatives in the Third Republic. In this respect, Gaullism has for many historians occupied a key place: movements have been categorized and judged according to whether or not they anticipated the Fifth Republic.

Schematically, the story goes something like this. French political culture was fundamentally democratic. Historians disagree whether this culture matured during the Revolution, with the consolidation of the Third Republic, with the alleged end of the religious conflict during the Great War, or perhaps even with the appearance of the PSF.

Whatever the case, there was no political future outside this dominant culture. The alternative Catholic culture, like that of extremists of left and right, either chose marginality or success through compromise with Republicanism.[49] Likewise, according to Annie Kriegel, the Communist Party in the 1920s was a 'counter-society'; it was in, but not of, French society. It became a mass force only when it embraced the Popular Front.[50] Again, for Bertrand Joly the numerical weakness of the *fin-de-siècle* nationalist leagues hardly justifies the historiographical attention lavished on them,[51] while for Jean-Paul Thomas the Croix de feu broke through only when it became the 'democratic' PSF.[52]

Yet, the story continues, if French political culture was fundamentally democratic, its parliamentary political system was cut off from the people, for it was still based on notables and clients. The people were tempted by the rewards available in the corrupt parliamentary system, but they were half-aware of its deficiencies. That was another reason why they periodically turned to extremism, or rather to movements in which a minority of extremists attempted, unsuccessfully, to manipulate the legitimate discontent of ordinary citizens. The Communist Party acted as a 'tribune' for the workers, and functioned ultimately to include them in the Republic. As for the leagues, they reflected the desire for a stronger executive, even if during the Boulanger and Dreyfus Affairs and on 6 February 1934, extremists had attempted to manipulate this good sense.[53]

Jean-Paul Thomas explicitly links developments in the late Third Republic to this longer-term 'modernization' of the right. He cites Berstein's concept of political

[49] Serge Berstein, 'Nature et fonction des cultures politiques', in *Les Cultures politiques en France* (Paris, 1999), 7–31 at 20.

[50] Annie Kriegel, *Aux Origines du communisme français, 1914–1920 contribution a l'histoire du mouvement ouvrier français* (Paris, 1970).

[51] Bertrand Joly, *Nationalistes et conservateurs en France* (Paris, 2008), 141—2

[52] Jean-Paul Thomas, 'Le Parti social français (PSF), obstacle à la radicalisation des droites. Contribution historique à une réflexion sur les droites, la radicalité et les cultures politiques françaises', in *À Droite de la droite. Les Droites radicales en France et en Grande-Bretagne au XXe siècle* (Lille, 2012), 243–73 at 255–6.

[53] Michel Winock, *La Fièvre hexagonale. Les Grandes crises politiques de 1871 a 1968* (Paris, 1984), 196, 237–8.

culture, and argues that PSF had a dual role as a barrier to fascism and as a means to integrate the extreme right into democratic conservatism. He bases this argument especially on the continuities between the PSF and de Gaulle's Rassemblement du peuple français (RPF), founded in 1947, and on the role of key PSF figures in shaping the constitution of the Fifth Republic.[54]

Jean-Pierre Rioux takes the narrative into the Fourth Republic. Like the subjects of this book, Rioux assumes that the Third Republic suffered from objective defects that required 'technical solutions'. Its governments were weak, vulnerable to lobbies, and more concerned with political manoeuvres than with the people's aspiration for peace, prosperity, and strong government (we may detect the assumption of a unitary national psychology here). The government of Pierre Mendès France in 1954–1955 potentially offered a left-wing answer to the people's desire to be governed effectively, but ultimately de Gaulle established a strong executive, responsive to the nation and electorate as a whole. The Fifth Republic reduced the power of notables, while giving a greater role to competence.[55] Similar ideas underlay Jean Charlot's classic works on Gaullism, which argued that at last France had produced in the 1960s a two-party system responsive to the people rather than to activists.[56] The election of François Mitterrand in 1981 initially seemed to confirm that France had at last become a 'mature' two-party democracy, in which 'alternance' between right and left was possible.[57]

Three years later the emergence of the National Front (FN) potentially challenged this optimistic view, and certainly confidence has been dented. The Republic has not succeeded in integrating all groups, particularly those who are adversely affected by globalization.[58] Yet by conceiving globalization as an external force to which France reacts (rather than helping to globalize the economy), it has proved possible to deploy again the idea that extremism is really a surface phenomenon. Thus, the Front national reflects the frustration of electors, especially working-class electors, who demand inclusion. Take, for instance, Matthias Bernard's recent history of the right and extreme right. He argues that beyond 'conjunctures', a 'chasm' exists between the FN and the parliamentary right. They may have collaborated at the local and regional level, but that is because the Front 'ultimately adopted the same attitude as its more or less distant predecessors (Jean-Louis Tixier-Vignancour, but also the interwar leaguers and the Antidreyfusard nationalists), which also decided to privilege the ballot box over the street. It has occupied a part of the ground of the RPR [Rassemblement du people français] and the UDF [Union démocratique française]. It moderates its discourse, and it even attracts cadres trained in the traditional right'.[59]

[54] Jean-Paul Thomas, 'Droite et rassemblement' du PSF au RPF, 1936–1948. Hommes, réseaux, cultures: Rupture et continuités d'une histoire politique', thèse de doctorat, IEP, Paris, 2002, 308–9; Thomas, 'Le Parti social français', 243–73.

[55] Jean-Pierre Rioux, *La France de la IVe République* (Paris, 1980).

[56] Jean Charlot, *Histoire politique du gaullisme* (Paris, 1983).

[57] Michel Winock, *La France politique: XIXe–XXe siècle* (Paris, 1999), 430.

[58] Pascal Perrineau, 'The conditions for the re-emergence of an extreme-right wing in France: the National Front, 1984–1998', in Nicholas Atkin and Franck Tallett (eds), *The Right in France* (London, 1997).

[59] Bernard, *La Guerre des droites*, 9–10, 201.

In this book I have explored some of the problems with the above narrative of conservative politics. First, methodologically speaking, one can hardly deny the continuities between, say, Gaullism and the PSF. Yet one may in principle establish continuities (or discontinuities) between any two movements, for party members, voters, and sympathizers were never clear about goals, and potentially shared many things with sympathizers of other parties. To make one such continuity the baseline from which to judge all other developments is to impose a preconceived pattern on the past and to ignore the complexities of particular contexts.

For instance, in a critique of Jean-Paul Thomas' argument, Sean Kennedy rightly points out that there were as many discontinuities as continuities between the PSF and RPF: the RPF lacked the well-organized social sections of the PSF, while La Rocque's visceral dislike of the elective principle contrasted with de Gaulle's plebiscitary democracy.[60] Only Thomas' assumption that Gaullism was both uniformly democratic and represented the *outcome* of French history makes the similarities more important than the differences, and indeed allows him to ignore the many contradictions and ambiguities of the RPF. Thomas argues that only a 'long-term' approach allows historians to understand the meaning of the PSF, an ahistorical method that does little justice to the way in which contemporaries saw matters. As Kennedy points out, while some former PSF activists admired the RPF's anti-communism, others denounced de Gaulle as a divider of the French people and friend of the Communists.[61] Kennedy counters that the real heir of the Croix de feu and PSF is actually the Front national, and inevitably it is easy for him to point to continuities. Once again, there are also major differences. For instance, the Front should be understood in the context of a breakdown of Socialism and Communism and of important mutations in racial and gender politics. And while the Front is hostile to cultural pluralism, it does not appear to share the leagues' antipathy to political democracy.

Secondly, Vichy occupies a problematic position in the democratic narrative of conservative politics. Jean-Paul Thomas' view that the PSF integrated the hitherto anti-democratic right into the Republic confronts the problem that PSF supporters, along with all the conservative tendencies discussed in this book, along with a significant part of the left, rallied in 1940 to Vichy. Certainly, historians have made many concessions to Robert Paxton's claim that Vichy derived from French precedents. However, they simultaneously reiterate the view that Vichy represented the reactivation of a French tradition of extreme rightism and traditionalism that would have remained marginal had it not been for the special circumstances of 1940—an argument that Rémond had advanced.[62] In effect, Vichy remains a 'parenthesis'. Paxton's view that Vichy represented a mutation of the Republican tradition has found little favour, and Gérard Noiriel's discussion of the Republican origins of Vichy remains extremely controversial.[63] This is not to contradict my

[60] Kennedy, *Reconciling France*, 252–3.
[61] Kennedy, *Reconciling France*, 264.
[62] Rémond, *Les Droites*, 231–7; Peschanski, 'Vichy au singulier', 639–61.
[63] Noiriel, *Les Origines républicaines de Vichy*.

argument, stated at the beginning of this chapter, that Vichy was not the logical outcome of Third Republican conservative politics. My point is rather that Gaullism was not either, and neither is the Front national. In a sense, *all* movements and regimes derive from exceptional circumstances, but they also re-work an eclectic range of pre-existing ideas and practices, French and non-French, and they create something new in the process. Neither Vichy nor the Front national derive their meaning from measurement against an external process of modernization or globalization.

Readers may object that by privileging the importance of crowd theory in conservative political culture I have replaced the modernization narrative with a meta-category of my own. The charge is all the more plausible, given that the influence of crowd theory and its associated concepts—national character, the elite–mass dichotomy, and modernization—may be traced into the constitution of the Fifth Republic and, moreover, that of the European Union. Both institutions privilege the role of experts over parliament; the former was founded on a supposedly uniquely French 'grandeur', while the latter has often been presented as part of a competition between continental blocs. Stereotypes traceable to crowd theory remain all too evident in journalistic, political, and indeed academic discourses. There are nevertheless important counter tendencies. From the 1970s, sociologists and historians such as Charles Tilly developed new ways of understanding the motives and behaviour of those who participated in 'social movements', while political scientists and electoral strategists abandoned generalizations about the 'mass' for analysis of the aspirations of a segmented electorate with specific goals and aspirations, and advertisers started from the notion that people were sceptical of their claims.

Crowd theory is not the key to conservative politics; I have privileged it only as a new perspective. Crowd theory was useful to conservatives—and indeed the left—precisely because it was an empty category and an unfalsifiable one. It persisted because it could explain any set of circumstances, and could be integrated into projects that from other angles were radically different. Similarly, 'modernization' is still useful to politicians as a way to present as technical and unavoidable projects that are really ideological and contingent. Insofar as other concepts have displaced crowd theory and modernization, it is because they appear more 'useful' to politicians—not because they are 'truer'. While I hope to have shown that crowd theory was important to a range of conservative groups, it cannot explain the actual strategies and world views of historical actors. Only careful contextual analysis can do that. Liberated from the necessity of searching for precursors of de Gaulle, Pétain, or Le Pen, historians are free to ask new questions and provide new insights.

Further Reading

All the secondary works, newspapers, and archival source used in the writing of this book may be in the footnotes, and this guide lists only major works that directly concern the history of the right and centre under the Third Republic. It does not include the immense number of specialist journal articles and other essays on conservative politics.

GENERAL WORKS

On the political history of the period, two works remain essential: Jean-Marie Mayeur, *La Vie politique sous la Troisième République* (1984)* and Georges and Édouard Bonnefous, *Histoire politique de la Troisième République*, 7 vols (1956–1967).

On conservative politics, René Rémond, *Les Droites en France*, fourth revised edition (1982) remains the compulsory starting point, but Jean-François Sirinelli, *Histoire des droites en France*, 3 vols (1992) supersedes it in terms of research, and occasionally method. Mathias Bernard, *La Guerre des droites. Droite et extrême droite en France de l'affaire Dreyfus à nos jours* (2007) is the best single volume study, even if the evidence presented suggests as much cooperation as 'war' between right and extreme right. The best general study of the nationalist right is Pierre Milza, *Fascisme français, passé et présent* (1987).

CONTEXT

One of the major arguments of my book is that the meanings of conservative politics can only be understood in relation to detailed knowledge of context, and it would not have been possible to write this book without incorporating the insights of a great many published works. It is impossible to list all of them, but certain of them must be mentioned because they are methodologically as well as empirically important to my book. Jackie Clarke, *France in the Age of Organization* (Leamington Spa, 2011) unpicks and historicizes 'modernization' narratives, without falling into the trap of 'special paths'. Robert Nye, *Masculinity and Male Codes of Honor in Nineteenth-Century France* (Oxford, 1993) is essential for understanding gender in the period. I am also much indebted to his *The Origins of Crowd Psychology: Gustave Le Bon and the Crisis of Mass Democracy in the Third Republic* (London, 1975). Special mention is also due to another product of that historiographical period: Bonne Smith, *Ladies of the Leisure Class: The Bourgeoisie of Northern France in the Nineteenth Century* (Princeton, 1981). Contemporary readers might doubt the psychoanalytic dimension of Smith's argument, but as a discussion of parapolitical women's social action, and of the hidden gender conflicts within the conservative world, it remains unmatched.

MONARCHISM

Rather surprisingly, monarchist movements in the early Third Republic have received relatively little attention from Francophone scholars. Three works in English have not

* All works published in Paris, unless otherwise stated.

been superseded: Robert R. Locke, *French Legitimists and the Politics of Moral Order* (New Jersey, 1974); Stephen Kale, *Legitimism and the Reconstruction of French Society 1852–1883* (Baton Rouge, 1992); John Rothney, *Bonapartism After Sedan* (New York, 1969). Orleanism in its declining years has yet to find its historian, but historians may usefully turn to Alan Grubb, *The Politics of Pessimism: Albert de Broglie and Conservative Politics in the Early Third Republic* (Newarck 1996). On one strand of Legitimism, Philippe Levillain, *Albert de Mun. Catholicisme français et catholicisme romain du syllabus au ralliement* (Rome, 1983), provides fascinating insights.

Monarchists' encounter with Boulangism has received more attention: Philippe Levillain, *Boulanger, fossoyeur de la monarchie* (1982); W.D. Irvine, *The Boulanger Affair Reconsidered* (Oxford, 1989); and Bertrand Joly, *Nationalistes et Conservateurs En France: 1885–1902* (2008), all make important contributions.

On Action Française, Eugen Weber, *Action française: Royalism and Reaction in Twentieth-Century France* (Stanford, 1962) remains the only general history of the neo-Royalist movement, rather than of Maurrassian ideas, in which respect, Michael Sutton, *Nationalism, Catholicism, Positivism: The Politics of Charles Maurras and French Catholicism, 1890–1914* (Cambridge, 1982), is more useful, as is Jacques Prévotat, *Les catholiques et l'Action française. Histoire d'une condamnation* (2001). The most important—indeed brilliant—work on royalism in the Third Republic is Bruno Goyet, *Un Rôle en politique. Henri d'Orléans, Comte de Paris* (2001).

THE PARLIAMENTARY RIGHT AND CENTRE

In recent years, exhaustive studies of the main parliamentary conservative movements have appeared, most of them originating in doctoral theses, and some of them unpublished. They are largely political in focus, but evoke broad social and intellectual developments as explanatory devices. On the centre, see Rosemonde Sanson, *L'Alliance républicaine démocratique. Une Formation du centre (1901–1920)* (Rennes, 2003). On the Fédération républicaine, Jean Vavasseur-Desperriers, 'Cultures, structures, stratégie d'une organisation de la droite parlementaire entre les deux guerres. La Fédération républicaine de 1919 à 1940', thèse d'état, Lille III, 1999, has not been published. In terms of interpretation, W.D. Irvine, *French Conservatism in Crisis: The Republican Federation of France* (Baton Rouge, 1979) remains essential. Jean-Noël Jeanneney, *François de Wendel en République. L'Argent et le pouvoir* (1976) is a fine biography of a key figure, even if the author's desire to dismantle the left's caricature of Wendel distracts him from the wider question of the importance of money in politics. For Christian Democracy, see Jean-Claude Delbreil, *Centrisme et démocratie chrétienne en France. Le Parti démocrate populaire des origines au M.R.P* (Publications de la Sorbonne, 1990) and the excellent Jean-Marie Mayeur, *L'Abbé Lemire. Un Prêtre démocrate 1853–1928* (1968).

Although it does not exclusively concern party politics, and deals with the moderate left too, Gilles Le Béguec, 'L'Entrée au Palais-Bourbon. Les Filières privilégiées d'accès à la fonction parlementaire, 1919–1939', thèse pour le doctorat d'état, Paris X Nanterre, 1989, is fundamentally important. A sample of specialist work on moderate conservatism may be found in François Roth (ed.), *Les Modérés dans la vie politique française (1870–1965)* (Nancy, 2000).

THE NATIONALIST AND EXTREME RIGHT

On the pre-1914 nationalist leagues, Zeev Sternhell, *La Droite révolutionnaire (1885–1914). Les Origines françaises du fascisme* (1978) is the most complete, but may now be read in conjunction with Joly, *Nationalistes et conservateurs*.

The interwar leagues have been the subject of major studies and enormous controversy in recent years, starting with Robert Soucy, *French Fascism: The First Wave, 1924–1933* (New Haven, 1986) and *French Fascism: The Second Wave* (Newhaven, 1995). Monumental, but fascinating, is Jean Philippet, 'Le Temps des ligues. Pierre Taittinger et les Jeunesses patriotes', thèse pour le doctorat, IEP Paris, 2000. Michel Dobry (ed.), *Le Mythe de l'allergie française au fascisme* (2003) is perhaps more important for its methodological reflections than for its empirical work. Samuel Kalman, *The Extreme Right in Interwar France: The Faisceau and the Croix de Feu* (Aldershot, 2008) compares the ideologies of the Croix de feu and Faisceau.

On the Croix de feu, see Albert Kéchichian, *Les Croix de feu à l'age du fascism*. Two other books, Jacques Nobécourt, *Le colonel de La Rocque (1885–1946), ou les pièges du nationalisme chrétien* (1997), and Sean Kennedy, *Reconciling France Against Democracy: The Croix de feu and the Parti Social Francais, 1927–1945* (Montreal, 2007), deal with both the Croix de feu and the PSF. Jean-Paul Thomas, 'Droite et rassemblement du PSF au RPF, 1936–1948. Hommes, réseaux, cultures. Rupture et continuités d'une histoire politique', thèse de doctorat, IEP Paris, 2002, in contrast, deals with the PSF alone, and argues that it was not an extremist party.

On the PPF, see Jean-Paul Brunet, *Jacques Doriot, du communisme au fascisme* (1986), and on the PPF itself, Laurent Kestel, *La Conversion politique. Doriot, le PPF, et la question du fascisme français* (2012).

On the Vichy regime, Olivier Wieviorka, *Les Orphelins de la République. Destinées des députés et des sénateurs français, 1940–1945* (2001) includes valuable discussion of the fate of conservatives under Vichy, while Julian Jackson's *France: The Dark Years* (Oxford, 2001) provides the most nuanced discussion of the political orientation of the regime.

Two books appeared too late for me to incorporate their findings in the book. Nimrod Amzalak, *Fascists and Honorable Men: Contingency and Choice in French History* (Basingstoke, 2011) parallels my own approach, while Gabriel Goodliffe, *The Resurgence of the Radical Right in France: From Boulangism to the Front National* (Cambridge, 2012), develops the view that the radical right was a response to industrialization, modernization, and globalization.

REGIONAL STUDIES

Conservative politics have been discussed in several 'total' regional histories, such as Marcel Vigreux, *Paysans et notables du Morvan au XIXe siècle jusqu'en 1914* (Château-Chinon, 1987). Conservatives have also merited studies in their own right. Among the best are Michel Denis, *Les Royalistes de la Mayenne et le monde moderne (XIXe–XXe siècles)* (Klincksieck, 1977); Jean Quellien, *Bleus, blancs, rouges. Politique et élections dans le Calvados 1870–1939* (Caen, 1986); David Bensoussan, *Combats pour une Bretagne catholique et rurale. Les Droites bretonnes dans l'entre-deux-guerres* (2006); Philippe Secondy, *La Persistance du midi blanc. L'Hérault (1789–*1962) (Perpignan, 2006), and Mathias Bernard, *La Dérive des modérés. La Fédération républicaine du Rhône sous la Troisième République* (1998).

OTHER ASPECTS

Although there is now a massive literature on the role of women in conservative parties and especially the extreme right, there are few book-length studies. Bonnie Smith's work on Catholic women, already mentioned, sets the standard. The publication of Magali Della Sudda, 'Une Activité politique féminine avant le droit de suffrage en France et en Italie', thèse de doctorat, EHESS Paris, 2007, on the Ligue patriotique des françaises, will fill a major gap. On Vichy, Francine Muel-Dreyfus, *Vichy et l'éternel féminine* (1996), and Miranda Pollard, *Reign of Virtue: Mobilizing Gender in Vichy France* (Chicago, 1998) are important. Christine Bard, *Un Siècle d'antiféminisme* (1999) provides relevant material on conservatism.

Julian Wright, *The Regionalist Movement in France 1890–1914* (Oxford, 2003) shows that regionalism was not simply a concern of the reactionary right, while Éric Phélippeau, *L'Invention de l'homme politique moderne. De Mackau, l'Orne et la République* (2002) is the best work on methods of political organization. Jean Garrigues, *Les Patrons et la politique* (2002) explores the links between business and conservative Republicans in the early years of the Third Republic. While there is much scholarly work on social policy, which provides important context for this book, the contribution of the working class to conservative politics has barely been studied—on that subject, we await the doctorate of Joe Starkey, 'Working-class conservatism in France, 1932–40', PhD thesis, Cardiff University, forthcoming 2015.

In addition to those mentioned above, certain biographies provide essential insights into the history of conservatism: Allen Douglas, *From Fascism to Libertarian Communism: Georges Valois against the Third Republic* (Berkeley, 1992), François Monnet, *Refaire la République. André Tardieu, une dérive réactionnaire, 1876–1945* (1993), and Thibaud Tellier, *Paul Reynaud. Un Indépendant en politique* (2005) are three of the best.

In the line of recent work on political culture, three books show the way: Jessica Wardhaugh, *In Pursuit of the People: Political Culture in France, 1934–39* (Basingstoke, 2009), Susan B. Whitney, *Mobilizing Youth: Communists and Catholics in Interwar France* (Chicago, 2009), and Laura Lee Downs, *Histoire des colonies de vacances* (2009). Each of these books demonstrates that left and right both participated in a common culture and conceived it differently.

Index

[1] Charles-Brun, followed the contemporary custom of writing under a name composed of part of his first name hyphenated with part or all of his surname. In this and other cases, I have used the name that the individual was known by, along with alternatives.